The **Rough Guide** to

Sweden

written and researched by

James Proctor and Neil Roland

ROUGH GUIDES

www.roughguides.com

Contents

The Swedish winter
colour section following
p.184

Food and drink
colour section following
p.312

◄◄ Midnight sun over Lake Mälaren ◄ Lighthouse, Stockholm archipelago

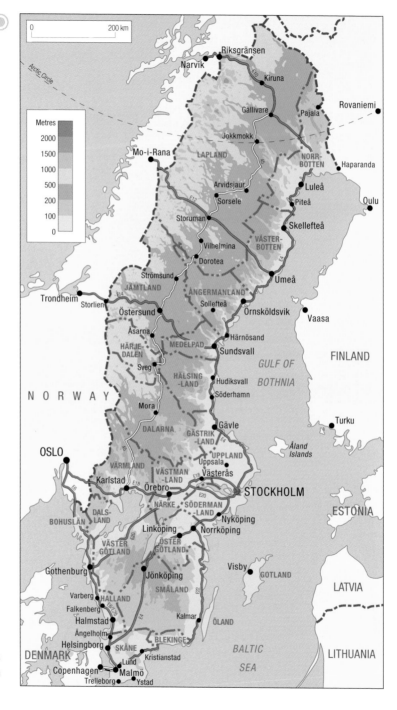

Introduction to
Sweden

The mere mention of Sweden conjures up resonant images: snow-capped peaks, reindeer wandering in deep green forests and the 24-hour daylight of the midnight sun. But beyond the household names of ABBA, IKEA and Volvo, Sweden is relatively unknown. The largest of the Scandinavian countries, with an area twice that of Britain (and roughly that of California), but a population of barely nine million, Sweden is still one of Europe's best-kept secrets. Its cities are safe, carefree places where the cheap public transport runs on time and life is relaxed, while the countryside boasts pine, spruce and birch forest as far as the eye can see and crystal-clear lakes perfect for a summer afternoon dip – not to mention possibly the purest air you'll ever breathe. The country's south and west coasts, meanwhile, feature some of the most exquisite beaches in Europe – without the crowds.

Forget anything you've heard about Sweden's reputedly high **prices** – over recent years, the Swedish *krona* has depreciated significantly against most other Western currencies, putting Sweden within the scope of most visitors' budgets. For accommodation, there's a range of decent hotels, guesthouses and hostels to suit every pocket, and many hotels drop their prices in summer (and at weekends all year round).

Many tourists come to Sweden looking forward to wild sex and easy pick-ups – and most return disappointed. Somehow, over the years, the open Swedish attitude to nudity and sexuality has become confused with sex. Contrary to popular belief, Sweden isn't populated solely with

5
∎

▲ Reindeer

Fact file

• Sweden is the **third largest country** in western Europe – behind only France and Spain – stretching 1600km from north to south. If the country were pivoted around on its southernmost point, the top of the country would reach as far south as Naples in Italy.

• More than half of Sweden's land surface is covered with **forest** – mostly coniferous – punctuated by an astonishing **100,000 lakes**.

• The **Swedish parliament** has one chamber, and its 349 members are elected by **proportional representation**, with ballots held every four years on the third Sunday in September. At 45 percent, the country has one of the highest proportions of **female MPs** in the world.

• Although the **Sámi**, the indigenous population of Swedish Lapland, constituted the only distinct minority of any size before World War II, today twenty percent of Sweden's inhabitants are of foreign extraction.

• There is no translation for the Swedish word **lagom**, one of the most commonly used terms in the language. Roughly speaking, it means "just the right amount, not too much but not too little", a concept that is the very essence of Swedishness.

people waiting for any opportunity to tear off their clothes and make passionate love under the midnight sun. People may talk about sex openly, but when it comes down to it the Swedes can be rather puritanical. **Nudity**, though common, is quite unrelated to sex: go to a beach in Sweden on a hot summer's day and you'll doubtless see people sunbathing naked, but this state of affairs is certainly not an invitation for a love-in. However, the Swedes' **liberal** and open attitude to virtually every aspect of life is certainly one of their most enviable qualities; people are generally left to do their own thing, providing it doesn't impinge on the rights and freedoms of others. In Sweden, rights go hand in hand with duties, and there's a strong sense of civic obligation (count how few times you see people dropping litter, for example), which in turn makes for a well-rounded and stable society.

Where to go

Sweden is principally a land of forests and lakes. Its towns and cities are small by European standards and are mostly located in the southern third of the country, where the majority of Swedes live. Of the cities, serenely beautiful Stockholm is supreme. Sitting elegantly on fourteen different islands, where the waters of Lake Mälaren meet the Baltic Sea, the city boasts some fantastic architecture, fine museums and by far the best culture and nightlife in the country. In fact, the capital's wide, tree-lined boulevards, the narrow medieval streets of Gamla Stan, Stockholm's Old Town, and its modern, state-of-the-art buildings make it one of the most beautiful cities in Europe. The 24,000 islands which comprise the Stockholm archipelago begin just outside the city limits and are a perfect antidote to the urban bustle, offering endless opportunities to explore unspoilt island villages and, of course, to go swimming. On the west coast, Gothenburg, the country's second city, is also one of Sweden's most appealing destinations. Gothenburgers have a reputation for being among the friendliest people in Sweden, and the city's network of canals and spacious avenues are reminiscent of Amsterdam, whose architects designed it.

The south is the most cosmopolitan part of the country, owing to the proximity of Denmark and the rest of the European continent, and its surprisingly varied western coast has bustling towns all the way

▲ Stockholm

Jugendstil – Swedish style

Forget any notion of **Swedish design** and style consisting solely of IKEA flatpacks and stripped-pine simplicity. One of the country's most splendid periods for architecture and design was the end of the nineteenth century and the first decade of the twentieth – the era of Art Nouveau or **Jugendstil**.

This free-flowing style was employed to decorate the facades of urban landscapes across Europe, but the luxuriant curves and organic shapes were never so resonant as in nature-loving Sweden. Towns across the country still boast a wealth of beautiful examples from this elegant era: Stockholm's Östermalm area is rich in Jugendstil, while in Gothenburg, the curves and curls are most

apparent in Vasastan. In Malmö, Helsingborg and Lund the best houses – often cream-stuccoed with green paintwork – are peppered with images of quirky faces, rising suns and stylized flowers.

---

along its length. **Helsingborg**, near the Danish island of Zeeland and across the water from where Hamlet's Elsinore is situated, is small yet breezily continental; to the north lies the Bjäre peninsula, offering some of the country's best cycling and hiking, with the home of Swedish tennis, **Båstad**, nestling at the peninsula's base. Just over 50km south of Helsingborg is the glorious ancient university seat of **Lund**, while nearby **Malmö**, Sweden's third city, heaves with youthful nightlife around its medieval core. The south coast is brimming with chocolate-box villages and a few cultural surprises; inland, southern Sweden boasts some handsome lakes, the two largest of which, **Vänern** and **Vättern**, provide exceptional fishing and splendid backdrops to some beautiful towns,

▲ Hiker on the Kungsleden trail

not least the evocative former royal seat and the monastic centre after **Vadstena**; and **Karlstad**, the sunshine capital of Värmland, a rugged province ideal for river-rafting trips. To the east of the mainland lie the islands of **Öland** – featuring some stunning scenery – and **Gotland**, justifiably raved about as a haven for summer revelry, especially within the medieval walls of its unspoilt Hanseatic city, Visby.

Central Sweden and Swedish Lapland represent the most quintessentially "Swedish-looking" part of the country. In the centre lies **Dalarna**, an area of rolling hills and villages that's home to **Lake Siljan**, one of Sweden's most beautiful lakes. From Dalarna, the private Inlandsbanan train line strikes north through some of Sweden's most beautiful scenery, with reindeer – and occasionally bears – having to be cleared off the track as the trains make their way from village to village. To the east, the other train line linking the north with the south runs close to the **Bothnian coast**. It's along this eastern shoreline that most towns and cities of the north are located: **Sundsvall**, **Umeå** and **Luleå** are all enjoyable, lively places in which to break your journey on the long trek northwards. Equally, the **High Coast** north of Sundsvall is an excellent introduction to northern Sweden, with its array of pine-clad islands and craggy inlets, set against a patchwork of flower meadows and rolling hillsides.

▼ Jämtland

Midsummer mayhem

An atmosphere akin to Mediterranean *joie de vivre* takes over Sweden during the **midsummer solstice** (the weekend closest to June 24), when maypoles are erected as giant fertility symbols in gardens and parks across the country. Midsummer is not a time for staying in towns – everyone heads to the countryside and coasts, with Dalarna, the island of Öland and the shores of the Bohuslän coast being just a few of the most popular spots. Aided in no small part by copious quantities of **alcohol**, the population's national characteristics of reserve and restraint dissolve over midsummer weekend. Long trestle tables draped in white cloths and sagging under the weight of multiple varieties of herring, potatoes with dill, and gallons of *akvavit* are set up outside, and parties go on through the light night with dancing to the strains of accordions and fiddles.

Both train lines eventually meet in the far north of Sweden, inside the **Arctic Circle** and in the home of the Lapps or **Sámi** – Sweden's (and Scandinavia's) indigenous people. The further north you travel into **Swedish Lapland**, the more isolated the towns become – you'll often be covering vast distances in these regions just to get to the next village, and you shouldn't be surprised if you drive for hours without seeing a soul. This is the land of reindeer, elk and bears, of swiftly flowing rivers and coniferous forest, all traversed by endless hiking routes. The **Kungsleden**, a trail that stretches for 500km from Abisko to Hemavan, passes through some of Sweden's wildest and most beautiful terrain, offering the chance to experience nature in the raw. Two of Sweden's northernmost towns, **Kiruna** and **Gällivare**, make excellent bases for exploring the region's **national parks**, which can all be reached easily by train or bus, and for visiting the world-famous **Icehotel** in nearby Jukkasjärvi. Swedish Lapland is also where you will experience the **midnight sun**: in high summer the sun never sets, allowing you to read the newspaper outdoors or play golf at midnight. In midwinter the opposite is true, and the complete darkness (not to mention temperatures as low as –30°C) can make this one of the most magical parts of the country to travel through, as the sky is lit up by the multicoloured patterns of the **northern lights**, or aurora borealis.

When to go

n general, **May to September** is the best time to visit Sweden – north or south. **Summer** weather in Sweden is similar to that in southern Britain, though there are more hours of sunshine and less rain; the average July temperature in Stockholm, for example, is the same as that in London. Most Swedes take their summer holiday between mid-June and mid-August, which is when the weather is at its best and festivals are thick on the ground. Generally, if southern Sweden is having a hot summer, it'll be miserably cold and rainy in the north – and vice versa.

▲ Skier in Riksgränsen

By the end of August, the leaves in northern Sweden start to change colour and night frosts are not uncommon; the first snows fall in September. In Stockholm, snow starts to fall in October but doesn't generally settle; by November, though, the ground is usually covered in a blanket of snow, which will last until the following March or even April, when there can still be snow showers. **Winters** in the south of Sweden are often mild, and the southern province

► Husky dog, Lapland

of Skåne can escape snow completely. By the end of March or beginning of April, temperatures slowly start to rise; the official definition of the arrival of spring is five consecutive days with temperatures above zero. Bear in mind, though, that if you're heading north in late spring you're likely to encounter snow until well into May.

11

Daylight is in short supply in winter. In December, it doesn't get light in Stockholm until around 9.30am, and it's normally dark again by 3pm. North of the Arctic Circle – in Kiruna, for example – there's 24-hour darkness from mid-December to mid-January, and the merest glow of light at noon during the months immediately either side. Conversely, at the height of summer there's no part of Sweden which is **dark** for any length of time; in the far north there's 24-hour daylight and midnight sun from the end of May to the end of June, and April and July are very light months. Even the south of the country only experiences a few hours of darkness: in Stockholm it doesn't get properly dark at all in June

Northern lights

Also known by their Latin name, *aurora borealis*, the **northern lights** are visible all across northern Sweden during the dark months of winter. These spectacular displays of green-blue shimmering arcs and waves of light are caused by solar wind, or streams of particles charged by the sun, hitting the atmosphere. The colours are the characteristic hues of different elements when they hit the plasma shield that protects the Earth: blue is nitrogen and yellow-green oxygen. Although the mechanisms which produce the aurora are not completely understood, the displays are generally more impressive the closer you get to the poles – low temperatures are also rumoured to produce some of the most dramatic performances. **Gällivare** and **Kiruna**, both well inside the Arctic Circle, are arguably the best places in Sweden to catch a glimpse of the aurora, particularly during the coldest winter months from December to February. Although displays can range from just a few minutes to several hours, the night sky must be clear of cloud to see the northern lights from Earth.

▲ Forest in Vasterbotten

– from 11pm or midnight there's a sort of half-light, with the sun only just below the horizon, which lasts just a few hours, and come 3am it's bright daylight again.

Average daily temperatures (°C) and precipitation (mm)

	Jan	Mar	May	June	July	Aug	Oct	Dec
Jokkmokk								
°C	-17	-8	6	12	14	12	1	-14
mm	30	24	35	48	78	74	41	32
Umeå								
°C	-9	-4	7	13	15	14	4	-7
mm	49	41	41	44	53	78	65	56
Östersund								
°C	-7	-4	7	12	13	12	4	-6
mm	27	23	35	57	76	60	37	31
Stockholm								
°C	-3	0	11	16	17	16	8	-1
mm	39	26	30	45	72	66	50	46
Gothenburg								
°C	-2	1	11	15	16	16	9	0
mm	62	50	51	61	68	77	84	75
Visby								
°C	-1	0	10	14	16	16	8	1
mm	48	32	29	31	50	50	50	51
Lund								
°C	-1	2	11	15	17	17	9	1
mm	54	44	43	54	66	63	60	65

things not to miss

It's not possible to see everything Sweden has to offer in one trip, and we don't suggest you try. What follows is a selective taste of the country's highlights, from snowmobiling to sampling a smorgasbord. They're arranged in five colour-coded categories, which you can browse through to find the very best things to see and experience. All highlights have a page reference to take you straight to the guide, where you can find out more.

01 Snowmobiling See *Swedish winter* colour section • Snowmobiling across Lapland is an exhilarating way to see Sweden in winter.

02 **Sámi culture, Lapland** Page **366** • Sights such as Jokkmokk market and Fatmomakke village in Lapland are monuments to the thriving culture of Sweden's indigenous population.

03 **Lund Cathedral** Page **189** • This twelfth-century cathedral in Sweden's principal university town is the finest Romanesque building in northern Europe.

04 **Swimming in a lake** Page **44** • Amongst Sweden's 100,000 lakes, you're bound to find one you can call your own.

05 Renaissance buildings, Kalmar Page 224 • Perfectly preserved architecture in Sweden's most beautiful town square.

06 Smorgasbord See *Food and drink* colour section • Eat until you drop: the smorgasbord is a perfect way to sample Sweden's excellent cuisine.

07 Vasa ship, Stockholm Page 80 • After lying in mud for centuries at the bottom of Stockholm harbour, the mighty Vasa warship has now been restored to her former glory.

08 **Walking the Kungsleden trail** Page **379** • Hiking the Kungsleden trail in northern Sweden is the best way to experience nature in the raw.

09 **South coast beaches** Pages **198** & **208** • Stretches of white sandy beaches and clear, warm waters are perfect places to relax in the summer sun.

10 **Smögen** Page **149** • Great bars and restaurants on the Smögen jetty – a classic place to chill for Sweden's young crowd.

12 Herring See *Food and drink* colour section • The quintessential Swedish dish best enjoyed with a cold beer or a shot of *akvavit*.

13 Gothenburg's Konstmuseum Page 133 • The Fürstenberg Galleries boast some of Sweden's finest late-nineteenth-century paintings.

11 Koster islands Page 152 • Unspoilt, car-free islands perfect for exploring by bicycle.

14 **Gammelstad, Luleå** Page **307** • Proudly listed on the UNESCO World Heritage list, Gammelstad is Sweden's largest church town.

16 **Orsa Grönklitt bear park cabin** Page **325** • Europe's biggest bear park is the perfect place to see Sweden's greatest predator in its natural habitat.

15 **Birka** Page **96** • Get to grips with Sweden's stirring Viking past on this Stockholm island

17 River-rafting, Värmland
Page **162** • Build your own raft and glide down the graceful Klarälven river taking in some of Sweden's scenery.

18 Bohuslän coast Page **143** •
Sweden's most enchanting stretch of coastline with smooth rocky outcrops pefect for sunbathing.

19 Jokkmokk winter market Page **368** • The Jokkmokk winter market sells everything from bearskins to candlesticks.

20 **Stockholm archipelago** Page **97** • No visit to Stockholm is complete without a trip to one of the 24,000 islands that make up the archipelago, at its most beautiful around the island of Gällnö.

21 **Visby** Page **259** • Explore the cobbled lanes and medieval churches of this ancient walled city.

22 **Inlandsbanan** Page 318 • A trip on the Inlandsbanan through northern Sweden is one of Europe's great railway journeys.

23 **Icehotel** Page 378 • One of the most unusual structures in Europe, the Icehotel is a masterpiece of snow and ice sculpture.

24 **Crossing the Arctic Circle** Page 367 • Don't leave Sweden without crossing the Arctic Circle, 66° 33' north.

25 **Gamla Stan, Stockholm** Page **69** • Gamla Stan in Stockholm is one of Europe's best-preserved medieval cities.

26 **Having a sauna** See *Swedish winter* **colour section** & page **44** • The perfect end to a long day, a Swedish sauna traditionally ends with a roll in the snow.

27 **Europe's last wilderness** Page **349** • Wild, rugged and remote, Sweden's far north is about as far from civilization as you can get.

28 **Midnight sun** Page **367** • From late May to mid-July the sun never sets in northern Sweden.

Basics

Basics

Getting there

Given the extremely long distances and journey times involved in reaching Sweden overland, flying will not only save you considerable amounts of time – but money, too. The main gateways are Stockholm and Gothenburg, as well as Copenhagen in neighbouring Denmark, just a twenty-minute train ride from Malmö.

Air fares are generally cheaper when booked as far in advance as possible. Midweek travel is less expensive than weekend departures.

Flights from North America

Five airlines operate **from the US** to Sweden: SAS (Scandinavian Airlines) from New York (Newark) and Chicago, Continental and Malaysia Airlines from New York (Newark), Delta from Atlanta and US Airways from Philadelphia. Less expensive tickets can sometimes be found on European airlines routing via their home hub, for example British Airways via London or Icelandair via Keflavík, the latter very often being a source of reasonable fares to Sweden. From **New York**, a return ticket midweek **fare** to Stockholm (8hr) will cost around US$900 in high season, US$740 in low season. From **Chicago** (9hr), prices are roughly US$150 more than from New York; from the **West Coast** (journey time at least 12hr), you'll pay around US$200–300 more.

There are no direct flights **from Canada**, so the best way of reaching Sweden is from **Toronto** via Helsinki with Finnair (summer only). Several other airlines also operate flights from Toronto and Vancouver to European cities, with connections on to Stockholm. **Fares** from Toronto (journey time 9–13hr depending on connections) are Can$1100–1300 in high season, Can$850–1050 in low season. From Vancouver (13–18hr), they're around Can$500 higher.

Flights from the UK and Ireland

Flights for Stockholm, Gothenburg and Copenhagen leave from several **UK airports**; in winter there are also direct flights from London Heathrow to Kiruna (available only through Discover the World; see p.29). **Flying to Sweden** with Ryanair is usually the cheapest way of getting there. Single fares can be a low as £10 (sometimes even less than that), though in peak season a return price of £50–100 is more realistic, depending on how early the booking is made. The other main **airline** serving Sweden is SAS whose return tickets start around £100. The Scandinavian low-cost operator, Sterling, is also an option; its fares are generally midway between those of Ryanair and SAS. **From Ireland**, there are only services from Dublin and fares are roughly the same as from the UK.

Flights from Australia, New Zealand and South Africa

There are no direct flights to Sweden from Australia, New Zealand or South Africa and by far the cheapest option is to find a discounted airfare to London and arrange a flight to Sweden from there. All air fares to London **from Australian east coast gateways** are similarly priced, with the cheapest deals via Asia starting around $1800. From Perth or Darwin, flights are around $100 less. **From New Zealand** reckon on NZ$2200 as a starting point from Auckland, NZ$250 more from Wellington. **From South Africa**, count on around ZAR6000 for the cheapest return from Cape Town.

Airlines and agents

bmi US ☎1-800/788-0555, UK ☎0870/607 0555 or 0870/607 0222, Republic of Ireland ☎01/283 0700, Australia ☎02/8644 1881, New Zealand ☎09/623 4293, South Africa ☎11/289 8111; ⊛www.flybmi.com.

British Airways US & Canada ☎ 1-800/AIRWAYS, UK ☎ 0844/493 0787, Republic of Ireland ☎ 1890/626 747, Australia ☎ 1300/767 177, New Zealand ☎ 09/966 9777, South Africa ☎ 114/418 600; ⓦ www.ba.com.

City Airline UK ☎ 0870/220 6835, ⓦ www.cityairline.com.

Continental Airlines US & Canada ☎ 1-800/523-3273, UK ☎ 0845/607 6760, Republic of Ireland ☎ 1890/925 252, Australia ☎ 1300/737 640, New Zealand ☎ 09/308 3350, International ☎ 1800/231 0856; ⓦ www.continental.com.

Delta US & Canada ☎ 1-800/221-1212, UK ☎ 0845/600 0950, Republic of Ireland ☎ 1850/882 031 or 01/407 3165, Australia ☎ 1300/302 849, New Zealand ☎ 09/9772232; ⓦ www.delta.com.

easyJet UK ☎ 0905/821 0905, ⓦ www.easyjet.com.

Finnair US ☎ 1-800/950-5000, UK ☎ 0870/241 4411, Republic of Ireland ☎ 01/844 6565, Australia ☎ 1300/798 188, South Africa ☎ 11/339 4865/9; ⓦ www.finnair.com.

Icelandair US & Canada ☎ 1-800/223-5500, UK ☎ 0870/787 4020; ⓦ www.icelandair.net.

Malaysia Airlines US ☎ 1-800/5529-264, UK ☎ 0871/423 9090, Republic of Ireland ☎ 01/6761 561, Australia ☎ 13 26 27, New Zealand ☎ 0800/777 747, South Africa ☎ 11-8809 614; ⓦ www.malaysiaairlines.com.

Ryanair UK ☎ 0871/246 0000, Republic of Ireland ☎ 0818/303 030; ⓦ www.ryanair.com.

SAS (Scandinavian Airlines) US & Canada ☎ 1-800/221-2350, UK ☎ 0871/521 2772, Republic of Ireland ☎ 01/844 5440, Australia ☎ 1300/727 707; ⓦ www.scandinavian.net.

Sterling UK ☎ 0870/787 8038, ⓦ www.sterlingticket.com.

US Airways US & Canada ☎ 1-800/428-4322, UK ☎ 0845/600 3300, Republic of Ireland ☎ 1890/925 065; ⓦ www.usair.com.

Booking flights online

The sites listed below are useful for online bookings though the best deals are usually found on the specific airline's own website.

ⓦ www.expedia.co.uk (in UK), ⓦ www.expedia.com (in US), ⓦ www.expedia.ca (in Canada)

ⓦ www.lastminute.com (in UK)

ⓦ www.opodo.co.uk (in UK)

ⓦ www.orbitz.com (in US)

ⓦ www.travelocity.co.uk (in UK), ⓦ www.travelocity.com (in US), ⓦ www.travelocity.ca (in Canada), ⓦ www.travelocity.co.nz (in New Zealand)

ⓦ www.travelonline.co.za (in South Africa)

ⓦ www.zuji.com.au (in Australia)

Fly less – stay longer! Travel and climate change

Climate change is perhaps the single biggest issue facing our planet. It is caused by a build-up in the atmosphere of carbon dioxide and other greenhouse gases, which are emitted by many sources – including planes. Already, **flights** account for three to four percent of human-induced global warming: that figure may sound small, but it is rising year on year and threatens to counteract the progress made by reducing greenhouse emissions in other areas.

Rough Guides regard travel as a **global benefit**, and feel strongly that the advantages to developing economies are important, as are the opportunities for greater contact and awareness among peoples. But we also believe in travelling responsibly, which includes giving thought to how often we fly and what we can do to redress any harm that our trips may create.

We can travel less or simply reduce the amount we travel by air (taking fewer trips and staying longer, or taking the train if there is one); we can avoid night flights (which are more damaging); and we can make the trips we do take "climate neutral" via a carbon offset scheme. **Offset schemes** run by **climatecare.org**, **carbonneutral.com** and others allow you to "neutralize" the greenhouse gases that you are responsible for releasing. Their websites have simple calculators that let you work out the impact of any flight – as does our own. Once that's done, you can pay to fund projects that will reduce future emissions by an equivalent amount. Please take the time to visit our website and make your trip climate neutral, or get a copy of the *Rough Guide to Climate Change* for more detail on the subject.

www.roughguides.com/climatechange

Sunvil
discovery

real **sweden**

• Flexible tailor-made holidays
• City breaks
• Canal cruises
• Character accommodation

call **020 8758 4722**

or visit **www.sunvil.co.uk**

ATOL 808   AITO   AITO TRUST

By train

Getting to Sweden by **train** is much more expensive. There are no through tickets and the total of all the tickets you'll need is likely to cost around £300–400). Hence, it's worth buying a rail pass instead; a global **InterRail** pass (from £205) or Eurail pass (from US$795) are the best options. **From London**, trains to Sweden go via Brussels, Cologne, Hamburg and Copenhagen. A typical journey will involve changing trains four or five times and takes around 24 hours.

Train information

Rail Europe US ☎1-888/382-7245, Canada ☎1-800/361-7245, UK ☎0844/848 4064, Australia ☎03/9642 8644, South Africa ☎11/628 2319; ⓦwww.raileurope.com.
Sweden Booking ☎0046/498 20 33 80, ⓦwww .swedenbooking.com. The general agent for Swedish rail tickets and passes.

Package holidays

Don't be put off by the idea of an inclusive **package**, as it can sometimes be the cheapest way of doing things, and a much easier way of reaching remote areas of northern Sweden in winter. City breaks are invariably less expensive than if you arrange the same trip independently. There are also an increasing number of operators (see below) offering **special-interest holidays** to Sweden, particularly Arctic expeditions.

Specialist operators

North America

Abercrombie & Kent ☎1-800/554 7016, ⓦwww.abercrombiekent.com. Top-end tours of Scandinavia by land and sea.
Contiki Tours ☎1-888/CONTIKI, ⓦwww .contiki.com. Budget tours of Scandinavia for 18- to 35-year-olds.
Passage Tours ☎1-800-548-5960, ⓦwww .passagetours.com. Specializes in Scandinavia. Offers escorted and unescorted tours and cheap weekend breaks to Sweden.
Scanam World Tours ☎1-800/545-2204, ⓦwww.scanamtours.com. Specializes in mid-range Scandinavian tours and cruises for groups and individuals. Also offers cheap weekend breaks.
Scantours ☎1-800/223-7226, ⓦwww .scantours.com. Major Scandinavian holiday specialists offering upmarket vacation packages and customized itineraries, including cruises and city sightseeing tours.

UK

Discover the World ☎01737/218800, ⓦwww.discover-the-world.co.uk. This long-established, professional and upmarket company know the country like the back of their hand. They are the only company selling a direct flight from London Heathrow to Kiruna and the world's largest tour operator to Icehotel in Jukkasjärvi.
Enjoy Sweden ☎01908/288 777, ⓦwww .enjoysweden.co.uk. The UK's only dedicated tour operator to Sweden, offering wilderness tours in Lappland, visits to the bear park in Dalarna and a variety of summer activities such as sailing along the Bohuslän coast.
Scantours ☎020/7554 3530, ⓦwww.scantours .co.uk. Mid-priced holidays to various regions of Sweden, including Gotland, cruises on the Göta canal, and trips out to lakes and mountains.
Taber Holidays ☎01274/875 199, ⓦwww .taberhols.co.uk. A wide range of Swedish holidays from this Yorkshire-based tour operator – everything from walking tours in the Stockholm archipelago to northern lights tours in the Torne Valley.

Viking Trails ☎46/8 25 25 29, ⓦwww.vikingtrails .co.uk. Sweden-based travel company specializing in mid-priced biking, hiking, kayaking, canoeing and sailing trips in the greater Stockholm area.

Australia

Bentours Australia ☎02/9241 1353, ⓦwww .bentours.com.au. The leading specialist to Sweden

offering air, ferry and rail tickets and a host of (often upmarket) escorted and independent tours throughout Scandinavia.

Explore Holidays Australia ☎02/9423 8080, ⓦwww.exploreholidays.com.au. Wholesaler of mid-priced trips to Sweden, including Stockholm mini-breaks.

Getting around

The public transport system in Sweden is one of Europe's most efficient. There's a comprehensive train network in the south of the country; in the north travelling by train isn't quite so easy, as many loss-making branch lines have been closed. However, it's still possible to reach the main towns in the north by train, and where train services no longer exist, buses generally cover the same routes.

Look out for city and regional **discount cards**, which often give free use of local transport, free museum entry and other discounts.

By train

Other than flying, **train** travel is the quickest and easiest way of covering Sweden's vast

SWEDISH
RAIL NETWORK

- - - Rail lines
——— Inlandsbanan

Riksgränsen
Abisko
Kiruna
Gällivare
Jokkmokk
Murjek
Boden
Arvidsjaur Älvsbyn
Sorsele
Luleå
Jörn
Storuman
Bastuträsk
Vilhelmina
Dorotea
Vännäs
Umeå
Strömsund
Mellansel
Due to open
Storlien
Långsele
Örnsköldsvik
Östersund
Sollefteå
Ullånger
Bräcke
Härnösand
Åsarna
Ånge
Sundsvall
Sveg
Hudiksvall
Bollnäs
Söderhamn
Orsa
Mora
Rättvik
Malung
Leksand
Gävle
Falun
Borlänge
Torsby
Uppsala
Västerås
Karlstad
Örebro
STOCKHOLM
Kristinehamn
Eskilstuna
Nynäshamn
Strömstad
Mariestad
Nyköping
Norrköping
Skövde
Linköping
Borås
Jönköping
Gothenburg
Visby
Nässjö
Västervik
Gotland
Varberg
Värnamo
Falkenberg
Växjö
LATVIA
Halmstad
Laholm
Öland
Båstad
Kalmar
BALTIC
Ängelholm
Hässleholm
SEA
Helsingborg
Karlskrona
Karlshamn
Kristianstad
LITHUANIA
Malmö
Lund
Simrishamn
DENMARK
Trelleborg
Ystad

INLANDSBANAN

NORWAY

FINLAND

GULF OF
BOTHNIA

ESTONIA

Arctic Circle

0   200km

expanses. The service is generally excellent and prices are not that high. At holiday times (see p.49) and between mid-June and mid-August, trains are often heavily booked; it's worth making reservations (often compulsory) as far in advance as you can. The national train operator is SJ (☎0771/75 75 75, ⓦwww.sj.se) which runs an extensive network across the whole of Sweden. For train and connecting bus information visit ⓦwww.resplus.se. Many station names in Sweden carry the letter C after the name of the city, for example: Stockholm C; this is a "railspeak" abbreviation of Central.

Tickets

Individual train tickets are rarely cost-effective and visitors doing a lot of touring by train may be better off buying a **train pass** such as InterRail. A one-country InterRail pass for Sweden allows up to eight days' travel in one month and starts at £149. Full details can be found at ⓦwww.interrailnet.com. If you do need to buy an individual ticket, it's worth knowing that the sooner you buy it the cheaper it will be. The cheapest tickets, limited in number, cost 99kr on all SJ routes and are available up to ninety days before departure. **Reserved seats** on Swedish trains are not marked, so although it may appear that a seat is free it may not be so.

The Inlandsbanan

If you're in Sweden for any length of time, travelling at least part of the summer-only **Inlandsbanan** (Inland Railway; ☎0771/53 53 53, ⓦwww.grandnordic.se), which runs through central and northern Sweden, is a must. The route takes in some of the country's most unspoilt terrain – kilometre after kilometre of forests, and several lakes (the train usually stops at one or two of them for passengers to take a quick dip), and offers a chance to see real off-the-beaten-track Sweden. For more information, see p.318. The length of the operating season varies from year to year; check the website for the latest details.

By bus

Although bus travel is a little less expensive than going by train, **long-distance buses** are generally less frequent, and so much slower that they aren't a good choice for long journeys. Most long-distance buses are operated by one of two companies, Swebus (☎0200/218 218, ⓦwww.swebusexpress.se) and Säfflebussen (☎0771/15 15 15, ⓦwww.safflebussen.se). Departures on Friday and Sunday cost more than on other days; a standard single ticket from Stockholm to Gothenburg, for example, costs from 299kr, but around 100kr more on Friday and Sunday.

Regional buses are particularly important in the north, where they carry mail to isolated

Journey times and distances

	Gävle	Gothenburg	Halmstad	Helsingborg	Karlstad
Gävle	-	7.40	8.30	9.20	5.00
Gothenburg	545	-	2.10	3.00	3.40
Halmstad	6.37	145	-	1.10	5.40
Helsingborg	717	229	87	-	6.30
Karlstad	325	249	405	485	-
Kiruna	1029	1636	1729	1809	1417
Luleå	761	1306	1399	1479	1087
Malmö	768	280	138	66	536
Örebro	262	282	377	453	108
Östersund	400	870	961	1040	638
Stockholm	172	471	492	572	300
Sundsvall	214	759	852	932	540
Umeå	490	1034	1128	1208	815

areas. Several companies operate daily services, and their fares are broadly similar to one another's (usually 250–350kr for a 1–2hr journey). Major routes are listed in the "Travel Details" section at the end of each chapter, and you can pick up a comprehensive timetable at any bus terminal.

By plane

The main players on the Swedish domestic airline market are: SAS (⊕0770/727 727, ⓦwww.sas.se); Skyways (⊕0771/95 95 00, ⓦwww.skyways.se); Norwegian (⊕0770/45 77 00, ⓦwww.norwegian.se) and Nextjet (⊕08/639 8538, ⓦwww.nextjet.se). When booked well in advance, one-way fares on most routes begin at 450kr.

By ferries and boats

In a country with such an extensive coastline and many lakes, it's only natural that domestic ferry services in Sweden are many and varied. The main route is between Visby, on the Baltic island of Gotland, and Nynäshamn, on the mainland near Stockholm and Oskarshamn. High-speed catamarans as well as regular ferries operate on both routes. Departures are very popular in summer and you should try to book ahead.

Many of the various archipelagos off the coast – particularly the Stockholm archipelago with its 24,000 islands – have ferry services which link up the main islands in the

group; see p.97 for more details. There's also an extensive archipelago off Luleå which is worth visiting; details of boat services there are given on p.309.

By car

As far as road conditions go, **driving** in Sweden is a dream. Traffic jams are rare (in fact in the north of the country yours will often be the only car on the road), roads are well maintained and motorways, where they exist, are toll-free. The only real **hazards** are reindeer (in the north) and elk (everywhere), which wander onto the road without warning. It's difficult enough to see them at dusk, and when it's completely dark all you'll see is two red eyes as the animal leaps out in front of your car. If you hit an elk or deer, not only will you know about it (they're as big as a horse), you're bound by law to report it to the police.

To drive in Sweden you'll need your own full license; an international driving license isn't required. **Speed limits** are 110kph on motorways, 90kph on dual carriageways and many other roads, 50kph in built-up areas, and 70kph elsewhere if unsigned; for cars towing caravans, the limit is 80kph. Fines for speeding are levied on the spot. You must drive with your headlights on 24 hours a day. Studded tyres for driving on snow and ice are allowed between October 1 and April 30, longer if there's still snow on

Kiruna	Luleå	Malmö	Örebro	Östersund	Stockholm	Sundsvall	Umeå
13.50	10.00	9.50	4.00	5.10	2.20	3.00	6.30
21.20	17.30	3.30	3.50	12.00	5.50	10.30	14.00
22.10	18.20	1.40	5.20	13.20	6.20	11.20	14.50
23.00	19.20	0.50	6.00	14.10	7.10	12.10	15.40
18.40	14.50	7.00	1.30	9.00	4.00	7.40	11.20
-	4.00	23.30	17.40	12.20	16.00	11.00	7.30
344	-	19.30	13.50	8.40	12.10	7.10	3.40
1860	1529	-	6.40	14.40	7.40	12.40	16.10
1354	1023	514	-	8.20	2.30	6.50	10.20
998	667	1091	578	-	7.30	2.30	5.00
1263	933	622	191	572	-	5.10	8.40
877	547	982	477	188	386	-	340
602	271	1258	752	396	661	-	275

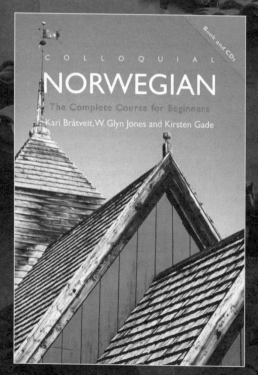

the ground; when in use they must be fitted to all wheels.

Be extremely attentive when it comes to **parking**. Under Swedish law you aren't allowed to park within 10m of a road junction, whether it be a tiny residential cul-de-sac or a major intersection. Parking is also prohibited within 10m of a pedestrian crossing, and in bus lanes and loading zones. In city centres, parking isn't permitted on one night each week to allow for cleaning (see the rectangular yellow street signs with days and times in Swedish, below the "no stopping" sign on every street). In winter the same applies to allow for snow clearance.

Swedish **drink-driving laws** are among the strictest in Europe, and random breath tests are commonplace. Basically, you can't have even one beer and still be under the limit; the blood alcohol level is 0.2 percent. If you're found to be over the limit you'll lose the right to drive in Sweden, face a fine (often) and a prison sentence (not infrequently).

The cost of **petrol** (*bensin*) is in line with the European average (about 15kr per litre). At filling stations, you either pay at the pump with a credit card or inside at the till – choose the pumps marked "Kassa" for this.

Car rental agencies

Avis US ☎ 1-800/331-1212, Canada ☎ 1-800/879-2847, UK ☎ 0844/581 8181, Republic of Ireland ☎ 021/428 1111, Australia ☎ 13 63 33 or 02/9353 9000, New Zealand ☎ 09/526 2847 or 0800/655 111, South Africa ☎ 11/923 3660; ⓦ www.avis.com.
Budget US ☎ 1-800/527-0700, Canada ☎ 1-800/268-8900, UK ☎ 0870/156 5656,

Australia ☎ 1300/362 848, New Zealand ☎ 0800/283 438; ⓦ www.budget.com.
Europcar US & Canada ☎ 1-877/940 6900, UK ☎ 0845/758 5375, Republic of Ireland ☎ 01/614 2800, Australia ☎ 1300/131 390; ⓦ www .europcar.com.
Hertz US & Canada ☎ 1-800/654-3131, UK ☎ 0870/040 9000, Republic of Ireland ☎ 01/870 5777, Australia ☎ 13 30 39, New Zealand, ☎ 0800/654 321, South Africa ☎ 21/935 4800; ⓦ www.hertz.com.
Holiday Autos US & Canada ☎ 0866/392 9288, UK ☎ 0870/400 4482, Republic of Ireland ☎ 01/872 9366, Australia ☎ 1300/554 432, New Zealand ☎ 0800/144 040, South Africa ☎ 11/234 0597; ⓦ www.holidayautos.co.uk. Part of the LastMinute.com group.

Cycling

Some parts of the country were made for **cycling**: Stockholm, the southern provinces, and Gotland in particular are ideal for a leisurely bike ride. Many towns are best explored by bike, and tourist offices, campsites and youth hostels often rent them out from around 150kr a day. There are a lot of cycle paths in towns, which are often shared with pedestrians. Sweden has a large number of signposted **cycle trails**; one of the most popular is the Sweden Trail (Sverigeleden), which stretches all the way from Helsingborg in the southwest to Karesuando on the Finnish border, taking in many of the country's main sights. Svenska Cyckelsällskapet (Swedish Cycling Association), Torneågatan 10, S-164 79 Kista, Stockholm (☎ 08/751 62 04, ⓦ www.svenska -cykelsallskapet.se) has more information.

Accommodation

Finding somewhere cheap to stay in Sweden isn't difficult. There's an extensive network of youth hostels (of an exceptionally high standard) and campsites, while hotels and guesthouses are common in towns and cities. Self-catering accommodation is generally restricted to youth hostels and campsites, where cabins are often equipped with kitchens.

Accommodation prices in Sweden vary according to the day of the week or the season. Pricing falls into two main categories: the higher price is charged for stays from Sunday to Thursday outside of the summer peak (generally mid-June to mid-Aug); the lower rate is charged on Fridays and Saturdays. This lower rate is also applied every day during the summer peak. Remember though that this rule does not apply across the board and there are some places that actually charge higher prices in summer in line with most other countries; this is usually the case with hotels on the west coast. When we give two price codes in the guide, the higher price is the non-summer weekday price, the lower one the summer and weekend price. Single rooms, where available, usually cost between sixty and eighty percent of the price.

Youth hostels

Youth hostels in Sweden (*vandrarhem*) turn up in the unlikeliest of places. There

are over three hundred of them dotted across the country, in converted lighthouses, old castles and prisons, historic country manors, schoolrooms and even on boats. Quite simply, they offer some of the best accommodation in the country. Forget any preconceptions about youth hostelling: in Sweden, large dormitories are few, and rooms usually sleep four to six people.

The majority of hostels are run by STF (**Svenska Turistföreningen**; ☏08/463 22 70, ⓦ www.svenskaturistforeningen.se). Throughout the guide, we have given the non-members' rate for dorm beds and a price code for double rooms. The members' reduction is 50kr a night per person. To stay at an STF hostel it's best to have your own sheets, although they can be rented for around 50kr. You are allowed to use a sleeping bag provided you put a sheet between it and the mattress to keep the latter clean.

Accommodation prices

The hotels listed in the guide have been graded according to the following price codes, based on the cost of the least expensive double room available. When two codes are given, the first one is for double rooms during high season and the second one applies for the rest of the year. For more details and information on hostel prices, see opposite.

❶ 500kr and under. A private double room in a hostel.

❷ 501–700kr. A double room in a simple B&B-type establishment.

❸ 701–900kr. A room in an upmarket hotel at the weekend, or a room in a mid-range hotel from Monday to Friday – both generally outside Stockholm.

❹ 901–1200kr. A room in an upmarket hotel at the weekend, or a room in a mid-range hotel from Monday to Friday – both within Stockholm.

❺ 1201–1500kr. A room in a smart hotel in Stockholm, from Monday to Friday.

❻ 1501–2000kr. A luxury room in a top-end Stockholm hotel.

❼ 2001kr and over. The most expensive hotels in Stockholm and some of the leading ski resorts.

Apart from the STF hostels there are a number of independently run hostels, usually charging similar prices; we've mentioned the most useful in the text, and tourist offices will have details of any other local independent hostels.

Fell stations and cabins

Fell stations (*fjällstationer*) provide top-notch, hostel-like accommodation along mountain hiking routes; prices vary and are given in the guide. They're usually better equipped than the average youth hostel: rooms are private rather than dorms and each fell station has a sauna, a shop and a kitchen.

Mountain cabins (*fjällstugor*), of which there are around ninety, are often no more than simple huts out in the wilds and are wonderful for getting away from it all. Run by the STF, they generally are often located at convenient intervals along popular walking routes. Both fell stations and mountain cabins allow you to use a sleeping bag without a sheet underneath.

Hotels and guesthouses

Hotels and **guesthouses** (usually family-run bed and breakfast establishments) needn't be expensive, and although there's little chance of finding any kind of room for under 500kr a night, you can often find good-value hotel rooms in summer, especially between mid-June and mid-August, when business people who would otherwise fill the hotels during the week are on holiday. If you turn up at some of the larger hotels after 6pm in summer without a booking, you may find they drop their prices even lower than their usual discount rate. The only parts of the country where summer discounts don't apply are in some of the popular holiday destinations in southern Sweden such as Båstad, where prices can actually go up in summer. Nearly all hotels include a huge self-service buffet breakfast in the price, which will keep you going for much of the day.

Campsites, cabins and self-catering

Practically every town or village has at least one **campsite**, and they are generally of a high standard. To pitch a tent at any of them you'll need the Camping Card Scandinavia, which costs 125kr and is issued at the first site you visit; contact the Swedish Camping Site Owners' Association (ⓦwww.camping.se). It costs 100–200kr for two people to pitch a tent at an official campsite. Most sites are open from June to September, some – including around two hundred in winter sport areas – throughout the year. For details on camping rough, see p.43.

Many campsites also boast **cabins**, each of which is usually equipped with bunk beds, a kitchen and utensils, but not sheets. Self-catering in cabins is a good way to keep costs down. Cabins start around 500kr per night for a two-bed number. As usual, it's wise to ring ahead to secure one. Sweden also has a whole series of cabins for rent in spots other than campsites, often in picturesque locations such as in the middle of the forest, by a lakeshore or on the coast. For information and to make a booking, contact the local tourist office.

Food and drink

There's no escaping the fact that eating and drinking is going to take up a large slice of your budget in Sweden – though no more so than in any other northern European country. Note that although tipping in Swedish restaurants is not expected, it is customary to round the bill up to the nearest 20kr or so.

Swedish food – based largely on fish, meat and potatoes, and very varied in preparation – is always tasty and well presented and, at its best, is delicious. Unusual specialities generally come from the north of the country and include reindeer, elk meat and wild berries, while herring and salmon come in so many different guises that fish fiends will always be content. Vegetarians too should have no problems, with plenty of non-meat options available, especially in the bigger towns; elsewhere the choice may be limited to pizzas and salads. Alcoholic drinks are available in most establishments, with lager-type beers and imported wines providing no surprises; the local spirit *akvavit*, however, is worth trying at least once. It comes in dozens of weird and wonderful flavours, from lemon to cumin-and-dill.

Eating well and **eating cheaply** needn't be mutually exclusive aims in Sweden. The best strategy is to fuel up on breakfast and lunch, both of which offer good-value options. A good way to keep costs down when eating out is to resist the temptation to order a starter – throughout Sweden portions are generous and most main dishes are large enough to fill even the emptiest stomach. **Breakfast** is often included in the cost of a night's accommodation, and most restaurants have **lunchtime specials** (*Dagens Rätt*) that time and again are the best-value meals you'll find.

Food

Sweden's various **salmon** dishes are among the very best the cuisine has to offer – they're divine either warm or cold, and a mainstay of any Swedish *smorgasbord* worth its salt. **Herring** is mostly served marinated, but don't let that put you off as it tastes surprisingly good. **Sauces** feature prominently in Swedish cooking, often flavoured with dill or parsley; alternatively there are many delicious creamy concoctions too.

Wild berries appear in many dishes, especially the lingonberry, which is something like a cranberry, and makes a good accompaniment to Swedish meatballs, a combination praised by many a Swede as a delicacy of the country. You'll also be able to taste orange-coloured sweet cloudberries, which grow in the marshes of Lapland and are delicious with ice cream.

Breakfast

Breakfast (*frukost*) is almost invariably a help-yourself buffet in the best Swedish tradition; you can go up to the serving table as many times as you like and eat until you're fit to explode. Youth hostels charge around 50kr for breakfast; if you stay in a hotel, it'll be included in the price of your accommodation.

Coffee is something the Swedes excel at, and is always freshly brewed, strong and delicious. A coffee costs 20–25kr and the price will often buy you more than one cup. For coffee, head for the local *konditori*, a coffee and cake shop of the first order. You should try at least one *konditori* while you're in Sweden; coffee and cake will typically set you back 70–80kr. Swedes are not tea drinkers and tea isn't generally up to much.

Snacks and light meals

For **snacks** and **light meals** you're really looking at the delights dished up by the *gatukök* (street kitchen) or *korvstånd* (sausage stall). A **gatukök** is often no more than a hole in the wall – generally conspicuous by the snaking queue and gaggle of teenagers it attracts – serving sausages, burgers, chips, soft drinks and sometimes pizza slices or chicken pieces. Chips with a sausage or burger generally comes to around 75kr. The **korvstånd** usually limits itself to sausages (hotdogs are usually around 25kr), though some have chips and burgers as well.

Self-catering

For the cheapest eating it's hard to beat the supermarkets and market stalls. Of the supermarket chains, ICA and CoopKonsum have the biggest range of produce but most supermarkets in Sweden are small local affairs selling just the basics and a few other bits and pieces. If it's choice you're after, and you're in one of the bigger towns and cities, you should try the food hall in the department store Åhléns, which has a much wider selection than the average supermarket. Alternatively, head for the indoor or outdoor markets, which often have fresher produce than the supermarkets, and at lower prices.

Fish is always excellent value, especially salmon. Pork and beef aren't too bad either, but chicken is slightly more expensive. Sweden is a country rich in **cheeses**, all of which are reasonably good value and make great sandwich fillers; the range runs from stronger ripened cheeses such as Västerbotten and Lagrad Svecia to milder types like Grevé and Herrgårdsost. Prästost, a medium-strong cheese akin to a mature Cheddar, is also a particular favourite here.

There are also loads of different yoghurts and varieties of *filmjölk* to choose from, which are all very healthy and inexpensive. Fruit and vegetables are expensive but not exorbitantly so. Pasta, rice, potatoes, eggs, onions and bacon are relatively inexpensive.

Restaurants

Swedes eat their main meal of the day at lunchtime; do likewise and you'll save lots of cash. You don't have to restrict yourself to eating out at lunchtime; many restaurants also offer special deals in the evening, and even if they don't you're bound to find something on their menu that will fit your pocket. Remember that Swedish portions are generous and that, accordingly, you may not have room for a starter as well.

An evening meal in a mid-range restaurant will cost you 150–250kr without alcohol. A three-course meal naturally costs more; expect to pay something in the region of 350–600kr, and add around 55kr for a strong beer, or 250kr for an average bottle of wine. Dishes usually have some sort of salad accompaniment and come with bread. Bear in mind that Swedes eat early; lunch will be served from 11am, dinner from 6pm. It's always a good idea to **book a table** to avoid disappointment, particularly during the summer months of June to August when tables can be at a premium. **Smoking** is not allowed in restaurant or pubs.

At lunchtime, go for the **Dagens Rätt** or set dish of the day, which costs between 65kr and 85kr and is one way to sample Swedish *husmanskost* (home-cooking). You'll also find various pizza and pasta dishes on offer in Italian restaurants, and basic meals in Thai and Chinese restaurants (sometimes a buffet-type spread). Most cafés also offer some sort of *Dagens Rätt* but their standard of cooking is often not as good as in restaurants.

While you're in Sweden you should sample a **smorgasbord**, available in the larger restaurants and in hotels for around 350kr – expensive, but good for a blowout. If you're a traditionalist you should start with *akvavit*, drink beer throughout and finish with coffee. Coffee will be included in the price, but alcohol won't.

Many of the **traditional Swedish dishes** on offer in most restaurants are listed on p.428. **Prices** given in the guide are for a main course dish in the evening unless otherwise stated.

Drinks

Drinking in Sweden can be expensive, but there are ways of softening the blow. Either forgo bars and buy your booze in the state-run liquor shops, the **Systembolaget**, or seek out the happy hours (usually called After Work in Swedish) offered at many pubs and bars. The timing of happy hours is usually set to coincide with people finishing work so keep your eyes peeled for signs either in bar windows or on the pavement outside. Drinking outdoors is frowned upon and you're not allowed to take alcohol onto a train or the street for your own consumption (drinking alcohol purchased on trains or pavement cafés is permitted).

The Systembolaget

In any Swedish town or city, the **Systembolaget** is the only shop that sells wine, strong beer and spirits. It's run by the state, is only open office hours (generally Mon–Wed & Fri 10am–6pm, Thurs till 7pm, Sat 10am–2pm), and until quite recently kept all its alcohol on display in locked glass cabinets. Quite unthinkable just a couple of years ago in alcohol-obsessed Sweden, a number of stores have now gone self-service, giving buyers the chance to actually fondle the hard stuff before purchasing.

The system is designed to make Swedes think about how much they drink, and the price of hard liquor is accordingly high – 70cl of whisky costs about 250kr; a bottle of wine is around 65kr. However, debate over the future of the system rumbles on and Sweden is coming under increasing pressure from the European Commission to liberalize the sale of alcohol and open up the market to free competition.

What to drink

Beer is the most common alcoholic drink in Sweden, although it can be expensive. Whether you buy beer in a café, restaurant or a bar, it'll cost roughly the same, on average 45–55kr for half a litre of lager-type brew.

Unless you specify a type, the beer you get in a bar will be *starköl* (also referred to as *storstark*), the strongest Class IV beer with an alcohol content of 5.6 percent by volume. Outside bars and restaurants, Class IV is only available in the Systembolaget, where it's around a third of the price you'll pay in a bar. *Mellanöl*, a Class III brew, costs slightly less than a *starköl* because it contains less alcohol; once again, it's not available in the shops, only at the Systembolaget and in

bars and restaurants. Class II or *folköl* is very similar in strength to *mellanöl* though contains slightly less alcohol. Cheapest of all is the Class I *lättöl*, the beer served with *Dagens Rätt* at lunchtime. It's palatable with food, though it contains virtually no alcohol; Pripps and Mariestad are the two main brands. *Folköl* and *lättöl* are the only beers available in supermarkets.

Wine in restaurants is pricey; a bottle will set you back something like 250kr, and a glass around 45kr. It's also worth trying the **akvavit** or schnapps, which is made from potatoes, served ice-cold in tiny shots and washed down with beer. If you're in Sweden at Christmas, don't go home without having sampled **glögg**: mulled red wine with cloves, cinnamon, sugar and more than a shot of *akvavit*.

Where to drink

You'll find pubs and bars in all towns and some villages. In Stockholm and the larger cities the trend is towards British and Irish-style pubs although the atmosphere inside never quite lives up to the original. Elsewhere – particularly in the north of the country – you'll come across more down-to-earth drinking dens. Drink is no cheaper here, and the clientele is predominantly male and usually drunk. They can be intimidating places for outsiders, especially in small provincial villages, where drinking seems to be the main way of coping with eight months of winter.

In the summer, **café-bars** spill out onto the pavement, which is a more suitable environment for children and handy if all you want is a coffee. When you can't find a bar in an out-of-the-way place, head for the local hotel – but be prepared to pay for the privilege. Bar **opening hours** are elastic and drinking-up time is generally some time after midnight. Since June 2005, **smoking** has been banned in all of Sweden's restaurants, bars, cafés and nightclubs.

The media

Stockholm is the centre of the Swedish media world. All national radio and television stations are broadcast from the capital, and the country's four main daily newspapers are also based there. However, every region or city also has its own newspaper, for example Göteborgsposten in Gothenburg or Norrbottens tidning in Lapland. In remote parts of the country, particularly in the north, these local media really come into their own; in winter, people depend on them for accurate and up-to-date information on everything from local political machinations to snow depths in the vicinity.

Newspapers

Assuming you don't read Swedish, you can keep in touch with world events by buying **English-language newspapers** in the major towns and cities, sometimes on the day of issue, more usually the day after. Municipal libraries across the country often have good selections of foreign broadsheets but they can sometimes be a little out of date. The main Swedish papers are *Dagens Nyheter* and *Svenska Dagbladet* and the tabloids, *Expressen* and *Aftonbladet*. You may also come across *Metro*, a free newspaper available at train and tube stations, which has lots of "what's on" information; its listings are in Swedish only, but will be comprehensible enough if you don't speak the language.

TV and radio

Swedish TV won't take up much space on your postcards home. There are two state channels, SVT1 and SVT2, operated by Sveriges Television (SVT), worth watching if only for the wooden in-vision continuity announcers. TV3 is a pretty dire cable station,

and Sweden's only terrestrial commercial station is the somewhat downmarket TV4. TV5 is a cheesy cable channel available in most hotels that seems to show nothing but a string of American sitcoms. On all the channels, foreign programmes are in their original language, which makes for easy viewing; SVT1 and SVT2 show a lot of excellent BBC documentaries and comedy programmes.

On the **radio**, you'll find pop and rock music on P3 and classical music on P2 – all operated by state broadcaster, Sveriges Radio (Swedish Radio; ⓦwww.sr.se for frequencies). There are also an increasing number of commercial stations in towns and cities across Sweden. You'll find **news in English** courtesy of Radio Sweden (Swedish Radio's international arm; ⓦwww.sr.se/rs). Their English-language current affairs programmes about Sweden can be heard weekdays in Stockholm on 89.6MHz FM and are also available as podcasts. The BBC World Service (ⓦwww.bbc.co.uk /worldservice) can also be heard on 6195, 9410 and 12095kHz short wave.

Festivals

Swedish festivals are for the most part organized around the seasons. Most celebrations are lively events, as Swedes are great party people – once the beer begins to flow. The highlight of the year is the Midsummer festival, when the whole country gets involved, and wild parties last well into the early hours. The date of Midsummer's Day varies from year to year but is the Saturday closest to the actual summer solstice.

Major festivals and events

Valborgsmässoafton (April 30). Walpurgis Night. One of the most important festivals in Sweden, heralding the beginning of spring with bonfires and songs.

Labour Day (May 1). A none-too-thrilling marching day for the workers' parties.

Swedish National Day (June 6). In existence since 1983, though a bit of a damp squib even though it's now a public holiday; worthy speeches are delivered in the evening and the king often puts in an appearance at Skansen in Stockholm.

Midsummer (June 21–23). The biggest and best celebration anywhere in Sweden, with festivities centred around the maypole, an old fertility symbol, which is erected at popular gatherings across the country. The maypole is raised in June because it's often still snowing in northern Sweden in May. There's much dancing and drinking into the night – and severe hangovers the next morning.

Crayfish parties (throughout Aug). Held in the Aug moonlight across the country to say a wistful farewell to the short Swedish summer. Competitions are often held to establish the season's best and tastiest crayfish.

Surströmming (late Aug). In coastal areas of northern Sweden, particularly along the High Coast, parties are held at which people eat *surströmming* (see p.293), a foul-smelling fermented Baltic herring which is something of an acquired taste – though a quintessentially Swedish experience.

Eel parties (Sept). Held in the southern province of Skåne, often along a sandy beach. This region is known for its smokehouses and the smoked eel they produce.

St Martin's Eve (Nov 10). The people of Skåne get together to eat goose – the traditional symbol of the province.

Nobel Prize Day (Dec 10). Official ceremonies are held in Stockholm as the winners of the annual Nobel prizes are awarded. Although this is not a public festival, it is a key date in the Swedish calender.

St Lucia's Day (Dec 13). Led by a girl with a crown of candles, this is a procession of children who sing songs as they bring light into the darkest month. For many Swedes, this is a welcome highlight during the ever-shortening days of Dec and a chance to look forward to Christmas and the longer nights of January and onwards.

Sports and outdoor activities

Sweden is a wonderful place if you love the great outdoors, with fantastic hiking, fishing and, of course, winter-sports opportunities. Best of all you won't find the countryside overcrowded – there's plenty of space to get away from it all, especially in the north. You'll also find Swedish lakes and beaches refreshingly relaxed and always clean.

Skiing and winter pursuits

During the winter months, **skiing** – a sport which began in Scandinavia – is incredibly popular, and in the north of Sweden people even ski to work. The most popular ski resorts are Åre, Idre, Sälen and Riksgränsen; these and many others are packed out during the snow season when prices hit the roof. If you do intend to come to ski, it is essential to book accommodation well in advance or take a package holiday.

In northern Sweden you can ski from the end of October well into April, and at Riksgränsen in Lappland you can ski under the midnight sun from late May to the end of June when the snow finally melts. Riksgränsen is also the place to head for if you're into **snowboarding**. Kiruna is a good bet as a base for other winter pursuits, whether you fancy **dog sledding**, snowmobile riding, a night in the world's biggest igloo

(*Icehotel* at Jukkasjärvi, see p.378), or **ice fishing**. Bear in mind, though, that the area around Kiruna is one of the coldest in the country, and temperatures in the surrounding mountains can sink to -50°C during a really cold snap.

Hiking

Sweden's Right of Public Access, *Allemansrätten*, means you can **walk** freely right across the entire country (see box below for more details). A network of more than forty long-distance footpaths covers the whole of Sweden, with overnight accommodation available in mountain stations and huts. The most popular route is the **Kungsleden**, the King's Route, which can get rather busy in July at times, but is still enjoyable. The path stretches for 460km between Abisko and Hemavan, passing through some spectacular landscape in the wild and isolated northwest of the country; the trail also takes in Sweden's

The countryside – some ground rules

In Sweden you're entitled by law to walk, jog, camp, cycle, ride or ski on other people's land, provided you don't cause damage to crops, forest plantations or fences; this is the centuries-old **Allemansrätten** or Everyman's Right. It also allows you to pick wild berries, mushrooms and wild flowers (except protected species), fish and swim, where there are no nearby houses. But this right brings with it certain obligations: you shouldn't get close to houses or walk across gardens or on land under seed or crops; pitch a tent on land used for farming; camp close to houses without asking permission; cut down trees or bushes; or break branches or strip the bark off trees. Nor are you allowed to drive off-road (look out for signs saying "*Ej motorfordon*", no motor vehicles, or "*Enskild väg*", private road); light a fire if there's a risk of it spreading; or disturb wildlife.

It's common sense to be wary of frightening reindeer herds in the north of Sweden; if they scatter it can mean several extra days' hard work for the herders. Also avoid tramping over the lichen – the staple diet of reindeer – covering stretches of moorland. As you might expect, any kind of hunting is forbidden without a permit. National parks have special regulations which are posted on huts and at entrances.

highest mountain, Kebnekaise (2078m). For more information, see p.383.

Canoeing and rafting

There are almost one hundred thousand lakes and thousands of kilometres of rivers and canals in Sweden. Needless to say, on summer afternoons taking to a **canoe** is a popular pastime; two excellent areas for this are Strömsund (see p.351) and the Stockholm archipelago (see p.97). Another excellent alternative is to get hold of a **raft** and glide down the Klarälven river in Värmland (see p.162); one of the companies offering these tours even allows you to build your own raft before departure.

Saunas and swimming in lakes

Most public swimming pools and hotels, even in the smallest towns, will have a **sauna**. They're generally electric and extra steam is created by tossing water onto the hot elements. The temperature inside ranges from 70°C to 120°C. Traditional wood-burning saunas are often found in the countryside and give off a wonderful smell. Public saunas are always single-sex and nude; you'll often see signs forbidding the wearing of swimming costumes, as these would collect your sweat and allow it to soak into the wooden benches inside. Take a paper towel to sit on; these are often available in the changing rooms. It's common practice to take a cold shower afterwards or, in the winter, to roll in the snow to cool off. Otherwise in the countryside, people often take a dip in a nearby lake. As Sweden boasts around 100,000 **lakes** and one of the lowest population densities in Europe, you needn't worry about a spot of skinny-dipping.

Golf and fishing

Golf has become incredibly popular in Sweden in recent years and there are now over three hundred courses in the country. Most are concentrated in the south and are playable year-round, but it's also possible to play north of the Arctic Circle in the light of the midnight sun. For more information, contact the Swedish Golf Federation (Klevinge Strand 20, S-182 57 Danderyd; ☏08/622 15 00, ⓦwww.golf.se).

Sweden is an ideal country for **anglers**. Salmon are regularly caught from opposite the Parliament building right in the centre of Stockholm, because the water is so clean and fishing there is free. Fishing is also free along the coastline and in the larger lakes, including Vänern, Vättern (particularly good for salmon and char) and Mälaren. In the north of the country, Tärnaby (see p.357) offers top-class mountain fishing for char and trout; and nearby Sorsele (see p.358) is good for fly-fishing for trout, char and grayling. For salmon fishing, the river running up through the Torne Valley (see p.348) is one of the best places. In most areas you need a permit for freshwater fishing, so ask at local tourist offices.

Culture and etiquette

In many ways, Sweden is a model country: society is liberal, people are prosperous and the social and economic position of women is one of the most advanced in the world. As a result, most visitors find Sweden an easy country to visit. Swedes, in general, are an efficient nation – planning meticulously and booking ahead to ensure they get what they want, when they want. Accordingly, spontaneity and flexibility are not high on the agenda in Sweden, which can sometimes create a mistaken impression of rudeness to the outsider. Honesty and straight-talking are two highly-cherished sides of the Swedish character; a promise in Sweden is just that. Haggling over prices is not the done thing. On meeting, friends of both sexes usually hug, rather than kiss, each other. In more formal situations, people shake hands whilst saying their name.

In line with the liberal reputation Sweden gained during the 1970s as a result of countless soft porn films, nudity is widely accepted. In changing rooms, people are uninhibited about their bodies and don't feel the need to cover up with a towel. Nude lake swimming and sunbathing are common practice across the country. If other people are around, show them consideration, but you're unlikely to meet opposition.

Travel essentials

Costs

Although often considered the most expensive country in Europe, Sweden is in fact cheaper than all the other Nordic countries and no more expensive than, say, France or Germany. If you don't mind having your main meal of the day at lunchtime – like the Swedes – or having picnics under the midnight sun with goodies bought from the supermarket, travelling by the efficient public transport system and going easy on the nightlife, you'll find Sweden isn't the financial drain you might expect.

Accommodation is good value: youth hostels are of a very high standard and charge around 200kr per night for non-members; hotels offer special low prices to tourists in summer; and campsites are plentiful and cheap. **Admission prices** to museums and galleries are also low or nonexistent. At most places there are also reductions of around thirty to fifty percent for children and senior citizens, and younger children often get in for free.

Restaurant eating can work out a good deal if you stick to the *Dagens Rätt* (dish of the day), served at lunchtime from Monday to Friday in most restaurants and cafés, and generally consisting of salad, a main meal (often a choice between two or three dishes), bread, a drink and a coffee for 65–85kr all-in. What will cost you more in Sweden than elsewhere in mainland Europe is **alcohol**: a strong beer in a bar costs 45–55kr, making a beer only slightly more expensive than in London; a bottle of wine in a restaurant will set you back around 250kr.

Put all this together and you'll find you can exist – camping, self-catering, hitching, no drinking – on a fairly low budget (around

£25/$45/€30 a day), though it will be a pretty miserable experience and only sustainable for a limited period of time. Stay in hostels, eat the *Dagens Rätt* at lunchtime, get out and see the sights and drink the odd beer or two and you'll be looking at doubling your expenditure. Once you start having restaurant meals with wine, taking a few taxis, enjoying coffees and cakes and staying in hotel accommodation, you'll probably spend considerably more (£70–85/US$130–160).

Crime and personal safety

Sweden is in general a **safe** country to visit, and this extends to women travelling alone. However, it would be foolish to assume that Stockholm and the bigger cities are free of petty crime, fuelled as elsewhere by a growing number of drug addicts and alcoholics after easy money. Keep tabs on your cash and passport (and don't leave anything valuable in your car when you park it) and you should have little reason to visit the police. If you do, you'll find them courteous, concerned and, perhaps most importantly, usually able to speak English.

As for offences *you* might commit, a big no-no is drinking alcohol in public places (which includes trains). Being drunk in the streets can get you arrested, and drunk driving is treated especially rigorously (see p.35). Drugs offences, too, meet with the same harsh attitude that prevails throughout the majority of Europe.

Although **racism** is not a major problem in Sweden, it would be wrong to say it doesn't exist. It stems mainly from a small but vocal neo-Nazi movement, VAM (their full name translates as "White Aryan Resistance"), who occasionally daub slogans like "*Behålla Sverige Svenskt*" (Keep Sweden Swedish) on walls in towns and cities and on the Stockholm metro. Although there have been several racist murders and many attacks on dark-skinned foreigners over the past couple of years, it's still the exception rather than the rule. Keep your eyes and ears open and avoid trouble, especially on Friday and Saturday nights when drink can fuel these prejudices.

Electricity

The supply is 220V, although appliances requiring 240V will work perfectly well. Plugs have two round pins. Remember that if you're staying in a cottage out in the wilds, electricity may not be available.

Entry requirements

European Union, American, Canadian, Australian and New Zealand citizens need only a valid **passport** to enter Sweden, and can stay for up to three months. Once the three months are up, EU nationals can apply for a **resident's permit** (uppehåll-stillstånd) to cover longer visits. For further information on where to obtain the permits, contact the Swedish embassy in your home country.

Swedish embassies abroad

Australia 5 Turrana St, Yarralumla, ACT 2600 Canberra ☎02/6270 2700, ⓦwww .swedenabroad.com.
Canada 377 Dalhousie St, Ottawa, ON K1N 9N8 ☎613/244-8220, ⓦwww.swedenabroad.com.
Republic of Ireland 13–17 Dawson St, Dublin 2 ☎01/671 5822, ⓦwww.swedenabroad.com.
UK 11 Montagu Place, London W1H 2AL ☎020/7917 6400, ⓦwww.swedenabroad.com.
US 2900 K St NW, Washington, DC 20007 ☎202/467-2600, ⓦwww.swedenabroad.com.

Gay and lesbian travellers

Swedish attitudes to **gay men** and **lesbians** are remarkably liberal – on a legal level at least – when compared to most other Western countries, with both the government and the law proudly geared towards the promotion of gay rights and equality (the official age of sexual consent is 15 whether you are gay or straight).

In 1995, Sweden introduced its registered-partnership law, despite unanimous opposition in parliament from the right-wing Moderates and Christian Democrats. Ten years on, in July 2005, the Swedish parliament granted lesbians the right to artificial insemination.

Paradoxically, the acceptance of gays and lesbians in society as a whole can at best be described as sporadic, and in fact homosexuality was regarded as a psychological disease in Sweden until 1979. Outside the cities, and particularly in the north of the country where the lumberjack mentality rules supreme, there can still be widespread embarrassment and unease whenever the subject is mentioned in public.

There are very few gay bars and clubs in Sweden though gay community life in general is supported by the state-sponsored Riksförbundet för Sexuellt Likaberättigande, or RFSL (National Association for Sexual Equality; Sveavägen 57–59, PO Box 350, 101 26 Stockholm; ☎08/501 62 900, 🖥www .rfsl.se), founded in 1950 as one of the first gay rights organizations in the world. The website 🖥www.qx.se has useful information about gay and lesbian happenings in Sweden, and listings of bars and discos where they do exist.

Health

EU nationals can take advantage of Sweden's **health services** under the same terms as residents of the country. For this you'll need a European Health Insurance Card, available in the UK through post offices and Department for Work and Pensions offices. Citizens of non-EU countries will be charged for all medical services, although US visitors will find that medical treatment is far less expensive than they are accustomed to at home. Even so it is advisable to take out travel insurance (see opposite). Note that you need a doctor's prescription even to get minor painkillers in Sweden, so bring your own supplies.

There's no **local doctor** system in Sweden. Instead, go to the nearest hospital with your passport (and Health Insurance Card, if applicable) and they'll treat you; the casualty department is called *Akutmottagning* or

Vårdcentral. The fee for staying in hospital overnight depends on the care you need.

For **dental treatment**, foreign citizens generally have to pay in full for treatment. You can spot a dental surgery by looking out for the sign "Tandläkare" or "Folktandvården". An emergency dental service is available in most major towns and cities out of hours – look in the windows of the local pharmacy for contact telephone numbers.

Insurance

Even though EU health-care rights apply in Sweden, you'd do well to take out an insurance policy before travelling to cover against theft, loss and illness or injury. Before paying for a new policy, however, it's worth checking whether you are already covered: some all-risks home insurance policies may cover your possessions when overseas, and many private medical schemes include cover when abroad.

A typical policy usually provides cover for the loss of baggage, tickets and – up to a certain limit – cash or cheques, as well as cancellation or curtailment of your journey. Most of them exclude so-called **dangerous sports** unless an extra premium is paid: in Sweden this can mean skiing, whitewater rafting, windsurfing and trekking, though probably not kayaking or hiking.

Many policies can be chopped and changed to exclude coverage you don't need – for example, sickness and accident benefits can often be excluded or included at will. If you do take **medical coverage**, ascertain whether benefits will be paid as treatment proceeds or only after return home, and whether there is a 24-hour medical emergency number. If you need to make a claim, you should keep receipts for

---

Rough Guides travel insurance

Rough Guides has teamed up with Columbus Direct to offer you tailor-made travel insurance. Products include a low-cost backpacker option for long stays; a short break option for city getaways; a typical holiday package option; and others. There are also annual multi-trip policies for those who travel regularly. Different sports and activities (trekking, skiing, etc) can usually be included.

See our website (🖥www.roughguides.com /shop) or call UK ☎0870/033 9988, Australia ☎1300/669 999, New Zealand ☎0800/559 911, or worldwide ☎+44 870/890 2843.

medicines and medical treatment, and in the event you have anything stolen, you must obtain an official statement from the police.

Internet

Internet cafés are surprisingly thin on the ground in Sweden, and only really exist in the larger cities. However, there are sometimes terminals operated by the internet provider, Sidewalk Express, in train stations, Pressbyrån newsagents and 7-Eleven food stores, access is from 19kr per hour. As an alternative, try the local tourist office or **library**.

Mail

The Swedish **post office** is a thing of the past. Postal services are instead to be found in local supermarkets and filling stations; look for the blue postal sign outside (a yellow horn and crown on a blue background) which are open longer hours than the traditional post office used to be. You can buy **stamps** (*frimärken*) at most newspaper kiosks, tobacconists, hotels, bookshops and stationers' shops, as well as at supermarkets and petrol stations. Note that **Swedish addresses** are always written with the number after the street name. In multi-floor buildings, the ground floor is always counted as the first floor.

Maps

The most useful map of **Stockholm** can only be bought in the city itself: the Stockholm Map (Stockholmskartan) is available from any office of the local transport authority, Storstockholms Lokaltrafik. This map has the advantage of showing all bus and metro routes in the capital, and includes a street index. For maps of the whole country, go for Hallwag's Sverige/Sweden (1:8,000,000). There are also regional maps produced by Kartförlaget (1:250,00 and 1:400,000), which are excellent.

If you're staying in one area for a long time, or are **hiking** or walking, you'll probably need something more detailed still, with a minimum scale of 1:400,000 – though preferably much larger for serious trekking. The Fjällkartan series covering the northwestern mountains are good; these maps, produced by Lantmäteriverket, at a scale of 1:100,000, are unfortunately rather expensive, both in Sweden and abroad. The best and cheapest place to **buy** maps of Sweden is online at ⓦwww.kartbutiken.se.

Money

The Swedish **currency** is the *krona* (kr; plural *kronor*). It comes in coins of 1kr, 5kr and 10kr, and notes of 20kr, 50kr, 100kr, 500kr and 1000kr. There's no limit on the amount of Swedish and foreign currency you can take into Sweden. At the time of going to print, the exchange rate was around 11.50kr to £1, 6kr to US$1 and 9kr to €1.

The cheapest and easiest way of accessing money whilst you're in Sweden is from ATMs with your **debit card**. There will be a flat transaction fee for withdrawals, which is usually quite small, but no interest payments.

Credit cards are a very handy backup source of funds, and can be used either in ATMs or over the counter. Mastercard, Visa, American Express and Diners Card are accepted just about everywhere for goods or cash.

Traveller's cheques are a safe and simple way of carrying your money, although there can be a hefty commission when you come to change them. Some places charge per cheque, others per transaction, so it's common sense to take large denominations with you, or to try to change as much as you feel you can handle in one go.

Banks (Mon–Wed & Fri 9.30am–3pm, Thurs 9.30am–4/5.30pm; in some cities, banks may stay open to 5.30pm every weekday) have standard exchange rates but commissions can vary enormously. The best place to change money is at the yellow **Forex** offices (ⓦwww.forex.se), which offer more *kronor* for your currency. You'll find Forex branches in Sweden's main cities as well as at major airports.

Mosquitoes and ticks

Mosquitoes are common throughout Sweden and it's sensible to protect yourself against bites. Although Swedish mosquitoes don't carry diseases, they can torment your every waking moment from the end of June, when the warmer weather causes them to hatch, until around mid-August. They are found in their densest concentrations in the north of the country, where there's swampy ground, and are most active early in the morning and in the late afternoon/early evening; the best way to protect yourself is to wear thick clothing (though not dark colours, which attract them) and apply mosquito **repellent** to any exposed skin. When camping, make a smoky fire of (damp) peat if feasible, as mosquitoes don't like smoke. Don't scratch mosquito bites (*myggbett*); treat them instead with Salubrin or Alsolsprit creams, or something similar, available from local chemists.

Ticks (*fästingar*) are fast becoming a big problem in Sweden due to a succession of milder winters. The country has one of the highest rates of tick-borne encephalitis in Europe, a disease which causes fever and nausea, and in a third of cases spreads to the brain; it causes lasting damage in forty percent of people infected. A third of all ticks also carry the bacteria which cause Lyme disease, an illness which can lead to inflammation of the brain and nerves. The insects, which burrow painlessly into the skin, are prevalent predominantly on the east coast and islands and are active from March to November. Their preferred habitat is warm, slightly moist undergrowth, bushes and meadows with long grass. In addition to vaccination, sprays, roll-ons and creams are available in local pharmacies; eating large amounts of garlic is also effective in keeping ticks away.

Opening hours and public holidays

Shop **opening hours** are generally from 9.30am to 6pm on weekdays and 9.30am to 4pm on Saturdays. In larger towns, department stores remain open until 7pm or longer on weekdays, and some are also open on Sundays between noon and 4pm. Museums and galleries operate various opening hours, but are generally closed on Mondays outside the summer months. Banks, offices and shops are closed on public holidays (see below). They usually also close or have reduced opening hours on the eve of the holiday.

Phones

In the land of Ericsson, **mobile phones** work virtually everywhere and almost every Swede has at least one. Consequently,

Public holidays in Sweden

New Year's Day	January 1
Epiphany	January 6
Good Friday	March/April
Easter Sunday	March/April
Easter Monday	March/April
Labour Day	May 1
Ascension Day	Fortieth day after Easter Sunday
Whit Sunday	Seventh Sunday after Easter
National Day	June 6
Midsummer's Eve	Always on a Friday
Midsummer's Day	Saturday closest to the summer solstice
All Saints' Day	Closest Saturday to November 1
Christmas Eve	December 24
Christmas Day	December 25
Boxing Day	December 26
New Year's Eve	December 31

public payphones have all but disappeared. Mobile coverage in the south of the country is virtually a hundred percent. In the north there is good coverage along the main roads and the coast, and even the most remote village in Norrland has some kind of network coverage; with international roaming this means you can use your phone virtually wherever you happen to be. In order to avoid roaming charges, you can buy a Swedish SIM card from any newsagent (*pressbyrån*) for around 150kr (ask for a *startpaket*).

Time

Sweden conforms to **Central European Time** (CET), which is always one hour ahead of Britain and Ireland. For most of the year Sweden is six hours ahead of New York; nine hours behind Sydney and eleven hours behind Auckland. Clocks go forward by one hour in late March and back one hour in late October (on the same days as in Britain and Ireland).

Tourist information

All towns – and some villages – have a **tourist office** from where you can pick up free town plans and information, brochures,

Making international calls to and from Sweden

To **call Sweden from abroad**, dial your country's international access code followed by 46 for Sweden, then dial the area code (without its first 0) and the number. To **call abroad from Sweden**, dial 00 followed by the required country code (see below), then the area code (without its first 0) and the number.

Useful country codes

Sweden ☏46
Britain ☏44
Ireland ☏353
US ☏1

Australia ☏61
Canada ☏1
New Zealand ☏64

timetables and other literature. Most offices have internet access. During the summer they're open until late evening; out of season it's more usual for them to keep shop hours, and in the winter they're normally closed at weekends. You'll find full details of individual offices throughout the guide.

Travellers with disabilities

Sweden is, in many ways, a model of awareness in terms of **disabled travel**, with assistance forthcoming from virtually all Swedes, if needed. Public transport throughout the country is also geared up for people with disabilities. Wheelchair access is usually available on trains (InterCity trains have wide aisles and large toilets, and often have special carriages with hydraulic lifts), and there are lifts down to the platforms at almost every Stockholm metro station. In every part of the country there'll be some taxis in the form of minivans specially converted for disabled use.

Accommodation suitable for people with disabilities is often available: most hotels have specially adapted rooms, while some chalet villages have cabins with wheelchair access. Any building with three or more storeys must, by law, have a lift installed, while all public buildings are legally required to be accessible to people with disabilities and have automatic doors. Generally, hotels, hostels, museums and other public places are very willing to cater to those with disabilities. For more information, contact De Handikappades Riksförbund, (Katrinebergsvägen 6, Box 47305, S-100 74, Stockholm; ☏08/685 80 000, ⊛www.dhr.se).

Travelling with children

Sweden is an exemplary country when it comes to **travelling with children**. Most hotels and youth hostels have family rooms and both men's and women's toilets – including those on trains – usually offer baby-changing areas. Always ask for children's discounts as many activities, particularly during the summer months, are geared towards families.

Guide

Guide

1

Stockholm and around

CHAPTER 1 # Highlights

✳ **Gamla Stan, Stockholm**
Wander through the narrow streets and alleyways of the Old Town for a taste of medieval Stockholm. See p.69

✳ **Vasa museum, Stockholm**
Fascinating seventeenth-century warship raised from Stockholm harbour and painstakingly restored to her former glory. See p.80

✳ **Drottningholm, Stockholm**
Take a boat trip to the Rococo-inspired home of the Swedish royal family, beautifully set on the shores of Lake Mälaren. See p.95

✳ **Birka, Lake Mälaren** Get to grips with Viking history in Sweden's oldest town. See p.96

✳ **Gällnö island, Stockholm archipelago** Walk through deep green forest and swim from the shores of an island edged by purple reeds and carpets of wildflowers. See p.100

✳ **Utter Inn, Västerås**
A night spent underwater in this mini-oil-rig-cum-hotel in Lake Mälaren is one of Sweden's most unusual accommodation choices. See p.105

✳ **Island beaches, Västerås**
The chain of islands in Lake Mälaren offer the perfect opportunity to chill out and work on your all-over tan. See p.108

✳ **Gamla Uppsala** Royal burial mounds and a beautiful medieval church add mystery to this ancient pagan settlement. See p.114

▲ Stockhom Old Town

Stockholm and around

Without a shadow of a doubt, **Stockholm** is one of the most beautiful cities in Europe. Built on no fewer than fourteen **islands**, where the fresh water of Lake Mälaren meets the brackish Baltic Sea, clean air and open space are in plentiful supply here. One-third of the area within the city limits is made up of water, while another third comprises parks and woodlands, including the world's first urban national park, where you can swim and fish just minutes from the city centre. Broad boulevards lined with elegant buildings are reflected in the deep blue water, and rows of painted wooden houseboats bob gently alongside the cobbled waterfront. Yet Stockholm is also a hi-tech metropolis, with futuristic skyscrapers and a bustling commercial heart. The modern centre is a consumer's heaven, full of stylish shops and a myriad of bars and restaurants – of which Stockholm has more per capita than most other European capitals. Quality of life is important to Stockholmers – a seat on the T-bana and elbow room on even the most crowded shopping street are regarded as virtual birthrights. As a result, the capital is one of Europe's saner cities and a delightful place in which to spend time.

Move away from Stockholm, and it's easy to appreciate its unique geographical location. Water surrounds the city and – although you can travel by train and bus – it's worth making the effort to ply the serene waters of Lake Mälaren or the Stockholm archipelago by boat. The **archipelago** is made up of a staggering 24,000 islands, islets and rocks, as the Swedish mainland slowly splinters into the Baltic Sea; it's a summer paradise for holidaying city dwellers, as the islands are easily and cheaply accessible from the centre. A boat trip inland along Lake Mälaren is also a must, either to the Viking island of **Birka**, where you can see the remains of Sweden's most important medieval trading centre and a dizzying array of ancient finds, or to **Drottningholm**, the seventeenth-century royal residence situated right on the lakeside. Another easy excursion on Lake Mälaren leads to the impressive castle of **Gripsholm** at Mariefred; also within reach on a day-trip are the ancient Swedish capital and medieval university town of **Uppsala** and one of the country's oldest settlements, **Sigtuna**, complete with its rune stones and ruined churches; there are frequent train services to both from Stockholm's Central Station, as well as the occasional boat. Lakeside **Västerås**, with its fascinating mix of the new and old – including a sixth-century royal burial mound – is also worth exploration and is easily reached by regular trains from Stockholm.

Stockholm

"It is not a city at all. It is ridiculous to think of itself as a city. It is simply a rather large village, set in the middle of some forest and some lakes. You wonder what it thinks it is doing there, looking so important."

Ingmar Bergman

At times, **STOCKHOLM**'s status as Sweden's most contemporary, forward-looking city seems at odds with the almost pastoral feel of its wide open spaces and ageing monumental buildings. First impressions of the city can be of a distant and unwelcoming place, and it comes as no surprise that many provincial Swedes regard it with disdain. But don't be put off: on a Friday or Saturday night you'll see its other side, when Stockholmers let their hair down, and the night air is abuzz with conversation.

Gamla Stan (Swedish for "Old Town") was the site of the original settlement of Stockholm, first mentioned in ancient documents as a town in 1252. Today the area is an atmospheric mixture of buildings surrounded on all sides by a latticework of medieval lanes and alleyways. Close by is the tiny island of **Skeppsholmen**; conveniently, the island is also the site of the two most central youth hostels (see p.65). To the north of the Old Town, the district of **Norrmalm** swaps tradition for a thoroughly contemporary feel: you'll find shopping malls, huge department stores and conspicuous, showy wealth. Central Station and the lively **central park**, Kungsträdgården, are located here too. Most of Stockholm's **museums and galleries** are spread across this area and two others: to the east, the more residential **Östermalm**, with its mix of grand avenues and smart houses; and to the southeast, the green park island of **Djurgården**. Here the extraordinary seventeenth-century warship, **Vasa**, rescued and preserved after sinking in Stockholm harbour, and **Skansen**, the oldest and best of Europe's open-air museums, both receive loud and deserved acclaim. The island of **Södermalm**, or plain "Söder" (as its right-on inhabitants call it), was traditionally the working-class area of Stockholm, but today is known for its cool bars and restaurants and lively street life. Indeed, any visit to Stockholm is not complete without sampling one of the growing number of eateries in this neighbourhood – an ideal place to watch, and join, the city's population at play. To the west of the centre, the island of **Kungsholmen** is fast becoming a rival to its southern neighbour for trendy restaurants and drinking establishments.

Arrival and information

All Scandinavian Airlines flights and most international and domestic services arrive at **Arlanda airport** (☎08/797 60 00, ⓦwww.arlanda.se/en), an inconvenient 45km north of Stockholm. High-speed trains operate all day long every fifteen minutes from the two dedicated **Arlanda Express** stations beneath the airport (Arlanda Norra for Terminal 5, Arlanda Södra for the other terminals), the trip to Central Station in Stockholm taking just twenty minutes (220kr one-way, 420kr return valid one month, 240kr one-way for two adults valid Sat & Sun all year and daily mid-June to Aug; ⓦwww.arlandaexpress.com). Trains to Uppsala and Gävle leave from the Arlanda Central station which is also beneath the airport. **Airport buses**, Flygbussarna, call at all terminals and run all day to Stockholm's long-distance bus station, Cityterminalen, every ten to fifteen minutes (40min; 99kr single, 179kr return; ⓦwww.flygbussarna.se). **Taxis** from the airport into town (30–40min) should cost around 495kr and are an affordable alternative for a group. If you pick up a **rental car** and drive into central Stockholm you will be subject to the new **congestion charge**; cameras register vehicles automatically and your credit card will be debited accordingly. The charge is 10–20kr and is payable Monday to Friday 6.30am to 6.29pm. Foreign registered vehicles are exempt.

Some domestic flights and all flights with Brussels Airlines arrive at the more central **Bromma airport**, which is connected to Cityterminalen by Flygbussarna – buses run in connection with flight arrivals and departures (20min; 69kr single, 130kr return). Ryanair's Stockholm flights arrive at **Skavsta airport**, 100km to the south of the capital close to the town of Nyköping, and at **Västerås**, 100km to the west of Stockholm; Skavsta and Västerås buses operate in connection with flight arrival and departure times (both routes 1hr 20min; 150kr one-way, 249kr return).

By **train**, you'll arrive at **Stockholm Central Station** (the station is also known as Stockholm C, which is an abbreviation of "Central" in railspeak throughout Sweden), a cavernous structure on Vasagatan in the central Norrmalm district. Inside, there are several Forex money exchange offices and cash machines. All branches of the **Tunnelbana** ("T-bana"), Stockholm's efficient metro system, meet at T-Centralen, the T-bana station directly below the main station.

By **bus**, your arrival point will be the huge glass structure known as **Cityterminalen** (☎08/762 59 97), a hi-tech terminal adjacent to Central Station

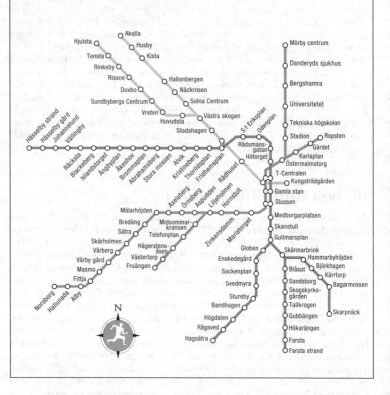

which handles all bus services. There's also a Forex office here, and you can get to the northern end of Central Station's main hall using a series of escalators and walkways.

Information

At the start of any visit to Stockholm it's worth heading for Sverigehuset (Sweden House) at Hamngatan 27 in Norrmalm, home to the city's **tourist office** (Mon–Fri 9am–7pm, Sat 10am–5pm, Sun 10am–4pm; ☎08/508 285 08, ⓦwww .stockholmtown.com) which hands out fistfuls of free brochures, and carries *What's On*, a useful free listings and entertainments guide. You'll also be able to buy the Stockholm Card (see opposite), which can be invaluable if you're planning to visit more than a couple of museums.

From the tourist office it's a ten-minute walk south through Kungsträdgården and then over Strömbron bridge to Slottsbacken 10 in Gamla Stan, where the ⚜ **Sweden Bookshop** (Mon–Fri 10am–6pm, Sat 11am–4pm; ☎08/453 78 00, ⓦwww.swedenbookshop.com) run by the **Swedish Institute** (ⓦwww.si.se) has an unsurpassed stock of English-language books on Sweden and Sweden-related gifts and souvenirs.

City transport

At first, Stockholm can be a confusing place, winding and twisting its way across islands, over water and through parkland. To get your bearings, the best bet is to **walk**: it takes about half an hour to cross central Stockholm on foot, from west to east or north to south. Sooner or later though, you'll probably want to use some form of **transport**. While routes are easy enough to master, it's best to avoid paying per trip on the city's transport system which can prove very expensive, and make use instead of the **passes** and **discount cards** available (see box below).

Storstockholms Lokaltrafik (**SL**; ⓦwww.sl.se) operates a comprehensive system of buses and underground trains, which extends well out of the city centre. Their main information office is the **SL-Center** at Sergels Torg (Mon–Fri 7am–6.30pm, Sat & Sun 10am–5pm), just by the entrance to T-Centralen. It stocks timetables for the city's bus and T-bana systems and archipelago boats. Up-to-date information on the public transport system in English can also be obtained by phoning ⓣ08/600 10 00.

The Tunnelbana

The quickest and most useful form of transport is the **Tunnelbana** (T-bana; ⓦwww.sl.se), Stockholm's metro system, which comprises three main lines (red, green and blue) and a smattering of branches. It's the swiftest way to travel between Norrmalm and Södermalm, via Gamla Stan, and it's also handy for trips out into the suburbs – to ferry docks and distant youth hostels, campsites and museums. Station entrances are marked with a blue letter "T" on a white background, and displays above each platform give the final destination of each train. From Sunday to Thursday trains operate from around 5am until around midnight, but on Fridays and Saturdays – as well as the evening before a public holiday – there are services all through the night (roughly every 30–40min). The Tunnelbana is something of an artistic experience too, as many of the stations look like Functionalist sculptures:

Travelcards and tickets

Travelcards represent excellent value for money. There are several to choose from: a **one-day travelcard** (valid 24 hours: 100kr); a **3-day** travelcard (200kr), a **7-day travelcard** (260kr) and a **30-day travelcard** (690kr). All cover unlimited travel by bus and T-bana plus travel on ferries to Djurgården. When you buy them you must specify whether you want your card to be valid from the exact time of purchase, or alternatively, whether you want it for use on a specific date. In this case the card is valid from midnight of your chosen day until 4.30am of the following night. Discounts apply for under-19s and over-65s. Travelcards cannot be bought at T-bana stations. Instead get them from Pressbyrå newsagents or the SL-Center.

Alternatively, you can buy a strip of sixteen reduced-price SL **ticket coupons** known as *rabattkuponger* (180kr) from bus drivers or at any T-bana station. These are valid on the T-bana and the buses; you'll have to stamp at least two for each journey.

The Stockholm Card

If you're planning to visit several museums, the best pass to have is the **Stockholm Card**, which gives unlimited travel on the T-bana, city buses and the Djurgården ferry, as well as free entry to around 75 museums and free sightseeing boat trips. Cards are sold undated and are stamped on first use, after which they're valid for 24, 48 or 72 hours (330/460/580kr respectively). The card is available from the tourist office or at ⓦwww.stockholmtown.com/stockholmcard.

T-Centralen is like a huge papier-mâché cave, and Kungsträdgården is littered with statues, spotlights and fountains. Other stations to look out for are Akalla (which displays ceramic images of daily life), Rissne (with maps of the world, each region labelled with key historical events and their dates) and Midsommarkransen (featuring massive wooden sculptures of garlands of flowers).

Buses and ferries

Buses are often less direct than the metro because of the city's layout – route maps are available from the SL-Center (see p.59). Tickets are bought from the driver; board buses at the front and get off at the back or in the middle. **Night buses** replace the T-bana after midnight, except on Friday and Saturday (and the night before a public holiday), when it runs all night. Incidentally, in an effort to cut pollution, Stockholm's buses have been running on ethanol since the 1980s. They're also pushchair- and pram-friendly; a special area halfway down the bus is set aside for these.

Ferries provide access to the sprawling archipelago, and sail from outside the *Grand Hotel* on Strömkajen (see p.97 for more details); they also link some of the central islands: Djurgården is connected with Nybroplan in Norrmalm (a small square behind the *Grand*) via the Vasa museum and Skeppsholmen (early May to late Aug only), and with Skeppsbron in Gamla Stan (year-round). **Cruises** on Lake Mälaren leave from outside Stadshuset on Kungsholmen, and **city boat tours** leave from outside the *Grand Hotel*, as well as from round the corner on Nybroplan. **Travelcards** are valid for ferries linking the central islands, which run roughly every fifteen minutes (7.30am–7pm) though not for longer trips out into the archipelago. Tickets for these boats cost up to 120kr, depending on how far you are going. They can be bought from the offices of the ferry company that operates the majority of sailings into the archipelago, Waxholmsbolaget (Ⓦwww .waxholmsbolaget.se), on Strömkajen in front of the *Grand Hotel*, or on the boats themselves. If you are intending to spend a week or so exploring Stockholm's different islands, the **archipelago pass** (*båtluffarkort*; see p.97) allows five days' unlimited travel for 340kr (plus a refundable 40kr deposit).

Bikes, taxis and cars

Bike rental is centrally available from *Djurgårdsbrons Sjöcafé* at Galärvarvsvägen 2 (Ⓣ08/660 57 57), just over the bridge that leads to Djurgården, or from Servicedepån-Cykelstallet at Scheelegatan 15 on Kungsholmen (Ⓣ08/651 00 66, Ⓦwww.cykelstallet.se); reckon on paying 250kr per day. There are several **taxi ranks** around the city (including one outside Central Station); you can also ring one of the three main operators: Taxi Stockholm (Ⓣ08/15 00 00, Ⓦwww .taxistockholm.se), Taxi Kurir (Ⓣ08/30 00 00, Ⓦwww.taxikurir.se) or Taxi 020 (Ⓣ020/20 20 20, Ⓦwww.taxi020.se). The meter will show around 45kr when you get in and will then race upwards at an alarming speed: 84kr for every 10km during the day (124kr per 10km on Fri & Sat nights and public holidays). A trip across the city centre will cost 100–200kr. If **driving**, be extremely careful when **parking**: see p.35 for advice. For **car rental**, see "Listings" on p.94 and be aware of the congestion charge in central Stockholm (see p.57).

Canoes and kayaks

The dozens of **canoes** and **kayaks** you see being paddled around Stockholm are testimony to the fact that one of the best ways to see the city is from the water. *Djurgårdsbrons Sjöcafé*, at Galärvarvsvägen 2 (Ⓣ08/660 57 57), is the best place in town to rent boats. It costs 300kr to rent a canoe per day, or 75kr per hour.

For canoes in the archipelago, try Skärgårdens Kanotcenter at Vegabacken 22 on Vaxholm (℡08/541 377 90, ⓦwww.kanotcenter.com), or ask locally on the other islands – corner shops often have a couple of canoes or boats for rent.

Accommodation

Stockholm has plenty of **accommodation** to suit every taste and pocket, from elegant upmarket hotels with waterfront views to youth hostels in unusual places – two are on boats and another is in a former prison. From mid-June to mid-August it is always a good idea to book your accommodation in advance, either directly with the hotel or hostel or through ⓦwww.stockholmtown .com/hotels.

Hotels and pensions

Summer in Stockholm means a buyer's market for **hotel** rooms as business travel declines; double rooms can cost as little as 545kr. The cheapest choices on the whole are found to the north of Cityterminalen in the streets to the west of Adolf Fredriks kyrka. Don't rule out the more expensive places, however: there are some attractive weekend and summer prices that make a spot of luxury nearer the waterfront a little more affordable. All of the following establishments include breakfast in the price, unless otherwise stated.

Greater Stockholm

The following hotels are marked on the map on pp.62–63.

Bema Upplandsgatan 13 ℡08/23 26 75, ⓦwww.hotelbema.se. Bus #47 or #65 from Central Station. A 10min walk from the station, this small pension-style hotel has twelve en-suite rooms with beechwood furniture and modern Swedish decor. ❹/❸

Best Western Time Vanadisvägen 12, Norrmalm ℡08/545 473 00, ⓦwww.timehotel.se. Odenplan T-bana. Newly built hotel with around 150 contemporary, brightly decorated airy rooms featuring wooden floors and French balconies. Rooms on the top floor have their own terrace. ❻/❹

Diplomat Strandvägen 7C ℡08/459 68 00, ⓦwww .diplomathotel.com. Östermalmstorg T-bana or buses #47 or #69. Owned by the Malmström family for four generations, this is one of the city's top hotels, offering individually decorated rooms with wonderful views over Stockholm's inner harbour. Although the suites in this Art Nouveau town house don't come cheap, they represent much better value than the cheaper double rooms at the *Grand*. ❼/❼

Hellsten Luntmakargatan 68, Norrmalm ℡08/661 86 00, ⓦwww.hellsten.se. Rådmansgatan T-bana. Dating from 1898, the original bourgeois family apartments in this building have been lovingly restored; some still have their tile stoves and antiques whilst others have been given an Asian-style make-over. ❻/❻

Micro Tegnérlunden 8, Norrmalm ℡08/545 455 69, ⓦwww.hotelmicro.se. Rådmansgatan T-bana. Windowless cabin-style basement rooms with bunk beds and shared facilities, all decked out in bright marine colours, give this new budget hotel a strangely maritime feel. Basic, maybe, but certainly a great money-saving option. ❸/❷

Pensionat Oden City Kammakargatan 62, Norrmalm ℡08/796 96 00, ⓦwww.pensionat.nu. Bus #47 or #65 from Central Station. One of the three Pensionat Oden guesthouses where nineteenth-century charm is the key. All fifteen rooms enjoy high ceilings and a sense of spaciousness and elegance unusual for such a central location. Reception though is not always staffed and personal attention can be a bit hit and miss. ❸

Pensionat Oden Vasastan Odengatan 38, Norrmalm ℡08/796 96 00, ⓦwww.pensionat.nu. Rådmansgatan T-bana. Second-floor hotel in a good central location, offering just seven elegant rooms where the decor is 1940–50s retro. Excellent value for money, though personal service could be better. ❸

Rex Luntmakargatan 73, Norrmalm ℡08/16 00 40, ⓦwww.rexhotel.se. Rådmansgatan T-bana. The original pine floors and sweeping staircase from 1866 have been lovingly restored to create a sense of style and elegance throughout this tasteful hotel,

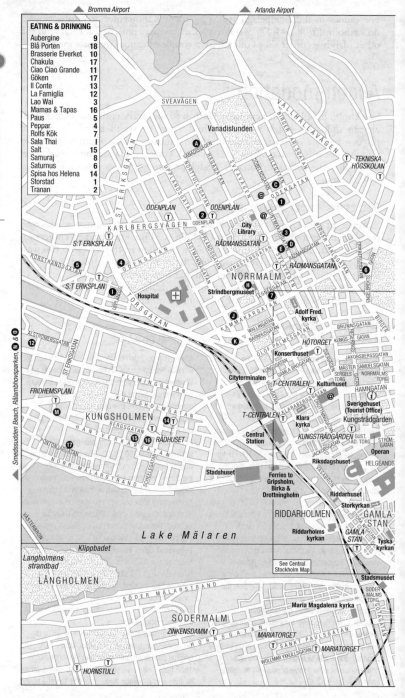

EATING & DRINKING

Aubergine	9
Blå Porten	18
Brasserie Elverket	10
Chakula	17
Ciao Ciao Grande	11
Göken	17
Il Conte	13
La Famiglia	12
Lao Wai	3
Mamas & Tapas	16
Paus	5
Peppar	4
Rolfs Kök	7
Sala Thai	1
Salt	15
Samuraj	8
Saturnus	6
Spisa hos Helena	14
Storstad	1
Tranan	2

Ropsten & Lidingö

Silja Line Terminal
(ferries to Helsinki, Turku
& Mariehamn)

Tallink Ferry to Estonia

Kaknästornet

B

Stadium

N

STADION

STADION

ÖSTERMALM

KARLAPLAN

F

G

LADUGÅRDSGÄRDET

ÖSTERMALM-
STORG

9
11
8
10

13

Historiska Muséet

Thielska
Galleriet

DJURGÅRDSBRUNNVÄGEN

Royal Theatre
of Drama

L

STRANDVÄGEN

KUNGSTRÄDGÅRDEN

Djurgårdsbrunnsviken

ROSENDALSVÄGEN

Waxholm
boats

Nordiska Muséet

Nationalmuseum

Vasamuséet

Skansen

DJURGÅRDEN

HOLMEN

Östasiatiska Muséet

Arkitekturmuséet

Estonia
Memorial

Kungliga
Slottet

Moderna Muséet

18

SKEPPSHOLMEN

Q P

KASTELLHOLMEN

Gröna
Lunds
Tivoli

See Southern
Stockholm Map

KARL JOHANS
TORG

All year

BECKHOLMEN

SLUSSEN

ABBA the Museum

Saltsjön

KATARINAVÄGEN

Viking Line Terminal
(ferries to Helsinki,
Turku & Mariehamn)

Katarina kyrka

ACCOMMODATION	
Af Chapman	Q
Ängby Camping	N
Backpackers Inn	F
Bema	J
Best Western Time	A
Bredäng Camping	O
City Packpackers	K
Diplomat	L
Fridhemsplan Hostel	M
Gärdet Hostel	G
Hellsten	D
Micro	H
Östermalm Citycamping	B
Pensionat Oden City	J
Pensionat Oden Vasastan	C
Rex	E
Skeppsholmen Hostel	P
Wasa Park	I

0   500m

whose rooms are topped off with granite bathrooms. ⑥/⑤

Wasa Park St Eriksplan 1, Norrmalm ☎08/545 453 00, ⓦwww.wasaparkhotel.se. Sankt Eriksplan

T-bana. A clean, simple budget hotel dating from the early 1900s; a bit out of the centre but cheap. Although there are no en-suite facilities, every room has a TV. ③/③

Central Stockholm

The following hotels are marked on the map on p.68.

Art Johannesgatan 12, Norrmalm ☎08/402 37 60, ⓦwww.arthotel.se. Hötorget T-bana. Run by Sweden's arts committee, this stylish hotel has welcomed artists for decades though its doors are now also open to the general public. Rooms are rather small but tastefully decorated with Nordic fittings and lots of bright colours. ⑥/④

Central Vasagatan 38 ☎08/566 208 00, ⓦwww.profilhotels.se. T-Centralen T-bana. A friendly, modern and comfortable place on one of Stockholm's main streets, whose city centre location is arguably its best feature. Rooms may be a little uninspiring but the hotel is hard to beat for easy access to the train station and the Arlanda Express to the airport. ⑥/⑤

First Reisen Skeppsbron 12 ☎08/22 32 60, ⓦwww.firsthotels.com/reisen. Gamla Stan or Slussen T-bana. One of Stockholm's classic hotels, tracing its history back to the eighteenth century. Rooms are decked out with handsome wood-panelling and all have bathtubs (not the norm in Sweden). The more expensive options even have their own Jacuzzi, private saunas and balconies with wonderful views over the waterfront. ⑥/⑥

Grand Södra Blasieholmshamn 8, Norrmalm ☎08/679 35 00, ⓦwww.grandhotel.se. Kungsträdgården T-bana. Set in a late nineteenth-century waterside building overlooking Gamla Stan, this is Stockholm and Scandinavia's most refined hotel, providing the last word in luxury, with prices to match. It's only worth it if you're staying in the best rooms however (notably the rooftop suite with its own turret); the *Diplomat* has suites with a view for the same price as a double here. Rooms are beyond our price codes: a double costs 5890kr, whilst summer and weekend discounts reduce things to a mere 4190kr. ⑦

Lady Hamilton Storkyrkobrinken 5 ☎08/506 401 00, ⓦwww.ladyhamiltonhotel.se. Gamla Stan T-bana. Traditional hotel in a building dating from the 1470s, with charming rooms tastefully decorated in old-fashioned Swedish style – lots of antique furniture and folk artefacts. Curiously, though, for a top-range hotel, breakfast is not included in the room rate. ⑦/⑥

Lord Nelson Västerlånggatan 22 ☎08/506 401 20, ⓦwww.lordnelsonhotel.se. Gamla Stan T-bana. This cosy hotel – the narrowest in Sweden at just

5m wide – is stuffed full of naval antiques and curiosities including an original letter from Nelson to Lady Hamilton. Rooms are small with ship's teak floorboards and lots of mahogany and brass. Better value than the *Lady Hamilton*. ⑥/⑥

Mälardrottningen Riddarholmen ☎08/545 187 80, ⓦwww.malardrottningen.se. Gamla Stan T-bana. Moored off the island of Riddarholmen, this elegant white ship was formerly the gin palace of American millionairess Barbara Hutton. Its cabin-style rooms are a little cramped, but make a fun change from the city's mainstream hotels and offer good value for such a central location. ⑤/④

Nordic Light Vasaplan 7, Norrmalm ☎08/505 630 00, ⓦwww.nordiclighthotel.com. T-Centralen T-bana. The last word in Nordic design – each room is individually decorated in shades of white and steely grey – but sadly the emphasis is on looks rather than comfort. Lapland's amazing northern lights may have been the inspiration but the result is painfully contemporary. ⑦/⑥

Nordic Sea Vasaplan 2–4, Norrmalm ☎08/505 630 00, ⓦwww.nordicseahotel.com. T-Centralen T-bana. As with its more expensive sister hotel opposite, the focus here is on bold designs and colours – maritime blues and greens predominate. Be sure to ask to see your room on check-in since some are tiny and only have views of the train station. The superb buffet breakfast is one of the best in Sweden. ⑦/⑥

Queen's Drottninggatan 71A, Norrmalm ☎08/24 94 60, ⓦwww.queenshotel.se. Hötorget T-bana. Extensively renovated hotel with individually decorated en-suite rooms taking their decorative cue from the turn of the last century. A perfect location for Stockholm's central shopping district. ⑥/⑤

Rica Gamla Stan Lilla Nygatan 25 ☎08/723 72 50, ⓦwww.rica.se. Gamla Stan T-bana. Like other hotels in the Old Town, this one doesn't come cheap. However, it's wonderfully situated in an elegant medieval building, with stylish yet old-fashioned rooms in 1700s Swedish design; all 51 are individu-ally decorated with antiques, and feature paintings of Swedish royals from centuries past. ⑦/⑥

Sven Vintappare Sven Vintappares Gränd 3 ☎08/22 41 40, ⓦwww.hotelsvenvintappare.se. Gamla Stan T-bana.

Tucked away in a narrow alley between Västerlånggatan and Stora Nygatan, this charming building, which dates from 1607, is classic Gamla Stan. It's named after Sven Staffansson, the winemaker to King Gustav III, and has just seven rooms, all decorated in Swedish Gustavian style. The bathrooms are to die for: their granite floors and marble walls completing the sense of royal elegance. ❻

STOCKHOLM AND AROUND | Accommodation

Southern Stockholm

The following hotels are marked on the map on p.83.

Alexandra Magnus Ladulåsgatan 42 ☏08/455 13 00, ⓦwww.alexandrahotel.se. Medborgarplatsen T-bana. The en-suite rooms in this small neighbourhood hotel are simply yet brightly decorated with contemporary Scandinavian furnishings. Its peaceful Södermalm location is perfect if you're looking for a somewhere quiet and residential. ❹/❹

Anno 1647 Mariagränd 3 ☏08/442 16 80, ⓦwww.anno1647.se. Near Slussen on Södermalm; Slussen T-bana. This hotel is a real treat: located in a seventeenth-century building handy for the Old Town, with pine floors and period furniture, it is an oasis of elegance and Gustavian charm and has perfect views of the colourful roofs and buildings of Gamla Stan. ❻/❹

Columbus Tjärhovsgatan 11 ☏08/503 112 00, ⓦwww.columbushotell.se. Medborgarplatsen T-bana. Although the exterior looks almost school-like, the rooms in this building dating from 1780 ooze old-fashioned charm, and high ceilings and generously sized windows create an agreeable sense of space. ❻/❹

Pensionat Oden Söder Hornsgatan 66B ☏08/796 96 00, ⓦwww.pensionat.nu. Mariatorget T-bana. This is a good-value guesthouse in the heart of Söder, with 22 tastefully decorated rooms at excellent prices. High ceilings, wood panelling (in some rooms) and heavy drapes help create a feeling of old-fashioned elegance. All rooms have TV. ❹/❹

Rival Mariatorget 3 ☏08/545 789 00, ⓦwww.rival.se. Mariatorget T-bana. Owned by Benny Andersson of ABBA. The singer designed the hotel himself in a combination of 1930s and contemporary Swedish style to recapture the former glamour of the building. Combining a cinema, bistro, café and even a bakery, the luxurious *Rival* has become one of Söder's preferred meeting places as well as a classy place to stay. Rooms look out over the courtyard and many have balconies. ❻

Tre Små Rum Högbergsgatan 81 ☏08/641 23 71, ⓦwww.tresmarum.se. Mariatorget T-bana. A clean, modern option in the heart of Södermalm; the seven, simple basement rooms with shared bathrooms are very popular, so book in advance. A help-yourself breakfast from the kitchen fridge is available, and bike rental is also possible. In terms of quality and price, this hotel is one of the best deals in the city. ❸

Zinkensdamm Zinkens Väg 20 ☏08/616 81 10, ⓦwww.zinkensdamm.com. Hornstull or Zinkensdamm T-bana. Comfortable, well-appointed and homely hotel rooms, all en suite, with tasteful wallpaper and wooden floors located in a separate wing of the youth hostel (see p.66). ❻/❺

Youth hostels and private rooms

Stockholm has a wide range of good, well-run **hostels**, nearly all in the city centre or within easy access of it, and costing from 150kr a night per person per bed. It's also possible to reserve a double room in Stockholm's hostels from 480kr. There are no fewer than seven official STF youth hostels in central Stockholm, two of which – *Af Chapman* and *Fridhemsplan* – are among the best in Sweden. There are also a number of independently run places, which tend to be slightly more expensive. The prices we give for STF hostels are for non-members; youth hostel members pay 50kr less.

Another good low-cost option is a **private room**, generally in a family house; to book one, contact the Hotelltjänst agency, Nybrogatan 44 (☏08/10 44 37, ⓦwww.hotelltjanst.com), close to Östermalmstorg square in Östermalm. A double room with access to a fridge and cooking facilities costs 700kr per night (two-night minimum stay applies); a two-person **apartment** costs 1000kr.

STF hostels

The following hostels are marked on the map on p.63 & p.83.

Af Chapman Flaggmansvägen 8, Skeppsholmen ☏ 08/463 2266, ⓦ www .stfchapman.com. Kungsträdgården T-bana or bus #65 direct from Central Station. See map, p.63. This square-rigged 1888 ship – a landmark in its own right – has views over Gamla Stan that are unsurpassed at the price. Newly renovated and looking smarter and more shipshape than ever, this is one of the best places to stay in Stockholm, though without an advance reservation the chances of a space in summer are slim. Closed second week of Jan. Dorm beds 235–330kr, double rooms ❷

Backpackers Inn Banérgatan 56, Östermalm ☏ 08/660 75 15, ⓦ www.backpackersinn.se. Karlaplan T-bana, exit Valhallavägen, or bus #4. See map, p.63. A fairly central school residence, with three hundred beds in a combination of fourteen-bed bright, south-facing dorms and smaller four-bed dorms. Late June to mid-Aug only. Dorm beds 200kr, double rooms ❷

Fridhemsplan Sankt Eriksgatan 20, Kungsholmen ☏ 08/653 88 00, ⓦ www.fridhemsplan.se. Fridhemsplan T-bana. See map, p.63. The latest jewel in the STF crown, this vast modern hostel can take 390 people and has TVs and internet connection points in all rooms. Closed Christmas and New Year. There are no dorms here – accommodation is in two-, three- or four-bed rooms. A (hotel quality) bed in any of these costs 250kr, double rooms ❷

Gärdet Sandhamnsgatan 65, Östermalm ☏ 08/463 22 99, ⓦ www.stfturist.se/gardet. See map, p.63. A new and well-appointed addition to STF's Stockholm hostels in the Östermalm district. Karlaplan T-bana. Accommodation is in 1–4 bed en-suite rooms with cooking facilities. Dorm beds 250kr, double rooms ❷

Långholmen Kronohäktet, Långholmen ☏ 08/720 85 00, ⓦ www.langholmen.com. See map, p.83. Hornstull T-bana then follow the signs. On the island of Långholmen, Stockholm's grandest STF hostel is set in the former prison building dating from 1724. The cells are converted into smart private and dormitory rooms, still with their original, extremely small windows. A great location, with beaches and buses to Kungsholmen nearby, the whole of Södermalm on the doorstep, and fantastic views of Stockholm and of Lake Mälaren. Dorm beds 270kr, double rooms ❷

Skeppsholmen Flaggmansvägen 8, Skeppsholmen ☏ 08/463 22 66, ⓦ www.stfchapman.com. Kungsträdgården T-bana or bus #65 direct. See map, p.63. Right in the centre and immensely popular, this former craftsman's workshop is of a similar standard to *Af Chapman*, at the foot of whose gangplank it lies; there are no kitchen or laundry facilities. Dorm beds 235–330kr, double rooms ❷

Zinkensdamm Zinkens Väg 20, Södermalm ☏ 08/616 81 00, ⓦ www.zinkensdamm.com. Hornstull or Zinkensdamm T-bana. See map, p.83. A huge hostel with 490 beds in an excellent location for exploring Södermalm, though it's a 30min walk from the city centre. Kitchen and laundry facilities available (also see "Hotels and pensions"). Dorm beds 260kr, double rooms ❷

Independent hostels

The following hostels are marked on the map on p.63, p.68 & p.83.

Castanea Kindstugatan 1, Gamla Stan ☏ 08/22 35 51, ⓦ www.castaneahostel .com. Gamla Stan T-bana. See map, p.68. It doesn't come any cheaper than this to stay in the heart of the Old Town. This hostel is perfectly located amid Gamla Stan's narrow cobbled streets and is a firm favourite among travellers. Rooms are stylishly decorated in modern Scandinavian style with wooden floors. Dorm beds 220kr, double rooms ❷

City Backpackers Upplandsgatan 2A ☏ 08/20 69 20, ⓦ www.citybackpackers .se. T-Centralen T-bana. See map, p.63. Friendly hostel with hundred beds, only 5min from the Central Station. The owners and staff have travelled widely and specialize in catering for backpackers; facilities include all-day free high-speed wireless internet access, cable TV and a sauna. Twin-bed rooms are available for 650kr, but eight-bed dorms for 230kr per person, or four-bed dorms for 280kr are more economical. Slightly higher prices Fri & Sat.

Red Boat Mälaren Södermälarstrand, Kajplats 6, Södermalm ☏ 08/644 43 85, ⓦ www.theredboat .com. Slussen T-bana. See map, p.83. Housed in an old Göta canal steamer, this hostel enjoys a fantastic location overlooking the City Hall. Cabins are compact but comfortable and clean. There are no cooking facilities on board due to the risk of fire. Double cabin ❷

Campsites

With the nearest year-round sites a good half an hour out of the city centre, **camping** out of season in Stockholm can prove rather inconvenient. However, a summer-only city campsite does exist in Östermalm. Pitching a tent costs from 155kr. This being Sweden, all sites listed are well equipped with modern service buildings providing showers and laundry facilities.

Ängby Camping ☎08/37 04 20, ⓦwww .angbycamping.se. Ängbyplan T-bana (take the green line towards Hässelby); turn left when leaving the station. West of the city on the lakeshore. Open all year, but phone ahead to book mid-Sept to April.

Bredäng Camping ☎08/97 70 71, ⓦwww .camping.se/a04. Bredäng T-bana (take the red line towards Norsborg). Southwest of the city with views over Lake Mälaren. Open mid-April to mid-Oct.

Östermalm Citycamping Fiskartorpsvägen 32, Östermalm ☎08/10 29 03. Stadion T-bana. The most centrally located of all Stockholm's campsites but only open mid-June to mid-Aug. Adjacent to the Östermalm sportsground and walkable from the city centre in around 30min.

The City

Visitors have been enchanted by Stockholm for the past 150 years, though the sights and museums have changed radically during that time: back in those days there were country lanes, great orchards, grazing cows and even windmills in the centre of the city; the downside was the lack of pavements (until the 1840s) or piped water supply (until 1858), and the presence of open sewers, squalid streets and crowded slums. In the twentieth century, a huge **modernization** programme was undertaken as part of the Social Democratic out-with-the-old-and-in-with-the-new policy: Sweden, and particularly the capital, Stockholm, was to become a place fit for working people to live. Old areas were torn down as "a thousand homes for a thousand Swedes" – as the project was known – were constructed. The result, unfortunately, can be seen only too clearly around Sergels Torg in Norrmalm: five high-rise monstrosities and an ugly rash of soulless concrete buildings that blot the city-centre landscape. There was even a plan to tear down the whole of the Old Town and build a modern city in its stead, a scheme that was thankfully quickly rescinded.

Stockholm is now, for the most part, a bright and elegant place, and with its great expanses of open water right in the centre, it offers a spectacular city panorama unparalleled anywhere in Europe. Seeing the sights is a straightforward business: everything is easy to get to, opening hours are long, and the pace of life relaxed.

For most visitors the first stop is the Old Town, **Gamla Stan**, a medieval jumble of cobbled streets and narrow alleyways huddled together on a triangular-shaped island. Gamla Stan is sandwiched between Stockholm's modern centre, **Norrmalm**, home to the capital's main area of shops as well as the train and bus stations, and the fashionable southern island of **Södermalm**, whose grids of streets lined with lofty stone buildings create an altogether more homely ambience than the grand and formal buildings of the city centre. It's here, south of the main city, that you'll find some of the city's most enjoyable bars and restaurants, as well as a couple of popular beaches on the neighbouring island of Långholmen. In this city of islands, you'll find more waterside greenery and relaxation opportunities on **Djurgården**, a vast area of parkland right on the edge of the modern city. Stockholm boasts an amazing range and number of **museums**, found in most districts of the city; we've described the most interesting ones in detail. The many **churches** are also worthy of your attention as you amble round the city.

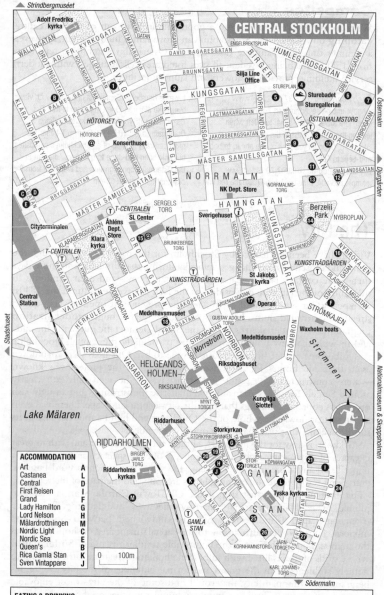

CENTRAL STOCKHOLM

ACCOMMODATION

Art	A
Castanea	L
Central	D
First Reisen	I
Grand	F
Lady Hamilton	G
Lord Nelson	H
Mälardrottningen	M
Nordic Light	C
Nordic Sea	E
Queen's	B
Rica Gamla Stan	K
Sven Vintappare	J

0   100m

EATING & DRINKING

Berns	14	East	5	Konditori Kungstornet	2	Riche	12
Bistro Ruby & Grill Ruby	23	F12	18	Le Rouge	21	Sturekatten	8
Café Art	25	Gråmunken	19	Operakällarens bakficka	17	Sawadee	1
Café Panorama	15	Grodan	6	Örtagården	7	Torget	4
Chokladkoppen	22	Hermitage	20	PA & Co	10	Wayne's	3
Den Gyldene Freden	27	KB	13	Pontus by the sea	24	Wedholms Fisk	16
Dubliner	11	Kleins	26	Prinsen	9		

Old Stockholm: Gamla Stan and around

Three islands – Riddarholmen, Staden and Helgeandsholmen – make up the **oldest part of Stockholm**, a cluster of seventeenth- and eighteenth-century buildings backed by hairline medieval alleys. It was on these three adjoining polyps of land that Birger Jarl erected a fortification in 1255, an event that was to herald the beginnings of the present city. Rumours abound as to the derivation of the name "Stockholm", though it's now widely believed to mean "island cleared of trees", since the trees on the island that is now home to Gamla Stan were probably felled to make way for the settlement. Incidentally, the words *holm* (island) and *stock* (log) are still in common use today. You can experience a taste of Stockholm's medieval past at the excellent **Medeltidsmuseum**, at the northern end of the two bridges – Norrbron and Riksbron – which lead across to Gamla Stan.

Although strictly speaking only the largest island, Staden, contains **Gamla Stan**, this name is usually attached to the buildings and streets of all three islands. Once Stockholm's working centre, nowadays Gamla Stan is primarily a tourist city with many an eminently strollable area, in particular around the **Kungliga Slottet** (royal palace), **Riksdagshuset** (parliament building) and **Storkyrkan** (cathedral). The central spider's web of streets – best approached over the bridges of Norrbron or Riksbron – is a sprawl of monumental buildings and high airy churches which form a protective girdle around the narrow lanes. Some of the impossibly slender alleys lead to steep steps ascending between battered walls, others are covered passageways linking leaning buildings. The tall, dark houses in the centre were mostly owned by wealthy merchants, and are still distinguished by their intricate doorways and portals bearing coats of arms. The main square of the Old Town is **Stortorget**, an impressive collection of tall pastel-coloured stone buildings with curling gables which saw one of the medieval city's most ferocious battles, the Stockholm Bloodbath (see p.395). It's easy to spend hours wandering around here, although the atmosphere these days is not so much medieval as mercenary: there's a dense concentration of antique shops, art showrooms and chi-chi cellar restaurants. Not surprisingly, this is the most exclusive part of Stockholm in which to live. Off the western shore of Gamla Stan, the tiny islet of **Riddarholmen** houses not only one of Stockholm's most beautiful churches, **Riddarholmskyrkan**, the burial place for countless Swedish kings and queens over the centuries, but also the Baroque **Riddarhuset** (House of the Nobility), a reminder of the glory days of the Swedish aristocracy.

Riksdagshuset and the Medeltidsmuseum

Perched on Helgeandsholmen, a small oval-shaped island wedged between Norrmalm to the north and Gamla Stan to the south, **Riksdagshuset**, the Swedish parliament building (late June to late Aug guided tours in English Mon–Fri noon, 1, 2 & 3pm, rest of the year Sat & Sun 1.30pm; free) is where Sweden's famous welfare state was shaped and formed during the postwar years of the 1940s and 1950s. The building was completely restored in the 1970s, just seventy years after it was built, and the original, columned facade (viewed to best effect from Norrbron) is rarely used as an entrance today; the main entrance is on Riksgatan, the short street between the bridges of Riksbron and Stallbron. It's the glassy bulge at the back (which you see when coming into Stockholm from the south by train) that is the hub of most activity, and where you're shown round on **guided tours**. This being Sweden, the seating for the 349 members is in healthy, non-adversarial rows, grouped by constituency and not by party, and it is has even been known for some politicians to breastfeed their children in the chamber.

In front of the Riksdag, accessed by a set of steps leading down from Norrbron, is the **Medeltidsmuseum** (Museum of Medieval Stockholm; Ⓦ www .medeltidsmuseet.stockholm.se), where medieval ruins, tunnels and parts of Stockholm's city walls dating from the 1530s, discovered during excavations under the parliament building, have been incorporated into a walk-through underground exhibition. Due to reopen in early 2010 following extensive renovation (check the website for the latest details), there will be reconstructed houses to poke around, alongside a selection of models, pictures, boats and skeletons.

Kungliga Slottet

Cross Norrbron or Riksbron from the Riksdagshuset and up rears the most distinctive monumental building in Stockholm, **Kungliga Slottet** (Royal Palace; Ⓦ www.royalcourt.se) – a low, square, yellowy-brown construction, with two arms that stretch down towards the water. Stockholm's old Tre Kronor (Three Crowns) castle burnt down at the beginning of King Karl XII's reign (1697–1718), leaving his architect, Tessin the Younger (see p.397), a free hand to design a simple and beautiful Baroque structure in its stead. Finished in 1754, the palace is a striking achievement: uniform and sombre outside, but with a magnificent Rococo interior that's a swirl of staterooms and museums. Its sheer size is quite overwhelming and it's worth focusing your explorations on one or two sections of the palace.

The rooms of state used for royal receptions are known as the Palace **Apartments** (mid-May to mid-Sept daily 10am–4pm; Feb to mid-May and mid-Sept to Dec Tues–Sun noon–3pm; 90kr). They hold a relentlessly linear collection of furniture and tapestries, all too sumptuous to take in and inspirational only in terms of their colossal size. The **Treasury** (same times; 90kr), on the other hand, is certainly worth a visit for its ranks of jewel-studded crowns. The oldest one was made in 1650 for Karl X, while the two smaller ones belonged to princesses Sofia (1771) and Eugéne (1860).

Also worth catching is the **Armoury** (June–Aug daily 10am–5pm; Sept–May Tues–Sun 11am–5pm, Thurs until 8pm; 60kr; Ⓦ www.livrustkammaren.se), which is not so much about weapons as ceremony – with suits of armour, costumes and horse-drawn carriages from the sixteenth century onwards. Also on display is the stuffed horse of King Gustav II Adolf, who died in the Battle of Lützen in 1632, and the king's blood- and mud-spattered garments, retrieved after the enemy had stripped him on the battlefield.

Nearby, two other museums are worth a quick look if you're a real palace junkie: the **Museum Tre Kronor** at Slottskajen in front of the Kunliga Slottet (same times and price as Apartments; Ⓦ www.royalcourt.se) contains part of the older Tre Kronor castle, its ruins underneath the present building, while the **Royal Coin Cabinet**, Slottsbacken 6 (mid-June to mid-Aug daily 9am–5pm, rest of the year daily 10am–4pm; 50kr, free on Mon; Ⓦ www.myntkabinettet.se), is home to a stash of coins, banknotes and medals from across the centuries, as well as a number of silver hoards from Viking days.

The Apartments, Treasury and Museum Tre Kronor offer a combined entry ticket costing 130kr.

Gamla Stan: Stortorget and around

South of the Royal Palace, the streets suddenly narrow and darken and you're into Gamla Stan proper. The highest point of the old part of Stockholm is crowned by **Storkyrkan** (May–Sept daily 9am–6pm; Oct–April daily 9am–4pm; 25kr), in Trångsund, built in 1279, and almost the first building you'll stumble upon. Pedantically speaking, Stockholm has no cathedral, but this rectangular brick church is now accepted as such, and the monarchs of Sweden married and were crowned here. Storkyrkan gained its present shape at the end of the fifteenth century following a series of earlier alterations and additions, but was given a Baroque remodelling in the 1730s to better fit in with the new palace taking shape next door. The interior is marvellous: twentieth-century restoration has removed the white plaster from its red-brick columns, giving a warm colouring to the rest of the building. Much is made of the fifteenth-century Gothic sculpture of St George and the Dragon (see p.394), certainly an animated piece but easily overshadowed by the royal pews – more like golden billowing thrones – and the monumental black-and-silver altarpiece. Fans of organ music will enjoy the recitals that often take place on Thursdays at 8pm (50kr).

Stortorget, Gamla Stan's main square, one block south of Storkyrkan along either Trångsund or Källargränd, is a handsome and elegantly proportioned space crowded with eighteenth-century buildings. In 1520, Christian II used the square as an execution site during the "Stockholm Bloodbath" (see p.395), dispatching his opposition en masse with bloody finality. Now, as then, the streets **Västerlånggatan**, **Österlånggatan**, **Stora Nygatan** and **Lilla Nygatan** run the length of the Old Town, although today their time-worn buildings harbour a succession of art-and-craft shops and restaurants. Happily, the consumerism here is largely unobtrusive, and in summer buskers and evening strollers clog the narrow alleyways, making it an entertaining place to wander or to stop for a bite to eat. There are few real targets, though at some stage you'll probably pass **Köpmantorget** square (off Österlånggatan), where there's a replica of the George-and-Dragon statue inside the Storkyrkan. Take every opportunity, too, to wander up side streets, where you'll find fading coats of arms, covered alleys and worn cobbles at every turn.

On Kindstugatan, just off Västerlånggatan, is the **Tyska kyrkan** (German Church; May–Aug daily noon–4pm; Sept–April Sat & Sun noon–4pm; free). Once belonging to Stockholm's medieval German merchants, the church served as the meeting place of the Guild of St Gertrude. A copper-roofed red-brick building atop a rise, it was enlarged in the seventeenth century when Baroque decorators got hold of it: the result, a richly fashioned interior with the pulpit dominating the nave, is outstanding. The royal gallery in one corner – designed by Tessin the Elder – adds to the overall elegance of this church, one of Stockholm's most impressive.

Riddarhuset and Riddarholmen

From Storkyrkan, it's a five-minute stroll west along Storkyrkobrinken to the handsome, seventeenth-century Baroque **Riddarhuset** (Mon–Fri 11.30am–12.30pm; 50kr; Ⓦwww.riddarhuset.se), or House of the Nobility. Its Great Hall was used by the Swedish aristocracy for two hundred years for parliamentary debate until a law was passed in 1865 to create Sweden's current two-chamber parliament. The nobility's coats of arms – around two and a half thousand of them – are splattered across the walls. Take a peek at the Chancery downstairs, which stores heraldic bone china by the shelf-load and has racks full of fancy signet rings – essential accessories for the eighteenth-century noble-about-town.

Riddarhuset shouldn't really be seen in isolation. It's only a matter of seconds to cross the bridge onto **Riddarholmen**, and thus to **Riddarholmskyrkan** (June–Aug daily 10am–5pm; rest of the year daily 10am–4pm; 30kr). Originally a Franciscan monastery, the church has been the burial place of Swedish royalty for over six centuries. Since Magnus Ladulås was sealed up here in 1290, his successors have rallied round to create a Swedish royal pantheon. Amongst others, you'll find the tombs of Gustav II Adolf (in the green marble sarcophagus), Karl XII, Gustav III and Karl Johan XIV, plus other innumerable and unmemorable descendants. Walk around the back of the church for stunning views of Stadshuset, the City Hall and Lake Mälaren. In winter, the lake often freezes from here right up to the Västerbron bridge, a couple of kilometres further west, and people skate and take their dogs for walks along the ice.

Skeppsholmen, Kastellholmen and the Nationalmuseum

Off Gamla Stan's eastern reaches lies the island of **Skeppsholmen** (a 10min walk from Stortorget: cross Strömbron, turn right and cross Skeppsholmbron; you can also take a ferry from Nybroplan, see p.60, or bus #65 from Central Station), home to two of Stockholm's best youth hostels. However, it's the eclectic clutch of **museums**, the first of which, the National Art Museum, is actually just before Skeppsholmsbron, that draw most people here. There's little else to detain you on Skeppsholmen or on the tiny, adjacent **Kastellholmen**, connected by a bridge to the south. The Swedish Navy built camps here in the nineteenth century, and some of the abandoned old barracks are still visible.

Nationalmuseum

As you approach Skeppsholmsbron on the way to Skeppsholmen, you'll pass the striking waterfront **Nationalmuseum** (National Art Museum; June–Aug Tues 11am–8pm, Wed–Sun 11am–5pm; Sept–May Wed & Fri–Sun 11am–5pm, Tues & Thurs until 8pm; 100kr; ⓦ www.nationalmuseum.se), overlooking the Royal Palace. This impressive collection of Swedish and European fine and applied arts from the late medieval period to the present day is contained on three floors.

Changing exhibitions of prints and drawings take up the **ground floor** as well as several permanent frescoes by Swedish painter Carl Larsson which adorn the six wall panels of the museum's lower staircase. There is also a museum shop and a decent café, plus lockers to leave your bags in on the ground floor.

The **first floor** is devoted to applied art, and those with a penchant for royal curiosities will be pleased to find beds slept in by kings, cabinets leaned on by queens and plates eaten off by nobles, mainly from the centuries when Sweden was a great power. There's modern work alongside the ageing tapestries and

▲ Nationalmuseum

furniture, including Art Nouveau coffeepots and vases, and a collection of simply and elegantly designed wooden chairs.

It's the **second floor** that's most engaging, however – there's a plethora of European and Mediterranean sculpture, along with some mesmerizing sixteenth- and seventeenth-century Russian icons. The **paintings** on this floor include works by El Greco, Canaletto, Gainsborough, Gauguin, Rembrandt and Renoir. Something of a coup for the museum is Rembrandt's *Conspiracy of Claudius Civilis*, one of his largest monumental paintings. Depicting a scene from Tacitus's *History*, the bold work shows a gathering of well-armed chieftains. There are also some fine works by Swedish artists from the sixteenth to early twentieth centuries – most notably paintings by the nineteenth-century masters Anders Zorn and Carl Larsson. Another, by Carl Gustav Pilo, a late eighteenth-century painter, depicts the coronation of Gustav III in Gamla Stan's Storkyrkan; it's worth noting the white plaster columns depicted in the painting, which have today been replaced by red brick.

Skeppsholmen's museums

On Skeppsholmen itself, Stockholm's **Moderna Muséet** (Modern Art Museum; Tues 10am–8pm, Wed–Sun 10am–6pm; 80kr; ⓦwww.modernamuseet.se) is one of the better modern art collections in Europe, with a comprehensive selection of work by some of the twentieth century's leading artists divided into three periods: 1900–39, 1940–69 and 1970 to the present day. Take a look at Dali's monumental *Enigma of William Tell*, showing the artist at his most conventionally unconventional, and Matisse's striking *Apollo*. Look out also for Picasso's *Guitar Player* and *Spring*, plus a whole host of Warhol, Lichtenstein, Kandinsky, Miró, Magritte and Rauschenberg. Next door is the **Arkitekturmuséet** (Architecture Museum; same times; 50kr; ⓦwww.arkitekturmuseet.se), serving up a taste of Swedish architecture through the ages in one of the most inspired buildings in the city – there are lots of glass walls and bright, airy exhibition space. The permanent exhibition, Architecture in Sweden – Function, Design and Aesthetic through the Ages, outlines some of the core themes of pan-Swedish architectural styles, and is housed alongside a number of temporary displays on construction styles.

A steep climb up the northern tip of the island brings you to **Östasiatiska Muséet** (Museum of Far Eastern Antiquities; Tues 11am–8pm, Wed–Sun 11am–5pm; 60kr; ⓦwww.ostasiatiska.se). A visit here is half a day well spent: you'll be rewarded by an array of objects displaying incredible craftsmanship, including many from China, the favourite hunting ground of Swedish archeologists. The two main exhibitions, "The Middle Kingdom" and "China before China", tackle 5000 years of imperial Chinese history through a series of engaging artefacts, including just about anything you care to mention in porcelain. There are fifth-century Chinese tomb figurines, intricate ceramics from the seventh century onwards and fine Chinese paintings on paper and silk. Alongside these, take a look at the astounding assembly of sixth-century Buddhas, Indian watercolours, gleaming bronze Krishna figures and a magnificent set of Samurai armour, a gift from the Japanese crown prince in the 1920s.

Norrmalm and Kungsholmen

Immediately to the north and west of Gamla Stan, modern Stockholm is split into two distinct sections. **Norrmalm**, to the north, is the commercial heart of the city, a compact area full of shops and offices, restaurants, bars and cinemas, always bustling with people and street life – unfortunately, it also has a high count of ugly modern buildings. To the west, **Kungsholmen** has a very different feel, with wider, residential streets, larger parks, select shops and Stockholm's town hall. Norrmalm is easy to get to on foot; Kungsholmen is best reached by T-bana (either Rådhuset or Fridhemsplan T-bana stations). If you want to walk there, take Stadshusbron bridge from close to the Central Station across to the island.

Gustav Adolfs Torg and around

Down on the waterfront, beside Norrbron, is **Gustav Adolfs Torg**, more a traffic island than a square these days, with the nineteenth-century **Operan** (Opera House; ⓦwww.operan.se) its proudest, most notable – and ugliest – building. It was here, in an earlier opera house on the same site, that King Gustav III was shot at a masked ball in 1792 by one Captain Ankarström. The story is recorded in Verdi's opera *Un ballo in maschera*, and you'll find Gustav's ball costume, as well as the assassin's pistols and mask, displayed in the Palace Armoury in Gamla Stan (see p.70). The opera's famous restaurant, *Operakällaren* (see p.88), which faces the water, is hellishly expensive, its trendy café, *Bakfickan*, less so.

A statue of King Gustav II Adolf marks the centre of the square, between the Opera and the Foreign Ministry opposite. Look out too for fishermen pulling salmon out of **Strömmen**, the fast-flowing stretch of water that winds its way through the centre of the city. Since the seventeenth century, Stockholmers have had the right to fish this outlet from Lake Mälaren to the Baltic; landing a catch here isn't as difficult as it looks, and there's usually a group of hopefuls on one of the bridges around the square.

Just off the square, at Fredsgatan 2, and surrounded by several government ministries, is **Medelhavsmuséet** (Museum of Mediterranean and Near Eastern Antiquities; Tues–Thurs noon–8pm, Fri–Sun noon–5pm; 80kr; ⓦwww.medelhavsmuseet.se). Its enormous display on Egypt includes several whopping great mummies; the most attractive pieces, though, are the bronze weapons, tools and domestic objects from the time before the Pharaohs. The Cyprus collections are also huge, the largest such assemblage outside the island itself, depicting the island civilization over a period of six thousand years. A couple of rooms examine Islamic culture through pottery, glass and metalwork, as well as decorative elements from architecture, Arabic calligraphy and Persian miniature painting.

Walking back towards the Opera House and continuing across the main junction onto Arsenalsgatan, you'll soon come to **St Jakobs kyrka** (Tues, Wed & Sat 11am–4pm, Thurs & Fri 11am–6pm, Sun 10am–7pm). Curiously, although the church is located in a prime location, it's often overlooked by visitors to the city. It stands on the site of an earlier chapel of St James (Jakob in Swedish) and was completed some 52 years after the death of its founder, Johan III. Although the church's doors are impressive – check out the south door with its statues of Moses and St James on either side – it's the great, golden pulpit that draws most attention. The date of the building's completion (1642) is stamped high up on the ceiling in gold relief. Organ recitals are held here, generally on Fridays at 5pm (free).

Kungsträdgården

One block east of Saint Jakobs kyrka and the Opera House, Norrmalm's eastern boundary is marked by **Kungsträdgården**, the most fashionable and central of the city's numerous parks, reaching northwards from the water as far as Hamngatan. The mouthful of a name literally means "the king's gardens", though if you're expecting perfectly designed flowerbeds and rose gardens you'll be sadly disappointed – it's a pedestrianized paved square, albeit in the form of an elongated rectangle, with a couple of lines of elm trees, and its days as a royal kitchen garden are long gone. Today the area is Stockholm's main meeting place, especially in summer, when there's almost always something going on – free music, live theatre and other performances take place on the central open-air stage. There are also several popular **cafés**: the open-air one off Strömgatan at Kungsträdgården's southern edge is popular in spring as a place for winter-weary Stockholmers to lap up the sunshine. In winter, the park is as busy as in summer: the **Isbanan** (early Nov to early March Mon, Wed & Fri 8.30am–6pm, Tues & Thurs 8.30am–8pm, Sat & Sun 10am–6pm; skate rental 40kr), an open-air ice rink at the Hamngatan end of the park, rents out skates. Stockholm's tourist office is here too, at the corner of Hamngatan and Kungsträdgårdsgatan in Sverigehuset (see p.58 for details).

North of the park, Hamngatan runs east to **Birger Jarlsgatan**, the main thoroughfare that divides Norrmalm from Östermalm, which has become a Mecca for increasingly trendy eating and drinking in recent years.

Sergels Torg to Hötorget

At the western end of Hamngatan, past the enormous NK department store, lies **Sergels Torg**, the ugliest square in modern Stockholm. It's an open-air meeting area and venue for impromptu music performances or demonstrations, centred around **Kulturhuset** (June–Aug Tues–Fri 11am–6pm, Sat & Sun 11am–4pm; Sept–May Tues–Fri 11am–7pm, Sat & Sun 11am–5pm; free, but fees for exhibitions), whose windows overlook the milling concrete square below. Inside this building, devoted to contemporary Swedish culture, are temporary art-and-craft exhibitions and a great design store. The *World News Café* (Tues–Fri 2–6pm, Sat noon–4pm) on the first floor is not only stuffed with foreign newspapers and magazines but also offers the chance to watch foreign news broadcasters both via the internet and on television – especially handy when it's wet and windy outside. As you come in, check with the information desk for details of poetry readings, concerts and theatre performances. At the *Panorama* **café** on the top floor (Tues–Fri 11am–7pm, Sat 11am–6pm, Sun 11am–5pm; see p.87), you can indulge in delicious apple pie and custard, and take in the best **views** of central Stockholm.

Down the steps, below Sergels Torg, is **Sergels Arkaden**, a set of underground walkways that are home to buskers, brass bands and demented lottery ticket vendors. There are political rallies and demonstrations too, or oddball games including the ever-popular *klädsträcket*, where graduation students run around shivering in their underwear or less, having tied their clothes together in a line to see whose line is longest – somehow a very Swedish pastime. There's also an entrance to **T-Centralen**, the central T-bana station, as well as a gateway to Stockholm's other main department store, Åhléns, not quite as posh as NK, and an easier place to find your way around.

A short walk along Klarabergsgatan, west of Kulturhuset, brings you to the **Central Station** and **Cityterminalen**, the main hub of Stockholm's transport. The area around here is given over to unabashed consumerism, but there's little to get excited about in the streets surrounding the main drag, **Drottning-gatan**, just run-of-the-mill shops selling clothing and twee gifts, punctuated by a *McDonald's* and the odd sausage stand. There is one highlight, however, in the **Klara kyrka** (daily 10am–5pm), just to the south of Klarabergsgatan. Hemmed in on all sides, with only the spires visible from the streets around, the church is particularly delicate, with a light and flowery eighteenth-century painted interior and an impressive golden pulpit. Out in the churchyard, a memorial stone commemorates the eighteenth-century Swedish poet Carl Michael Bellman, whose popular, lengthy ballads are said to have been composed extempore; his unmarked grave is somewhere in the churchyard.

Three blocks further up Drottninggatan in the cobbled square, **Hötorget**, you'll find a daily open-air fruit, vegetable and flower market (roughly 9am–5pm), as well as the wonderful **Hötorgshallen** (Mon–Thurs 10am–6pm, Fri 10am–6.30pm, Sat 10am–4pm), an indoor market boasting a tantalizing array of Middle Eastern sights and smells. The tall building across the square, PUB, is a former department store where **Greta Garbo** began her working life as a sales assistant in the hat section. Although she died in New York in 1990, it wasn't until 1999 that her ashes were returned to Stockholm and buried in the Skogskyrkogården cemetery in Enskede in the south of Stockholm (take the T-bana green line to the station called Skogskyrkogården to visit). Fittingly, Hötorget is also home to Stockholm's biggest cinema complex, Filmstaden Sergel; to the east, **Kungsgatan**, running across to Stureplan and Birger Jarlsgatan, has most of the rest of the city's cinemas (see p.93), interspersed with agreeable little cafés and bars.

North of Hötorget

From Hötorget, the city's two main streets, **Drottninggatan** and **Sveavägen** – the latter with some excellent restaurants and bars – run parallel uphill and north as far as Odengatan and the Stadsbiblioteket (City Library), set in a little park. In secluded gardens on Sveavägen, not far north of Hötorget, sits eighteenth-century **Adolf Fredriks kyrka** (Mon 1–7pm, Tues–Sat 10am–4pm, Sun 10.30am–4pm), its churchyard popular with lunching office workers. Although the church has a noteworthy past – the French philosopher Descartes was buried in the church's cemetery for eleven years before his body was taken back to France in 1661 – it would have remained unremarkable were it not for one of the most tragic, and still unexplained, events in modern Swedish history: the murder of the former prime minister **Olof Palme** in 1986 (see box below).

The assassinations of Olof Palme and Anna Lindh

Adolf Fredriks kyrka is of immense significance to modern Swedes, as it is the final resting place of **Olof Palme**; a simple headstone and flowers mark his grave. The then prime minister of Sweden was gunned down in front of his wife on February 28 1986, while they were on the way home from the Riviera cinema on Sveavägen. As with most Nordic leaders, Palme's fame was his security, and he had no body guards with him when he died. A simple **plaque** on the pavement, often respectfully bedecked with flowers, now marks the spot, near the junction with Olof Palmes Gatan, where the prime minister was shot; the assassin escaped up a nearby flight of steps.

Sweden's biggest-ever murder enquiry was launched, and as the years went by, so the allegations of police cover-ups and bungling grew. When **Christer Pettersson**, a smalltime criminal, was convicted for the murder in July 1989, most Swedes thought that was the end of the story, but his release just five months later for lack of evidence only served to reopen the bitter debate, with consequent recriminations and resigna-tions within a much-derided police force. Although the finger of suspicion used to be most often pointed at Kurdish extremists, right-wing terror groups or even a hitman from within the police itself, recent theories have suggested that the corrupt regime in South Africa was behind the killing; Palme was an outspoken critic of apartheid, leading calls for an economic blockade against Pretoria.

Palme's death sent shockwaves through a society unused to political extremism of any kind, and has sadly led to a radical rethink of the open-government policy Sweden had pursued for decades. Although government ministers now rarely go unescorted, Sweden was rocked by the news in September 2003 that a second leading politician had been murdered on home soil; Foreign Minister Anna Lindh was fatally stabbed in a Stockholm department store by a man with mental illness who was later arrested and imprisoned (see p.404).

Continuing north along Drottninggatan, you'll soon come to the intriguing **Strindbergsmuséet** (Strindberg Museum; Tues–Sun noon–4pm, March–Oct Tues until 7pm; 40kr; Ⓦwww.strindbergsmuseet.se) at no. 85. Housed in the "Blue Tower", the last building in which the writer August Strindberg lived in Stockholm, it provides an illuminating insight into the author's curious life. The house, which was the writer's home between 1908 and 1912, is so carefully preserved that you must put plastic bags over your shoes on entering to protect the floors and furnishings. The study is a dark and gloomy place just as he left it on his death; he always wrote with the Venetian blinds and heavy curtains closed against the sunlight. Upstairs, his library is a musty room with all the books firmly behind glass, which is a great shame as Strindberg was far from a passive reader. He underlined heavily and criticized in the margins as he read, though rather less eruditely than you'd expect – "Lies!", "Crap!", "Idiot!" and "Bloody hell!" tended to be his favourite comments. Good English notes are supplied free of charge, and the nearest T-bana stop is Rådmansgatan.

Heading further north, the city gradually peters out into a number of parks and gardens. The closest to town, only a twenty-minute walk along Sveavägen from Adolf Fredriks kyrka, is **Vanadislunden** at no. 142. Inside the park is a water sports and activities centre, **Vilda Vanadis** (mid-May to mid-Sept daily 10am–6pm; 60kr; ☎08/34 33 00), containing an outdoor pool and water slides. To get there from the centre, you can either walk from the T-bana at Rådmansgatan (use the Handelshögskolan exit from the T-bana), or take bus #2 from Norrmalmstorg or Stureplan towards Norrtull.

Kungsholmen: Stadshuset

The island of **Kungsholmen** and the Stadhuset (City Hall) are only a matter of minutes from the Central Station, across Stadshusbron. Finished in 1923, **Stadshuset** (June–Aug guided tours daily hourly 10am–4pm; rest of year daily 10am & noon; 60kr; Ⓦwww.stockholm.se/cityhall) is one of the landmarks of modern Stockholm and one of the first buildings you'll see when approaching the city from the south by train. Its simple if somewhat drab exterior brickwork is no preparation for the intriguing detail inside. If you're a visiting head of state you'll be escorted from your boat up the elegant waterside steps; for lesser mortals, the only way to view the innards is on one of the guided tours, which reveal the kitschy Viking-style legislative chamber and impressively echoing Golden Hall. Whilst here, it's worth climbing the steps to the top of the **tower** (June–Aug daily 9am–5pm; May & Sept daily 10am–4pm; 20kr) for a wonderful aerial view of the city centre and Lake Mälaren. The Stadshuset is also the departure point for **ferries** to Drottningholm, Birka, Mariefred and Gripsholm, Sigtuna and Uppsala (see "Around Stockhom", p.94).

Venture further into Kungsholmen and you'll discover a rash of great new bars and restaurants (see p.86), and an excellent **beach** at Smedsudden (bus #4 to Västerbroplan, then a 5min walk). There's also the popular park, **Rålambshovsparken**; head through it to get to Smeduddsbadet, where you can swim in Lake Mälaren and enjoy fantastic views of the City Hall and the Old Town.

Östermalm

East of Birger Jarlsgatan, the streets become noticeably broader and grander, forming a uniform grid as far as Karlaplan. **Östermalm** was one of the last areas of central Stockholm to be developed; the impressive residences here are as likely to be consulates and embassies as fashionable homes. The first place to head for is **Nybroplan**, a square at the water's edge, a ten-minute walk just east along Hamngatan from Sergels Torg (from Gamla Stan, it's a 15min stroll from Strömbron, or take the T-bana to Östermalmstorg or bus #2) and marked by the white-stone **Kungliga Dramatiska Teatern**, Stockholm's showpiece theatre, and more commonly known as Dramaten. The curved harbour in front is the departure point for all kinds of archipelago **ferries** and tours (see p.97), including a summertime ferry operated by Strömma Kanalbolaget that makes the short journey to Djurgården via Skeppsholmen (late May to late Aug daily 7am–10pm; late April to late May & late Aug to mid-Sept Sat & Sun 7.30am–7pm; every 15min; 35kr one-way, 60kr return).

From the theatre continue up the hill of Sibyllegatan and you'll reach **Östermalmstorg**, an elegant square that's home to the somewhat ritzy **Östermalmshallen** (Mon–Thurs 9.30am–6pm, Fri 9.30am–6.30pm, Sat 9.30am–4pm), a wonderful indoor food market. Although it looks very similar to Norrmalm's Hötorgshallen, the items here are more akin to what you might find in a smart delicatessen, along with various oddities including reindeer hearts and the wicked-smelling *surströmming* (fermented Baltic herring). Wander round at lunchtime and you'll spot well-heeled ladies and gents sipping Chardonnay and munching on shrimp sandwiches.

Historiska Muséet

As you wend your way around Östermalm's well-to-do streets, sooner or later you're bound to end up at the circular **Karlaplan**, a handy T-bana and bus interchange full of media types coming off shift from the Swedish Radio and Television buildings at the eastern end of Karlavägen. From here, it's a short walk down Narvavägen – or you can jump on a #44 bus – to the **Historiska Muséet** at nos. 13–17 (Museum of National Antiquities; May–Sept daily 10am–5pm; Oct–April daily 11am–5pm, Thurs until 8pm; 50kr; ⓦ www.historiska.se); from Norrmalm, hop on bus #56, which runs there from Central Station via Stureplan and Linnégatan.

The most wide-ranging historical display in Stockholm, it covers a period of ten thousand years from the Stone Age to the Middle Ages with extensive displays of battles, beliefs and trading patterns. The **Viking** section is particularly engaging and informative in its efforts to portray Scandinavia's former inhabitants not as warriors but as farmers and tradesmen. Exhibits feature a mass of weapons, coins and boats, including jewellery and bones from Birka (see p.96). It's the **Gold Room**, though, with a magnificent 52kg of gold and 200kg of silver including fifth-century gold collars and other fine pieces of jewellery that really steals the show. Elsewhere, the prehistory section includes displays on the idealized Stone Age household (flaxen-haired youth amid stripped-pine benches and rows of neatly labelled herbs). Upstairs, there's a worthy collection of medieval church art and architecture, with odds and ends gathered from all over the country, evocatively housed in massive vaulted rooms. If you're moving on from Stockholm to Gotland, be sure to take in the reassembled bits of stave churches uncovered on the Baltic island – some of the few examples that survive in Sweden.

Millesgården

Northeast of the city centre, Lidingö is a commuter island close to the ferry terminals serving Finland and Estonia. The residential district of Stockholm's well-to-do, the island is home to the startling **Millesgården** at Carl Milles Väg 2 (mid-May to Sept daily 11am–5pm; Oct to mid-May Tues–Sun noon–5pm; 80kr; ⓦ www.millesgarden.se), the outdoor sculpture collection of **Carl Milles** (1875–1955), one of Sweden's greatest sculptors and art collectors. To get to

Millesgården, take the T-bana to Ropsten, then the rickety Lidingöbanan train over the bridge to Torsvikstorg, and walk down Herserudsvägen.

Phalanxes of gods, angels and beasts sit on terraces carved into the island's steep cliffs, many of the animated, classical figures also perching precariously on soaring pillars, which overlook the distant harbour. A huge *Poseidon* rears over the army of sculptures, the most remarkable of which, *God's Hand*, has a small boy delicately balancing on the outstretched finger of a monumental hand. Those who've been elsewhere in Sweden may find much of the collection familiar, as it includes copies and casts of originals adorning countless provincial towns. If this collection inspires, it's worth tracking down three other pieces by Milles in the capital – his statue of Gustav Vasa in the Nordic Museum on Djurgården; the *Orpheus Fountain* in Norrmalm's Hötorget; and, out at Nacka Strand (Waxholm boat from Strömkajen), the magnificent *Gud på Himmelsbågen*, a claw-shaped vertical piece of steel topped with the figure of a boy, forming a stunning entrance marker to Stockholm harbour.

Djurgården and around

East of Gamla Stan and south of Östermalm, occupying a forested island in Stockholm harbour, **Djurgården** (pronounced "Yoor-gorden") is Stockholm's most enjoyable city park. This finger-shaped island stretches over three kilometres in length from Djurgårdsbron bridge in the west (linking it to Strandvägen in Östermalm) to Blockhusudden point in the east. Royal hunting grounds throughout the sixteenth to eighteenth centuries, Djurgården is a perfect place to escape the bustle of the capital amongst the groves of pines and spruce, and is also home to some of Stockholm's finest **museums**.

A full day is just about enough to see everything on Djurgården. You can walk here through the centre along Strandvägen, but it's quite a hike – around half an hour on foot from Sergels Torg to the Djurgårdsbron bridge across to the island. Using public **transport**, take bus #44 from Karlaplan; from Norrmalm, buses #47 and #69; or from Gamla Stan, the ferries from Skeppsbron (all year; see p.60) or Nybroplan (May–Aug only; see p.60).

The Nordic Museum, Skansen and Gröna Lunds Tivoli

Starting with the palatial **Nordiska Muséet** (Nordic Museum; June–Aug daily 10am–5pm; Sept–May Mon–Fri 10am–4pm, Wed until 8pm, Sat & Sun 11am–5pm; 60kr; ⓦwww.nordiskamuseet.se), just over Djurgårdsbron from Strandvägen, is the best idea, if only because it provides a good grounding to what has made the Swedish nation tick over generations. The displays are a worthy attempt to represent the last five hundred years of Swedish cultural history in an accessible fashion with household furniture, items of clothing and other bits and bobs for perusal. On the ground floor of the cathedral-like interior, you can't fail to spot Carl Milles's phenomenal statue of Gustav Vasa, the sixteenth-century king who drove out the Danes (for more, see p.395).

However, it's **Skansen** (daily: Oct–April 10am–4pm; May & Sept 10am–8pm; June–Sept 10am–10pm; 40–100kr depending on time of year; ⓦwww.skansen .se), a ten-minute walk south along Djurgårdsvägen from the Nordiska Muséet, that most people come for: a vast open-air museum with 150 reconstructed buildings, from a whole town to windmills and farms, laid out on a region-by-region basis. Each section boasts its own daily activities – including traditional handicrafts, games and displays – that anyone can join in. Best of the buildings are the warm and functional *Sámi* dwellings, and the craftsmen's workshops in the old-town quarter. You can also potter around a **zoo** (containing Nordic animals such as brown bears and elk, as well as non-native species such as lemurs, monkeys and parrots), and an **aquarium** with poisonous snakes and turtles. Partly because of the attention paid to accuracy, and partly due to the admirable lack of commercialization, Skansen manages to avoid the tackiness associated with similar ventures in other countries. Even the snack bars dole out traditional foods and in winter serve up great bowls of warming soup.

Immediately opposite Skansen's main gates and at the end of the #44 bus route (bus #47 also goes by), **Gröna Lunds Tivoli** (daily: late April to Sept noon–10pm; 70kr; an optional all-day *åkband* pass costs 280kr for unlimited rides or alternatively you can pay per ride; ⓦwww.gronalund.com) is not a patch on its more famous namesake in Copenhagen, though decidedly cleaner and less seedy. The talk of the place is still the ominous Fritt Fall, a hair-raising vertical drop of around 80m in a matter of seconds, and the Fritt Fall Tilt, which involves being catapulted face-first towards the ground from on high – do lunch later. At night the emphasis shifts as the park becomes the stomping ground for hundreds of Stockholm's teenagers.

Vasaméseet

Housed in an oddly shaped building close to Nordiska Muséet, **Vasaméseet** (Vasa Museum; daily: June–Aug 8.30am–6pm; Sept–May 10am–5pm, Wed until 8pm; 95kr; ⓦwww.vasamuseet.se) is without question head and shoulders above Stockholm's other museums.

The *Vasa* warship, the pride of the Swedish fleet, was built on the orders of King Gustav II Adolf, but sank in Stockholm harbour on her maiden voyage in 1628. A victim of engineering miscalculation and insufficient maritime knowledge, the *Vasa's* hull was simply too narrow to withstand even the slightest swell which, when coupled with top-heavy rigging, made her a maritime disaster waiting to happen. On August 10 she went down with all hands barely a few hundred metres from her moorings. Preserved in mud for over three hundred years, the ship was raised along with twelve thousand objects in 1961, and now forms the centrepiece of a purpose-built hall on the water's edge.

The museum itself is built over part of the old naval dockyard. Impressive though the building is, nothing prepares you for the sheer size of the **ship**: 62m long,

▲ The Vasa

the main mast originally 50m above the keel, it sits virtually complete in a cradle of supporting mechanical tackle. Surrounding walkways bring you nose-to-nose with cannon hatches and restored decorative relief, the gilded wooden sculptures on the soaring prow designed to intimidate the enemy and proclaim Swedish might. Carved into the ship's stern, the resplendent figures of two naked cherubs complete with podgy stomachs and rosy cheeks, proudly bearing the Swedish crown between them, are truly remarkable for their fine detail and garish colours. Adjacent **exhibition halls** and presentations on several levels take care of all the retrieved items, which give an invaluable insight into life on board – everything from combs to wooden barrels for preserving food supplies. There are reconstructions of life on board, detailed models of the *Vasa*, displays relating to contemporary social and political life, and a fascinating film of the rescue operation; between June and August there are also hourly English-language guided tours, which run less frequently at other times of the year.

The Estonia Memorial

Adjacent to the museum, a more recent reminder of the power of the sea deserves your attention. Located on the Stockholm waterfront, the three 2.5-metre-high granite walls of the **Estonia Memorial**, arranged in a triangle, bear the engraved names of the 852 people who died on board the *Estonia* ferry, which sank in the Baltic Sea in September 1994 while crossing from the Estonian capital, Tallinn, to Stockholm. The inscription reads simply "their names and their fate, we shall never forget".

Following the disaster, an official three-nation investigation involving Sweden, Finland and Estonia was launched to try to determine the cause of the tragedy. After much deliberation, and to great derision from the relatives of those who died on the ferry, the investigators declared that poor design by the original German shipbuilders of the huge hinges which held the bow door in place was to blame for the accident. The shipyard immediately refuted the claim and said that fault lay squarely with the ferry operator, Estline, for shoddy maintenance of the vessel. Following the publication of the official accident report, a number of conspiracy theories have surfaced, most alarmingly suggesting that the Russian mafia had weapons on board, exploding a bomb on the car deck once it became clear that Swedish customs had been tipped off about their illicit cargo and imminent arrival in Stockholm. The wreck of the *Estonia* now lies on the sea bed southwest of the Finnish Åland islands, covered in a protective layer of concrete to prevent plundering.

Thielska Galleriet

At the far eastern end of Djurgården, known as Blockhusudden, (bus #69 from Norrmalm), **Thielska Galleriet** (Thiel Gallery; Mon–Sat noon–4pm, Sun 1–4pm; 50kr; ⓦ www.thielska-galleriet.se) is one of Stockholm's major treasures, a fine example of both Swedish architecture and Nordic art. The house was built by Ferdinand Boberg at the turn of the twentieth century for banker and art connoisseur Ernest Thiel, and turned into an art gallery after he sold it to the state in 1924. Thiel knew many contemporary Nordic artists personally and gathered an impressive collection of paintings over the years, many of which are on show today. There are works by Carl Larsson, Anders Zorn – most notably his portraits and female nudes – Edvard Munch, Bruno Liljefors and August Strindberg, whose paintings of wild Swedish landscapes are displayed. The museum enjoys a dramatic setting at the very tip of Djurgården; indeed the views out over Stockholm harbour and across to the district of Nacka on the southern shore warrant a trip out here.

The Kaknäs TV tower

It's possible to walk from Djurgården to Stockholm's famous **Kaknästornet** (Kaknäs TV tower; daily: Jan–March Mon–Wed 10am–6pm, Thurs–Sat 10am–9pm, Sun 10am–6pm; April & May Mon–Sat 10am–9pm, Sun 10am–6pm; June–Aug 9am–10pm; Sept–Nov 10am–9pm; Dec Mon–Sat 10am–11pm, Sun 10am–9pm; 30kr), in an adjoining stretch of parkland known as Ladugårdsgärdet – head eastwards across the island on Manillavägen, and over Djurgårdsbrunnskanalen (a canal), and you'll see the tower in the distance. At 155m, this is one of the tallest buildings in Scandinavia, providing excellent views (up to 60km on a clear day) over the city and archipelago, and there's a restaurant about 120m up for an elevated cup of coffee. Bus #69 from Norrmalm will also take you directly here.

Southern Stockholm: Södermalm and Långholmen

Whatever you do in Stockholm, don't miss the delights of the city's southern island, **Södermalm**, whose craggy cliffs, turrets and towers rise high above the clogged traffic interchange at Slussen. The perched buildings are vaguely forbidding, but venture beyond the main roads skirting the island and a lively and surprisingly green area unfolds, one that is at heart emphatically working class. On foot from Gamla Stan, head south along any of the parallel streets that head towards Kornhamnstorg or Järntorget squares, and continue past the Slussen T-bana station where Götgatan, Södermalm's main north–south thoroughfare, begins. To get here by public **transport**, you can either take bus #2 from Norrmalm, #3 from Kungsholmen or #53 from Central Station; get off either service at Folkungagatan; alternatively ride the T-bana to Medborgarplatsen or Mariatorget.

In Södermalmstorg, right by the Slussen T-bana station, is the rewarding **Stadsmuséet** (Stockholm City Museum; Tues–Sun 11am–5pm, Thurs until 8pm; free; ⓦ www.stadsmuseum.stockholm.se). The Baroque building, designed by Tessin the Elder and finished by his son in 1685, was once the town hall for this part of Stockholm; now it houses collections relating to the city's history as a seaport and industrial centre.

A mere ten-minutes' walk from Slussen along Stadsgårdsleden, Stockholm's latest attraction, set to become a veritable blockbuster, was taking shape inside one of the city's former waterfront customs warehouses as we went to press. **Abba the Museum** at Stora Tullhuset, Stadsgården (check ⓦ www.abbamusem.se for opening times; 245kr) will be the first ever museum dedicated to ABBA in Sweden when it opens its doors in June 2009. Featuring a whopping 6500 square metres of floor space, four floors of exhibitions, stages on the water in the harbour and quayside marquees, the museum will trace the story of ABBA by recreating, amongst other things, the stage at the Eurovision Song contest in Brighton, the helicopter used in Arrival and the Polar recording studio where the group put down many of their music tracks. Visitors will be able to ogle the supergroup's stage costumes, strut their stuff in the Voulez-Vous disco and even sing ABBA songs and record their own music videos.

An altogether more sobering experience, however, awaits just ten-minutes' walk to the south; the Renaissance-style **Katarina kyrka** at Högbergsgatan 13 (Mon–Fri 11am–5pm, Sat & Sun 10am–5pm; Oct–March closed Mon) stands on the site where the victims of the so-called "Stockholm Bloodbath" (see p.395) – the betrayed nobility of Sweden who had opposed King Christian II's Danish invasion – were buried in 1520. They were burned as heretics outside the city walls, and it proved a vicious and effective coup, Christian disposing of the

STOCKHOLM AND AROUND

SOUTHERN STOCKHOLM

DJURGÅRDEN

BECKHOLMEN

Saltsjön

S a l t s j ö n

Viking Ferries to Finland

VÄRMDÖVÄGEN
KANALVÄGEN

Hammarby Sjö

SÖDRA HAMMARBYHAMNEN

HAMMARBYHAMNEN

Patricia Boat (Restaurant & Nightclub)
ABBA the Museum
Slussen Bus Station

GAMLA STAN

Stadsmuseet
Slussen
Katarina kyrka
Sofia kyrka

Maria Magdalena kyrka

Forsgrenska Badet

Medborgar Platsen

Götgatan

Söderledstunneln

Skanstull

Skanstullsbron

Johanneshovsbron

Erikdalsbadet

Björngårdsgatan
Pendeltåg Station
Mariatorget

Södersjukhuset (Hospital)

Årstaviken

Lake Mälaren

Zinkensdamm
Sports Arena

Open Air Theatre

Tantolunden Park

Zinkensdamm

Hornstull

Långholmen

Reimersholm

Liljeholmsbadet

ÅRSTA HOLMAR

N

0   500m

ACCOMMODATION
Alexandra   I
Anno 1647   D
Columbus   H
Långholmen Hostel A
Pensionat Oden Söder C
Red Boat Mälaren   B
Rival   E
Tre Små Rum   G
Zinkensdamm   F

EATING & DRINKING
Akkurat   3
Blå Dörren   1
Blå Lotus   20
Bröderna Olsson   12
Crêperie Fyra Knop 9
Dionysos   16
Fenix   8
Gondolen   2
Gröne Jägaren   14
H2O/Eld   11
Hosteria Tre Santi 22
Indira   17
Kvarnen   11
Lasse i Parken   4
O'Leary's   5
Roxy   21
Sacré Coeur   18
Sidetrack   7
Sjögräs   6
Snaps   10
Soldaten Svejk   13
String   15
Tre Indier   19

▶ Main Line South, also Pendeltåg to Nynäshamn for Ferry to Gotland opposition in one fell swoop. In 1723 a devastating fire tore through the church, reducing it to ruins, an event that was repeated in 1990 when the building fell victim to another tragic blaze. Painstaking rebuilding work was finally completed five years later when the building reopened.

It's worth wandering westwards to **Mariatorget**, a spacious square where the influence of Art Nouveau on the buildings is still evident. This is one of the most desirable places for Stockholmers to live, close to the stylish bars and restaurants that are the favourite haunts of Stockholm's young and terminally hip, in particular Benny Andersson's *Rival* hotel and bar (see p.65).

Södermalm is also the place to come for **swimming pools**, as there are three in fairly close proximity: Forsgrénskabadet in Medborgarplatsen (℡08/508 403 15; Medborgarplatsen T-bana); Erikdalsbadet, Hammarby Slussväg 20, (℡08/508 402 50; Skanstull T-bana), which has an open-air pool; and the wonderful little Liljeholmsbadet, Bergsundsgatan 2, (℡08/668 67 80; Hornstull T-bana), a pool in a boat-like pontoon contraption that floats in Lake Mälaren and has nude swimming for women on Mondays, for men on Fridays. The water here is never cooler than 30°C, and there's an excellent sauna and terrace from where you can look out over the waters of the lake. It's best to call all three pools beforehand to check on opening hours.

Although you'll probably end up in one of Söder's bars or restaurants (see p.89) when night falls, it's best to get your bearings during the day, as the grids of streets become confusing in the dark. The main streets to aim for are **Götgatan**, **Folkungagatan**, **Bondegatan** and **Skånegatan**.

Sweden's fab four: ABBA

Overturning odds of 20–1, Anni-Frid Lyngstad, Benny Andersson, Björn Ulvæus and Agnetha Fältskog first came to the world's attention as they stormed to victory in April 1974 at the Eurovision Song Contest with *Waterloo*. ABBA went on to become the biggest-selling group in the world, topping the charts for a decade with hits like *Dancing Queen* (performed to celebrate the marriage of Swedish King Carl Gustaf to German commoner Silvia Sommerlath in 1976), *Mamma Mia* and *Money Money Money*, and became second only to Volvo as Sweden's biggest export earner. The winning combination led to a string of number-one hits and even a film, *ABBA – The Movie,* released to popular acclaim in 1978.

However, the relentless workload of recording and touring took its toll; frictions within the group surfaced and the two couples – Agnetha and Björn, and Anni-Frid and Benny – divorced and ABBA called it a day in 1983. News of the split was broken by the Swedish newspaper, *Dagens Nyheter* – Agnetha had casually dropped the bombshell into a conversation and to this day carries the blame for the break-up. Having withdrawn from public life, she now lives as a virtual recluse on the island of Ekerö in Lake Mälaren. Anni-Frid, on the other hand, married a German prince, lives in Switzerland and spends her time championing environmental causes. After a spell in Henley-on-Thames, near London, during the 1980s, Björn is now back in Stockholm where he co-owns the domestic airline, Nextjet, and writes and produces music with Benny, who's now opened his own hotel on Södermalm, *Rival* (see p.65). Together they've worked on a string of musicals including *Chess* and *Mamma Mia,* which uses 27 ABBA songs to tell the tale of the relationship between a mother and her daughter. Even more remarkable, though, is the number of new Swedish groups who've made the big time thanks to ABBA opening the world's eyes to Swedish music: Roxette, The Cardigans, The Wannadies, Ace of Base, Whale and Army of Lovers to name but a few.

ABBA may be no more, but their memory and their music live on: to tremendous popular acclaim, Sweden's first ever museum dedicated to the supergroup, ABBA the Museum, is set to open in June 2009 near Slussen on Södermalm (see p.82).

Långholmen

True to its name, which means "long island", **Långholmen** is a skinny sliver of land that lies off the northwestern tip of Södermalm, crossed by the mighty Västerbron bridge linking Södermalm with Kungsholmen. There are a couple of popular **beaches** here: **Långholmens strandbad** to the west of the bridge, rocky **Klippbadet** to the east and – over the bridge from here – at **Smeddsudden**, on Kungsholmen. Leafy and peaceful, Långholmen is a delightful place to take a walk; on the way you'll also get some stunning views of the city towards Stadhuset and Gamla Stan. Get to Långholmen by taking the T-bana to Hornstull and then following signs to the youth hostel, or on bus #4, which crosses Västerbron on its way from Södermalm, Kungsholmen, Norrmalm and Östermalm – incidentally, this bus ride is an excellent way of seeing a lot of the city for very little cost.

One of the better places to stay in the city is the **youth hostel** (see p.66), sited in what used to be Långholmen's large prison building. There's a **café** here in the summer; you can sit outside in the former exercise yard, which is full of narrow, bricked-up runs with iron gates at one end.

Eating

Eating out in Stockholm needn't be expensive – observe a few rules and you'll manage quite well. If money is tight, switch your main meal of the day to lunchtime, when on weekdays almost every café and restaurant offers an excellent-value set menu, known as *Dagens Rätt*, for 70–90kr. For evening meals, don't assume that Italian and Chinese places will be the least expensive; more often than not they're overpriced and serve food that's pretty tasteless. You're much better off seeking out one of Stockholm's many Swedish restaurants, where you're likely to find an extensive menu of traditional fare as well as some good international dishes. In fact, the culinary craze in Stockholm for French dishes with a hint of Swedish home cooking is still going strong, and can lead to some surprising and delicious combinations.

Of the indoor **markets**, Hötorgshallen in Hötorget (see p.76) is cheaper and more varied than the posher and downright expensive Östermalmshallen (see p.78). **Hötorgshallen** is awash with small cafés and ethnic snacks stalls, but for **fruit and vegetables**, buy either from the cheaper open-air market outside, or from the summer stalls outside most T-bana stations, especially in the suburbs (conveniently, the ones outside Slussen and Brommaplan T-bana stations are open all year). Pleasant for a wander, **Östermalmshallen** has all kinds of unusual eats; however, most of what's on sale here can be bought at lower prices from the city's most central **supermarket**, in the basement of Åhléns department store at Sergels Torg. There are also several other central supermarkets: try the Coop stores in Järntorget in Gamla Stan and at Katarinavägen 3–7 at Slussen.

Cafés and restaurants

Day or night, the main areas for decent eating are: in the city centre, the triangle marked out by Norrmalmstorg, Birger Jarlsgatan and Stureplan; in Östermalm, Grev Turegatan; and in Södermalm, around Folkungagatan, Skånegatan and Bondegatan. In Kungsholmen, restaurants are more spread out, so it helps to know your destination before you set off. Several places in Gamla Stan are also worth checking out, though they tend to be a little expensive. For the best choice in terms of price and variety, head for Södermalm, where you'll find the more trendy and chic **cafés** and **restaurants** and a broader range of cuisines. Being organized is the name of the game in Sweden, and to be sure of a table you should always **book ahead** at places for which we've given telephone numbers.

In recent years, a rash of good daytime **cafés** has appeared, where you can sit over coffee and cake and just watch the world go by. The best ones are *Waynes* and *Sturekatten* in the city centre; *Chokladkoppen* in Gamla Stan; *Saturnus* in Östermalm; and in Södermalm, the studenty *String* and *Lasse i Parken*.

Stockholm City

The following cafés and restaurants are marked on the map on pp.62–63.

Aubergine Linnégatan 38 ☎08/660 02 04. Östermalmstorg T-bana. Upmarket place with minimalist decor, modern art on the walls and trendy wooden tables, on one of Östermalm's busiest streets. The separate bar menu brings prices within reach and below the 200kr mark – Caesar salad, for example, is 125kr. Otherwise it's classic French-inspired pork, lamb, steaks and fish for 200–300kr.

Blå Porten Djurgårdsvägen 64. Bus #44 & #47. The best café in all of Stockholm is on Djurgården in a glass-walled building overlooking a courtyard, where outdoor seating is arranged around an old fountain. The open sandwiches and lunches here are Provençal influenced and include a wide choice of quiches, pies, salads and soups, including vegetarian options. Mains around 100–150kr.

Brasserie Elverket Linnégatan 69 ☎08/661 25 62. Karlaplan T-bana. A stylish, airy theatre restaurant serving tasty oysters, escargots and mussels as well as other French treats in the 95–185kr range. It's also *the* place for weekend brunch (Sat & Sun 11am–4pm) and is renowned for its wide range of salads, various scrambled egg concoctions, sausages from all over the world and waffles, alongside more mainstream salmon variations. A spacious lounge with maroon and black walls creates a relaxing atmosphere for after-dinner drinks.

Chakula Pontonjärgatan 28 ☎08/654 90 30. Fridhemsplan T-bana. This African restaurant (*chakula* is Swahili for "food") with its ornate wooden wall carvings is a real find. Run by Swedes who've lived and worked in Africa, the food is superb: lots of cinnamon, cloves and ginger in dishes which originate in Kenya, Tanzania and South Africa. Reckon on 145–220kr for a main course.

Ciao Ciao Grande Storgatan 11 ☎08/667 64 20. Östermalmstorg T-bana. A safe bet for dependable, tasty and relatively inexpensive Italian food, including really excellent pizzas, in the heart of pricey Östermalm. Pizzas go for 75–125kr, pasta dishes 125–155kr and meat mains weigh in around 240kr.

Göken Pontonjärgatan 28 ☎08/654 49 28. Fridhemsplan T-bana. This small friendly neighbourhood restaurant is big on pink: bar front, curtains and door drapes all make the boys wink and it's a firm favourite with Stockholm's gay crowd. An excellent choice for modern Swedish food, such as reindeer fillet with roast vegetables and juniper risotto for 219kr, but more mainstream burgers (145kr) and steaks (189kr) are also available. Sat & Sun brunch (noon–3pm) is inordinately popular.

Gondolen Stadsgården 6 ☎08/641 70 90. Slussen T-bana. At the top of the Katarina lift. The breath-taking views over Stockholm from this high-level place right on the seafront are half the reason for coming here. Gondolen is divided into three restaurants; of the two inside, the one closest to the kitchen is dramatically cheaper (main dishes from the eclectic menu, usually featuring a wide variety of fish and game, go for about 185kr). The third part, upstairs, is an open-air summer grill-restaurant.

Il Conte Grevgatan 9 ☎08/661 26 28. Östermalmstorg T-bana. This sophisticated Italian restaurant with linen tablecloths, subtle lighting and leather chairs is said to be the best Italian in town; pasta mains, such as linguine ai frutti di mare, are 135–195kr. Meat dishes such as beef medallions with rosemary and marsala sauce cost 265–295kr.

La Famiglia Alströmergatan 45 ☎08/ 650 63 10. Fridhemsplan T-bana. One of Kungsholmen's better Italian places, intimate and cosy with chequered tablecloths and candles; Frank Sinatra once ate here. Expensive, but portions are generous. Pasta dishes cost around 135kr, grilled meat dishes 195–230kr and a three-course set menu with either lamb or salmon is 275kr. Closed Sun.

Lao Wai Luntmakargatan 74 ☎08/673 78 00. Rådmansgatan T-bana. Sweden's first East Asian restaurant, and still decidedly good. Stark white walls decorated only by a giant piece of bamboo add a touch of simplicity to this compact restaurant with barely half a dozen tables. Authentic vegetarian Sichuan Chinese and Taiwanese main courses for 165–185kr, such as soya meatballs stuffed with shiitake mushrooms, Chinese cabbage and broccoli.

Mamas & Tapas Scheelegatan 3 ☎08/653 53 90. Rådhuset T-bana. Time and again voted one of Stockholm's best eateries and *the* place to come for authentic and reasonably priced Spanish cuisine. It's a fun venue, complete with paintings of flamenco dancers adorning the walls. Tapas from 35kr, paella 98kr and a good-value mixed meat platter including pork, steak, lamb, chorizo and vegetables for 158kr.

Örtagården Nybrogatan 31 ☎08/662 17 28. Östermalmstorg T-bana. Top-notch, though still affordable, predominantly vegetarian fare dished up under huge chandeliers in Art Nouveau surroundings. Dozens of different salads, hot main courses and soups. The extensive lunch buffet is excellent value at 85kr and is available until 4pm. Open Mon–Fri until 9.30pm, Sat & Sun until 8.30pm.

Paus Rörstrandsgatan 18 ☎08/34 44 05. Sankt Eriksplan T-bana. Bright and airy neighbourhood restaurant replete with linen tablecloths, arty paintings on the white tiled walls and a pleasant bar decked out with more Mediterranean-style tiling. The menu is modern Swedish at its most accomplished – for example, Arctic char, veal fillet or duck breast from 245kr, whilst the simpler bar menu has bouillabaisse at 155kr and corn-fed chicken with mushrooms for 165kr.

Peppar Torsgatan 34 ☎08/34 20 52. Sankt Eriksplan T-bana. Attractive Cajun and Creole restaurant, with decent-sized portions at fair prices – mains are 150–300kr. Dozens of posters pinned to the walls help create an agreeable, studenty rock-and-roll atmosphere which complements the southern American food perfectly.

Rolfs Kök Tegnérgatan 41 ☎08/10 16 96. Rådmansgatan T-bana. Since it opened in the 1980s, this popular French-style restaurant with its open kitchen, long wooden benches and dozens of chairs suspended on the walls has become well established on the Stockholm restaurant scene. With turbot for 375kr, cod with cauliflower at 245kr, osso bucco 265kr and confit of pork 205kr, for example, dining doesn't come cheap, but it's certainly accomplished and tasty.

Sala Thai Sankt Eriksplan 1 ☎08/30 86 23. Sankt Eriksplan T-bana. Sweden's first Thai restaurant is still going strong and is just as good as ever. The food is authentically spicy with mains, such as delicious yellow chicken curry, all around 160kr. Try to catch the extensive and excellent value all-you-can-eat buffet (Fri–Sun 1pm–8.30pm; 198kr). A smaller lunch buffet (85kr) is also served on weekdays.

Salt Hantverkaregatan 34 ☎08/652 11 00. Rådhuset T-bana. On the island's main road and resembling the interior of an off-beat summer cottage with elk antlers and triangular road signs on the walls, this is place to come for inspired modern Swedish home cooking (120–198kr per dish), including elk burgers with chips (140kr) and the classic potato pancakes known as *raggmunk* served with fried pork and lingonberries (120kr).

Samuraj Kommendörsgatan 40 ☎08/663 68 68. Karlaplan T-bana. Tucked away in a quiet residential street of Östermalm, this good and dependable Japanese place is known for its fine food and friendly staff with mains such as grilled salmon in teriyaki sauce (138kr) at the lower end of the price range (up to around 200kr). Lunch here is particularly good value at 75kr.

Saturnus Erikbergsgatan 6. Rådmansgatan T-bana. Stockholm's answer to a French patisserie-cum-boulangerie with signs in French on the brightly painted walls and a subtle Parisian atmosphere, albeit at 60 degrees north. Excellent range of sandwiches for 50–100kr, salads for 110kr and the biggest and best cinnamon buns in town which are made for sharing.

Spisa hos Helena Scheelegatan 18 ☎08/654 49 26. Rådhuset T-bana. Swedish home cooking with a hint of Mediterranean flavours is the order of the day at this stylish neighbourhood restaurant offering fine dining in the heart of Kungsholmen. Established 1996, it's a favourite among locals who rave about the whitefish roe with almond potatoes (119kr) and the succulent steaks with thyme (225kr).

Central Stockholm

The following cafés and restaurants are marked on the map on p.68.

Bistro Ruby and Grill Ruby Österlånggatan 14 ☎08/20 57 76. Gamla Stan T-bana. *Bistro Ruby* is a long-established and justifiably popular French place in the heart of the Old Town, tastefully done up in Parisian style with red walls covered with artwork. Mains, such as steak frites or tenderloin with mustard cream, cost 169–325kr. Next door, though in the same building, is Grill Ruby, which serves up TexMex and American-style charcoal grills of meat and fish (169–420kr) and Sat brunches (1–5pm).

Café Art Västerlånggatan 60–62. Gamla Stan T-bana. A delightful fifteenth-century cellar-café with vaulted ceilings offering sandwiches, salads, pancakes, waffles, baked potatoes and quiche plus good coffee and cakes.

Café Panorama Sergels Torg 3. T-Centralen T-bana. Top-floor café inside Kulturhuset with superb views over central Stockholm (try to get one of the window tables). Lunch is dependable and inexpensive, though it's the apple pie and vanilla sauce that's the real winner.

Chokladkoppen Stortorget 18. Gamla Stan T-bana. A fabulous, if rather cramped, café overlooking Gamla Stan's grand old square, specializing in gooey chocolate tart, apple pies and carrot cake. Also has tasty quiches and light lunch dishes and is justifiably popular with the city's gay lunchgoers and coffee drinkers.

Den Gyldene Freden Österlånggatan 51 ☎08/24 97 60. Gamla Stan T-bana. Opened in 1722, Stockholm's oldest restaurant (and a favourite haunt of poet Carl Michael Bellman in his day) is housed in a combination of vaulted cellars and regular serving rooms whose interiors are pure eighteenth century and adorned with elegant wall paintings. Service is impeccable but prices are a bit steep at around 350kr for traditional Swedish mains such as pike-perch. Better value are the home cooking dishes, for example Swedish meatballs, from 155kr. Closed Sun.

East Stureplan 13 ☎08/611 49 59. Östermalmstorg T-bana. Trendy to a T with classic wooden tables and two huge aquaria, this is the place for top quality cuisine from Japan, Korea, Thailand and Vietnam, with lots of sushi and sashimi on the menu. Try their delicious Peking duck served with pancakes and hoisin sauce for 184kr. Mains are in the range of 106–217kr, though a combination of sushi and sashimi costs 279kr.

F12 Fredsgatan 12 ☎08/24 80 52. T-Centralen T-bana. Sweden's most style-conscious restaurant with green walls and innovative suspended lighting resembling upside-down daffodils. A delicious mix of Swedish and international cuisine, for example, quail with split peas and mint (305kr) or turbot and sea urchin with parsley sprouts (385kr). Or, really push the boat out with the eight-course tasting menu for 1095kr.

Grodan Grev Turegatan 16 ☎08/679 61 00. Östermalmstorg T-bana. Ignore the chi-chi restaurant with chandeliers and ornate ceilings on the left and stick instead to the stylish bar-restaurant with its glass and chrome on the right where Swedish home cooking meets French with some stunning results: fish stew with shrimps and aioli (165kr), beef steak with horseradish and French fries (165kr) or potato pancake with pork and lingonberries (112kr).

Hermitage Stora Nygatan 11 ☎08/411 95 00. Gamla Stan T-bana. Vegetarian restaurant that describes its offerings as a journey through all the cuisines of the world and is well worth checking out for its hearty dishes. Food here is often spicy

and Asian-influenced. Buffet lunches go for 80kr and a set dinner 95kr.

KB Smålandsgatan 7 ☎08/679 60 32. Östermalmstorg T-bana. Excellent Swedish and Scandinavian food with plenty of seafood in posh 1930s surroundings with curious Alice in Wonderland-style drawings adorning the walls. A favourite haunt of authors and artists (KB is an abbreviation of Konstnärsbaren or "artist's bar"), this has been a Stockholm institution for decades. Reckon on over 160–260kr for a main course such as fish stew or steamed halibut, or why not try the assorted herring plate for 98kr.

Konditori Kungstornet Kungsgatan 28. Hötorget T-bana. Busy and rather small retro-style coffee house with wood panelling, dark green sofas and an upstairs jukebox which has been serving the masses since the 1930s. Excellent apple pie and vanilla sauce, cakes and pastries as well as substantial sandwiches.

Le Rouge Österlånggatan 17 ☎08/505 244 60. Gamla Stan T-bana. A gloriously OTT Moulin Rouge-style bistro, inspired by nineteenth-century Paris, where red is *de rigeur*: everything from drapes to the sofas are bright red. The frequently changing *plat du jour* is 160kr, a platter of barbecued meat is 250kr, burgers cost 140kr and there's also a couple of fish dishes at 235kr.

Operakällarens bakficka Operahuset, Gustav Adolfs Torg ☎08/676 58 09. Kungsträdgården T-bana. Attached to the ruinously expensive *Operakällaren* restaurant, this unpretentious neighbour is sound choice for reasonably priced Swedish home cooking served around the bar in this charming little eaterie which resembles the snug of a British pub, though there's a handful of regular tables, too. Classics such as meatballs in a cream sauce with cucumber salad (139kr) and mixed herring platter (147kr) are always on the menu.

PA & Co Riddargatan 8 ☎08/611 08 45. Östermalmstorg T-bana. Attracting Stockholm's in-crowd, this fashionable restaurant is done out as a chi-chi French brasserie complete with chandeliers. The menu changes frequently and is written up on the blackboard but usually features French classics such as escargots and onion soup as well as some good old Swedish favourites and a few inventive Asian numbers. Count on 200–250kr per dish.

Pontus by the Sea Skeppsbrokajen, Tullhus 2 ☎08/20 20 95. Gamla Stan T-bana. Housed in a former brewery whose copper vats still dominate the interior of this low wooden and glass structure, this waterfront brasserie specializes in seafood platters and champagne though it also serves French classics like minute steak, onion soup and lobster. Mains are in the region of 150–250kr per dish. Tremendous views of Stockholm harbour.

Prinsen Mäster Samuelsgatan 4 ⓣ08/611 13 31. Östermalmstorg T-bana. Dating from 1897, this traditional old place has long been the haunt of artists, musicians and writers enchanted by its soft lighting, glass panelling and wall etchings – and its top-notch Swedish home cooking. Mains include reindeer fillet with truffles and risotto (295kr), slow-braised lamb with artichoke (269kr) and dumplings with pickled chanterelles (189kr).

Riche Birger Jarlsgatan 4 ⓣ08/545 035 60. Östermalmstorg T-bana. In Strindberg's day, what is now *Riche* was built to be Stockholm's answer to a genuine Parisian bistro complete with glass-fronted verandah. Today, *Riche* is just that: an inordinately popular French brasserie serving a range of Swedish and French dishes such as smoked salmon with spinach (235kr), braised lamb (195kr) and duck à l'orange (285kr).

Sawadee Olofsgatan 6 ⓣ08/20 98 00. Hötorget T-bana. Attractive and extremely central Thai

restaurant with an extensive choice of main courses for 155–195kr, and reasonably priced drinks.

🏃 **Sturekatten** Riddargatan 4. Östermalmstorg T-bana. They don't come any more genuine than this traditional old café. With antique tables and chairs seemingly lifted from grandmother's sitting room, it has carpets on the floors and flowers in the windows. Tremendous cakes and pastries as well as filling sandwiches to boot make this café one of the most enjoyable the city has to offer.

Wayne's Kungsgatan 14. Hötorget T-bana. A popular café for smart city types and trendy young things who sip cappuccinos while pretending to read foreign newspapers.

Wedholms Fisk Nybrokajen 17 ⓣ08/611 78 74. Kungsträdgården T-bana. There's a neat and clean feel to this highly regarded fish restaurant with its stark white walls and mirrors. With starters over 200kr and main courses of fresh turbot for 495kr, monkfish 350kr and scallops at 395kr, prices are certainly not low, but the chefs know their stuff.

Southern Stockholm

The following cafés and restaurants are marked on the map on p.83.

Blå Dörren Södermalmstorg 6. Slussen T-bana. Unpretentious and popular beer hall-cum-restaurant with vaulted ceilings offering excellent Swedish traditional dishes (119–205kr) such as meatballs, steaks and *pytt i panna*.

Blå Lotus Katarina Bangata 21. Medborgarplatsen T-bana. Oriental decor from both Thailand and Turkey covers the walls of this hangout for a young alternative crowd. Extensive choice of teas and coffees as well as freshly made sandwiches with fillings varying from goat's cheese to salami, omelettes, quiches and soups; the home-made cakes are particularly good.

Bröderna Olsson Folkungagatan 84 ⓣ08/640 84 46. Medborgarplatsen T-bana. A fun American-style diner with the word "garlic" emblazoned across the black-and-white tiled walls in every conceivable language. Every dish is laced with garlic – there's even garlic beer. Main courses such as Thai-spiced garlic prawns or deep-fried garlic with halloumi cheese cost 127–229kr. There's also an extensive choice of vodkas and *akvavits*.

🏃 **Crêperie Fyra Knop** Svartensgatan 4 ⓣ08/640 77 27. Slussen T-bana, Götgatan exit. A rare treat in Stockholm – excellent, affordable galettes and crêpes for around 110kr, served in this French-owned and -run restaurant which consists of one intimate little room with rough maroon walls, battered wooden chairs and tables and an ancient Stella

Artois advertisement. There are only half a dozen tables so booking is essential.

Dionysos Bondegatan 56 ⓣ08/641 91 13. Medborgarplatsen T-bana. Tasteful though rather small Greek restaurant with a homely feel: it's been here since 1974. The food is accomplished: grilled halloumi for 70kr, souvlaki for 150kr. All mains are accompanied by potato wedges.

Hosteria Tre Santi Blekingegatan 32 ⓣ08/644 18 16. Skanstull T-bana. One of Södermalm's better and more upmarket Italian restaurants which is justifiably popular for its cosy and romantic interior and generous portions. Pasta dishes cost 135–155kr, meat mains are around 200kr, whilst fish costs 195–285kr; the accompanying home-made sauces are exceptionally good. Try the tasty scampi risotto for 195kr.

Indira Bondegatan 3B ⓣ08/641 40 46. Medborgarplatsen T-bana. Somewhat cramped, but the area's most popular Indian restaurant, with a good tandoori-based menu – if it's full upstairs, take the spiral staircase down to the basement for more seating. Main dishes from 95kr, though tandoori concoctions cost 110–130kr. Takeaway food available.

Kvarnen Tjärhovsgatan 4. Medborgarplatsen T-bana. Classic Stockholm beer hall with great Swedish home cooking – lunch for 75kr. Evening dishes such as salmon steak with dill potatoes and *pytt i panna* for 105–225kr. If your heart is set on eating reindeer whilst in Stockholm, look no further: it's always on the menu here, served with mushrooms and a creamy sauce (138kr).

Lasse i Parken Högalidsgatan 56. Hornstull T-bana. Daytime café housed in an eighteenth-century house, with a pleasant tree-lined garden that's very popular in summer. Serves classic Swedish dishes around the 200kr mark such as poached pike-perch. Also handy for the beaches at Långholmen. April–Sept daily 11am–5pm, June–Aug 11am–8pm; Oct–March Sat & Sun 11am–5pm.

Pelikan Blekingegatan 40. Skanstull T-bana. Atmospheric, working-class Swedish beer hall (from the entrance hall turn right) with excellent traditional food, such as *pytt i panna* for 132kr or meatballs for 156kr. Left of the entrance hall is a smarter restaurant with a more upmarket menu, though still based on Swedish home cooking. Mains 154–194kr.

Roxy Nytorget 6 ☏08/640 96 55. Medborgarplatsen T-bana. Gay-friendly restaurant with bare white walls and leather chairs, serving tasty Swedish food with a hint of the Mediterranean: squid in hot chilli and garlic sauce (67kr), rack of lamb (220kr) and Arctic char with fennel (235kr) are all good choices.

Sacré Coeur Skånegatan 83–85 ☏08/694 88 15. Medborgarplatsen T-bana. With orange and green walls hung with artsy photos, this fantastically good value Söder restaurant is an easy place to chill and enjoy some excellent food. The menu is French inspired: garlic escargots (73kr), wild duck with almond potato purée (179kr) and fried Arctic char with saffron risotto and vegetables marinated in lime (185kr) are all sound choices.

Sjögräs Timmermansgatan 24 ☏08/84 12 00. Mariatorget T-bana. A firm favourite for fine dining among Stockholm's foodies, the small yet carefully selected menu at this contemporary restaurant is a treat. Serving classic Swedish dishes such as duck breast or venison with a hint of fusion, particularly Caribbean, flavours, mains come in at 198–259kr. Stylish and airy Nordic interior with plenty of wood and glass and massive windows overlooking the street.

Snaps Götgatan 48 in Medborgarplatsen ☏08/640 28 68. Medborgarplatsen T-bana. Good, old-fashioned but reasonably priced Swedish food (mains 193–258kr) and an extensive range of schnapps (hence the Swedish name, *snaps*), set in a 300-year-old building. Very popular, especially in summer, when there's outdoor seating in the square.

Soldaten Svejk Östgötatan 35. Medborgarplatsen T-bana. Lively pub that draws in a lot of students. Simple, Eastern and Central European-inspired menu with dishes (schnitzel and various spicy sausages are always available) around the 120kr mark. Large selection of Czech beers; a Pilsner Urquell costs 48kr.

String Nytorgsgatan 38. Medborgarplatsen T-bana. If you fancy yourself as a writer, you'll fit in well at this retro studenty café with its brown plastic chairs and battered wooden tables. Good for a wide range of hot and cold sandwiches from 27kr, salads from 59kr, as well as muffins and carrot cake. There's a breakfast buffet on Sat & Sun (10.30am–1pm) for 65kr.

Tre Indier Åsogatan 92 ☏08/641 03 55. Medborgarplatsen T-bana. A lively Indian restaurant that's slightly tucked away, but well worth seeking out; it's located at the corner of the tiny street, Möregatan, and Åsögatan. There's an extensive menu and the curry dishes are genuinely tasty and well prepared. Mains go for 120–140kr each.

Drinking, nightlife and entertainment

There's plenty to keep you occupied in Stockholm, from pubs and clubs to the **cinema** and **theatre**. Many establishments have an unwritten dress code so it's best to leave your jeans and trainers at home if you want to get past the bouncers. Be prepared, too, to cough up around 20kr to leave your coat at the cloakroom, a requirement at many bars and pubs as well as at discos, particularly in winter. In addition to Friday and Saturday nights, Wednesday evening is a popular time for going out in Stockholm, with lots going on and queues outside the more popular places. Swedes, and especially Stockholmers, are fairly reserved, so don't expect to immediately get chatting to people – in fact it is positively fashionable to be cool and aloof. However, after a few drinks, it's usually easy enough to strike up conversation. Most clubs will open around 10pm – although they don't fill up for an hour or so – and close around 3am.

For **information** on what's happening in Stockholm, *What's On*, free from the tourist office, is particularly good for all kinds of listings. It contains day-by-day information about a whole range of events – gigs, theatre, festivals, dance – sponsored by the city, many of which are free and based in Stockholm's many parks. There's also a free Saturday supplement to the *DN* newspaper, *På stan* – get someone to translate if your Swedish isn't up to it – that details all manner of entertainments, from the latest films to club listings; it's also available in bars and restaurants.

Popular venues in summer for music are Kungsträdgården and Skansen, where there's always something going on. **Kulturhuset** in Sergels Torg has a full range of artistic and cultural events – mostly free.

Bars, brasseries and pubs

As elsewhere in Sweden, the majority of Stockholmers do their drinking and eating together, and all of the places listed below also serve food. If you just want to do some serious **drinking**, the capital certainly has enough establishments to choose from, nearly all open seven days a week. The scourge of Swedish nightlife – high alcohol prices – has been neutralized due to increased competition. In fact, drinking in Stockholm now costs roughly the same – and sometimes less – than in London; the tired old stories about beer in Stockholm requiring a second mortgage are quite simply no longer true. Over recent years, there's been a veritable explosion in the number of **bars and pubs** in the capital, in particular British- and Irish-style ones. **Beer prices** have dropped considerably and, on Södermalm especially, there are some very good deals. **Happy hours** or **After work**, as they're also known, at various places also throw up some bargains – watch out for signs outside bars and pubs advertising their particular times. Most places stay open until 1am during the week, 3am on Friday and Saturday. Gay bars are few and far between: those that do exist are listed below.

Stockholm City

The establishments below are marked on the map on pp.62–63.

Storstad Döbelnsgatan 44. Rådmansgatan T-bana. Light and airy lounge and bar with high ceilings that is a firm favourite for Stockholm's media pack and local celebrities. Packed with a credit-card-flashing crowd at weekends.

Tranan Karlbergsvägen 14. Sankt Eriksplan T-bana. An atmospheric old workers' beer hall in a basement. One of Stockholm's best and most popular drinking holes.

Central Stockholm

The establishments below are marked on the map on p.68.

Berns Berzelii Park, Nybroplan. Kungsträdgården T-bana. One of the chicest bars in town, with decor by the British designer Sir Terence Conran. Originally made famous by writer August Strindberg, who picked up character ideas here for his novel, *The Red Room*.

Dubliner Smålandsgatan 8. Östermalmstorg T-bana. One of the busiest Irish pubs in town, with live music most evenings.

Gråmunken Västerlånggatan 18. Gamla Stan T-bana. Cosy café-bar that's usually very busy, and sometimes has live jazz to jolly things along.

Kleins Kornhamnstorg 51. Gamla Stan T-bana. One of the most popular bars in Gamla Stan, though its tiny dimensions mean it can get a bit cramped. Definitely worth a look.

Torget Mälartorget 13. Gamla Stan T-bana. This elegant place is Stockholm's main gay bar, good for a drink at any time of the evening and always busy.

Southern Stockholm

The establishments below are marked on the map on p.83.

Akkurat Hornsgatan 18. Slussen T-bana. This famous spot is known for its 280 different whiskies and extensive beer selection, including an impressive array of Belgian varieties. Often has live music at weekends.

Fenix Götgatan 40. Slussen T-bana, Götgatan exit. A loud and brash American-style bar that's always packed with clientele who are here for the sole purpose of drinking large quantities of beer.

Gröne Jägaren Götgatan 64. Medborgarplatsen T-bana. An inordinately popular, and at times, rather drunken bar with some of the cheapest beer in the capital – the clientele is predominantly male and talk here is mainly of women, football and cars.

H2O/Eld Tjärhovsgatan 4. Medborgarplatsen T-bana. In the basement underneath the *Kvarnen* beer hall, these trendy bars are always popular. *H2O*, decorated entirely in blue and white ceramic tiles and resembling a public toilet, is the better of the two, where hanging out at the bar is the

in thing to do. *Eld* has a resident DJ most nights of the week, and both attract Stockholm's well-dressed, well-heeled and well-tipsy.

Kvarnen Tjärhovsgatan 4. Another busy beer hall on the same site as *H2O/Eld*; this one, at ground level, is a favourite haunt of football fans supporting Hammarby, who come here to celebrate their team's every win and defeat. If you're looking for a quintessentially Södermalm, working-class experience, here's a good bet.

O'Learys Götgatan 11–13. Medborgarplatsen T-bana. Södermalm's most popular Irish pub is good for watching sport on the widescreen TV before stumbling back to the nearby Slussen T-bana.

Pelikan Blekingegatan 40. Skanstull T-bana. This fantastic old beer hall is full of character – and characters – and is one of the city's most satisfying and relaxing places for an evening's drinking.

Sidetrack Wollmar Yxkullsgatan 7. Mariatorget T-bana. Dark and intimate British-style pub popular with gay leather and denim boys.

Clubs

The **club scene** in Stockholm is limited. Cover charges aren't too high at around 100kr, but beer gets more expensive as the night goes on, reaching as much as 85kr a glass. In Stockholm, as in the rest of Sweden, the gay scene is small; we've listed what the city has to offer below.

Aladdin Barnhusgatan 12–14. T-Centralen T-bana. One of the city's most popular dance-restaurants with five bars and three dancefloors, close to the Central Station, often with live bands. Fri & Sat until 3am.

Berns Berzelii Park, Nybroplan. Kungsträdgården T-bana. A Stockholm institution – a nightclub, bar and restaurant all in one. It's the stunning mix of nineteenth-century Baroque, contemporary design and beautiful people that creates such a buzz. Make sure you're dressed up to get in. Fri & Sat until 4am with contemporary and 1980s tunes.

Crazy Daizy Fleminggatan 2–4. Rådhuset T-bana. Very popular club with 30 and 40-somethings with a mix of disco and live music.

Guantanamero Upplandsgatan 2. T-Centralen T-bana. A mix of Latin, Cuban, salsa and R&B really draws the crowds, especially Stockholm's large Spanish-speaking community, to this unpretentious club on Sat nights.

Lino Riddarkällaren, Södra Riddarholmshamnen 19. Gamla Stan T-bana. Undoubtedly the best gay club in town with three dancefloors (one outside which is heated in winter) offering you picture-perfect views

of Lake Mälaren as you groove the night away to a buzzing mix of house, trance and 1980s & 1990s. Sat only.

Mosebacke Mosebacke torg 3, Södermalm. Slussen T-bana. One of the longest-established clubs in town; every night sees a different type of club or event taking place – everything from jazz to new bands, R&B to disco. In short, if it's in Stockholm, it's here.

Patricia Stadsgårdskajen, Slussen. Slussen T-bana. Formerly the royal yacht of Britain's late Queen Mother, today a restaurant-disco-bar with fantastic views of the city across the harbour and chart and 1980s music. The menu, with a huge variety of imaginative main courses (fajitas and Cajun steaks are always available) is quite simply terrific and booking is essential. Gay on Sun.

Sturecompagniet Sturegatan 4. Östermalmstorg T-bana. Long established as one of Stockholm's leading (and biggest) nightspots, playing house and techno, with three floors of bars; something for everybody and worth a look, although it can get packed and the queues to get in are frighteningly long. Expensive beer.

The White Room Jakobsbergsgatan 29. T-Centralen Hötorget. Playing a vibrant mix of 1990s music, this club right in the city centre is always packed at weekends. Be young, beautiful and trendy and let the champagne flow.

Live music: rock, pop and jazz

When there's live **rock** and **jazz** music at bars and cafés, it will mostly be provided by local bands, for which you'll pay around 100kr entrance. Most international big names make it to Stockholm, playing at a variety of seated halls and stadiums – tickets for these are, of course, much more expensive. The main **large venue** is the Stockholm Globe Arena in Johanneshov (Gullmarsplan T-bana; ☎0771/31 00 00, ⓦwww.globen.se).

Cirkus Djurgårdsslätten 43–45 ☎08/587 987 00, ⓦwww.cirkus.se. Bus #44 and #47. Occasional rock, R&B performances, classical concerts and theatre.

Engelen Kornhamnstorg 59 ☎08/505 560 00, ⓦwww.wallmans.com. Gamla Stan T-bana. Live jazz, rock or blues nightly until 3am, but arrive early to get in.

Fasching Kungsgatan 63, Norrmalm ☎08/534 829 64, ⓦwww.fasching.se. Hötorget T-bana. Local and foreign contemporary jazz, and a good place to go dancing too.

Nalen Regeringsgatan 74 ☎08/505 292 00. T-Centralen T-bana. Once *the* place to hear music in the city (even the Beatles were booked to play here), now offering rock with a smattering of jazz and swing.

Södra Teatern Mosebacke torg 3 ☎08/531 994 90, ⓦwww.mosebacke.se. Slussen T-bana. This is one of the best places in the capital for world music, hip-hop, rock and pop – if it's happening anywhere, it's happening here.

Stampen Stora Nygatan 5 ☎08/20 57 93, ⓦwww.stampen.se. Gamla Stan T-bana. Long-established and rowdy jazz club, both trad and mainstream, with blues and 1950s and 1960s rock too.

Classical music

Classical music is always easy to find in Stockholm. There's generally something on at one of the following venues: Konserthuset in Hötorget, Norrmalm (☎08/786 02 00, ⓦwww.konserthuset.se); Berwaldhallen, Strandvägen 69, Östermalm (☎08/784 18 00, ⓦwww.berwaldhallen .se); and Musikaliska Akademien, Blasieholmstorg 8, near the National Art Museum (☎08/407 18 00, ⓦwww.musakad.se). **Organ music** can be heard at Adolf Fredriks kyrka, Holländargatan 16, Norrmalm; St Jakobs kyrka in Kungsträdgården, Norrmalm; Gustav Vasa kyrka in Odenplan; and Storkyrkan in Gamla Stan – consult *What's On* (see p.58). Operan, on Gustav Adolfs Torg, is Stockholm's main **opera** house (☎08/791 44 00, ⓦwww.operan.se); for less rarefied presentations, check out the programme at Dramaten, Nybroplan, Östermalm (☎08/667 06 80, ⓦwww.dramaten.se).

Theatre, cinema and cultural events

Stockholm has dozens of **theatres**, but naturally most productions are in Swedish. For **English-language performances** check out Sweden's oldest English-language theatre company, Stockholm Players (ⓦwww.stockholmplayers.se), established in the 1920s. If you want other tickets, it's worth waiting for reduced-price standby tickets, available from the kiosk in Norrmalmstorg.

Cinema-going is an incredibly popular pastime in Stockholm. The largest venue in the city centre is Filmstaden Sergel in Hötorget (☎08/562 600 00, ⓦwww.sf.se), but there are also a good number of cinemas the entire length of Kungsgatan between Sveavägen and Birger Jarlsgatan, which are always very lively on Saturday night. Tickets cost around 85kr and films are never dubbed into Swedish.

Finally, **Kulturhuset** (☎08/508 31 508, ⓦwww.kulturhuset.stockholm.se) in Sergels Torg has a full range of artistic and cultural events, most of them free; the information desk on the ground floor has free programmes.

Listings

Airlines British Airways ⓦwww.ba.com; Continental ⓦwww.continental.com; Delta Air Lines ⓦwww.delta.com; Icelandair ⓦwww.icelandair.se; Ryanair ⓦwww.ryanair.com; SAS ⓦwww.sas.se; US Airways ⓦwww.usairways.com.

Airport enquiries Arlanda ⓦwww.arlanda.se; Bromma ⓦwww.lfv.se/bromma; Skavsta ⓦwww.skavsta-air.se; Västerås ⓦwww.vasterasflygplats.se.

Bookshops English-language books are available at Akademibokhandeln, corner of Regeringsgatan and Måster Samuelsgatan; and Sweden Bookshop, Slottsbacken 10 in Gamla Stan.

Bus enquiries For SL bus information see "SL travel information" below; for long-distance bus information try Swebus Express ⓦwww.swebusexpress.se and Säfflebussen ⓦwww.safflebussen.se.

Car rental Avis ⓦwww.avis.se; Europcar ⓦwww.europcar.se; Hertz ⓦwww.hertz.se.

Health care CityAkuten, Apelbergsgatan 48 ☎08/412 29 60.

Embassies and consulates Australia, Sergels Torg 12 ☎08/613 29 00, ⓦwww.sweden.embassy.gov.au; Canada, Tegelbacken 4 ☎08/453 30 00, ⓦwww.canadaemb.se; Ireland, Östermalmsgatan 97 ☎08/661 80 05, Ⓔswedenembassy@dfa.ie; New Zealand – use the Australian Embassy; UK, Skarpögatan 6–8 ☎08/671 30 00, ⓦwww.britishembassy.se; US, Dag Hammarskjöldsväg 31 ☎08/783 53 00, ⓦhttp://stockholm.usembassy.gov.

Emergencies Ring ☎112 for police, ambulance or fire services.

Exchange Forex exchange offices at Central Station, Cityterminalen, Vasagatan 14, Sverigehuset tourist office, Terminal 2 & 5, Arlanda airport and Skavsta airport. More information at ⓦwww.forex.se.

Gay information RFSL (National Association for Sexual Equality), Sveavägen 57 ☎08/457 13 00, ⓦwww.rfsl.se. The free newspaper, *QX* (ⓦwww.qx.se), available at gay bars and clubs, is handy for listings. Gay beaches are at Freskati (turn left out of the Universitetet T-bana, then walk past Pressbyrån, under the bridge and towards the trees); and at Kärsön (Brommaplan T-bana then any bus towards Drottningholm palace. Get off at the stop over the bridge and walk to the right along the water's edge).

Internet access Sidewalk Express have dozens of internet points across Stockholm, for example, at Central Station, Cityterminalen and most 7 Eleven supermarkets. See ⓦwww.sidewalkexpress.se for complete listings. 19kr per hour.

Laundry Self-service laundry at Västmannagatan 61 (Mon–Fri 8.30am–6.30pm, Sat 9.30am–3pm; ⓦwww.tvattomaten.se).

Left luggage There are lockers at Central Station and the Cityterminalen bus station.

Lost property Klara Östra Kyrkogatan 6, ☎08/600 10 00.

Pharmacy 24hr service at Klarabergsgatan 64, ☎08/454 81 30.

Police Kungsholmsgatan 37 ☎08/401 01 00.

Radio English-language programming from Radio Sweden as well as broadcasts from the BBC can be heard on 89.6 FM.

Travel information (SL) Bus and T-bana information on ☎08/600 10 00, ⓦwww.sl.se.

Around Stockholm

Such are Stockholm's attractions that it's easy to overlook the city's surroundings, yet if you did so you'd be missing some of Sweden's most fascinating sights. One hour from the city centre stands **Drottningholm**, the country's greatest royal palace, while a little further out in Lake Mälaren is the World Heritage site of **Birka**, with its magnificent Viking remains. The stunning **archipelago** makes another excellent waterborne day-trip, with dozens of pine-clad islands, all served by regular ferries. Alternatively, west of the capital, the little lakeside village of **Mariefred**, containing another great castle, **Gripsholm**, is not only accessible by a fine boat ride on Lake Mälaren but also by train. On the opposite shore, lively **Västerås** is readily reached by train from Stockholm. North of Stockholm, **Sigtuna** is one of Sweden's oldest towns and, even today, is full of ruined medieval churches and runes tones. Just to the north, the charming university town of **Uppsala** can be reached from both central Stockholm and Arlanda airport, and can, in principle, be visited on a day-trip from the former, or as a first destination in any Swedish tour from the latter, though it really merits a longer stay.

Drottningholm and Birka

Just to the west of the capital on the banks of Lake Mälaren, the stately royal residence of **Drottningholm** affords sweeping views across the water. Less than an hour away from Stockholm, the palace makes a relaxing day-trip and can be coupled with a visit to the dizzying array of ancient finds at the Viking town of **Birka**, on the nearby island of Björkö.

Drottningholm

Even if your time in Stockholm is limited, try to see the architecturally harmonious royal palace of **Drottningholm** (May–Aug daily 10am–4.30pm; Sept daily noon–3.30pm; Oct–April Sat & Sun noon–3.30pm; 70kr; Ⓦwww .royalcourt.se). The best way to reach the palace is by **ferry** (May to early Sept daily 9.30am–6pm, hourly; early Sept to late Oct Sat & Sun 2 daily; 90kr one-way, 120kr return), which leaves from Stadshusbron on Kungsholmen and takes just under an hour each way. Otherwise, take the T-bana to Brommaplan and then any bus towards Drottningholm (the bus stop is marked as such) – a less thrilling ride, but covered by the Stockholm Card and the SL travelcards, unlike the ferry.

Beautifully located on the shores of leafy **Lovön**, an island 11km west of the centre, Drottningholm is perhaps the greatest achievement of the two architects **Tessin**, father and son. Work began in 1662 on the orders of King Karl X's widow, Eleonora, with Tessin the Elder modelling the new palace in a thoroughly French style – giving rise to the stock comparisons with Versailles. Apart from anything else, it's considerably smaller than its French contemporary, utilizing false perspective and trompe l'oeil to bolster the elegant, though rather narrow, interior. On Tessin the Elder's death in 1681, the palace was completed by his son, then already at work on Stockholm's Kungliga Slottet.

Inside, good English notes are available to help you sort out the riot of Rococo decoration in the rooms, which largely date from the time when Drottningholm was bestowed as a wedding gift on Princess Louisa Ulrika (a sister of Frederick the Great of Prussia). No hints, however, are needed to spot the influences in the Baroque "French" and the later "English" **gardens** that back onto the palace. Since 1981, the Swedish royal family has lived out at Drottningholm, instead of in the city centre, using it as a permanent home. This move has accelerated efforts to restore parts of the palace to their original appearance, and the monumental **grand staircase** is now once again exactly as envisaged by Tessin the Elder. Another sight worth visiting is the Slottsteater (**Court Theatre**), nearby in the palace grounds (May daily noon–4.30pm; June–Aug daily 11am–4.30pm; Sept 1–3.30pm; obligatory guided tours every

30min; 60kr; ⓦ www.dtm.se). It dates from 1766, but its heyday was a decade later, when Gustav III imported French plays and theatrical companies, making Drottningholm the centre of Swedish artistic life. Take the guided tour and you'll get a florid but accurate account of the theatre's decoration: money to complete the building ran out in the eighteenth century, meaning that things are not what they seem – painted papier-mâché frontages are *krona*-pinching substitutes for the real thing. The original backdrops and stage machinery are still in place though, and the tour comes complete with a display of eighteenth -century special effects including wind and thunder machines, trapdoors and simulated lighting. Also within the extensive palace grounds is a **Chinese Pavilion** (May–Aug daily 11am–4.30pm; Sept daily noon–3.30pm; 60kr), a sort of eighteenth-century royal summerhouse.

Birka

Björkö (the name means "island of birches"), in Lake Mälaren, is known for its rich flora, good beaches and ample swimming opportunities, but most of all for the Viking town of **BIRKA** (ⓦ www.raa.se/birka), which is a UNESCO World Heritage site. Sweden's oldest town, founded around 750AD, Birka was once the most important Viking trading centre in the northern countries, benefiting from its strategic location near the mouth of Lake Mälaren on the portage route to Russia and the Byzantine Empire. Tradesmen and merchants were drawn to the prosperous and rapidly expanding village, and the population soon grew to around one thousand. The future patron saint of Scandinavia, **Ansgar**, came here in 830 as a missionary at the instruction of the Holy Roman Emperor, Louis I, and established a church in an attempt to Christianize the heathen Swedes. They showed little interest and the Frankish monk preached on the island for just over a year before being recalled. Birka reached its height during the tenth century before sliding into decline: falling water levels in Lake Mälaren, the superior location of the Baltic island of Gotland for handling Russian-Byzantine trade and the emergence of nearby rival Sigtuna all led to its gradual disappearance after 975.

In Viking times, Björkö was actually two separate islands, with the main settlement located in the northwest corner of the one further north. As the land rose after the last Ice Age, the narrow channel between the two islands vanished, resulting in today's single kidney-shaped island; remains of jetties have been found where the channel would have been, as well as a rampart which acted as an outer wall for the settlement. The developed nature of Viking society is evident from modern finds: scissors, pottery and even keys have all been excavated. Among the remains of Viking-age life, the most striking is Birka's graveyard, which is the largest Viking-age burial ground in Scandinavia with around four hundred burial mounds, some accompanied by standing stones. Totally surrounding the site of the former village, the graveyard can be found outside the rampart by turning right from where the boat arrives. Major excavations began on the island in 1990 and the **Birka museum** (open in connection with boat arrivals and departures) now displays historical artefacts as well as scale models of the harbour and craftsmen's quarters.

Getting there

From Stockholm, Strömma Kanalbolaget sail from Stadshusbron outside the Stadshuset on Kungsholmen (May to early Sept daily 9.30am & 2.45pm; also July to mid-Aug daily 1.15pm; 1hr 45min; ⓦ www.strommakanalbolaget.com). Tickets can be bought on board and cost 200kr one-way or 270kr return which includes entry to the museum.

The Stockholm archipelago

If you've admired the view from the top of the Kaknästornet TV tower, you'll already have had a tantalizing glimpse of the **Stockholm archipelago**. In Swedish the word for archipelago is *skärgården* – literally "garden of skerries" and a pretty accurate description: the array of hundreds upon hundreds of pine-clad islands and islets is the only one of its kind in the world. Most of the little-known islands are flat and are wonderful places for **walking**; we've picked out the most rewarding islands for strolls and hikes, and have suggested a few trails which are a good way to take in the sweeping sea vistas and unspoilt nature here. The archipelago, though, holds another secret, little known even to most Swedes – many of **ABBA**'s most famous hits were written out here, on the island of Viggsö where the famous foursome owned a couple of summer cottages (see p.100).

Island practicalities

Getting to the islands is easy and cheap, with Waxholmsbolaget (☎08/679 58 30, ⓦwww.waxholmsbolaget.se) operating the majority of the passenger-only sailings into the archipelago; their boats leave from Strömkajen in front of the *Grand Hotel* and the National Museum. Tickets are very reasonable: Grinda, for example, is 85kr one-way, whereas Finnhamn, one of the furthest islands, is 120kr. Pay on the boat or at the Waxholmsbolaget office on Strömkajen. If you're planning to visit several islands, it might be worth buying the **Båtluffarkort** (Archipelago Card; 340kr, plus a 40kr refundable deposit on return of the card), which gives five days' unlimited travel on all Waxholmbolaget lines. There is usually a small charge for taking a bicycle.

Boats operate a fixed route calling at a dozen or so different islands in various parts of the archipelago; timetables posted on the quayside or available free from Waxholmsbolaget give full details of routes and timings. If you're waiting for the boat out in the archipelago, you must raise the semaphore flag on the jetty to indicate that you want to be picked up; torches are kept in the huts on the jetties for the same purpose at night. **Departures** to the closest islands (around 4 daily) are more frequent than those to the outer archipelago since journey times are correspondingly longer; if there's no direct service, connections can often be made on the island of Vaxholm.

In some parts of the archipelago, it's possible to visit a couple of islands on the same trip by taking the ferry to your first port of call, then **rowing** across to a neighbouring island, from where you return to Stockholm by the ferry again – we've detailed these options in the text. Since the ferries do not necessarily call at adjacent islands, rowing from one island to another can avoid the time-consuming backtracking and detours which would otherwise be necessary to switch between different ferry routes. For this purpose, there'll be a row-boat either side of the water separating you from your destination. When you use the boats, you have to ensure there's always one left on either side – this entails rowing across, attaching the other boat to yours, rowing back to your starting point, where you leave one boat behind, and then rowing across one last time.

Accommodation

There are few hotels in the archipelago but it does have plenty of well-equipped and comfortable **youth hostels**, all of which are open in the summer (May–Sept); we list the available hostels in the accounts of individual islands.

It's also possible to rent summer **cottages** on the islands for 3500–6000kr a week for four people – for more information on prices, contact the tourist office in Stockholm, where you can also pick up their *Bed & Breakfast in Stockholm's Archipelago* brochure. For summer stays, you'll need to book well in advance – at least six months before – or you may well find that you've been pipped to the post by holidaying Swedes.

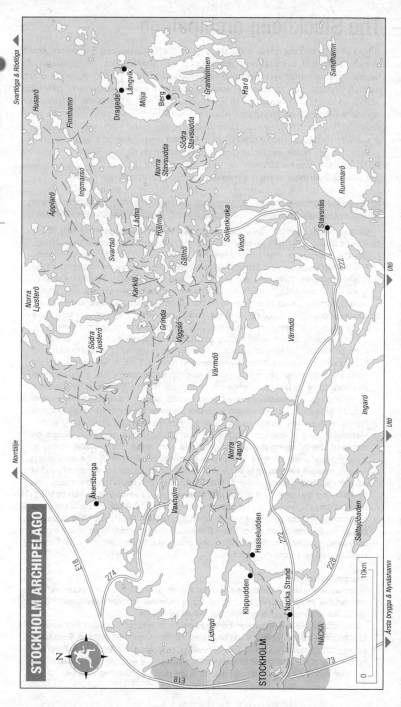

STOCKHOLM ARCHIPELAGO

N

Svartöga & Rödlöga

Nortälje

Utö

Utö

Ärsta brygga & Nynäshamn

Husarö
Finnhamn
Dragede
Långvik
Möja
Berg
Granholmen
Harö
Ingmarsö
Äpplarö
Norra
Stavsudda
Södra
Stavsudda
Runmarö
Sandhamn
Svartsö
Lådna
Hjälmö
Gällnö
Sollenkroka
Vindö
Stavsnäs
Karklö
Grinda
Viggsö
Värmdö
222
Norra
Ljusterö
Södra
Ljusterö
Akersberga
Vaxholm
Norra
Lagnö
Värmdö
Ingarö
E18
274
Hasseludden
Klippudden
222
228
Saltsjöbaden
Lidingö
Nacka Strand
NACKA
STOCKHOLM
E18
73

0   10km

From November to April, life in the archipelago can be tough, with the winter ice stretching far out into the Baltic and throwing boat timetables into confusion. But in summer the archipelago is at its best: the air is heavy with the scent of fresh pine, and seemingly endless forests are reflected in the deep blue of the sea. It's worth bearing in mind that when it's cloudy in Stockholm, chances are the sun is shining somewhere in the islands.

The central archipelago

The easiest section of the archipelago to reach, and consequently the most popular with day-tripping Stockholmers, the **central archipelago** is the islands at their most stunning: hundreds of rocks, skerries, islets and islands jostle for space in the pristine waters of the Baltic, giving the impression of giant stepping-stones leading back to the mainland. Navigating this maze of islands certainly takes experience, and at times boats here are forced to cut their speed to chug through narrow sounds and passageways. This is especially true on the narrow approach to **Vaxholm**, the first and most popular island in the central archipelago, whose charms lie in strolling the town's couple of main streets and browsing in the handful of small shops. Nearby **Grinda** can also be busy, though it does boast a number of sandy and rocky beaches to help disperse the summer crowds. For a more back-to-nature experience, head for **Gällnö** and, particularly, its neighbour **Karklö**. Tranquil, unspoilt havens of peace and solitude, the simple pleasures of walking through the forest, **nude sunbathing** (very popular in the archipelago) or swimming in the sea are the main attractions. **Svartsö**, on the other hand, is a little more developed than its southerly neighbours, with a number of small settlements and a shop selling provisions in addition to large expanses of forest and coastline to enjoy. One of the best **walks** can be found on **Ingmarsö**, in terms of appearance very similar to neighbouring Svartsö, leading through untouched forest to a narrow sound, where row-boats will take you over to tiny **Finnhamn**, a small hilly island with fine sea views – in terms of distance from Stockholm, this is one of the last inhabited islands of the archipelago.

Vaxholm

The island of **Vaxholm** lies only an hour from the capital by boat, and is a popular weekend destination for Stockholmers. Its eponymous town has an atmospheric wooden harbour, whose imposing fortress once guarded the waterways into the city, superseding the fortifications at Riddarholmen. Having successfully staved off attacks from the Danes and the Russians in the seventeenth and eighteenth centuries, the fortress is now an unremarkable museum of military bits and pieces (daily: June noon–4pm; July & Aug 11am–5pm; 50kr; Ⓦwww.vaxholmsfastning .se). However, since all boats to and from Stockholm dock at Vaxholm, it's often swarming with visitors, so do yourself a favour – stay on the boat and seek out one of the archipelago's quieter islands, which are quite frankly more worthy of your attention.

Grinda and Viggsö

Another firm favourite, though again a much-overrated destination, is **Grinda** (1hr 20min from Stockholm by boat), a thickly wooded island typical of the central archipelago, with some sandy beaches. It's particularly popular with families and so can be busy, particularly at weekends. In its favour, Grinda has frequent boat connections, a pleasant **youth hostel** (Ⓣ08/542 490 72, Ⓦwww .grindawardshus.se; late April to late Oct; 250kr dorm beds; double rooms ❷) on the south coast, east of the southern jetty, several ad hoc **campsites**, a **restaurant** and a **café** in the centre of the island. To enjoy the sunshine on summer afternoons, head for beaches on the southern side of the island, as the tall trees on the northern side block out the sun. Boats dock at two jetties on the island, at its southern (Södra Grinda) and northern ends (Norra Grinda); a walk between the two takes thirty to forty minutes.

On the approach to Södra Grinda, you'll pass a tear-shaped island tightly sandwiched in the narrow channel between Grinda and the much larger Värmdö to the south: this unassuming rocky outcrop topped by dense pine forest is **Viggsö**, the place where **ABBA** composed *Dancing Queen, Fernando* and several other chart-topping hits; shots of the island were also used in *ABBA The Movie*. Agnetha and Björn bought a summer cottage on Viggsö in 1971, closely followed in 1974 by Benny and Frida, who became neighbours on the other side of the island, the sound of piano music drifting across the treetops a sure sign that one or other couple had sailed their boat out from Stockholm to spend a few days away from the city. In fact, the members of the group often retreated to the island throughout their career, and the two men would spend days at a time in Björn's yellow wooden outhouse hammering away at a battered upright piano and strumming an old guitar, producing some of the greatest pop hits the world has ever known – the restorative calm of Viggsö was at the very heart of much of ABBA's music-making.

Gällnö and Karklö

A beautiful low-lying island covered with thick pine forest, **Gällnö** (1hr 30min–2hr from Stockholm by boat) is the archipelago at its best. Home to just thirty people, a couple of whom farm the land near the jetty, Gällnö has been designated a nature reserve: you can spot deer in the forest or watch eider ducks diving for fish. The idyllic **youth hostel** (☎08/571 661 17, ⓦwww.gallno.se; mid-May to Sept; dorm beds 230kr, double rooms ❶), surrounded by low-hanging trees, is easy enough to find; the track leading to it is well signposted from the tiny main village, where there's also a small **shop** selling provisions. From here, there's the choice of two **walks**: either head east through the forest for Gällnönäs, from where you can pick up boats back to Stockholm or further out into the islands, or alternatively, continue past the youth hostel, following signs for Brännholmen until you arrive at a small bay popular with yachties. Look for the hut where the toilet is, as one of its walls bears a map and sign on the outside showing the path leading from here to the row-boats – these enable you to cross the narrow sound (around 15m wide) separating Gällnö from its neighbour, Karklö. When you head across, remember to leave one boat on either side of the sound (see p.97).

Karklö (2hr from Stockholm by boat) is one of the most unspoilt islands in the archipelago and, combined with Gällnö, makes for an excellent day-trip from Stockholm. There are no shops or roads here, only tracks which meander across the island and around farmers' fields, connecting the spot where the row-boats are moored with the main jetty on the other side, where the boats from Stockholm dock. The paths can be difficult to find at times, so it's best to ask directions in the main village, which is close to the row-boat moorings.

Svartsö

North of Gällno (2–3hr from Stockholm by boat), **Svartsö** is busier than its neighbour, though it's never overrun with visitors and there's plenty of space to unwind and sunbathe on the rocky shores – particularly on the western edge of the island. With its fields of grazing sheep, thick virgin forest and crystal-clear lakes, Svartsö has a more pastoral feel than some of the other surrounding islands, where forest predominates, and there are also good roads which make it ideal for cycling or walking. From the northern jetty, where most boats from Stockholm arrive, there's a pleasant walk – lasting about ninety minutes – which takes you along the road towards the two lakes in the centre of the island. Just before you arrive at the lakes, turn right into the path that follows the lakeside, passing a few houses on the way. The road then becomes a track which heads into the forest. Continue past a couple of hayfields in a forest clearing, and eventually you'll glimpse the sea through the trees at the forest edge; this is an ideal place to sunbathe nude or stop for a picnic. Past a farmhouse and a couple of barns, the track eventually turns into a road again; from here it's another twenty- to thirty-minutes' walk to the village of **Alsvik**, with its post office and **shop** where you can buy snacks and refreshments – ferry connections back to the capital also depart from here.

Ingmarsö and Finnhamn

Ingmarsö (2hr 30min–3hr from Stockholm by boat) is an excellent island for walkers. Most boats dock at the northern jetty (Norra Ingmarsö), and from here you can do an enjoyable roundabout **walk** that takes you across the island and onto neighbouring Finnhamn, from where you can catch a boat back. Follow the main road away from the northern jetty, and after about fifteen minutes, turn left at the signpost marked "Båtdraget" and "Femsund". Before making this turn you may want to continue straight ahead for five minutes to the island's **supermarket** to stock up on provisions, before retracing your steps to the signpost. The road to Femsund eventually turns into a track – marked by blue dots on tree trunks – which strikes out through the forest heading for Kålmårsön. After about an hour, the path skirts a wonderfully isolated lake, where you can swim and sunbathe, before passing through more unspoilt forest and emerging at a small bay filled with yachts. Look carefully here for the continuation of the path – still marked with blue dots – which will take you to rowing-boat moorings at the narrow sound (around 20m wide) between here and Finnhamn. If you fail to locate the path, follow the coast round to the right for roughly ten to fifteen minutes while facing the yachts in the bay. It takes about two and a half hours to get to the sound from the northern jetty. Row over to Finnhamn, remembering to leave one row-boat on either side of the sound (see p.97).

Although only a tiny island, **Finnhamn** is often busy because of its popular **youth hostel** (℡08/542 462 12, ⓦwww.finnhamn.se; dorm beds 295kr, double rooms ❷), which is set in a dramatically located yellow building complete with waterfront sauna, and perched on rocks looking out to sea. To walk from the row-boat moorings to the main jetty and the youth hostel takes around forty minutes; the journey time back to Stockholm is around two hours. During summer, the café by the jetty serves up simple snacks and refreshments. If the crowds are too much here, head southeast from Finnhamn's tiny main village for the adjoining islet of Lilla Jolpan, where there are some good bathing opportunities.

The northern archipelago

Though similar in nature to their counterparts in the central archipelago, the islands in the northern stretches of the *skärgård* are far fewer in number. As a result, the appearance of the **northern archipelago** is very different: characterized by open vistas and sea swells rather than narrow sounds and passageways, the islands here are very much at the mercy of the sea and weather. The most interesting to make for are **Svartlöga** and **Rödlöga**, which are perfect for those seeking to get away from it all – if you're looking for your very own clearing in the forest or rocky beach, you won't go far wrong.

Svartlöga and Rödlöga

Lying far out in the Baltic towards Finland, Svartlöga and Rödlöga have untouched nature in plenty. **Svartlöga** is the only island in the archipelago whose forest is totally deciduous, and was one of the few to escape Russian incursions in 1719 during the Great Northern War. There are several good rocky beaches on which to relax after the long journey here. Neighbouring **Rödlöga** is a much tinier red-granite affair, with no roads – just leafy paths, overgrown hedgerows thick with wild roses, and wonderful secluded beaches. The boat journey from Stockholm to both islands takes roughly four hours (they are only 10min apart and the same boat calls at both islands), or ninety minutes from Furusund, a coastal town which can be reached from central Stockholm in about two hours by a cominbation of T-bana and bus: from Danderyds sjukhus T-bana, take bus #676 to Norrtälje, where you change to the #632 to Furusund.

The southern archipelago

Although sharing more in appearance with the denser central archipelago than its more barren northern counterpart, the **southern archipelago** is much quieter in terms of visitor numbers, because it's harder to reach from central Stockholm. The one notable exception is **Sandhamn**, a yachting Mecca which draws sailors from all across Sweden and the surrounding Baltic Sea countries. Though enjoyable, Sandhamn is often overrun with visitors and prices are inflated as a result. It's the much larger **Utö**, further to the south, which remains the southern archipelago's most likeable destination, with good opportunities for swimming and cycling.

Sandhamn

With its fine harbour, the island of **Sandhamn** (2hr from Stockholm by boat) has been a destination for seafarers since the eighteenth century and remains so today, attracting large numbers of yachts of all shapes and sizes. The main village is a haven of narrow alleyways, winding streets and overgrown verandahs. If you fancy staying overnight there are a couple of options: an exclusive and rather swanky **hotel**, *Seglarhotellet Sandhamn* (℡08/574 504 00, Ⓦwww.sandhamn.com; ❼), catering for wealthy yachties, and *Sandhamns Värdshus* (℡08/571 530 51, Ⓦwww .sandhamns-vardshus.se; ❹), a much smaller and altogether more agreeable bed-and-breakfast establishment – both places serve excellent seafood.

Utö

Far out in the southern reaches of the archipelago, **Utö** is flat and thus ideal for cycling around; it's not bad for bathing and picnics either. There are excellent views from the island's windmill on Kvarnbacken hill, ten-minutes' walk southwest of the jetty. It takes three and a half hours to get here by boat from Stockholm. The comfortable **youth hostel** (℡08/504 203 00, Ⓦwww.uto-vardshus.se; May–Sept; dorm bed 270kr, double rooms ❷) is near where the ferry docks, and has three elegant wooden verandahs overlooking the sea.

Around Lake Mälaren

Freshwater **Lake Mälaren** dominates the countryside west of Stockholm, and provides the backdrop to some of the capital region's most appealing destinations – all suitable for day-trips. Frequent **train services** run to **Västerås**, a modern and thoroughly enjoyable city on the northern shore of the lake, which is about an hour from Stockholm, and also boasts some excellent sandy **beaches** on a couple of islands just beyond the harbour. Closer to the capital, however, it's the enchanting lakeside village of **Mariefred** that really steals the show with its magnificent castle, **Gripsholm**. Trains link both Mariefred and Västerås, making it possible to complete a circuit around the lake without having to return to Stockholm – total travel time for this circuit is around four and a half hours.

Mariefred

If you've only got time for one boat trip outside Stockholm, make it to **MARIEFRED**, a tiny, quintessentially Swedish village about an hour west of the city, whose peaceful attractions are bolstered by one of Sweden's finest castles. A couple of minutes up from the quayside and you're strolling through narrow streets where the well-kept wooden houses and little squares haven't changed much in decades.

Steam-train fans will love the **Railway Museum** at the railway station in Läggesta (alight here for Mariefred), an adjoining small village five-minutes' bus ride south of Mariefred – you'll probably have noticed the narrow-gauge tracks running all the way to the quayside. There's an exhibition of old rolling stock and workshops, given added interest by the fact that narrow-gauge **steam trains** still run between Mariefred and **Läggesta**, a twenty-minute ride away on the Östra Sörmlands Järnväg railway (Ⓦ www.oslj.nu). These trains leave Mariefred roughly hourly between 11am and 5pm (late May to late June & mid-Aug to Sept Sat & Sun; late June to early Aug daily; ℡0159/210 00; 90kr return, half price for rail pass holders). From Läggesta, it's possible to pick up the regular SJ train back to Stockholm; check for connections at the Mariefred tourist office. Of course, you could always come to Mariefred from Stockholm by this route too (see p.104).

Gripsholms slott

Lovely though Mariefred is, it's really only a preface to seeing **Gripsholms slott**, the imposing red-brick castle built on a round island just to the south (mid-May to mid-Sept daily 10am–4pm; 70kr; Ⓦ www.royalcourt.se). Walk up the quayside, and you'll see the path to the castle running across the grass by the water's edge.

▲ Gripsholms slott

In the late fourteenth century, Bo Johnsson Grip, the Swedish high chancellor, began to build a fortified castle at Mariefred, although the present building owes more to two Gustavs – Gustav Vasa, who started rebuilding in the sixteenth century, and Gustav III, who was responsible for major restructuring a couple of centuries later. Rather than the hybrid that might be expected, the result is rather pleasing – an engaging textbook castle with turrets, great halls, corridors and battlements. There are optional English-language **guided tours** (mid-May to mid-Sept daily 1pm; 10kr extra) lasting one hour, on which the key elements of the castle's construction and history are pointed out: there's a vast portrait collection that includes recently commissioned works depicting political and cultural figures as well as assorted royalty and nobility; some fine decorative and architectural work; and, as at Drottningholm, a private theatre, built for Gustav III. It's too delicate to be used for performances these days, but in summer, plays and other events are staged out in the castle grounds; more information can be obtained from Mariefred's tourist office (see below). Even **ABBA** have put in an appearance here – in February 1974 Gripsholm was used as the cover shot for their *Waterloo* album.

Practicalities

To get to Mariefred by public transport, take the **train** from Stockholm to Läggesta, from where connecting buses and, at certain times of year, steam trains (see p.103) shuttle passengers into Mariefred. In summer, you can get here from Stockholm on a **steamboat**, the *S/S Mariefred*, which leaves from Klara Mälarstrand, near Stadshuset on Kungsholmen (late May to mid-June & mid-Aug to early Sept Sat & Sun 10am; mid-June to mid-Aug Tues–Sun 10am; 3hr 30min each way; 160kr one-way, 220kr return; Ⓦwww.mariefred.info); buy your ticket on board. The **tourist office** is in the fine eighteenth-century timber Rådhuset, the building with the large spire on top that's easily visible from the quay (June & Aug Mon–Fri 10am–6pm, Sat 11am–5pm; also July Sun 11am–5pm; early to mid-Sept Mon–Sat 10am–3pm; Ⓣ0159/296 99, Ⓦwww.mariefred.se).

Mariefred warrants a night's stay, if not for the sights – which you can exhaust in half a day – then for the pretty, peaceful surroundings. For **accommodation**, *Gripsholms Värdhus*, Kyrkogatan 1 (Ⓣ0159/347 50, Ⓦwww.gripsholms-vardhus .se; Ⓞ), a beautifully restored inn (the oldest in Sweden), is a wonderfully luxurious option overlooking the castle and the water – rooms here are gloriously opulent and elegant. At the other end of the scale, the youth hostel, *Djurgårdsporten*, is basic but centrally located at Djurgårdsgatan 2 (Ⓣ0159/124 15, Ⓦwww.imariefred .nu/djurgardsporten; dorm beds 200kr, double rooms Ⓞ).

As for **eating**, treat yourself to lunch in *Gripsholms Värdhus*. The food is excellent (mains cost 165–300kr) and the restaurant enjoys terrific views over to Gripsholm. Two other good spots are the classy *Strandrestaurangen* on the lakeside near the church, which serves up delicious lunches for 75kr and seafood mains (115–225kr) in the evening, and *Gripsholms slottspaviljong* (May–Aug only), in the park between the castle and the town centre, with meaty mains for 95–175kr. For **coffee** and cakes, head for *Fredmans konditori* in the main square, opposite the town hall at Kyrkogatan 11.

Västerås and around

Capital of the county of Västmanland and Sweden's sixth biggest city, **VÄSTERÅS** is an immediately likeable mix of old and new. Today, the lakeside conurbation carefully balances its dependence on ABB, the industrial technology giant, with a rich history dating back to Viking times. If you're looking for a place that's lively and cosmopolitan, yet retains cobbled squares, picturesque wooden houses and even a sixth-century royal burial mound, you won't go far wrong here. Västerås also boasts some of Lake Mälaren's best **beaches**, all a short ferry ride from the city centre.

Arrival and information

As the train pulls into Västerås, the first thing you'll notice is a sea of bicycles neatly standing in racks right outside the **train station** on Södra Ringvägen; arriving by **bus**, you'll be dropped at the adjacent terminal. The **airport**, served by Ryanair flights from London Stansted, is just 6km east of the city, from where **bus** #941 (Ⓦwww.vl.se) runs to the centre in connection with Ryanair flights (20kr).

From immediately opposite the train station, Kopparbergsvägen leads up to the town centre and the **tourist office** at no. 1, barely a two-minute walk away (Mon–Fri 10am–6pm, Sat 10am–3pm; also July to mid-Aug Sun 10am–2pm; ☏021/39 10 00, Ⓦwww.vasterasmalarstaden.se). There's internet access, too, at the tourist office.

Accommodation

There's plenty of choice of accommodation in Västerås and prices are quite reasonable. However, there's also a chance here to opt for somewhere altogether more unusual to stay (see below).

Arkad Östermalmsgatan 25 ☏021/12 04 80, Ⓦwww.hotellarkad.se. Individually designed rooms ranging from contemporary Swedish to nineteenth-century classic. Excellent sauna suite incorporating darts and pool. Good value for money, especially in summer and at weekends. ❺/❸

Elite Stadshotellet Storatorget ☏021/10 28 00, Ⓦwww.vasteras.elite.se. This classic Jugendstil hotel opened in 1907 and oozes old-world charm with its sweeping staircases, elaborate chandeliers and elegant rooms where contemporary and antique meet. Superb location in the main square at the heart of everything. ❺/❸

First Plaza Karlsgatan 9A ☏021/10 10 10, Ⓦwww.firsthotels.com/plaza. Known locally as the "Skyscraper", this 25-storey glass-and-chrome structure is the last word in Scandinavian chic. Rooms are light and airy, featuring stylish, contemporary Swedish design and have panoramic views of the city and Lake Mälaren. The summer/weekend rate is particularly good value. ❻/❹

🏃 **Hotell Hackspett** Vasaparken ☏021/39 10 00, Ⓦwww.vasterasmalarstaden.se. A fabulous one-room treehouse 13m off the ground in the largest oak tree in Vasaparken. The cost is 1150kr per person on a B&B basis or 1500kr per person for half-board, bookable through the tourist office.

Klipper Kungsgatan 4 ☏021/41 00 00, Ⓦwww.klipperhotel.se. This centrally located option overlooking the lazy Svartån river in the old town offers charming rooms done out in early nineteenth-century style. Make your own bed and forego breakfast and a double room costs just 495kr. ❸

Lövudden Lövudden, ☏021/18 52 30, Ⓦwww.lovudden.se. Västerås's youth hostel, complete with sauna and wonderful lake views, is 5km west of the city on Lake Mälaren; bus #25 (Mon–Sat roughly hourly, Sun 3 daily). Dorms sleep a maximum of six people and there's an onsite kitchen. Dorm bed 200kr, double rooms ❶

🏃 **Utter Inn** Lake Mälaren ☏021/39 10 00, Ⓦwww.vasterasmalarstaden.se. A platform about 1km out into the lake, not unlike a mini oil rig, whose one and only bedroom is actually underwater. Whilst not for the claustrophobic, a night spent underwater is certainly memorable. The cost is 1150kr per person on a B&B basis or 1500kr per person for half-board, bookable through the tourist office who will also arrange boat transport to the platform.

Västerås Vasagatan 22 ☏021/18 03 30, Ⓦwww.hotellvasteras.se. Modern if rather cramped rooms in this well-located hotel in town right in the city centre. A worthwhile 100kr extra gets you a superior room with a balcony overlooking one of the main shopping streets. ❸/❷

The City

From the tourist office, it's a short stroll up Köpmangatan to the twin cobbled squares of Bondtorget and Storatorget. The slender lane from the south-western corner of Bondtorget leads to the narrow **Svartån river**, which runs right through the centre of the city; the bridge over the river here (known as Apotekarbron) has great views of the old wooden cottages which nestle eave-to-eave along the riverside. Although it may not appear significant (the Svartån is actually much wider further upstream), the river was a decisive factor in making Västerås the headquarters of one of the world's largest engineering companies, **Asea-Brown-Boveri** (ABB), which needed a ready source of water for production; if you arrived by train from Stockholm you'll have passed their metallurgy and distribution centres on approaching the station. Back in the square, look out for the striking sculpture of a string of cyclists, the *Asea Stream*, which is supposed to portray the original workers of ABB as they made their way to work; today the sculpture is also a reminder of the impressive fact that Västerås has over 300km of bicycle tracks and is a veritable haven for cyclists.

North of the two main squares, the brick **Domkyrkan** (Mon–Fri 8am–5pm, Sat & Sun 9.30am–5pm) dates from the thirteenth century, although its two outer aisles are formed from a number of chapels built around the existing church during the following two centuries. The original tower was destroyed by fire, leaving Nicodemus Tessin the Younger (who also built the Kungliga Slottet in Stockholm, see p.70) to design the current structure in 1693. The highly ornate gilded oak triptych above the altar was made in Antwerp, and depicts the suffering and resurrection of Christ. To the right of the altar lies the tomb of Erik XIV, who died an unceremonious death imprisoned in Örbyhus castle in 1577 after eating his favourite pea soup – little did he realize it was laced with arsenic. Local rumour has it that the king's feet had to be cut off in order for his body to fit the coffin, which was built too small. Today though, his elegant, black-marble sarcophagus rests on a plinth of reddish sandstone from Öland.

Beyond the cathedral is the most charming district of Västerås, **Kyrkbacken**, a hilly area that stretches just a few hundred metres. Here, steep cobblestone alleys wind between well-preserved old wooden houses where artisans and the petit bourgeoisie lived in the eighteenth century. Thankfully, the area was saved from the great fire of 1714 – which destroyed much of Västerås – and the wholesale restructuring of the 1960s. At the top end of Djäknegatan, the main street of the district, look for a narrow alley called Brunnsgränd, along which is a house bearing the sign "Mästermansgården": it was once the abode of the most hated and ostracized man in the district – the town executioner.

A quick walk past the restaurants and shops of Vasagatan in the city centre will bring you to Storagatan, and eventually to the eye-catching modern **Stadshuset** in Fiskatorget – the building is a far cry from the Dominican monastery which once stood on this spot. Although home to the city's administration, the Stadshuset is best known for its 47 bells, the largest of which is known as "the Monk" and can be heard across the city at lunchtimes.

Across the square, the old town hall has been transformed into an **art museum** (Västerås Konstmuseum; June–Aug Tues–Fri 11am–4pm, Sat & Sun noon–4pm; rest of the year Tues–Fri 10am–5pm, Sat & Sun noon–5pm; free). It's worth a quick look for its contemporary collections of Swedish and other Nordic art – don't expect too much though. Continue across Slottsbron to the **castle**, today home to a dull collection of local paraphernalia inside the **county museum** (Västmanlands Länsmuseum; Thurs–Sun noon–4pm; free). The best exhibit lies just inside the entrance: the most lavish female burial in Sweden, in the form of a Viking boat grave from nearby Tuna, Badelunda; the boat was buried in clay for hundreds of years, which accounts for its remarkable state of preservation. The gold jewellery worn by the woman found in the boat dates from the Roman Iron Age, and is also on display.

Eating and drinking

Västerås has easily the best **restaurants** of any town around Lake Mälaren. You'll find all kinds of cuisine, from Thai to Greek, traditional Swedish- to British-style pub food. The city also has a lively **drinking scene**, including one cocktail bar 24 floors up, from where there are unsurpassed views of the lake.

Atrium Smedjegatan 6 ☏021/12 38 48. Dine amid Greek busts, Ionic columns and Olympic torches at this smart Greek restaurant serving moussaka (109kr), souvlaki (165kr) and a range of grilled meat dishes (from 125kr).

Bellman Storatorget 6 ☏021/41 33 55. The smartest restaurant in town with eighteenth-century furniture and linen tablecloths. Count on 125–199kr per dish, such as grilled catfish in red pepper sauce (172kr) or marinated lamb with chanterelle mushrooms (199kr), although lunch is considerably less expensive.

Bill o Bob Storatorget 5 ☏021/41 99 21. This pub restaurant with curious stained-glass windows covers all corners: everything from venison in juniper sauce (238kr) and beef in bearnaise sauce (192kr) to bacon burgers (124kr).

Bishops Arms Storatorget. Enjoyable British-style pub attached to the *Elite Stadshotellet*, with a large selection of beers and single malt whiskies. Pub food also available.

Brogården Storagatan 42. Vaulted riverside café with a range of decent sandwiches, quiches and cakes offering good views of the water and Västerås's old wooden houses.

Kalle på Spången Kungsgatan 2. Snug and cosy café with tabletop candles serving up great baguettes, pasta salads, lasagne and soup as well as cakes and a good choice of coffees.

Karlsson på taket Karlsgatan 9A ☏021/10 10 98. Chi-chi café-restaurant on the 23rd floor of the *First Plaza*. Not as expensive as you might imagine and the views are fantastic. Reckon on around 175–255kr per main dish, for example roast lamb, duck confit or rib-eye steak.

The *Sky Bar* upstairs has great cocktails and an unsurpassed view of the city.

Limone Storagatan 4 ☏021/41 75 60. Stylish though rather expensive modern Italian restaurant with high-backed leather chairs and painted walls, serving top-notch pasta starters at 94kr and regular meat mains, for example, beef in green pepper sauce for around 245kr.

Piazza di Spagna Vasagatan 26 ☏021/12 42 10. The best Italian in town and a very popular place for lunch. Don't be put off by the rather gloomy interior, the food here is perfectly nice and locals rave about the place. Pizzas cost 79–129kr whilst mains such as pepper steak (199kr) or thyme-marinated monkfish (205kr) are fairly priced.

Spicy Hot Sturegatan 20A ☏021/18 17 40. This understated interior with simple wooden tables and chairs is inordinately popular: excellent Thai curries and stir fries cost 89kr, and there's a range of vegetarian dishes. Takeaway prices 20kr less.

Tabazco Storagatan 36 ☏021/21 91 90. With 1960s stripy wallpaper and flower-power lamps, locals flock to this retro lounge restaurant for superb tapas (32–45kr) and Mediterranean grilled meats and fish: chicken breast (169kr), duck breast (198kr) and halibut (225kr). The restaurant is set back from the road in the courtyard.

Varda Vasagatan 14 ☏021/14 81 50. Chi-chi lounge restaurant with floor-to-ceiling windows and a stylish, contemporary interior that really draws the crowds. Try the roast reindeer (258kr) or the baked salmon (198kr) before retiring to the lounge to loll on the leather sofas by candlelight.

Around Västerås: the Anundshög burial mound

Whilst in Västerås, try not to miss nearby **Anundshög**, the largest royal burial mound in Sweden at 60m in diameter and 14m high, just 6km northeast of the city. Dating from the sixth century, the mound is said to be the resting place of King Bröt-Anund and his stash of gold. Although the mound has not been excavated, it's widely thought to contain the remains of a cremation burial and a stone cist. Anundshög was also used for sessions of the local *ting*, or Viking parliament, and several other smaller burial mounds nearby suggest that the site was an important Viking meeting place over several centuries. Beside the main mound lie a large number of **standing stones** arranged end-to-end in the shape of two ships measuring 53m and 50m in diameter. The nearby **rune stone** dates from around 1000 AD though it's not thought to be connected to the burial mound. The stone's inscription, when translated, reads "Folkvid erected all these stones for his son, Hedin, brother of Anund. Vred carved the runes."

To get here, take **bus** #12 from the centre of town to its final stop, Bjurhovda, from where it's a fifteen-minute walk – it's a good idea to ask for precise details at the tourist office in Västerås before setting out, as Anundshög is not signposted from the bus stop. Alternatively, take the new daily "museum bus" which leaves from Fiskartorget square near the art museum (mid-June to mid-Aug, hourly noon–4pm; 50kr)

Beaches and boat trips on Lake Mälaren

It's easy to forget that Västerås is situated on Lake Mälaren, as the centre of town is removed from the waterfront. Yet it's very easy to get out onto the lake, with **boat trips** operating to Västeråsfjärden and Ridöfjärden, the sections of the lake south of the city, which hold a string of small islands blessed with great **beaches**.

The closest island to Västerås is **Östra Holmen**, which is the easternmost of three islets located immediately off the coast. Noted for its three excellent **nudist beaches** on the southern shore, it's popular with locals who come here to enjoy the wide open views of Lake Mälaren and to explore the island's undisturbed shoreline – an easy circular walk of around 2km. *M/F Elba* sails here hourly (late May to early Sept daily 10.15am–5.45pm; 10min; 50kr return; Ⓦ www.rederimalarstaden.se) from Färjkajen quay in the harbour, southwest of the train station.

Further south, sitting roughly halfway between the northern and southern shores of the lake, the much larger island of **Ridön** traces its history back to Viking times, when it was home to a small fishing community. Today, Ridön is a peaceful haven of forest, sheltered coves ideal for **swimming**, and paths which lead around the entire coast. A country lane winds its way across the centre of the island from west to east; there's a small **café** and wooden bell tower at the point where this lane meets the path leading up from the ferry jetty. There are several daily sailings to Ridön from Färjkajen quay (May–Sept 7am–6.30pm roughly every 2hr; 40 min; 100kr return; Ⓦ www.rederimalarstaden.se).

En route, the boats call in at two smaller islands, **Almö–Lindö** and tiny **Skåpholmen** (both 90kr return), perfect for seekers of total solitude. Of these two uninhabited islands, cashew nut-shaped Almö-Lindö, which the boat reaches first, is the better bet since it's larger, has more varied terrain and some good swimming beaches – though no facilities. **Skåpholmen** is a skinny sliver of an island just off the southern shore of its larger neighbour. Its main attraction is total seclusion – if you're keen to spend a people-free day and are looking for your very own island where you can cast off your clothes and amble at will around the shoreline or through the forest – a quintessentially Swedish experience – this is the place to make for as you're likely to be the only person here: once again, there are no facilities.

Uppsala and around

First impressions as the train pulls into **UPPSALA**, only an hour northeast of Stockholm, are encouraging, as the red-washed castle looms up behind the railway sidings with the cathedral dominant in the foreground. A medieval seat of religion and learning, Uppsala clings to the past through its cathedral and university, and a striking succession of related buildings in their vicinity. The city is regarded as the historical and religious centre of the country, and attracts day-trippers seeking a

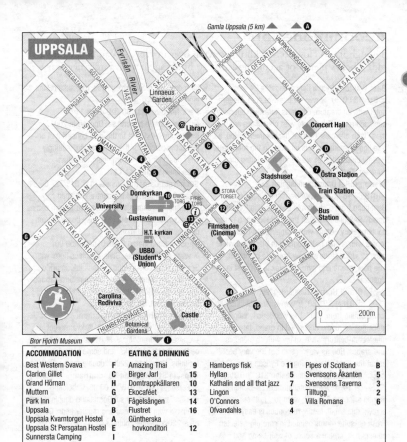

Gamla Uppsala (5 km) ▲ ▲ A

UPPSALA

ACCOMMODATION		EATING & DRINKING					
Best Western Svava	F	Amazing Thai	9	Hambergs fisk	11	Pipes of Scotland	B
Clarion Gillet	C	Birger Jarl	15	Hyllan	5	Svenssons Åkanten	5
Grand Hörnan	H	Domtrappkällaren	10	Kathalin and all that jazz	7	Svenssons Taverna	3
Muttern	G	Ekocaféet	13	Lingon	1	Tilltugg	2
Park Inn	D	Fågelsången	14	O'Connors	8	Villa Romana	6
Uppsala	B	Flustret	16	Ofvandahls	4		
Uppsala Kvarntorget Hostel	A	Güntherska					
Uppsala St Persgatan Hostel	E	hovkonditori	12				
Sunnersta Camping	I						

lively alternative to Stockholm as well as travellers looking for a worthwhile stop on the long trek north.

Arrival and information

The quickest way to get from Stockholm to Uppsala is by SJ train from the Central Station. As we went to press, Uppsala's new **Resecentrum** was taking shape on Kungsgatan, combining the existing **train** and **bus stations** into one neat travel interchange. There's cuurently internet access with Sidewalk Express inside the train station and at *Burger King*, Dragarbrunnsgatan 34. Whether you arrive by train or bus, the first sight that meets you outside is an erotic statue of a man with an oversized penis by local sculptor and painter, Bror Hjorth (see p.112). From here it's a fifteen-minute walk west to the **tourist office** at Fyris Torg 8 (Mon–Fri 10am–6pm, Sat 10am–3pm; end June to mid-Aug same hours plus Sun 11am–3pm; ☎018/727 48 00, ⊛www.uppland.nu), where you can pick up bundles of leaflets about the city. Uppsala can also be easily reached from Arlanda, Sweden's main **airport**; trains connect Arlanda C station with Uppsala (daily every 20min; 20min; 120kr) whilst bus #801 also runs to the city (daily every 15–30min; 40min; 100kr).

Accommodation

Though it's so close to Stockholm, staying over in Uppsala can be an attractive idea. There's plenty of accommodation so booking ahead is rarely necessary.

Best Western Svava Bangårdsgatan 24 ☏018/13 00 30, ⓦwww.hotelsvava.com. Modern hotel with all creature comforts, including specially designed rooms for people with disabilities and those with allergies. Outside the summer period, a free light evening meal is included in the room rate. Heavily discounted at weekends and during the summer. ❹/❸

Clarion Gillet Dragarbrunnsgatan 23 ☏018/68 18 00, ⓦwww.clarionhotelgillet.se. Benefiting from a change of owners, this former dowdy SAS pile has been transformed into a contemporary beauty with Scandinavian designer rooms with stylish bathrooms with black and white tiles, all just a stone's throw from the cathedral. The pool, sauna and gym complex is the best in Uppsala. ❻/❹

🏃 **Grand Hörnan** Bangårdsgatan 1 ☏018/13 93 80, ⓦwww.grandhotellhornan .com. Dating from 1907, this wonderfully elegant place boasts rooms decorated in grand, late nineteenth-century style, many with chandeliers and drapes. Rooms vary in size but the very best are at the front, overlooking the Fyrisån river. ❻/❺

🏃 **Muttern** St Johannesgatan 31C ☏018/51 04 14, ⓦwww.hotellmuttern.se. Curiously named after the Swedish word for "nut" (as in screw), this small, family-run option is easy to like. Fresh en-suite rooms painted in carefully selected colours help create a sense of well-being and

harmony. The reasonable prices, too, aid a restful night's sleep. ❹/❸

Park Inn Storgatan 30 ☏018/68 11 00, ⓦwww.uppsala.parkinn.se. Opened in 2001, this trendy hotel next to the new concert hall is perfectly located for the train station. Invitingly cosy designer rooms containing the latest Scandinavian chic. ❻/❹

Sunnersta Camping Graneberg ☏018/727 60 84. Located 7km south of the centre and open May–Aug, the campsite also has two-person cabins by Lake Mälaren for rent (❶). Take bus #20 from outside the train station.

Uppsala Kungsgatan 27 ☏018/480 50 00, ⓦwww.profilhotels.se. Style-concious hotel with Scandinavian colours and designs taking pride of place, resulting in eye-catching natural fabrics and woods which help make this hotel one of Uppsala's best. ❻/❸

Uppsala Kvarntorget Vandrarhem Kvarntorget 3 ☏018/24 20 08, ⓔkvarntorget @uppsalavandrarhem.se. Most rooms have regular beds, rather than bunks, and some have private facilities. Dorm beds 220kr; double rooms ❶

Uppsala St Persgatan Vandrarhem St Persgatan 16 ☏018/10 00 08, ⓔbokning @uppsalavandrarhem.se. Dorms and double rooms available with bunk beds and regular beds. Dorm beds 220kr; double rooms ❶

The City

From the train and bus stations, it's best to make the new **concert hall** your first port of call, barely a five-minute walk away on Storgatan just the other side of the train tracks. A mammoth structure of brushed steel and glass, whose facade resembles the keys of a giant piano keyboard, it's certainly divided local opinion; many people believe it's little more than a huge carbuncle. Be that as it may, venture inside and take the escalators to the top floor for a superb **view** of the entire city. From the concert hall, Vaksalagatan leads back under the train tracks and up towards the great **Domkyrkan**, Scandinavia's largest cathedral (daily 8am–6pm; free; ⓦwww.uppsaladomkyrka.se) and the centre of the medieval town. Built as a Gothic boast to the people of Trondheim in Norway that even their mighty church, the Nidarosdom, could be overshadowed, it loses out to its rival only on building materials – local brick rather than imported stone. The echoing interior remains impressive, particularly the French Gothic ambulatory, flanked by tiny chapels and bathed in a golden, decorative glow. One chapel contains a lively set of restored fourteenth-century wall paintings that recount the legend of St Erik, Sweden's patron saint: his coronation, subsequent crusade to Finland, eventual defeat and execution at the hands of the Danes. The Relics of Erik are zealously guarded in a chapel off the nave: poke around and you'll also find the tombs of the Reformation rebel Gustav Vasa and his son Johan III, and that of the botanist Linnaeus (see p.112), who lived in Uppsala. Time and fire have led to the rest of the cathedral being rebuilt, scrubbed and painted to the extent that it resembles a museum more than a thirteenth-century place of worship; even the characteristic twin spires are late nineteenth-century additions.

The other buildings grouped around the Domkyrkan can all claim a purer historical pedigree. Opposite the west end of the cathedral, the onion-domed **Gustavianum** (Tues–Sun 11am–4pm; 40kr) was built in 1625 as part of the university, and is much touted by the tourist office for the masterpiece of kitsch that is the **Augsburg Art Cabinet** – a treasure chest of black oak containing all manner of knick knacks presented to Gustav II Adolf by the Lutheran councillors of Augsburg in 1632 – and the world's first ever thermometer from 1745 owned by none other than Anders Celsius, inventor of the temperature scale. Whilst here be sure to make it up to the top floor to see the perfectly preserved **anatomical theatre** from 1660 where convicts' bodies were once carved up in the name of science, until the church stepped in to end the practice. The same building houses a couple of small collections of Egyptian, Classical and Viking antiquities.

The current **University** building (Mon–Fri 8am–4pm) is the imposing nineteenth-century Renaissance-style edifice opposite Gustavianum. Originally a seminary, today it's used for lectures and seminars and hosts the graduation ceremonies each May. Among the more famous alumni are Carl von Linné (Linnaeus; see p.112) and Anders Celsius. No one will mind you strolling in for a quick look, but the rest of the building is not open to the public.

From the university, Övre Slottsgatan leads south to the **Carolina Rediviva** (mid-May to Sept Mon–Thurs 9am–6.30pm, Fri until 5.30pm, Sat 10am–5pm, Sun 10am–4pm; rest of the year Mon–Fri 9am–8pm, Sat 10am–5pm; mid-May to Sept 20kr, otherwise free), the university library and one of Scandinavia's largest, with around five million books. On April 30 (Valborgsmässoafton) each year the students meet here to celebrate the official first day of spring (usually in the snow), all wearing the traditional student cap that gives them the appearance of disaffected sailors. Take a look in the **manuscript room**, where there's a collection of rare letters and other paraphernalia. The beautiful sixth-century Silver Bible is on permanent display, as is Mozart's original manuscript for *The Magic Flute*.

After this, the **castle** (guided tours mid-June to Aug Tues–Sun 1pm & 3pm; 70kr) up on the hill, built by Gustav Vasa in the mid-sixteenth century, is a disappointment. Certainly significant chapters of Sweden's history were played out here over the centuries: the Uppsala Assembly of 1593, which established the supremacy of the Lutheran Church, took place in the Hall of State, where also, in 1630, the Parliament resolved to enter the Thirty Years' War. Sadly though, much of the castle was destroyed in the 1702 fire that also did away with three-quarters of the city, and only one side and two towers – the L-shape of today – remain of what was once an opulent rectangular palace. Inside, admission also includes access to the castle's art museum but, quite frankly, it won't make your postcards home.

The Linnaeus Garden

Seeing Uppsala – at least its compact older parts – will take up a good half-day; afterwards, take a stroll along the Fyrisån river that runs right through the centre of town. In summer, there are several places here that are good for an hour or two's sunbathing, and there's enough greenery to make for a pleasant wander. One beautiful spot is the **Linnaeus Garden** (May–Sept Tues–Sun 11am–8pm; 50kr includes the museum; Ⓦ www.linnaeus.uu.se) over the river on Svartbäcksgatan, which contains around 1300 varieties of plants. These are Sweden's oldest botanical gardens, established in 1655 by Olof Rudbeck the Elder, and relaid by Linnaeus

Carl Von Linné

Born in Småland in 1707, **Carl von Linné**, who styled himself Carolus Linnaeus, is undoubtedly Sweden's most revered scientist: any Swedish town of a decent size has a street named Linnégatan, one of Gothenburg's most appealing districts (see p.137) is named after him. His international reputation was secured by the introduction of his **binomial classification**, a two-part nomenclature that enabled plants and animals to be consistently named and categorized into families; it was Linnaeus who invented the term *homo sapiens*, for example. Only very recently has the basis of his classifications been undermined by genetic methods, resulting in the complete realignment of certain plant families.

In 1732, while still a university student, he secured funds from the bishop of Växjö to undertake a botanical expedition to Lapland. His later expeditions to the Baltic islands of Öland and Gotland, and the mainland provinces of Västergotland and Skåne, were to provide the cornerstones for the creation of his ground-breaking system of plant classification. In 1754 he acquired an estate at **Hammarby**, 13km southeast of Uppsala, and built a house there. Today, the beautiful homestead, with lush gardens (May–Sept Tues–Sun 11am–8pm) including a collection of Siberian plants and a gene bank for the fruit species of the Lake Mälaren region, is managed by the university (May–Sept Tues-Sun 11am–5pm; 50kr including the garden). A special service, the Linnébuss, leaves Uppsala train station for Hammarby every hour (late May to mid-Sept daily 11am–5pm; 80kr; ⓦwww.ul.se/linnebussen) calling at the Linnaeus garden and the cathedral on the way where you can hop on and off. Tickets can be bought onboard and give free entrance to the garden.

(see box above) in 1741 with perennials and annuals either side of the central path; some of the species he introduced and classified still survive here. Incidentally, you can see the garden behind Linnaeus's head on the 100kr note. The adjoining **museum** (May–Sept Tues–Sun 11am–5pm; 50kr includes the garden) was home to Linnaeus and his family from 1743 to 1778, and attempts to evoke his life through a partially restored library, his writing room and even the bed where he breathed his last. While you're in Uppsala, you may also wish to visit the great man's former house at Hammarby, south of town (see box above).

The Bror Hjorth museum

Travelling around Sweden, you can't help but spot the work of Uppsala-born sculptor and painter, **Bror Hjorth** (1894–1968), a former professor of drawing at the Swedish Royal Academy of Fine Arts, who's considered one of Sweden's greatest artists. A modernist with roots in folk art, his numerous public art commissions can be seen right across the country – perhaps most strikingly in the church in Jukkasjärvi in Lapland (see p.377). His former home and studio in Uppsala have now been turned into a **museum** (Thurs–Sun noon–4pm, also mid-June to mid-Aug Tues & Wed noon–4pm; 30kr, free on Fri) containing the largest and most representative collection of his work in the country. Buses #6 and #7 run from the city centre to the museum, located a ten-minute ride west of the centre at Norbyvägen 26.

Eating, drinking and nightlife

In keeping with its status as one of Sweden's largest cities and major university centres, Uppsala boasts an impressive range of sophisticated **restaurants** and **bars**. Almost all of them are located in the grid of streets bordered by the Fyrisån river, St Olofsgatan and Bangårdsgatan, and since it can be busy in Uppsala in summer, booking a table is worthwhile.

Cafés and restaurants

Amazing Thai Bredgränd 14 ⓣ018/15 30 10. This small and friendly place has even won awards from the Thai state for its tasty food, which is widely regarded as the best in town: stir fries from 99kr, curries from 109kr or a three-course set menu for a tremendously good value 139kr.

Birger Jarl Nedre Slottsgatan 3 ⓣ018/71 17 34. This rambling wooden structure immediately below the castle has a meat-heavy menu dominated by several different types of burgers (130kr) and steaks. It's an entertaining place to spend an evening as there's often live music while you eat. Wed–Sat only.

Domtrappkällaren St Eriks Gränd 15 ⓣ018/13 09 55. One of the most chi-chi places in town, with an old vaulted roof and a great atmosphere. Main dishes such as reindeer fillet with asparagus and chanterelle mushrooms or home-prepared gravadlax with potato salad go for 135–275r; excellent lunch upstairs from 85kr.

Ekocaféet Drottninggatan 5. The most environmentally aware café in town and a student favourite serving eco-everything. The environs fit the bill too: green wooden chairs and benches with multi-coloured cushions beside a battered old upright piano.

Fågelsången Munkgatan 3. Plying the masses with caffeine since 1954, this agreeable café has become an Uppsala institution over the years, renowned for its terrific selection of pastries and cakes as well as good-value sandwiches: a cheese and ham ciabatta costs just 62kr.

Güntherska hovkonditori Östra Ågatan 31. Gloriously old-fashioned café serving simple lunch dishes for around 70kr, and a mouthwatering selection of cakes and pastries.

Hambergs fisk Fyris Torg 8 ⓣ018/71 21 50. A smartly tiled seafood restaurant with a trio of dried fish hanging in the window. It serves a good selection of Mediterranean fish which is imported directly from France, as well as the usual Swedish classics like salmon. Particularly popular at lunchtime. Reckon on 150–250kr per dish.

Lingon Svartbäcksgatan 30 ⓣ018/10 12 24. Come here for upmarket Swedish home cooking and dine in genteel surroundings that resemble an elegant country manor. Mains are in the 185–239kr range and feature classics such as fried Baltic herring, oxtail and slices of reindeer with horseradish. Rear terrace in summer.

Ofvandahls Sysslomangatan 3–5. Near the old part of town, this lively café with antique furniture and fittings opened in 1878. Don't leave town without trying the home-made cakes.

Svenssons Åkanten St Eriks Torg ⓣ018/15 01 50. The wonderful riverside summer-only restaurant beside the Saluhallen market hall has great views and is a firm favourite with Uppsala folk. Lots of barbecue dishes such as chicken breast (155kr) and rack of lamb (195kr) as well as lighter salads (from 85kr). The starter of whitefish roe on grilled brioche with red onion and dill (120kr) is heavenly.

Svenssons Taverna Sysslomangatan 14 ⓣ018/10 09 08. This is one of Uppsala's most popular eateries, specializing in deep-pan pizzas served on a wicker basket tray from 159kr. There are also a couple of other Asian-inspired meat dishes such as barbecued duck breast (165kr) and salmon tournedos (155kr). Large outdoor seating area in the shade of huge beech and oak trees.

Tilltugg Vaksalagatan 24 ⓣ018/12 97 01. A style-concious lounge bar with white leather chairs and a bar dressed in mosaic tiles serving a terrific range of tapas for 20–60kr, ranging from olives to garlic scampi. A plate of mixed warm tapas goes for 90kr.

Villa Romana St Persgatan 4 ⓣ018/12 50 90. A decent Italian restaurant with elegant old wallpaper and a nice wooden floor serving pasta dishes such as linguine with tiger prawns and fennel for 149–175kr and meat and fish mains courses, including grilled swordfish with risotto, at 175–255kr.

Bars, clubs and live music

By evening Uppsala's large student population makes its presence felt and more often than not the city centre is abuzz with life. The most popular places for a drink are all within easy walking distance of each other and are listed below.

Birger Jarl Nedre Slottsgatan 3. A fun and popular place for a drink and a good bet for live music, usually on Fri & Sat eve.

Flustret Svandammen 1. This fancy twin-towered Tivoli-style building has consistently been one of the busiest drinking holes in town since the 1950s, attracting students and locals alike. A pub and nightclub rolled into one that really rocks on Fri & Sat nights.

Hyllan St Eriks Torg. The contemporary brick and steel surrounds of this urban loft bar would fit perfectly in New York. Located in the roof space of the Saluhallen, this is Uppsala at its most sophisticated.

Kathalin and all that jazz Roslagsgatan 1. Uppsala's premier spot for live jazz (Fri–Sun nights) located in the converted goods sheds known as Östra Station behind the main train station.

O'Connors Storatorget 1. A first-floor Irish pub with food, tucked away above the fast-food joint, *Jalla*, that's a good place to start the evening. It's quite astounding just how many people can crowd into this pub – always busy and fun.

Pipes of Scotland Kungsgatan 27. At the corner of St Olofsgatan and Kungsgatan and the latest addition to the pub scene and inordinately popular. People flock here for the After Work happy hour (Mon–Fri 4.30–7pm) when there's also a buffet.

Gamla Uppsala

Five kilometres to the north of Uppsala, three huge royal **burial mounds** dating back to the sixth century mark the original site of the town, **Gamla Uppsala** (ⓦ www.raa.se/gamlauppsala). According to legend, they are the final resting places of three ancient kings – Aun, Egil and Adlis. Though the site developed into an important trading and administrative centre, it was originally established as a pagan settlement and a place of ancient sacrificial rites by the Svear tribe. In the eleventh century, the German chronicler, Adam of Bremen, described the cult of the *æsir* (the Norse gods Odin, Thor and Freyr) practised in Uppsala: every ninth year, the deaths of nine people would be demanded at the festival of Fröblot, the victims left hanging from a nearby tree until their corpses rotted. Two centuries later, the great medieval storyteller, Snorri Sturluson of Iceland, depicted Uppsala as the true home of the Ynglinga dynasty (the original royal family in Scandinavia who also worshipped Freyr), a place where grand sacrificial festivals were held in honour of their god.

The pagan temple where these bloody sacrifices took place is now marked by the Christian **Gamla Uppsala kyrka** (daily 9am–4pm), which was built over pagan remains when the Swedish kings first took baptism in the new faith. Built predominantly of stone yet characterized by its rear nave wall of stepped red-brick gabling, this is one of the most breathtakingly beautiful churches in Sweden, with an understated simplicity at the very heart of its appeal. Although what survives of the church today is only a remnant of the original cathedral, the relics inside more than compensate for the downscaling. In the porch are two impressive collecting chests, one made from an oak log and fitted with iron locks, which dates from the earliest days of the church. Entering the nave, look out for the cabinet on the left containing a superb collection of church silver, including a fourteenth-century chalice and a censer from the 1200s. Nearby, in the nave wall, a stone memorial to Anders Celsius, inventor of the temperature scale that bears his name, is a worthy tribute. Outside, if you haven't yet set eyes on a genuine rune stone in Sweden, look carefully in the church walls at the back to find a perfectly preserved example from the eleventh century.

The burial mounds and the Historical Centre

Southeast of the church, the **tinghög** or parliament hill (the only mound not fenced in) was once the site of the local *ting* where, until the sixteenth century, a Viking parliament was held to deliberate on all matters affecting Uppsala. Immediately west of here, a path leads around the three main mounds, the first of which, **östhögen** – the east mound – dates from around 550. Following the 1846–47 excavations of Gamla Uppsala, this hill yielded the site's most astonishing artefacts: the cremated remains of a woman – possibly a priestess for the god Freyr – buried in magnificent wool, linen and silk clothing, as well as a necklace bearing a powerful image of a Valkyrie. The adjacent central mound, **mitthögen**, is thought to be around fifty years older than its neighbour but has still to be excavated. Finally, the western **västhögen** has been dated from the late sixth century, and following excavations in 1874 revealed male bone fragments and jewellery commensurate with high status.

The finds are proudly displayed at the entrance to the new and enjoyable **Gamla Uppsala Historical Centre** (May to Aug daily 11am–5pm; Sept to mid-Dec & Jan–April Wed, Sat & Sun noon–3pm; 50kr), a brave and successful attempt to portray early Swedish history in a wider non-Viking context. You can gawp at an archeologist's dream – gold fragments, ancient pieces of glass and precious ivory game pieces – as well as ambling through exhibitions illustrating the origin of local myths. There's also a full account of Uppsala's golden period, which ended in the thirteenth century.

Practicalities

Buses #2 and #110 from Vaksalagatan in Uppsala drop you at the Gamla Uppsala terminus, in reality nothing more than a bus stop next to a level crossing opposite the Historical Centre. From the bus stop cross the busy Stockholm–Uppsala mainline at the level crossing to reach the site; from the Centre paths lead to the church and burial mounds. If the munchies strike after an afternoon of pillaging and plundering, there's a good **restaurant** nearby: *Odinsborg* (℡018/32 35 25; May–Sept daily 10am–6pm; Oct–April Sat & Sun 11am–4pm), halfway between the Historical Centre and the church, was built in the Swedish National Romantic style and serves a buffet lunch for 165kr, and a few other main courses such as salmon (119kr) or schnitzel (199kr), though nothing else – it is precisely this absence of touristy adornments that has helped Gamla Uppsala remain so mysterious and atmospheric.

Sigtuna

For more ancient history, look no further than **SIGTUNA**, 40km south of Uppsala, a compact little town that dates all the way back to Viking times, with extensive ruined churches and rune stones right in the centre. Apart from its ruins, it looks like any other old Swedish town with cobbled streets and squares. Scratch the surface though, and you'll understand what made Sigtuna so important. Founded in 980 by King Erik Segersäll, Sigtuna grew from a village to become Sweden's first town. Fittingly, it contains Sweden's oldest street, Storagatan; the original, laid out during the king's reign, still lies under its modern-day counterpart. Sigtuna also boasts three intriguing **ruined churches** dating from the twelfth century.

Two of the most impressive ruins, the churches of **St Per** and **St Olof**, lie along Storagatan itself. Much of the west and central towers of St Per's still remain from the early 1100s; experts believe it likely that the church functioned as a cathedral until the diocese was moved to nearby Uppsala (see p.108). The unusual formation of the vault in the central tower was influenced by church design then current in England and Normandy. Further east along Storagatan, St Olof's has impressively thick walls and a short nave, the latter suggesting that the church was never completed.

Close by on Olofsgatan (daily 9am–5pm) is the very much functioning **Mariakyrkan**, constructed of red brick during the mid-thirteenth century to serve the local Dominican monastery. Inside, the walls and ceiling are richly adorned with restored paintings from the fourteenth and fifteenth centuries.

The Sigtuna district contains more rune stones than any other area in Sweden – around 150 of them have been found to date – and several can be seen close to the ruins of the church of St Lars along Prästgatan. Further along the main road, Storagatan, the **Sigtuna museum** at no. 55 (daily noon–4pm; closed Mon Sept–May; 20kr; ⓦ www.sigtunamuseum.se) includes material on Sigtuna's role as Sweden's foremost trading centre. Coins bear witness to the fact that this was the first town in the land to mint coins, in 995, plus there's booty from abroad: gold rings and even an eleventh-century clay egg, from Kiev.

Practicalities

To reach Sigtuna from Uppsala or Stockholm, take either the train to Märsta, from where **buses** #570 and #575 run the short distance to the town – the total journey time is around 45 minutes.

Sigtuna's **tourist office** is at Storagatan 33 (June–Aug Mon–Sat 10am–6pm, Sun 11am–5pm; Sept Mon–Fri 10am–5pm, Sat & Sun 11am–4pm; Oct–May Mon–Fri 10am–5pm, Sat 11am–4pm, Sun noon–4pm; ℡08/594 806 50, ⓦhttp://sal.sigtuna.se/turism). Should you decide to stay overnight, there's a delightful little **youth hostel**, *Fågelsångens vandrarhem* (℡073/404 43 40, ⓔfagelsangensvandrarhem@hotmail.com; no dorm beds; ❶, 100kr extra for sheets), right in the town centre by the main square at Fågelsångsvägen 3; with only two rooms, booking ahead is essential. However, total luxury is also available at *Sigtuna Stadshotell*, Stora Nygatan 3 (℡08/592 501 00, ⓦwww.sigtunastadshotell.se; ❼), in an exclusive five-star design hotel stuffed full of period fittings from the early 1900s.

There are a couple of places to **eat** located off the main street: the atmospheric *Tant Bruns kaffestuga* café, at Laurentii gränd 3, specializes in home-made bread and is housed in a seventeenth-century building with outdoor seating in summer; *Farbror Blå* (℡08/592 560 50) at Storatorget 4, next to the town hall, serves excellent Swedish home cooking. Also worth a look is the floating *Båthuset* on Strandpromenaden, a pontoon supporting a little wooden restaurant dishing up delicious fish and beef mains for around 150kr. The best place to **drink** is *The Corner Pub*, Stationsgatan 3, a ten- to fifteen-minute bus ride away opposite the train station in Märsta, which also has bar meals and an impressive range of beers and whiskies.

Travel details

Trains

Stockholm to: Gällivare (2 daily; 15hr); Gävle (hourly; 1hr 20min); Gothenburg (hourly; 3hr by X2000, 5hr by InterCity); Karlstad (9 daily; 2hr 30min); Kiruna (2 daily; 16hr); Läggesta (for Mariefred; hourly; 35min); Luleå (2 daily; 13hr); Malmö (hourly; 4hr 30min); Mora (2 daily; 4hr); Östersund (3 daily; 6hr); Sundsvall (9 daily; 3hr 20min); Umeå (1 daily; 11hr 30min); Uppsala (every 20min; 40min); Västerås (hourly; 1hr).
Läggesta to: Stockholm (hourly; 35min).
Uppsala to: Gällivare (2 daily; 14hr); Gävle (hourly; 40min); Kiruna (2 daily; 15hr); Luleå (2 daily; 12hr); Mora (2 daily; 3hr); Östersund (3 daily; 5hr); Stockholm (every 20min; 40min); Sundsvall (9 daily; 2hr 35min); Umeå (daily; 11hr).
Västerås to: Stockholm (hourly; 1hr); Gothenburg (6 daily; 4hr); Luleå (1 daily; 15hr).

Buses

Märsta to: Sigtuna (every 20min; 20min)
Stockholm to: Gothenburg (10 daily; 7hr); Gävle (2 daily; 4hr 30min); Helsingborg (2 daily; 8hr 30min); Jönköping (2 daily; 5hr); Kalmar (2 daily; 6hr); Malmö (2 daily; 10hr); Norrköping (hourly; 1hr 20min); Umeå (1 daily; 9hr 20min); Östersund (1 daily; 8hr 30min).

Ferries

For details of Stockholm city ferries, see p.60; for the services to the archipelago, see p.97; for Birka see p.96.

International trains

Stockholm to: Copenhagen (2 daily; 5hr); Narvik (1 daily; 19hr); Oslo (2 daily; 6hr).
Uppsala to: Narvik (1 daily; 18hr 30min).

Gothenburg and around

CHAPTER 2 # Highlights

❋ **Café life on Avenyn, Gothenburg** Sip a coffee at the laid-back pavement cafés on Gothenburg's main street – perfect for people-watching. See p.128

❋ **Fürstenberg galleries, Gothenburg** The highlight of the city's grand Konstmuseum, housing paintings by Sweden's finest nineteenth- and early twentieth-century artists. See p.133

❋ **Marstrand** This glorious fortress island on the Bohuslän coast buzzes with activity in the summer, when the yachting set joins the sea bathers. See p.144

❋ **Fiskebäckskil** This picture-perfect fishing village on the Bohuslän coast is home to painter Carl Wilhelmson's studio. See p.146

❋ **Kosteröarna** These unspoilt islands off Strömstad are the perfect place to chill. Cycle through the forest or relax on the beach. See p.152

❋ **Karlstad** This shimmering lakeside town on Lake Vänern is known for its long hours of sunshine, great beaches and laid-back inhabitants. See p.157

❋ **Rafting on the Klarälven river, Värmland** Build your own raft and glide down one of Sweden's most enchanting rivers. See p.162

▲ Avenyn

2

Gothenburg and around

O f all the cities in southern Sweden, the grandest is the western port of **Gothenburg**. Designed by the Dutch in 1621, the country's second largest city boasts splendid Neoclassical architecture, masses of sculpture-strewn parkland and a welcoming and relaxed spirit. The cityscape of broad avenues, elegant squares, trams and canals is not only one of the prettiest in Sweden, but also the backdrop to long-established art and youth scenes, and a well-developed café society. There is a certain resentment on the west coast that Stockholm wins out in the national glory stakes, but Gothenburg's easier-going atmosphere – and its closer proximity to western Europe – makes it first choice as a place to live for many Swedes. Talk to any Gothenburger and they will soon disparage the more frenetic lives of the "08-ers" – 08 being the telephone code for Stockholm. Gothenburg has a buoyancy of its own though – thanks to its highly visible student population – that inspires you to explore.

The regions to the north and east of the city are prime targets for domestic tourists. To the north, the craggy **Bohuslän coast**, with its uninhabited islands, tiny fishing villages and clean beaches, attracts thousands of holiday-makers along its entire length. The coast is popular with the sailing set, and there are many guest harbours along the way from Gothenburg. One highlight is the glorious fortress island of **Marstrand**, which makes for an easy and enjoyable day-trip from Gothenburg, while further north, the **Koster** islands offer splendid isolation and abundant birdlife.

To the northeast of the city, the vast and beautiful lakes of **Vänern** and **Vättern** provide the setting for a number of historic towns, fairytale castles and some splendid inland scenery, all of which are within easy reach of Gothenburg. The lakes are connected to each other (and to the east and west coasts) by the cross-country **Göta Canal**, allowing you to take a lovely trip by boat all the way from Gothenburg to Stockholm. Other agreeable waterside towns vie for your attention: the picturesque medieval kernel of **Mariestad**, on Vänern's eastern shore, and the huge military fortress at **Karlsborg**, on the western shore of Lake Vättern, both make worthwhile stops. The lake region's main town is **Karlstad**, a thoroughly likeable place that sits snugly on Vänern's northern shore, and is the perfect jumping-off point for **river-rafting** trips through the rural province of **Värmland**.

Trains and buses provide most of the region with a regular, efficient service; the only area you may find difficult to explore without a car is the Bohuslän coast. Accommodation is never a problem, with plenty of hotels, hostels and campsites in each town.

Gothenburg

With its long history as a trading centre, GOTHENBURG (Göteborg in Swedish; pronounced "Yur-te-borry") is Scandinavia's biggest seaport and a truly cosmopolitan city. Founded on its present site in the seventeenth century by Gustav II Adolf, Gothenburg was the Swedes' fifth attempt to create a centre free from Danish control – the Danes had enjoyed control of Sweden's west coast since the Middle Ages, and extracted extortionate tolls from all vessels entering the country. Sweden's medieval centre of trade had been 40km further up the Göta River than present-day Gothenburg, but to avoid the tolls it was moved to a site north of the present location. It wasn't until Karl XI chose the island of Hisingen, today the site of the city's northern suburbs, as the location for Sweden's trading nucleus that the settlement was first called Gothenburg. This, however, fell to the Danes during the battle of Kalmar (1611–13) and it was left to Gustav II Adolf to find the vast ransom demanded for its return. Six years later, when it had finally been paid off, he founded the city of Gothenburg where the main square is today.

Although Gothenburg's reputation as an industrial and trading centre has been severely eroded in recent years – clearly evidenced by the stillness of its shipyard cranes – the British, Dutch and German traders who settled here during the eighteenth and nineteenth centuries left a rich architectural and cultural legacy. The city is graced with terraces of grand merchant's houses featuring carved stone, stucco and painted tiles. The influence of the Orient was also strong, reflecting the all-important trade links between Sweden and the Far East, and is still visible in the chinoiserie detail on many buildings. This trade was monopolized for over eighty years during the nineteenth century by the hugely successful Swedish East India Company, whose Gothenburg auction house, selling exotic spices, teas and fine cloths, attracted merchants from all over the world.

Today the city remains a business centre, but the flashy hotels in the centre are much less striking than the restrained opulence of the older buildings, which echo not only Gothenburg's bygone prosperity but also the understated tastes of its citizens. In the 1960s building boom, parts of the city lost their grandest old buildings, but the new apartment blocks that replaced them, while lacking the beauty of their predecessors, are far less hideous than their equivalents in other European cities. Gothenburgers themselves have a justified reputation for friendliness and there's a relaxed geniality among many of the city's inhabitants, making this one of the few places in Sweden where the locals may strike up a conversation with you, rather than vice versa.

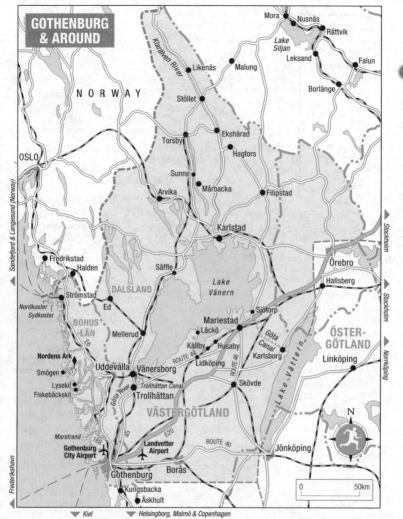

Arrival and information

All **trains** arrive at **Centralstation**, which forms one side of Drottningtorget. Long-distance **buses** use **Nils Ericsons Terminalen**, beside the train station, which can be reached by an undercover walkway. Gothenburg has two **airports**: Ryanair flights arrive at **Gothenburg City** (also known as Säve), 17km north of the city, and all other airlines use **Landvetter**, 25km east of the city. Both airports are connected to Nils Ericsons Terminalen by **bus** (from City airport after each flight arrival; 30min; 60kr; from Landvetter daily every 15–20min; 30min; 75kr).

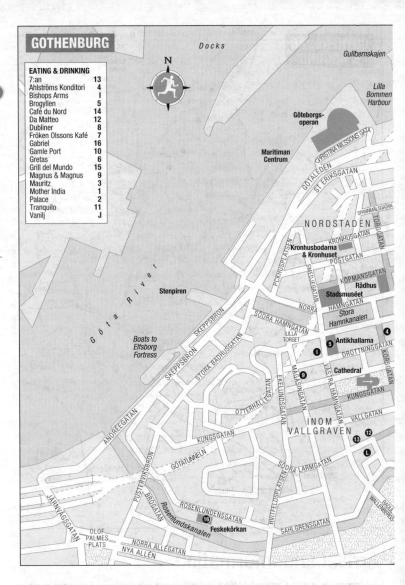

GOTHENBURG

EATING & DRINKING

7:an	13
Ahlströms Konditori	4
Bishops Arms	1
Brogyllen	5
Café du Nord	14
Da Matteo	12
Dubliner	8
Fröken Olssons Kafé	7
Gabriel	16
Gamle Port	10
Gretas	6
Grill del Mundo	15
Magnus & Magnus	9
Mauritz	3
Mother India	1
Palace	2
Tranquilo	11
Vanilj	J

Stena Line (☎031/704 00 00, ⓦwww.stenaline.se) operates ferries from Fredrikshavn in Denmark, which dock just twenty-minutes' walk from the city centre, close to the Masthuggstorget tram stop on lines #3, #9 and #11; their services from Kiel in Germany put in close to the arching Älvsborgsbron bridge, a couple of kilometres west of the centre – take lines #3 or #9 into town from Jægerdorffsplatsen.

Gothenburg has two **tourist offices**; the one handiest for those arriving by train or bus is in Nordstan, the indoor shopping centre near Centralstation

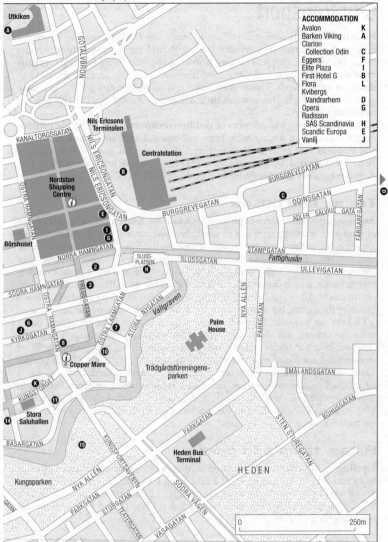

Gothenburg City Airport

ACCOMMODATION

Avalon	**K**
Barken Viking	**A**
Clarion	
Collection Odin	**C**
Eggers	**F**
Elite Plaza	**I**
First Hotel G	**B**
Flora	**L**
Kvibergs	
Vandrarhem	**D**
Opera	**G**
Radisson	
SAS Scandinavia	**H**
Scandic Europa	**E**
Vanilj	**J**

(Mon–Sat 10am–6pm, Sun noon–5pm). The main office, however, is on the canal front at Kungsportsplatsen 2 (May Mon–Fri 9.30am–6pm, Sat & Sun 10am–2pm; June & mid- to late Aug daily 9.30am–6pm; July to mid-Aug daily 9.30am–8pm; Sept–April Mon–Fri 9.30am–5pm, Sat 10am–2pm; ☎031/61 25 00, ⓦwww.goteborg.com), just five-minutes' walk from the train station across Drottningtorget and down Stora Nygatan. Both offices provide information, a room-booking service, and the useful *Göteborgsguiden* detailing events, music and nightspots in town.

City transport

It's easy to **walk** to almost anywhere of interest in Gothenburg. The streets are wide and pedestrian-friendly, and the canals and the grid system of avenues make orientation simple. The city is one of the best in Europe for **cycling**: most main roads have cycle lanes, and motorists really do seem to give way to those on two wheels. The tourist office can provide you with the excellent *cykelkarta*, which clearly shows all the cycle routes throughout the city, and out to the archipelago.

That said, access to some form of **public transport** is always handy, particularly if you end up staying away from the centre. The **tram** system is efficient and frequent, and more easily negotiated than buses for travel within the city. Both are operated by Västtrafik (T0771/41 43 00, Wwww.vasttrafik.se/en). A free **transport map** is available at both tourist offices.

Trams and buses

The most convenient form of public transport is the **tram**: a colour-coded system of tram lines serves the city and its outskirts – you can tell at a glance which line a tram is on, as the route colour will appear on the front. Trams run daily every few minutes from 5am to midnight, with a reduced service running after midnight on Friday and Saturday nights. Gothenburg also has a fairly extensive **bus** network, which uses much the same routes, but pedestrianization in the city centre can lead to some odd and lengthy detours. You shouldn't need to use buses much in the centre, but useful routes are detailed in the text where necessary.

Tickets are available from vending machines onboard the trams and direct from bus drivers, and allow you to travel for up to ninety minutes. Fares are a standard 25kr for adults, while 7- to 16-year-olds go for half price. If you are staying for a couple of days and travelling around the city quite a bit, it's better value to buy **carnets** from the Tidpunkten travel information offices at Brunnsparken, Drottningtorget and Nils Ericsonsplatsen, or from Pressbyrån newsagents or 7 Eleven supermarkets. A ten-trip carnet, known as *Maxirabatt 100*, costs 100kr. Stick these in the machines on a tram or bus, and press twice for an adult, once for a child.

Bikes, taxis and cars

Cycling in the city is easy and popular; there's a comprehensive series of cycle lanes and bike racks. You can rent a bike from Cykelkungen at Chalmersgatan 19 (T031/18 43 00, Wwww.cykelkungen.se; 120kr per day) or, alternatively, the *Slottskogens* and *Stigbergssliden* hostels (see p.127). **Taxis** can be summoned by calling Taxi Göteborg on T031/65 00 00 or Taxi Kurir on T031/27 27 27;

The Gothenburg Pass

A boon if you want to pack in a good bit of sightseeing, the **Gothenburg Pass** provides unlimited bus and tram travel within the city; free entry to all the city museums and the Liseberg Amusement Park; free boat trips to the Elfsborg fortress; and a fifty-percent reduction on day-trips to Fredrikshavn in Denmark with Stena Line. The Gothenburg Pass comes with a second card, which entitles the holder to free parking in roadside spaces (but not at privately run or multistorey car parks). You can buy the card from either of the tourist offices or online at Wwww.goteborg.com (225kr for a 24hr pass, 310kr for a 48hr pass).

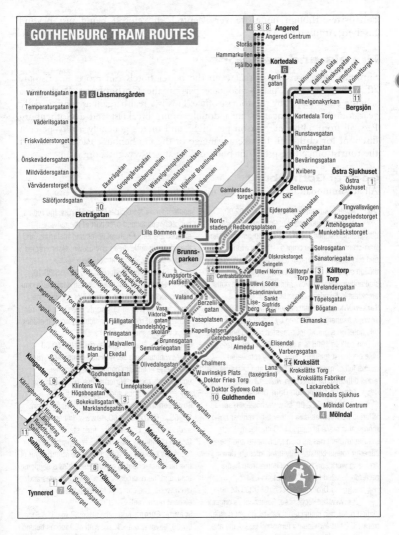

GOTHENBURG TRAM ROUTES

you can also pick one up at the rank at Centralstation. For information on **car rental**, see p.142.

Accommodation

Gothenburg has plenty of good **accommodation** to choose from, with no shortage of comfortable **youth hostels** and **private rooms**. You should have little trouble finding accommodation whenever you turn up, though in summer it's a good idea to book ahead if you are on a tighter budget, or if you want to stay in the most popular youth hostels. There are several

125

campsites, though none are very central, the closest being just beyond Liseberg Amusement Park.

Hotels and pensions

Summer reductions mean that even the better hotels can prove surprisingly affordable, and most places also take part in the **Gothenburg Package**, a scheme coordinated by the tourist office. This is a real bargain as it offers daily, year-round accommodation in a double room, breakfast and a Gothenburg Pass, all from 540kr per person per night, and there's generally a fifty-percent discount for **children**. To take advantage of the Gothenburg Package, contact the tourist office (see p.122) or book online at Ⓦ www.goteborg.com.

Central Gothenburg

All accommodation listed below is marked on the map on pp.122–123.

Avalon Kungstorget 9 ☎031/751 02 00, Ⓦ www.avalonhotel.se. Gothenburg's latest design hotel, stuffed full of pop art, mosaic pillars and lime-green and orange drapes – there's even a pool and sun terrace on the roof (open April–Sept). Rooms, though stylish to a T, can be a little on the cramped side and impractical. However, this is the best buffet breakfast in Sweden – superlative. **❼/❺**

Barken Viking Gullbergskajen ☎031 63 58 00, Ⓦ www.liseberg.se. Moored by the Opera House, this hotel on a grand, four-masted sailing ship built in Denmark in 1906 is a charismatic and comfortable choice. It features cosy, newly renovated rooms full of maritime furnishings and beautiful wood panelling on the cabin walls. **❼/❺**

Clarion Collection Odin Odinsgatan 6 ☎031/745 22 00, Ⓦ www.hotelodin.se. Offering designer studios rather than regular hotel rooms, this place is unique in Gothenburg. Each mini-apartment has its own kitchenette and the superior rooms boast a fully fitted kitchen, dining area and work space – a real home from home perfectly located for the train station. **❻/❺**

Eggers Drottningtorget ☎031/333 44 40, Ⓦ www.hoteleggers.se. Gothenburg's original station hotel, this characterful establishment dating from 1820 has individually furnished bedrooms and a wealth of original features including stuccoed ceilings and cut-glass chandeliers. Believed to have been used during World War II for secret discussions between British and Nazi military negotiators, it's also reputed to be haunted. **❻/❹**

Elite Plaza Västra Hamngatan 3 ☎031/720 40 00, Ⓦ www.elite.se. The magnificent facade of this opulent hotel hides a stunning blend of contemporary and classic decor, with majestic vaulted ceilings and mosaic floors complemented by striking modern paintings. Worth pushing the boat out for. **❼/❺**

First Hotel G Nils Ericsonsplatsen 4 ☎031/62 72 00, Ⓦ www.firsthotels.se. The last word in

contemporary Nordic design and luxury, the rooms, curiously suspended over part of the railway station, are full of natural fibres and materials, and the predominantly green and brown decor creates a wonderfully calming atmosphere. **❼/❺**

Flora Grönsakstorget 2 ☎031/13 86 16, Ⓦ www.hotelflora.se. Stylish designer rooms with wooden floors, flat-screen TVs and the latest Scandinavian chic at this newly opened family-run hotel. The loft rooms are particularly cosy, featuring velux windows in the roof. **❺/❹**

Opera Norra Hamngatan 38 ☎031/80 50 80, Ⓦ www.hotelopera.se. A family-owned and -run mid-range hotel with comfortable, if rather uninspiring, rooms. Nevertheless, good value for money at weekends and in summer. **❺/❹**

Radisson SAS Scandinavia Södra Hamngatan 59–65 ☎031/758 50 00, Ⓦ www.gothenburg .radisson.com. Opposite the train station, with a facade of hideous pink panels, and glass lifts and fountains making up the interior, the atrium foyer of this business-oriented option resembles a shopping mall, and the bedrooms are all pastel shades and birch wood. The complex is also home to an elegant restaurant. **❼/❺**

Scandic Europa Köpmansgatan 38 ☎031/751 65 00, Ⓦ www.scandic.se. With 460 rooms behind an amorphous facade adjoining the Nordstan shopping centre, this is one of the largest hotels in the country. The interior is very plush, with lots of marble and – unusually for Sweden – the bathrooms have bathtubs. A huge buffet is served for breakfast. **❼/❹**

Vanilj Kyrkogatan 38 ☎031/711 62 20, Ⓦ www.hotelvanilj.se. Housed in a former snuff factory from the 1800s, all 32 rooms in this small and friendly hotel are a delight: contemporary and elegant but with a touch of old-fashioned charm. At this price, they get snapped up fast, so book early. **❹/❸**

Southern Gothenburg

All accommodation listed below is marked on the map on p.135.

City Lorensbergsgatan 6 ⓣ 031/708 40 00, ⓦ www.cityhotelgbg.se. It's hard to get more central at these prices. Excellently located in a parallel street to Avenyn, rooms are nothing special, though they are all bright and airy with high ceilings and perfectly comfortable. Share facilities and you can save a further 200–300kr. ④/③

Gothia Towers Mässansgata 24 ⓣ 031/750 88 00, ⓦ www.gothiatowers.com. Inside the mirrored towers just opposite Liseberg is a subtle, well-designed, contemporary hotel, with wonderful uninterrupted views over the city from the upper floors. Substantial summer and weekend reductions make this an affordable option. ⑥/⑤

🎿 **Lilton** Föreningsgatan 9 ⓣ 031/82 88 08, ⓦ www.hotellilton.com. This cosy, ivy-covered fourteen-bedroom place with individually decorated rooms, each with flatscreen TV, is one of Gothenburg's hidden gems. It's quiet and friendly, with splendid National Romantic and Art Nouveau buildings close by, and even has its own courtyard of roses and peonies. ⑤/④

Maria Erikssons Pensionat Chalmersgatan 27A ⓣ 031/20 70 30, ⓦ www.mariaspenionat.nu. With just ten pleasant-enough rooms, this place is well positioned on a road running parallel with Avenyn. Rooms with shared facilities cost 100kr less. Breakfast is not included. ④

Vasa Viktoriagatan 6 ⓣ 031/17 36 30, ⓦ www.hotelvasa.se. What this plain but comfortable hotel lacks in glamour is more than made up for by the geniality of its owners and its excellent position in Vasastan, close to Avenyn and even closer to Haga. There's a sauna and solarium, too. ⑤/④

Youth hostels and private rooms

The cheapest accommodation option is staying in one of the **youth hostels** around the city; these are open all year unless otherwise stated. **Private rooms** are another good, economical alternative, and can be booked through the tourist office (around 250kr per person in a double room, 300kr for a single). For stays of a week or more, it's worth contacting SGS Veckobostäder, Utlandagatan 24 (ⓣ031/333 63 90, ⓦwww.sgsveckobostader.se), who rent out **furnished rooms** and **flats**, with access to kitchen facilities, from 2100kr a week per unit.

Hostels

Göteborgs Minihotel Tredje Långgatan 31 ⓣ 031/24 10 23, ⓦ www.minihotel.se. This uninspiring building with simple, unadorned rooms is nevertheless well placed for the alternative scene around the Linné area. It's possible to choose between regular beds or bunks. Dorm beds 150kr, double rooms ①

Kvibergs Vandrarhem Lilla regementsvägen 35 ⓣ 031/43 50 55, ⓦ www.vandrarhem.com. Northeast of the city centre but just 10min by tram #6, #7 or #11 from Centralstation and offering a little taste of the countryside. No dorm beds but cosy single and double rooms which cost a little less during Sept–May. ①

Masthuggsterrassen Masthuggsterrassen 10H ⓣ 031/42 48 20, ⓦ www.mastenvandrarhem. com. Up the steps from Masthuggstorget (tram #3, #4 or #11) and a couple of minutes' walk from the terminal for the Stena Line ferry from Denmark. Dorm beds 190kr, and decent-sized double rooms ①

🎿 **Slottsskogen** Vegagatan 21 ⓣ 031/42 65 20, ⓦ www.sov.nu. Superbly appointed and well-designed STF hostel with 165 beds, a TV in every room and washbasin in most. Onsite sauna, solarium and billiards available. Just 2min walk from Linnégatan and not far from Slottsskogen Park; take tram #1 or #2 to Olivedalsgatan. Dorm beds 195kr, double rooms ①

Stigbergsliden Stigbergsliden 10 ⓣ 031/24 16 20, ⓦ www.hostel-gothenburg.com. This excellent hostel, built in 1830 as a seamen's house, is well placed for ferries to Denmark as it's just west of the Linné area down Första Långgatan. All rooms have basins, and there's disabled access, laundry facilities and a pleasant back courtyard. Dorm beds 200kr, double rooms ①

Cabins and campsites

Two of the following campsites also provide **cabins**, which are worth considering, especially if there are more than two of you. Facilities are invariably squeaky clean and in good working order – there's usually a well-equipped kitchen too – but you'll have to pay extra for bedding. Prices for cabins are given below; if you want to **camp**, you'll pay around 120kr per night for two people in July or August, or 60kr the rest of the year.

Askim Strand ☏031/28 62 61, ⊛www.liseberg .se. Set beside sandy beaches 12km from the centre (bus #80 towards Snipen and alight at Askimsbadet), this campsite also has two-bed cabins (④). Open late April to early Sept.
Kärralunds Timmerbyn Olbergsgatan 9 ☏031/84 02 00, ⊛www.liseberg.se. 4km from the centre, close to Liseberg Amusement Park (tram #5 to Welandergatan, direction Torp) and set

among forest and lakes, the site offers two-bed cabins (⑤); huge discounts outside June–Aug.
Lilleby Havsbad ☏031/56 22 40, ⊛www .lillebycamping.se. About 1hr from the city centre in Torslanda (bus #121 from Centralstation and change to #23 towards Silvik at Torslanda torg), this splendid seaside location is some compensation for the trek. May–Aug only.

The City

You should allow around two or three days to see Gothenburg's attractions; nearly everything of interest in the city is south of the **Göta River** and, unless you fancy a trip to the **Volvo factory** on the northern island of **Hisingen**, there's no real need to cross the water. At the heart of the city is the historic **old town**: this is the best place to start your sightseeing, although Gothenburg's attractions are by no means restricted to this area. Tucked between the Göta River to the north and the zigzagging Rosenlundkanalen to the south, the old town's tightly gridded streets are lined with impressive facades, interesting food markets and a couple of worthwhile museums, most notably the **Stadsmuseum** and, up by the harbour, the **Maritiman**, a repository of all things nautical. Just across the canal that skirts the southern edges of the old town is **Trädgårdsföreningen** park, in summer full of colourful flowers and picnicking city dwellers.

Heading further south into the modern centre, **Avenyn** is Gothenburg's showcase boulevard, alive with flashy restaurants and bars. However, it's the roads

▲ Sightseeing boat

off Avenyn that are the area's most interesting, with alternative-style café-bars and some of Gothenburg's best museums, including the **Konstmuseum** (Art Museum) further south in **Götaplatsen**. For family entertainment day or night, the classic **Liseberg Amusement Park**, just to the southeast of the Avenyn district, has been a meeting place for Gothenburgers since the 1920s.

In Vasastan, a small district to the west of Avenyn, crammed with intricately decorated late nineteenth-century apartment buildings and peppered with appealing little cafés, you'll find the **Röhsska Museum** of applied arts. Vasastan stretches west to **Haga**, the old working-class district, now a haven for the trendy and moneyed. Haga Nygatan, the main thoroughfare, leads on to Linnégatan, the arterial road through **Linné**. Fast establishing itself as the most vibrant part of the city, it's home to the most interesting evening haunts, with new cafés, bars and restaurants opening up alongside long-established antique emporiums and sex shops. Further out, the rolling **Slottskogsparken** park holds the **Naturhistoriska Museet** (Natural History Museum), as well as being an alluringly pretty place to sunbathe.

The old town and the harbour

The **old town** is divided in two by the **Stora Hamnkanalen**, to the north of which is the harbour, where the impressive shipyards make for a dramatic backdrop. The streets south of the canal stretch down to Rosenlundskanalen and are perfect for a leisurely afternoon stroll, with some quirky cafés, food markets and antique and junk shops, along with the excellent Stadsmuseum. Straddling the Stora Hamnkanalen is the stately main square, **Gustav Adolfs Torg**, a good starting point for sightseeing around the old town; you should be able to see the whole area in a day.

Gustav Adolfs Torg

At the centre of **Gustav Adolfs Torg**, a copper statue of Gustav II Adolf points ostentatiously to the spot where he reputedly declared: "Here I will build my city." This isn't the original German-made statue of the city founder however: that one was kidnapped on its way to Sweden and, rather than pay the ransom demanded, the Gothenburgers commissioned a new one.

To the east of the square, with the canal behind you, stands the **Rådhuset**, which isn't a town hall as the name suggests, but has housed the criminal law courts since 1673. The dull Neoclassical facade is dramatically improved by an extension designed by the ground-breaking Functionalist architect Gunnar Asplund in 1937.

North to the harbour

Heading north from the square along Östra Hamngatan, you'll pass Sweden's biggest shopping centre, the amorphous **Nordstan** (Mon–Fri 10am–7pm, Sat 10am–6pm, Sun 11am–5pm; Ⓦ www.nordstan.se). Packed with glitzy boutiques and branches of just about every Swedish chain store you choose to mention, it's Gothenburg's most ostentatious show of wealth. If you have time to spare and haven't yet seen the city's impressive **Centralstation**, take a short detour along Burggrevegatan to Drottningtorget. Dating from 1856, this is the oldest train station in the country and its period facade fronts a grand and marvellously preserved interior – take a look at the wooden beam-ends in the ticket hall, each one carved in the likeness of the city-council members of the day.

Back on Östra Hamngatan, it's a five-minute stroll north to Lilla Bommen harbour, where Gothenburg's industrial decline is juxtaposed with its artistic regeneration to dramatic visual effect. To the west, beyond the harbour, redundant

Nya Elfsborg

Boats leave from Lilla Bommen, near the Opera House, for the popular excursion to the island fortress of **Nya Elfsborg** (early May to Aug daily every 90min 9/10am–4/5pm; 30min; 140kr), built in the seventeenth century to defend the harbour and the city; the surviving buildings have been turned into a museum and café. On the half-hour guided tours of the square tower, chapel and prison cells (included in the price of the boat trip) you'll hear about violent confrontations with the Danes, and some of the methods used to keep prisoners from swimming away – check out the set of iron shackles weighing over 36kg.

shipyard cranes loom across the sky, making a sombre background to the industrially themed bronze and pink-granite sculptures dotted along the waterfront. A couple of minutes' walk to the west is the striking modern **Göteborgsoperan** (Opera House; daily noon–6pm; guided tours late June to mid-Aug daily 3pm; ☏031/10 80 00, ⓦwww.opera.se); you can look inside, though you'd be better off spending your time continuing to wander along the waterfront.

North along the riverbank from Göteborgsoperan is **Utkiken** (Lookout Point; June–Aug daily 11am–4pm; rest of the year Mon–Fri 11am–4pm; 30kr); designed by the Scottish architect Ralph Erskine (who also designed the Sydney Opera House) in the late 1980s, this 86-metre-high office building resembles a half-used red lipstick. Its top storey offers panoramic views of Gothenburg and the harbour, and there's a café, too.

Walking west along the quay, it's just a couple of minutes to **Maritiman** (March & Nov Fri–Sun 10am–4pm; April, May & Oct daily 10am–4pm; June–Sept daily 10am–6pm; 80kr; ⓦwww.maritiman.se), the city's engaging maritime museum, which comprises nineteen boats, including the 1915 lightship, *Fladen*, a submarine and a freighter which once sailed regularly from Gothenburg across the North Sea to the east coast of England, each giving a glimpse of how seamen lived and worked on board. The most impressive ship is a monstrous naval destroyer, *Småland*, which saw active service until 1979. There's a rather good café on another of the ships, the ferry *Dan Broström*, with outdoor seating available on the upper deck.

The Kronhuset and the Stadsmuseum

From Maritiman, it's a short walk southwest to Gothenburg's oldest secular building, **Kronhuset**, on Kronhusgatan (Mon–Fri 11am–4pm, Sat & Sun 11am–2pm). Built by the Dutch in 1642 as an artillery depot for the city's garrison, it was where 5-year-old Karl XI was proclaimed king in 1660. Picturesquely set in the eighteenth-century wings that flank the original building is **Kronhusbodarna** (Mon–Fri 10am–5pm, Sat 10am–2pm), a cluster of small, pricey shops specializing in making gold, silver and glass ornaments and jewellery. The silversmith here can sell you a replica of the city's oldest key, but your money would be better spent at the atmospheric vaulted *Café Kronhuset* (Mon–Fri 10am–7pm, Sat & Sun 11am–6pm), which is renowned for its excellent open sandwiches with toppings of egg, prawns, salmon and roast beef.

A couple of blocks further south, the **Stadsmuseum**, Norra Hamngatan 12 (City Museum; Tues–Sun 10am–5pm, Wed 10am–8pm; 40kr; ⓦwww.stadsmuseum.goteborg.se) is Gothenburg's biggest and best museum. It is located in the Ostindiska Huset, which housed the offices, goods store and auction house of the enormously influential **Swedish East India Company**. Envious of the major maritime nations, two Gothenburg-based industrialists, Colin Campbell and Niklas Sahlgren, set up the firm in the early eighteenth century. Granted the sole Swedish rights to trade with China in 1731, the company monopolized all Swedish trade with the Far East for over eighty years, on condition that the bounty – tea, silk, porcelain, spices and arrack (an East Indian schnapps used to make Swedish punch) – had to be sold and auctioned in Gothenburg. As a result, Chinese influence pervaded Gothenburg society, and wealthy financiers adorned their homes and gardens with Chinese motifs. By 1813, unrest caused by the French Revolution and competition from British and Dutch tea traders meant profits slid, and the company lost its monopoly. The headquarters, however, remain an imposing reminder of the power and prestige the company – and Gothenburg – once had. Elsewhere in the museum, other main exhibits focus on Gothenburg's Viking past and include the remains of a longboat, the only one from this period on display in Sweden, as well as a thorough account of the founding of Gothenburg in 1621 and its development through the centuries.

South of Stora Hamnkanalen

Crossing Stora Hamnkanalen from the Stadsmuseum, you'll come to **Lilla Torget**. In itself, the square is nothing to get excited about, but, having nodded at the statue of Jonas Alströmer – the man who introduced the potato to Sweden in the eighteenth century – continue a couple of minutes' walk west to the quayside, **Stenpiren** (Stone Pier). It was from here that hundreds of emigrants said their last goodbyes before sailing off to a "New Sweden" in the United States, in 1638. The granite **Delaware Monument** marking Swedish emigration was carted off to America from Gothenburg in the early part of the nineteenth century, and it wasn't until 1938 that celebrated sculptor Carl Milles cast a replacement in bronze, which stands here looking out to sea.

Back in Lilla Torget, it's only a short walk down Västra Hamngatan, which leads off from the southern side of the square, to the city's cathedral; on the way, at no. 6, you'll pass **Antikhallarna** (May–Aug Mon–Fri 10am–5pm; Sept–April Mon–Fri 10am–6pm; Aug–May also Sat 10am–2pm), a clutch of pricey antique shops. There's a small amount of affordable stuff here, towards the back along with the tat, but it's the grand mid-nineteenth-century building that warrants your attention, with its fantastic gilded ceiling and regal marble stairs leading up to the second floor, where there's a decent café.

A few blocks south of Antikhallarna, and left off Västra Hamngatan, is the Neoclassical cathedral, **Domkyrkan** (Mon–Fri 8am–6pm, Sat 9am–4pm, Sun 10am–3pm), built in 1815 – the two previous cathedrals were destroyed by fires in 1721 and 1802. Four giant sandstone columns stand at the portico, and inside, the altarpiece is a picture of gilded opulence. The plain white walls concentrate the eye on the unusual post-Resurrection cross – devoid of a Jesus, and with his gilded grave clothes strewn around, it summons images of an adolescent's bedroom floor. Another quirky feature is the twin glassed-in verandas that run down either side of the cathedral; looking like glamorous trams with net curtains, they were actually designed for the bishop's private conversations.

Continuing east past the cathedral and north towards Stora Hamnkanalen, the leafy square known as **Brunnsparken** soon comes into view, with Gustav Adolfs Torg just across the canal. The sedate house facing the square is now a snazzy restaurant and nightclub called *Palace* (see p.141), but in 1752 the building was home to Pontus and Gothilda Fürstenberg, the city's leading arts patrons. They opened up the top floor as an art gallery and later donated their entire collection – the biggest batch of Nordic paintings in the country – to the city's **Konstmuseum**. As a tribute to the Fürstenbergs, the museum made over the top floor into an exact replica of the original gallery.

West from Stora Nygatan along Rosenlundskanalen

Following the zigzagging Rosenlundskanalen that marks the southern perimeter of old Gothenburg – a moat during the days when the city was fortified – makes for a fine twenty-minute stroll, past pretty waterside views and a number of interesting diversions. Just southeast of Brunnsparken, **Stora Nygatan** wends its way south along the canal's most scenic stretch; to one side are Neoclassical buildings all stuccoed in cinnamon and cream, and to the other is the green expanse of well-groomed **Trädgårdsföreningen** park (daily: July–Sept 10am–8pm; Oct–June 7am–6pm; July–Sept 50kr, otherwise free). The main entrance is located just across the canal from Stora Nygatan, close to Kungsportsplatsen. There are a number of attractions to visit in the park, the most impressive of which is the 1878 **Palm House** (same times as park; July–Sept 100kr). Designed as a copy of London's Crystal Palace, and looking like a huge English conservatory, it contains a wealth of very un-Swedish plant life, including tropical, Mediterranean and Asian flowers. Further on is the **Rosarium** which, with nearly three thousand varieties of rose, provides a myriad of colours throughout the year. During summer the place goes into overdrive, with lunchtime concerts and a special children's theatre (details are available at the tourist office).

Continuing west from the park, you'll pass **Kungsportsplatsen**, in the centre of which stands a useful landmark, a sculpture known as the "Copper Mare" – though it's immediately obvious if you look from beneath that this is no mare. A few minutes further on, and one block in from the canal at Kungstorget, stands **Stora Saluhallen** (Mon–Fri 10am–6pm, Sat 10am–2pm), a pretty, barrel-roofed indoor market built in the 1880s. Busy with shoppers perusing the forty-odd stalls and shops and full of atmosphere, it's a great place to wander, as is the market outside.

Five-minutes' walk west of here is Gothenburg's oldest food market, the Neo-Gothic **Feskekôrka**, or "Fish Church" (Tues–Thurs 9am–5pm, Fri 9am–6pm, Sat 10am–2pm), whose strong aromas may well hit you long before you reach the door. Despite its undeniably ecclesiastical appearance, the nearest this 1874 building comes to religion is the devotion shown by the fish-lovers who come to buy their dinner here. Inside, every kind of seafood, from cod to crustaceans, lies in gleaming, pungent silver, pink and black mounds, while in a gallery upstairs there's a tiny but excellent restaurant (see p.139).

Avenyn and around

Running all the way from Rosenlundskanalen southeast to Götaplatsen is the wide, cobbled length of Kungsportsavenyn. Known more simply as **Avenyn**, this "avenue" teems with life and is Gothenburg's showiest thoroughfare. The ground floor of almost every grand old nineteenth-century home has been converted into a café, bar or restaurant, which the young and beautiful inhabit whilst sipping overpriced drinks and posing at tables that, from mid-spring to September, spill out onto the street. Avenyn is arguably one of the best places in the city for people-watching, and no visit to Gothenburg is complete without a stroll down it. At the southern end of the avenue on **Götaplatsen** is the fascinating **Konstmuseum**, which contains a fine collection of international art from various periods.

Götaplatsen

At the top of Avenyn, **Götaplatsen** is modern Gothenburg's main square, in the centre of which stands Carl Milles's **Poseidon** – a giant, nude, bronze body-builder with a staggeringly ugly face. The size of the figure's penis caused moral outrage when the sculpture first appeared in 1931, and it was subsequently dramatically reduced to its current, rather pathetic proportions, totally out of keeping with a statue that's seven-metre high. Today, although from the front *Poseidon* appears to be squeezing the living daylights out of what looks like a massive fish, if you climb the steps of the **Concert Hall** to the right and view the statue from an angle, it becomes clear that Milles won the battle over *Poseidon*'s manhood to stupendous effect, as the enormous fish appears to be the original penis.

Konstmuseum

Behind *Poseidon* stands Götaplatsen's most impressive attraction, the superb **Konstmuseum** (Art Museum; Tues & Thurs 11am–6pm, Wed 11am–9pm, Fri–Sun 11am–5pm; 40kr; ⓦ www.konstmuseum.goteborg.se), its massive, symmetrical facade reminiscent of the fascist architecture of 1930s Germany. This is one of the city's finest museums, and it's easy to spend half a day absorbing the diverse and extensive collections, the highlights of which are picked out below.

On the ground floor, the **Hasselblad Center** (ⓦ www.hasselbladcenter.se) contains excellent photographic exhibitions, while on the floor above, the work of contemporary Scandinavian painters and sculptors is displayed. Another room on the same floor contains works by the celebrated masters of French Impressionism, and the next couple of floors hold a range of minor works by Van Gogh, Gauguin and Pissarro, a powerful and surprisingly colourful Munch and a couple of Rodin sculptures. Moving on to floor five, you'll find Italian paintings from 1500 to 1750, including works by Canaletto and Francesco Guardi, as well as Rembrandt's *Knight with Falcon* and Rubens' *Adoration of the Magi*.

Best of all, however, and the main reason to visit, are the **Fürstenberg Galleries** on the sixth floor: these celebrate the work of some of Scandinavia's most prolific and revered early twentieth-century artists; well-known works by Carl Larsson, Anders Zorn and Carl Wilhelmson reflect the seasons and landscapes of the Nordic countries, and evoke a vivid picture of Scandinavian life at that time. Paintings to look out for include Larsson's *Lilla Suzanne*, which touchingly depicts the elated face of a baby and is one of his most realistic works; Anders Zorn's *Bathers*, flushed with a pale pink summer glow and exemplifying the painter's feeling for light and the human form; and the sensitive portraits by Ernst Josephson, most notably his full-length portrait of Carl Skånberg – easily mistaken for the young Winston Churchill. The Danish artist Peter Kroyer's marvellous *Hip Hip Hooray* again plays with light, and a couple of works by Hugo Birger also deserve your attention. One depicts the interior of the original Fürstenberg Gallery (see p.132), while his massive *Scandinavian Artists' Breakfast in Paris*, dominating an entire wall, puts some faces to the artists' names – a pamphlet in the room will help identify them. Also worth a look is an entire room of Larsson's bright, fantastical wall-sized paintings.

A delightful little park, **Näckrosdammen** ("Waterlily Park"), lies just behind the museum; with its late-spring rhododendrons and big pond full of ducks, it's a lovely place for a stroll.

Liseberg and around

Southeast of Avenyn is the Liseberg Amusement Park, alive both during the day and at night throughout the summer. In its shadow to the south is one of Gothenburg's most engaging museums, **Universeum**, which is particularly fascinating for children, while the absorbing **Världskulturmuséet** (Museum of World Culture) is just next door.

Liseberg Amusement Park

Just a few minutes' walk southeast from Götaplatsen, **Liseberg Amusement Park** (daily: late April–May & Sept 3pm–10pm; June 1pm–10pm; July & Aug 11am–midnight; 70kr, under-7s free; all-day ride pass 290kr, or buy tickets as you go – a coupon costs 20kr, each attraction requires 1–3 coupons; ⓦwww.liseberg.se) is a riot of party lights and bubblegum-pink paintwork. Opened in 1923, this is Scandinavia's largest amusement park, and with its flowers, trees, fountains and clusters of lights, it's great fun for adults as well as children, and leagues away from the neon and plastic mini-cities that constitute so many theme parks around the world. The old and the young dance to live bands most evenings, and although louder and more youth-dominated at night (especially on Sat), it's all good-humoured. Pride of place at Liseberg goes to "Kanonen", an ambitious roller coaster which reaches its top speed just two seconds after being fired bullet-like from its start point, before plummeting 24m at a ninety-degree angle. If you're around between mid-November and late December, head for the enjoyable **Christmas market**, where stalls selling handicrafts and presents are lit by around three million fairy lights. This being Sweden, the commercialism is remarkably low-key, and the smell of glögg (mulled wine), roast almonds and freshly made waffles which pervades the air adds to the enjoyment. This is also a good place to sample the traditional Swedish *julbord*, a Christmas **smorgasbord** full of hams, cheeses and heavenly cakes (booking required for the *julbord*, ☎031/733 03 00).

Universeum and Museum of World Culture

Just a few steps from Liseberg, at Södra Vägen 50, the city's science and environment museum, **Universeum** (late June to late Aug daily 10am–7pm; rest of the year daily 10am–6pm; 145kr; ⓦwww.universeum.se), is well worth an hour or so of your time. Designed by Gothenburg architect Gert Wingårdh, and contained within a splendidly organic building with soaring glass, wood and concrete walls, it couldn't be more in contrast to the fairy lights and pink paint of the amusement park reflected in its vast windows. Water is a major theme (the complex holds the world's largest recirculating water system, processing three million litres a day), and once inside, you can walk some 3km through various different environments – Swedish mountain streams, rainforest, open ocean complete with sharks and stingrays – all of which feel extremely authentic; expect to emerge dripping. There's also an interactive "explora zone" for kids to discover robots, models and all kinds of techno-logical wizardry, plenty of information in English, and a **café** with good-value meals and organic coffee.

Next door to Universeum, at Södra Vägen 54, is the unusually interesting **Världskulturmuséet** (Museum of World Culture; Tues & Fri–Sun noon–5pm, Wed & Thurs noon–9pm; 40kr; ⓦwww.varldskulturmuseet.se). A glass and concrete colossus complete with a four-storey glass atrium, the building has been awarded one of Sweden's most prestigious architectural prizes for its innovative design. Through a series of changing exhibitions, the museum aims to reflect the depth and variety of world culture – recent displays have focused on sexuality in India, human trafikking around the world and the native people who live along the Orinoco. The café-cum-restaurant here, *Tabla*, serves up an impressive range of international and Swedish dishes, as well as the coffee and cakes.

Vasastan

Back at Avenyn, you can take one of the roads off to the west and wander into the **Vasastan** district, where the streets are lined with fine nineteenth-century and National Romantic architecture, and the cafés are cheaper, more laid-back and much more charismatic than the city centre. The area also boasts Gothenburg's collection of applied arts, the **Röhsska Museum**, and several fine University buildings.

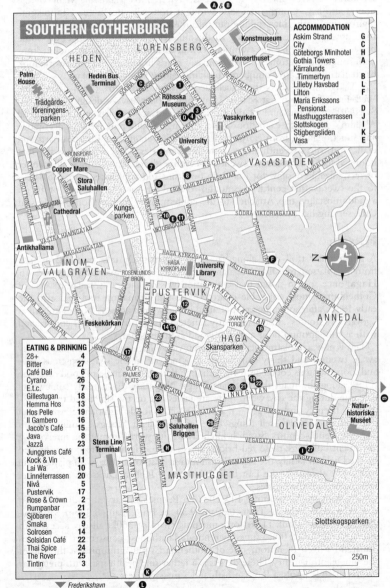

Vasagatan and the Röhsska Museum

Along Vasagatan, the main street through the district, and parallel **Engelbrekts-gatan** to the south, you'll come across solid, stately and rangy buildings that epitomize Gothenburg's nineteenth-century commercial wealth and civic pride. White-stuccoed or red-and-cream brick facades are decorated with elaborate ceramic tiles, intricate stone-and-brick animal carvings, shiny metal cupolas and classical windows. With the detail spread gracefully across these six-storey terraces, the overall effect is of restrained grandeur. Many of the houses also have Continental-style wrought-iron balconies; it's easy to imagine high-society gatherings spilling out into the night on warm summer evenings. In contrast, interspersed among all this nineteenth-century swagger are some perfect examples of early twentieth-century National Romantic architecture, with rough-hewn stone and Art Nouveau swirls in plaster and brickwork; look particularly at the low-numbered buildings along Engelbrektsgatan.

At Vasagatan 37–39 is the excellent **Röhsska Museum** (Tues noon–8pm, Wed–Fri noon–5pm, Sat & Sun 11am–5pm; 40kr; ⓦ www.designmuseum.se), Sweden's main museum of design, fashion and applied arts and an aesthetic Aladdin's cave, with each floor concentrating on different areas of decorative and functional art, from early-dynasty Chinese ceramics to European arts and crafts from the sixteenth and seventeenth centuries. Most arresting is the first floor, which is devoted to twentieth-century decor and features all manner of recognizable designs for domestic furniture and appliances from the 1910s to the twenty-first century – enough to send anyone over the age of 10 on a giddy nostalgia trip. Attached to the contemporary design shop is a pleasant **café**, serving light lunches.

Haga

A ten-minute stroll west along Vasagatan (alternatively take tram #2 or #13 from Vasaplatsen to Olivedalsgatan) is the city's oldest working-class suburb, **Haga**; once so run-down that demolition was on the cards, today it's one of Gothenburg's most enjoyable quarters. The transformation took place in the early 1980s, after someone saw potential in the web of artisans' homes known as "governor's houses", distinctive early nineteenth-century buildings constructed with a stone ground floor and two wooden upper storeys.

Haga is now a miniature version of Greenwich Village, with well-off and socially aware twenty- and thirty-somethings hanging out in the style-conscious cafés and shops along its cobbled streets. Although there are a couple of good cafés (see p.139) along the main thoroughfare, **Haga Nygatan**, this is really somewhere to come during the day, when there are tables out on the street and the atmosphere is friendly and villagey – if a little self-consciously fashionable. Apart from the boutiques, which sell things like Art Deco light fittings, calming crystals and nineteenth-century Swedish kitchenware, it's worth noting the intervening apartment buildings; these red-brick edifices were originally almshouses funded by the Dickson family, the city's British industrialist forefathers who played a big part in the success of the East India Company – Robert Dickson's name is still emblazoned on the facades.

Next door to the beautiful F.D. Dickson People's Library, at Södra Allégatan 3, is **Hagabadet** (Mon–Thurs 6.30am–9.30pm, Fri 6.30am–8.30pm, Sat 9am–7pm, Sun 10am–7pm; 115kr for a morning swim or 360kr all-day access with sauna; ⓣ 031/60 06 00), a superbly renovated bathhouse constructed with funds donated by Sven Renström, one of Gothenburg's philanthropists at the end of the nineteenth century. These days it is a rather fine health spa, with pretty Art Nouveau-style pools, a Roman bath and a massage area.

Linné

To the west of Haga, the cosmopolitan district of **Linné** is named after the botanist Carl von Linné, who created the system for classifying plants used the world over (see p.112). To get there, turn south off Haga Nygatan into Landsvägsgatan, which joins up with Linnégatan – the main thoroughfare. In recent years, so many stylish cafés and restaurants have sprung up along the main drag that Linné is now considered Gothenburg's "second Avenyn", although without the attitude; the street is lined with Dutch-inspired nineteenth-century architecture, tall and elegant buildings interspersed with steep little side roads. However, it's the main roads leading off Linnégatan, prosaically named First Long Street (Första Långgatan), Second Long Street (Andra) and so on up to Fourth (Fjärde), that give the area its real character; the not-very-long Second and Third streets contain a mix of dark antique stores, basement cafés and upfront sex shops.

On the left as you head up Linnégatan towards Järntorget is the forbidding building where King Oskar II had his private apartment – and his women. Directly opposite is a modern apartment block that's worth a second glance; it replaced a property whose republican owner so hated both the monarchy and the morals of the king that he had a run of colourful ceramic panels depicting the devil installed, facing the royal apartment. Sadly, the Gothenburg propensity for doing away with its own past meant the "devil building", as it was known, was recently demolished, but two of the grotesque panels have been incorporated into the new apartment block.

Slottskogsparken

Slottskogsparken, a five-minute walk south from Linnégatan (or take tram #13 or #2 to Linnéplatsen), is a huge, tranquil expanse of parkland with farm animals and birdlife, including pink flamingoes in summer. The rather dreary **Naturhistoriska Muséet** (Natural History Museum; Tues–Sun 11am–5pm; 40kr; Ⓦ www.gnm.se), within the grounds of the park, prides itself on being the city's oldest museum, dating from 1833. Its endless displays of stuffed birds are particularly depressing after seeing the living ones outside; the most worthwhile item is the world's only stuffed blue whale, which was killed in 1865.

On the south side of Slottskogsparken are the impressive **Botaniska Trädgården** (Botanical Gardens; daily 9am–dusk; voluntary 20kr), a vast glasshouse akin to London's Kew Gardens; Ⓦ www.goteborg.se/botaniska), which, at almost two square kilometres, are the biggest in Europe. The gardens hold some sixteen thousand species of plants; highlights are some of Sweden's biggest orchids, the summer flower plantations and the adjoining arboretum.

West to the Gothenburg Archipelago

On a fine day, Gothenburgers make for the nearest **coastal islands**, where bathing in the sea and sun are a real pleasure and it's hard to imagine you're so close to a city. One of the best ways of exploring the area is by bike, taking in some industrial heritage on your way out to the beaches of the **Gothenburg archipelago**.

Around 5km west of the city centre is **Saltholmen**, at the tip of Gothenburg's most westerly peninsula. Outcrops of smooth rocks provide a multitude of hidden sun-worshipping areas, where **nude bathing** is quite the norm. The zone around to your left, on the south side of the peninsula, has become a recognized gay bathing area. Climbing to Saltholmen's highest point, the views are quite idyllic, with boats flecking the water and the offshore islands stretching out into the distance.

From Saltholmen, regular ferries make the short trips to the most popular islands, stopping first at **Brännö**, an island mainly given over to summerhouses converted from fishermen's shacks, and crowded with Gothenburgers through high season. **Styrsö** is the next island, with three hamlets where most of its residents live all year. The furthest of the main islands is **Vrångö**, which has one small village and a perfect lagoon with a great beach: on leaving the boat, turn left, follow the short path and you'll find a spit of flat stone forming one side of the lagoon.

Tram #11 runs all the way to Saltholmen, and the ferries cost 25kr (free with tram ticket). There's a delightful little outdoor **café** at Saltholmen selling coffee, cake, ice cream and light snacks.

Eating

Gothenburg has a multitude of eating places, catering for every budget and for most tastes; among the best to try are the pan-European eateries which draw on Swedish staples such as good breads, exceptional herring and salmon and, in summer, glorious soft fruits. However, cafés and restaurants are not the only place to satisfy a hunger; bustling, historic **Saluhallen** at Kungstorget is a delightful sensory experience, with a great choice of meats, fish, fruits, vegetables and a huge range of delectable breads. Alternatively, **Saluhallen Briggen**, on the corner of Tredje Långgatan and Nordhemsgatan in the Linné area, specializes in good-quality meats, fish, cheese and mouthwatering deli delights. For excellent fresh fish, **Feskekôrka** (see opposite) is an absolute must. For a superb **delicatessen**, head for Delitalia, Övre Husargatan 21, a terrific Italian place in the Linné area selling anything you could want for a picnic. The conveniently located **Coop Konsum** supermarket at Kungsportsavenyn 26–28 (daily until 11pm) sells a wide range of fruits, fish and meats, and also has a good deli counter.

Cafés and konditori

During the past few years, **café life** has really come into its own in Gothenburg, the profusion of new places throughout the city adding to the more traditional **konditori**. Cafés also offer a wide range of light meals and are fast becoming the best places to go for good food at reasonable prices.

Central Gothenburg

Ahlströms Konditori Korsgatan 2. Dating from 1901, this traditional café/bakery is very much of the old school, as are many of its patrons. The original features have been watered down by modernization, but it's still worth a visit for its good selection of cakes, quiches plus *Dagens Rätt* at 79kr. Closed Sun.

Brogyllen Västra Hamngatan 2. High ceilings and chandeliers add an old-world charm to this pleasant *konditori* which is one of the best places in town for watching the world go by – large windows look out on the canal.

Da Matteo Södra Larmgatan 14. In the Victoria-passagen arcade, this homely café is a perfect example of Gothenburg's foray into cool little Italian-style coffee houses. There's outdoor seating

here too, with blankets to wrap over your knees for those chilly spring and autumn days.

Fröken Olssons Kafé Östra Larmgatan 14. Ecological coffee, lactose-free drinks, vegetarian and vegan meals are the speciality at this right-on café decked out in orange tiles and swirly wallpaper. Look out also for the truly enormous cheesecakes in silver cake trays. Outdoor seating at the rear.

Mauritz Kaffe Fredsgatan 2. Very small and unassuming, this place is run by the founder's great grandson; the family have been importing coffee into Gothenburg since 1888. Come here for espresso and cappuccinos standing at the bar, and drinks served with apple buns or homebaked rye rolls with grevé cheese. Closed Sun.

Vanilj Kyrkogatan 38. A light and airy modern café with wooden floors, serving up the biggest and best cinnamon buns in town as well as a wide range of pies, salads and breads. Outdoor seating in summer in the rear courtyard.

Southern Gothenburg

Café Dali Vasagatan 42. Popular with students, and set in an orange-painted basement, this is a friendly, stylish place for sandwiches and really good chocolate cake.

Jacob's Café Haga Nygatan 10. *The* place to sit outside and people-watch; inside, the decor is fabulous, with some fine Jugendstil furniture. The food is equally impressive: quiches, baked potatoes, salads, ciabattas, cheesecake and other home-made cakes.

Java Vasagatan 23. There's a Parisian feel to this studeny coffee house that's stood the test of time.

It offers breakfasts at 30kr, a wide range of coffees, and decor that includes a collection of thermos flasks dotted among shelves of books; all in all, a good Sun-morning hangout.

Junggrens Café Avenyn 37. With chandeliers and wall paintings of old Gothenburg, this atmospheric and convivial place has been here since 1898. Hard to beat for its prime location at the top of Avenyn.

Solsidan Café Linnégatan 42. Lovely café with outdoor seating that's very popular with Linné locals, serving delicious cakes and lunches, or plenty of pasta salads.

Tintin Engelbrektsgatan 22. One of the very few cafés in Gothenburg open around the clock, this busy place is popular with a younger crowd and dishes up mounds of food and coffee at low prices.

Restaurants

If you want to avoid paying over the odds, it's generally best to steer clear of Avenyn itself and to eat your main meal at **lunchtime**, when you can fill up on *Dagens Rätt* deals for 75–90kr. Some of the best deals are to be found in the Haga and Linné districts.

Central Gothenburg

Café du Nord Kungstorget 3. Serving the best meatballs in town: four of them with mashed potato and lingonberries costs just 65kr. Alternatively, buy them individually (10kr each) and add green salad (25kr), mash (13kr) and lingonberries (5kr). Also has tuna or Greek salads for 60kr and sandwiches for 55kr.

Gabriel Feskekôrka fish hall ☎031/13 90 51. Excellent upstairs fish restaurant, though prices seem particularly high when you can see the real cost of the ingredients below; a fishy smorgasbord here is around 300kr. Closed Sun.

🏃 **Grill del Mundo** Kungsparken 1 at the foot of Avenyn ☎031/701 70 70. A fantastic range of grilled meats from cuisines around the world – everything from Argentinian steaks to grilled chicken from Lebanon for 120–275kr. Plus good desserts with a world flavour such as Congolese chocolate mousse or Italian pannacotta, around 120kr. Sit in the dappled light of ancient beech trees overlooking the canal.

Magnus & Magnus Magasinsgatan 8 ☎031/13 30 00. Consistently voted one of Sweden's best restaurants, this intimate little place oozes sophistication. Against a backdrop of velvet drapes and fresh flowers, diners are teased with a list of ingredients: duckling, orange, pumpkin, onion, for example, and the results are mouthwatering. Two courses 445kr, three courses 555kr.

🏃 **Mother India** Köpmansgatan 27 ☎031/15 47 41. This tiny basement Indian restaurant is tucked away down a side street opposite the Nils Ericsson Terminalen and beside the *Scandic Hotel*. Well worth hunting down for authentically tasty curries (59–79kr) and other treats at reasonable prices, and a good range of vegetarian options such as paneer balti at 69kr.

🏃 **Tranquilo** Kungstorget 14 ☎031/13 45 55. Mexican food is the order of the day at this funky restaurant with live DJs playing loud salsa sounds. Grilled meats and fish cost around 250kr, or there's chicken Caesar salad for 140kr and a tasty seafood and avocado salad at 169kr.

Southern Gothenburg

28+ Götabergsgatan 28 ☎031/20 21 61. Very fine French-style gourmet restaurant, whose name refers to the fat percentage of its renowned cheese, also sold in the shop near the entrance. Service is excellent, though prices are high with main dishes, such as side of pork with red onion purée and duck liver at 325–435kr, and set menus from 845kr. Closed Sun.

Bitter Linnégatan 59 ☎031/24 91 20. Upmarket Swedish home cooking at great-value prices: the classic of the week is 126kr, fish gratin costs 149kr and fried herring 196kr. The whitefish roe on a quiche of Västerbotten cheese with red-onion chutney is heavenly (124kr).

Cyrano Prinsgatan 7 ☎031/14 31 10. A superb Provençal-style bistro with a cosy, candlelit ambience and a good range of French classics: escargots (from 64kr), moules marseillaises (105kr) and frogs' legs in pernod (105kr). A set three-course menu costs 240kr, or there's the choice of a salad, wood-fired pizza and desert for 165kr.

E.t.c. Vasaplatsen 4 ☎031/13 06 02. This cool, elegant grey-painted basement is the best place in town for superb home-made pasta (119–138kr), such as tagliatelle with grilled scampi and leeks. It also has good meat and fish dishes in the range of 195–235kr: the roast lamb en croûte with goats cheese and polenta is particularly good.

Hemma Hos Haga Nygatan 12 ☎031/13 40 90. Very popular though rather cramped restaurant serving upmarket Swedish food for 139–230kr per main dish, including an excellent fish soup with saffron and marinated lamb with artichoke purée.

Hos Pelle Djupedalsgatan 2 ☎031/12 10 31. This sophisticated wine bar and restaurant off Linnégatan offers modern Swedish fare. There are three-course menus for 350kr where the starter and dessert (each consisting of three small dishes) is set, allowing you to choose the main: fried haddock with celeriac and walnuts is especially tasty.

Il Gambero Övre Husargatan 5 ☎031/13 78 38. On a long street at the end of Linnégatan, this excellent Italian eatery is decked out with Venetian face masks. The servings are generous and the service very obliging: meat mains such as lamb fillet with truffle risotto are 215–235kr, whilst pasta is a more reasonable 115–125kr. Try the superb gnocchi with mushrooms and Parma ham. Also has takeaway pasta dishes for 99kr.

Jazzå Andra Långgatan 4B ☎031/14 16 90. Pleasant bar and restaurant attracting a young crowd with a limited menu including Cajun pork (125kr), fried monkfish (175kr) and seafood soup (125kr). Occasional jazz and blues nights.

Kock & Vin Viktoriagatan 12 ☎031/701 79 79. An excellent choice for classic Swedish food with a hint of the Mediterranean, served amid airy surrounds and chandeliers. Starters such as the delicious breaded herring with whitefish roe and creme of pickled lemons go for 165–195kr, whilst mains are around the 250kr mark.

Lai Wa Storgatan 11 ☎031/711 02 39. Established in 1975, this is the best Chinese in town with dependable meat mains like beef with bamboo shoots and a good number of vegetarian dishes, including stir-fried vegetables with glass noodles in a satay sauce for 98kr.

Linnéterrassen Linnégatan 32 ☎031/24 08 90. Upmarket Swedish home cooking served in a beautifully restored wooden house with wall panelling and chandeliers, or on the extensive open-air terrace. Exceptional value with mains in the range of 95–230kr, including a herring platter with *akvavit*, meatballs, fish gratin and pan-fried pork with onions and potatoes.

Rumpanbar Linnégatan 38 ☎031/775 83 00. A popular, Mediterranean-style place with a great tiled interior and huge windows, serving excellent pizzas (from 92kr), pasta (from 102kr) and good meat and fish dishes too (129–159kr).

Sjöbaren Haga Nygatan 25 ☎031/711 97 80. Small and cosy fish and shellfish restaurant with sensible prices located on the ground floor of a former city governor's home. The range of fish is superb. Highlights include a delicious platter of smoked and *gravad* salmon (119kr) and a succulent cod gratin (139kr).

Smaka Vasaplatsen 3 ☎031/13 22 47. This elegant restaurant with a striking blue interior is one of Gothenburg's culinary gems; the moderately priced traditional local fare, with mains for 98–215kr, is enjoyed by a lively, young crowd. Try the divine salmon tartare starter with capers and mustard-topped prawn roe (98kr).

Solrosen Kaponjärgatan 4a ☎031/711 66 97. The oldest vegetarian restaurant in Gothenburg, this is the place to come for well-prepared veggie and vegan delights: the set dish of the day including the salad buffet costs 75kr (70kr for the vegan alternative). Or, the salad buffet alone is an excellent-value 55kr.

Thai Spice Andra Långgatan 8 ☎031/42 30 35. Not only is the Thai food at this agreeable neighbourhood Thai place genuinely tasty and spicy, but the prices are also quite exceptional: any dish with chicken is just 69kr, add 6kr for beef or prawns. Try the lunch buffet, too, for just 70kr. Closed Tues.

Nightlife and entertainment

There's an excellent choice of places to **drink**, and even the hippest bars often serve food and so have a bit of a restaurant atmosphere. Although it's not uncommon for Gothenburgers to drink themselves to oblivion, the atmosphere around the bars is generally non-aggressive.

The city also has a brisk **live music scene** – jazz, rock and classical – as well as the usual cinema and theatre opportunities. Pick up the Saturday edition of the *Göteborgs-Posten* newspaper, whose weekend supplement, *Två Dagar*, has the latest listings of bars, concerts and clubs.

Bars and pubs

We've listed some of the city's most popular **pubs** and **bar-restaurants** below. The bar scene along Avenyn notwithstanding, the atmosphere is generally a bit low-key in the city centre at night. Having first sampled the delights of Avenyn, head for the area around Järntorget in Haga where there are great places to drink into the early hours.

Central Gothenburg

7:an Södra Larmgatan 7. Pronounced *shoo-ann* and meaning simply "number seven", this is one of the city's better beer halls, located close to Stora Saluhallen. The interior is dark, intimate and old-fashioned in feel – a quintessential Gothenburg experience.

Bishops Arms Västra Hamngatan 3. Attached to the glamorous *Elite Plaza* hotel (see p.126), this pub boasts a wide range of beers. It's all faux "olde Englishe" inside, but nicely done and a cut above similarly styled places around the country.

Dubliner Östra Hamngatan 50b. For some time, Swedes have been overtaken with a nostalgia for all things old and Irish (or at least a Swedish inter-pretation of what's old and Irish), this being the most popular exponent.

Gamle Port Östra Larmgatan 18. The city's oldest watering hole, with cosy leather chairs in the downstairs pub and a loud and raucous disco upstairs playing 1980s music and techno.

Gretas Drottninggatan 35 ☏ 031/13 69 49. Gay bar, restaurant and nightclub all rolled into one that is *the* gay nightspot in town (Fri & Sat only). Occasional drag shows and other live performances.

Palace Södra Hamngatan 2. The rather splendid former home of the Fürstenbergs and their art gallery (see p.131) is a very popular spot, particularly on Thurs when over 27s gravitate here for a night of 1970s and 1980s hits.

Southern Gothenburg

Gillestugan Järntorget 6. Cosy and panelled without being over the top, this bar has plenty of outdoor seating and offers full meals such as beef fillet or seafood burgers at reasonable prices.

Nivå Avenyn 9. Stylish, popular bar with a modern interior heavy on black-and-white tiling and several dancefloors for a fun mix of 1980s classics, disco and R&B.

Pustervik Järntorgsgatan 12. A popular bar and club off Järntorget where there's a good chance of live music – everything from up-and-coming new bands to big names.

Rose & Crown Avenyn 6. One of a bevy of British-oriented neighbourhood pubs that are very much in vogue with Gothenburgers; this one really goes overboard with a stylistic mishmash of British paraphernalia plus live sports matches, karaoke and a Saturday Night Fever 1970s disco.

The Rover Andra Långgatan 12. Run-of-the-mill Anglo-Irish pub selling Boddingtons, with other ales, lagers and cider on tap, plus a wide range of bottled beers. Lamb, steaks and fish dishes for around 150kr.

Clubs

Gothenburg's main **nightclubs** are mostly clustered in the city centre around Vasagatan, Avenyn and Storgatan. Opening days and times change, but generally all places listed below are open Friday and Saturday nights.

Bliss Magasinatan 3. Next door to *Uppåt Framåt*, this place is regularly filled to the gills with revellers over 28 and is currently one of the hottest clubs in town with a mix of live music and DJs – be prepared to queue.

Klara Viktoriagatan 1. The best of all the more alternative nightspots, this long-established and eminently likeable bar has live music which varies each night.

Respekt Järntorget 7. Though rather unappealing on the outside, this rambling place covers one square kilometre and boasts a number of different dancefloors where people come to dance to every-thing from disco and hip-hop to soul and R&B. Occasional live music.

Trädgår'n Nya Allén 11. One of the city's liveliest haunts, this hip club offers five bars, a casino, a disco playing house and party favourites and show bands.

Uppåt Framåt Magasingatan 3. A trendy club and bar that's really drawing the crowds from across town for its live music nights and resident DJs playing house music.

Valand Vasagatan 41. The oldest of the traditional nightclubs in town, it boasts two dance floors as well as four bars, and is always crowded.

Vasastan Viktoriagatan 2A. A suave spot where confident twenty- and thirty-somethings enjoy a mellow atmosphere.

Live music

Gothenburg's large student community means there are plenty of local **live bands** which tend to play in a cluster of bars in the city centre. The best nights to catch a live performance are Friday and Saturday. **Classical music** concerts are held regularly in the Konserthuset, Götaplatsen (☎031/726 53 90, ⓦwww .gso.se), and occasionally at Stadsteatern, Götaplatsen (☎031/708 71 00, ⓦwww .stadsteatern.goteborg.se; programme details can be obtained from the tourist office). For opera, head to the renowned Göteborgsoperan at Christina Nilssons gata at the harbour (☎031/13 13 00, ⓦwww.opera.se).

Jazzhuset Erik Dahlbergsgatan 3 ☎031/13 35 44. Puts on trad and Dixieland jazz, and swing, and is something of a pick-up joint for executives.

Nefertiti Hvitfeldtsplatsen 6 ☎031/711 15 33. The premier place for jazz in Gothenburg with modern jazz, big-band and folk music as well as reggae, blues and soul.

Sticky Fingers Kaserntorget 7 ☎031/701 07 17. A rock club supporting local talent, which hosts live bands several nights a week.

Storan Kungsparken 1 at the foot of Avenyn ☎031/60 45 00. Hosts bands which are big on the club scene. Enter at the back of the theatre building.

Cinema

There are plenty of **cinemas** around the city, and English-language films (which make up the majority of what's shown) are always subtitled in Swedish, never dubbed. The most central complexes are Bio Palatset, Kungstorget 2 (☎031/774 22 90), and Bergakungen, at Skånegatan 16B (☎0771/11 12 13). For a great **art-house cinema**, check out Hagabio at Linnégatan 21 (☎031/42 88 10).

Listings

Airlines City Airline ⓦwww.cityairline.com; Ryanair ⓦwww.ryanair.com; SAS ⓦwww .scandinavian.net; Sterling ⓦwww.sterling.dk.

Airport Gothenburg City Airport ☎031/92 60 60, ⓦwww.goteborgcityairport.se; Landvetter ☎031/94 10 00, ⓦwww.lfv.se.

Buses City bus information from Västtrafik on ☎0771/41 43 00, ⓦwww.vasttrafik.se. Long-distance buses: SwebusExpress ⓦwww .swebusexpress.se; Säfflebussen ⓦwww .safflebussen.se.

Car rental Avis ⓦwww.avis.se; Europcar ⓦwww .europcar.se; Hertz ⓦwww.hertz.se.

Dentist Akuttandvården, Odinsgatan 10 ☎031/80 78 00.

Doctor Sahlgrenska Hospital at Per Dubbsgatan (☎031/342 10 00). City Akuten, a private clinic, has doctors on duty 8am–6pm at Drottninggatan 45 (☎031/10 10 10).

Emergency services Ambulance, police, and fire brigade are on ☎112.

Exchange Forex exchange offices Centralstation, Avenyn 22, Nordstan shopping centre and Kungsportsplatsen. More information at ⓦwww .forex.se.

Gay information RFSL Stora Badhusgatan 6 ☎031/13 83 00, ⓦwww.rfsl.se.

Internet access Sidewalk Express have lots of internet points across Gothenburg, for example, at Centralstation and at most 7 Eleven supermarkets. See ⓦwww.sidewalkexpress.se for complete listings. 19kr per hour.

Laundry At Nordstan Service Centre inside the Nordstan shopping centre.

Left luggage Lockers at Centralstation.

Pharmacy Apoteket Vasen, Götgatan 12, in Nordstan shopping centre ☎031/80 44 10. Daily 8am–10pm.

Police Spannmålsgatan 6 ☎031/739 20 00.

Swimming The biggest and best pool is Valhallabadet, Valhallagatan 3 (☎ 031/61 19 56), next to the Scandinavium sports complex.

Train information SJ trains ☎ 0771/75 75 75, ⓦ www.sj.se.

Around Gothenburg

North of Gothenburg, the rugged and picturesque **Bohuslän coast**, which runs all the way to the Norwegian border, attracts countless tourists each summer, the majority of them Scandinavian and German. The crowds don't detract, though, from the area's wealth of natural beauty – pink-and-black-striped granite rocks, coves, islands and hairline fjords – nor from the many fishing villages that make this stretch of coastline well worth a few days' exploration. The most popular destination is the island town of **Marstrand**, with its impressive fortress and richly ornamental ancient buildings, but there are several other attractions further up the coast that are also worth visiting, not least the buzzing summer destination of **Smögen** and the nearby wildlife park, **Nordens Ark**. Further north, **Strömstad**, a pleasant seaside town close to the Norwegian border, is also worth a stop before heading inland.

Northeast of the city, the region of **Västergötland** encompasses the southern sections of Sweden's two largest lakes, **Vänern** and **Vättern**. Here the scenery is gentler, and a number of attractive lakeside towns and villages make good bases from which to venture out into the forested countryside and onto the **Göta Canal**, which connects the lakes with each other, and runs from the North Sea to the Baltic. There are a number of ways to journey along the canal, from cross-country cruises to short ferry rides. The use of **bikes** is a great alternative for exploring Västergötland, by means of the countless cycling trails, empty roads and the canal towpaths; nearly all tourist offices, youth hostels and campsites in the region rent out bikes, for around 150kr per day.

The Bohuslän coast

A chain of **islands** linked by a thread of bridges and short ferry crossings make up the region of **Bohuslän** where, despite the summer crowds, it's still easy enough to find a private spot to swim. Sailing is also a popular pastime among the many Swedes who have summer cottages here, and all the way along the coast you'll see yachts gliding through the water. Another feature of the Bohuslän landscape you can't fail to miss is the large number of **churches** throughout the area. The region has a long tradition of religious observance, fuelled in the early nineteenth century by the dogmatic Calvinist clergyman Henric Schartau, who believed that closed curtains were a sign of sin within – even today, many island homes still have curtainless windows. The churches, dating from the 1840s up to the early twentieth century, are mostly white, simple affairs, and look like windmills without sails. Once you've seen the inside of one you've mostly seen them all, but the few that are exquisite or unusual have been highlighted in the guide. Each church is usually open between 10am and 3pm, but the clergyman invariably lives next door and will be happy to unlock the building at other times.

Getting around

There's just one single-track **train** line in Bohuslän: running north from Gothenburg through industrial **Uddevalla**, it terminates in **Strömstad**, from where there's are regular **ferries** to Sandefjord (the location of Ryanair's Oslo Torp airport) and Langesund in Norway. Alternatively, there are direct buses between Gothenburg and **Marstrand**, and between **Smögen** or **Lysekil** and Uddevalla.

Heading **northwards** from Strömstad involves first backtracking to Uddevalla from where you can pick up connections for Mariestad and Karlstad. However, if you really want to explore Bohuslän's most dramatic scenery and reach its prettier villages, you'll need a car. From Gothenburg, the **E6** motorway is the quickest road north, with designated scenic routes leading off it every few kilometres.

Marstrand

About 50km northwest of Gothenburg, the island of **Marstrand** buzzes with activity in the summer, as holiday-makers come to sail, bathe and take one of the highly entertaining historical tours around its impressive **castle**, Carlstens fästning. With ornate wooden buildings lining the bustling **harbour**, Marstrand is a delightful place to visit and as an easy day-trip from Gothenburg, it shouldn't be missed.

The town's colourful **history** – as so often in Sweden – mainly revolves around fish. Founded under Norwegian rule in the thirteenth century, it achieved remarkable prosperity through herring fishing during the following century, when the ruling king, Håkon of Norway, obtained permission from the pope to allow fishing in the town even on holy days. Rich herring pickings, however, eventually led to greed and corruption, and Marstrand became known as the most immoral town in Scandinavia. The murder of a cleric in 1586 was seen as an omen: soon after, the whole town burned to the ground and the herring mysteriously disappeared from its waters, neither the fish nor Marstrand's prosperity to return until the 1770s. Around this time, the king announced an open-door policy, or *porto franco*, for Marstrand, which for the first time allowed foreigners to settle in Sweden. Unfortunately, in 1808 the fish disappeared for good, and in his anger, the king abolished *porto franco*. Meanwhile the town, without its main source of income, fell behind Gothenburg in importance, and by the 1820s, the old herring salting-houses had been converted into bathhouses as Marstrand reinvented itself as a fashionable bathing resort.

Arrival and information

Bus #312 leaves from Nils Ericson Terminalen in Gothenburg for Marstrand hourly (7.25am–6.40pm; 1hr). By **car**, take the E6 north out of Gothenburg, and then Route 168 west, leading right to the ferry stop; cars are not permitted on Marstrand, so you must park at the ferry quay on the island of Koön and travel across to Marstrand as a foot passenger (every 15min; 5min; 20kr).

The **tourist office**, at Hamngatan 33 (early June Mon–Sat 11am–5pm, Sun noon–4pm; late June to Aug Mon–Fri 10am–6pm, Sat & Sun 11am–5pm; ☏0303/600 87, ⓦwww.marstrandshamn.nu), is close to the harbour where the ferries dock.

Accommodation

The island's *Båtellet* **youth hostel** (☏0303/600 10, ⓔmarstrandsvarmbadhus @telia.com; dorm beds 225kr, double rooms ❷) is wonderfully set in an old bathhouse in Kungsplan square and looks out onto idyllic islands; the rooms are nothing special but the facilities are good, and include a sauna, laundry, a swimming pool and a restaurant (see p.146). To get there, turn right from the ferry pier and follow the water's edge from the harbour as far as you can go.

Of the several very pleasant **hotels** on the island, the *Grand* (☏0303/603 22, ⓦwww.grandmarstrand.se; ❻) at Rådhusgatan 2, just 50m from the tourist office and left through the park, is a real classic. Expertly refurbished, this very fine hotel lives up to its name, but ask for a room away from the street – loud late-night revellers can keep you awake otherwise. The more standard but still very pleasant *Hotel Nautic* (☏0303/610 30, ⓦwww.hotellnautic.com; ❹), at Långgatan 6, has a lovely setting, surrounded by water and sailing boats.

The Town

Turning left when you leave the ferry, head up cobbled Kungsgatan and past the *Grand Hotel* (see above). After about a minute, you'll arrive at a small square, surrounded by beautiful wooden houses painted in pastel hues; the locals play *boules* here beneath the shade of a huge, ancient beech tree. Across the square is the squat, white **St Maria kyrka**, whose interior is simple and unremarkable. From here, all the streets, lined with wooden villas, climb steeply to the castle.

Carlstens fästning (early to mid-June & mid- to late Aug daily 11am–4pm; mid-June to mid-Aug 11am–6pm; rest of the year Sat & Sun 11am–4pm; 70kr including guided tour; for English-language tours, book ahead on ☏0303/602 65; ⓦwww.carlsten.se) is an imposing sweep of stone walls solidly wedged into the rough rock above. You could easily spend half a day clambering around the castle walls and down the weather-smoothed rocks to the sea, where there are always plenty of places to bathe in private. The informal **tours** take 45 minutes, and guides will explain about Carlstens' most noted prisoner-resident, **Lasse-Maja**, a thief who got rich by dressing as a woman to seduce and rob wealthy farmers. A sort of Swedish Robin Hood, Maja was known for giving his spoils to the poor. Incarcerated here for 26 years, Lasse-Maja ingratiated himself with the officers by deploying his cooking skills in a kitchen not renowned for its cuisine. His culinary expertise eventually won him a pardon: when the new king – who was reputed to hate Swedish cooking – visited, Lasse-Maja had the foresight to serve him French food. Some tours include climbing the hundred-metre-high towers, built in 1658. The views from the top are stunning, but you have to be fit to get up there: the steep, spiral climb is quite exhausting.

Eating, drinking and nightlife

For a daytime **coffee**, the most atmospheric place is the café in the old officers' mess at the fortress. Marstrand doesn't have **drinking** haunts as such; instead, people tend to drink with their meals in the places listed below.

Marstrand is nowadays known as something of an **eating** Mecca, though the privilege of dining here mostly comes at considerable cost, with main dishes at 150–250kr, though there are one or two cheap eats too.

Bröderna Arvidssons Fisk Kyrkogatan 25, at the harbour. Those in the market for cheap eats are well catered for at this very good smoked fish stall. Serves fish and chips as well as burgers, sausages and ice cream, plus fresh fish and seafood.

Drott *Båtellet* youth hostel ☎0303/618 70. Attractive spot serving very pleasant lunches and dinners in an old bathhouse with delightful views (see p.145 for directions). Daily pasta dishes for around 100kr, and meat or seafood meals from 150kr.

Lasse-Maja Krog Hamngatan 31, at the harbour ☎0303/611 22. Named after Marstrand's infamous prisoner (see p.145), this spot is very popular with locals and tourists alike (May–Aug only). Located in a cheerful old house, its wide-ranging meat and fish menu has main courses from 150kr, as well as pizzas at around 100kr.

Marstrands Wärdshus Hamngatan 23, at the harbour ☎0303/603 69. Very popular for its sunny quayside terrace with basic wooden tables, where you can eat deliciously fresh seafood for 150–250kr. Open from Easter to Sept.

Societetshuset Långgatan 1, by the youth hostel ☎0303/606 00. Three restaurants within one classic old house, all serving a good range of meat and fish dishes in an old-fashioned atmosphere, though prices are high. Reckon on 250kr for a main dish.

Tenan Rådhusgatan 2, in the *Grand Hotel* ☎0303/603 22. A charming option overlooking the bandstand at the front of the hotel. The speciality is garlic-fried crayfish which has been served here for decades. Reckon on 250kr per dish.

Fiskebäckskil

FISKEBÄCKSKIL is one of the most attractive villages along the entire length of the Bohuslän coast. Peppered with imposing old wooden houses perched high up on rocky rises, many with fancily carved porchways and intricate glazed verandas, it also boasts several attractions that are well worth exploring.

Arriving by road from the south, you'll find the remarkably stylish **art café**, *Saltarvet* (mid-June to mid-Aug Wed–Sun noon–6pm; ☎0523/222 70), just on the right where the road enters the village at Saltängen. Its galleries display constantly changing exhibitions of contemporary Swedish artists.

Fiskebäckskil's most famous son is the artist **Carl Wilhelmson** (1866–1928), who was born in a cottage near the marina. He made his name nationally with his powerful, evocative portraits and landscapes, which beautifully reflect west-coast Swedish life at the end of the nineteenth century. In 1912, he had a strikingly elegant cottage built close to his birthplace, with splendid views over the waters towards Lysekil, its double-height windows letting the famous Nordic light flood in. Reproductions of his work line the walls (the originals are mostly in Gothenburg's Konstmuseum or the Nationalmuseum in Stockholm, the subjects often being the scenery just outside these windows. The most poignant of the prints, *On The Hill* (the original of which is in Gothenburg's Konstmuseum), shows a scene from Wilhelmson's childhood. Aged 9, he had stood unnoticed behind a group of old men sitting on a rock in Fiskebäckskil, while they discussed a hurricane which had wrecked twenty ships the day before, killing his father, a sea captain. When they became aware of the boy's presence, they asked him not to say anything, and he kept the secret from his mother, who only learnt of her husband's death from the post-boat captain a month later.

Not far away, close to the marina, the **church** (daily 10am–9pm) has an opulent yet almost domestic feel about its interior. There are chandeliers, gold-plated sconces, etched-glass mirrors with hand-carved wood frames and fresh flowers at the ends of each pew. The luxuriance of the decor is thanks to donations from Bohuslän's richest eighteenth-century landowner, Margaretha Huitfeldt, who also paid for the wrought-iron and sheet-metal spire, crowned with a gold-plated weathercock. The wooden, barrel-vaulted ceiling is worth a glance, too: it's covered in eighteenth-century murals, the oddest aspect of which is the scattering of angels' heads. Outside, in the graveyard close to the main door, is Wilhelmson's rather plain grave, his likeness carved into the granite tombstone. More unusual is the grave in the far corner, where an English officer and a German soldier, who died in the Great North Sea Battle of 1916, were buried together.

Practicalities

Although Fiskebäckskil lies around 50km due north of Marstrand, the fragmented nature of the coast hereabouts makes it difficult to reach without first heading back to the mainland in order to proceed northwards. Once back on the E6, the easiest approach is via Herrestad and then Route 161 southwest via Bökenäs. By **public transport** from Marstrand, the easiest way is to take bus #312 to Kungälvsmotet then bus #841 to Bökenäs skola, where you change again for the #845 to Fiskebäckskil – although this sounds rather complicated, it's actually quite straightforward as the buses connect with each other. The journey is generally possible two or three times a day but since timings change you should always check Ⓦ www.vasttrafik.se before setting out or ask in a tourist office.

Though Fiskebäckskil is a quiet, hidden-away sort of place, it does have a fine **hotel**: the stylish *Gullmarsstrand Hotel* (Ⓣ 0523/66 77 88, Ⓦ www.gullmarsstrand .se; ❼) is right on the water, next to the Lysekil ferry pier. Fiskebäckskil has a couple of excellent eating opportunities. The art café, *Saltarvet*, is also a lovely spot for a light lunch – enjoyed while you look out through the glass walls onto the picturesque natural harbour. The *Gullmarsstrand Hotel* (see above) boasts an excellent if expensive **restaurant** (reckon on around 250kr for a main dish), but for a really exceptional meal, head to *Brygghuset* (Ⓣ 0523/222 22) on the marina below the church, which does good fish dishes for 245–275kr – the grilled halibut with rhubarb, mango and chives is sensational.

Lysekil and around

The largest coastal town in this area is **LYSEKIL**, at the tip of a peninsula with the Gullmar fjord twisting to the east and the Skagerrak to the west. While the journey into town by Route 162 does not reveal it as immediately attractive, Lysekil does have plenty to recommend it. From the tourist office (see p.148), it's a five-minutes' walk through the village to **Havets Hus** at Strandvägen 9 (daily: mid-June to late Aug 10am–6pm; Feb to mid-June & late Aug to early Nov 10am–4pm; 90kr; Ⓦ www.havetshus.se), an amazing museum of marine life featuring no fewer than forty aquaria. The chief attraction, though, is an eight-metre-long underwater tunnel, containing 140,000 litres of saltwater and home to dozens of enormous fish, including sharks, that swim over and around you. Fish with such delightful names as the "lesser spotted dogfish" and "the topknot" mingle with varieties more usually associated with lemon-wedges in restaurants, and children can enjoy feeling the slimy algae or starfish in the touch pool.

From Havets Hus, continue west along the shore and you'll reach the best **beach** in town, Pinnevik, in about ten minutes. From here, a walking trail heads west across to the rocky headland, Stångehuvud, made of the local pink granite,

Bohusgraniten, where it's also possible to sunbathe and swim; maps are available at the tourist office (see below).

The villas en route to Havets Hus, with their intricately carved eaves, porticoes and windows, are worth a look, too. Lysekil was a popular bathing resort in the nineteenth century, and these ornate houses are a reminder of the time when the rich and neurotic came to take the waters. The bizarre, castellated rough granite house on the inland side of the main road was built as home for a Herr Laurin, then Lysekil's wealthiest man; it now plays host to the offices of the local newspaper. A better-known local figure of the past is **Carl Curman**, a self-styled health guru. Of the town's ornate, mustard-and-chocolate-brown Hansel-and-Gretel houses on the waterside of the main road, his was the most fancy (a bronze bust of him stands behind it, at the water's edge). In his day, Curman managed to convince his patients that sunbathing on the exposed rock was dangerous, as "the amount of air must be regulated", and persuaded them that it was in the interests of their health to pay to use the bathhouses, which he conveniently owned. Today, the classic old bathhouses, along the waterfront, are a popular place for segregated **nude bathing** (free).

Walk up any set of steps from the waterfront and you'll reach the **church** (daily 11am–7pm; shorter hours Sept–May), the town's most imposing landmark and visible for miles around. It's hewn from the surrounding pink granite, with beaten copper doors and windows painted by early twentieth-century artist Albert Eldh.

Practicalities

From Fiskebäckskil, an hourly passenger ferry runs all day (15min; 38kr) and sails to Lysekil from the end of Kaptensgatan. To get here **by car**, head back out of Fiskebäckskil in an eastward direction (towards Bökenäs) for 10km, then take Route 161 and the regular all-day free car ferry (between Finssbo and Skår; 10min) across to the town. Express **buses** #840 and #841 come here from Gothenburg (8 daily; 1hr 45min). By **car from Gothenburg**, take Route 161, which leads off the E6 at Herrestad, west of Uddevalla.

Lysekil's **tourist office** (mid-June to Aug Mon–Sat 10am–6pm, Sun 11am–3pm; ☎0523/130 50, ⓦwww.lysekilsturist.se) is located at Södra Hamngatan 6, the main road along the waterfront. If you want to **stay**, there's a hostel, *Strand Vandrarhem* (☎0523/797 51, ⓦwww.strandflickorna .se; dorm beds 260kr, double rooms ❷), at Strandvägen 1, which is pleasingly placed on the waterfront next to Havets Hus. Another attractive place is the grand old *Stadshotellet* (☎0523 140 30, ⓦwww.stadshotellet-lysekil .se;❹) on Kungstorget, which faces the appealing town park. The best and most characterful option, ⚓ *Havshotellet* (☎0523/797 50, ⓦwww.strandflickorna .se; ❻/❻), at Turistgatan 13, is in an archetypal red-and-white house from 1905 with a cosy interior full of period furnishings. On the other side of the enormous granite boulder that lies behind the hotel, the two luxury waterfront rooms *Havsateljen* (❼) and *Badpaviljongen* (❼), built on stilts over the sea, are perfect for a special occasion.

Lysekil has plenty of mid-range family **restaurants** serving big portions with a choice of fish and meat dishes. One good option is *Rosvik* (☎0523/100 54), in Rosvikstorget just back from the waterfront, where daily specials of halibut and plaice go for 200kr. For a cheaper fish supper and a beer, *Pråmen* (☎0523/134 52), a pontoon **restaurant-bar** floating in Södra Hamnen, is a pleasant spot, with views back towards Fiskebäckskil and dishes from 150kr. Up in the town centre at Kungsgatan 32, *Café Kungsgatan* is the best option for light meals, salads and sandwiches.

North to Nordens Ark and Smögen

From Lysekil, head back along Route 162 and turn left (west) for Nordens Ark, a wildlife sanctuary near Åby. It's a twenty-minute drive north from Lysekil, and on the way you'll pass a couple of notable churches, in particular the one at **Brastad**, an 1870s Gothic building with an oddly haphazard appearance: every farm in the neighbourhood donated a lump of its own granite towards the construction, but none of the bits matched.

Don't be put off by the yeti-sized puffin plonked at the entrance to **Nordens Ark** (daily: mid-June to mid-Aug 10am–7pm; Sept & April to mid-June 10am–5pm; Jan–April 10am–4pm; 150kr; Ⓦwww.nordensark.se), on the Åby fjord. This non-profit-making place is a wildlife sanctuary for endangered animals, where animal welfare takes priority over human voyeurism. Red pandas, lynxes, snow leopards and arctic foxes are among the rare creatures being bred and reared in a mountainous landscape of dense forest and grassy clearings that's kept as close as possible to the animals' natural habitat. The enclosures are so large, and the paths and bridges across the site so discreet, that it's a good idea to bring a pair of binoculars with you to ensure against disappointment.

Smögen

From Lysekil, to reach the old fishing village and island of **SMÖGEN**, 15km west of Nordens Ark along the coast, you'll have to return on Route 162, then take Route 171, as there is no crossing over the Åby fjord. By **bus** it's a straightforward journey (1hr 15min) involving a change of buses in Hallinden (first take the #850 from Lysekil, then the #860 from Hallinden to Smögen). Smögen is linked to the mainland and its neighbour, Kungshamn, by bridge.

Smögen is one of the most picturesque and enjoyable destinations in the whole of Bohuslän. Today, the village is an attractive mix of shops and boutiques in old seafront wooden houses, fronted by a quay that runs for several hundred metres that's famous across Sweden and known as the Smögenbryggan. Smögen first hit the big time in the late 1960s as tourists began to discover its unassuming charms. Then, during the 1970s, it became the number one summer destination for Swedish teens and twenty-somethings who came here to party all night long in the countless bars that once lined the jetty. Things are quieter now and Smögen, though still busy, is once again regaining its dignity – the town is at its most animated between July and mid-August. When it comes to **beaches**, most people take the boat (every 30min; 10min; 100kr return) from the harbour to the tiny, low-lying island of **Hallö** where the smooth, flat rocks that make up the entire island, which is also a nature reserve, are perfect for sunbathing and swimming.

The **tourist office** (Mon–Fri 10am–6pm, also mid-June to mid-Aug Sat & Sun 10am–5pm; Ⓣ0523/66 55 50, Ⓦwww.sotenasturism.se) is back on the mainland in Kungshamn, at Bäckevikstorget 5 opposite the bus station. For **accommodation**, there is a **youth hostel**, ⚡ *Makrillvikens* (Ⓣ0523/315 65, Ⓦwww .makrillviken.se; dorm beds 250kr, double rooms ❷), at Makrillgatan, in a former wooden bathhouse set well back from the crowds amid rocky outcrops of granite, with open sea views and a sauna right on the waterfront. Alternatively, *Smögens Havsbad* (Ⓣ0523/66 84 50, Ⓦwww.smogenshavsbad.se; ❺/❻), at Hotellgatan 26, is a stylish hotel, ten-minutes' walk from the quay and the summertime hubbub, but note that prices go up in summer, unlike in much of the rest of Sweden. In an attractive fin-de-siècle house bordered by granite boulders, the rooms are more modern than you might expect; there's a fine spa and lounge, and also a good **restaurant** and bar with superb sea views.

You'll find plenty of places for a cheap bite, though the real culinary draw is the terrace of open-fronted **fishmongers' shops** selling mounds of shrimp, crab and all manner of smoked seafood. The most popular **restaurant** in the village is *Skärets Krog* (☎0523/323 17), by the water at Madenvägen 1; it's a loud but thoroughly enjoyable place, particularly on a balmy summer evening, and is renowned for its excellent fish dishes which cost around 250kr. *Lagergrens*, close by at no. 12, is a more laid-back establishment, good for a drink and simpler mains like Caesar salad, spare ribs or pizzas. By far the best **café** in the village is *Coffeeroom* (June–Aug) at Sillgatan 10, just 50m from the foot of Storgatan. They serve a breakfast buffet, excellent home-baked bread, cakes, warm baguettes and pies, though their speciality is giant, warm cinnamon buns.

Strömstad

Around 100km north of Smögen, the once fashionable eighteenth-century spa resort of **STRÖMSTAD** has an air of faded grandeur, though thanks to its regular **ferry** link with Sandefjord in Norway, it's pretty lively all year round, particularly so at Easter (especially Maundy Thurs) and in June and July, when the tiny town is full to the brim with holidaying Norwegians and their caravans. Aside from its close proximity to the Koster Islands (see p.152), the town boasts a couple of quite remarkable public buildings that are well worth a look; everywhere of interest is easily accessible from the train station and the ferry terminal.

Arrival, information and accommodation

Strömstad can be reached by direct **train** from Gothenburg. From Smögen there are two main ways of getting to the town: either by **bus** #860 to Håby and then by bus #871 or #880, or by bus #860 to Munkedal and then by train, either way a journey of a couple of hours which is possible several times daily. Travelling by car, take Route 174 back to the E6 and then head north. The **train station** (also the departure point for Strömstad's buses) and the **ferry terminal** are both within a few hundred metres of each other on the main road into town from the south, Uddevallavägen. There are two ferries to Norway from Södra Hamnen: ColorLine (☎0526/620 00, ⓦwww.colorline.se) operate to Sandefjord, whilst Kystlink (☎0525/140 00, ⓦwww.kystlink.com) sail to Langesund with onward connections to Hirtshals in Denmark; ferries to the Koster Islands depart from Norra Hamnen, 200m to the north, on the other side of the rocky promontory, Laholmen (see below).

The **tourist office** (May to mid-June & mid- to end Aug Mon–Fri 9am–6pm, Sat & Sun 10am–4pm; mid-June to mid-Aug Mon–Sat 9am–8pm, Sun 10am–8pm; Sept–April Mon–Fri 9am–5pm; ☎0526/623 30, ⓦwww.stromstadtourist .se) on the quay has full details of ferry times and **internet** connection (20kr per 15min).

Accommodation

Although Strömstad sees plenty of tourists from Norway, there's generally lots of accommodation to go round. **Private rooms** can be booked at *alabohuslan.se* (☎0706/88 89 57).

Crusellska hemmet Norra Kyrkogatan 12 ☎0526/101 93, ⓦwww.crusellska.com. A real find, this elegant youth hostel is decorated in early 1900s style and even boasts its own spa and rose garden. It's closed from Dec to Feb. Dorm beds for 230kr and double rooms ❷

Daftö FerieCenter 5km south of Strömstad along Route 176 ☎0526/260 40, ⓦwww.dafto.com.

A busy campsite popular with holidaying Norwegians complete with a variety of different sized cottages (from ❶) which is open mid-March to mid-Dec.

Krabban Södra Bergsgatan 15 ☎0526/142 00, ⓦwww.hotellkrabban.se. A cosy place with a maritime decor in the town centre. Rooms are decked out with homely wallpaper and have wooden floors. Rooms with shared facilities cost 100kr less. ❹

Hotel Laholmen Laholmen ⊕ 0526/197 00, ⓦwww
.laholmen.se. Sitting atop the rocky promontory in the
town centre, this modern plush hotel enjoys a prime
waterfront position between Strömstad's two
harbours. Try for a room with a balcony to appreciate
the hotel's elevated location. ❻/❺

Roddaren Fredrikshaldsvägen 2 ⊕ 0703/58 79 19,
ⓦ www.roddaren.se. An independent hostel 10min
walk east along the road fronting Stadshuset,
Fredrikhaldsvägen. Open late June to mid-Aug; no
dorm beds, double rooms ❷

The Town

Although you wouldn't guess it from its run-of-the-mill exterior, inside Strömstad's **church**, a few minutes' walk from the train station, there's an eclectic mix of unusual decorative features, including busy frescoes, model ships hanging from the roof, gilt chandeliers and 1970s brass lamps. During the summer, numerous concerts ranging from jazz to gospel are held here; they're free and usually begin at 8pm. The town's arts venue is **Lokstallet Konstgalleri** (July daily 11am–5pm; Aug Tues–Sun 11am–5pm; April–June & Sept–Dec Thurs–Sun 11am–5pm; Jan–March Fri–Sun 11am–5pm; 20kr; ⊕ 0526/146 95), at Uddevallavägen 1. Right opposite the ferry terminal at Södra Hamnen, it holds some striking contemporary art exhibitions in a former engine shed.

Strömstad's most bizarre building, which overlooks the whole town, is the massive, copper-roofed **Stadshuset** (town hall), the product of a millionaire recluse. Born to a Strömstad jeweller in 1851, Adolf Fritiof Cavalli-Holmgren became a financial whizz-kid, moved to Stockholm and was soon one of Sweden's richest men. When he heard that his impoverished home town needed a town hall, he offered to finance the project, but only on certain conditions: the building had to be situated on the spot where his late parents had lived, and he insisted on complete control over the design. By the time the mammoth structure was completed in 1917, he was no longer on speaking terms with the city's politicians, and he never returned to see the building he had battled to create, which had been topped with a panoramic apartment for his private use. Much later, in 1951, it was discovered that his obsessive devotion to his parents had led him to design the entire building around the dates of their birthdays – January 27 and May 14 – and their wedding day – March 7. The dimensions of the over one hundred rooms were calculated using combinations of the numbers in the dates, as were the sizes of every window, every flight of stairs and every cluster of lamps. Furthermore, in all his years of dealing with city officials, he only ever responded or held meetings on these dates. Built entirely from rare local apple-granite (so named because it contains circular markings), the town hall is open to the public. Adolf's portrait, which bears a false date (unsurprisingly, one of his three favourites), can be seen in the main council chamber, and despite his animosity towards the city administration, Adolf still chose to be buried in the graveyard at Strömstad's church – his rough-hewn granite tombstone is by far the grandest here, its inscription translating as "From Strömstad town, with grateful thanks to this most memorable son".

Eating, drinking and nightlife

Strömstad has a good number of places to eat and drink, most of which are easily found by just wandering around near the harbour area. There are also a number of fishmongers doubling as **fish-snack cafés**. Excellent value is *Skaldjurscafé*, hidden away behind *The Cod* in a row of red wooden sheds by the harbourside. For 100kr, you can get a plateful of prawns with bread.

Nightlife in Strömstad has really come on in recent years. The nightclubs inside *Hotel Laholmen* and *The Cod* are open all year, whilst there's generally live music at *Prämen* between June and August. *Skagerack* in the centre, opposite the church, in a tired-looking wedding cake of a building, is where the Stockholm elite once partied; it's also worth a look in summer (June–Aug).

Cafés and restaurants

The Cod Torskholmen ☎0526/615 00. A few metres towards the centre from the ColorLine terminal, this is one of the best eating places in town and has a range of seafood dishes: fish gratin (198kr), fish and chips with king prawns (179kr) and pan-fried redfish with coriander (225kr).

Pråmen ☎0526/135 09. On the boat opposite *The Cod*, moored in Södra Hamnen opposite the train station and specializing in seafood at slightly cheaper prices to its neighbour.

Göstases Strandpromenaden, ☎0526/107 78. A great maritime pub with outdoor seating overlooking the harbour. Also serves a few light seafood dishes. Open daily June–Aug, occasional weekends out of season.

Kaffe Kompaniet Södra Hamngatan 12. Wide range of unusual coffees and delicious cakes in this characterful building which has been serving the masses since 1882.

Kaffedoppet Järnvägstorget. A characterful *konditori* by the station serving a no-nonsense range of filling open sandwiches and a small selection of home-made cakes and buns. Seating upstairs, too, with a balcony.

Rökeriet Torskholmen ☎0526/148 60. Smart harbourside restaurant which smokes its own fish. With outdoor seating and a balcony, it's the perfect spot to enjoy fresh seafood: smoked salmon at 149kr, fish soup 119kr and fried plaice for 199kr are good choices.

The Koster Islands

Sweden's two most westerly inhabited islands, Nordkoster and Sydkoster, have a combined population of three hundred and enjoy more sunshine hours than almost anywhere else in the country. To get to **Kosteröarna** (ⓦwww.kosteroarna .com), as they're known in Swedish, pick up the **catamaran** (May–Sept 120kr return, rest of the year 65kr; 35–55min; timetable available on the website) at Norra Hamnen, outside Strömstad's tourist office.

The boat stops first at **Nordkoster** (35min), the more rugged of the pair; the island is a grand **nature reserve** bursting with wild flowers, which takes a couple of hours to walk around. It's just another five minutes on the ferry to **Långegärde**, the first stop on **Sydkoster**, an island three times the size of its neighbour. You could stay on another fifteen minutes to reach **Ekenäs**, the only settlement of any size, but it doesn't make much difference where you disembark as one spot is much like any other here on the islands.

No vehicles are allowed on either Nordkoster or Sydkoster other than the curious, motorized buggy bikes with wooden trays in front for carrying provisions. There are no dramatic sights on the islands – the pleasure of being here lies in losing yourself in an atmosphere of complete calm, the silence broken only by the screeching of birds. Cycling in the sun, along the easy paths through wild-flower meadows is another delight; once in a while you can have refreshments at the smattering of small cafés and ice-cream parlours. During the summer, there are also **bird- and seal-watching expeditions** (170k); more information is available from Strömstad's tourist office).

Practicalities

Wherever you disembark from the ferry, you'll be met by a sea of **bikes** to rent, all for 80kr a day (100kr with gears); they're the best way to explore the gently undulating landscape of Sydkoster. A free **map** of the islands is available at Strömstad tourist office, but you don't really need one: all the tiny tracks lead to coves and also interconnect, so finding your way around should be simple.

Camping on the islands is restricted to just one site on Nordkoster, *Reservatet* (☎0526/204 66); there are **cabins** for rent at *Kostergården* (☎0526/201 23; ❶) 800m from the ferry stop at Kilesand on the south island. There's also one **hotel**

on Sydkoster, and surprisingly stylish it is too: ♨ *Sydkoster Hotell Ekenäs* (☎0526/202 50, ⊛www.sydkoster.com; ⊙), at Ekenäs, is just 100m from the harbour and is open from March to December. It has a variety of rooms ranging from regular doubles to better value and very nicely appointed mini-suites (1900kr) and apartments (3400kr) sleeping up to eight. There's a good **restaurant** here too (main courses 150–200kr), which serves its own delicious home-pressed fruit and berry juices. Ekenäs is also the place to find the excellent *Kosters rökeri* (June–Aug daily 10am–6pm), a smoked fish and seafood emporium whose lines include delicious cod, salmon, mackerel and shrimps. Alternatively, there's a good **café**, *Sundets Skaldjurscafé*, where the boat comes in at Långegärde. Located in a big red wooden house, it serves meat and fish dishes, as well as light bites like *pytt i panna*, home-baked toasted bread and shrimp (known locally as "Toast Koster"), and mussel soup.

The Göta Canal

The giant waterway that is the **Göta Canal** leads from the mouth of the Göta river on the western seaboard to **Vänern**, Sweden's largest lake, via the **Trollhättan Canal**, then links up with another formidable lake, **Vättern**, before running right through southeastern Sweden to the Baltic Sea. Centuries ago, it was realized that Vänern and Vättern could be linked as part of a grand scheme to create a continuous waterway across the country from Gothenburg to the Baltic. This would not only make inland transport easier, but also provide a vital trade route – a means of both shipping iron and timber out of central Sweden, and of avoiding Danish customs charges levied on traffic through the Öresund. It was not until 1810 that Baron Baltzar von Platen's hugely ambitious plans to carve out a route from Gothenburg to Stockholm were put into practice by the Göta Canal Company. Sixty thousand soldiers took 22 years to complete the mammoth task, and the canal opened in 1832, shortly after Von Platen's death.

It's thanks to the Trollhättan Canal that shipping from ports along Lake Vänern's shores has access to the sea at Gothenburg, and every year millions of

---

The Göta Canal by boat

The section of the **Göta Canal** between Vänern and Vättern is an extremely popular tourist destination, with a seemingly endless range of options for boat trips along the canal available through the upmarket Göta Kanal Rederiaktiebolag (☎031/80 63 15, ⊛www.gotacanal.se) at Pusterviksgatan 13 in Gothenburg and, more affordably, Mariestads Skärgårdstrafik, Slussvägen 105 in Sjötorp (☎0501/514 70, ⊛www .gotakanal.net). Many involve a mixture of cycling and relaxing on the boats, though others include canoeing, riding Icelandic ponies, and even ice-skating trips on the canal in winter. Prices vary dramatically, depending on the length of trip and what is included, such as accommodation, bus transfers, museum entry and guided tours. For example, a five-hour trip through sixteen locks on M/S Bellevue, between Sjötorp (north of Mariestad) and Töreboda, costs a good-value 375kr. It runs Wednesday and Saturday from mid-May to August, and includes a bus back to where you started; there's a restaurant and café on board and children under 7 travel free. More glamorous, and correspondingly more expensive, is a two-day trip from Motala to Söderköping (or vice versa; return to starting point by bus included) on *M/S Diana*. It costs from 3975kr per person including full board and one night on the boat, with a stop at Berg with its impressive flight of locks.

tonnes of timber, paper pulp and oil are transported by this route. For the visitor, however, it's the eastern and northern shores of the lake – a province known as **Västergötland** – that contain most of the region's attractions, notably **Läcko castle** and the pretty town of **Mariestad**, both easily reached from Gothenburg. With more time, you can cut across to the western shore of Lake Vättern; the colossal fortress at **Karlsborg** is particularly worth a detour.

Lake Vänern

The Trollhättan canal's raison d'être is **Lake Vänern** (ⓦwww.vanerland.com), the largest lake in Western Europe, covering a whopping 5600 square kilometres (almost four times the size of Greater London). The map of Sweden is totally dominated by this tremendous body of water, which stretches 140km up to Karlstad in the province of Värmland. Travelling around the lake you could be forgiven for thinking you're on the coast: the endless vistas of water and sky really do resemble those of the sea. Indeed, such is its size that the Swedish Met Office even produces a shipping forecast for the lake.

Vänern was created after the last Ice Age about ten thousand years ago. Very slowly, as the land began to rise following the retreat of the ice, islands formed in the extensive waters which once covered this part of southern Sweden; with further landrise, today's familiar pattern of forest and lake gradually took shape. Consequently, Vänern – and neighbouring Vättern – contain several species of marine life left over from the Ice Age, and not normally found in freshwater lakes.

Läckö Slott

Heading along Vänern's east coast, make your first port of call **Läckö Slott** (June–Aug daily 10am–6pm; 80kr; May & Sept daily 11am–5pm; 50kr; ⓦwww.lackoslott.se), just 25km to the north of uneventful Lidköping. To get here by public transport, first take the train from Gothenburg to Lidköping, then change to bus #132 (every 2hr; 35min).

Officially billed as being on its own island, but surrounded by water on just three sides, Läckö is everyone's idea of a fairytale castle, its turrets and towers all creamy white as if dipped in yoghurt. The castle dates from 1290, but was last modified and restructured by Lidköping's chancellor, Count Magnus Gabriel de la Gardie, when he took it over in 1652. Inside, there is a wealth of exquisite decoration, particularly in the apartment that belonged to the count's wife, Princess Marie Euphrosyne. There are celebrated annual art exhibitions here in summer (June–Aug) and there's a daily guided tour in English at 3.30pm. Läckö's charms are no secret, so if you visit during summer, be prepared for the crowds.

Mariestad

Back in Lidköping, it's barely 45 minutes by train to lakeside **MARIESTAD**, renowned for its splendid medieval quarter and harbour area. What lifts the town beyond mere picture-postcard status is the extraordinary range of building styles crammed into the centre – Gustavian, Carolean, Neoclassical, Swiss-chalet style and Art Nouveau – a living museum of architectural design.

It's also worth taking a look at the late-Gothic **cathedral**, on the edge of the centre, whose construction at the end of the sixteenth century was fuelled by spite. Duke Karl, who named the town after his wife, Maria of Pfalz, was jealous of his brother, King Johan III, and so built the cathedral to resemble and rival the king's Klara kyrka in Stockholm. Karl ensured the new building was endowed with over-the-top Baroque features and some odd niceties – note the stained-glass windows depicting mint-green and yellow wheat sheaves, painted with spiders and crop insects, and the dramatic Baroque pulpit, covered in cherubs with silver or black bodies, all dressed in gold wreaths.

Once you've inspected Mariestad's fine architecture, there is little else to do in town. Better prospects are offered at the nearby island of **Torsö**, which is connected to the mainland by a bridge and has good fishing and bathing opportunities (fishing equipment is available to rent at the tourist office, see below). To reach Torsö, head up Strandgatan past Snapen, from where the route is signposted; it's a fifteen-minute bicycle ride (bike rental available from the tourist office; see below), or **bus** #511 runs here from the bus station in Mariestad. Perhaps best of all, Mariestad is also an ideal base from which to **cruise** up Lake Vänern to the start of the Göta Canal's main stretch at **Sjötorp**. There are 21 locks between Sjötorp and Karlsborg, the most scenic section being up to **Lyrestad**, just a few kilometres east of Sjötorp and 20km north of Mariestad on the E20. Canal cruises cost 375kr, no matter where you choose to disembark; a free bus will return you to your starting point (contact Mariestad's tourist office for details or try ☏0501/514 70 or ⓦwww .gotakanal.net. For more, see box, p.153).

Practicalities

The **train station** is in a beautiful Art Nouveau building about five-minutes' walk from the harbour, though rail services here are limited. The adjoining **bus station** has handy Swebus services to Gothenburg, Karlstad, Örebro and Stockholm; for details see ⓦwww.swebusexpress.se. The particularly helpful **tourist office** is a five-minute walk away, inside the Stadshus in the main square at Kyrkogatan 2 (June–Aug Mon–Fri 9am–5pm, Sat 10am–3pm; Sept–May Mon–Fri 9am–5pm; ☏0501/75 58 50, ⓦwww.turism.mariestad.se).

The harbourside STF **youth hostel** (☏0501/104 48; Sept–May advance reservations necessary; dorm beds 210kr, double rooms ❶), is hugely popular with its galleried timber outbuildings and an excellent garden café (June–Aug). The oldest **hotel** is the 1698 *Bergs Hotell* (☏0501/103 24, ⓦwww.bergshotel .com), ❷), in the old town at Kyrkogatan 18. The interior is quite basic, with no en-suite rooms, though it's comfortable enough and quiet. Rather more luxurious is the *Stadshotellet* at Nygatan 10 (☏0501/138 00, ⓦwww .stadtshotelletmariestad.com; ❺/❹), just five-minutes' walk away close to the train station. The nearest **campsite** is *Ekuddens*, 2km down the river (☏0501/106 37, ⓦwww.ekuddenscamping.se; May to mid-Sept); alternatively you can stay on Torsö at *Torsö Camping* (☏0501/213 02, ⓦwww.torso .nu/tbif; mid-June to mid-Aug).

In the new town area, Mariestad's trendiest **coffee-house** hangout is *Café Ströget* at Österlånggatan 10, a laid-back place that's popular with young locals. The liveliest **bar-restaurants** are *Buffalo* (☏0501/149 30) at Österlånggatan 16 and *Hjortens källare krog* (☏0501/122 21) opposite the train station at Nygatan 21; the latter also has occasional live music. For atmosphere, though, there's nothing to beat the lovely alfresco *Hamnkrogen i Laxhall*, in the northwest corner of Torsö island; it's only open in summer (May–Aug daily 10am–9pm; ☏0501/221 20), but with superb fish dishes served overlooking the water it's definitely worth a trip.

Karlsborg

Despite the great plans devised for the fortress at **KARLSBORG**, around 70km southeast of Mariestad on the western shores of Lake Vättern, it has become known over the years as one of Sweden's greatest follies. By the early nineteenth century, Sweden had lost Finland – after six hundred years of control – and had become jumpy about its own security. In 1818, with the Russian fleet stationed on the Åland Islands and within easy striking distance of Stockholm, Baltzar von Platen (see p.153) persuaded parliament to construct an inland fortress at Karlsborg, capable of sustaining an entire town and protecting the royal family and the treasury – the idea being that enemy forces should be lured into the country, then destroyed on Swedish territory. With the town pinched between lakes Vättern and Bottensjön, the Göta Canal – also the brainchild of von Platen and already under construction – was to provide access, but while von Platen had the canal finished by 1832, the fortress was so ambitious a project that it was never completed. It was strategically obsolete long before work was finally abandoned in 1909, as the walls were not strong enough to withstand modern weaponry. However, parts are still used today by the army and air force, and uniformed cadets mill around, lending an air of authenticity to your visit.

The complex, which is as large as a small town, can seem austere and forbidding, but you are free to wander through and enter the **museum** of military uniforms (daily: mid-May to mid-June & early Aug to end Aug 10am–4pm; mid-June to early Aug 10am–6pm; 40kr), and the **guided tour** (80kr), with special sound and smoke effects, is a must for children.

Practicalities

There's no train service to Karlsborg, but there are regular **bus** services (#500) from Mariestad via Skövde, from where the #400 runs directly to the centre. By road, take Route 201 from Mariestad, which brings you to Storgatan when you reach town. The **tourist office** (late June to early Aug daily 9.30am–6pm; ☎0505/173 50, Ⓦwww.karlsborgsturism.se) is at Ankarvägen 2, close to the fortress. **Bikes** can be rented from Mellgrens at Strandvägen 59 (☎0505/101 80), which has excellent models for 100kr per day. Karlsborg has one of the most delightful family-run hotels you'll find in Sweden, and a couple of good places to eat. Its stylish **hotel**, *Kanalhotellet*, is at Storgatan 94 (☎0505/121 30, Ⓦwww.kanalhotellet.se; ❸). Built in 1894 when the present owner's grandparents returned from America after working for President Cleveland at the White House, the dining room, with stately dark panels, oil portraits and glinting chandeliers, overlooks the Göta Canal. The STF **youth hostel** (☎&Ⓕ0505/446 00; dorm beds 190kr, double rooms ❶) is at the fortress entrance (signposted "*Fästningen*"), and Karlsborg's **campsite** is on the banks of Lake Bottensjön (☎0505/120 22; April–Sept), 2km north along Storgatan.

The **restaurant** at the *Kanalhotellet* is as fine as its rooms, with classic local Swedish dishes for around 200kr – try the speciality chilled char fresh from Lake Vättern – and sumptuous breakfasts. Another good eating option is *Idas Brygga* (☎0505/131 11) just opposite the hotel at Skepparegatan 9, which serves Swedish home-cooking; the lemon pepper smoked salmon with cider vinegar mustard (185kr) is terrific. With a canal backdrop, it's a romantic spot for dinner, and there's live music in the evenings. To fill up on a tight budget, try *Pizzeria San Remo* (☎0505/100 34) on Storgatan 47, a somewhat uninspired but inexpensive place in the former train station, with pizzas from around 70kr and a range of salads.

North to Värmland

From Mariestad it's an easy journey of around 75km along Route 26, hugging the northeastern shores of Lake Vänern, to unremarkable Kristinehamn, and a further 50km on the E18 to the shimmering lakeside city of **Karlstad**. The capital of the surrounding province of Värmland, it sits amid an extensive area of sweeping forests, fertile farmland and lazy rivers once used to float timber into Vänern, and now an excellent way of seeing this most peaceful part of western Sweden.

Karlstad

"Wherever I look I see fire – fire in the houses, fire in the air, fire everywhere. The whole world is burning. There is thundering, crackling, shouting, hissing and howling."

The recollections of Karlstad's most famous son, the poet Gustaf Fröding, on the Great Fire of 1865.

Sitting elegantly on the northern shore of Lake Vänern, **KARLSTAD** is named after King Karl IX, who granted the place its town charter in 1584.

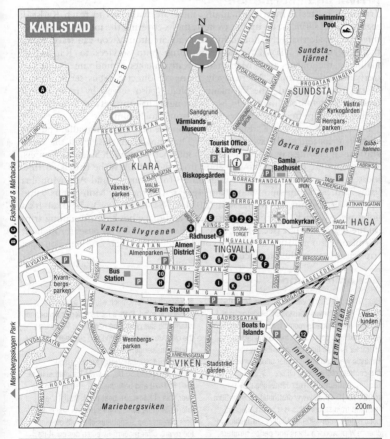

KARLSTAD

ACCOMMODATION		EATING & DRINKING			
Best Western Savoy	**I**	Freden	**H**	Ankdammen	**12**	Habibi	**11**	Rådhuskafeet	**5**
Clarion Collection Drott	**J**	Ibis Karlstad City	**D**	Bishops Arms	**E**	Harry's	**1**	Tom-Yam	**10**
Clarion Plaza	**K**	Karlstad SweCamp		Blå	**2**	Koriander	**7**	Valfrids	**9**
Elite Stadshotellet	**E**	Bomstad-Baden	**B**	Fontana di Trevi	**6**	Leprechaun	**8**		
First Camp Karlstad		Karlstad Vandrarhem	**A**	Glada Ankan	**3**	Pråmen	**4**		
Skutberget	**C**	Scandic Karlstad City	**F**						
		Solsta	**G**						

Since then, the town has been beset by several disasters: devastating **fires** ripped through the centre in 1616 and 1729, but it was in 1865, when fire broke out in a bakery on the corner of Östra Torggatan and Drottninggatan, that Karlstad suffered its worst calamity: virtually the entire town, including the cathedral, burned to the ground – of the 241 buildings that made up the town, only seven survived the flames. Sweden had not experienced such a catastrophe in living memory, and a national emergency fund was immediately set up to help pay for reconstruction. Building began apace, with an emphasis on wide streets and large open squares to act as firebreaks and so prevent another tragedy. The result is an elegant and thoroughly likeable town that's full of life, and is the perfect base from which to tour the surrounding country and lakeside.

Arrival and information

Travelling by **train** from Gothenburg, there are two ways to reach Karlstad: regular direct services run up the western shore, covering the journey in around three hours; alternatively, though much more circuitously, you can travel along the eastern shore via Mariestad, connecting onto services to Karlstad at Hallsberg; the journey from Mariestad to Karlstad takes around three hours and thirty minutes by train. Alternatively, there are direct Swebus services from Mariestad to Karlstad. The Värmland capital is also served by international **trains** between Stockholm and Oslo (it's roughly halfway between the two), as well as the more frequent services to and from Stockholm.

The modern centre of Karlstad is built upon the island of **Tingvalla**. The **bus station** is located at the western end of Drottninggatan; close by is the **train station** on Hamngatan where there's also internet access with Sidewalk Express. At the opposite end of the town centre from the stations is the **tourist office**, located in the library at Västra Torggatan 26 (mid-June to mid-Aug Mon–Fri 9am–7pm, Sat 10am–6pm, Sun 10am–4pm; rest of the year Mon–Thurs 9am–6pm, Fri 9am–5pm, Sat 10am–3pm; ☎054/29 84 00, ⓦ www.karlstad.se). It's a good place to pick up general information and make bookings for rafting trips on the Klarälven river (see p.162); they also have timetables for buses throughout Värmland (also available at ⓦ www.kollplatsen.com), which can help you plan trips elsewhere in the province.

Accommodation

Best Western Savoy Västratorggatan 1A ☎054/15 66 40, ⓦ www.savoy-karlstad.se. Modern chain hotel with comfortable rooms featuring wooden floors and light decor. What the rooms lack in character is more than compensated by the fantastic weekend and summer prices which make this central hotel a sound choice. ❹/❸

Clarion Collection Drott Järnvägsgatan 1 ☎054/10 10 10, ⓦ www.drotthotel.se. Just 50m from the train station, this is a smart, elegant hotel dating from 1909 and full of old-fashioned charm. With wooden floors and period furniture, many rooms are decked out in tasteful yellows and blues. The daily evening buffet is free to residents. ❺/❸

Clarion Plaza Västratorggatan 2 ☎054/10 02 00, ⓦ www.choicehotels.se. Large, modern, plush four-star hotel very much with the business traveller in mind; there's modern Nordic decor and a fantastic sauna offering panoramic views over the city. Attractive weekend and summer rates are worth considering. ❻/❸

Elite Stadshotellet Kungsgatan 22 ☎054/29 30 00, ⓦ www.karlstad.elite.se. Built in 1870 and beautifully located next to the river, this is Karlstad's best hotel. Whilst the interior with its sweeping staircases and chandeliers conjures up sumptuous old-style elegance, the rooms offer modern Swedish design at its very best: mosaic-tiled bathrooms with stylish round sinks, drapes of light grey and wonderful airy ceilings. ❺/❸

First Camp Karlstad Skutberget Skutberget ☎054/53 51 20, ⓦ www.firstcamp.se/karlstad.

A seven-kilometre drive west out of the town along the E18, located beyond Ikea, beside Lake Vänern. Open all year. The daily Badbussen, bus #56 (mid-June to mid-Aug hourly 9.45am–8.15pm; 20min), runs from Storatorget via the bus station to the campsite.

Freden Fredsgatan 1A ☎054/21 65 82, ⓦwww .fredenhotel.com. Cheap and cheerful place close to the bus and train stations, whose rooms all share facilities, though they do have washbasins. Breakfast costs an extra 30kr (small) or 50kr (large) and is brought to the room. Youth hostel-style double rooms with bunks are also available for 430kr. ②/①

Ibis Karlstad City Västra Torggatan 20 ☎054/17 28 30, ⓦwww.ibishotel.com. Good-value hotel in the centre of town with modern, comfortable en-suite rooms, boasting a large breakfast buffet (70kr extra per person). ③/②

Karlstad Swecamp Bomstad-Baden Bomstad-Baden ☎054/53 50 68, ⓦwww.bomstadbaden.se. Beautifully situated on the lakeshore and open all year. The daily Badbussen, bus #56 (mid-June to mid-Aug hourly 9.45am–8.15pm; 20min), runs from Storatorget via the bus station to the campsite.

Karlstad Vandrarhem Kasernhöjden 19 ☎054/56 68 40, ⓔkarlstad.vandrarhem @swipnet.se. The town's elegant, new STF youth hostel with top-quality beds is set in a grand former military building located just 1km from the centre (bus #6 also comes here). Dorm beds 245kr, double rooms ②

🏃 **Scandic Karlstad City** Drottninggatan 4 ☎054/770 55 00, ⓦwww.scandichotels .com. Built in 2005, this elegant place is Karlstad's pride and joy. One of the most stylish hotels in town, its Nordic minimalist decor and warm wooden floors represent Swedish design at its best; rooms 608–620 have their own south-facing balcony and cost just 200kr extra – well worth it. ④/③

Solsta Drottninggatan 13 ☎054/15 68 45, ⓦwww.solstahotell.se. A good, central option with cable TV in all rooms and access to a fridge, microwave and kettle for self-catering. Free bicycle hire is included in the price. ③/②

The Town

It's best to start your wanderings around town in the large and airy market square, Storatorget. The Neoclassical **Rådhuset**, on the square's western side, was the object of much local admiration upon its completion in 1867, just two years after the great fire; local worthies were particularly pleased with the two stone Värmland eagles that adorn the building's roof, no doubt hoping the birds would help ward off another devastating blaze.

In front of the town hall, the rather austere **Peace Monument**, unveiled in 1955, commemorates the peaceful dissolution of the union between Sweden and Norway in 1905, which was negotiated in the town; when translated, the inscription reads "feuds feed folk hatred, peace promotes people's under-standing". Across Östratorggatan, the nearby **Domkyrkan** was consecrated in 1730, although only its arches and walls survived the flames of 1865. Its most interesting features are the altar, made from Gotland limestone with a cross of Orrefors crystal, and the font, also crystal.

Continuing east along Kungsgatan and over the narrow Pråmkanalen into Hagatorget square, the road swings left and changes its name to Nygatan ahead of the longest arched **stone bridge** in Sweden, Östra Bron. Completed in 1811, this massive construction is made up of twelve arches and spans 168m across the eastern branch of the Klarälven river, known as Östra Älvgrenen. It's claimed the bridge's builder, Anders Jacobsson, threw himself off the bridge and drowned, afraid his life's achievement would collapse; his name is engraved on a memorial stone tablet in the centre of the bridge. On sunny days, the nearby wooded island of **Gubbholmen**, reached by crossing Östra Bron and turning right, is a popular place for soaking up the rays and an ideal place for a picnic. Heading back towards town, turn right into Tage Erlander-gatan from Östra Bron, and carry on until you reach the old bathhouse, **Gamla Badhuset**, on Norra Strandgatan, which functioned as a spa and swimming baths until 1978; the building's exterior is worth a quick glance for its impressive red stonework. Nearby, at the junction of Norra Strandgatan and Västratorggatan, is the Bishop's Residence, **Biskopsgården**, dating from 1781 and, as such, one of the handful of buildings in Karlstad not destroyed in the great fire. A two-storey yellow wooden building with a mansard roof, it owes its survival to the massive elm trees on its south side which formed a natural firebreak, and to the sterling firefighting efforts of the bishop of the time, which gave rise to the local saying "the bishop swore and doused the flames whilst the governor wept and prayed". The only other houses which survived are located in the Almen district of town, next to the river at Älvgatan; though their facades are all nineteenth century, the oldest parts of these wooden buildings date from the century before.

From Biskopsgården, a two-minute stroll north along Västratorggatan leads to Sandgrundsudden point and **Värmlands Museum** (mid-June to mid-Aug daily 10am–5pm; rest of the year Wed till 8pm; 40kr; ⓦwww.varmlandsmuseum .se), a comprehensive account of the province's life and times with engaging displays devoted to the discovery of iron during the 1500s and emigration to the United States during the latter half of the nineteenth century; one third of the population of Värmland left Sweden for a fresh start in the New World as a result of grinding poverty and poor prospects at home. The museum also houses a sizeable collection of local art. Look out especially for Karlstad artist, Stefan Johansson: his watercolour of the harbourside in the Faroese capital, Tórshavn, is particularly pleasing.

Mariebergsskogen and the nature centre

Originally based on the Skansen open-air museum in Stockholm, **Mariebergsskogen** (daily 7am–10pm; free; ⓦwww.mariebergsskogen.se), 2km southwest of the centre, was established in 1920 when a number of old wooden buildings from across Värmland, including a smoking house, windmill and storehouse, were relocated here. Today, as well as the original open-air museum, the **Lillskogen** section (daily 9am–4pm; free) contains a children's animal park with rabbits, cows, pigs and goats. However, it's the **Naturum Värmland** nature centre (Tues–Sun 11am–5pm; free), built right on the water's edge overlooking Mariebergsviken bay, that really makes a trip here worthwhile. The centre was designed to accentuate the closeness to nature: glass exterior walls offering cinemascope views out over the surrounding trees and the lake help create the impression that you really are out in the wilds. Aimed predominantly at children, it provides a fascinating insight into local flora and fauna as well as the different landscapes found in the province, from marshland to dense forest. For grown-ups, it's the excellent and informative short film (in Swedish only) about the province's wildlife which includes the wolf, wolverine, lynx and bear that is the real highlight. From the train or bus stations, head west to Klaraborgsgatan, which becomes Jungmansgatan a bit further south; turn right off this street into Hööksgatan and then left into Långövagen, which runs parallel to Mariebergsviken bay, into the park – reckon on around 25 minutes on foot from the centre, or take bus #3 from the bus station.

The beaches

The Karlstad region is renowned throughout Sweden for its relatively long hours of sunshine, something which the locals make the most of during the summer months. The **sandy beach** by the campsites at Bomstad, 7km west of the city along the E18, extends for several kilometres and is known as the Värmland Riviera. It benefits from the sheltered waters of Kattfjorden, one of

Vänern's northern bays, and the shallow waters here heat up quickly during the long summer days making swimming deliciously enjoyable. Adjoining to the east, **Skutberget** offers smooth **rocks** which gently slope down to the lake. There's also an unofficial – though popular – **nudist beach** here, located at the western end of the beach by *First Camp Karlstad Skutberget*. From the Skutberget car park, walk to the lakeshore and then follow the walking path to the right for about five minutes until you come to a couple of wooden cottages in the trees; the word Nakenbad painted on the rocks below denotes the naked area.

Eating, drinking and nightlife

Eating and **drinking** in Karlstad are a joy. There's a good selection of **restaurants**, specializing in everything from Thai and TexMex to vegetarian dishes. **Bars** are thick on the ground, too; the *Bishops Arms* and the *Leprechaun* are especially popular and packed out most nights, particularly at weekends.

Bars, cafés and restaurants

Ankdammen Magasin 1, Tynäsgatan, in the Inre Hamnen harbour ☎054/18 11 00. This open-air café-restaurant has a large wooden jetty that catches the afternoon sun, and is a nice place for coffee and a snack. Late May to mid-Aug only.

Bishops Arms Kungsgatan 22. Classic British-style pub enjoying a great location overlooking the river, with outdoor seating in summer and a wide range of beers.

Blå Kungsgatan 14 ☎054/10 18 15. Despite its name meaning "blue", this restaurant is big on brown: everything from the walls and the carpets to the chairs is brown and ultra-stylish. The food, too, is modern in approach: woodpigeon confit (275kr), bean ragout with lamb (249kr) or scallops with chilli and lime (169kr) are all excellent. A great location overlooking the main square.

Fontana di Trevi Järnvägsgatan 8 ☎054/21 05 00. Karlstad's best Italian restaurant, with suspended brass lanterns, plenty of greenery and a beamed ceiling that create an intimate and romantic atmosphere. Prices here are really quite respectable: pizzas cost from 83kr, while there are mains such as an excellent breast of chicken stuffed with spinach and mozzarella for 179kr.

Glada Ankan Kungsgatan 12 ☎054/21 05 51. A lively first-floor restaurant with a balcony overlooking the main square, which serves mostly plenty of TexMex treats such as enchiladas (119kr) and pasta with grilled Mexican chicken (129kr). Also burgers (135kr), salmon fillet (165kr) and tuna steak (159kr). However, the Wiener schnitzel is exceptionally good and just 159kr.

Habibi Drottninggatan 7 ☎054/18 00 05. Attractive Lebanese restaurant with a truly enormous selection of hot and cold meze such as garlic chicken livers with hummus (69kr) and bean

salad (69kr) in the range of 59–89kr, as well as more substantial mains like mixed grill with bulgur wheat for 215kr.

Harry's Kungsgatan 16 ☎054/10 20 20. There's a wooden Red Indian figure to welcome guests, half-built brick walls and chandeliers at every turn. It's one of Karlstad's most popular eateries with fillet of salmon (182kr), tuna nicoise (95kr), chicken salad (129kr) and croque monsieur (98kr) all on the menu. The nightclub upstairs is one of the town's most popular hangouts.

Koriander Västratorggatan 14 ☎054/21 00 54. The first-floor eatery at this newly opened, chi-chi restaurant-cum-bar specializes in Värmland produce such as salmon from Lake Vänern and locally caught elk (mains cost 145–245kr) – there's even ice cream made from Värmland bees' honey. Outdoor seating on the roof and takeaway is available, too.

Leprechaun Östratorggatan 4, just across the road from the train station. Karlstad's best Irish pub and a firm favourite, particularly for its After Work (Mon–Fri 3–7pm) when there's cheap beer and eats such as fish and chips (69kr). An impressive array of whiskies is also available.

Prämen Älvgatan 4 ☎054/10 11 63. A restaurant, bar and café on a boat moored close to the main square, with good views over the river and the centre. Serving uncomplicated grilled dishes such as TexMex chicken (163kr), barbecued chicken fillet (159kr) or a variety of steaks (from 210kr). Choose from the open-air deck upstairs or the smarter restaurant on the deck at street-level.

Tom-Yam Drottninggatan 35 ☎054/18 51 00. A small and friendly Thai restaurant with just a handful of tables downstairs (more upstairs), making it a good idea to either arrive early or book to avoid disappointment. Authentic Thai food served up by a friendly Swedish guy and his Thai wife: seafood red curry (149kr), chicken with roast cashews in oyster sauce (142kr) or an exceptional beef massamam curry (149kr). Now open at lunchtime, too.

Valfrids Östratorggatan 8 ☏054/18 30 40. A long-established and well respected lounge restaurant that's big on style, with black-and-white leather chairs and stripy wallpaper. Here Swedish

food meets the best of Italian and French cuisine: wild boar is 240kr, veal saltimbocca with sage risotto costs 240kr, too, or there's an excellent braised pheasant for 195kr.

Wayne's Coffee Tingvallagatan 8 ☏054/15 29 29. Elegant café in the corner of the main square. In summer there's outdoor seating, making this the premier spot for people-watching.

Around Karlstad

Karlstad's importance as an inland port is in no small measure due to the sheer scale of **Lake Vänern**. The city makes an ideal base from which to explore the northern reaches of the lake and see some of the twenty-two thousand islands and skerries off Karlstad, which comprise the largest freshwater **archipelago** in Europe. You can do both by taking a **boat trip** on the charming old steamer *M/S Vestvåg* (☏054/21 99 43, ⓦwww.tillsjoss.se), which sails from Karlstad's Inre Hamn, southeast of the train station, (late June to late Aug Tues–Sat 3pm; 100kr return; 1hr 45min) out into the archipelago. Incidentally, the fresh smell of roasting coffee that fills the air down by the harbour comes from the nearby Löfbergs Lilla factory, which produces one of Sweden's most popular blends. Karlstad's also a good place from which to sail down one of the longest waterways in Scandinavia, the **Klarälven River**. Another interesting day-trip from Karlstad is a visit to the house, at nearby Mårbacka, where the Nobel-prize-winning author **Selma Lagerlöf** once lived and wrote many of her books.

To explore more of this unspoilt corner of northern Värmland, home to bears, wolves and lynx, pretty Ekshärad makes a perfect base. Not only are there direct buses to and from Karlstad, but the village also has a decent **youth hostel** (☏0563/405 90; ⓦwww.wardshusetpilgrimen.se; dorm beds 200kr; double

Rafting on the Klarälven River

The five-hundred-kilometre long **Klarälven River** begins over the border in Norway near Lake Femunden, entering Sweden at Långflon in the north of Värmland at slightly over half of its course. The Klarälven was one of the last Swedish rivers where timber was floated downstream to sawmills; the practice only ceased here in 1991. Branäs Sverigeflotten (☏0564/402 27, ⓦwww.sverigeflotten.com) and Vildmark i Värmland (☏0560/140 40, ⓦwww.vildmark.se) now operate **trips** along the river on sixteen-square-metre **timber rafts**, each of which holds two people; it's a good idea to book ahead no matter which company you choose. Their prices are roughly the same: a four-day trip with Vildmark costs from 2020kr and three days with Sverigeflotten is 1850kr, but travelling with the former you get to build the raft yourself, supervised by one of their staff, using the three-metre-long logs and the rope provided; no other materials are allowed.

Once you're under way, you'll find the water flows at around 2km per hour, which gives you time to swim, fish and study the countryside and animals along the river (beavers and elk are plentiful). At night, you sleep in a tent either on the raft (which is moored) or on the riverbank. With Vildmark you need to assemble on day one at **Gunnerud** beside Route 62 south of **Ekshärad**; to **get there**, take bus #300 from Karlstad bus station and tell the driver you're going to the rafts (Mon–Fri 3 daily, Sat & Sun 2 daily; 2hr 15min; ⓦwww.kollplatsen.com). Travelling with Sverigeflotten, you need to call in advance to find out where to meet; a bus leaves the riverside *Byns Camping* in Ekshärad (☏0563/407 76) at 9.30am for the start point (either Ransby or Värnäs).

▲ Selma Lagerlöf's house

room ❶) located on the main road at Klarälvsvägen 35. The attached **restaurant** serves a range of meat and fish dishes for around 150kr. Whilst here, check out the ornately decorated eighteenth- and nineteenth-century wrought-iron crosses in the church graveyard beside the main crossroads.

Mårbacka: the home of Selma Lagerlöf

About 40km north of Karlstad by bus is **Mårbacka** (mid-May to early July & mid- to late Aug daily 10am–4pm; early July to mid-Aug daily 10am–5pm; 70kr; ⓦ www.marbacka.com), the house where the author **Selma Lagerlöf** was born and died. The first woman winner of the Nobel Prize for Literature, in 1909, Lagerlöf is arguably Sweden's best-known author of her generation and is familiar to every Swede. Her fantastical prose was seen as a revolt against the social realism of late nineteenth-century writing; commissioned to write a geography book for

Swedish children, Lagerlöf came up with *The Wonderful Adventures of Nils*, a saga of myth and legend infused with affection for the Swedish countryside, which became compulsory reading at every school in the country. Lagerlöf never married, but had a long-term relationship with another woman, though this wasn't generally acknowledged until their love letters were published some fifty years after Lagerlöf's death. The first woman to gain membership of the Swedish Literary Academy, her be-hatted features now appear on 20kr notes, which Swedes affectionately refer to as "Selmas".

The house, complete with portico supporting a wonderfully long balcony, was completely rebuilt after Lagerlöf won the Nobel Prize. Upstairs is her **study**, much as she left it, along with a panelled library and an extensive collection of her work. Mårbacka is not easy to reach, but with some careful advance planning it's generally possible to get there and back by public transport on Tuesdays and Fridays by first taking the train to Sunne and then bus #215 to Mårbacka. However, timings and days of operation can change and it's essential to check the latest situation with Värmlandstrafiken (℡0771/32 32 00; ⓦwww .kollplatsen.com) or ask at the tourist office in Karlstad. Driving from Karlstad is much more straightforward: take Route 62 north towards Ekshärad and take the signed left turn for Mårbacka just before the village of Ransäter.

Travel details

Trains

Gothenburg to: Kalmar (1 daily; 4hr); Karlskrona (2 daily; 4hr 20min); Karlstad (5 daily; 2hr 50min); Lidköping (2 daily; 1hr 35min); Luleå (1 daily; 19hr); Malmö (hourly; 3hr); Mariestad (2 daily; 2hr 15min); Stockholm (hourly; 3hr by X2000, 5hr InterCity); Strömstad (9 daily; 2hr 30min); Umeå (1 daily; 14hr 30min); Östersund (1 daily; 12hr).
Karlstad to: Gothenburg (5 daily; 2hr 50min); Stockholm (9 daily; 2hr 30min).
Mariestad to: Gothenburg (2 daily; 2hr 15min).
Strömstad to: Gothenburg (9 daily; 2hr 30min).

Buses

Gothenburg to: Falun (2 daily; 8hr); Gävle (1 daily; 10hr); Karlstad (6 daily; 4hr); Malmö (16 daily; 3hr); Mariestad (6 daily; 2hr 30min).
Karlstad to: Falun (1 daily; 4hr); Gothenburg (6 daily; 4hr); Stockholm (10 daily; 4hr).

Mariestad to: Karlstad (Mon–Fri 3 daily, Sat 2 daily, Sun 1 daily; 2hr); Örebro (Mon–Fri 2 daily, Sat & Sun 1 daily; 1hr 30min); Jönköping (Mon–Thurs & 4 daily, Fri 5 daily, Sat 2 daily, Sun 3 daily; 2hr).

International trains

Gothenburg to: Copenhagen via Kastrup airport (12 daily; 4hr); Oslo (3 daily; 4hr).
Karlstad to: Oslo (4 daily; 3hr).

International ferries

Gothenburg to: Frederikshavn (4–8 daily; 2hr by catamaran, 3hr 15min by ferry); Kiel (1 daily; 14hr).
Strömstad to: Langesund (1 daily; 3hr); Sandefjord (5 daily; 2hr).

International buses

Gothenburg to: Copenhagen via Kastrup airport (10 daily; 4hr); Oslo (10 daily; 4hr).
Karlstad to: Oslo (8 daily; 3hr).

3

The southwest

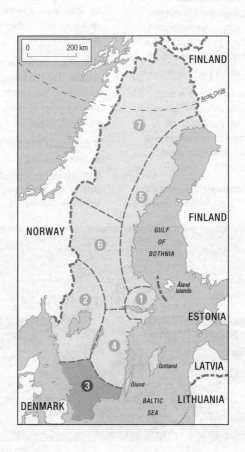

CHAPTER 3 # Highlights

✳ **Varberg Fortress** Stay in one of the old prison cells in the splendid youth hostel set within the fortress, which dominates the landscape of the west coast. See p.169

✳ **Café Utsikten, Båstad** The sweeping views of golden sand, turquoise water and pine forest from this hilltop café are some of the most idyllic in Sweden. See p.180

✳ **Hallands Väderö** A boat trip to this unspoilt island off the Bjäre peninsula offers a chance to commune with nature – and spot seals. See p.181

✳ **Lund cathedral** Beneath the finest Romanesque cathedral in Northern Europe lies the eerie crypt where Finn the Giant is said to have been turned to stone. See p.189

✳ **Lilla torg, Malmö** This beautiful cobbled square in the city centre is a fine place to down a beer or two and rest your feet and mind. See p.195

✳ **Sandhammaren beach, Skåne** Visit the miles of seamless, fine sands beneath the hot skies of Sweden's southern coast. See p.208

✳ **Karlskrona** A riot of Baroque architecture and a rich naval past make this seaside town one of the most enticing in southern Sweden. See p.212

▲ Varberg bathing house

The southwest

T he southwestern provinces of Halland, Skåne and Blekinge were on the frontiers of **Swedish–Danish conflicts** for more than three hundred years. In the fourteenth to seventeenth centuries, the flatlands and fishing ports south of Gothenburg were constantly traded between the two countries, and the presence of several fortresses still bear witness to the area's status as a buffer in medieval times.

Halland, a finger of land facing Denmark, has a coastline of smooth, sandy beaches and bare, granite outcrops, punctuated by a number of small, distinctive towns. The most charismatic of these is the old bathing resort of **Varberg**, dominated by its tremendous thirteenth-century fortress; also notable is the small, beautifully intact medieval core of **Falkenberg**, while the regional capital, **Halmstad**, is popular for its extensive beaches and nightlife.

Further south, in the ancient province of **Skåne**, the coastline softens into curving beaches backed by gently undulating fields. This was one of the first parts of the country to be settled, and the scene of some of the bloodiest battles during the medieval conflict with Denmark. Although Skåne was finally ceded to Sweden in the late seventeenth century, Danish influence died hard and is still evident in the thick Skåne accent – often incomprehensible to other Swedes and the butt of many a joke – and in the province's architecture. Today Skåne is known as the breadbasket of Sweden and its landscapes are those of slabs of yellow rape, crimson poppies and lush green fields contrasting with charming white churches and black windmills. In the north of the province, **Båstad**, is renowned for glamorous living through its close links to the tennis set. One of Sweden's best areas for **walking** and **cycling**, the **Bjäre peninsula** lies to the west of Båstad and comprises forested hill ranges, spectacular rock formations and dramatic cliffs. To the south of the town, both **Helsingborg**, with its laid-back, cosmopolitan atmosphere, and bustling **Malmö**, Sweden's third city, have undergone some dramatic changes in the last decade. Helsingborg's harbour has been transformed by an influx of stylish bars, while Malmö has seen the most significant development in recent Swedish history – the completion of the sixteen-kilometre-long **bridge** linking the city to Copenhagen, and thus Sweden to the rest of Europe via the Öresund Strait.

Just north of Malmö, the university town of **Lund**, with its wealth of classic architecture, has a distinctive bohemian atmosphere that contrasts with Malmö's more down-to-earth heritage, whilst east from Malmö, you'll encounter the pretty medieval town of **Ystad** on the south coast, and then the splendid countryside of **Österlen**, whose pastoral scenery is studded with Viking monuments, such as the "Swedish Stonehenge" at **Ales Stennar** and

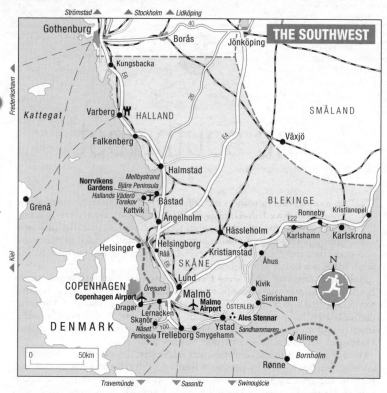

the southwest's most alluring beaches. Beyond here to the east, the ledge of land running to the Baltic is **Blekinge** province. Among its several small and not particularly distinguished resorts, **Karlskrona** stands out, a Baroque beauty built on a number of islands.

Getting around

South of Gothenburg, **trains** hug the coast and stop at all towns as far as Malmö before continuing over the Öresund bridge to Kastrup airport and Copenhagen. From Malmö there's a branch line southeast to Ystad and a mainline northeast to Kristianstad and on to Karlskrona whilst **buses** fill in the gaps. With no really steep hills, the southwest is wonderful country for **cycling and walking**: there are several recognized hiking trails in the area and bike rental outlets are numerous.

Varberg and around

More atmospheric than any other town in Halland, the fashionable little nineteenth-century bathing resort of **VARBERG** boasts surprisingly varied sights – its imposing fortress the most striking – a laid-back atmosphere and plenty of good places to eat. The rocky coastline becomes sandier heading south out of town and there are plenty of opportunities for bathing and windsurfing.

Arrival and information

Varberg is a handy entry point to southern Sweden: a twice-daily Stena Line **ferry** sails here from Grenå in Denmark (4hr) and regular **trains** run up and down the coast between Gothenburg and Malmö or Copenhagen. From the **train** and **bus stations**, turn right down Vallgatan, and you'll find the town centre off to the left and the fortress to the right. The **tourist office** is at Kyrkogatan 39, just off the main square (April to mid-June & mid-Aug to Sept Mon–Fri 10am–6pm, Sat 10am–3pm; mid-June to mid-Aug Mon–Sat 9.30am–7pm, Sun 1–6pm; Oct–March Mon–Fri 10am–5pm; ☏0340/868 00, ⓦwww.turist.varberg.se), where you can pick up a free map of the town and access the internet. Varberg itself is easy to get around on foot, but to explore the coast around the town you can **rent a bike** from Erlan Cykel och Sport at Västra Vallgatan 41 (☏0340/144 55; 100kr a day), or Fridbergs Cykel och Sport at Östra Långgatan 47 (☏0340/61 12 55; 85kr a day), both of which are in the centre.

Accommodation

There's a wide variety of really good **places to stay** in Varberg – some of them representing excellent value. The west coast can be busy in summer so it pays to book well in advance, no matter where you choose to stay.

Apelviken Sanatorievägen 4 ☏0340/64 13 00, ⓦwww.apelviken.se. Varberg's main campsite is an easy 2km walk south of the fortress along Strandpromenaden. There are also cabins for rent at 630kr per night in peak season.
Clarion Collection Fregatten Hamnplan ☏0340/67 70 00, ⓦwww.cchotelfregatten.se. Varberg's twin-turreted former cold storage warehouse has been converted into a swanky hotel overlooking the harbour with well-appointed, modern rooms. An evening buffet is included in the room rate. ❺/❹
Gästis Borgmästaregatan 1 ☏0340/180 50, ⓦwww.hotellgastis.nu. Dating from 1786 and excellent value as the price includes an evening meal and afternoon coffee. Rooms in this family-run hotel are individually decorated and mix old and new styles. ❺/❹

Varberg Norrgatan 16 ☏0340/161 25, ⓦwww.hotellvarberg.nu. Another family-run hotel, this one is from 1899, with rooms on the spartan side and uninspiring modern furnishings. ❹
Varbergs Fästning Off Strandgatan ☏0340/868 28, ⓦwww.turist.varberg.se/vandrarhem. Housed in the former prison at the fortress, accommodation is in the original cells complete with spy-hole in the door though only nos. 7, 13 & 19 have windows. Regular doubles are available in the building next door. ❶
🚶 **Varbergs Stadshotell** Kungsgatan 24–26 ☏0340/69 01 00, ⓦwww.varbergsstadshotell.com. Top-quality luxury rooms at this centrally located hotel in the main square. However, it's the beautifully appointed Asian-style spa on the top floor with saunas and even a vitality pool for water massage that makes a stay here worthwhile. ❻/❺

The Town

All of Varberg's sights are concentrated along or near the seafront, although in summer the main square, Stortorget, throngs with **markets** and pavement cafés. The thirteenth-century moated **fortress**, set on a rocky promontory, is Varberg's most prominent attraction. It was home to the Swedish king Magnus Eriksson, who signed important peace treaties with Denmark here in 1343 aimed at preventing further incursions into Swedish territory. The great bastions were added for protection by the Danish king Christian IV in the seventeenth century; ironically, they were completed just in time for him to see the fortress fall permanently to Sweden in 1645. The entrance is on the fortress's seaward side, either through the great archways towards the central courtyard or by a side route, the uneven stone steps which lead up to a delightful terrace **café**.

Tours (late June to mid-Aug daily 11am–4pm on the hour; 40kr) in English will take you into the dungeons and among the impressive cocoa-coloured buildings that make up the inner courtyard. It's the **museum**, though, that deserves most of your attention (late June to mid-Aug daily 10am–6pm; 50kr; mid-Aug to late June Mon–Fri 10am–4pm, Sat & Sun noon–4pm; ⓦwww.lansmuseet.varberg .se). The most unnerving exhibit is **the Bocksten Man**, a murder victim who was garrotted, drowned, impaled (three stakes were thrust through his body, in the belief this would stop his spirit seeking out his murderers) and thrown into a local bog around 1350, where he remained until 1936 when a farmer dug him up while planting crops. His entire garb preserved by the acidity of the bog, the Bocksten Man sports the Western world's most complete medieval costume, including a cloak, a hood, shoes and stockings. In addition to the skeleton, an unnerving Madame Tussaud-like figure with thick, ringleted blond hair now forms the centrepiece of the exhibition and provides a truly arresting idea of what the Bocksten Man really looked like. An engaging film with English subtitles runs through the carbon-14 dating procedure used to establish the man's age.

Elsewhere in the museum check out the sensitive work of Richard Bergh, Nils Kreuger and Karl Nordström, the so-called **Varberg School**. These three artists linked up in the last years of the nineteenth century and developed a plein-air style which reflected the moods and atmosphere of Halland and Varberg in particular. Night scenes of the fortress beneath the stars show the strong influence of van Gogh; in other paintings, the misty colours create a melancholy atmosphere.

Overlooking the sea, and painted custard and cream, the 1850 **fortress prison** seems like a soft option next to the looming fortress in whose shadow it lies. The first Swedish prison built after the American practice of having cells for individual inmates was begun, it housed lifers until 1931, when the last one ended his days here. Today you can stay in a private **youth hostel** in the fortress, which has been carefully preserved to retain most of its original features (see p.169).

A couple of fine remnants from Varberg's time as a spa resort are within a minute of the fortress. On the side of the fortress facing the town is the grand **Societetshuset**, a wedding-dress-like confection of cream-and-green carved wood, set in its own small park. This was where upper-class ladies took their meals after bathing in the splendid 1903-built **Kallbadhuset** (Cold Bathhouse) nearby, just to the north of the fortress and overlooking the harbour; there's now a pleasant **café** here. Beautifully renovated to its original splendour, this dainty bathhouse has single-sex nude bathing areas and is topped at each corner by Moorish cupolas.

Eating and drinking

There are plenty of good places to eat in Varberg, mostly along Kungsgatan, which runs north of the main square. It's a good idea to book a table since Varberg is a popular holiday spot in summer.

Blå Dörren Kafé Norrgatan 1. The best café in town, with home-made cakes to die for and delicious breakfasts too, all in a friendly setting.

🏃 **Grappa** Brunnsparken ☎0340/179 20. Next door-but-one to the tourist office, this intimate, candlelit restaurant is the place to come for Mediterranean food in Varberg: the three-course menu for 300kr is good value. Try the fresh figs with prosciutto cooked gratin style with gorgonzola (84kr) or the tasty lamb marinated with rosemary served with goats cheese (229kr).

Harry's Kungsgatan 18. The most popular place to drink in town with a large open-air terrace that really draws the crowds. Live music in summer and regular happy hours.

Societets Restaurang In Societets Parken, directly behind the fortress ☎0340/67 65 00. There are three restaurants here, but *Bodegan* is the best, with occasional live music and a bar menu of burgers (69kr), barbecued meats (from 179kr) and grilled fish dishes (from 194kr). Mid-June to mid-Aug only.

Thai Thai La La Kungsgatan 28 ☏ 0340/808 70. This marvellously named Thai restaurant just off the main square serves up tasty Southeast Asian cuisine, such as stirfried chicken with Thai basil or beef masaman curry, all for just 68kr.

Zorba Västra Vallgatan 37 ☏ 0340/ 132 20. Close to the tourist office on Varberg's main road, this Greek restaurant is worth seeking out for its delicious Hellenic specialities for around 160kr, though the interior furniture is uninspiringly flatpack.

Beaches around Varberg

Halland's **coastline** becomes less rocky the further south you go, turning into open beaches at Falkenberg (see below). Although it's still a little rocky around Varberg, there are several excellent spots here for bathing; for the best ones, head south, to the left of the fortress as you face the sea, down Strandpromenaden. In summer, this stretch of the track, built in 1912 as a route from the fortress to the sanatorium 4km beyond, is filled with an assortment of strolling couples, roller skaters and cyclists. After about five minutes, two separate-sex **nudist beaches** are signposted, called Goda Hopp ("High Hopes", the men's area) and Kärringhålan ("Old crone's gap"). A little further along, at **Apelviken**, is a small sandy beach popular with families, beside the eponymous campsite (see p.169).

Falkenberg

It's a twenty-minute train ride south from Varberg to the decidedly likeable medieval town of **FALKENBERG** (falcons were once used for hunting here, hence the name), with some lively museums and a gloriously long beach. It's a well-preserved little town that really comes alive in July and August, when most of the tourists arrive.

Falkenberg has a long-standing reputation as a centre for **fly-fishing** on the Ätran river. A succession of wealthy **English gentlemen** came here throughout the nineteenth century; one such devotee, London lawyer William Wilkinson, went so far as to write a book about the experience, *Days In Falkenberg* (1894). In it, he described the place where the well-to-do visitors stayed as "an ancient inn with a beautiful garden leading down to the river". This building, one of the few here to have escaped the dozen or so town fires which devastated the town over the centuries (most recently in the 1840s), now houses *Falkmanska Caféet*, the best café in town (see p.173).

These upper-class Englishmen brought considerable wealth with them, and had a tremendous influence on the town. Predictably enough, they made no attempt to adapt to local culture: Falkenbergers had to learn English, and throughout the latter half of the nineteenth century, baby boys here were named Charles instead of the Swedish Karl, while the most popular girls' name was Frances, after Wilkinson's daughter. English influence can be seen even today: near the post office there is a British telephone box donated by Oswaldtwistle, the English town with which Falkenberg is twinned.

Arrival and information

Regular **buses** and **trains** drop you close to the town centre on Holgersgatan; from there it's a couple of hundred metres along to the **tourist office** at no. 11 (June–Aug Mon–Sat 9.30am–6pm, Sun 1–6pm; Sept to mid-June Mon–Fri 10am–5pm; ☏0346/88 61 00, ⊛www.falkenbergsturist.se) with internet access. To **rent bikes**, which make trips to the beaches easier, try Hertings Cykel at Plankagårdsvägen 3 (☏0346/ 100 68).

Accommodation

Like neighbouring Varberg, Falkenberg is a popular destination for holidaying Swedes so it pays to book early if you're intending to come here during the Swedish holiday season of mid-June to mid-August. At other times, there's no need to book ahead.

Elite Strandbaden Havsbadsallén 2A ☎0346/71 49 00, ⓦwww.strandbaden.elite.se. A plush modern hotel lacking any design niceties but with uninterrupted views of the sea. Rooms are spacious and very well appointed. ⑤/④

Grand Hotellgatan 1 ☎0346/144 50, ⓦwww .grandhotelfalkenberg.se. This elegant, waterside hotel overlooks the historic Tullbron bridge and enjoys the best location in Falkenberg in terms of views. The economy rooms, though smaller than the regular doubles, cost several hundred *kronor* less and are certainly worth considering since the standard is still high. ⑤/④

Hwitan Storgatan 24 ☎0346/820 90, ⓦwww .hwitan.se. Overlooking a picturesque open courtyard surrounded by low-built houses dating from 1703, the rooms here are cosy and intimate with period furnishings. ④

Steria Arvidstorpsvägen 28 ☎0346/155 21, ⓦwww.hotelsteria.se. The cheapest hotel in town with frilly curtains and flowery bedspreads, a 10min walk away from the river. ②

Skrea Camping *Sommarvägen* ☎0346/171 07, ⓦwww.skreacamping.se. A comfortable youth hostel and campsite together on the beachfront. Get here by following Strandvägen to the beach. Open all year. No dorm beds, double room ①

The Town and around

The **old town**, to the west of the curving river, comprises a dense network of low, wooden cottages and cobbled lanes. Nestling among them is the fine twelfth-century **St Laurentii kyrka**, its ceiling and interior walls awash with seventeenth- and eighteenth-century paintings. It's hard to believe that this gem of a church was – in the early twentieth century – variously a shooting range, a cinema and a gymnasium; indeed its secular usage saved it from demolition after the Neo-Gothic "new" church was built at the end of the nineteenth century. When St Laurentii kyrka was reconsecrated in the 1920s, its sixteenth-century font and silverware were traced to, and recovered from, places all over northern Europe.

Falkenberg is full of quirky **sculptures** which make for amusing viewing. Right outside Falkenberg Museum you'll find a diverting piece called *Wall*, which you may not realize is a sculpture at all. Per Kirkeby, a celebrated Danish artist, built the two brick walls here for a major exhibition in 1997, to close off the wide space below the museum building down to the river. A series of entrances and window openings are designed to let shadows fall at striking angles – though predictably, the more conservative locals loathe the piece. The most fun sculpture is one taking up the whole wall at the corner of Nygatan and Torggatan in the centre: *Drömbanken*, by Walter Bengtsson, is a witty, surrealist explosion of naked women, cats, mutant elks, bare feet and beds.

The town also boasts the rather unusual **Fotomuseum Olympia** (Tues–Thurs 2–6pm, Sun 2–5pm; 40kr) at Sandgatan 13A, home of Falkenberg's first purpose-built cinema which opened in 1912. It has over one thousand cameras and a remarkable collection of cinematic paraphernalia, including some superb local peasant portraits taken in 1898. The oldest pictures on show are English and date back to the 1840s. There's also an impressive section on Sweden's well-loved author Selma Lagerlöf at her home in Mårbacka (see p.163). For a completely different experience, head to the Carlsberg Sverige **brewery** at Årstadvägen 164 (usually twice weekly tours July & Aug only; ☎0346/72 12 53, ⓦwww.alltommalt.se; free; book tours through the tourist office), where Sweden's popular beer, Falcon, has been brewed since 1896, and is available for sampling at the end of the tour.

Skrea Strand and Klitterbadet

Over the river and fifteen-minutes' walk south from town, **Skrea Strand** is a fine, two-kilometre stretch of sandy beach. At the northern end, a relaxing diversion is the large bathing and tennis complex of **Klitterbadet**, which has a fifty-metre pool plus a shallow children's pool nearby, a vast sauna, Jacuzzi and steam rooms. At the southern end of the long beach, all the way down past the busy wooden holiday shacks, lie some secluded coves; in early summer the marshy grassland here is full of wild violets and clover.

Eating, drinking and nightlife

The birthplace of Sia Glass – a popular **ice cream** made by Sweden's oldest family firm, established in 1569 – and **Falcon beer**, Falkenberg caters well to the tastebuds. Although the variety of food on offer isn't huge, the town's restaurants and bars are of a standard to make eating and drinking here a pleasant experience.

Falkmanska Caféet Storgatan 42. This welcoming café is the best in town. Housed in one of Falkenberg's oldest buildings, dating from the 1690s, it features a stripped wood floor, mellow furnishings and a lovely garden. A wide range of open sandwiches and decadent home-made cakes. Closed Sun.

Gustaf Bratt Brogatan 1 ☎ 0346/103 31. Built as a grain warehouse in 1860 and complete with wooden beams and chandeliers, this popular restaurant has as range of tasty fish and meat dishes for 159–239kr: the fish gratin with flounder and prawns is excellent (199kr), as is reindeer steak with goats cheese (219kr). There are pizzas, too, for 75kr.

Harry's Rådhustorget 3A. Enjoying a prime location in the main square, this American-style bar is always packed with drinkers and in summer there's outside seating, too.

Laxbutiken Heberg ☎ 0346/511 10. Located 9km south of Falkenberg, exit 49 off the E6. Fans of salmon really should make the effort to come to this salmon restaurant housed in a white building near the village of Heberg. They serve up an array of superb dishes, all around 180kr, with salmon exclusively as the main ingredient. June–Aug only, daily 10am–7pm

Royal Thai Storgatan 25 ☎ 0346/805 99. A friendly place with a wide variety of good-value Southeast Asian mains: beef or chicken dishes cost 100kr; add another 18kr for prawns. The lunch buffet (68kr) consists of five different dishes and is available until 2.30pm.

Zätas Storgatan 37 ☎ 0346/142 00. An airy and rather stark bistro that's popular with the town's younger generation, dishing up Mediterranean-style mains (149–208kr) such as a tangy salmon fillet marinated in lime and coriander served with spinach and lentils (162kr), as well as more mainstream burgers (118kr).

Halmstad and around

The principal town in Halland, **HALMSTAD** was once a grand walled city and an important Danish stronghold. Today, although most of the original buildings have disappeared, the town makes a pleasant enough stop on the long haul south from Gothenburg, thanks to the extensive – if rather crowded – **beaches** not far away, and a range of really good places to eat.

In 1619, the town's **castle** was used by the Danish king Christian IV to entertain his Swedish counterpart, Gustav II Adolf; records show that there were seven solid days of festivities. The bonhomie, however, didn't last much longer, and Christian was soon building great stone-and-earth fortifications around the city, all surrounded by a moat, with access afforded by four stone gateways. However, it was a fire soon after, rather than the Swedes, that all but destroyed the city; the only buildings to survive were the castle and the church. Undeterred, Christian took the opportunity to create a contemporary Renaissance town with a grid of

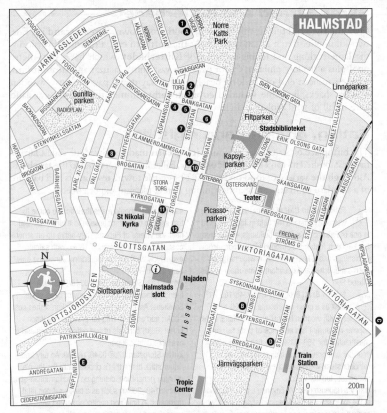

ACCOMMODATION		EATING & DRINKING					
Best Western Grand	D	Börje Ollssons		Harry's	9	The Pull's Pub	4
Clarion Collection		Skafferi	7	Lilla Helfwetet	6	Svea	12
Norre Park	A	Fridbergs konditori	1	Neely's Thai Corner	10	Tre Hjärtan	11
Continental	B	Fridolfs	8	Pio & Co	2	Yoss	3
Hagöns Camping	C	Gastons	5				
Patrickshills							
Vandrarhem	E						

straight streets; today the main street, Storgatan, still contains a number of impressive merchants' houses from that time. After the final defeat of the Danes in 1645, Halmstad lost its military significance, and the walls were torn down. Today, just one of the great gateways, Norre Port, remains, the moat has been filled in and a road, Karl XIs vägen, runs directly above where the water would have been.

Arrival and information

It takes 25 minutes to get here from Falkenberg by train. From the **train station**, follow Bredgatan west to the Nissan river, then walk north along Strandgatan to the bridge across to the centre of town. The helpful **tourist office** (May, June & mid-Aug to late Aug Mon–Fri 9am–6pm, Sat 10am–3pm; late June to mid-Aug Mon–Sat 9am–7pm, Sun 11am–6pm; Sept–April Mon–Fri 10am–5pm;

T035/13 23 20, Wwww.halmstad.se/turist) is within the castle on the opposite river bank and has internet access.

Accommodation

There's a good selection of good-quality accommodation available in Halmstad. However, it's worth remembering that the town centre is a fifteen- to twenty-minute walk from the train station, which may influence your choice of somewhere to stay.

Best Western Grand Stationsgatan 44 T035/280 81 00, Wwww.grandhotel.nu. Cosy, traditional and ideally located for the train station, this hotel dates from 1904 and is full of old-world charm. Rooms are spacious with parquet flooring and a mix of period and contemporary furnishings. ⑥/④
Clarion Collection Norre Park Norra vägen 7 T035/21 85 55, Wwww.norrepark.se. Overlooking the beautiful Norre Katt park, this hotel is reached through the Norre Port arch. Rooms are elegantly decorated in turn-of-the-century style: all have high ceilings, potted plants in the window and most have wooden floors. ⑤
Continental Kungsgatan 5 T035/17 63 00, Wwww.continental-halmstad.se. Just 2min walk from the train station, this elegant building was

built in 1904 in the early *Jugendstil* and National Romantic styles. It's the most beautiful hotel in town with a bright, well-preserved interior and classy rooms to match. Prices rise at weekends. ④/⑤
Hagöns Camping Östra Stranden T035/12 53 63, Wwww.hagonscamping.se. Located 3km to the east of the town centre, this pleasant campsite is located beside a sandy beach and a nature reserve. There are also four-berth cabins. ③
Patrickshills Vandrarhem Neptunigatan 3 T035/18 66 66, Wwww.patrickshill.se. A modern, central and comfortable summer-only (mid-June to mid-Aug) youth hostel. Each room has its own toilet whilst showers are communal. Access to four kitchens on site. Dorm beds 175kr, double rooms ①

The Town

At the centre of the large, lively market square, **Stora torg**, is Carl Milles's *Europa and the Bull*, a fountain with mermen twisted around it, all with Milles's characteristically muscular bodies, ugly faces and oversized nipples. Flanking one side of the square is the grand **St Nikolai kyrka** (daily June–Aug 8.30am–6pm; Sept–May 8.30am–3pm). Dating from the fourteenth century, its monumental size bears witness to Halmstad's former importance, although the only signs of the town's medieval origins which remain are the splodges of bare rock beneath the plain, brick columns. Adjacent to the church, at Kyrkogatan 7, the **Värdshuset Tre Hjärtan** (Three Hearts) restaurant (see p.177) is a vast, proud building with a crossbeamed ceiling; its name derives from the three hearts that make up the town's emblem, Christian IV having granted the town the right to use it in gratitude for their loyalty to Denmark. It's worth taking your coffee and cake upstairs, where the beams and ceiling are beautifully hand-painted, and photographs of nineteenth-century Halmstad adorn the walls.

Not far from Österbron Bridge in the town centre, **Halmstad Castle** is a striking, coral-red affair half hidden by trees, which contains the tourist office (see opposite). Moored in front is **Najaden**, a fully rigged sailing ship built in 1897 and once used for training by the Swedish navy (early June to Aug Tues & Thurs 6–8pm, Sat 11am–3pm; free). With children in tow, a reasonable though not outstanding diversion is a trip to the **Tropic Center**, a few minutes along the river from the tourist office at Strandgatan 19 (daily: July 10am–6pm; Aug–June 10am–5pm; 70kr; Wwww.tropikcenter.se), where snakes, monkeys, crocodiles and spiders are on display in a sort of miniature menagerie.

Leading north from the square, pedestrianized **Storgatan** – the main thoroughfare for restaurants and nightlife (see p.176) – is a charming street, with some creaking old houses built in the years following the 1619 fire; the great stone arch of **Norre Port** marks the street's end. To the right is the splendid **Norre Katt park**, a delightful, shady place that slopes down towards the river and is dotted with mature beech, copper beech and horse-chestnut trees, with great weeping willows by the water. The town's most serene spot is at the park's centre, where there's a lily pond crossed by a bridge. A popular **café**, *Rotundan*, housed in an ornate former bandstand, overlooks the spot (June–Aug daily 11am–8pm).

The Halmstad Museum and Hallandsgården

At the northernmost edge of the park, by the river, is the fine **Halmstad Museum** (Tues–Sun noon–4pm, Wed until 8pm; 40kr; ⓦ www.hallmus.se). While the archeological finds and history of Halland on the top floor are unlikely to set many pulses racing, the museum's collection of regional art, in particular that of the **Halmstad Group**, is definitely worth a look. A body of six local artists from the 1920s who championed Cubism and Surrealism in Sweden, the Halmstad Group comprised brothers Eric and Axel Olson, their cousin Waldemar Lorentzon and three others who all worked together in an artistic alliance for fifty years. The group's members had studied in Berlin and Paris and were strongly influenced by Magritte and Dalí, producing work that caused considerable controversy from the 1920s to the 1940s and sometimes working collectively on projects – an almost unheard-of practice in Swedish art. A changing exhibition of their work is on display in the museum.

Close by, on Galgberget (Gallows Hill), is a collection of a dozen or so typically Halland buildings which were moved to the site in 1925 to form a miniature outdoor museum, **Hallandsgården** (mid-June to mid-Aug noon–6pm; guided tours 2pm daily; free), including a windmill from Morup and a schoolhouse from Eldsberga.

Martin Luther Church

A kilometre east of the centre on Långgatan, one of the main roads out of town, stands the gleaming 1970s **Martin Luther Church** (daily 9am–3pm). The first church in Scandinavia to be assembled entirely of steel – it is known by locals as the Tin Factory – this unique creation looks from the outside like a clumsily opened sardine can, with jagged and curled edges, and stained glass. Inside it's just as unusual: all the walls are a rust-orange version of the outer skin, and there are some striking ornaments. The building is famed for its acoustics, and holds occasional concerts (details from the tourist office).

Eating and drinking

People congregate in the trendy restaurants, bars and clubs along cobbled, pedestrianized **Storgatan**, many of which have shaded outdoor areas along the street. **Lilla torg**, just behind Storgatan, also swarms with people on summer evenings. Prices can be steep, but there are also plenty of cheaper cafés and light meal options. Tylösand is a night-time spot for people who've been on the beach during the day.

Börje Olssons Skafferi Storgatan 23. A large, airy Italian café and deli with a great quiche buffet (89kr) as well as a tasty range of takeaway ciabatta sandwiches (50kr).

The Bull's Pub Bankgatan 5. Very popular, modern English-style bar, rather than pub, with live music and after-work specials that bring people from across town. Also serves light meals and has outdoor seating in summer.

Fribergs Konditori Norra vägen 9. Traditional coffee house overlooking the park with black-and-white pictures of Halmstad adorning the interior. A nice relaxed atmosphere and a good place for a coffee and slice of cake.

Fridolfs Brogatan 26 ☏ 035/21 16 66. There's a maritime feel to the interior of this cosy neighbourhood restaurant, though the back-garden eating area is equally tempting. The food is a classic mix of French and Swedish: beef cooked gratin style with goats cheese or poached plaice, for example. Mains are 185–289kr.

Gastons Storgatan 31 ☎035/10 84 80. Describing itself as a "gourmet's oasis", the food at this stylish bistro with Art Deco ceilings and lighting is spectacular and imaginative: venison with pastrami and mushrooms (245kr), Arctic char with cloudberry salsa, coriander and chilli (229kr), whilst their pasta aragosta with grilled lobster, giant prawns and mussels in a creamy sauce is the talk of the town (149kr).

Harry's Storgatan 22. Massively popular pub attesting to the delight taken by some Swedes in all things American. It also does reasonably priced steaks and burgers, as well as a couple of fish dishes.

Lilla Helfwetet Hamngatan 37 ☎035/21 04 20. Meaning "Little Hell", this stylish place with gloriously high ceilings and lots of neon is located in a former turbine engine room by the river. Classics such a grilled sirloin steak, grilled halibut or grilled lamb fillet go for 200–300kr, whilst the three-course set Lucifer menu featuring moules marinière, chicken saltimbocca and ice cream is a good value 375kr.

Neely's Thai Corner Brogatan 2 ☎035/16 90 90. Great little Thai place opposite the bus station serving authentic Thai favourites for either 75kr or 79kr to take away or

eat in. The daily lunch buffet is served until 3pm and costs an amazing 59kr.

Pio & Co Storgatan 37 ☎035/21 06 69. A lovely, intimate place with brick walls and antique wooden chairs, where the speciality is fish served on wooden planks with clouds of mashed potato. The menu consists of modern Swedish dishes (165–289kr).

Svea Rådhusgatan 4 ☎035/295 86 07. Don't rule out this trendy little restaurant because it's inside the Scandic Hotel. The Swedish bistro food is decent and it's a fun place after work when locals come here for a drink or three. Baltic herring, steaks, burgers and enormous prawn sandwiches are usually on the menu (mains around 129kr).

Tre Hjärtan Kyrkogatan 7 ☎035/10 86 00. This brick and timber building from the early 1700s in the main square is more inspiring than the food on the menu: standard meat and fish mains for 165–220kr, as well as pasta dishes (80–100kr) and pizzas (70kr or 80kr).

Yoss Storgatan 35 ☎035/18 76 49. This chi-chi French-Italian bistro whose walls are covered in posters and paintings has some of the best prices in town: mains go for 129–179kr and include ovenbaked chicken in a blue cheese sauce, marinated lamb with herbs and delicious whitefish roe with sour cream and onions.

Around Halmstad: the beaches

Eight kilometres west of the town centre, Halmstad's most popular **beach** is at **Tylösand** (bus #10 runs here hourly from town), which in July and August becomes packed with bronzing bodies, as do the surrounding bars and restaurants in the evenings. There's a smuggler's cove to wander around at **Tjuvahålan**, signposted directly off the beach, and plenty of excellent spots for bathing, including **Svärjarehålan** around the headland to the east, where a bathing beach has been adapted for the disabled. To reach less crowded areas, head 45-minutes' walk north from Tjuvahålan to **Frösakull** and **Ringenäs**, the latter of which is popular for windsurfing.

The best beach to the east of town is at **Östra Stranden**, where there is also a large, well-equipped campsite. It's reached by crossing the river from Stora torg and heading along Stationgatan past the train station, then turning southeast for a couple of kilometres down Stålverksgatan. Bus #63 runs here hourly from the town centre; get off at the stop called "Hästskon" at the corner of Sommarvägen and Ryttarevägen (shown on the free map from the tourist office) and walk west through the forest towards the sea. The long beach – sandy and less crowded than at Tylösand – is excellent for children as the waters are particularly shallow here. A little further south is **Hagön**, a secluded **nudist beach** which is principally, though not exclusively, gay (same stop on bus #63); privacy is afforded by the deep hollows between the dunes, behind which is a nature reserve.

Båstad

The people of this province speak a guttural dialect which betrays their Danish origin; a peculiarity so marked that the Swedes playfully say that the Skåne folk "are born with gruel in their throats." They have a great difficulty in managing the letter 'r' ... They consider themselves as quite a separate nationality – as indeed they really are; for the typical Skåne man is neither a Swede nor a Dane, but distinct from both.

From Unknown Sweden (1925) by James Steveni.

Thirty-five kilometres south of Halmstad, a journey of around twenty minutes by train, lies **BÅSTAD** (pronounced bow-sta). The northernmost town in the ancient province of **Skåne**, its character is markedly different from other towns along the coast. Cradled by the **Bjäre peninsula** (see p.180), which bulges westwards into the Kattegat (the waters between Sweden and Danish Jutland), Båstad is Sweden's **tennis centre**, where the Swedish Open is played at the beginning of July – the centre court down by the harbour has been newly rebuilt and is truly impressive. The town also boasts the Drivan Sports Centre, one of Sweden's foremost sports complexes, as well as an extremely beautiful setting, with forested hills on the horizon to the south.

There is a downside, though, which can blunt enthusiasm for the place. Ever since King Gustav V chose to take part in the 1930 national tennis championship and Ludvig Nobel (nephew to Alfred of the Nobel Prize) gave financial backing to the tournament, wealthy retired Stockholmers have flocked here, bringing an ostentatious smugness to the town for the annual competition held during the second week of July. The locals themselves, however, are quite down-to-earth, and most view this arrogance as a financial lifeline. Despite all this, Båstad isn't a prohibitively expensive place to stay, and makes a good base from which to explore the peninsula.

Arrival and information

Until the delayed rail tunnel through the Hallandsås ridge of hills outside Båstad is complete and the town's new **train station** opens in 2012, it remains a lamentably long walk of around half an hour up Köpmangatan into the town centre from the existing station. Båstad's **tourist office** (mid-June to mid-Aug Mon–Fri 10am–5pm, Sat 10am–3pm, Sun 11am–3pm; mid-Aug to mid-June Mon–Fri 10am–5pm, Sat 11am–2pm; ℡0431/750 45, ⓦwww.bastad.com) on the main square, has maps and information about the town and the Bjäre peninsula. The main place to **rent bikes** is Sven's Cykelaffär at Tennisvägen 31 (℡0431/701 26), which charges 90kr per day.

Accommodation

Accommodation in Båstad is plentiful, but to find somewhere to stay during the Swedish Open in July, you'll need to book months in advance. Unlike the rest of Sweden, prices increase dramatically during the summer as a result of the town's sporting endeavours.

Båstad Sporthotell Korrödsvägen ℡0431/685 00, ⓦwww.bmts.se. Next to the Drivan Sports Centre and a 20min walk from the centre back towards the train station and signposted off Köpmansgatan. Rooms are plains and on the small side but are en suite and sensibly priced. Also has two-berth cottages for rent (❸); double rooms ❷

Enehall Stationsterrasen 10 ℡0431/750 15, ⓦwww.enehall.se. Rooms are located in nine different houses grouped together just a few metres from the train station. Although simply furnished, all rooms are perfectly comfortable and clean ❹

Falken Hamngatan 22 ℡0431/36 95 94, ⓦwww .villafalken.com. This most charming and charismatic

Skåne summer card

An excellent money-saver if you're spending any significant time in Skåne is the **sommarkort** (summer card). For 450kr, it allows fifty journeys (maximum 3hr each) on all buses and Pågatåg and Öresund trains (though not Kustpilen) throughout the province between June 15 and August 15; up to two children under 7 travel free. To use it, insert the card into the card reader on trains and buses before every journey. You can buy the card from the Kundcenter at Lund or Helsingborg stations or Gustav Adolfs torg in Malmö, or online at ⓦwww.skanetrafiken.se.

B&B is wonderfully located just above the harbour in delightful gardens. A 1916-built villa, the house has been lovingly maintained and has a welcoming atmosphere. ❷

Hjorten Roxmansvägen 23 ℡0431/701 09, ⓦwww.hjorten.net. This homely pension just off the main road, Köpmansgatan, dates from 1910 and is the oldest in town. It represents good value for money, though the decor is a little frilly and fussy. Also offers the option of half-board. Open June–Aug only. ❸

Norrvikens Camping Kattviksvägen 347 ℡0431/36 91 70. In a pretty spot right by the sea, this site is a couple of kilometres west of the town centre. Open late March–Sept.

Pensionat Neptun Havsbadsvägen 18 ℡0431/36 91 30, ⓦwww.pensionatneptun.se. A pleasant, traditional wooden house with two enormous verandahs that's just 100m from the beach, offering youth hostel-style accommodation for just 250kr per dorm bed; double rooms ❶

Skansen Kyrkogatan 2 ℡0431/55 81 00, ⓦwww.hotelskansen.se. This beautifully designed hotel, set in a cream bathhouse with stylish annexe villas, offers excellent service and a great health spa (included in all room rates). Rooms in the tennis pavilion annexe and the neighbouring annexe cost several hundred *kronor* less. ❻

The Town

From the train station, it's a half-hour walk eastwards up Köpmansgatan to the central, old square and tourist office (see opposite). Once you get close to the centre, you'll see that the street's architecture is unusual for Sweden, and somewhat reminiscent of provincial France, with shuttered, low-rise shops and houses. In the square is the fifteenth-century **Sancta Maria Church**, a cool haven on a hot summer's day. The altar painting is unusual, depicting Jesus on his cross with a couple of skulls and haphazardly strewn human bones on the ground beneath. For a feel of real old Båstad, take a stroll down the ancient cottage-flanked Agardhsgatan, off Hamngatan and parallel with the seashore. To reach the **beach** head down Tennisvägen, off Köpmansgatan, and through a glamorous residential area until you reach Strandpromenaden, where you can take a lovely evening stroll as the sun sets on the calm waters. West of here, the old 1880s bathhouses have all been converted into restaurants and bars which owe much of their popularity to their proximity to the tennis courts where the famous tournament is played. Just a few steps further lies the harbour, thick with boat masts.

Eating, drinking and nightlife

In Båstad, **eating and drinking** is as much a pastime as tennis, and most of the waterside eating establishments and hotels here have two-course dinner offers, with menus changing weekly. Although it has a few **nightclubs**, Båstad is much more geared up for those who prefer to sip wine in restaurants; only teenagers fill the naff clubs along Köpmansgatan. *Madison's*, at Köpmansgatan 39 (℡0431/750 80), is the town's leading nightspot and a firm favourite which draws young crowds from right across the north of the province in season.

Café Utsikten Duvlinge Gård ℡ 0431/708 00. This countryside café, in an old farmhouse perched high on a hilltop above Båstad, enjoys some of the best views anywhere in Skåne and serves sandwiches and light snacks. From the train station, take Finsbovägen off to the right and then follow the signs up the steep hill for about 1km. Open daily 11am–9pm Easter–Sept; rest of the year Sat & Sun noon–6pm.

Coffee and the Bakery Köpmansgatan 4. A delightful café serving newly baked bread, ciabatta, soup, quiche and lovely coffees and cake in a fresh, country atmosphere.

Hamnkrogen Strandpromenaden ℡ 0431/724 77. Undoubtedly the best of the waterfront seafood places with a large wooden deck overlooking the marina. A plentiful choice of fish and meat specials which change frequently (125–150kr). A perfect place for a romantic dinner, watching the sun set over the sea.

Pepe's Bodega Hamngatan 6 ℡ 0431/36 91 69. A very popular place with Båstad's twenty-somethings, serving pizzas from 159kr and TexMex dishes such as burritos and fajitas for around 119kr. The food is good and, this being Båstad, along with basic stomach fillers, the bar also stocks champagne and cocktails.

Sand Kyrkogatan 2 ℡ 0431/55 81 09. Attached to *Hotel Skansen* with glorious views out over the sea, this is an excellent quality à la carte restaurant (mains around 265kr) serving up rack of lamb, steaks, plaice and pike-perch.

Sveas Skafferi Hamngatan 8. Down at the harbour, this is the place to come to fill up well, cheaply and alfresco. Excellent smoked mackerel and salmon are served on paper plates, as are home-baked pies and chocolate cake. A plate of fish with potato salad and greens costs around 100kr.

The Bjäre peninsula

Jutting into the Kattegat directly west of Båstad and deserving a couple of days' exploration, the **Bjäre peninsula**'s natural beauty has a magical quality to it. Its varied scenery includes wide fertile fields where potatoes and strawberries are grown, splintered red-rock cliff formations, and remote islands ringed by seals, thick with birds and historical ruins.

Travel information

The well-known **Skåneleden walking trail** runs around the entire perimeter of the peninsula and makes for a great bicycle ride, although having a bike with a choice of gears helps, as it's hilly in parts. **Public transport** around in the area is adequate, with **buses** connecting the main towns and villages. Bus #525 runs through the centre of the peninsula from Båstad to **Torekov**, and stops at the small hamlets of Hov and Karup on the peninsula's southern coast en route.

The northern coastline

Heading north out of Båstad along the coast road, it's just a couple of kilometres to **Norrvikens Trädgårdar** (Norrviken Gardens: May–Sept daily 10am–6pm; 60kr; ⓦ www.norrvikenstradgardar.net), a paradise for horticulturists and lovers of symmetry. With the sea as a backdrop, these fine gardens were designed by Rudolf Abelin at the end of the nineteenth century; he is buried in a magnificent hollow of rhododendrons near the entrance. The best walk is the "King's Ravine", ablaze in late spring and early summer with fiery azaleas and more blushing rhododendrons, and leading to a fine Japanese-style garden. At the centre of the grounds there's an open-air theatre with occasional productions (details available at the tourist office in Båstad).

Kattvik and around

Two to three kilometres further on is **KATTVIK**. Once a village busy with stone-grinding mills, it is now largely the domain of wealthy, elderly Stockholmers, who snap up the few houses on the market as soon as they are up for sale. Kattvik achieved its moment of fame when Richard Gere chose a cottage here as a venue for a summer romance, but these days there's little more than the friendly and peaceful ⚓ *Delfin Bed & Breakfast* (℡0431/731 20; ❶). With just three rooms (shared facilities) and breakfast with home-baked bread in the garden or on the terrace, it makes an idyllic base for exploring the region.

A kilometre from Kattvik off the Torekov road (follow the sign "*rökt fisk*") is Kai's fish **smokery**, an old farm where fish is smoked in little furnaces fired by sawdust from the nearby clog factory. Here you can have a taste of – and buy – the very best smoked fish in the area; as well as the usual mackerel and salmon, sample *horngädda* (garpike), a scaly fish with bright green bones, and *sjurygg* (lumpsucker), an extraordinarily ugly, seven-crested fish with oily, flavoursome flesh.

Heading north along the coast road or the signposted walking trail, the undulating meadows and beamed cottages you'll encounter have a rural and peculiarly English feel. To continue along the coast after taking the trail from Kattvik, follow the path for **Hovs Hallar nature reserve**, leading off at the T-junction (20min walk). Wandering across to the reserve from the car park, you can clamber down any of several paths towards the sea. The views are breathtaking – screaming gulls circling overhead and waves crashing onto the unique red-stone cliffs – though it's something of a tourist magnet during the summer.

Overlooking the cliffs, *Vårdshus Hovs Hallar* is a famed **restaurant** serving fine à la carte meals and lunch specials (daily noon–9pm; ℡0431/44 83 70, ⓦwww.hovshallar.com). Particularly popular is the Sunday lunch smorgasbord (noon–5pm), which mutates into a herring table the last Sunday of the month; reservations are recommended. There are pretty, four-bed **cabins** just behind the restaurant (same contact details; May–Aug 895kr per night for the cabins; Sept–April 630kr; double rooms ❹ all year).

Torekov and Hallands Väderö

On the peninsula's western coast, **TOREKOV** is just 5km from Hovs Hallar nature reserve. The village is named after a little girl later known as St Thora, who, so the story goes, was drowned by her wicked stepmother; the body was washed ashore and given a Christian burial by a blind man, who then miraculously regained his sight. It's a perfect place to chill, indeed, one odd sight is the daily ritual of elderly men in dressing gowns wandering along the pier – so sought after is the property here, these old boys promenade in bathrobes to set themselves apart from the visitors. The main reason to venture here though is to take one of the old fishing **boats** which regularly leave from Torekov's little harbour for the island nature reserve of **HALLANDS VÄDERÖ** (mid-June to early Aug hourly; May to mid-June and early Aug to late Aug Mon–Fri every 2hr; April, May & Sept also Sat & Sun every 2hr; 15min; mid-June to early Aug 100kr, otherwise 80kr return).

The island is a scenic mix of trees and bare rocks with isolated fishermen's cottages dotted around its edges, while the skies above are filled with countless birds – gulls, eiders, guillemots and cormorants. One particularly beautiful spot is at its southernmost tip, where weather-smoothed islets stand out amid the tranquil turquoise waters. If you're lucky, you may be able to make out the colony of seals which lives on the furthest rocks; there are organized "seal safaris" there (mid-June to early Aug Thurs 6pm; May to mid-June & early Aug to late Aug Sat 10am; 140kr; ℡0431/36 34 940, ⓦwww.vaderotrafiken.se). Also on the south of the island is the English graveyard, surrounded by mossy, dry-stone walls. It holds the remains of English sailors who were killed here in 1809, when the British fleet was stationed on the island in order to bombard Copenhagen during the Napoleonic Wars. Torekov Church would not allow them to be buried on its soil as the sailors' faith was, strangely, considered unknown.

Helsingborg and around

Long gone are the days when the locals of **HELSINGBORG** joked that the most rewarding sight here was Helsingør, the Danish town whose castle – Hamlet's celebrated Elsinore (Kronoborg castle) – is clearly visible, just 4km across the Öresund strait. Bright and pleasing, Helsingborg has a tremendous sense of buoyancy. With its beautifully developed harbour area, an explosion of stylish bars, great cafés and restaurants among the warren of cobbled streets, plus an excellent **museum**, it is one of the best town bases Sweden has to offer.

In the past, the links between Helsingborg and Copenhagen were less convivial than they are now. After the Danes fortified the town in the eleventh century, the Swedes conquered and lost it again on six violent occasions, finally winning out in 1710 under Magnus Stenbock's leadership. By this time, the Danes had torn down much of the town and on its final recapture, the Swedes contributed to the destruction by razing most of its twelfth-century castle – except for the five-metre-thick walled **keep** (*kärnan*), which still dominates the centre. By the early eighteenth century, war and epidemics had reduced the population to just seven hundred, and only with the onset of industrialization in the 1850s did Helsingborg experience a new prosperity. Shipping and the

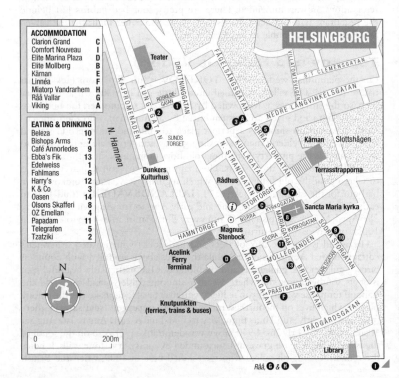

HELSINGBORG

ACCOMMODATION
Clarion Grand	C
Comfort Nouveau	I
Elite Marina Plaza	D
Elite Mollberg	B
Kärnan	E
Linnéa	F
Miatorp Vandrarhem	H
Råå Vallar	G
Viking	A

EATING & DRINKING
Beleza	10
Bishops Arms	7
Café Annorledes	9
Ebba's Fik	13
Edelweiss	1
Fahlmans	6
Harry's	12
K & Co	3
Oasen	14
Olsons Skafferi	8
OZ Emellan	4
Papadam	11
Telegrafen	5
Tzatziki	2

Teater

Dunkers Kulturhus

Rådhus

Magnus Stenbock

Acelink Ferry Terminal

Knutpunkten (ferries, trains & buses)

Kärnan   Slottshågen

Terrasstrapporna

Sancta Maria kyrka

Library

N

0   200m

Råå, **G** & **H** ▼

railways turned the town's fortunes round, as is evident from the formidable late nineteenth-century commercial buildings in the centre and some splendid villas to the north, overlooking the Öresund.

Arrival, information and city transport

Unless approaching by car on the E6, chances are you will arrive at the harbourside **Knutpunkten**, the vast, glassy hulk of which incorporates the Scandlines **ferry** and **train** terminal. On the ground floor, behind the main hall, is the **bus station**, whilst the **train station** is one floor downstairs and the **ferry terminal** one floor upstairs. There are two Forex **currency exchange** offices: one at ground level, the other upstairs (see Ⓦwww.forex.se for opening times). There's also internet access here with Sidewalk Express, who can also be found at 7-Eleven, Järnvägsgatan 19. The ACE link passenger-only ferry from Helsingør is just outside at Hamntorget, 200m away. A third ferry company, HH-Ferries (cars and passengers), uses Sundsterminalen, off Oceangatan, about 300m southeast of Knutpunkten. Between all three companies, there are an astonishing 125 ferry departures for Helsingør every day.

Outside Knutpunkten, heading north (left) and then right into the lower reaches of Stortorget, the **tourist office** (mid-June to mid-Aug Mon–Fri 9am–8pm, Sat 9am–5pm, Sun 10am–3pm; mid-Aug to mid-June Mon–Fri 10am–6pm, Sat 10am–2pm; ☏042/10 43 50, Ⓦwww.helsingborg.se) is inside the Rådhuset at the corner of Stortorget and Drottninggatan. This is the place to pick up a copy of *Destination Helsingborg*, an events guide with sections in English or the very comprehensive *Helsingborg Helsingør Two Countries – One Destination* (free).

Central Helsingborg is all within easy walking distance of the centre, but for the youth hostel you may want to catch a **bus**. Tickets bought on board cost 20kr and are valid for two changes within an hour.

Accommodation

There are plenty of central **hotels**. The most glamorous are around Stortorget, while cheaper establishments are to be found opposite Knutpunkten and along the roads leading away from it. All the following include breakfast in the price.

Clarion Grand Stortorget 8–12 ☏042/38 04 00, Ⓦwww.grandissimo.se. Built in 1926, this is one of Helsingborg's biggest and grandest hotels. The interior is a successful blend of modern and classic design with good-sized rooms in a superbly central location. The lobby area, always full of life, contains a number of restaurants, a piano bar, café and even an outlet of Pressbyrån. ❺/❹

Comfort Nouveau Gasverksgatan 11 ☏042/37 19 50, Ⓦwww.hotelnouveau.se. This lacks the grandeur of other Stortorget hotels, but is pretty central and has all the comforts of the top hotels, including a swimming pool and a sauna. Serves exceptionally good breakfasts. ❺/❹

Elite Marina Plaza Kungstorget 6 ☏042/19 21 00, Ⓦwww.elite.se. Right at the harbourside, next to Knutpunkten. Taking inspiration from the sun, wind and water, the newly renovated rooms at this modern and well-equipped hotel are bright, airy and contemporary in design and some have sea views. ❺/❻

Eilte Mollberg Stortorget 18 ☏042/37 37 00, Ⓦwww.elite.se. Every inch a premier hotel, with a grand nineteenth-century facade, though rooms are simpler, smaller and more homely than at the sister hotel, the Marina Plaza. ❹/❷

Kärnan Järnvägsgatan 17 ☏042/12 08 20, Ⓦwww.hotelkarnan.se. Opposite Knutpunkten, this comfortable staff-owned hotel prides itself on home-from-home rooms, though the floral curtains and stripy designs in some rooms may be a little hard to live with. There's a also small library-cum-bar and sauna. ❺/❹

Linnéa Prästgatan 2–4 ☏042/37 24 00, Ⓦwww.hotell-linnea.se. Good value, central option in an elegant building from 1887, with cosy, agreeable rooms with period furnishings as well as ten-percent discounts for bookings made via their website (mark your request "booking with discount"). ❺/❸

Miatorp Vandrarhem Planteringsvägen 71
ⓣ042/13 11 30, ⓦwww.miatorp.nu. A 20min walk
south of the centre along Södergatan, Västra
Sandgatan and finally Planteringsvägen; all rooms
at this STF hostel are modern, clean and en suite.
Dorm beds 300kr, double room ❶.
Råå Vallar Kustgatan in the district of Råå, 2km
south of town ⓣ042/18 26 00, ⓦwww
.nordiccamping.se. Take bus #1 from the town
centre. This campsite is well located for

Helsingborg's nudist beach which is just to the
northwest of the site at the foot of Högastensgatan.
🏃 Viking Fågelsångsgatan 1 ⓣ042/14 44 20,
ⓦwww.hotellviking.se. This is the place to
try first. Very appealing, quiet old hotel with beautifully appointed period rooms in a splendid location
close to some of the finest buildings in town. Room
15 has its own private Jacuzzi and costs about
500kr more than a regular double. Excellent service
and a cosy atmosphere. ❺/❹

The Town

The most obvious starting point is on the waterfront, by the bronze **statue** of former Skåne governor, Magnus Stenbock, on his charger. With your back to the Öresund and Denmark, to your left is the **Rådhus** (town hall), a heavy-handed, Neo-Gothic pile, complete with turrets and conical towers. The extravagance of provincial nineteenth-century prosperity, and the architect's admiration for medieval Italy, make it worth seeing inside (ask about tours at the tourist office), in particular for the many fabulous stained-glass windows, which tell the history of the town. The ones to look out for are those in the entrance hall, depicting Queen Margareta releasing her rival, Albert of Mecklenburg, in Helsingborg in 1395, and the last window in the city-council chamber, showing Jean Baptiste Bernadotte arriving at Helsingborg in 1810, having accepted the Swedish crown. When he greeted General von Essen at the harbour, farce ensued as their elaborate gold jewellery and medals became entangled in the embrace. The original wall and ceiling frescoes were deemed too costly to restore and were painted over in 1968, though have now been uncovered.

Crossing over the road towards the Kattegat from the Magnus Stenbock statue, you'll see the **harbour**, divided in two by the new bridge to the pier. To the north of the bridge, at Kungsgatan 11, is the exceptional city museum **Dunkers Kulturhus** (Tues–Sun 10am–5pm, Thurs until 8pm; exhibitions 70kr; ⓦwww .dunkerskulturhus.se). The white-brick building contains a first-rate museum exploring the city's history. The centre is named after Henry Dunker, a local man and pioneer of galoshes – he developed the process for keeping rubber soft in winter and non-sticky in summer and his brand, Tretorn, became a world leader until the factories closed in 1979. When he died in 1962, he left 58 million *kronor* to set up a foundation and this museum is a major recipient. If you're expecting traditional exhibitions, its dramatic special sound-effects and lighting certainly come as a surprise. The history of Helsingborg, with water as the theme, from Ice Age to present day is tremendous fun, though there's no explanation in any language so it's more sensory than educational; the history of the town's social, economic and military history has far more explanation in English though. There are also some **galleries** showing temporary art exhibitions year round. The museum contains a fine **restaurant**, overlooking the Öresund, and a bistro serving light meals.

To the north of the bridge, a chain of stylish contemporary apartment blocks has transformed the area from wasteland into a residential haven with sea views. The ground floor of each block is a bar-cum-café-restaurant, with hip colour schemes and plenty of steel columns and beams. The area is made for strolls on summer evenings, interspersed by sipping wine and serious eating by candlelight (see p.186).

The Swedish winter

The Swedish winter is not to be taken lightly.
In the north, the cold sets in during October
and lasts until May, and temperatures are
often as low as -30°C; in the south of the
country things are not so extreme, though
it can nevertheless snow at any time
between November and May.
Swedes go to great lengths,
however, to point out that a
cold, snowy winter is far better
than a mild, grey one: a cover
of snow on the ground acts as
a reflector for the little light
there is, and goes a long way
to brightening things up during
December and January, when
daylight is in short supply.
North of the Arctic Circle,
the sun doesn't rise at all in
midwinter.

The Winterswede and the Summerswede

Winter mountain biking, Abisko ▲

Traditional Sámi winter footwear ▼

Wrapping up warm, Swedish style ▼

Unsurprisingly, the long, dark winters have a tangible effect on the **Swedish psyche**. During the winter months, you'll find that people are generally quieter and more withdrawn, and protect themselves from the rigours of the cold and dark by deliberately socializing indoors, often choosing to light **candles** throughout the home to create a sense of cosiness. You'll even see candles burning in public buildings and shops to brighten up the gloomiest time of year. It's during winter that Seasonal Affective Disorder, or **S.A.D.**, causes widespread depression, affecting roughly one in five people. Although you're unlikely to suffer during a short visit in winter, you're likely to encounter gloomy faces and a general sense of inertia throughout the winter months. S.A.D. is caused by a lack of daylight which leads to an increase in the production of the sleep-related hormone, melatonin, secreted from a gland in the brain. Naturally people do all they can to alleviate the effects of winter; for example, during the period of 24-hour darkness in northern Sweden, the **Winterswede** creates a semblance of day and night by switching on bright lights during what would be daytime, and using low-lighting during the evening hours. Once spring arrives, there's a notable bounce in people's step, and the **Summerswede** prepares to emerge from months of enforced hibernation – you'll see people sitting in lines on park benches in the sunshine, faces tilted to the sky, making the most of the return of the sun. **Festivals** and **revelries** are thick on the ground in spring and summer, and outdoor life is lived to the full, including picnics under the midnight sun, beach parties lasting late into the night and an exodus to the countryside as people take up residence in their forest or lakeside log cabins to enjoy the brief yet intense summer months.

Surviving the winter

Swedes cope by wearing several **layers of clothes**, preferably made of cotton, which is good at keeping out the chill. You'll also need snug-fitting gloves or mittens, a good woolly hat and thick socks – thirty to fifty percent of body heat is lost from the feet and head. Bring boots or stout shoes with soles that can grip onto the finely polished, compacted snow that covers streets and pavements in winter. It's also important to eat **hearty meals** to provide your body

▲ Icehotel bar, Jukkasjärvi

▼ Driving in wintry conditions

Winter activities

As winter can last up to eight months, the locals try to make the most of it – it's no coincidence that some of the world's greatest skiers, for example, are Swedish. However, as a visitor, there's only a limited number of places where you can go skating on frozen lakes or take a dip in an icehole after a sauna. The best options for winter fun are **ice-skating** on Lake Storsjön in Östersund (see p.337), **snowboarding** around Riksgränsen (see p.382) and **long-distance skiing** at Sälen (see p.326). **Winter resorts** such as Åre (see p.341) buzz with activity during the coldest times of the year. However, the winter destination to end them all is undoubtedly the world-famous **Icehotel**, tucked away inside the Arctic Circle near Kiruna, where dog-sledding and snowmobiling trips (see p.379) in 24-hour darkness and subzero temperatures conspire to leave a lasting impression of winter Swedish-style.

▼ Snowboarding

with enough energy to keep warm. Be aware, too, of **icicles** hanging from roofs and gutters, and marked by pavement signs reading "Varning Takras": sooner or later they'll come crashing to the ground, and you don't want to be underneath when that happens.

Driving on snow and ice

Although many Swedish **roads** are gritted and ploughed in winter, it's rare that they're completely free of snow and ice. In order to drive in such treacherous conditions, all vehicles registered in Sweden must be fitted with studded **winter tyres** between December 1 and March 31; embedded with dozens of small metal spikes and studs, these special tyres are designed to grip compacted snow and ice as the car is driven. Once the snow melts, winter tyres do terrible damage to the regular road surface, and are therefore only permitted between October 1 and April 30 (longer if snow is still present). Foreign-registered cars are exempt from the requirement to be fitted with studded tyres, but it's extremely inadvisable to drive in winter without them – it's far better to rent a local car if you visit during the cold months. Although Swedish drivers in the north of the country often take shortcuts across **frozen lakes**, venturing onto ice, either in a car or on foot, isn't advisable; if you choose to follow suit, first ask the advice of local people as to whether the ice will hold your weight, and make sure you stick to the existing well-worn tracks across the ice. **Vägverket** (Swedish Road Administration, Ⓦwww.vv.se) maintain up-to-the-minute information about road conditions throughout Sweden on their website; click on the läget på vägarna link.

Off-piste in Swedish Lapland ▲

Snow-covered trees, Värmland ▼

Kärnan and around

Returning to the bottom of **Stortorget** – the central "square", so elongated that it's more like a boulevard – it's a short stroll upwards to the steps leading to the remains of the medieval **castle**, dominated by the massive castellated bulk of the **keep** (kärnan), surrounded by some fine parkland (daily: April, May & Sept Tues–Fri 9am–4pm, Sat & Sun 11am–4pm; June–Aug daily 11am–7pm; Oct–March Tues–Sun 11am–3pm; 20kr). The keep and Sancta Maria kyrka (see below) were the sole survivors of the ravages of war, but the former lost its military significance once Sweden finally won the day. It was due for demolition in the mid-nineteenth century, only surviving because seafarers found it a valuable landmark. What cannon fire failed to achieve, however, neglect and the weather succeeded in bringing about: the keep was a ruin when restoration began in 1894. It looks like a huge brick stood on end and is worth climbing today more for the views than the scant historical exhibitions within.

From the parkland at the keep's base, it's just a few steps to a charming **rose and magnolia garden**, exuding scent and colour all summer. To the side of this, you can wander down a rhododendron-edged path, Hallbergs Trappor, to the **Sancta Maria kyrka** (Mon–Fri 8am–4pm, Sat & Sun 9am–4pm), which squats in its own square by a very French-looking avenue of beech trees. Resembling a basilica, and Danish Gothic in style, the church was begun in 1300 and completed a century later. Its rather plain facade belies a striking interior, with a clever contrast between the early seventeenth-century Renaissance-style ornamentation of its pulpit and gilded reredos, and the jewel-like contemporary stained-glass windows.

Walking back to Stortorget, you arrive at **Norra** and **Södra Storgatan** (the streets that meet at the foot of the stairs to the *kärnan*), which comprised Helsingborg's main thoroughfare in medieval times and so are lined with the oldest of the town's merchants' houses. As you head up Norra Storgatan, the 1681 **Henckelska house** is hidden behind a plain stuccoed wall; once you have pushed your way through the trees that have grown over the entrance archway, you'll see a rambling mix of beams and windows, with a fine little topiary garden hidden beyond a passage to the right. The garden was laid out in 1766 for the future wife of King Gustav III, who was to spend one night at the beautiful eighteenth-century **Gamlegård house** opposite.

Back on Södra Storgatan, take the opening to the left of the old cream brick building at no. 31, opposite the modern Maria Församling House, to find a real historical gem. After a fairly arduous climb of 92 steps, you'll find a handsome nineteenth-century **windmill**, which you're free to enter using a narrow ramp. Around the windmill are a number of exquisite farm cottages, and inside the

---

Ferries to Helsingør

For a taste of what the locals traditionally do for fun, buy a **foot passenger ferry** ticket to Helsingør. Scandlines' ferries run every 20min (50kr return; children aged 4-11 half-price; ⓦ www.scandlines.se); ACE link's vessels (55kr return; ⓦ www.acelink.se) go every half-hour; while HH-Ferries also run every 30min and are the cheapest (48kr return; ⓦ www.hhferries.se). Tickets are available at each company's terminal. Try to go on Scandlines' Swedish boat, *Aurora*, as it has better restaurants and bars than the Danish ones (*Hamlet* and *Tycho Brahe*); you can see in the timetable which ship operates which departure. The idea is to go back and forth all night on the same ticket; the only reason to get off at Helsingør, apart from having a closer look at **Kronoborg Castle**, is to buy cheaper drink, although duty-free can also be bought, but not consumed, on the boat.

low (120cm) doors is a treasure trove of items from eighteenth-century peasant interiors: straw beds, cradles, hand-painted grandmother clocks and the like. A further reward for your climb is the fact that one house, built in 1763 and brought to this site in 1909, serves **waffles**: it's *Möllebackens Våffelbruk* (May–Aug daily noon–8pm). Established in 1912, they still use the original recipes.

Eating and drinking

The city has a good range of excellent **restaurants**, including a host of stylish **bar-restaurants** along the restored harbourfront. These places can seem samey, though, and it's the older restaurants that continue to provide the variety. During the day, there are some great **cafés** and *konditori*.

Cafés

Café Annorledes Södra Storgatan 15. A friendly café with a genteel 1950s atmosphere known for its extremely reasonable breakfasts (48kr) featuring porridge, yoghurt, eggs and cheese.

Ebba's Fik Bruksgatan 20. The most fun café in town: its enthusiastic owners have collected an amazing jumble of 1950s furnishings, and the jukebox belts out mambo, bebop and jive. Every detail of the era – from crockery to menu board – is here. The cakes are very good and you can also get egg and bacon fryups and delicious home-made Swedish beefburgers too.

Fahlmans Stortorget 11. This classic bakery/café has been serving elaborate cakes and pastries since 1914 and is *the* place for decadent apple meringue pie – a meal in itself. Also try the chocolate and marzipan confections or filling sandwiches.

K & Co Nedre Långvinkelsgatan 9. The best of the laid-back cafés in town with 1960s-style plastic chairs and swirly wallpaper. Very friendly, serving great muffins, cakes and filling ciabattas and panini.

Bar and restaurants

Beleza Södra Storgatan 19 ☎042/21 80 22. A delightfully airy café-cum-restaurant housed in one of Helsingborg's first pubs from the early 1900s, complete with the original wall paintings. Pasta salads, quiches, lasagne (around 75kr) and a huge selection of muffins are the order of the day, whilst on Sun the Swedish-style brunch is a winner.

Bishops Arms Södra Storgatan 2. At the top end of Stortorget, this centrally located pub is a firm favourite among Helsingborgers for its relatively genuine British pub feel, and its extensive range of beers, most on tap.

Edelweiss Drottninggatan 15 ☎042/21 37 37. A fun German restaurant-cum-beerhall with a tremendous selection of real German beers such as Spaten, as well as Wiener schnitzel

(189kr), a mammoth plate of Bavarian sausages, sauerkraut and mashed potato (149kr) and other German staples (149–199kr). Regular live music. Closed Mon.

Harry's Järnvägsgatan 7. Very popular place for a drink at any time of evening or night. Rather more stylish than the usual Harry's, with soft leather armchairs and chandeliers throughout this cavernous place opposite Knutpunkten. There's a nightclub here on Thurs, Fri & Sat nights.

Oasen Bruksgatan 25 ☎042/12 80 74. This restaurant serves nothing but fondues: meat (195kr), fish (229kr) and Mexican (209kr). Their speciality is a totally wicked Toblerone fondue (89kr) with cointreau and brandy into which you dip marshmallows, bananas and other fruit. Closed Sun & Mon.

Olsons Skafferi Mariagatan 6 ☎042/14 07 80. An absolute must. Despite its Swedish name, this is the very best Italian restaurant in town. Not a pizza in sight: they simply offer wonderfully prepared fish, meat and pasta dishes (129–235kr) in a relaxed atmosphere using Italian bases with Swedish overtones. The asparagus and mushroom risotto with truffle and parmesan (169kr) is to die for.

OZ Emellan Kajpromenaden 2, Norra Hamnen ☎042/14 61 61. An airy, style-conscious brasserie with floor-to-ceiling windows overlooking the marina. Serves well-prepared à la carte meat and fish dishes such as duck breast (255kr) and roast lamb (245kr) or there's a three course set menu for 445kr. Outdoor seating in summer.

Papadam Bruksgatan 10 ☎042/12 16 00. Finally, decent Indian food has made it to Helsingborg. Balti dishes are 145kr, an excellent chicken curry with spinach is 115kr, whereas lunch (served until 3pm) is an exceptionally good-value 50kr.

Telegrafen Norra Storgatan 14. A long-term favourite, this cosy British-style pub with stained-glass windows, wooden floors and a bar lined with tattered old books can do no wrong – Swedes seem to love the mock-Britannia.

Tzatziki Roskildegatan 2 ☏042/13 21 85. With a predictably blue-and-white interior, the food here is anything but predictable – genuinely, tasty Greek specialities such as calamari, marinated chicken skewers and Greek yoghurt with honey and walnuts. There's also a large selection of meze (35–89kr); 159kr buys a plate large enough for two people.

Lund

"There is a very tangible Lund spirit – those with it have ... an ironic distance to everything, including themselves and Lund, a barb to deflate pompous self-importance", wrote the Swedish essayist Jan Mårtensson. His compatriot, poet Peter Ortman, for his part once described what he termed "Lund syndrome": "a mix of paranoia, exhibitionism and megalomania". Whatever it is about the place, there is indeed a special spirit to **LUND** – a sense of tolerance (it's more relaxed than other Swedish cities), and a belief that people should be judged by what they do, not by what they have.

A few kilometres inland and 54km south of Helsingborg, Lund's reputation as a glorious old **university city** is well founded. An ocean of bikes is the first image to greet you at the train station, and like Oxford in England – with which

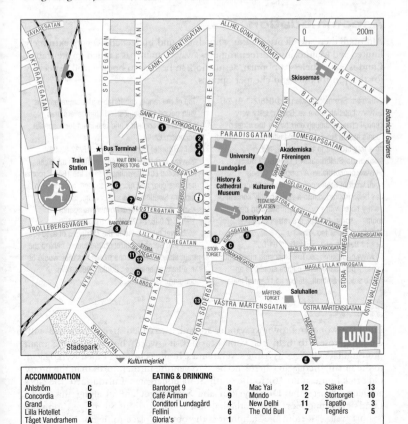

ACCOMMODATION		EATING & DRINKING					
Ahlström	C	Bantorget 9	8	Mac Yai	12	Stäket	13
Concordia	D	Café Ariman	9	Mondo	2	Stortorget	10
Grand	B	Conditori Lundagård	4	New Delhi	11	Tapatio	3
Lilla Hotellet	E	Fellini	6	The Old Bull	7	Tegnérs	5
Tåget Vandrarhem	A	Gloria's	1				

Lund is usually aptly compared – there is a bohemian, laid-back eccentricity in the air. With a twelfth-century Romanesque **cathedral**, medieval streets lined with a variety of architectural styles, and a wealth of cafés and restaurants, Lund is an enchanting little city that could well captivate you for a couple of days; it has a wide range of **museums**, a couple of them excellent, a mix of architectural grandeur, plus the buzz of student life. While Lund does lose much of its atmosphere during the summer months, some places remain open through June to August.

Arrival and information

Trains arrive at the western edge of the centre. **Buses** use the station south of Mårtenstorget, with many also stopping outside the train station. From the train station, the centre is two-minutes' walk, and everything of interest is within easy reach, with all the sights no more than ten minutes away. The **tourist office** is at Kyrkogatan 11, opposite the Domkyrkan (May & Sept Mon–Fri 10am–5pm, Sat 10am–2pm; mid-June to mid–Aug Mon–Fri 10am–7pm, Sat 10am–3pm, Sun 11am–3pm; Oct–April Mon–Fri 10am–5pm; ☎046/35 50 40, ⓦwww.lund .se); they can provide maps and copies of *i Lund*, a monthly diary of events with museum and exhibition listings. For internet, try 7-Eleven at Lilla Fiskaregatan 5.

Accommodation

Although there are plenty of luxury hotels in Lund, budget choices are extremely limited and Malmö, just thirteen minutes away by train, has a much greater range. Lund is, nevertheless, a popular destination, so be sure to book ahead, especially for the youth hostel and cheaper options.

Ahlström Skomakaregatan 3 ☎046/211 01 74, ⓦwww.hotellahlstrom.se. Good quality, very central cheapie though only two of the sixteen rooms en suite. No breakfast room: it's served on a tray brought to the room. ❸/❷
Concordia Stålbrogatan 1 ☎046/13 50 50, ⓦwww.concordia.se. A couple of streets southwest of Stortorget, this former student hostel has been upgraded into a very homely contemporary hotel with airy, modern Swedish designer rooms – some, though, are rather cramped. There's a sauna too. ❻/❺
Grand Bantorget 1 ☎046/280 61 00, ⓦwww.grandilund.se. This imposing nineteenth-century pink-sandstone edifice straddles an entire side of a small, stately and central square.

Top of the range, comfortable and unpretentious with period furnishings and chandeliers, this hotel oozes opulence and is perfect for a special occasion. ❼/❻
Lilla Hotellet Bankgatan 7 ☎046/32 88 88, ⓦwww.lillahotelletilund.se. Located in a typical, low-roofed Lund townhouse from the 1850s, rooms here are cosy and nicely appointed, decorated in modern Swedish style and colours. ❻/❹
Tåget Vandrarhem Vävaregatan 22 ☎046/14 28 20, ⓔtrainhostel @ebrevet.nu. Housed in the carriages of a 1940s train and accessed through the tunnel behind the train station, with bunks exactly as they would be in a train sleeping car. Bunks 200kr, own compartment ❶

The Town

Lund is a wonderful town to wander around, its cobbled streets festooned with climbing roses. To help get your bearings, it's worth noting that the main thoroughfare changes its name several times. In the centre, it's called Kyrkogatan; to the north, Bredgatan (there's no need to venture further north than the pretty old brick house at no. 16); to the south, Stora Södergatan. **Lundagård** (the city's academic heart), the **Domkyrkan** and **Stortorget** are all along this route. Lund's crowning glory is its cathedral; just 100m north of Stortorget, and only a short walk east from the station, it is the obvious place to begin.

The Domkyrkan

The magnificent **Domkyrkan** (Mon–Fri 8am–6pm, Sat 9.30am–5pm, Sun 9.30am–6pm; free) is built of storm-cloud charcoal and white stone, giving it an imposing monochrome appearance. Before going inside, have a look round the back of the building; on the way there, you'll notice the grotesque animal and bird gargoyles over the side entrances, their features blunted by eight centuries of weathering. At the very back, the most beautiful part of the exterior, the three-storey **apse** above the crypt, is revealed, crowned with an exquisite gallery.

The majestic **interior** is surprisingly unadorned, an elegant mass of watery-grey, ribbed stone arches and stone-flagged flooring. One of the world's finest master-pieces of Romanesque architecture, the cathedral was built in the twelfth century when Lund became the first independent archbishopric in Scandinavia, laying the foundation for a period of wealth and eminence that lasted until the advent of Protestantism. There are several striking features, such as the elaborately carved fourteenth-century choir stalls depicting Old Testament scenes, and the grotesque carvings hidden beneath the seats. The most vividly coloured feature is just to the left of the entrance, an amazing **astronomical clock** dating from the 1440s, which shows hours, days, weeks and the courses of the sun and moon in the zodiac. Each day at noon and 3pm, the clock also reveals its ecclesiastical Punch-and-Judy show, as two knights pop out and clash swords as many times as the clock strikes, followed by little mechanical doors opening to trumpet-blowing heralds and the Three Wise Men trundling slowly to the Virgin Mary.

The dimly lit and dramatic **crypt** beneath the apse has been left almost untouched since the twelfth century, and should not be missed. Here, the thick smattering of what look like tombstones is really comprised of memorial slabs, brought down to the crypt from just above; but there is one actual tomb – that of Birger Gunnarsson, Lund's last archbishop. A short man from a poor family, Gunnarsson chose the principal altar-facing position for his tomb, dictating that his stone effigy above it should be tall and regal. Two **pillars** here are gripped by stone figures – one of a man, another of a woman and child. Local legend has it that Finn the Giant built the cathedral for St Lawrence; in return, unless the saint could guess his name, Finn wanted the sun, the moon, or the saint's eyes. Lawrence was just preparing to end his days in blindness when he heard Finn's wife boasting to her baby, "Soon Father Finn will bring some eyes for you to play with." The relieved saint rushed to Finn declaring the name. The livid giant, his wife and child rushed to the crypt to pull down the columns, and were instantly turned to stone. Even without the fable, the column-hugging figures are fascinating to view.

Around the Domkyrkan: the museums

Just behind the cathedral, the **History and Cathedral Museum**, on Sandgatan (Tues–Fri 11am–4pm, Sun noon–4pm; 50kr; ⓦ www.luhm.lu.se), is for the most part rather dull unless you have a specialist interest in ecclesiastical history. The statues from Skåne's churches, in the medieval exhibition, deserve a look though, mainly because of the way they are arranged. The crowd of Jesuses hanging on crosses have an ominous quality worthy of Hitchcock, while in the next room all the Madonnas are paired off with the baby Jesuses.

A few minutes' walk away, on Tegnerplatsen, is the town's best museum, **Kulturen** (mid-April to Sept daily 11am–5pm; Oct to mid-April Tues–Sun noon–4pm; 70kr; ⓦ www.kulturen.com). It's easy to spend the best part of a day just wandering around this privately owned open-air museum, a virtual town of perfectly preserved cottages, farms, merchants' houses, gardens and even churches, brought from seven Swedish regions and encompassing as many centuries.

A few streets to the north, there's another stimulating attraction, the **Skissernas Museum** at Finngatan 2 (Museum of Sketches; Tues–Sun noon–4pm, Wed until 9pm; 50kr; ⓦwww. adk.lu.se), which houses a fascinating collection of around 25,000 preliminary sketches and original maquettes of works of art from around the world. An ever-changing selection of them is displayed; usually one room is full of work by all the major Swedish artists, while in another are sketches by international giants, such as Chagall, Matisse, Léger, Miró and Dufy; the best-known sculptural sketches here are by Picasso and Henry Moore. Outside, the sculptures on display include preliminary versions of pieces found in town squares all over Sweden, including those by Bror Marklund.

Botanical Gardens

An antidote to museum fatigue, the **Botanical Gardens** are as much a venue for picnicking and chilling out as a botanical experience (daily 6am–8pm, greenhouses noon–3pm; free). From Finngatan, the gardens are a few minutes' stroll away; head southeast down to the end of the street, then turn left into Pålsjövägen and right into Olshögsvägen. The greenhouses and rock gardens are the best areas to view; the rarest sights here are the Far Eastern paper-mulberry trees and the huge tulip trees – part of the same family as magnolias – with masses of flowers in June.

Eating and drinking

There are plenty of charming places to eat and drink in Lund, many of them associated with the university: certain **coffee houses** are institutions with the students helping keep prices low, especially for beer. For provisions, the **market** at Mårtenstorget, *Saluhallen*, sells a range of fish, cheeses and meats, including Lund's own tasty speciality sausage, *knake*.

Cafés

Café Ariman Kungsgatan 2. Attached to the Nordic Law Department, this classic left-wing coffee house is located in a striking red-brick building. It's frequented by wannabe writers and artists, with goatees, ponytails and blond dreadlocks predominating. Cheap snacks, coffee and cakes.

Conditori Lundagård Kyrkogatan 17. *The* classic student *konditori* from the days when this was the only student hangout in which to drink tea and smoke. A delightful institution with excellent caricatures of professors adorning the walls. Justly famous for its *spetkaka* meringues.

Mondo Kyrkogatan 23. In a quaint, beamed house with tiled interior walls, this pleasant little café serves bagels, baguettes, pasta salads and ciabattas. Does takeaway, too.

Restaurants

Bantorget 9 Bantorget 9 ☏046/32 02 00. This very chic restaurant with old painted ceilings and linen tablecloths is an established haven for gourmets. Well-prepared and succulent mains, such as pike-perch, char, veal or pork steak, cost around 265kr. The five-course set menu for 635kr is good value.

Fellini Bangatan 6 ☏046/13 80 20. Just opposite the train station, this stylish and popular Italian restaurant with red leather chairs has an excellent buffet lunch for 109kr; otherwise it's pizzas from 89kr and pasta from 129kr.

Gloria's Sankt Petri Kyrkogatan 9 ☏046/15 19 85. Serving TexMex and Cajun food, *Gloria's* sportsbar is very popular, particularly when there's a match on the big screen. Blackened chicken with corn salsa is 139kr, a scampi platter goes for 169kr and there are vegetarian dishes such as a feta schnitzel for 129kr.

Mac Yai Stora Fiskaregatan 15B ☏046/13 00 93. A plain and simple Thai restaurant which is very popular with the town's student population for its decent and generous Asian stir-fries and curries: every dish is 75kr, 5kr less for takeaways.

New Delhi Stora Fiskaregatan 15 ☏046/15 25 61. A really good Indian restaurant that's made more of an effort on interior decor than its Thai neighbour, but whose mains are slightly more expensive at 89kr. The chicken jalfrezi is a winner every time.

The Old Bull Bantorget 2. Traditional, carpeted British-style pub with solid metal tables which attracts a large student crowd during term time.

Stäket Stora Södergatan 6 ☏ 046/211 93 67. A step-gabled vaulted house built in 1570 is the characterful setting for this fondue- (from 170kr) and meat-oriented place. A mixed grill is 190kr, grilled duck breast 190kr and venison steak in juniper sauce costs 210kr.

Stortorget Stortorget 1. Housed in a National Romantic building that was formerly a bank, this trendy place has walls covered with black-and-white shots of musicians and actors and really pulls the crowds. Well established on the Lund bar scene, it's always busy and is a good place for a pre-dinner drink.

Tapatio Kyrkogatan 21 ☏ 046/32 44 70. Trendy, popular and very reasonable Mexican place serving fajitas, burritos and enchilladas from 129kr, whereas the excellent hot chicken stew with potatoes and salad costs 159kr. Also, a very good salmon steak with hot salsa and guacamole for 179kr.

Tegnérs Sandgatan 2 ☏ 046/13 13 33. Next to Akademiska Föreningen, the student union. Forget any preconceptions about student cafés being tatty, stale sandwich bars. Lunch for 74kr is self-service and you eat as much as you like from a delicious spread.

Malmö

Founded in the late thirteenth century, **MALMÖ** was once Denmark's second most important city, after Copenhagen. The high density of herring in the sea off the Malmö coast – it was said that the fish could be scooped straight out with a trowel – brought ambitious German merchants flocking to the city; the striking fourteenth-century St Petri kyrka in the city centre is heavily influenced by German styles. Eric of Pomerania gave Malmö its most significant medieval boost, when, in the fifteenth century, he built the castle, endowed it with its own mint, and gave Malmö its own flag – the gold-and-red griffin of his own family crest. It wasn't until the Swedish king Karl X marched his armies across the frozen Öresund to within striking distance of Copenhagen in 1658 that the Danes were forced into handing back the counties of Skåne, Blekinge and Bohuslän to the Swedes. For Malmö, too far from its own (uninterested) capital, this meant a period of stagnation, cut off from nearby Copenhagen. Not until the full thrust of industrialization, triggered by the tobacco merchant Frans Suell's enlargement of the harbour in 1775 (his jaunty bronze likeness, on Norra Vallgatan opposite the train station, overlooks his handiwork), did Malmö begin its dramatic commercial recovery. In 1840, boats began regular trips to Copenhagen, and Malmö's great Kockums shipyard was opened; limestone quarrying, too, became big business here in the nineteenth century.

During the last few decades of the twentieth century, Malmö found itself facing commercial crisis after a series of economic miscalculations, which included investing heavily in the shipping industry as it went into decline in the 1970s. But the past few years have witnessed a dramatic renaissance in the city's fortunes, reflected in the upbeat, thoroughly likeable atmosphere pervading the town today. With a very attractive medieval centre, a myriad of cobbled and mainly pedestrianized streets, full of busy restaurants and bars, Malmö has bounced back with plenty of style. Since the opening of the **Öresund bridge** linking the town to Copenhagen, the city's fortunes have been further improved, with Danes discovering what this gateway to Sweden has to offer, as opposed to the one-way traffic of Swedes to Denmark in the past.

Beyond the compact centre, Malmö is endowed with the stunning and dramatic **skyscraper**, the **Turning Torso** (see p.198). There's also a popular **beach**, and you'll discover some interesting cultural diversions south of the centre. These are located around **Möllevångstorget square**.

MALMÖ

ACCOMMODATION

Astoria	F
Baltzar	H
Best Western Royal	E
City Room & Apartments	J
Clarion Collection Temperance	I
Elite Savoy	A
Ibis Malmö	C
Mayfair	D
Malmö Camping & Feriecenter	G
Malmö City	K
Vandrarhem	
Radisson SAS Malmö	B

EATING & DRINKING

Årstiderna	2
Bishops Arms	1
Café Siesta	5
Café Slottsträdgården	20
Espresso House	15
Fagan's	18
Gazpacho	4
Gökbøet	9
Gustav Adolf	19
Harry's	10
Hollandia	21
Indian Side	12
Johan P	6
Krua Thai	26
Mando Steakhouse	14
Mello Yello	8
Moosehead	16
Nesta	25
Nyhavn	3
Paddy's	7
Rådhuskällaren	11
Salt & Brygga	23
Smak	17
Spot	22
Systrar & Bröder	24
Tempo	13
Trappaner	

Central Station

Bus Terminal

St Petri kyrka

Rådhus

Stortorget

Saluhallen

Form/Design Center

Sankt Pauli kyrka

Victoriateatern

Malmöhus

Kommendanthus

Kungsparken

Slottsparken

Mariedalspark

Library

250m

Folketspark, Möllevångstorget, ⑳, ㉕ & ㉖

Konsthall & ㉒, ㉓ & Ⓚ

Ribersborg Park, Kallbadhuset & Beaches

Öresund bridge, Ⓖ & ⑪

Arrival, information and city transport

The **train station** is where all trains arrive and depart. The frequent Pågatågen regional services to and from Helsingborg/Lund and Ystad use platforms 9–13 at the back. In the square immediately outside you'll find the main **bus terminal**.

The **tourist office** is inside Centralstation (June–Aug Mon–Fri 9am–7pm, Sat & Sun 10am–5pm; Sept–May Mon–Fri 9am–5pm, Sat & Sun 10am–3pm; ☏040/34 12 00, ⓦwww.malmo.se/turism). Here, you can pick up a wealth of free information, including the English-language listings brochure, *Malmö Guide*. Opposite the tourist office is a Forex **currency exchange** office.

City transport

Although the city centre is easy to walk around, its central squares and streets all interlinked, you'll need to use the city **bus** service to reach some of the sights and places to stay. Each ride costs 16kr (tickets valid for 1hr); a 200kr magnetic card (*rabattkort*) is also available, which reduces bus fares slightly and can be used by several people at the same time. All tickets are sold on the bus.

Several **taxi** companies in Malmö operate a fixed-price system within the city and surrounding area (see "Listings" for telephone numbers, p.201), but you should always agree the price before you start your journey. To give a rough idea of costs, a trip across the centre costs around 150kr.

Canal boat tours make a fun way of seeing the city; they leave daily from the canal opposite the *Elite Savoy* hotel (late April to Sept daily 11am–7pm; ⓦwww.rundan.se; 1hr; 85kr). Alternatively, **pedal boats** let you tour around the canal network at your own pace. They're moored at Amiralsbron (late-April to Sept daily 11am–7pm; ⓦwww.cityboats.se; 120kr per hr).

To strike out to the south of the city or further afield, **bike rental** is a good idea. The best place is Fridhems Cykelaffär at Tessins väg 13 (☏040/26 03 35): head down Citadellsvägen past Malmöhus, take the first left, Mariedalsvägen, then right into Tessins väg. Otherwise, try Cykelkliniken, Regementsgatan 12, across the canal from Gustav Adolfs torg (☏040/611 66 66) where a day's rental is around 100kr.

Accommodation

There are some really good and surprisingly affordable **hotels** in Malmö: the city is eager to attract tourists, and competition between the hotels can be fierce; most hotels can be booked online at ⓦwww.malmo.se/hotellbokning where special deals are sometimes also available.

Astoria Gråbrödersgatan 7 ☏040/786 60, ⓦwww.hotelastoria.nu. A few minutes from the train station across the canal, this is a good, modern, plain hotel which is worth checking out for its weekend and summer prices. ❺/❹

Baltzar Södergatan 20 ☏040/665 57 00, ⓦwww .baltzarhotel.se. Very central (between the two main squares), this is a swanky place done out in swags and flourishes that are more British than Swedish in design with chandeliers and handwoven carpets rather than polished wood floors throughout. ❻/❹

The Malmö Card

The very useful **Malmökortet** (Malmö Card; available for 1, 2 or 3 days; 130kr, 160kr or 190kr respectively) entitles you to free museum entry, free parking at public car parks and unlimited bus journeys within town. It also gives various other discounts on certain sights. Pick up *The Malmö Card* leaflet from the tourist office for full details or check ⓦwww.malmo.se/turist.

Best Western Royal Norra Vallgatan 94 ℡ 040/664 25 00, ⓦ www.bwhotelroyal.se. Exceptionally cosy rooms for a chain hotel (this was until recently a long-standing family-run place) whose modern interiors really are a home from home. As yet, the anonymous chain hotel feel has yet to pervade this winning little place. ❺/❸

City Room & Apartments Amiralsgatan 12 ℡ 040/795 94, ⓦ www.cityroom.se. Bargain-priced double rooms and small flats for rent in a newly renovated and centrally located building close to Konserthuset. All rooms have access to kitchen facilities, common rooms and balconies. ❷

Clarion Collection Temperance Engelbrektsgatan 16 ℡ 040/710 20, ⓦ www.choice.se. As you would expect at these rather steep prices, rooms are first-class, modern and classically Swedish in design with polished dark wood floors, cosy furnishings and top facilities including a sauna and solarium. ❻/❹

Elite Savoy Norra Vallgatan 62 ℡ 040/664 48 00, ⓦ www.savoy.elite.se. This is where Lenin, Bardot and Dietrich all stayed, with a brass plaque to prove it. Now part of the upmarket Elite chain, it's lost its edge but the rooms are big, very comfortable and the extensive breakfast is an experience in itself. ❻/❹

Ibis Malmö Stadiongatan 21 ℡ 040/672 85 70, ⓦ www.ibishotel.com. Although a 30–45min walk from the centre (bus #3 comes here), the prices at this simple yet functional place close to the sports stadium make up for the inconvenience. Book at least one month in advance and rooms cost just 500kr. ❸/❷

Malmö Camping & Feriecenter Strandgatan 101 in Limhamn ℡ 040/15 51 65, ⓦ www.camping.se /m08. Formerly known as Sibbarps Camping, this pleasant campsite is not far from the Öresund bridge and can be reached by bus #34 from town. Also has a number of cottages for rent (❷). Open all year.

Malmö City Vandrarhem Rönngatan 1 ℡ 040/611 62 20, ⓔ malmo.city@stfturist.se. This newly opened STF hostel has a variety of dorms sleeping up to six people. Sixteen rooms have en-suite facilities. Check-in is 4–7pm. Dorm beds 230kr, double room ❷

Mayfair Adelgatan 4 ℡ 040/10 16 20, ⓦ www .themayfairhotel.se. Very central luxury place and one of the finest of Malmö's more intimate hotels. Rooms are well furnished in cherry and Gustavian pastels. A sumptuous buffet breakfast is served in the vaulted cellar restaurant. ❺/❸

Radisson SAS Malmö Östergatan 10 ℡ 040/698 40 00, ⓦ www.malmo.radissonsas.com. Just beyond the Carolina Church, this hotel's blank and unimposing facade opens into a delightful interior. The stylish rooms are huge (the largest in Scandinavia), and breakfast is eaten inside one of the city's oldest houses, cunningly incorporated into the former apartment building. ❻/❺

The city centre

Heading south from the heavy-handed nineteenth-century opulence of the train station, with its curly-topped pillars and red-brick ornate arches, the **canal** is immediately in front of you. Dug by Russian prisoners in 1815, it forms a rough rectangle encompassing the **old town** to the south and the moated **castle** to the west. The castle is also surrounded by the first in a series of lovely, connecting **parks**. First off, though, head down Hamngatan to the main square. On the way you'll pass the striking sculpture of a twisted revolver, a monument to nonviolence, standing outside the grand 1890s building that is the former Malmö Exchange.

Stortorget and St Petri kyrka

The laying out of **Stortorget**, the proud main square, necessitated the tearing down of much of Malmö's medieval centre in the mid-sixteenth century. Among the elaborate sixteenth- to nineteenth-century buildings, the 1546 **Rådhus** draws the most attention. It's an impressive pageant of architectural fiddling and crowded with statuary: restoration programmes in the last century robbed the building of its original design, and the finicky exterior is now in Dutch Renaissance style. To add to the pomp, the red-and-gold flag of Skåne, of which Malmö is so proud, flaps above the roofs. The cellars, home to the *Rådhuskällaren* restaurant (see p.200), have been used as a tavern for more than four hundred years. To the south of the town hall, have a look inside **Apoteket Lejonet** (Lion Pharmacy – Swedish pharmacies are always named after creatures of strength): the outside is gargoyled and balconied, the inside a busy mix of inlaid woods, carvings and etched glass. From here, **Södergatan**, Malmö's main pedestrianized shopping street, leads down towards the canal. At the Stortorget end, there's a jaunty troupe of sculptured bronze musicians. On the opposite side of the square, the crumbling, step-gabled red-brick building was once the home of the sixteenth-century mayor and master of the Danish mint, Jörgen Kocks. Danish coins were struck in Malmö on the site of the present Malmöhus castle (see p.196), until irate local Swedes stormed the building and destroyed it in 1534. The cellars of Jörgen's pretty home contain the *Årstiderna* restaurant (see p.200), the only entry point for visitors today. In the centre of the square, a statue of Karl X, high on his charger, presides over the city he liberated from centuries of Danish rule.

A block east, on Göran Olsgatan behind the Rådhus, the dark, forbidding exterior of the Gothic **St Petri kyrka** belies a light and airy interior (daily 10am–6pm). The church has its roots in the fourteenth century, and, although Baltic in inspiration, has ended up owing much to German influences, for it was beneath its unusually lofty and elegantly vaulted roof that the German community came to pray – probably for the continuation of the "sea silver", the herrings that brought them to Malmö in the first place. The ecclesiastical vandalism, brought by the Reformation, of whitewashing over medieval roof murals started early at St Petri; almost the whole interior turned white in 1553. Consequently, your eyes are drawn not to the roof but to the pulpit and a four-tiered altarpiece, both of striking workmanship and elaborate embellishment. The only part of the church left with its original artwork was a side chapel, the **Krämare** (merchant's).

Lilla torg

Despite the size of Stortorget, it still proved too small to suffice as the town's sole main square, so in the sixteenth century **Lilla torg** was tacked on to its southwest corner, over a patch of marshland. With its half-timbered houses, flowerpots and cobbles, this is where most locals and tourists congregate. During the day, people come to take a leisurely drink in one of the many bars and wander around the summer jewellery stalls. At night, Lilla torg explodes in a

▲ Lilla torg bar

frenzy of activity, the venues all merging into a mass of bodies who converge from all over the city and beyond (see also "Eating and drinking", p.199). Head under the arch on Lilla torg to get to the **Form/Design Center** (Tues–Fri 11am–5pm, Thurs until 6pm, Sat 11am–4pm, Sun noon–4pm; free; ⓦwww .formdesigncenter.com). Built into a seventeenth-century grain store, it concentrates on Swedish contemporary design in textiles, ceramics and furniture. It's all well presented, if a little pretentious. The courtyard entrance contains several small trendy boutiques and there's a simple café.

From the end of the nineteenth century until the 1960s, the whole of Lilla torg was a covered market, and the sole remnant of those days, **Saluhallen**, is diagonally opposite the Form Design Center. Mostly made up of specialist fine food shops, Saluhallen is a pleasant, cool retreat on a hot afternoon, (see p.200).

Malmöhus and around

Take any of the streets running west from Stortorget or Lilla torg and you soon come up against the edge of **Kungsparken**, within striking distance of the fifteenth-century castle of **Malmöhus** (daily: June–Aug 10am–4pm; Sept–May noon–4pm; 40kr). For a more head-on approach, walk west (away from the station) up Citadellsvägen; from here the low castle, with its grassy ramparts and two circular keeps, is straight ahead over the wide moat. It's one of Sweden's least aesthetically pleasing castles, with mean windows and patched-up brickwork, but the inside is worth a peek.

After Sweden's destruction of Denmark's mint here in 1534, the Danish king Christian III built a new fortress two years later. This was only to be of unforeseen benefit to his enemies, who, once back in control of Skåne, used it to repel an attacking Danish army in 1677. For a time a prison (its most notable inmate the earl of Bothwell, Mary Queen of Scots' third husband), the castle declined in importance once back in Swedish hands, and it was used for grain storage until becoming a museum in 1937.

Once in the **museum**, pass swiftly through the natural history section, a taxidermal Noah's Ark holding no surprises; the most rewarding part of the museum is upstairs in the so-called **art museum**, part of the historical exhibition, where an ambitious series of furnished rooms covers most modern styles, from the mid-sixteenth-century Renaissance period through Baroque, Rococo, pastel-pale Gustavian and Neoclassical. A stylish interior from the *Jugendstil* (Art Nouveau) period is also impressive, while other rooms have Functionalist and post-Functionalist interiors, with some wacky colour and texture combinations. Other sections of the historical exhibition include a display of medieval skeletons from Malmö's churchyards, showing the signs of infection with contemporary diseases like leprosy and tuberculosis – less gruesome than you might imagine. It's more interesting to head into the castle itself, with its spartan but authentic interiors.

Just beyond the castle, to the west along Malmöhusvägen, is **Kommendanthuset** (Governor's House; same times as Malmöhus), containing a military museum with a fairly lifeless collection of neatly presented rifles, swords and photographs. A little further west, running off Malmöhusvägen, is a tiny walkway, **Banérskajen**, lined with higgledy-piggledy fishing shacks selling fresh and smoked fish – a rare little area of traditional Malmö that contrasts with the lively pace of the rest of the city.

Malmö is justifiably proud of its beautiful **parks**, a chain of which run southwards from the grounds of Malmöhus. Heading south from the castle, the first of these you encounter is Kungspark, with its graceful trees and classic sculptures, bordering the canal.

South of the centre

Tourists are still rarely encouraged to venture further south of the city than the canal banks that enclose the old town, but those who do are rewarded with the hip multicultural district around **Möllenvången** (see below). The buildings and areas off **Amiralsgatan**, to the southeast, give an interesting insight into Malmö's mix of cultures and its Social Democratic roots (the city has been at the forefront of left-wing politics for the last century, and was central to the creation and development of Sweden's Social Democratic Party). Around **Fersens väg**, several blocks west of Amiralsgatan, there are some charming enclaves of antique shops, cafés and quirky buildings, and the impressive Konsthall art exhibition centre.

There's plenty of pleasure to be had from simply strolling around the chain of **parks** that continues south of Kungsparken, with free guided tours of the flora and royal history connected with these appealing green swathes also available (ask at the tourist office). Just on the south side of the curving river is Slottsparken, with graceful, mature trees and places to picnic; further south is the largest of the parks, Pildammsparken, boasting several tranquil lakes.

South towards the Konsthall

Heading south from Malmöhus along Slottsgatan, first cross over Regementsgatan and then cut across three blocks east to cobbled Södra Förstadsgatan; at no. 4 is a splendid house designed in 1904, its National Romantic facade covered with flower and animal motifs. A little further along the same road at no. 18, the **Victoriateatern** is Sweden's oldest still-operating cinema, dating from 1912 – it's all fine Art Nouveau swirls of dark oak and bevelled glass.

Back on Fersens väg (the southward continuation of Slottsgatan after crossing Regementsgatan), you'll pass the city **theatre** on your right, with its amusing sculpture of tiers of people – the naked supporting the clothed on their shoulders. Arriving at St. Johannesgatan, head for the single-storey glass and concrete building at no. 7: the **Konsthall** (Art Hall; daily 11am–5pm, Wed until 9pm; free; Ⓦ www.konsthall.malmo.se), an enormous white-painted space showing vast modern works in regular temporary exhibitions; there's lots of room to stand back and take in the visual feast.

South to Möllevången

From the canal, head east along Regementsgatan and turn right into Amiralsgatan, from where it's a ten-minute walk south to **Folkets Park**, Sweden's oldest existing public park, which was once the pride of the community. Recently restored with an elegant new water feature at the Möllevången exit, Folkes Park contains a basic amusement park, and at its centre, a ballroom named the **Moriskan**, an odd, low building with Russian-style golden domes topped with crescents. Both the park and the ballroom are now privately owned, a far cry from the original aims of the park's Social Democratic founders. Severe carved busts of these city fathers are dotted all over the park. The socialist agitator August Palm made the first of his several historic speeches here in 1881, marking the beginning of a 66-year period of unbroken Social Democratic rule in Sweden.

More interesting than the giant twirling teacup fun rides in the park is the multicultural character of the city south from here. Strolling from the park's southern exit down Möllevången to **Möllevångstorget**, you enter an area populated almost entirely by people of non-Swedish descent, where Arab, Asian and Balkan émigré families predominate. The vast square is a haven of exotic food stores, side by side with shops selling pure junk and more recently established Chinese restaurants and karaoke pubs. On a hot summer afternoon it's easy to forget you're in Sweden at all, the more makeshift and ramshackle atmosphere around the bright fruit and veg stands contrasting with the clean, clinical order of the average Swedish neighbourhood. It's worth taking a close look at the provocative **sculpture** at the square's centre: four naked, bronze men strain under the colossal weight of a huge chunk of rock bearing carved representations of Malmö's smoking chimneys, while two naked women press their hands into the men's backs in support. It's a poignant image, marrying toil in a city founded on limestone-quarrying with the Social Democratic vision of the working man's struggle.

The Turning Torso and Malmö's beaches

From the western side of Malmöhus, Malmö's most breathtaking sight looms on the horizon: the **Turning Torso**. An easy walk north along Mariedalsvägen, crossing the canal over Varvsbron, leads you to Västra Varvsgatan, which streaks in a straight line to the city's Västra Hamnen district, home to the **skyscraper** that bears down on you as you approach. The tallest building in Scandinavia, this sleek, twisting tower of steel curves 90° clockwise as it rises to a height of 190m above the ground. It was designed to reshape the city skyline that had been dominated for decades by the massive Kockum shipyard crane, and now houses luxury flats and penthouses. An exhibition centre next door (daily 10am–6pm), including a film show of the building process, gives an idea of what it's like to live in the Twisting Torso with its truly fantastic views of the Öresund bridge and neighbouring Denmark.

Separated from the Turning Torso by delightful Ribersborg **park**, Malmö's long stretch of sandy **beach** stretches several kilometres to the old limestone-quarrying area of Limhamn to the southwest. Fringed by dunes and grassland,

▲ The Öresund bridge

The Öresund bridge

Linking Malmö with Copenhagen in Denmark (and thus Sweden with the rest of continental Europe), the elegant **Öresund bridge** was finally completed in 1999, after a forty-year debate. From Lernacken, a few kilometres south of Malmö, the bridge runs to a four-kilometre-long artificial island off the Danish coast, from where an immersed tunnel carries traffic and trains across to the mainland – a total distance of 16km. The bridge itself has two levels, the upper for a four-lane highway and the lower for two sets of train tracks, and comprises three sections: a central high bridge, spanning 1km, and approach bridges to either side, each over 3km long. The latest project which began in 2005, with expected opening in December 2010, is **Citytunneln** (ⓦ www.citytunneln .com), an underground rail tunnel and terminal which will speed trains right into the heart of Malmö from Denmark, avoiding the lengthy detour services currently make through the city's suburbs on existing tracks.

Stockholmers who played down the bridge's importance, fearing it would draw attention to Sweden's west coast, away from the capital, were, it seems, justified. It has fulfilled its promise to make Malmö the ultimate gateway into Sweden, and significantly raised the city's fortunes.

the beaches, popular with young families as the water remains shallow for several metres out to sea, are numbered according to the jetty which gives access into the water. At jetty #1, the **Ribersborgs kallbadhus** (contact for opening hours ☏040/26 03 66, ⓦ www.ribban.com) is a cold-water bathhouse offering separate-sex **nude bathing** areas and sauna; bus #32 runs here from the centre of town. The last jetty, #10, denotes Malmö's popular **nudist beach**.

Eating and drinking

Between Malmö's many **eating places** you're bound to find something to whet your appetite. Over recent years the influx of immigrants (and second-generation Swedes) has created a demand for all types of cuisine, not just traditional Swedish. Most of Malmö's restaurants, brasseries and cafés are concentrated in and around its three central squares, with Lilla torg attracting the biggest crowds. For cheaper eats and a very un-Swedish atmosphere, head south of the centre to Möllenvångstorget, the heart of Malmö's immigrant community.

Cafés

Café Siesta Hjorttackegatan 1. A newly renovated little café with stark white walls and leather stools serving light Mediterranean-style lunches such as a tasty goats cheese terrine with parma ham (56kr) as well as a good selection of home-made cakes and open sandwiches.

Café Slottsträdgården An appealing garden café surrounded by flowers and exotic plants located in the park south of the Malmöhus overlooking an old black windmill. The home-made carrot and chocolate cakes are excellent.

Espresso House Skomakaregatan 2. Close to both Stora and Lilla torg. Part of the excellent chain, this one serves great chocolate cake, muffins and ciabattas, and a delicious Oriental *latte* flavoured with cardamom. There's another popular branch at Södra Förstadsgatan 11, just south of the city.

Gustav Adolf Gustav Adolfs torg 43. Long established and stylishly renovated with chandeliers and black wallpaper with motifs of birdcages, this is still a popular spot, in a grand, white-stuccoed building. As well as coffee and cakes, it serves pasta dishes, a couple of fish mains and a good brunch buffet.

Hollandia Södra Förstadsgatan 8. South of Gustav Adolfs torg, across the canal. Classic, pricey *konditori* with marble busts, chandeliers and a window full of breads and pastries. The speciality of the house is moutwatering chocolate cake.

Nesta Södergatan 22. A wonderfully central location for this genuine Italian café serving all manner of freshly brewed Italian coffees makes it hard to resist. Italian biscuits and cakes are also available – and there's a small area of outdoor seating in the pedestrian street outside.

Systrar & Bröder Östra Rönneholmsvägen 26.
Superb breads, cakes and a full range of baguettes
plus a great-value breakfast buffet for just 65kr are
on offer at this hip joint with leatherette bench
seats and a 1960s ambience.

Restaurants

Årstiderna Frans Suellsgatan 3 ☎040/23 09 10.
This fine old basement restaurant with rough brick
walls and period furniture is within the former
home of Malmö's sixteenth-century mayor Jörgen
Kock. Pricey but worth the splash for its creative
marriage of traditional Swedish ingredients such as
cured salmon (165kr) and a succulent pepper-fried
fillet of beer (240kr).

Gazpacho Västergatan 16 ☎040/12 09 08. On a
quiet street, only a few minutes' walk from the
Stortorget action, this attractive choice with
contemporary art adorning its maroon walls has a
reputation for excellent tapas (25–47kr). With
around forty varieties on the menu, most guests
choose five or so to make a meal.

Gökboet Lilla torg 3 ☎040/611 21 99. With a name
that means "cuckoo's nest", this compact place has
a friendly, youthful atmosphere and excellent prices:
Mexican enchilladas for 65kr, delicious pasta 68kr,
salads 58kr and baked potatoes 59kr. Check out the
old-fashioned tiled stove in the corner once common
in all Swedish homes.

Indian Side Lilla torg 7 ☎040/30 77 44.
Stylish Indian brasserie with outdoor seating
under gas heaters that is always packed: all the
classics are here such as rogan josh and chicken
tikka masala at quite respectable prices. Reckon on
145kr for a main course, 24–75kr for a starter.

Johan P Saluhallen, Lilla torg ☎040/97 18 18.
With its black-and-white chequer-tiled walls, this
place has a good reputation for totally delicious fish
dishes and is inordinately popular at lunchtime
when bookings are essential. The selection of fresh
fish is the best in the city, although it doesn't come
cheap: steamed turbot is 398kr, seafood lasagne
298kr and fish soup 165kr.

Krua Thai Möllevångtorget 14 ☎040/12 22
87. In the big square south of the city centre,
this informal and unlicensed restaurant serves the
best Thai food in town with mains such as pad thai
or massamam curry for a reasonable 69kr.

Mando Steakhouse Skomakaregatan 4
☎040/780 00. All meat at this inordinately
popular steakhouse with curious copper-plated
interior walls comes from local farms and is grilled
over lava stones to give it a special barbecue
flavour. Mains cost 132–179kr.

Nyhavn Möllevångtorget 8 ☎040/12 88 30. A
Danish restaurant run by a Danish-Turkish émigré.
Chief among the offerings are *smørrebrod* with
all manner of possible toppings, plus rich Danish
meals, all for around 150kr. Outdoor seating
available.

Rådhuskällaren Stortorget 1 ☎040/790 20.
This restaurant is housed in the long vaulted
cellars of the gloriously decorated town hall. The
emphasis here is on modern Swedish dishes given
an international twist such as Cajun blackened
salmon with pak choi (169kr). Main dishes cost
135–269kr.

Salt & Brygga Sundspromenaden 7
☎040/611 59 40. Superb location by the
water's edge in Västra Hamnen with superb views
of the Öresund bridge. Everything on the menu
here is organic and exceptionally tasty: pink lamb
chops with carrots and potatoes, smoked organic
salmon, and, in season, even a delicious nettle
soup. A three-course set menu is 395kr.

Smak St Johannesgatan 7 ☎040/50 50 35. Inside
the Konsthall building, this relaxed café-restaurant
does a good line in vegetarian, meat and fish
dishes at lunchtime. It's also a very popular place
for weekend brunch.

Spot Stora Nygatan 33 ☎040/12 02 03. An
extremely popular and chic Italian trattoria with
tiled walls and floor serving good Italian fare at
sensible prices: pasta carbonara for 75kr, for
example, or pasta with pesto and bacon, also 75kr.
The pizzas are baked in a wood-fired oven and are
accordingly tasty.

Trappaner Tegelgårdsgatan 5 ☎040/57 97 50.
Widely regarded as one of the very best restaurants in southern Sweden, this stylish place with
stark white walls and linen tablecloths is perfect
for a special occasion. Top-notch gourmet dishes
based on modern French cuisine: monkfish with
beetroot or fillet of venison, for example, are
295kr; a three-course set menu here costs a
reasonable 495kr.

Nightlife and entertainment

Long gone are the days when the only entertainment in Malmö was watching
rich drunks become poor drunks at the blackjack table in the Centralstation
bar. Nowadays there are some decent **live-music** venues and **discos**, most
of which are cheaper to get into than their European counterparts. The
best places to see live music are *Palladium*, Södergatan 15 (☎040/10 30 20,

@www.paladium.nu), with a variety of Scandinavian R&B and rock bands, and *Jeriko*, Spånggatan 8 (℡040/10 30 20, @www.jeriko.nu) which specializes in jazz and world music.

Classical music performances take place at the Malmö Konserthus, Föreningsgatan 35 (℡040/34 35 00; @www.mso.se), home of the Malmö Symphony Orchestra, and at Musikhögskolan, Ystadvägen 25 (℡040/32 54 50); check with the tourist office for programme details.

In August Malmö plays host to the annual **Malmöfestivalen** (@www.malmofestivalen.se), one of the biggest in Sweden. Sprawling across the city from the parks around Malmöhus to Stortorget and Gustav Adolfs torg, the festival's grand opening, always on a Friday, is marked by a giant crayfish party in Stortorget, when thousands of people bring their own crayfish and akvavit to sing and dance the night away. Over the eight days, there's free music and entertainment at twenty or so locations across the city. Food from across the world is served up from a multitude of stalls: Pakistani, Somali and Bosnian dishes alongside more traditional elk kebabs and Swedish pancakes.

Bars

For **drinking**, Lilla torg is where mainstream Malmöites and tourists head in the evenings. The square buzzes with activity, as the smell of beer wafts between the old, beamed houses, and music and chatter fill the air. With a largely twenty- and thirty-something crowd, the atmosphere is like that of a summer carnival – orange-jacketed bouncers keep the throng from suffocating. It doesn't make a huge difference which of the half a dozen or so bars you go for – expect a wait to get a seat.

Bishops Arms Norra Vallgatan 62. This is a cosy but rather staid pub with a heavy-handed insistence on looking British. However, it does have an impressive range of beers on tap.

Fagan's Per Weijersgatan 4. Malmö's leading Irish pub with lots of whiskeys and Irish beers available. Happy hour is Mon–Fri 4–7pm. Fri and Sat nights attract a large crowd for the live music on offer.

Harry's Södergatan 14. People start arriving here from 3pm onwards to make the most of the happy hours which run Mon–Fri until 7pm. In line with other *Harry's* throughout Sweden, this is a popular place for an evening drink or three.

Mello Yello Lilla torg 1. A popular haunt for the 25-plus age group. Gets very drunken as the night progresses.

Moosehead Lilla torg 1. With rough brick walls and a gorgeous stucco cornice, this stylish bar is definitely one of the most fun places to drink in town and a firm favourite with the twenty-something fraternity – even in winter when people huddle under gas heaters outside.

Paddy's Kalendegatan 7. Definitely more bar than pub with black-and-white pictures of Irish writers adorning the walls, this is a stylish and laid-back place for a drink right in the centre of town.

Tempo Södra Skolgatan 30. This compact little bar close to Möllevångstorget is always packed with students and would-be musicians who come here to relax and enjoy the music chosen by the resident DJ.

Listings

Buses Skånetrafiken ℡0771/77 77 77.
Car rental Avis, Skeppsbron 13 @www.avis.se; Europcar, Mäster Nilsgatan 22 @www.europcar.se; Hertz, Jorgen Kocksgatan 1B @www.hertz.se.
Doctor On call ℡1177.
Internet access Sidewalk Express have several internet points across Malmö, for example, at Central Station and at the 7 Eleven supermarkets

at Baltzargatan 22 and Södra Förstadsgatan 78A. See @www.sidewalkexpress.se for complete listings. 19kr per hour.
Pharmacy Apoteket Gripen, Bergsgatan 48 (daily 8am–10pm).
Taxis Taxi 97 ℡040/97 97 97, Taxi Kurir ℡040/700 00, Taxi Skåne ℡040/33 03 30.
Train enquiries SJ ℡0771/75 75 75.

Southern Skåne: from Malmö to Ystad

Leaving Malmö, the Pågatåg train and the E65 highway cut southeast directly towards Ystad (see p.204). However, if you take the train, you'll miss the remarkable Viking-style settlement at **Foteviken**. With time to spare, and particularly with your own transport, the museum and nearby Skanör are definitely worth a visit.

Foteviken Viking Museum

From Malmö, it's 25km southwest along the E6 and Route 100 to Höllviken, on the way to Skanör (see p.202). Höllviken itself has nothing to detain you, but signs here point the way to the **Foteviken Viking Museum**, just 500m away (June–Aug daily 10am–4pm; Sept–April Mon–Fri 10am–4pm; **guided tours** in English at 11.30am, 1 & 2.30pm; 60kr; ☏040/33 08 00, ⓦwww .foteviken.se). An ancient coastal village and reputedly also a pagan sacrificial site, **Foteviken** was a market town and centre for herring fishing during Viking times. Today, the whole area has been transformed into a working **Viking-style village** comprising houses, workshops, a sacrificial temple and shipyard – a virtually self-sufficient settlement with an astonishing ring of authenticity. The idea was to show the way of life here in the twelfth century, but more than this, the place has become a Mecca for people from all over Europe who want to live as Vikings, together with a not inconsiderable number of characters, sporting wild beards and lots of beads, who firmly believe they *are* Vikings.

The resulting atmosphere is that of a hippy commune in a time warp. Everyone dresses entirely in home-spun garments of loose, coarse linen, coloured with dyes made from local grasses and herbs. The villagers' simply crafted footwear is made from leather which they cure themselves, and if you wander into the **cure-houses** you'll see the pelts of locally caught mink – along with elk and wild-boar hides donated by local abattoirs. Dotted around the ever-growing village are ant-hill-like **kilns** and **clay ovens** used to bake bread and fire the bowls from which the villagers eat.

There are currently twenty or so complete houses, though it is intended that the village will eventually comprise thirty or forty homes. Among the highlights is a **weavers' cottage** containing the village's answer to the Bayeux Tapestry: a wall-hanging here depicts the Battle of Foteviken of June 4, 1134, in which King Nils of Denmark is seen trying to reconquer Skåne from the rebellious pretender Erik Emune. And it's worth heading down to the shore, where longships, based on the designs of excavated wrecks, are built.

You can stay here in a four-berth **cabin** (☏040/33 08 06, Ⓔbokning @foteviken.se; ❷), while in the **café and restaurant** you can sample modern interpretations of Viking fare, such as smoked salmon and hog roast.

Skanör and the Näset peninsula

With a distinctly well-heeled population, the appropriately golf-club-shaped **Näset peninsula**, marking the southwest tip of the country, is well known for its many golf courses. Heading west from Foteviken, you cross the Falsterbo Canal (dug by Swedes during World War II to bypass occupied Danish coastal waters), before arriving in the early medieval town of **SKANÖR**, which was once an important commercial centre, and founded as part of the Hanseatic commercial system. In the early twentieth century, Skanör became a fashionable bathing resort for wealthy Malmö families. Aside from the admirably pretty houses, there's not much to see in Skanör, but its **beaches** are superb: long ribbons of white sand bordering an extensive **bird and nature reserve**. At the

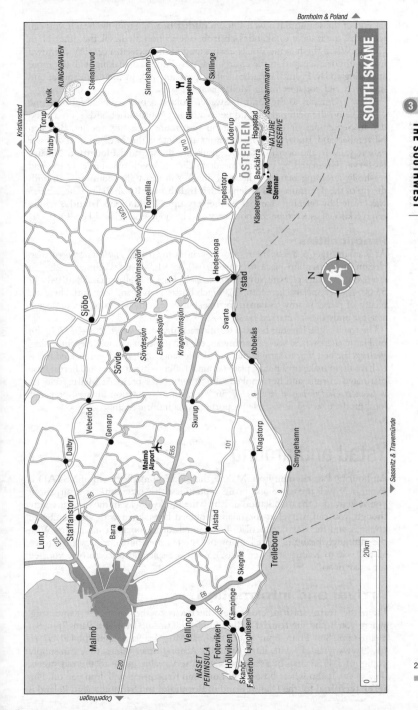

SOUTH SKÅNE

Bornholm & Poland ▲

Kristianstad ▲

Copenhagen ▲

Sassnitz & Travemünde ▶

KUNGAGRAVEN

Stenshuvud

Simrishamn

Skillinge

Kivik

Torup

Vitaby

Glimmingehus

Löderup

Sandhammaren

ÖSTERLEN

Hagestad

Backåkra

NATURE RESERVE

Tomelilla

Ingelstorp

Ales Stennar

Käseberga

19/20

Snogeholmssjön

Hedeskoga

Sjöbo

13

Ystad

Sövdesjön

Ellestadssjön

Krageholmssjön

Sövde

Svarte

Abbekås

Veberöd

Genarp

Skurup

Klagstorp

9

Dalby

Smygehamn

101

Malmö Airport

E65

Staffanstorp

Bara

Alstad

9

Lund

80

Skegrie

Trelleborg

20km

NÄSET PENINSULA

Vellinge

Fotevikën

Höllviken

Kämpinge

E6

Skanör

Falsterbo

Ljunghusen

100

E20

Malmö

N

0

203

3

far end of the seashore is a well-known **nudist beach**. From the beach, you can see across the reserve to Skanör's **church**, one section medieval, the other High Gothic. When the herring stocks disappeared in the sixteenth century, the town lost its importance, and so the church was never updated, making it all the more appealing today. From the harbour, it's a pleasant walk to the town square and the lovely old cottages lining Mellangatan.

A few kilometres to the south is Sweden's oldest nature reserve, **Nabben**, one of twelve on the peninsula. It's home to a huge population of birds – on a good day in September or October you can spot more than fifty species. Between November and January it's all off-limits to protect the birds and, to a lesser extent, seals. To the north of the peninsula lies the splendid **Flommen Nature Reserve**, dominated by wetland meadows carpeted with blue butterfly iris, and sea-holly sprouting between the sand dunes. You can walk southwards, towards the tip of the peninsula, to Sweden's oldest **lighthouse**, Kolabacken, whose beam was created by burning charcoal. At the very tip is **Maklappen Island**, a nature reserve known as a refuge for both grey and harbour seals (closed Feb–Oct).

Practicalities

At Rådhustorget 6, a few metres from Skanör's town hall, *Hotell Gässlingen* is an elegant and charming place to **stay** (☎040/45 91 00, ⓦwww.hotel-gasslingen .com; ❻). Another pleasant, small hotel is *Spelabäcken*, at Mellangatan 58 (☎040/47 53 00, ⓦwww.spelabacken.com; ❺), which boasts a sauna and solarium. There are plenty of places nearby to **camp** for free, but be careful not to pick a protected area for birds: they're marked by signposts.

The town's little harbour boasts a terrific **restaurant**, *Fiskrögeri* (☎040/47 40 50) on Hamngatan, where you can savour superb fish dishes in a simple, elegant setting. Perhaps the best way to sample the remarkable range of smoked and pickled fish is to have them make up a picnic plate (around 120kr) – in particular, try herring roe marinated in rum, and hot smoked salmon with black bread. At Mellangatan 13, is *Skanörs Gästgifvaregård* (☎040/47 56 90), with its reputation for well-prepared, local produce served in sizeable proportions in a historic setting.

Ystad and around

An hour by Pågatåg train from Malmö, the medieval market town of **YSTAD** is exquisitely well preserved and boasts a prettiness that may come as a surprise if you've arrived at the train station down by the murky docks. In the historic centre though, you can marvel at the quaint, cobbled lanes, lined with cross-timbered cottages, and the town's chocolate-box central square, oozing rural charm. With the stunningly beautiful coastal region of Österlen stretching northeast from town all the way to Kristianstad (see p.209), Ystad is a splendid place to base yourself for a day or so.

Arrival and information

From the **train station**, cross over the tracks to the square, St Knuts torg, where you'll find the **tourist office** (mid-June to Aug Mon–Fri 9am–7pm, Sat 10am–6pm, Sun 11am–6pm; rest of the year Mon–Fri 9am–5pm; ☎0411/57 76 81, ⓦwww.ystad.se) with internet access. Among other things, they can supply copies of a 1753 map of Ystad that's still a serviceable guide to the old streets. The square is also where buses from Lund and Kristianstad will drop you off. The **ferry terminal** for the Danish island of Bornholm and Swinoujscie in Poland is

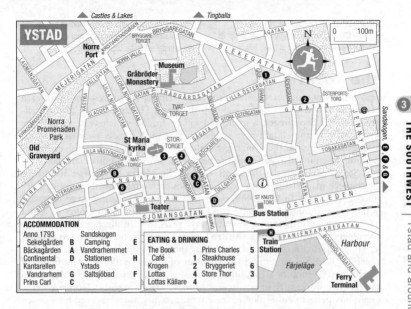

300m southeast of the train station. **Bikes** – a great way to see the surrounding cycle-friendly landscape – can be rented from Roslin Cykel, Jennygatan 11 (℡0411/123 15), just east of the bus and train terminals.

Accommodation

There are several good and reasonably priced **hotels** in town, and one at the beach, listed below. Prices are considerably less than Malmö so if money is tight, staying here and travelling up to Malmö will save lots. Ystad also has two youth hostels, quite unusual for such a small place.

Anno 1793 Sekelgården Långgatan 18 ℡0411/739 00, ⓦwww.sekelgarden.se. The best place to stay in town, this small family-run hotel in a merchant's house of 1793 is friendly and informal, with a great sauna and a cobbled courtyard filled with flowers and trees. There are en-suite rooms in both the main house and the old tannery at the back, and excellent breakfasts are served under the trees or in the charming dining room. ❸

Bäckagården Dammgatan 36 ℡0411/198 48, ⓦwww.backagarden.nu. A small-scale guesthouse in a beautiful, converted private townhouse just behind the tourist office and complete with a tranquil garden. ❸/❷

Continental Hamngatan 13 ℡0411/137 00, ⓦwww.hotelcontinental-ystad.se. Classic hotel touted as Sweden's oldest, with a grand lobby of marble, and crystal chandeliers, plus bright, comfortable rooms with parquet floors. The breakfast buffet is a treat. ❹

Kantarellen Vandrarhem Fritidsvägen 9 ℡0411/665 66, ⓦwww.turistlogi.se. A great location for this STF hostel on the beach at Sandskogen, 2km east of the town centre and reached by buses #304, 322 & 392. Dorm beds 230kr, double room ❶; Sept to mid-June advance bookings only.

Prins Carl Hamngatan 8 ℡0411/737 50, ⓦwww.hotellprinscarl.com. An elegant, family-run, non-smoking place dating from 1888 with rooms adapted for people with disabilities or allergies. ❸/❷

Sandskogens Camping ℡0411/192 70, ⓦwww.sandskogenscamping.se. Next to the *Kantarellen* youth hostel and reached by the same buses (see above). Beautiful location overlooking a large sandy beach.

Vandrarhemmet Stationen Spanienfararegatan 25 ℡0708/57 79 95, ⓦwww.turistlogi.se. Independent hostel located in the railway station with comfort-able, high-ceilinged rooms. Dorm beds 200kr, double rooms ❶.

Ystads Saltsjöbad Saltsjöbadsvägen 6 ℡ 0411/136 30, ⓦ www.ysb.se. Renowned for its beachside position, just east of town, this large, 100-year-old hotel (with endless modern extensions) has a sauna, pool (summer only), and a restaurant in the original saltwater bathing house. ④

The Town

Leaving the train or bus stations or the ferry terminals, head west until you reach Hamngatan, where you take a right up the street. This brings you to the well-proportioned **Stortorget**, a grand old square around which twist picturesque streets. West of the church here is Mattorget, a small square, away from which leads Lilla Västergatan, the main street in the seventeenth and eighteenth centuries; strolling down it today, you'll see the best of the town's Lilliputian cottages.

In Stortorget itself, the thirteenth-century **St Maria kyrka** is a handsome centrepiece (daily 10am–4pm), with additions dating from nearly every century since it was built. In the 1880s, these rich decorative features were removed, as they were thought "unsightly", and only the most interesting ones were put back during a restoration programme forty years later. Inside, the Baroque early seventeenth-century pulpit is worth a look for the fearsome face carved beneath it, while opposite is the somewhat chilling medieval crucifix, placed here on the orders of Karl XII to remind the preacher of Christ's suffering. The figure of Christ wears a mop of actual human hair – sacrificed by a local parishioner in the nineteenth century, in an attempt to make it look realistic. Notice also the green box pews to either side of the entrance, which were reserved for women who had not yet been received back into the church after childbirth.

Not far from Stortorget, up Lilla or Stora Norregatan, is **Norreport**, the original northern arched entrance to the town. From here, you can stroll through **Norra Promenaden**, an avenue lined with mature horse-chestnut trees and surrounded by parkland. Here you'll find a white pavilion, built in the 1870s to house a genteel café and a dance hall with a brass band. Today, the café here, *Café Promenaden* is something of a favourite spot for funeral teas (the small park borders on a graveyard), with many of Ystad's older residents wanting to be remembered at the place where most of them first met and danced with their loved ones.

Another short stroll from Stortorget, past Garvaregränd's art-and-craft workshops (one of which, Krukmakaren, is in a fantastically higgledy-piggledy house on the right), then up Klostergatan, brings you to the town's thirteenth century **monastery**, now a simple **museum** (June–Aug Mon–Fri 10am–5pm, Sat & Sun noon–4pm; rest of the year Tues–Fri noon–5pm, Sat & Sun noon–4pm; 30kr; ⓦ www.klostret.ystad.se). The collection is pretty standard local history

The Night Bugler of Ystad

Staying in Ystad, you'll soon get acquainted with a tradition that harks back to the seventeenth century: from a room in the church's watchtower, a night watchman sounds a **bugle** every fifteen minutes from 9.15pm to 1am. The haunting sound isn't disturbing, though it's audible wherever you stay in the centre. The sounding through the night was to assure the town that the watchman was still awake (until the mid-nineteenth century, he was liable to be executed if he slept on duty); however, the real purpose of this activity was as a safeguard against the outbreak of **fire**. The idea was that if one of the thatched cottages went up in flames, the bugle would sound repeatedly for all to go and help extinguish the blaze. The melancholic bellowing only ceased during World War II, though then the residents complained they couldn't sleep in the unbroken silence. If you look carefully from Stortorget, you can just see the instrument appear at little openings in the tower walls each time it's played.

paraphernalia, but given piquancy by its medieval surroundings. After the monks were driven out during the Reformation, the monastery declined and was used, among other things, as a hospital and a distillery, before becoming a museum in the early twentieth century. The museum has a small **café** serving coffee and cake for 30kr. Brightly painted low cottages line the streets around here; a brief stroll down the most picturesque of these, **Vädergränd**, off Lilla Östergatan and just one block up from the *Book Café* (see below), makes for a worthwhile foray. Look particularly at no. 4 – the 1727 Gamla Handtwerfargården, a grocery in a time-warp.

Eating, drinking and entertainment

There is a fair selection of places to eat in Ystad, with some atmospheric **cafés** and fine **restaurants**; most of the latter are on or around Stortorget. Ystad stages its annual **opera festival** through most of July at Ystad Teater at Sjömansgatan 13. You can get information on performances and book tickets at the tourist office.

The Book Café Gåsegränd. Down a tiny, cobbled street off Stora Östergatan, this precariously leaning wooden house has books – all in English – to read while you feast on the home-baked focaccia or sample one of the varieties of coffee. The gardens are delightful too, and retain their layout from 1778.

Krogen Stora Östergatan 47 ⓣ 0411/155 66. The latest addition to the eating scene in Ystad, this bright and airy modern place serves tasty fish and meat dishes and is renowned for its herring trilogy starter which is truly delicious. Mains are around 150kr.

Lottas Stortorget 11 ⓣ 0411/788 00. Justifiably the most popular restaurant in town, packed each evening in summer and serving beautifully presented, scrumptious fish and meat dishes such as schnitzel, chicken fillets and fried perch around the 150kr mark.

Lottas Källare Stortorget 11 ⓣ 0411/788 00. In the cellars below *Lottas* restaurant this cosy bar offers several English beers including the so-called "Manchester United".

Prins Charles Hamngatan 8 ⓣ 0411/55 51 24. Next door to the *Prins Carl Hotel*, this English-style pub and restaurant serves meat and fish dishes in the evenings, with live music on Fri and Sat nights.

Steakhouse Bryggeriet Långgatan 20 ⓣ 0411/699 99. The rough, beamed interior dominated by two copper beer casks creates a welcoming ambience at this meatlover's treat. The well-cooked steaks and other meat mains are 119–186kr and the house speciality is a delicious pork schnitzel with cucumber and fries.

Store Thor Stortorget 1 ⓣ 0411/185 10. Located in the cellars of the fourteenth-century Rådhuset, and adding a breath of life to Stortorget in summer when tables are brought into the square itself. At weekends, and out of the high season, the more elegant surroundings inside serve as a fitting backdrop to the less touristy Swedish menu. Tapas from 24kr, pasta dishes from 139kr, burgers and salads (around 130kr) are the order of the day.

Österlen and the southeast coast

The landscape of the southeastern corner of Skåne, known as **Österlen**, is like a Mondrian painting: horizons of sunburst-yellow fields of rape running to cobalt-blue summer skies, punctuated only by white cottages, fields of blood-red poppies and the odd black windmill. Along with the vivid beauty of its country-side, Österlen has a number of engaging sights, notably picture-perfect villages, plenty of smooth, sandy beaches, and the Viking ruin of **Ales Stennar**. It's not surprising the area has lured writers and artists to settle here more than anywhere else in Sweden.

Unfortunately, **getting around** this part of the country isn't straightforward without your own transport; the only major road, Route 9 to Kristianstad via uninteresting Simrishamn, bypasses the most interesting southeastern corner of

Österlen. The whole area is poorly served by buses and there are no trains. If you haven't got a car, the best way to get around is to use a combination of public transport, walking and cycling.

From Ystad to Ales Stenar

There are two ways to get to Ales Stennar from Ystad: either take **bus** #322 or #392 (20min) or rent a bike and follow the coastal cycle track for the twenty-kilometre journey. The track runs through an area of pine forest opening onto white sandy beaches, with excellent bathing opportunities. Near Kåseberga is **Ales Stennar**, an awe-inspiring Swedish Stonehenge. Believed to have been a Viking meeting place, it consists of 56 **stones** forming a 67-metre-long boat-shaped edifice, prow and stern denoted by two appreciably larger **monoliths**. The site was hidden for centuries beneath shifting sands, which were cleared in 1958; even now, the bases of the stones are concealed in several metres of sand. It's difficult to imagine how these great stones, not native to the region, might have been transported here. Ales Stennar stands on a windy, flat-topped hill, which most of the tourists snapping away don't bother to climb; once at the top, though (it's a steep, 10min hike), there's a majestic timelessness about the spot that more than rewards the effort.

Hagestad Nature Reserve and Sandhammaren beach

For a day in really splendid natural surroundings, it's hard to beat the **Hagestad Nature Reserve**, the best of the three reserves around the village of **Backåkra**, a signposted drive 5km east of Kåseberga. Thousands of pines were planted here in the eighteenth and nineteenth centuries to bind the sandy earth, and, together with oaks and birches, they make up a densely forested area; the clumps of gnarled, stunted oaks are particularly distinctive. It's especially beautiful in midsummer when orchids and heathers colour the forest floor; if you're lucky, you may also see elk, badgers and roe deer, while buzzards and golden orioles are often sighted above. The reserve is also the home of the most glorious **beach** in Skåne, known as **Sandhammaren**: walk along any path towards the sea and you'll soon reach a bright white ribbon of sand – marked "Sandhammaren" on signs – backed by steep dunes and lapped by turquoise waters.

In the midst of the nature reserve, uphill on heathland towards Backåkra is an old farmstead (signposted from Backåkra) once owned by **Dag Hammarskjöld**, United Nations secretary-general in the 1950s. His love of the Skåne coast led him to buy the farm and the surrounding sixty acres in order to save it from developers. Killed in a plane crash in Zambia in 1961, Hammarskjöld willed the farm and its contents to STF, which now runs the house as a **museum** (daily mid-June to mid-Aug noon–5pm; ☏0411/52 60 10). It contains amazing pieces of art from all over the world, including an ancient Egyptian painting of the jackal-headed god Anubis, Greek bronzes from 200 BC and contemporary pieces by the Wakefield sculptor Barbara Hepworth, Picasso and Matisse.

Practicalities

Backåkra village has a well-equipped STF **youth hostel**, in an old school house with a bus stop right outside (☏0411/52 60 80, ✉backakra @swipnet.se; dorm beds 230kr, double room ❶; April–Oct); you also can **rent bikes** here. At **Löderups Strandbad**, just west of Backåkra, is a beautifully situated **campsite** (☏0411/52 63 11), with a **café** and **restaurant** at Gökvägen.

Kristianstad

Twenty kilometres inland, quiet **KRISTIANSTAD** (pronounced "cri-shan -sta") is eastern Skåne's most substantial historic centre and a convenient gateway to Sweden's southern coast. Dating from 1614, when it was created by Christian IV, Denmark's seventeenth-century "builder-king", during Denmark's 44-year rule here, it's the earliest and most evocative of his Renaissance towns. With beautifully proportioned central squares and broad, gridded streets flanking the wide river, it was a shining example of the king's architectural preoccupations. Christian nurtured plans to make the fortified town one of Denmark's most important, and it wasn't until the mid-nineteenth century that the fortifications were finally levelled, allowing the town to spill beyond the original perimeter. The late-nineteenth century saw the creation of Parisian-style boulevards, pleasant to wander through today, though the many bland buildings erected during the 1960s and 1970s have left the town with a rather dull appearance.

With its beautiful little **Tivoli Park** containing a fine Art Nouveau theatre, a historic **film museum** and a most elegant **cathedral**, Kristianstad can easily detain you for a relaxed day-long visit.

Arrival and information

The SkåneExpressen #4 **bus** from Ystad (1hr 30min) stops outside the **train station**, Kristianstad C, on Västra Boulevarden. This is also the terminus for trains from Malmö and Copenhagen. The **tourist office** (mid-June to mid-Aug Mon–Fri 10am–7pm, Sat 10am–3pm, Sun 10am–2pm; mid-Aug to mid-June Mon–Fri 10am–5pm, Sat 11am–3pm; ☎044/13 53 35, ⓦwww.kristianstad.se /turism), with internet terminals, is located in Stora torg, a five-minute walk from the station; to get here, turn right out of the train station and then take the second left. **Bikes** can be rented for 100kr per day at Cykelcentralen, Kanalgatan 22 (☎044/21 35 07).

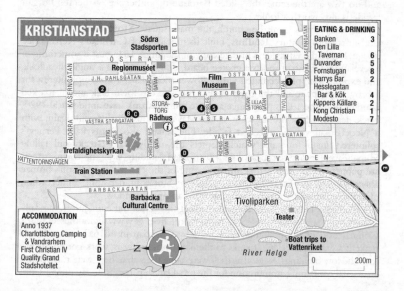

Accommodation

There's rarely a big demand for accommodation in Kristianstad, so arriving in summer without a reservation shouldn't pose a problem. The centre of town is compact and most hotels are located within easy reach of the town's attractions and restaurants.

Anno 1937 Västra Storgatan 17 ⊤044/12 61 50, ⓦwww.hotelanno.se. A rather cramped hotel over two storeys housed in a building dating from the turn of the last century – with annoyingly low ceilings. Rooms are comfortable but lack any real style. ⑤/③

Charlottsborgs Camping & Vandrarhem Jacobs väg 34 ⊤044/21 07 67, ⓦwww .charlottsborgsvandrarhem.se. Located 3km west of the town centre and reached by bus #2. A combined campsite and youth hostel, where campers can use all the hostel facilities including the TV and lounge room. Dorm beds 150kr and cottages for two people ①

First Christian IV Västra Boulevarden 15 ⊤044/20 38 50, ⓦwww.firsthotels.com. The most glamorous hotel in town, just south of Stora torg,

located in a rather splendid building that was once home to a bank, retaining its original fireplaces and parquet floors; the old bank vaults are now a washroom and a wine cellar. ⑤

Quality Grand Västra Storgatan 15 ⊤044/28 48 00, ⓦwww.choicehotels.se. This modern, modest-looking place offers excellent friendly service and well-equipped en-suite rooms, with supremely comfortable beds, wooden floors and some attractive weekend and summer prices. ④/⑤

Stadshotellet Nya Boulevarden 8 ⊤044/10 02 55, ⓦwww.stadshotelletkristianstad.se. The lobby is all panelled opulence in this old Freemasons' Hall; the rooms, though, are a let down with cheap, modern decor that is rather out of keeping with the rest of the building. ④/⑤

The Town

The most obvious starting point for a visit to town is the 1618 **Trefaldighet-skyrkan** (Holy Trinity Church; daily 9am–5pm), right opposite the train station. It symbolizes all that was glorious about Christian IV's Renaissance ideas: the grandiose exterior has seven magnificent spiralled gables, and the building's high windows allow light to flood the white interior. Inside, the most striking features are the elaborately carved pew ends: each is over 2m tall, and no two are the same; the gilded Baroque magnificence of the 1630 organ facade is also worth a look.

Diagonally across from the church, the main square, **Stora torg**, contains the late nineteenth-century **Rådhus**, built in imitation of Christian's Renaissance design. Inside the entrance, a bronze copy of the king's 1643 bust is something of a revelation: Christian sports a goatee beard, one earring and a single dreadlock, and exposes a nipple decorated with a flower motif, itself a source of interest for a baby elephant round the royal neck. Opposite the town hall, and in marked contrast to it, the 1920s post office and the old Riksbank have an identical 1920s brick design; while the adjacent 1640s Mayor's House is different again, with a Neoclassical yellow-stuccoed facade. The square also boasts Palle Pernevi's splintered *Icarus* fountain, which depicts the unfortunate Greek soul falling from heaven into what looks like a scaffolded building site. The town's streets are peppered with modern **sculptures**; one of the best is Axel Olsson's bronze *Romeo & Julia* at Östra Storgatan 3, close to Storatorg, depicting an accordion player serenading a woman emerging from an open window.

Behind the old bank is the **Regionmuséet** (Regional museum; June–Aug daily 11am–5pm; Sept–May Tues–Sun noon–5pm; free; ⓦwww.regionmuseet.m.se). Construction of the building was started by Christian in 1616; he intended to make it a grand palace, but, thanks to the bloody Skåne wars, work got no further than the low buildings. As soon as they were built, the stables here were turned into an arsenal containing ammunition for the pro-Danish partisans. Today, the museum is home to permanent exhibitions about the town's military and industrial past. There's also an **art gallery** showing good contemporary exhibitions. Walking back through the town centre, a few minutes east of the Stora torg is the **Film Museum**, Östra Storgatan 53 (late June to mid-Aug Tues–Sat 1–4pm; rest of the year Sun noon–5pm; free), with a bronze model of an early twentieth-century movie camera standing outside its door. This was Sweden's oldest film studio, though little is made of the fact that it closed down within eighteen months of opening in 1909. In order to compete with the other film companies, Svenska Biografteatern, which became the more famous Svensk Filmindustri, had to move to Stockholm in 1911. Fun black-and-white films from the museum's extensive collection are shown in the newly renovated cinema on site.

Wander down any of the roads to the right and you'll reach **Tivoliparken**, known locally as the "English Park", with avenues of horse-chestnut and copper beech trees. In its centre is a fine Art Nouveau **theatre**, a stylish white building whose designer, Axel Anderberg, also designed the Stockholm Opera. Just beyond here, on the lakeshore, boats leave for two-hour tours (May–Aug daily 11am, 2pm & 6pm; 100kr; Ⓦ www.flodbaten.se) of the nearby marshes and wetlands, a UNESCO World Heritage site known as **Vattenriket** and renowned for its rich vegetation as well as extensive bird and marine life. Weekday departures must be booked in advance through the tourist office or the website.

Eating, drinking and nightlife

Eating in Kristianstad throws up several opportunities, though the prettiest café, *Fornstugan* (see below) is only open during the short summer season. Otherwise, there's a fair range of restaurants clustered around the central square.

Banken Östra Storgatan 27 ☏044/10 20 23. In the old Riksbanken building, this is one of the most popular of the town's restaurant-cum-bars. The simpler pub menu features staples such as lasagne, chilli con carne and burgers (99–135kr), whereas the more upmarket restaurant menu has more substantial mains like pork fillet or venison (130–225kr). There's 20 percent off all food Mon–Wed 5–7pm.

Den Lilla Tavernan Nya Boulevarden 6B ☏044/21 63 04. The city's only Greek restaurant with a classic blue-and-white interior, serving a wide range of main courses such as calamari (72kr), moussaka (109kr) and wicked tiropitaki cheese pastries (52kr).

Duvander Hesslegatan 6. A classic and central *konditori* with high ceilings and ornate cornices which has been serving cakes and meringues since 1934. Also has pasta salads, sandwiches and soup.

Fornstugan Tivoli Park. An atmospheric and elaborately carved Hansel-and-Gretel lodge in the middle of the park which is Kristianstad's most pleasant outdoor café. Serves waffles, coffee and cakes (June–Aug daily 10am–5pm, stays open later if there are park concerts).

Kippers Källare Östra Storgatan 9 ☏044/10 62 00. An atmospheric choice in a building that dates from 1615 and was once regularly frequented by Danish King Christian IV. The rustic dining area is located in the original vaulted cellar and is beautifully lit. They specialize in well-prepared steaks, game and poultry dishes; dinner costs about 185-265kr.

Modesto Västra Storgatan 54 ☏044/12 06 30. A great modern bistro with plain white walls ablaze with modern art serving fantastic tapas with a Swedish edge including meatballs, grilled char and garlic mushrooms (70–80kr). Also more substantial meat dishes, like rack of lamb, for 130–325kr. Closed Sun.

Bars and entertainment

For loud rock **music**, try *Harry's Bar*, Östra Storgatan 9 (not belonging to the chain *Harry's*), with a thirty-something crowd and a very popular beer garden. The largest selection of beers in town is to be found at the attractive *Hesslegatans kök och bar*, at Hesslegatan 1A, whose interior is hung with black lanterns and features motifs of horsemen with their mounts. Another decent place for a late-night drink is *Kong Christian*, Tivoligatan 12, a rather unusually named Irish theme bar.

The town hosts two annual festivals: **Kristianstadsdagarna** is a huge seven-day cultural festival in the second week of July, and the annual **Kristianstad and Åhus Jazz Festival** (Ⓦwww.bluebird.m.se) is spread between the two neighbouring towns throughout June and October; details of both can be obtained at the tourist office.

Into Blekinge: Karlskrona

The province of **Blekinge** is something of a poor relation to Skåne in terms of tourism. Tourist offices here put out an endless stream of glossy brochures touting the region's attractions, but in truth, even Swedes themselves admit Blekinge remains the forgotten corner of the south. The landscape is much the same as in northeastern Skåne: forests and hills, with grassland fringing the sea. The only real place of interest is the handsome town of **Karlskrona**, the provincial capital, which merits, say, a day or so of your time.

Karlskrona and around

KARLSKRONA really is something special. Set on the largest link in a chain of breezy islands, this fine example of Baroque exuberance, founded by Karl XI in 1680, is unique in southern Sweden. No sooner had the base for the Swedish Baltic fleet been chosen (the seas here are ice-free in winter), than architects from across the country were dispatched to draw up plans for the town's grid of wide avenues and grand buildings. These were to provide the classical purity and

KARLSKRONA

EATING & DRINKING

Café Tre G	1
Fox and Anchor	E
Kofferdins Packhus	A
Michelangelo	4
Montmatre	2
Nivå	3
Nya Skafferiet	5
Systrarna Lindkvists Café	7
Två Rum Och Kök	6

ACCOMMODATION

Aston	D
Clarion Collection Carlscrona	A
First Camp Dragsö	B
First Ja	F
First Statt	E
Siesta	G
STF Vandrarhem Karlskrona	C

0   200 m

Baroque splendour commensurate with a town destined to become Sweden's second city. Built to accommodate the king's naval parades, Karlskrona's original layout has survived intact, a fact which has earned it a place on UNESCO's World Heritage list, despite the anonymous blocks plonked between the town's splendid churches. Today, cadets in uniform still career around its streets, many of which are named after Swedish admirals and battleships; the town's biggest museum is, unsurprisingly, dedicated to maritime history (see p.215).

Don't despair, though, if you're not a fan of things naval, for Karlskrona has plenty more to offer: a picturesque **old quarter**, around the once-busy fishing port at Fisktorget; and good **swimming** off the nearby island of Dragsö (see p.217). If you're around during the first week of August, you'll witness the whole town come alive for a huge **sailing festival** with boats lining the harbour and a party atmosphere with a fair, live music, food stalls and entertainment late into the evening from Friday to Sunday.

Arrival and information

The **train** and **bus stations** are opposite each other, 200m north of Hoglands Park. From either station, the **tourist office**, at Stortorget 2, just behind Frederikskyrkan (June–Aug daily 9am–8pm; Sept–May Mon–Fri 9am–6pm, Sat 10am–4pm; ☏0455/30 34 90, ⓦwww.karlskrona.se/tourism), is an ten-minute stroll away: head south up Landbrogatan, with the park on your left, then proceed along Rådhusgatan to the main square, Stortorget. There's internet access here, too. For **bike rental**, head for Sportkompagniet at Hantverkaregatan 9 (☏0455/147 60).

Accommodation

The sailing festival notwithstanding, Karlskrona and Blekinge don't see hordes of tourists, even during the summer months, hence, there's little need to reserve a bed in advance.

Aston Landbrogatan 1 ☏0455/194 70, ⓦwww.hotellaston.se. This simple but comfortable place has been recently renovated. Rooms are rather small but pleasingly decorated in maritime style with wall pictures of lighthouses and the sea. ④/③

Clarion Collection Carlscrona Skeppsbrokajen ☏0455/36 15 00, ⓦwww.choice.se. A pleasant hotel close to the station in a contemporary glass-fronted building. Rooms are well appointed but it can get very noisy during the sailing festival. The weekend and summer prices are exceptionally good value. ⑥/③

First Camp Dragsö Dragsövägen, Dragsö island ☏0455/153 54, ⓦwww.firstcamp.se. A pleasant waterside campsite that's about around 2.5km from the centre of town. Catch bus #7 from the bus station to Saltö, the island before Dragsö, from where it's a 1km walk across the bridge. Also has cabins for rent (②).

First Ja Borgmästaregatan 13 ☏0455/555 60, ⓦwww.firsthotels.se. Bizarrely built over a shopping mall with modern, agreeable rooms, though some are rather cramped and curiously shaped with odd corners and low ceilings. The

likeable decor is maritime inspired with plenty of blues and whites and ships' bells. Free coffee and biscuits are available. ⑥/④

First Statt Ronnebygatan 37 ☏0455/555 50, ⓦwww.firsthotels.se. The Empire-style design rooms in this 1890 building on the main shopping street are aimed at the luxury end of the market. Fantastic reductions for weekend and summer stays which make this hotel a real bargain. ⑥/③

Siesta Borgmästaregatan 5 ☏0455/801 80, ⓦwww.hotellsiesta.com. Just off Stortorget, this really quite agreeable little hotel has just renovated all its rooms. Standards have gone up and rooms are now decorated in contemporary colours and designs and represent good value for money. ④/③

STF Vandrarhem Karlskrona Drottninggatan 39 and Bredgatan 16 ☏0455/100 20. Two central locations – though only the Drottninggatan hostel is open all year. Bredgatan operates June–Aug only; check-in and reception is at Drottninggatan. Dorm beds here are 230kr, en-suite double rooms ①. The Drottninggatan hostel has shared facilities but is accordingly cheaper with dorm beds 190kr; double room ①.

The Town

The centre of Karlskrona today occupies the island of **Trossö**, connected to the mainland by the main road, Österleden (the E22). Climb uphill past Hoglands Park, named after an eighteenth-century battle between the Swedish and Russian navies (Hogland is an island in the Gulf of Finland), to the main square, **Stortorget**, at the highest point and geographical centre of the island. It's a vast and beautiful space, dominated by two complementary **churches**; both were designed by Tessin the Younger and are stuccoed in burnt orange with dove-grey stone colonnades.

▲ Fredrikskyrkan, Karlskrona

The more interesting of the churches is the circular, domed **Trefaldighet-skyrkan** (Mon–Fri 11am–3pm, Sat 9.30am–2pm; guided tours can be requested here). Built for the town's German merchant community in 1709, its most remarkable feature is its domed ceiling, painted with hundreds of rosettes. The altar is also distinctive, with golden angelic faces peering out of a gilded meringue of clouds. In the crypt are the remains of two of Karlskrona's most revered men, Count Hans Wachtmeister, responsible for much of the building of the town in the late seventeenth century; and Johan Törnström, the Admiralty sculptor, who made most of the fabulous ship figureheads on show at the Maritime Museum (see below). **Fredrikskyrkan**, a few steps away, is an elegant, light-flooded church with towers, but holds fewer surprises inside (Mon–Fri 11am–3pm, Sat 9.30am–2pm). Housed in the former water town beside the square at Drottninggatan 28, the new **Museum Lionardo da Vinci Ideale** (℡0455/255 73, ⓦwww.museumldv.com) is definitely worth a look. It contains a mesmerising painting of da Vinci by van Gogh along with other elements of the art collection of Bosnia's Kulenovic family, never before exhibited, which stretches over 500 years from the Renaissance period to the present day. Annoyingly, admission can only be arranged by telephoning or emailing in advance.

The Admiralty Church

From Stortorget, head between the churches and walk past the pseudo-medieval castellated waterworks down Södra Kungsgatan. The wide, cobbled street is divided down the centre by the boulder-like stone walls of a tunnel, where a train line (disused) once ran from the main station up to the harbour. The leafy square ahead is **Amiralitetstorget**; perched at its centre is the huge, apricot-and-grey-painted wooden bell tower of the Admiralty Church. To see the church itself (signposted "Kungliga Amiralitetskyrkan"), head down Vallgatan on the left of the square, passing the symmetrical austerity of the Marine Officers' School; just before you reach the harbour, the beautifully proportioned, entirely wooden **Admiralty Church** is up on the right. This simple elegant structure, Sweden's biggest wooden church, was built in 1685.

Outside the entrance, take a look at one of the city's best-known landmarks: the wooden statue of **Rosenbom**, around which hangs a sorrowful tale. Mats Rosenbom, one of the first settlers on Trossö island, lived nearby with his family and earned his keep in the shipyard. However, after a fever killed six of his children and left him and his wife too ill to work, he applied for, and was granted, a beggar's licence. One New Year's Eve, while begging at the homes of leading townspeople, he became somewhat drunk from the festive wine on offer and forgot to raise his hat to thank the wealthy German figurehead carver, Fritz Kolbe. When admonished for this, Rosenbom retorted, "If you want thanks for your crumbs to the poor, you can take my hat off yourself!" Enraged, Kolbe struck him between the eyes and sent him away, but the beggar, unable to make it home, froze stiff and died in a snowdrift by the church. Next morning, Kolbe found the beggar frozen to death and, filled with remorse, carved a figure of Rosenbom which stands at the spot where he died. It's designed so that you have to raise his hat yourself to give some money.

Stumholmen: The Marinmuseum

The best museum Karlskrona has is set on the island of **Stumholmen**, connected to the mainland by road and just five-minutes' walk east of Stortorget, down Kyrkogatan. As soon as you cross the bridge onto

Stumholmen, there's a large sign indicating all the buildings of interest here. To the left, the prizewinning **Marinmuseum** (Maritime Museum; June–Aug daily 10am–6pm; Sept–May Tues–Sun 11am–5pm; free; ⓦ www.marinmuseum .se) has a facade like a futuristic Greek temple. A portrait of Carl XI, who had the navy moved from Stockholm to Karlskrona in 1680, features in the hallway, a pet lion at his feet gazing up at the king's most unappealing, bloated face. Down a spiral staircase from here is a transparent underwater tunnel offering a view of hundreds of fish in the murky depths. The best room, though, contains the **figureheads** designed and made by the royal sculptor to the navy, Johan Törnström. King Gustav III declared that ships of the line should be named after manly virtues, and so have male figureheads, while frigates have female ones. Among the finest is one made for the ship *Försiktigheten* (*Prudence*; 1784) – a metre-long foot, perfectly proportioned complete with toenails. There's a pleasant, though unambitious, **café** here too, serving light meals for around 100kr.

The harbour and Fisktorget

From the waterside, at the end of Amiralitetstorget, the divide between the picturesque town and the continuing military presence is most apparent: to the left are the old white lighthouse and the archipelago, and the pink-and-white-stuccoed county governor's residence (Länsresidens); to the right, however, mud-coloured military vessels fill the old quayside, and "Forbidden to Enter" signs abound. For more of a feel of old Karlskrona, wander west past the military hardware towards the **Björkholmen** area. Here, a couple of early eighteenth-century wooden houses survive, homes that the first craftsmen at the then new naval yard built for themselves. All the streets running from north to south are named after types of ships, while those from west to east are named after admirals. Nearby **Fisktorget**, once the site of a fish market, is pleasant for a stroll. Nowadays the boats here are mainly pleasure yachts, and there are a couple of pleasant cafés. You'll also find the dull **Blekingemuseum** at the harbourfront (June–Aug daily 10am–6pm, rest of the year Tues–Sun 11am–5pm, Wed until 7pm; free), housed in the 1705 wooden home built for Count Wachtmeister – the pleasant summer-time café is more appealing than the exhibits on shipbuilding and the like. Just behind the museum and a few steps inland at Borgmästaregatan 17, housed in the town's striking former cinema, the new **Konsthall** (Tues–Sun noon–5pm, Wed until 7pm; free; ⓦ www.karlskrona.se/konsthall) is the place to look for temporary exhibitions of modern art as well as occasional dance and music productions.

Eating and drinking

Karlskrona is surprisingly poor for good restaurants – most proper eating places are along Ronnebygatan – and, even more strangely given its location, has almost nothing in the way of decent fish places. A couple of the town's **cafés** stand out from the rest.

Café Tre G Landbrogatan 9, opposite Hoglands Park. With black-and-white photographs hung on the walls, this stylish café does a good range of baked potatoes and pasta salads as well as cakes and sandwiches. The city's only café open on a Sun.

Fox and Anchor Norra Smedjegatan 1, ☎ 0455/229 10. British-style drinking den serving real pub grub: burgers (115kr), fish & chips (89kr) and steaks (89–225kr). Also has a large selection of whiskies and beers.

Kofferdins Packhus Skeppsbrokajen ☎ 0455/36 15 41. A gourmet restaurant attached to the *Clarion Collection Carlscrona* hotel serving a mouthwatering selection of perfectly cooked modern Swedish food such as whitefish roe on thickly sliced potato wedges (134kr), a succulent pork fillet, rolled and stuffed with chorizo and a deliciously creamy salmon and seafood soup. Mains are around 187kr.

Michelangelo Ronnebygatan 29 ☎0455/121 95. With copies of Renaissance paintings on the rough brick walls, the scene is set for an elegant dinner at this smart Italian restaurant with a good choice of fine cuisine: meat and fish dishes, such as grilled pork with fig compote, are 165–199kr, though there's also pasta for 139kr and fondues at 239kr.

Montmartre Ronnebygatan 18 ☎0455/31 18 33. With rough brick walls and velvet drapes, this candlelit bistro is the cosiest of all the Italian places in town. The menu contains all your favourite Italian dishes, plus huge pizzas for 64–79kr, pasta at 79kr and meat mains like steak marinated in garlic at 129–189kr.

🎿 **Nivå** Stortorget ☎0455/103 71. Semi-circular glass-fronted steakhouse perfectly situated on the edge of the main square with great views of the Baroque splendour all around. Burgers from 115kr, steaks from 140kr though there's also a couple of fish dishes, for

example, grilled tuna or baked halibut, for around 200kr.

Nya Skafferiet Rådhusgatan 9 ☎0455/171 78. A really good deli and café combined. Here, you can buy luscious air-dried hams, meats, cheeses and exotic pickles for picnics as well as filled baguettes, freshly baked croissants, great coffees and the best hot chocolate in town.

Systrarna Lindkvists Café Borgmästaregatan 3, across from the tourist office. Coffee is served in fine old gilded china cups, with silver teaspoons and sugar tongs, at this rather genteel establishment that's all wood-panelling and elderly ladies talking in hushed tones.

Två Rum Och Kök Södra Smedjegatan 3 ☎0455/104 22. As the Swedish name implies, a romantic little place featuring two rooms and one kitchen. The whole place is decked out with models of fishing boats, fishing nets and yet more maritime paintings on the walls: one room is for à la carte dining with meat and fish dishes, including reindeer fillet with chanterelle mushrooms (at a pricey 199–265kr plus), while the other is the fondue room – red wine, garlic, TexMex, French herb as well as the popular Asian (198kr).

Dragsö

Karlskrona is surrounded by a plethora of small islands whose simple pleasures revolve around soaking up the summer sun on the smooth rocks which pass as beaches here or taking a dip in the surprisingly warm waters of the southern Baltic. The easiest island to reach, **Dragsö,** is barely five minutes northwest of the town centre by ferry from Fisketorget (June to late Aug 4 daily) aboard *M/S Gåsefjärden*. This tiny island is predominantly one long beach which is very popular at weekends with locals. For something to eat there's a simple restaurant and café at the harbour, *Dragsövikens Restaurang*, whose menu consists of light snacks and sandwiches. If you don't want to take the ferry to Dragsö, it's also possible to **walk** here in about thirty minutes. From Fisketorget head west along the harbourside, taking Björkholmsvägen across the neighbouring Saltö, then follow Strandvägen along the coast northwards towards Dragsöviken, the sound between Saltö and Dragsö, before turning left into Dragsövägen which will lead you onto the island itself; this route is clearly shown in the Karlskrona guide available from the tourist office.

Travel details

Trains

In addition to the services below, hourly trains operate up and down the west coast between Gothenburg and Malmö calling at all main towns; many continue over the bridge to Copenhagen.

Karlskrona to: Gothenburg (2 daily; 4hr); Kristianstad (hourly; 1hr 30min); Malmö (hourly; 3hr).

Kristianstad to: Karlskrona (hourly; 1hr 30min); Malmö (hourly; 1hr 15min).

Malmö to: Ystad (hourly; 50min).

Ystad to: Malmö (hourly; 50min).

International trains

Gothenburg to: Copenhagen via Kastrup airport (hourly; 4hr).

Karlskrona to: Copenhagen via Kastrup airport (hourly; 3hr 40min).

Kristianstad to: Copenhagen via Kastrup airport (hourly; 2hr).

Malmö to: Berlin (1 daily; 8hr 30min); Copenhagen via Kastrup airport (every 20min; 35min); Narvik (1 weekly; 28hr).

Buses

Båstad to: Torekov (6 daily; 30min).
Malmö to: Skanör (6 daily; 50min).

International ferries

Helsingborg to: Helsingør, Denmark (every 20min; 25min).

Karlskrona to: Gdynia, Poland (2 daily; 10hr 30min).

Trelleborg to: Rostock, Germany (3 daily; 5hr 45min); Sassnitz, Germany (5 daily; 4hr)

Varberg to: Grenå, Denmark (2 daily; 4hr).

Ystad to: Rønne, Bornholm (2–3 daily; 1hr 25min); Swinoujscie, Poland (2 daily; 6hr 30min–9hr).

The southeast

CHAPTER 4 # Highlights

✳ **Kalmar Slott** Visit the exquisite interior of this sensational, twelfth-century castle that has been beautifully remodelled into a Renaissance Palace. See p.224

✳ **Kullzénska Caféet, Kalmar** Tuck in to scrumptious cakes amid the wonderful faded gentility of this eighteenth-century home. See p.227

✳ **House of Emigrants, Växjö** The exhibition of the poignant stories of millions of Swedes forced to emigrate to the United States in the nineteenth century is an essential stop on any visit to Småland. See p.234

✳ **Vadstena** This atmospheric town on the eastern shores of Lake Vättern is home to the massive abbey founded by Sweden's first female saint, Birgitta. See p.243

✳ **Nyköping** Visit the thirteenth-century capital in this great provincial town before taking a cruise out into the stunning archipelago offshore. See p.255

✳ **Visby, Gotland** Visit the remarkable walled city of the former Hanseatic League stronghold and take in the party along with the thousands of young Swedes who visit this superb Baltic island every summer. See p.259

✳ **Sjaustrehammaren beach, Gotland** Get back to nature on this unspoilt sandy beach near Ljugarn, backed by pine forest and open flower meadows. See p.267

▲ Stortorget, Kalmar

4

The southeast

Although a less obvious target than the coastal cities and resorts of the southwest, Sweden's **southeast** certainly repays a visit. Inland, the provinces of Sörmland (also known as Södermanland), Östergötland and Småland boast impressive castles, ancient lakeside sites and numerous glassworks amid the forests of the so-called "Glass Kingdom", while off the east coast, Sweden's largest Baltic islands offer beautifully preserved medieval towns and fairytale landscapes. Train transport, especially between the towns close to the eastern shore of Lake Vättern and Stockholm, is good; speedy, regular services mean that you could see some places on a day-trip from Stockholm.

Småland, in particular, encompasses a varied geography and some stridently different towns. **Kalmar** is a very likeable stop; a glorious historic fortress town, it deserves more time than its tag as a jumping-off point for the island of Öland suggests. Inland, great swathes of dense forest are rescued from monotony by the many **glass factories** that continue the county's traditional industry, famous the world over for its design and quality, though today drowning in its own marketing hyperbole. In **Växjö**, the largest town in the southeast, two superb museums deal with the art of glass-making and the history of Swedish emigration: agricultural reforms that denied peasants access to common land, combined with a series of bad harvests, led to more than a million Swedes – a sixth of the population – emigrating to America between 1860 and 1930. At the northern edge of the province and perched on the southernmost tip of Lake Vättern, **Jönköping** is known as Sweden's Jerusalem for its remarkable number of Free Churches; it's also a great base for exploring the beautiful eastern shore of Vättern.

The idyllic pastoral landscape of **Östergötland** borders the eastern shores of the lake and reaches as far east as the Baltic. One of its highlights, and popular with domestic tourists, is the small lakeside town of **Vadstena**, its medieval streets dwarfed by austere monastic edifices, a Renaissance palace and an imposing abbey, brought into being by the zealous determination of Sweden's first female saint, Birgitta. To the northeast, the delightful coastal town of **Nyköping**, which is barely a stone's throw from one of Ryanair's main bases, Skavsta airport, rewards visitors handsomely with its laid-back seaside atmosphere and impressive castle.

Just off the southeast coast lie Sweden's two largest islands, Öland and Gotland: adjacent slithers of land with unusually temperate climates for their latitudes. They were domestic tourist havens for years, but now an increasing number of foreigners are discovering their charms – lots of summer sun, delectable beaches and some impressive historic (and prehistoric) sights. **Öland** – the smaller island

THE SOUTHEAST

and closer to the mainland – has a mix of shady forests and flowering meadows that make it a tranquil spot for a few days' exploration. **Gotland**'s well-known highlight is its Hanseatic medieval capital, **Visby**, a city pervaded by a carnival atmosphere in summer when ferry-loads of young Swedes come to sunbathe and party. The rest of the island, however, is little visited by tourists, and all the more magical for that.

Kalmar

Delightful, breezy **KALMAR**, set on a huddle of islands at the southeastern edge of Småland province, has treasures enough to make it one of southern Sweden's most delightful towns. Chief among its highlights are the **Länsmuseum**, home to an exhibition on the sunken warship, the *Kronan*, and an exquisite fourteenth-century **castle**, Scandinavia's finest preserved Renaissance palace. The town is also perfectly sited for reaching the Baltic island of Öland (see p.227), which is just 6km away across the connecting bridge.

Arrival and information

Kalmar's **train station** is on Stationsgatan, at the southern end of the new town on the island of Kvarnholmen. The **bus terminal**, used by Öland buses, is a few steps to the west. Within spitting distance of both stations is the **tourist office**, Ölandskajen 9 (May, June & Sept Mon–Fri 9am–5pm, Sat 10am–1pm; July to mid-Aug Mon–Fri 9am–9pm, Sat & Sun 10am–5pm; Oct–April Mon–Fri 9am–5pm; ☎0480/41 77 00, ⒲www.kalmar.se/turism). They stock an English booklet, with maps, for a worthy **self-guided tour** around the town (30kr) and also have internet access.

Kalmar can be explored easily enough on foot but if you wish to strike out into the surrounding countryside you can rent a **bike** from Team Sportia, Södravägen 2 (☎0480/212 44; 100kr a day).

Accommodation

Kalmar has several really attractive central **hotels** with good summer discounts, though there's little to choose from in terms of price. Undoubtedly, the Baroque splendour of the main square is the location of choice.

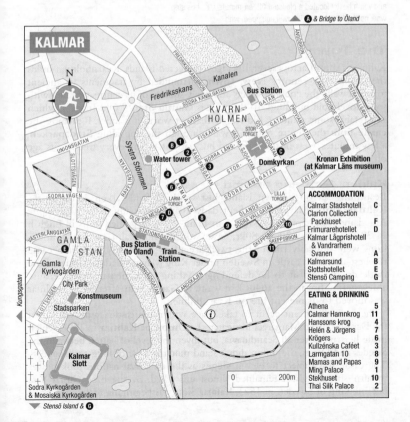

KALMAR

▲ Ⓐ & Bridge to Öland

Kanalen

Fredriksskans

Bus Station

KVARN-HOLMEN

Water tower

Domkyrkan

Kronan Exhibition
(at Kalmar Läns museum)

GAMLA STAN

Bus Station (to Öland) **Train Station**

Gamla Kyrkogården

City Park

Konstmuseum

Stadsparken

Ⓘ

Kalmar Slott

Södra Kyrkogården & Mosaiska Kyrkogården

▼ Stensö Island & Ⓖ

ACCOMMODATION

Calmar Stadshotell	C
Clarion Collection Packhuset	F
Frimurarehotellet	D
Kalmar Lågprishotell & Vandrarhem Svanen	A
Kalmarsund	B
Slottshotellet	E
Stensö Camping	G

EATING & DRINKING

Athena	5
Calmar Hamnkrog	11
Hanssons krog	4
Helén & Jörgens	7
Krögers	6
Kullzénska Caféet	3
Larmgatan 10	8
Mamas and Papas	9
Ming Palace	1
Stekhuset	10
Thai Silk Palace	2

0   200m

Calmar Stadshotell Stortorget 14 ℡ 0480/49 69 00, ⓦ www.profilhotels.se. Dating from 1906, this lovely old building with a stuccoed facade in Art Nouveau style is a tasteful mix of old and new, though sadly many rooms have cheap carpets and unstylish furnishings, detracting from the elegance of the public areas. ❺/❹

Clarion Collection Packhuset Skeppsbrogatan 26 ℡ 0480/570 00, ⓦ www.hotelpackhuset.se. Housed in a former waterfront storehouse, the wooden beams of this rambling old building add to the cosiness of the compact modern rooms, many of which have views out over the harbour. There's an evening buffet included in the rates. ❺/❸

Frimurarehotellet Larmtorget 2 ℡ 0480/152 30, ⓦ www.frimurarehotellet.com. Rather grand hotel, set in a castle-like building from 1878 owned by the Freemasons (hence the name: *frimurare* is Swedish for "freemason") and offering sumptuous rooms with period furniture. ❺/❹

Kalmar Lågprishotell & Vandrarhem Svanen Rappegatan 1, Ängö island ℡ 0480/129 28, ⓦ www.hotellsvanen.se. A combined budget hotel and youth hostel located a pleasant fifteen-minute walk north of the centre; it's well equipped, with laundry facilities and a shop for basic provisions. The youth hostel has dorm beds (195kr) and simple double rooms (❷). In the hotel section, all rooms have a toilet, though it's another 100kr for one with a private shower. ❷

Kalmarsund Fiskaregatan 5 ℡ 0480/48 03 80, ⓦ www.kalmarsundhotel.se. Part of the Best Western chain and a bit lacking in elegance, but with friendly, efficient service, comfortable en-suite rooms and an altogether contemporary feel. There's a sauna and roof garden too. ❻/❹

Slottshotellet Slottsvägen 7 ℡ 0480/882 60, ⓦ www.slottshotellet.se. The prettiest, most regal and the priciest of Kalmar's hotels, overlooking the castle across the bridge. The authentic interior is extremely tasteful, with a charming conservatory area and a sauna and solarium for use by guests. ❻/❺

Stensö Camping Stensövägen, Stensö island ℡ 0480/888 03, ⓦ www.stensocamping.se. As well as camping, there are cabins here for rent (❶). The site is 3km from the centre; bus #401 heads out this way but it's 1.5km to walk from the closest bus stop.

The Town

Kalmar is spread across several bridge-connected islands. Kvarnholmen holds the seventeenth-century **New Town**; surrounded by fragments of ancient fortified walls, the cobbled streets and lively squares of its centre are lined with some lovely old buildings. To the west is **Gamla Stan** ("Old Town"), which still retains some winding old streets that are worth a wander. Reaching the **castle** from the centre entails a walk through the appealing **Stadsparken**, a few minutes' west of the train and bus stations, where every tree has its age on a plaque.

Kalmar Slott and around

Beautifully set on its own island, just south of Stadsparken, is the castle, **Kalmar Slott** (May, June & Sept daily 10am–4pm; July daily 10am–6pm; Aug daily 10am–5pm; Oct Sat & Sun 11am–3.30pm; guided tours in English 11.30am, 1.30 & 2.30pm; 80kr; ⓦ www.kalmarslott.kalmar.se). Its foundations were probably laid in the twelfth century; a century later, it became the best-defended castle in Sweden under King Magnus Ladulås. Today, if the castle doesn't appear to be defending anything in particular, that's because a devastating fire in the 1640s laid waste to Gamla Stan, after which Kalmar was moved to its present site on Kvarnholmen.

The most significant event to take place within the castle's walls was when the Danish Queen Margareta instigated the **Union of Kalmar** in 1397, which made her ruler over all Scandinavia, but given the level of hatred between the Swedes and Danes, the union didn't stand much chance of long-term success. The castle was subject to eleven **sieges** as the two rival nations took power in turn; surprisingly, it remained almost unscathed. By the time Gustav Vasa became king of Sweden in 1523, Kalmar Slott was beginning to show signs of wear and tear, and so the king set about rebuilding it, while his sons, who later became Eric XIV and Johan III, took care of decorating the interior. The result, a fine Renaissance palace, is still preserved in fantastic detail today.

Unlike many other southern Swedish castles, this one is straight out of a storybook, boasting turrets, ramparts, a moat and drawbridge and a dungeon. The fully furnished interior – reached by crossing an authentically reconstructed wooden **drawbridge** and going through a stone-arched tunnel beneath the grassy ramparts – is great fun for a wander. Among the many highlights is King Johan's bedroom, known as the **Grey Hall**. His bed, which was stolen from Denmark, is decorated with carved faces on the posts, but all their noses have been chopped off – he believed that the nose contained the soul and didn't want the avenging souls of the rightful owners coming to haunt him. The **King's Chamber** (King Eric's bedroom) is the most visually exciting – the wall frieze is a riot of vividly painted animals and shows a wild boar attacking Eric and another man saving him. Eric apparently suffered from paranoia, believing his younger brother Johan wanted to kill him. To this end, he had a secret door, which you can see cut into the extravagantly inlaid wall panels, with escape routes to the roof in the event of fraternal attack. Eric's suspicions may have been justified – Johan is widely believed to have poisoned him with arsenic in 1569.

The adjoining **Golden Room** with its magnificent ceiling should have been Johan's bedroom, but sibling hatred meant he didn't sleep here while Eric lived. There are a couple of huge and intriguing portraits: though Gustav Vasa was already of an advanced age when his was painted, he appears young-looking, with unseemly muscular legs. The royal artist had been ordered to seek out the soldier with the best legs and paint those, before attempting a sympathetic portrayal of Vasa's face. The portrait next to his is of Queen Margareta, her ghostly white countenance achieved in real life through the daily application of lead and arsenic. Isolated on another wall is King Eric's portrait, hung much higher up than the others: his family believed that the mental illness from which he supposedly suffered could be caught by looking into his eyes – even images of them.

The tour guides will tell you that the castle is rattling with ghosts, but for more tangible evidence of life during the Vasa period, the kitchen fireplace is good enough; it was built to accommodate the simultaneous roasting of three cows. There's a splendidly minimalist **café** just inside the walls, dominated by a wonderfully evocative oil painting of a moody chamber interior.

Having left the castle, wandering back towards the town centre along Slottsvägen will bring you to Kalmar's grotesque new **Konstmuseum** (Art Museum; daily 11am–5pm, plus Thurs till 8pm; 40kr; Ⓦwww.kalmarkonstmuseum.se), a monstrous cube of a building dressed in black wooden panels plonked unceremoniously in the middle of Slottsparken, where there's an emphasis on Abstract Expressionist work painted by Swedish artists in the 1940s and 1950s. The museum's collection contains several nineteenth- and twentieth-century Swedish nude and landscape paintings, including some fine works by Anders Zorn and Carl Larsson, though exhibitions change regularly. In addition, there are often temporary displays of contemporary art.

Gamla Stan

For a feel of Kalmar's quaint **Gamla Stan**, it's best to head into the small warren of cobbled lanes west of *Slottshotellet*, which overlooks Stadsparken and is only a minute's walk along Slottsvägen from the Konstmuseum. The old wooden cottages, painted egg-yolk yellow and wisteria blue, are at their prettiest on Gamla Kungsgatan and Västerlångatan. These little streets surround the attractive **Gamla kyrkogården** (old churchyard), where the seventeenth- and eighteenth-century gravestones have recently been restored.

The Domkyrkan

The elegantly gridded Renaissance New Town is laid out around the grand **Domkyrkan** in Stortorget (daily 9am–6pm); to get here from the Old Town, head back east along Södra vägen across the river, then carry on through Larmtorget and along Storgatan. Designed in 1660 by Nicodemus Tessin the Elder (as was the nearby Rådhus) after a visit to Rome, this vast and airy church in Italian Renaissance style is today a complete misnomer: Kalmar has no bishop and the church no dome. Inside, the altar, designed by Tessin the Younger, shimmers with gold, as do the *Faith* and *Mercy* sculptures around it. The huge Deposition painting above the altar depicts in unusually graphic detail Jesus being taken down from the Cross by men on ladders, his lifeless form hoisted down with ropes. The pulpit is also worth a look; its roof is a three-tiered confection crowned with a statue of Christ surrounded by gnome-like sleeping soldiers, below which angels brandish instruments of torture, while on the "most inferior" level, a quartet of women symbolize such qualities as maternal love and erudition.

The Kronan Exhibition

From Stortorget, it's a few minutes' walk south down Östra Sjögatan and then left into Ölandsgatan to the **Kalmar läns muséet**, Kalmar's regional museum (mid-June to mid-Aug daily 10am–6pm; mid-Aug to mid-June Mon–Fri 10am–4pm, Sat & Sun 11am–4pm; 50kr). The centrepiece of the museum is the awe-inspiring **Kronan exhibition** (Ⓦ www.regalskeppetkronan.se), housed in a refurbished steam mill. Built by the seventeenth-century British designer Francis Sheldon, the royal ship *Kronan* was once one of the world's three largest vessels; it had three complete decks and was twice the size of the *Vasa*, which sank off Stockholm in 1628 (see p.80).

The *Kronan* itself went down, fully manned, in 1676, resulting in the loss of 800 of its 842 crew. Its captain, Admiral Creutz, had received a royal order to attack and recapture the Baltic island of Gotland. Pursued by the Danish, Creutz, who had remarkably little naval experience – just one week at sea – was eager to impress his king and engage in combat. To this end, he ignored pleas from his crew and ordered the *Kronan* to turn and face the enemy. A gale caused the ship to heave, and water gushed into her open gun ports, knocking over a lantern, which ignited the entire gunpowder magazine. Within seconds, an explosion ripped the mammoth vessel apart.

It wasn't until 1980 that the whereabouts of the ship's remains were detected, 26m down off the coast of Öland, using super-sensitive scanning equipment. A salvage operation began, led by the great-great-great-great-grandson of the ship's captain; the Kronan exhibition displays the resulting finds as part of an imaginative **walk-through reconstruction** of the gun decks and admiral's cabin, complete with the sound of cannon fire and screeching gulls, while the moments leading up to the disaster have been pieced together brilliantly. The ship's **treasure trove** of gold coins is displayed at the end of the exhibition, but it's the incredibly preserved **clothing** – hats, jackets, buckled leather shoes and even silk bows and cufflinks – which bring this exceptional show to life. The site is still being periodically explored and yields around one thousand items each year. The most significant in recent years was a complete box of medical equipment, found in July 2001.

Eating, drinking and nightlife

There's a good range of places **to eat** in Kalmar. The liveliest night-time area is **Larmtorget**, with restaurants, cafés and pubs serving a wide variety of food.

Athena Norra Långgatan 8 ☎0480/280 88. A bright and airy Greek restaurant with tasty traditional fare such as moussaka (95kr) or pork souvlaki (115kr), as well as various salads (68–95kr) and pasta dishes (70–100kr).

Calmar Hamnkrog Skeppsbron 30 ☎0480/41 10 20. Built right by the water on squat stilts with great views out over the harbour, this swish but pleasantly informal place offers such delights as ovenbaked pike-perch (269kr), rack of lamb (269kr) and grilled plaice (285kr) with classy sauces.

🏃 **Hanssons krog** Norra Långgatan 1 ☎0480/104 21. This great restaurant resembles the interior of a cosy farmhouse and serves exceptionally tasty modern Swedish specialities with a touch of Provence, such as lamb steak with aubergine, thyme and dauphinois potatoes. The building dates from the late 1600s and although originally an inn, it has also served as a cinema and a girls' school. Plentiful outdoor seating in summer.

🏃 **Helén & Jörgens** Olof Palmesgatan 2 ☎0480/288 30. With an interior dominated by a bizarre ceiling painting of restauranteurs Helén and Jörgen surrounded by angels, this popular place has a simple but tasty menu: schnitzel, steaks, chicken breast and several fish dishes all go for 150–200kr. There are also three-course menus from 230kr.

Krögers Larmtorget 7 ☎0480/265 50. This noisy bar-restaurant with its fake stained glass windows and model ships is one of the most popular places in town. The food isn't exactly adventurous, but neither is it too expensive: burgers for 109kr, steaks 198kr and jacket potatoes for 79kr. There's a good choice of bottled beers too.

🏃 **Kullzénska Caféet** Kaggensgatan 26. This charming *konditori* occupying the first floor of a house dating from 1771 is easily Kalmar's best café. Its eight interconnecting rooms are awash with mahogany furnishings, Indian carpets and crumbling royal portraits. There's a wide selection of sandwiches, cakes and light lunch dishes – the coffee is particularly good.

Larmgatan 10 Södra Långgatan 6 ☎0480/865 25. A very genteel place with roped-back drapes, wall paintings and window flowers and a good range of simple home-cooked dishes like pork fillet with bearnaise sauce (148kr) and chicken breast with gorgonzola sauce (148kr), as well as stir fries and pasta dishes (108–128kr).

Mamas and Papas Kaggensgatan 1 ☎0480/300 32. A hip tapas bar by the city walls serving Swedish and Spanish tapas such as tortilla, garlic chicken, meatballs and potato pancakes: reckon on 45–65kr per tapa.

Ming Palace Fiskaregatan 7 ☎0480/166 86. Kalmar's premier Chinese restaurant, with a beautiful interior featuring a fish pond full of carp and goldfish. Chicken and beef favourites go for 118kr, other mains are 148kr. A set menu of three small dishes is a very reasonable 115kr.

Stekhuset Skeppsbron 1 ☎0480/42 38 58. This is the place to come to taste locally produced Swedish meat from the farms of Småland: steaks, such as a delicious fillet steak wrapped in bacon cooked in red wine sauce, are 159–235kr. There are also a number of fish dishes on the menu such as grilled swordfish, sea bass and salmon (189–215kr).

Thai Silk Palace Fiskaregatan 8 ☎0480/281 26. Reached through the passage marked "Koppartorget" off Fiskaregatan, this ornate Thai restaurant decorated with reclining Buddhas and lots of carved wood has over a hundred Thai and Chinese dishes on its menu, and also does takeaway.

Öland

Linked to mainland Sweden by a six-kilometre-long bridge, the island of **Öland**, with its unspoilt beaches, mysterious forests, pretty meadows and wooden cottages, has been drawing Swedes in droves for over a century. Although it's a popular destination in summer and holiday traffic can clog the road from the bridge north to the main town **Borgholm**, this long, splinter-shaped island retains a very likeable old-fashioned holiday atmosphere. The bathing opportunities are among the best in Sweden, and the island's attractions include numerous

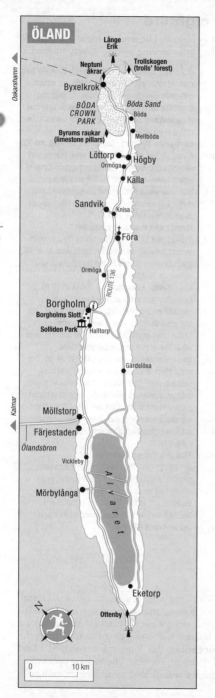

ruined castles, Bronze and Iron Age burial cairns, runic stones and forts, all set amid rich and varied fauna and flora and striking geography. Labyrinthine **walking trails** and **bicycle routes** wend their way past more than four hundred old wooden **windmills**, which give Öland a peculiarly Dutch air. The island is perfect for **camping**, and while you can pitch tent anywhere under the rules of *Allemansrätten* (see p.43), there are plenty of official sites. Almost all are open only between May and September, and are scattered the length of the island; for more details, visit Ⓦ www.camping-oland.com.

A royal hunting ground from the mid-sixteenth century until 1801, Öland was ruled with scant regard for its native population. Peasants were forbidden from chopping wood, owning dogs or weapons, and selling their produce on the open market. While protected wild animals did their worst to the farmers' fields, Kalmar's tradesmen exploited the restrictions on the islanders' trade to force them to sell at low prices. Danish attacks on Öland (and a ten-month occupation in 1612) made matters worse, with seven hundred farms being destroyed. A succession of disastrous harvests in the mid-nineteenth century was the last straw, causing a quarter of the population to pack their bags for a new life in America. In the twentieth century, mainland Sweden became the new magnet for Öland's young and, by 1970, the island's inhabitants had declined to just twenty thousand, around five thousand less than today's total.

Öland's geology varies dramatically due to the crushing movement of ice during the last Ice Age, and the effects of the subsequent melting process, which took place 10,000 years ago. To the south is a massive **limestone** plain known as **Alvaret**; indeed, limestone has been used here for thousands of years to build runic monuments, dry-stone walls and churches. The northern coastline is craggy and irregular, peppered with dramatic-looking **raukar** – stone stacks, weathered by the waves into jagged shapes. Among the island's **flora** are plants that are rare in the region, like the delicate rock rose and the cream-coloured wool-butter flower, both native to Southeast Asia and found in southern Öland. Further north are the twisted, misshapen pine sand oaks of the romantically named **Trollskogen** (trolls' forest).

Borgholm

As you walk the simple square grid of streets that makes up **Borgholm**, Öland's "capital", it becomes clear that tourism is the lifeblood of this small town. But despite being swamped by visitors each July, Borgholm is in no way the tacky resort it could be. Encircled by the flaking, turreted and verandahed villas that were the pride of the town during its first period as a holiday resort in the nineteenth century, most of the centre is a friendly, if bland, network of shops and restaurants lining the roads that lead down to the pleasant harbour.

Arrival and information

Buses terminate at Sandgatan, where you'll find Borgholm's **tourist office** (June & Aug Mon–Fri 9am–6pm, Sat 10am–4pm; July Mon–Fri 9am–6pm, Sat 9am–5pm, Sun 10am–4pm; Sept–May Mon–Fri 9am–5.30pm; ℡0485/890 00, ⓦ www.olandsturist.se), tucked away out of the hubbub at no. 25. The only place to **rent a bike** in the town is Hallbergs Hojjar, Köpmangatan 19 (℡0485/109 40).

Accommodation

It's imperative to book ahead if you're planning a visit to Öland during the June to August peak summer period, since the island is extremely popular with Swedish holidaymakers. Unlike elsewhere in Sweden, rooms prices go up in summer (the second price code listed below).

Borgholm Trädgårdsgatan 15 ℡0485/770 60, ⓦ www.hotellborgholm.com. Another central choice with smart rooms and pleasant gardens. The beautifully appointed top-floor double rooms with their wooden floors, French balconies and stone finishes are worth splashing out on. ④/⑤
Ebbas Vandrarhem Storgatan 12 ℡070/990 04 06, ⓦ www.ebbas.se. This spacious STF hostel, open May–Sept only, is right in the heart of town and boasts a delightful garden café. Dorm beds 290kr, doubles ②
Kapelludden Camping Sandgatan 27 ℡0485/56 07 70, ⓦ www.kapelludden.se. A family-oriented campsite (under 25s not allowed unless with children) that's open from late April–Sept and set on a small peninsula 5min walk from the centre. It has a number of overpriced cottages for rent (⑤).

Getting to Öland

The **bus** timetable, available from Kalmar's bus station and tourist office, is almost impossible to decipher – Ölanders mostly laugh when you refer to it. Buses #101 and #102 are safe bets, however, and run pretty well every hour from Kalmar bus station to **Borgholm**. If you don't want to go to Borgholm, ask at the bus station for the buses that stop at **Färjestaden**, the bus network hub, just by the bridge to the mainland.

Heading to Öland **by road**, take the Ängö link road to Svinö (clearly signposted), just outside Kalmar, from where the bridge takes you across onto Öland.

Strand Borgholm Villagatan 4 ☏ 0485/888 88,
ⓦ www.strandborgholm.se. Straddling one side of
the harbour and blandly styled like a modern
seaside hotel, its massive interior includes a small
shopping mall, a disco and nightclub. ④/⑤
Villa Sol Slottsgatan 30 ☏ 0485/56 25 52,
ⓦ www.villasol.nu. A central and tranquil

guesthouse located in a charming pale-yellow
house with stripped wooden floors and old
tiled fireplaces; rooms cost 200kr more
during mid-June to mid-Aug. The lush gardens
provide fresh fruit made into gorgeous jams for
breakfast. ③

④ The Town

The only real attraction in town is **Borgholms Slott**, several hundred metres
southwest of the centre (daily: April & Sept 10am–4pm; May–Aug 10am–6pm;
free). A colossal stone fortification with rows of huge arches and corridors open
to the skies, it's reached either through a nature reserve, signposted from the
town centre, or from the first exit south off Route 136. Built in the twelfth
century, the castle was fortified four hundred years later by King Johan III,
and given its present shape – with a tower at each corner – in the seventeenth
century. Regularly attacked, it eventually fell into disrepair, and when Borgholm
was founded in 1816, the castle was already a ruin.

Just a few hundred metres to the south of the castle is the present royal family's
summer residence, **Solliden Park**, an Italianate villa built in 1903 to a design
specified by the Swedish Queen Victoria (the present king's great-grandmother);
a huge, austere red-granite bust of her rises out of the trees at the entrance to
the car park. Of Austrian stock, Victoria loathed Sweden, and demanded the bust
face Italy, the country she most loved. The villa itself is not open to the public,
but the formal **gardens** can be visited (daily: mid-May to late June & mid-Aug
& Sept 10am–6pm; late June to mid-Aug 11am–6pm; gates close at 5pm; 60kr):
there's a very ordered Italian Garden, a colourful Dutch Garden and a simple
English-style one.

To see what the town looked like before the likes of the *Strand Hotel* were
built, head along Villagatan, the road to the left of the *Strand* as you face out
to sea; it's lined with classic wooden villas, their porches and eaves all fancy
fretwork. You can't drive along the street without authorization, though, as this
is the route used by the king and queen to reach their summer home.

Just to the north of the town centre is Öland's largest Bronze Age cairn,
Blå rör, a huge mound of stones excavated when a coffin was discovered in
1849. People have been turning up artefacts from time to time ever since:
in the 1920s, burnt bones, indicating a cremation site, were found, along with
bronze swords and tweezers – apparently common items in such tombs.

Eating, drinking and nightlife

There has traditionally been a pronounced summer-holiday feel to Borholm's
restaurants and bars, but in reality they're rather staid and run-of-the-mill.
Pizza places abound around Stortorget and down towards the harbour, cashing
in on the summer influx of tourists; the really good places, however, are the
long-standing, smart restaurants, which are very pricey.

Glasscafé Storgatan 10. A great place for a wide
range of home-made ice creams and sorbets, and
a pleasant eating area in the back garden with a
vine-covered verandah.
Hotel Borgholm Trädgårdsgatan 15 ☏ 0485/770 60.
This chi-chi hotel restaurant with walls covered in
modern art is the best place in town for fine
Swedish/pan-European food. A three-course set

menu featuring smoked salmon, guinea fowl and an
apricot dessert costs 565kr.
Mamma Rosa Södra Långgatan 2 ☏ 0485/129 10.
Beside the harbour, a smart pizza and pasta parlour
with a varied menu, including a decent selection of
traditional Italian meat dishes.
Pubben Storgatan 18. A cosy and extremely
popular pub run by the friendliest of owners, with

old radios and crystal sets for decor. As well as lager, stout and bitter, this popular bar specializes in whisky.

Robinson Crusoe Hamnvägen 1 ☎0485/777 58. Jutting into the harbour waters,

this restaurant-cum-bar is a fine place for a drink and the Swedish home cooking on the menu is certainly tasty, though watch what you order as the prices can be a little inflated.

Around Öland

Öland's most varied and interesting landscape is to be found towards the north, with no shortage of idyllic villages, dark woods and flowery meadows as you head up from Borgholm along the main road, **Route 136**. Though there aren't many proper hotels north of the Borgholm area, **campsites** are marked off the road every couple of kilometres; most of these high-standard sites are close to a beach. Public transport is limited to **buses** heading up Route 136 towards Byxelkrok; the road is safe for **cycling**, too, and there are plenty of tracks that lead off the main drag.

Föra to Böda Sand

At **Föra**, a village about 20km north of Borgholm, there's a good example of a typical Öland **church**, built in the medieval era (the font is the oldest part, dating from 1250). It doubled as a fortress, and was capable of accommodating a considerable garrison in times of war. A couple of kilometres north, a sign to **Knisa Mosse** leads to a peaceful nature reserve, centred on a shimmering lake, and to some Bronze Age burial mounds, though there's not much to see at the burial area itself.

Continuing north on Route 136, **Högby**, about 15km further on, has the only remaining tied church houses on the island, relics of the medieval Högby kyrka nearby; there's not a lot to see though. For a filling (though somewhat pricey) dining experience, head for the village of **Löttorp**, off Route 136, and follow the signs east for 4km down country lanes to the *Lammet & Grisen* restaurant, housed in a building like a Spanish hacienda (☎0485/203 50) at Hornvägen 35. The dishes on the menu tend to be spit-roasted lamb, pork and beef, though there is sometimes fish, too, such as grilled halibut (all mains around 365kr) – everything served with as much as you can eat from the buffet.

Continuing north and west off Route 136, following signs for Byrums Sandvik and Raukområde, you come to **Byrums raukar**, a striking sight: solitary limestone pillars formed by the eroding action of the sea, at the edge of a sandy beach. The best **beaches** are along the east coast; starting at Böda Sand, the most popular stretch is a couple of kilometres north at **Lyckesand**, with a **nudist beach** just to the north, the start of which is marked simply by a large boulder in the sea. Small lanes run east from the main road to the beaches, and there are many campsites signposted off Route 136.

At **Böda**, 50km north of Borgholm, is the large, well-equipped *Böda* STF **youth hostel**, at Mellböda (☎0485/220 38, @mikael.sten@telia.com; dorm beds 150kr, double rooms ❶; May–Sept), with a cosy kitchen and some private rooms. From the hostel, it's just 2km north to one of the island's best sandy beaches, **Böda Sand**. Take the narrow road heading east to reach the gently curving coastline of Böda bukten bay, which forms Öland's northeastern tip.

North of Böda Sand

There are some gorgeous areas of natural beauty in Öland's far north, and excellent walking to be had at the northeastern tip, threading through the twisted, gnarled, ivy-shrouded oak trees of **Trollskogen** ("trolls' forest").

The waters lapping against the rocky beaches of the north coast's western edge are of the purest blue; the **Neptuni åkrar** area here is covered with *blåelden* (viper's bugloss), lupin-like flowers whose brilliant blue rivals the sea beyond – they flower from late June to mid-July. The area's name, which was bestowed by Carl von Linné (see p.112), means "Neptune's ploughland" – the ridged land formation here looks like ploughed fields. Some 3km north of Neptuni åkrar on a tiny island at the very northern tip of Öland, **Långe Erik lighthouse** is a handsome obelisk built in 1845, and makes a good target for a walk or cycle ride.

The only town in this region is **BYXELKROK**, a quiet place with an attractive harbour that's used by **ferries** (☎0499/449 20, ⓦwww.olandsfarjan.se; mid-June to mid-Aug 2 daily; 2hr 20min) to and from Oskarshamn, on the mainland. *Solö Wärdhus* on the town's main road (☎0485/283 70, ⓦwww.wardshus.nu; ❷/❸) is a pleasant enough **guesthouse** whose prices rise in summer, whilst the best place to eat is *Sjöstugan* (☎0485/283 30; April–Aug), a restaurant and pub right by the shore. The restaurant specializes in salmon and flounder, but also serves pizzas.

Central Småland: Växjö and the Glass Kingdom

Back on the mainland, the thickly forested province of **Småland** makes up the southeastern wedge of Sweden. Although the scenery is appealing at first, the uniformity of the landscape means it's easy to become blasé about so much natural beauty. Småland is often somewhere people travel through rather than to – from Stockholm to Malmö and the south, or from Gothenburg to the Baltic coast. It does, however, have a few vital spots of interest of its own, alongside opportunities for hiking, trekking, fishing and cycling.

Historically, Småland has had it tough. The simple, rustic charm of the pretty painted cottages belies the intense misery endured by generations of local peasants: in the nineteenth century, subsistence farming failed, and the people were starving; consequently a fifth of Sweden's population left the country for America – most of them from Småland. While their plight is vividly retold at the House of Emigrants exhibition in **Växjö**, a town which makes an excellent base from which to explore the region, the province's main tourist attractions are its myriad **glass factories**. The bulk of these celebrated glassworks lie within the dense birch and pine forests that, together with a thread of lakes, make up the largely unbroken landscape between Kalmar and Växjö. Consequently, the area is dubbed **Glasriket**, or the "Glass Kingdom", with each glassworks signposted clearly from the spidery main roads.

Växjö and around

Founded by Saint Sigfrid in the eleventh century, **VÄXJÖ** (approximately pronounced "veck-shur"), 120km from Kalmar deep in the heart of Småland, is by far the handiest base hereabouts. Though its centre is fairly bland and quiet, Växjö, whose name derives from *väg sjö*, or "way to the lake", is within easy reach of some beautifully tranquil lake scenery. The town itself offers a couple of great **museums**, and once a year comes to life for the **Karl Oskar-dagar** (second weekend in Aug) – a long weekend of unbridled revelry in honour of

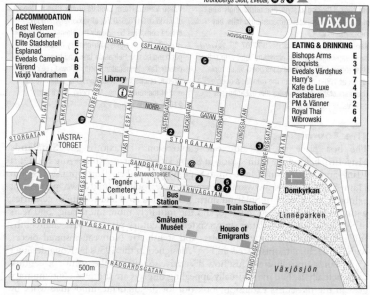

the character Karl-Oskar, created by author Wilhem Moberg, who symbolized the struggles of Småland's Swedish peasants in the nineteenth century. In reality, it means Växjö's youth drink themselves silly through the nights while daytime entertainment fills the streets.

Arrival and information

The **train** and **bus stations** are side by side in the middle of town. Växjö's **tourist office** is in the library at Västra Esplanaden 7 (June to mid-Sept Mon–Fri 9.30am–6pm, Sat 10am–3pm; mid-Sept to May Mon–Fri 9.30am–4.30pm; ☎0470/414 10, ⓦwww.turism.vaxjo.se) and also has internet access (otherwise try try *Everlast*, Sandsgärdsgatan 12). **Bikes** – useful for visiting the countryside around Växjö (see p.235) – can be rented from Smålands cykel, Västra Esplanaden 15 (☎0470/475 48).

Accommodation

Despite the fact that Växjö is a pleasant enough place, the town doesn't see mass tourism, so you should have no problem finding a room, even in the height of summer.

Best Western Royal Corner Liedbergsgatan 11 ☎0470/70 10 00, ⓦwww.royalcorner.se. Since becoming part of the Best Western chain, rooms here have been renovated and are now smart, comfortable and full of wooden panels, floors and fittings in keeping with the latest Swedish design trends. Extremely reasonable weekend and summer rates. ⑤/②

Evedals Camping Evedals Brunn ☎0470/630 34, ⓦwww.evedalscamping.com. Located beside Växjö youth hostel at Evedals Brunn. There's a decent

shop for stocking up on food, and four-person cabins for 750kr, including cooking facilities.

Elite Stadshotell Kungsgatan 6 ☎0470/134 00, ⓦwww.vaxjo.elite.se. The usual executive-class hotchpotch of shiny marble, potted palms and terrible carpets, but with a generous buffet breakfast included in the rates and an in-house English pub, the *Bishops Arms*. ⑤/③

Esplanad Norra Esplanaden 21A ☎0470/225 80, ⓦwww.hotellesplanad.com. A reasonable family-owned central hotel, whose compact rooms

233

are cosy, if lacking in style, and refreshingly free of the staid chain hotel sameness. No frills, but inexpensive. ④/❸

Värend Kungsgatan 27 ⓣ 0470/77 67 00, ⓦ www .hotellvarend.se. Another standard hotel with rather plain rooms, this one also does good-value triple rooms at 100kr more than the rate for a double. The respectable prices make this exceptionally good value for money. ❸/❷

Växjö Vandrarhem Evedals Brunn, 6km northeast of Växjö ⓣ 0470/630 70, ⓔ vaxjo.vandrarhem @telia.com. This beautifully maintained STF hostel is located in an eighteenth-century house in parkland beside Helgasjön lake and boasts its own beach. Take Linnégatan north, following signs for Evedal, or bus #1C from Växjö bus station to the end of the route (June–Aug only). Dorm beds 210kr, double rooms ❶.

The Town

The best place to kick off your exploration of Växjö is the **Smålands Museum**, behind the train station at Södra Järnvägsgatan 2 (June–Aug Mon–Fri 10am–5pm, Sat & Sun 11am–5pm; Sept–May Tues–Fri 10am–5pm, Sat & Sun 11am–5pm; 40kr; ⓦ www.smalandsmuseum.se), which holds two permanent exhibitions: a history of Småland during the nineteenth and twentieth centuries, with a section dedicated to Växjö, and the infinitely more interesting "500 Years of Swedish Glass". The latter shows sixteenth-century place settings, eighteenth- and nineteenth-century etched glass and stylish Art Nouveau-inspired pieces, with subtle floral motifs. "Trees in Fog", designed in the 1950s by Kosta designer Vicke Lindstrand, illustrates just how derivative so much of the twentieth-century work actually is. The most visually appealing displays are those of contemporary glass in the museum's extension; look out for the dramatic, innovative work by British-born glass maestro Richard Rackham.

House of Emigrants

Directly in front of Smålands Museum, in a plain building signposted "Utvandrarnas Hus", the inspired **House of Emigrants** (May–Aug Tues–Fri 9am–5pm, Sat & Sun 11am–4pm; Sept–April Tues–Fri 9am–4pm, Sat & Sun 11am–4pm; 40kr; ⓣ 0470/201 20, ⓦ www.utvandrarnashus.se) explores the intense hardship faced by the Småland peasant population in the mid-nineteenth century and their ensuing emigration.

The museum's **displays**, which include English-language translations and audio narratives, trace the lives of individual emigrants and recount the story of the industry that grew up around emigration fever. Most boats used by the emigrants left from Gothenburg and, until 1915, were British-operated sailings to Hull, from where passengers crossed to Liverpool by train to board the transatlantic ships. Conditions on board were usually dire: the steamer *Hero* left Gothenburg in 1866 with five hundred emigrants who shared their accommodation with nearly four hundred oxen and nine hundred pigs, calves and sheep. Walking through the exhibition, past models of crofters' huts in Småland and a sizeable replica of the deck of an emigrant ship, you're led on to displays on emigre life in America. One man who gets a special mention was known as Lucky Swede; he became America's most successful gold prospector in the Klondike before losing it all to his chorus-girl wife.

There's also a section on **women emigrants**, entitled "Not Just Kristina", a reference to a fictitious character in *The Emigrants*, a trilogy by one of Sweden's most celebrated writers, Wilhelm Moberg. Upon publication, it became the most-read Swedish history book in the country, and was made into a film starring Max von Sydow and Liv Ullman. On display here is Moberg's writing cabin, which was given to the museum after his death in 1973. Moberg would himself have emigrated, only his father sold a farrow of piglets to pay for his son to go to college in Sweden.

One of the saddest tales here is of Mauritz Ådahl who, like a fifth of those who left, returned to try and live again in his native land. Money pressure forced him to emigrate for a second time in 1912, and due to the English coal-miners' strike, which meant his ship could not sail, he took the much-publicized maiden voyage on the *Titanic*. Of the 1500 people killed in the *Titanic* disaster, several hundred were Swedish emigrants who, as third-class ticket holders, had no access to the deck until the lifeboats had all been taken. When his body was discovered twelve days later in the sub-zero waters, his watch had stopped at 2.34am, just as the *Titanic* vanished beneath the waves.

The museum's **Research Centre** (Tues–Fri 9am–4pm; ☎0470/201 20, ⓦwww.utvandrarnashus.se) charges remarkably good rates (150kr per half-day, 200kr full day) to help interested parties trace their family roots using passenger lists from ten harbours, microfilmed church records from all Swedish parishes and the archives of Swedish community associations abroad. If you want to use the centre's services during their peak season (May–Aug), it's especially worth booking ahead for an appointment with one of their staff.

The Domkyrkan

In the centre, on Linnégatan, the distinctive **Domkyrkan** (daily 9am–5pm; free), with its unusual twin green towers and apricot-pink facade, is certainly worth a look. The combined impact of regular restorations, the most recent in 1995, together with a catalogue of disasters, such as sixteenth-century fires and a 1775 lightning strike, have left little of note except an organ. There are, however, some brilliant new glass ornaments by two of the best-known contemporary Glass Kingdom designers: Göran Wärf's wacky alternative church font, and a stunning triptych altarpiece made entirely of glass and designed by Bertil Vallien. The cathedral is set in **Linnéparken**, named after Carl von Linné (see p.112), who was educated at the handsome school next door.

Out from the centre: Kronobergs slott

The ruin of **Kronobergs slott** has a beautiful and uncommercialized setting, on a tiny island in a lake, Helgasjön, 5km north of the centre of town. Heading there by car, follow signs for Evedal, and the castle will be signposted off the road; or take bus #1B from Växjö bus station (Mon–Sat hourly, less frequent on Sun). Though the bishops of Växjö had erected a wooden fortress here in the eleventh century, the present stone structure was built by Gustav Vasa in 1540. Although there's not much else to see when you get here, the journey is reason enough to make the trip. The grass-roofed *Ryttmästargården* **café**, directly opposite the castle and by the jetty where the boat arrives, is worth a visit for its eighteenth-century interior rather than its food. The jetty is used by Sweden's oldest wood-fired **steamer**, *Thor*, built in 1887, which makes regular excursions from here around Helgasjön and up to another lake, Asasjön – a delightful way to take in the pretty lakeland scenery (daily late June to late Aug; book tours at the café). The options include the so-called "lock gate trip" (*slusstur*) along the canal from Helgasjön to Asasjön, which enjoys picturesque scenery at a leisured pace (departures are generally on Wed, Sat & Sun; 2hr 30min; 125kr; timetables at ⓦwww.smalandsmuseum.se follow the *Ångaren Thor* link). For a glamorous all-day excursion (500kr), take the tour to the country manor house of Asa herrgård (most Sun at 10am), which includes lunch on board. Both trips can be booked on ☎0470/70 42 00 or at ⒺPreception@smalandsmuseum.se.

Eating and drinking

Växjö is a good place to try traditional **Småland cuisine**, which shows the influence of the forests and the poverty associated with the region, and is based around woodland berries, potatoes and game. Among local specialities are **isterband**, a flavoursome, spicy sausage usually served with potatoes and a dill sauce, and **krösamos**, potato pancakes with lingonberry sauce. The classic local dessert is **Smålands ostkaka**, a rich curd-cheese cake with warm cloudberry sauce.

Bishops Arms Kungsgatan 6. Like elsewhere in Sweden this fake English pub is attached to the town's *Elite* hotel and is an inordinately popular place for a drink. There are sometimes special After Work deals on beer – look out for the signs outside.

Broqvists Kronobergsgatan 14. This café just off Stortorget is nothing special to look at, but it's a Växjö institution nonetheless, as somewhere locals come to gossip or read the paper while enjoying a coffee and a slice of cake.

Evedals Värdshus Next to the youth hostel on Lake Helgasjön, Evedal ☎0470/630 03. The best food hereabouts, with Swedish specialities including grilled saithe with

scallops and fennel sauce, fresh from the local lake (209kr) or roast duck with apple and apple and lingonberry compote (239kr). Opening times vary; ring ahead.

Harry's Norra Järnvägsgatan 8. The locals love this American-style bar complete with its lifesize Red Indian figure, half-built brick arches and faux *Dieu et mon Droit* coat of arms hanging over the bar. As a result it's a good place to meet people and get under the skin of Växjö.

Kafe de Luxe Sandgärdsgatan 19 ☎0470/74 04 09. Sharing the same kitchen as *Wibrowski* next door, this great retro café is done out in 1960s style and belts out classic pop

IKEA

Among Swedish exports, only Volvo and ABBA spring to mind as readily as the furniture store **IKEA**, the letters standing for the name of its founder – **Ingvar Kamprad** (born 1926) – and his birthplace, Elmaryd, a farm in the Småland parish of Agunnaryd. Outside Sweden, the identity of IKEA's originator, now one of the world's richest men, is played down, and the firm is known for simple, modern design lines and prices that appeal to a mass market. Every item of furniture IKEA produces is assigned a fictional or real Swedish name; the styles of certain items are drawn from particular areas of the country, and are given a relevant name.

Founded in 1943 at Älmhult, a small town 50km southwest of Växjö, as a mail-order company, IKEA began producing furniture based on folk designs, which Kamprad had simplified. In the 1950s, Sweden's existing furniture-makers were sufficiently irritated by what they regarded as an upstart that they tried to pressure IKEA's suppliers into boycotting the company. Kamprad responded by importing furniture from abroad.

In his 1976 book, *Testament of a Furniture Dealer*, Kamprad wrote that from the outset, he wanted to promote "constructive fantasies": to change the world's view of design, rather than produce what people already believed they wanted. Having opened in Denmark in 1969, the company began expanding around the world, though it didn't enter the US market until 1985 or the UK until 1987. In 2006, IKEA opened its most northerly store in the world in Swedish Haparanda, drawing shoppers from across Lapland.

A number of biographies have been published on Kamprad, one of which (*The History of IKEA*) was authorized. They have revealed Kamprad's Nazi sympathies during World War II which he responds to by blaming his former political leanings on the folly of youth.

Today, if you pass through Älmhult, you can see the original IKEA store, built in 1958; the street on which it stands is called, appropriately enough, Ikeagatan. Ironically, IKEA's headquarters are no longer in Sweden, but in Leiden in the Netherlands, and Kamprad himself has lived in Switzerland since 1976.

tunes of an evening. Mains are 175–235kr and include poached halibut, tapas and roast lamb. Three-course special for 395kr.

Pastabaren Kungsgatan 3. Just steps from the train and bus stations, this basic diner is Växjö's cheapest place to fill up well. Vast pasta salads with tuna, cheese and ham or Greek pasta salad are excellent value at 52kr including bread. There are also huge baguettes (36kr), pizza (30kr per slice) and free coffee with food.

PM & Vänner Storgatan 24 ☎ 0470/70 04 44. A great bistro and an elegant fine-dining restaurant make up the two halves of this popular place. Bistro meals such as lasagne or fish stew go for around 200kr, whereas more sophisticated three-course affairs next door, featuring the likes

of lumpsucker roe, angler fish steak and rhubarb croissant, cost 599kr.

Royal Thai Norra Järnvägsgatan 10 ☎0470/458 06. Ornate Thai restaurant opposite the train station with carved bamboo pillars marking the entrance. An extensive menu with Thai, Chinese and Japanese food including chicken green curry (85kr), stir-fried chicken with cashews (75kr) and a popular lunch buffet with ten different dishes (75kr).

Wibrowski Sandgärdsgatan 19 ☎0470/74 04 10. This charming old pink-painted wooden house is where to come for ovenbaked pike, wild boar and roast lamb (from 175kr); the interior is simpler than you might expect given the ornate facade. Shares some of the same mains as *Kafe de Luxe* next door. Three-course menu for 485kr.

The Glass Kingdom

Glass-making in Sweden was pioneered by King Gustav Vasa, who'd been impressed by the glass he saw on a trip to Italy in the mid-sixteenth century. He initially set up a **glassworks** in Stockholm; however, it was Småland's forests that could provide the vast amounts of fuel needed to feed the furnaces, and so a glass factory was set up in the province in 1742. Called Kosta, after its founders, Anders Koskull, Georg Bogislaus and Stael von Holstein, it is still the largest glassworks in Småland today.

Visiting the glassworks

All of the fifteen glassworks (Ⓦ www.glasriket.se) still in operation in Småland give captivating **glass-blowing** demonstrations (Mon–Fri 9am–3pm). Several have permanent exhibitions of either contemporary glasswork or pieces from their history, and all have a shop. **Bus** services to the glassworks, or to points within easy walking distance of them, are extremely limited, and without your own transport it is almost impossible to see more than a couple in a day (though this will satisfy most people). While each glassworks has its individual design characteristics, **Kosta Boda** (Ⓦ www.kostaboda.se) is the easiest to reach from Växjö, has extensive displays and gives the best picture of what's available. To get there, take Route 25 to Lessebo, then follow signs to Kosta, or hop on the direct bus #218 from Växjö.

Kosta Boda glassworks

The **Kosta Boda** and Åfors glassworks are both operated by the same team. While two of Kosta's most celebrated and hyped designers, Bertil Vallien and Ulrica Hydman-Vallien, have their studios at Åfors, the bigger glassworks is at Kosta. The **historical exhibition** here (June to mid-Aug Mon–Fri 10am–6pm, Sat 10am–4pm, Sun noon–4pm; free) contains some of the most delicate fin-de-siècle glassware, designed by Karl Lindeberg; for contemporary simplicity, Anna Ehrner's bowls and vases are the most elegant. Among the most brilliantly innovative works are those by Göran Wärff – examples of his expressive work can also be found in Växjö's cathedral. Current design trends tend more towards colourful and rather graceless high kitsch; nonetheless, new designer sculptural pieces can go for astoundingly high prices. In the adjacent shop, Ulrica Hydman-Vallien's commercialized designs go for around 2500kr, although for a single, traditional *akvavit* glass you're looking at paying something like 150kr.

The **glass-making process** can be mesmerizing to watch, with a glass plug being fished out of a shimmering, molten lake (at 1200°C) and then turned and blown into a graphite or steel mould. With wine glasses, a foot is added during the few seconds when the temperature is just right – if the glass is too hot, the would-be stem will slide off or sink right through; if too cold, it won't stick. The piece is then annealed – heated and then slowly cooled – for several hours. It all looks deceptively simple and mistakes are rare, but it nevertheless takes years to become a *servitör* (glass-maker's assistant), working up through the ranks of stem-maker and bowl-gatherer.

Glassware is marketed with a vengeance in Småland – take a look at the often absurd hyperbole in the widely available *Kingdom of Crystal* magazine. If you want to buy glassware, don't feel compelled to snap up the first things you see: the same designs appear at most of the glassworks, testimony to the fact that the biggest factories by far, Kosta Boda and Orrefors, are now under the same umbrella ownership, while many of the smaller works have been swallowed up, too, even though they retain their own names. The **Glassriket Pass** (available at the tourist office in Växjö; 95kr) gives free entry to the glassworks (it generally costs 30kr to watch glassblowing) and discounts on some glassware products. It can therefore be a wise investment if you're out to buy.

Jönköping

Perched at the southernmost tip of Lake Vättern, northwest of Växjö along Route 30, **JÖNKÖPING** (pronounced "yurn-shurping") is one of the oldest medieval trading centres in the country, having won its town charter in 1284. Today, it's famous for being the home of the matchstick, the nineteenth-century manufacture and worldwide distribution of which made Jönköping a wealthy place. Despite the town's plum position on the lakeshore, its excess of high-rise offices and bland buildings in the centre detract from what is otherwise a pleasant place. At the very end of August, the town hosts a five-day **film festival** (Ⓦwww.filmfestival.nu). It's not pure art-house, but not mainstream Hollywood either, focusing on films from the rest of Scandinavia and across Europe, and it's undoubtedly the best time to be in town.

Arrival and information

At the lake's southern-most edge, the **resecentrum** contains the combined **train** and **bus station**, and the **tourist office** (daily Mon–Fri 9.30am–6pm, Sat 9am–2pm; June to mid-Sept also Sun 9.30am–2pm; ☎036/10 50 50, Ⓦwww.jonkoping .se/turist). For internet, there are a couple of terminals at the train station operated by Sidewalk Express, which can also be found at Pressbyrån, Bannarpsgatan 36.

Accommodation

There should be no problem getting accommodation in Jönköping, and especially in summer there are some good deals to be had at the central **hotels** which are keen to replace their normal business guests with tourists. Many slash their prices in summer by up to a half.

Clarion Collection Victoria F.E. Elmgrensgatan 5 ☎036/71 28 00, Ⓦwww.victoriahome.com. The best choice in town for style, atmosphere and value for money (rooms are at the top end of the price category). Afternoon coffee and cakes and an excellent buffet supper in the appealing atrium dining area are included, and the split-level sauna is the best in town. ⑤/⑧

Elite Stora Hotellplan ☎036/10 00 00, ⓦwww
.jonkoping.elite.se. Jönköping's most historic hotel,
built 1856–60 in Italian Renaissance Baroque
style. Rooms are decorated in Gustavian-style
pastels, and bathrooms here have that very
unusual Swedish commodity – bathtubs. Some
rooms have lake views. ⑤/③

Familjen Ericsson's City Västra Storgatan
25 ☎036/71 92 80, ⓦwww.cityhotel.nu.
Just 3min walk south from the train station, this is
a very comfortable choice, though plainer than
many other establishments in town. Rooms in the
nicer, newer, more modern section of the hotel cost
100kr more on weekdays, 200kr more at
weekends. ④/③

Grand Hotel Hovrättstorget ☎036/71 96 00,
ⓦwww.grandhotel-jonkoping.se. Built in 1904,
this rather elegant building is home to another of
the town's family-owned hotels. Rooms are airy

with wooden floors and offer exceptional value for
money. The location is great, too, right on the main
shopping street. ④/②

Jönköping SweCamp Villa Björkhagen
Friggagatan 31, Rosenlund ☎036/12 28 63,
ⓦwww.camping.se/f06. Roughly halfway
between the town centre and the youth hostel;
get here by walking east about 3km along the
lakeside Strandpromenaden (a continuation of
Norra Strandgatan) or on bus #1. Also has
cabins (③).

STF Vandrarhem Jönköping Odengatan 10,
Huskvarna ☎036/14 88 70, ⓔ148870@telia
.com. The nearest youth hostel is 6km to the
east in the neighbouring town of Huskvarna. Take
bus #1 from the Resecentrum and alight at the
stop marked "Esplanaden". Dorm beds 170kr,
double rooms ①.

The Town

Jönköping's restored historical core is the most interesting part of town
to explore. At its heart is the **Radiomuséet** (Radio Museum; Tues–Fri
10am–5pm, Sat 10am–2pm, June to mid-Aug also Mon 10am–5pm & Sun
11am–3pm; 20kr; ⓦwww.radiomuseet.com), Tandsticksgränd 16, dedicated

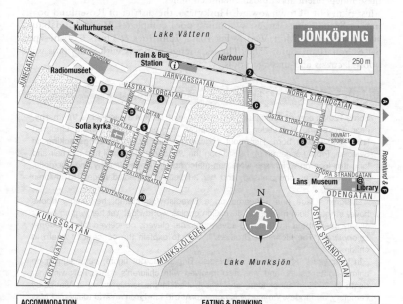

ACCOMMODATION				EATING & DRINKING			
Clarion Collection		Grand Hotel	E	Anna-Gretas Bar & Mat	9	Karlsons Bar &	
Victoria	D	Jönköping SweCamp		Bishops Arms	C	Matsal	4
Elite Stora	C	Villa Björkhagen	A	En Italienare & En Grek	10	Mackmakeriet	6
Familjen Eriksson's		STF Vandrarhem		Harry's	2 & 8	Mäster Gudmunds	
Pensionat	B	Jönköping	F	Hemma	7	Källare	3
				Jungle Thai	5	Saltkråkan	1

to the memory of Erik Karlson from nearby Huskvarna, who built his first radio receiver aged 14, and later opened one of Sweden's first radio stores just three months after the national broadcaster, *Sveriges Radio*, had taken to the air. The museum contains seemingly every type of radio, from early crystal sets to mobile phones.

The only other museum in town worth bothering with is **Jönköpings läns museum,** the county museum, at Dag Hammarskjöldsplats 2 on the east side of the canal between lakes Vättern and Munksjön (Tues–Sun 11am–5pm, Wed till 8pm; June to mid-Sept 40kr, otherwise free; Ⓦwww .jkpglm.se). A mishmash of oddities, with exhibits ranging from posters showing Swedish support for Che Guevara through garden chairs throughout the ages to samovars and doll's houses, the place is like a well-stocked junk shop. The best part is the well-lit collection of paintings and drawings by **John Bauer**, a local artist who enthralled generations of Swedes with his Tolkienesque representations of gnomes and trolls in the *Bland tomtar och troll*, a well-known series of Swedish children's books which were published around Christmas between 1907 and 1915. Upstairs is a constantly changing **art gallery** and a reference library (Tues–Fri 11am–noon & 1–3pm), the latter being worth a stop if you want to peruse the remarkable range of foreign-language **newspapers**.

Although there's little else to see in the town centre, it is remarkable for the sheer number of **Free Churches** – over twenty in the immediate vicinity; consequently, Jönköping has been dubbed "Sweden's Jerusalem". As the traditional Church watches its congregations diminish, people are turning instead to these independent and fundamentalist churches.

Just 3km out of town towards Huskvarna, the district of Rosenlund boasts one of Scandinavia's largest swimming pool complexes, **Rosenlundsbadet** at Elmiavägen 4 (Mon, Wed & Fri 10am–7pm, Tues & Thurs 6.30am–7pm, Sat & Sun 10am–5pm; 75kr). There's a range of pools with slides plus wave pools, Jacuzzis and massage pools.

Astrid Lindgren – creator of Pippi Longstocking

Some 120km east of Jönköping, and reachable on Routes 31 and 33, is **Vimmerby**, near where one of Sweden's most popular children's authors, **Astrid Lindgren** (1907–2002), was born. Her most endearing character, **Pippi Longstocking** (in Swedish, Pippi Långstrump), burst upon the world in 1945. Pippi had red hair and long thin legs on which she wore non-matching stockings. Wealthy and energetic, she could do as she pleased, and her adventures appealed hugely to children everywhere.

Lindgren's face has appeared on a Swedish 6kr stamp; her eighty books have, in total, sold more than 80 million copies worldwide. Yet her writing hasn't simply been about lighthearted adventures: her cleverly conceived tale, *Bröderna Lejonhjärta* ("The Lionheart Brothers"), tries to explain the concept of death to children.

In later years, she became a Swedish Brigitte Bardot figure, campaigning on animal-rights issues, and was also involved with children's rights. Following her death in 2002 in Stockholm, she was buried in the family grave in Vimmerby cemetery, and today, Vimmerby is home to **Astrid Lindgren's Värld** (daily mid-May to Aug 10am–6pm; 275kr, children under 13 165kr; Ⓦwww.astridlindgrensworld .com), a theme park where actors take on the roles of her most famous characters. Trains to Vimmerby run from Kalmar, as does bus #325 from Jönköping.

Eating, drinking and nightlife

Jönköping's most popular **eating** and **drinking** area is the harbour pier, though the rest of town has plenty of good, lively spots too. For a local food speciality, go for the **vätternröding** (Lake Vättern char), available from the little fish shop down by the harbour, or at any of the better restaurants. The char is brought here from the unusually cold and deep Lake Vättern, which can sustain fish normally found in the Baltic Sea.

Cafés, bars and restaurants

Anna-Gretas Bar & Mat Kapellgatan 19 ☎036/71 25 75. The oldest café in town and formerly the staple haunt of market traders, this popular place serves great Spanish food and an impressive range of tapas. Reckon on 65–100kr for tapas, and around 150kr for a main dish, including some juicy steaks.

Bishops Arms Hotellplan. Attached to the *Elite Stora* hotel, this is a good choice for a drink and is a firm favourite amongst the locals. There's an impressive selection of whiskies and beers.

En Italienare & En Grek Barnarpsgatan 35B ☎036/30 77 55. Well-priced, tasty Italian and Greek food (moussaka 160kr and pasta 115–145kr, pizzas from 85kr), good service and a decent location overlooking the attractive old tram depot in the university district. A fine spot for an evening drink, too, with outside tables in summer.

Harry's Brunnsgatan 13–15 and at Hamnen (by the pier). *Harry's* trademark half-built brick walls between the tables are well in evidence at the Brunnsgatan establishment. Both places are inordinately popular, though during the summer months, *Harry's Brygga* (at the pier) wins hands down in terms of atmosphere.

Hemma Smedjegatan 36 ☎036/10 01 55. The town's most popular venue for laid-back live music, with very friendly service and a relaxing terrace garden. There's also a decent menu of home cooking, including salmon and various steak dishes, from around 175kr.

Jungle Thai Trädgårdsgatan 9 ☎036/13 28 28. A welcome arrival in Jönköping, though the farmyard cartwheels which decorate the restaurant seem rather out of place. A good choice of Thai and other Asian dishes for around 120kr.

Karlsons Bar & Matsal Västra Storgatan 9 ☎036/71 21 60. This buzzing restaurant-cum-bar (with outdoor seating on the roof from May–Aug) attracts a wide age range and is popular for its After Work drinks specials. The menu features burgers, nachos and tapas as well as a few more substantial chicken and lamb dishes. Reckon on 160kr for a main course.

Mackmakeriet Smedjegatan 26A. The best café in town, friendly and housed in a wonderful eighteenth-century building with an original painted ceiling portraying two young girls sitting by a lake. Delicious fresh-filled baguettes plus a drink cost 44kr.

Mäster Gudmunds Källare Kapellgatan 2 ☎036/10 06 40. A fantastic old vaulted cellar restaurant from the 1600s serving very good, traditional Swedish fare including reindeer, wild boar and a vegetarian option. Three-course set menus from 297kr, otherwise mains, including *vätternröding*, at 169–199kr.

Saltkråkan Hamnen (end of the pier) ☎036/12 02 77. This old boat-based restaurant appeals to many Swedes, as it's featured in a long-running Swedish children's television programme. The lower deck has a bar, and the top a restaurant serving fine grilled meat and fish dishes. Summer only, usually May–Aug.

Along the shore of Lake Vättern to Vadstena

The eastern shores of **Lake Vättern** offer some of the most spectacular scenery in the region. The splendid little lakeside town of **Gränna**, with its fascinating museum of polar exploration, could be visited as a day-trip, after which you could press on to the highlight of the southeast: **Vadstena** and its magnificent sixteenth-century castle.

Gränna and around

"Instead of roaring factories with belching chimneys, the visitor to Gränna finds peaceful gardens, fruitful orchards and a soothing quietude in all parts of the town"

Allan Berggren, Gränna & Its Surrounds.

Forty kilometres north of Jönköping, the lakeside town of **GRÄNNA** is associated with the unlikely combination of pears, striped rock-candy and a gung-ho nineteenth-century Swedish balloonist (see below). In late spring, the hills around Gränna are a confetti of pear blossom, Per Brahe (see below) having encouraged the planting of pear orchards hereabouts – the Gränna pear is one of the best-known varieties in the country today. Approaching from the south, the beautiful Gränna Valley sweeps down to your left, with the hills to the right, most notably the crest of Grännaberget, which provides a majestic foil to some superb views over Lake Vättern and its island, Visingsö. On a hot summer's day, the trip here from Jönköping has something of the atmosphere of the French Riviera, evoked in particular by the winding roads, red-tiled roofs and the profusion of flowers in the old cottage gardens – not to mention the equal profusion of Porsche and Mercedes cars.

Per Brahe, one of Sweden's first counts, built the town in the mid-seventeenth century, using the symmetry, regularity and spaciousness of planning that he had learnt while governor of Finland. The charming main street, **Brahegatan**, was subsequently widened and remodelled, allowing the houses fronting it to have gardens, while the other main roads were designed so Brahe could look straight down them as he stood at the windows of his now-ruined castle, **Brahehus**. The gardens along Brahegatan remain mostly intact, and until the 1920s, there were no additions to the original street layout. Even now, there's very much a village feel to the little town.

A fine stroll with a fabulous vista over the lake takes you up to *Hembygdsstugan* café (May–Aug 10am–9pm), which should not be missed even though there's a climb of 243 steep steps to reach it: from the market square, walk across to the church then south for 200m to the steps in the hillside to your left. Outside seating affords a fabulous vista over the lake. Better still, you can explore inside a range of ancient grass and thatch-roofed buildings brought from the surrounding areas.

The Grenna Kulturgård: Andrée Expedition Polarcenter

Within the Grenna Kulturgård on Brahegatan is the fascinating **Polarcenter** (mid-May to Aug daily 10am–6pm; Sept to mid-May Mon–Fri 10am–4pm; 50kr), dedicated to Salomon August Andrée, the Gränna-born **balloonist** who led a doomed attempt to reach the North Pole by balloon in 1897. Born at Brahegatan 37, Andrée was fired by the European obsession of the day to explore and conquer unknown areas; with no real way of directing his balloon, however, his trip was destined for disaster from the start. After a flight lasting only three days, during which time it flew more than 800km in different directions, the balloon made a forced landing on ice just 470km from its departure point. The crew of three attempted to walk to civilization, but the movement of the ice floes meant they made no progress; after six weeks' trekking, they set up camp on a floe drifting rapidly southwards. Sadly, the ice cracked and their shelter collapsed, and with it their hopes. Finally they died from the effects of cold, starvation and trichinosis, caught after they ate the raw meat of a polar bear they had managed to spear. It would be another 33 years before their frozen bodies and their equipment were discovered by a Norwegian sailing ship. They were reburied in Stockholm at a funeral attended by a crowd of forty thousand. The museum exhibition poignantly includes a diary kept by one of the crew and film taken by the team, which makes for pitiful viewing: the men are seen with the polar bear they'd hunted, and other sequences show the three hopelessly pulling their sledges across the ice sheets.

The newly renovated museum has extended its remit to cover exploration of the polar region in general, with exhibitions centring on the Arctic and Antarctic historical expeditions, using Andrée as a springboard to a wider picture.

Practicalities

Bus #121 runs roughly every hour from Jönköping to Gränna. The **tourist office** (daily: mid-May to Aug 10am–6pm; Sept to mid-May 10am–4pm; ℡0390/410 10, Ⓦwww.grenna.se) is housed in the Grenna Kulturgård, Brahegatan 38, which also contains the museum (see above) and **library** with free internet access. Gränna's **youth hostel**, *Strandterrassen*, is located down at the harbour at the foot of Hamnvägen (℡0390/418 40; dorm beds 200kr, double room ❶).

The most sensational place to stay hereabouts is the historic country manor, **Västanå slott** (℡0390/107 00, Ⓦwww.vastanaslott.se; ❻ in the castle itself, ❺ in the wings; April–Dec), about 5km south of Gränna. Built in 1590 by Count Sten Bielke and owned in the seventeenth century by Per Brahe, this low, grey castle is owned and run by the formidable Rolf von Otter, a descendent of Bielke. There are no televisions in the rooms – but the sheer majesty of the antique-strewn furnishings and the fabulous lake views from the magnificent first-floor drawing room are worth the stay alone. Breakfast is served in the stunning dining room. Other than walking into town from here, you can order a **taxi** from Gränna Taxi (℡0390/121 00; 150kr).

There are several excellent **cafés** in Gränna, all of which are on Brahegatan. The best is *Fiket* at no. 43, with a quietly 1950s-themed interior where you can enjoy their speciality, a rich almond pastry, or their excellent Gränna *knäckebröd*, a crunchy, tasty crispbread made with linseed and sunflower and sesame seeds. For something more substantial, *Hamnkrogen*, at the harbour (℡0390/100 38), is a very pleasing **restaurant** specializing in well-prepared fish and meat meals from 125kr. Their prawn and salmon buffet (175kr; eve only) is well worth seeking out and there's outside eating in summer on the sunny terrace overlooking the lake.

Vadstena

With its beautiful lakeside setting, **VADSTENA**, which once served as a royal seat and important monastic centre, is a fine place for a day or two's stay. Sixty kilometres north of Gränna, the town's main attraction is its moated **castle**, designed in the sixteenth century by Gustav Vasa as part of his defensive ring protecting the Swedish heartland around Stockholm. The cobbled, twisting streets, lined with cottages covered in climbing roses, also contain an impressive fourteenth-century abbey, whose existence is the result of the passionate work of **Birgitta**, Sweden's first female saint (see p.245).

Arrival and information

There are no trains to Vadstena, though with careful planning it is possible to get here by **bus.** From Gränna, take bus #671 to Ödeshög (Mon–Fri 2 daily at 7.50am & 4.12pm; 30min) and then bus #610 from Ödeshög to Vadstena (9.10am & 5.12pm; 45min). The main **bus stop** is in the centre of town, between the castle and the abbey. By car, it's a straight run along the E4 and Route 50 north from Gränna.

The **tourist office** is located in the castle (May & Sept daily 10am–3pm; June–Aug daily 10am–6pm; Oct–April Mon–Fri 10am–2pm; ℡0143/315 70, Ⓦwww.vadstena.com).

▲ Vadstena Slott

Accommodation

Vadstena's STF **youth hostel** at Skänningegatan 20 (℡0143/103 02, Ⓔvandrarhem@sevadstena.se; dorm beds 230kr, double rooms ❶) is close to the lake, just up from the abbey. Advance booking is essential outside the mid-June to mid-August period.

Set in converted historic buildings and catering for glamorous tastes, the town's main **hotels** are fairly expensive, though there are a few bargains to be had. The *Vadstena Klosterhotel* (℡0143/315 30, Ⓦwww.klosterhotel.se; ❺/❸), in the 1369 nunnery next to the abbey, has atmospheric public areas, though the bedrooms are dated; the lower price applies daily from late June to mid-August. Opposite the castle is the rather ungainly *Vadstena Klosterhotel, Slottsflygeln*, set in a former mental hospital (reception is at the *Klosterhotel*, same telephone number; ❺). The best-value alternative to these is *Pensionat Solgården*, Strågatan 3 (May–Sept; ℡0143/143 50, Ⓦwww.pensionatsolgarden.se; ❷), a beautifully maintained villa from 1905 in a quiet, central position, whose rooms are named after famous artists such as Chagall and Matisse and feature prints of their work (300kr more for private facilities).

The Town

While Vadstena boasts numerous ancient sites and buildings, each with an information plate (in English), the two outstanding attractions here are the **castle** and the **abbey**. Vadstena is also made for romantic evening strolls, with wonderful lakeside sunsets and attractive streets of irregularly shaped houses.

Vadstena Slott

Those who've visited the castle at Kalmar will be familiar with the antics of Gustav Vasa and his troubled family, whose saga continues at **Vadstena Slott** (same hours as the tourist office; May to mid-Sept 55kr, otherwise 35kr; Ⓦwww.vadstena.com). With a grand moat and four round towers, each with a diameter of 7m, it was originally built as a fortification to defend against Danish attacks in 1545, but was then prettified to serve as a home to Vasa's mentally ill third son, Magnus. His elder brother, Johan III, was responsible for its lavish decorations, but fire destroyed them all just before their refurbishment was completed, and to save money they simply painted fittings and decor on the walls, including the swagged curtains that can still be seen today.

The castle's last resident was Hedvig Eleanor, the widowed queen of Karl X; after she died in the 1770s the castle was regarded as hopelessly unfashionable, and so no royal would consider living there. At the end of the seventeenth century, the building fell into decay and was used as a grain store; the original hand-painted wooden ceilings were chopped up and turned into grain boxes. Today, the interior is crammed with **portraits** mainly of the Vasa family, characterized by some very unhappy and unattractive faces. It's worth joining the regular English-language **tours** to hear all the Vasa family gossip (June & July daily 1.30pm; Aug daily 2pm; included in entry fee).

The abbey

Saint Birgitta specified that the **Klosterkyrkan** (abbey church; daily: May 10am–5pm; June & Aug 10am–7pm; July 9am–7pm; Oct–April 11am–3.30pm), easily reached by walking towards the lake from the castle, should be "of plain construction, humble and strong". Wide, grey and sombre, the lakeside abbey, consecrated in 1430, certainly fulfils her criteria from the outside; inside it has been embellished with a celebrated collection of medieval artwork. More memorable than the crypt containing the tombs of various royals is the statue of Birgitta, now devoid of the hands "in a state of ecstasy" – as the description puts it. To the right, the poignant "Door of Grace and Honour" was where each Birgittine nun entered the abbey after being professed – the next time they would use the door would be on their funeral day. Birgitta's bones are encased in a red velvet box, decorated with silver and gilt medallions, in a glass case down stone steps in the monks' choir stalls.

The **altarpiece** here is worth a glance, too: another handless Birgitta, looking rather less than ecstatic, is portrayed dictating her revelations to a band of monks, nuns and acolytes, while around her, representations of hell and purgatory depict finely sculpted faces of woe disappearing into the bloody mouth of what looks like a hippopotamus. Other than Birgitta's, a tomb to note inside the abbey is that of Gustav Vasa's mentally retarded son Magnus. His grand, raised tomb is flanked at each corner by obese, glum-faced cherubs, but the most impressive feature is the remarkably lifelike hands raised in prayer on the likeness of Magnus on the top.

Saint Birgitta

Birgitta (1303–73) came to the village of Vadstena as a lady-in-waiting to King Magnus Eriksson and his wife, Blanche of Namur, who lived at Bjälbo Palace. Married at 13, she gave birth to eight children, and had her first of many visions while living at the palace. Such was the force of her personality, she persuaded her royal employers (to whom she was vaguely related) to give her the palace in order to start a convent and a monastery. To obtain papal approval for the monastery, she set off for Rome in 1349, but the times were against her – the pope was in Avignon, France. She spent the next twelve years in Rome, having more visions, pressing for his return but dying before she could return to Vadstena. She was canonized in 1391, a final vision having already told her this would be the case. Her daughter, Katarina, carried on her work and brought about the building of the monastery and abbey; she too became a saint and her remains lie in the same coffin as her mother's.

Although now housing the *Vadstena Klosterhotel* (see p.244), the **monastery** and **nunnery** on either side of the abbey are open for tours. The most interesting part of the nunnery, housed in the thirteenth-century Bjälbo Palace, is the King's Hall, with an elegant lofty ceiling. On its conversion to a convent, Birgitta had the ceiling lowered to what she considered a more appropriate level for the nuns – it remains thus today.

The Hospitalsmuséet

Just beyond the gates of the abbey graveyard, at Lastköpingsgatan, the **Hospitalsmuséet** (Mental Hospital Museum; June & early Aug daily 11am–3pm; July daily 11am–4pm; 55kr) is based in what was Sweden's oldest mental hospital, dating from 1757 and once called Stora Dårhuset ("the big loony bin"). The display of terrifying contraptions used to control and "cure" the inmates includes a spinning chair, which difficult patients were tightly strapped to and spun until they vomited; an iron bath, in which patients were tied and then scalded; and a tub, used until 1880, in which patients were held down among electric eels. The most poignant displays on the first floor are the patients' own excellently drawn pictures, depicting the tortures inflicted on them. Also on display are moving photographs of inmates from the nineteenth century (extensive research having first been carried out to ensure that the people shown have no surviving relatives).

Eating and drinking

Vadstena's **eating** places are mostly expensive and not particularly trendy, but some are imbued with considerable historical atmosphere.

Gamla Konditoriet Storgatan 18. This classic, busy bakery and *konditori* in a fine seventeenth-century house is open every day for traditional cakes and sandwiches.

Klostercafé A few steps from the abbey at the water's edge, this is an elegant spot for coffee in a former vicarage. Munch on home-baked cakes outside or in the elegant interior. Closed in bad weather, and Sept–May.

Micasa Coffee & Kitchen Rådhustorget 9 ☎0143/141 01. The nearest Vadstena has to a trendy café, where you can eat quite cheaply. Come here for pies, baguettes, ciabatta and cakes, and a weekday lunch special for 75kr.

På Hörnet Skänningegatan 1 ☎0143/131 70. An understated neighbourhood pub that serves great

food, including marinated mushroom or cheese dishes and various types of herrings. Well worth seeking out, especially for a fine all-day brunch for around 100kr.

Rådhuskälleren Rådhustorget ☎0143/121 70. Informal restaurant set in the cosy cellars of the sixteenth-century courthouse, with main dishes like smoked whitefish (165kr) or chicken breast in a herb sauce (139kr). It's also a pub, particularly popular with locals on Fri and Sat eve.

Vadstena Valven Storgatan 18 ☎0143/123 40. This is the smartest restaurant in town with a lunch special (89kr), and fine dinners such as their speciality, Vättern char in a white wine sauce flavoured with truffles (205kr).

North of Vättern: Örebro

The lively and youthful town of **ÖREBRO** lies on the shores of the country's fourth largest lake, Hjälmaren, roughly two-thirds of the way between Stockholm and Karlstad. Örebro's development was dictated by its important strategic position: the main route from southwest Sweden to Stockholm, King Eric's Way, ran right through the centre, where a build-up of gravel made the river fordable (Örebro means "gravel bridge"). Nowadays, the E20 connects Gothenburg and Stockholm bypassing Örebro, but its centre is enjoyable and the town makes a good base for a day or so.

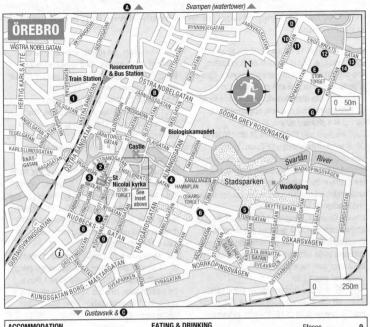

ACCOMMODATION		EATING & DRINKING				Efesos	9
Behrn	F	Gustavsvik	A Mano	13	Björnstugan	14	Harry's	4
Best Western City	G	Camping	C	Ågatan 3 Bar		Café		Pitchers	12
Clarion Örebro	E	Skomakaren	B	& Matsal	10	Stadsträdgården	5	Saigon Vietnam	8
Elite Stora	D	STF Vandrarhem		Bara Vara	7	Den Danske Kroen	1	Stallyktan	2
		Örebro	A	Bishops Arms	11	Drängen	6	Wobbler	3

Arrival and information

Örebro is just two hours from Stockholm, both on the **train** line which runs north of Lake Mälaren via Västerås, and on the E18 motorway which runs between Stockholm, Karlstad and Oslo. By **car** from Vadstena, take Route 50 north to the E18, from where it's a straight run to Örebro (the E18 joins up with the E20 about 15km west of the city which then runs directly there).

The **train station** is on Järnvägsgatan, north of the castle, whilst the **bus station** is alongside; both combining to form the Resecentrum travel centre. From Vadstena, take bus #612 or #661 north to Motala and change there for the train to Örebro. The **tourist office**, with every helpful and knowledgeable staff, is a fifteen-minute walk away, south along Östra Bangatan and then left into Änggatan at Olof Palmestorg (Mon–Fri 10am–6pm, Sat 10am–2pm, Sun noon–4pm; ☎019/21 21 21, ⓦ www.visitorebro.se). For **internet** access, head to *Pressbyrån* at Storgatan 3. The town centre is easily seen on foot but if you want to get a flavour of the surrounding countryside, it's a good idea to rent a **bike**; you can do this at the city library next to the tourist office (70kr per day).

Accommodation

There's currently a lot of money being invested in marketing Örebro across Sweden in an attempt to improve the city's profile and attract tourists. However, there's still a long way to go and at the moment, at least, you're unlikely to find it difficult to get a room. Indeed, in line with Örebrö's position as one of Sweden's biggest cities (in fact, seventh-largest), **hotels** here are thick on the ground.

Behrn Stortorget 12 ☏ 019/12 00 95, ⓦ www
.behrnhotell.se. One of the best deals in Örebro,
this comfortable hotel overlooking the main square
is perfectly placed. The antique furniture in the
otherwise thoroughly modern rooms makes for an
agreeable mix of old and new, and breakfast is
served in a pleasant atrium. ④/②

Best Western City Kungsgatan 24 ☏ 019/601 42
00, ⓦ www.cityhotelorebro.se. Rooms at this
business-oriented hotel, although perfectly adequate
and full of the latest Scandinavian designer touches,
are a little on the cramped side. Decor is typically
chain-hotel: anonymous white walls, wooden floors
and nondescript armchairs. ⑤/③

Clarion Örebro Kungsgatan 14 ☏ 019/670 67 00,
ⓦ www.choice.se. Well designed and stylish to a T,
this place has remarkable weekend and summer
discounts on its sumptuous bedrooms and wonderful
bathrooms done out with black-and-white
chequered tiles. ⑤/③

Elite Stora Drottninggatan 1 ☏ 019/15
69 00, ⓦ www.orebro.elite.se. The oldest
hotel in town – built in 1858 – with extremely
attractive suites and rooms, especially on the
top floor of the annexe. Said to be haunted by
the ghost of a young woman who hanged herself
over an arranged marriage. ⑤/③

Gustavsvik Camping Sommarrovägen
☏ 019/19 69 50, ⓦ www.gustavsvik.se. The
nearest campsite is 2km south of the centre at
Gustavsvik, open late-April to Sept. On site there's
also a large open-air swimming complex as well
as cabins to rent (③).

Skomakaren Järnvägsgatan 20 ☏ 019/611 90 35,
ⓦ www.hotellskomakaren.se. This hotel certainly
looks better inside than out, though it won't be the
highlight of your trip to Örebro. What counts in its
favour is the drastically reduced weekend and
summer rates and its handy location close to the
train station. ④/②

STF Vandrarhem Örebro Kaptensgatan 1 ☏ 019/31
02 40, ⓦ www.grenadjaren.se. A surprisingly pretty
nineteenth-century army barracks about 1.5km to
the north of town; take bus #31 and get off at the
stop called "Grenadjärstaden". Dorm beds 210kr;
double rooms ①.

The Town

The heart of Örebro comes as a pleasant surprise, its much-fortified thirteenth-century **castle** forming a magnificent backdrop to the water-lily-studded **Svartån River**. Aside from the town-centre attractions, **Lake Tysslingen**, a few kilometres west, makes for a good half-day excursion by bike (follow signs for "Garphyttan"). In late March, several thousand whooper swans settle here for two or three weeks to feed on their way up to northern Finland and make spectacular viewing from the lakeside (binoculars are essential).

Örebro Castle

The town's first defensive fort was built after a band of German merchants settled here in the thirteenth century, attracted by rich iron-mining. It was enlarged in the fourteenth century by King Magnus Eriksson, who lived here; Gustav Vasa's son Karl IX added fortifications and then, following in the footsteps of Vasa's other sons, turned it into a splendid Renaissance castle, raising all the walls to the height of the medieval towers and plastering them in cream-coloured stucco. When the Danes were no longer a threat, the town lost its importance, and **Örebro Castle** (entry on tours only: mid-June to mid-Aug daily in English at 2pm; 65kr) fell into disuse and subsequently became a storehouse and a jail. In the old **prison** on the fourth floor, you can see words scratched into the walls by Russian prisoners of war. Another room was used to hold suspected witches and was well furnished by King Karl as a **torture chamber**; at the time, fear of witchcraft was reaching fever pitch, and over four hundred women lost their heads here having survived attempts to drown them in the nearby river.

The fairy-tale exterior you see today is the result of renovation in the 1890s. Influenced by contemporary National Romanticism, the architects carefully restored the castle to reflect both Medieval and Renaissance grandeur. The same cannot be said for the interior, where the valiant guides face a real challenge: there's no original furniture left, and many of the rooms are used for conferences, hence the emphasis on the building being a "living castle".

Naturally, the castle is said to be riddled with ghosts, ranging from that of King Magnus Eriksson's wife Blanche (also known as Blanka in Swedish and said to be in torment for having murdered her son), to Engelbrekt, who had his head lopped off two years after he stormed the castle in 1434 and led a riot on behalf of farmers oppressed by harsh taxes. Among the few features of interest are some fine doors and floors, dating from as recently as the 1920s, the inlays depicting historical events at Örebro; and, in the main state room, a large **family portrait** of Karl XI and his family, their eyes all popping out as a result of using arsenic to whiten their faces.

St Nicolai kyrka
Just a few hundred metres south of the castle, **St Nicolai kyrka** (Mon–Fri 8.30am–5pm, Sat & Sun 11am–3pm), at the top of the very oblong Stortorget, dates from 1260. Extensive restoration in the 1860s robbed it of most of its medieval character, though recent renovations have tried to undo the damage. It was here in 1810 that the relatively unknown figure of Jean Baptiste Bernadotte, Napoleon's marshal, was elected successor to the Swedish throne. The descendants of the new King Karl Johan, who never spoke a word of Swedish, are the current royal family. Engelbrekt was also supposed to be buried here after his execution, but when his coffin was exhumed in the eighteenth century, it was empty, and his bones have never been recovered.

The Konsthall, Stadsparken and Wadköping
Immediately behind the castle at Olaigatan 17B, the **Konsthall** (Art Museum; Tues & Wed noon–6pm, Thurs noon–8pm, Fri noon–5pm, Sat & Sun noon–4pm; free) has a surprisingly spacious series of galleries, with temporary collections of contemporary Swedish art.

From the Konsthall, it's a pleasant stroll east along the waterside Olaigatan, crossing the Svartån River over Hamnbron bridge, to continue east along Kanalvägen to Örebro's stunning **Stadspark**, one of the most beautiful town parks in the country. Sunbathing locals flock here to picnic amid the park's most exceptional feature – the colour-coded border walks, each section bursting with a rainbow of flowers separated by tone.

A little further up the river, at the far end stands an open-air museum, **Wadköping** (mid-June to mid-Aug daily 11am–5pm; mid-Aug to mid-June Tues–Sun 11am–4pm; free; ⓦwww.orebro.se/wadkoping). An entire village of centuries-old wooden cottages and shops were brought to the site in the 1950s when urban planning was threatening the historical dwellings with demolition. A local man, Bertil Waldén, campaigned to save the better ones, and relocated them here at Wadköping on the banks of the river. The extremely pretty little "high street" is flanked with low eighteenth-century buildings on one side, and on the other with taller houses from after the town fire of 1854. Some of the cottages are now lived in again and there's a very good **café**.

Boat trips around Örebro
Given Örebro's easy access to Lake Hjälmaren just east of the town, you might want to consider taking a **boat trip** around the lake on *M/S Gustav Lagerbjelke* which operates from late June to mid-August. There are several options available but the most popular is the five-hour cruise out into Hjälmaren and through

the Hjälmarekanal with its many locks. Transport back to Örebro is by bus and the return ticket costs 295kr. Alternatively, shorter lunch cruises including a buffet cost a good-value 195kr. Details are available at ⓦ www.lagerbjelke.com and tickets can be bought at the tourist office. Another option is to hire your own **canoe** or **kayak** and paddle out yourself: both are available from KFUM Örebro Kanotcenter located out of town at Hästhagsvägen (☏019/26 04 00; 40kr per hr, 160kr per day). Give them a call and they'll help with pickup and dropoff. Useful waterway maps are available at the tourist office.

Eating, drinking and nightlife

Örebro boasts plenty of atmospheric **cafés** and **restaurants**, together with some popular **pubs**, all of which serve food and are a good bet for a quick bite to eat. For something a little different, you could try the popular prawn–eating dinners held aboard the boat which does trips on Lake Hjälmaren (250kr; advance bookings via the tourist office).

Cafés and restaurants

A mano Stallbacken ☏019/32 33 70. Off Kungsgatan in a quiet courtyard guarded by a statue of a horse, this style-conscious Italian place with small square tables facing a long leather bench serves classic Tuscan-inspired mains around 250kr. Try the halibut baked with spinach and parmesan in lobster jus.

Ågatan 3 Bar & Matsal Ågatan 3 ☏019/10 40 19. Just off Drottninggatan, a smart little restaurant with a heavy wooden interior and brown leather chairs creating a romantic atmosphere. They serve sophisticated, modern Swedish cuisine like wood pigeon with chanterelle mushrooms and char in lobster sauce. Reckon on around 229–249kr for a main course.

🏃 **Bara Vara** Köpmangatan 24. This justifiably popular place is where those in the know come for excellent cakes, muffins, ice cream, a good range of speciality coffees and a few light lunch dishes. Plenty of seating upstairs with a nice view of the shopping street below.

Café Stadsträdgården Stadsparken. Located in the greenhouses at the entrance to Stadsparken, and not to be confused with the newer restaurant next door, which isn't nearly as appealing. Serves delicious cakes, tasty pies and sandwiches, though its speciality is delicious home-made pastries.

Den Danske Kroen Kilsgatan 8 ☏019/611 20 69. Cosy atmosphere in an old, turreted house on the other side of the railway tracks from the rest of town, this Danish restaurant serves filling Danish *smørrebrød* (open sandwiches; from 89kr), but also has a range of meat dishes, including steaks, at 189kr. Makes a nice change from Swedish food.

🏃 **Drängen** Oskarsvägen 1 ☏019/32 32 96. A compact restaurant with intriguing farm-style decor including a bust that's half cow/half boy

(*drängen* means "farmhand"), this unpretentious place is one of the finer eating spots in town serving beautifully prepared dishes based on *husmanskost* such as chicken breast stuffed with cream cheese, herbs and spinach. Main courses 155–260kr.

Efesos Rudbecksgatan 28 ☏019/611 66 15. Renowned for its generous portions of tasty Greek fare, especially kebabs (99–149kr) and steaks (around 189kr). The interior here is plain and simple but that doesn't put the crowds off. Be sure to reserve a table as it's always busy.

Saigon Vietnam Rudbecksgatan 18 ☏019/10 08 75. Close to the Krämaren shopping centre, this dimly lit Vietnamese place is an excellent choice for lunch, when a variety of dishes go for 70kr. A full menu is offered, with mains in the evening from 138kr (vegetarian options from 118kr).

🏃 **Wobbler** Kyrkogatan 2 ☏019/10 07 40. Classic Swedish cooking with a modern twist in this bright and airy place with yellow walls, tiled floor and a separate tapas lounge. Elaborate mains (from 159kr) such as roast Hjälmare zander with pepper and charlotte vinaigrette, and tapas choices too (95kr or 145kr).

Bars

Bishops Arms Drottninggatan 1. Hugely popular for outdoor drinking, it serves a limited range of bar meals and is rightly known for an impressive selection of on-tap beers and ales.

Björnstugan Kungsgatan 3. An inordinately fashionable place for an evening drink or two, especially in summer. DJs play the latest chart music interspersed with a few golden oldies.

Harry's Hamnplan 1. Set in the old red-brick technical museum building on the riverside, 1min walk east of the castle, this is one of Örebro's most acclaimed bars; there's also a nightclub here on Fri and Sat eve till 2am. Closed Sun.

Pitchers Engelbrektsgatan 4. A long and narrow sportsbar with big screens showing the latest matches. Extremely busy, and popular with the town's sports followers.

Stallyktan Södra Strandgatan 3B. This excellent, rustic pub is a better choice for a quiet drink and dinner than most of the bigger venues. The lunch buffet here is a good-value 79kr.

East of Vättern: Norrköping and around

Although ranking only as Sweden's eighth largest city, enjoyable **Norrköping** punches well above its weight. It's the town's striking industrial heritage that draws people here – the old mills clustered around the Motala ström river, together with general youthful air, make for an appealing diversion. Based here, you could easily visit the **Kolmården Djurpark**, Sweden's premier zoo and safari park, as a day-trip; alternatively, the much underrated nearby town of **Nyköping**, with its ruined thirteenth-century castle, is equally demanding of your attention.

Norrköping

About eighty kilometres east of Lake Vättern, beyond the uninteresting town of Linköping, is one of Östergötland's most appealing destinations, **NORRKÖPING**, a dynamic, youth-oriented town which likes to call itself Sweden's Manchester. Like its British counterpart, Norrköping's wealth came from the textile industry, which was built up in the eighteenth and nineteenth centuries and kept things booming until the 1950s, when foreign competition began to undermine the town's share of the market. The last big mill closed its doors in 1992, but Norrköping retains one of Europe's best-preserved industrial landscapes, with handsome red-brick and stuccoed mills reflecting in the waters of its river, Motala ström.

Arrival and information

The **train** and **bus stations** are opposite each other in the **Resecentrum** travel centre on Norra Promenaden. From here, walk south down Drottning-gatan for five minutes, then take Prästgatan to the right to reach the helpful **tourist office** at Dalsgatan 9 (late June to mid-Aug Mon–Fri 10am–6pm, Sat 10am–5pm, Sun 10am–2pm; Sept to late June Mon–Fri 10am–5pm; ☏011/15 50 00, ⓦwww.upplev.norrkoping.se). Among other things, they'll be able to explain routes and times for the 1902 **vintage tram**, which circles around on a sightseeing tour during summer. **Internet** connection is available at Sidewalk Express in the train station.

Accommodation

Thanks largely to the booming local economy, Norrköping receives a lot of business trade during the week, and has a good array of **hotels** to cater for its often demanding visitors, though there are also a number of cheaper options available. Good weekend and summer deals are available as hotels try to fill otherwise empty rooms.

Centric Gamla Rådstugugatan 18–20 ☏011/12 90 30, ⓦwww.centrichotel.se. An inexpensive, comfortable hotel, 500m south of the train station. The reception in this stylish building from 1932 features a striking wall

fresco by Gothenburg artist Lars Gillies depicting Norrköping's central areas. ❸/❷

Elite Grand Tyskatorget 2, ☏011/36 41 00, ⓦwww.grandhotel.elite.se. This upmarket hotel from the early twentieth century is certainly the best in town, though it doesn't come cheap. Bang in the centre, its rooms are a stylish blend of classic and modern, and its staff go the extra mile to create a home-from-home feel. Amazing value at weekends and in summer. ⑤/③

Himmelstalunds Camping Campingvägen ☎011/17 11 90, ⓦwww.norrkopingscamping .com. Also has a number of cabins for rent (①). To get here, either walk west from the centre along the river, or take tram #3. Open all year though prebooking necessary from mid-Oct to March.

President Vattengränden 11 ☎011/12 95 20, ⓦwww.profilhotels.se/hotel/president. Straight out

of an IKEA catalogue, the designer rooms here are well equipped and full of the latest furniture. Tastefully done and extremely central. ⑤/③

Södra Södra Promenaden 142 ☎011/25 35 00, ⓦwww.sodrahotellet.se. A calm and pleasant alternative to the chain hotels, set in a sympathetically renovated 1920s house in a residential street formerly favoured by textile-mill owners. ③/②

Turistgården Vandrarhem Ingelstagatan 31 ☎011/10 11 60, ⓦwww.turistgarden.se. Norrköping's comfortable and centrally located STF hostel is just a few hundred metres behind the train station. Dorm beds 235kr, double rooms ①.

The Town

Norrköping's north–south central artery, **Drottninggatan** runs ruler-straight from the train station and crosses Motala ström, the small, rushing river that attracted the Dutch industrialist **Louis De Geer** (1587–1652) to the town in the early seventeenth century. He was known as the father of Swedish industry, and his paper mill, which still operates today, became the biggest factory in

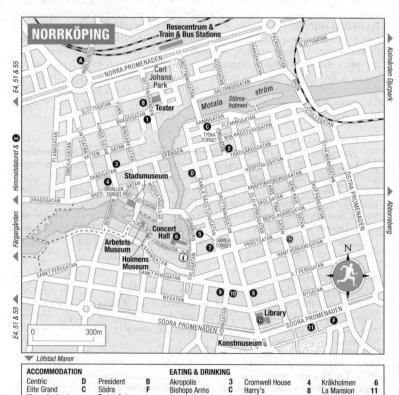

ACCOMMODATION				EATING & DRINKING					
Centric	D	President	B	Akropolis	3	Cromwell House	4	Kråkholmen	6
Elite Grand	C	Södra	F	Bishops Arms	C	Harry's	8	La Mansion	11
Himmelstalunds		Turistgården		Bomullsfabriken	1	Highlander Inn	10	Sing Thai	2
Camping	E	Vandrarhem	A	Café Kuriosa	9	Källaren Bacchus	5	Trädgårn	7

town. Many of Norrköping's buildings, and the trams, are painted in De Geer's colour of choice – a tortilla-chip yellow – which has become synonymous with the town.

Just a few steps down from the station, compact **Carl Johans Park** has 25,000 cacti, formally arranged in thematic patterns and interspersed with brilliantly coloured flowers and palm trees. Glance to the right from here (with the Resecentrum behind you) across Slottsgatan, and you'll see the splendid 1906 city **theatre**, with its Art Nouveau curves and double Ionic columns. Over the river, follow the tram lines up cobbled Drottninggatan and turn right into Repslagaregatan for **Gamlatorget**, overlooked by a charismatic Carl Milles sculpture of Louis De Geer with a bale of cloth slung over his shoulder.

At the southernmost tip of Drottninggatan, Norrköping's **Konstmuseum** (Art Museum; June–Aug Tues–Sun noon–4pm, Wed until 8pm; Sept–May Tues–Sun 11am–5pm, Tues & Thurs until 8pm; free) holds some of the country's best-known modernist works. Founded by a local snuff manufacturer at the turn of the twentieth century, the galleries offer a fine, well-balanced progression from seventeenth-century Baroque through to twentieth-century work. As you head back north from the art museum, the bunker-like concrete building to the right at Södra Promenaden 105 is the town **library**; more user-friendly than most, it has a range of newspapers from all over the world.

West of Gamlatorget

To the west of Gamlatorget lies the modern and stylish riverside **Concert Hall**, surrounded by trees and providing a lovely setting for the café, *Kråkholmen* (see p.254). It's worth stepping inside the Concert Hall for a moment, as its apparent modernity belies the fact that this was once one of De Geer's paper factories, though little remains now of its former incarnation. Continuing west from the Concert Hall, go through the impressive, eighteenth-century paper mill gates to the left, cross a wooden bridge behind the hall and you'll come to the small **Holmens museum** (Tues & Thurs 9am–12.30pm; free), depicting life in the town's paper mills. It's run on a voluntary basis by retired paper-mill workers; sadly, though, the exhibits aren't labelled in English. The best known of the mills, Holmens Pappersbruk, is still functioning just a few metres away.

West along the river on your right is the exceptionally well-presented **Arbetets museum** (Museum of Work; daily 11am–5pm, Sept–May also Tues until 8pm; free), housed in a triangular, yellow-stuccoed factory built in 1917. Known as *Strykjärnet* ("the iron") – though its shape and colour are more reminiscent of a wedge of cheese – the building was described by Carl Milles as Europe's most beautiful factory. The museum has seven floors of exhibitions on living conditions, workers' rights and day-to-day life in the mills. The most poignant (and the only permanent exhibit) tells the story of Alva Carlsson, who worked in the building for 35 years – a fascinating insight into working-class culture and the role of Swedish women in the first half of the twentieth century.

Over another little bridge is the excellent **Stadsmuseum** (City Museum; June–Aug Tues, Wed & Fri 10am–4pm, Thurs 10am–8pm; Sept–May Tues, Wed & Fri 10am–5pm, Thurs 10am–8pm; all year Sat & Sun 11am–4pm; free), set in an interconnecting (and confusing) network of old industrial properties. The most rewarding of its permanent exhibitions is a street showing various trades from the nineteenth century: there are workshops of a milliner, confectioner, chimney sweep and, in a back yard, a carriage maker. All are cleverly designed and well worth a wander.

Around Norrköping: Kolmården

If you've only got time for one excursion from Norrköping, make it to **Kolmårdens Djurpark** (May, June & mid-Aug to early Sept daily 10am–5pm; July to mid-Aug daily 10am–6pm; 290kr; ⓦ www.kolmarden.com), a safari park, zoo and dolphinarium which is one of Sweden's biggest attractions. Just 28km northeast of Norrköping and accessible by frequent trains, it's understandably popular with children, for whom there's a special section, and if your views on zoos are negative, it's just about possible to be convinced that this one is different. There are no cages; instead, sunken enclosures, rock barriers and moats prevent the animals from feasting on their captors. There's certainly no shortage of things to do, either: check out the cable-car ride over the safari park, dolphin shows (generally between one and four a day) and the working farm.

The adjacent **Tropicarium** (daily: May, June, Aug & Sept 10am–5pm; July 9am–7pm; Oct–April 10am–3pm; 80kr; ⓦ www.tropicarium.se) contains Sweden's largest collection of tropical plants and animals, spread out over two square kilometres. The interior really is extremely realistic, even featuring a mock-up of an alligator swamp which receives rain and thunderstorms every hour. The most popular attraction is the shark aquarium, with three different species of shark and hundreds of other tropical fish.

There's a **youth hostel** on site, *Varglyan* (ⓣ011/24 90 00; mid-June to mid-Aug only), which has five four-bed rooms (900kr per night) and four six-bed rooms (1200kr). Alternatively, you can **camp** at *Kolmårdens Camping* (ⓣ011/39 82 50, ⓦ www.firstcamp.se/kolmarden), 5km away at Bodaviken; there are four-bed cabins here (③), too.

Eating and drinking

There's a fair selection of **places to eat and drink** in Norrköping, some of which double as bars. Although in Swedish terms it's only a moderately sized town, the array of food on offer is unmatched for miles around.

Cafés, restaurants and bars

Akropolis Kungsgatan 35 ⓣ011/10 50 00. Very good Greek restaurant a few minutes' walk from the Stadsmuseum, with a wide menu of tasty food. A starter and a main course, for example aubergine dip and salmon fillet, go for 175kr.

Bomullsfabriken Dalsgatan 13 ⓣ011/13 44 00. Probably Norrköping's most popular restaurant since it opened in 2005. With an enjoyable outdoor seating area in summer, it's a great place for a drink or a bite to eat: the menu is an eclectic mix of Swedish and Mediterranean flavours. Try the grilled salmon with pastrami and cream of horseradish and avocado (179kr) or pork fillet with pineapple salsa, melon and chilli (189kr). Mains are 139–289kr.

Café Kuriosa Hörngatan 6. A super, central old-fashioned café with a little garden, serving home-made cakes, savoury pies and ice cream. Pie and salad costs 48kr. Try the fragrant Kuriosa tea, scented with apricots and vanilla.

Källaren Bacchus Gamlatorget 4 ⓣ011/10 07 40. The oldest restaurant in town, housed in a vaulted cellar from the mid-eighteenth century, this fantastic, atmospheric restaurant serves light eats and warm grills – try the fillet of chicken with sundried tomatoes in a sage sauce (171kr). The herring plate with trimmings (107kr) is another winner.

Kråkholmen Dalsgatan 15 ⓣ011/15 50 30. Outside the Concert Hall; enter through the hall, or round the back. The daily 75kr lunch menu here features salads, light dishes and home-cooked meals served against the backdrop of the crashing waters of Motala ström.

La Mansion Södra Promenaden 116 ⓣ011/16 70 20. A charming, sedate place for lunch or dinner, set in the preserved former home of a mill manager full of 1920s fixtures and fittings. Dinner menus offering dishes like grilled swordfish with mango sauce or glazed duck breast with fennel are around 250kr.

Sing Thai Trädgårdsgatan 15 ⓣ011/18 61 88. A good-value Thai restaurant right next to the town hall, open for both lunch (until 3pm) and dinner. The set lunch is 72kr, or 95kr lets you put three dishes together. Otherwise, in the evening, mains are 135–175kr.

Trädgårn Prästgatan 1 ⓣ011/10 07 40. This bar and grill is very popular, especially for outdoor eating in summer; the entrance is beneath an iron sign marked "VIP Paraden".

Bars

Bishops Arms Drottninggatan 2. Undoubtedly the most popular pub in Norrköping, this place has gone from strength to strength since opening in 1994 and boasts the biggest selection of beers and whiskies in town. Outdoor seating in summer.
Cromwell House Kungsgatan 36. Dark, faux-English pub full of stained glass and locals. Quite good-value grilled meat dishes cost 139–219kr.

Harry's Drottninggatan 63. One of the busier spots for a drink with the usual array of signature brick walls, well-polished floors – and well-oiled locals.
Highlander Inn St Persgatan 94. Norrköping's answer to a real Scottish pub that's well known for its large selection of beers and whiskies. It also serves light bar meals.
Pub Wasa Gamla Rådstugugatan 33. The upstairs is all done up like a ship's interior (hence the name) with little cannons pointing out of the windows. The atmosphere is friendly and there's live music most nights from 11pm.

Nyköping and around

Northeast of Norrköping lies the province of **Södermanland**, also abbreviated as Sörmland. Its capital, the diminutive but historic **NYKÖPING**, is the nearest town to Stockholm and home to Skavsta airport (used by Ryanair and now Sweden's third largest). If you're looking for a taste of provincial Sweden before pushing on to the capital, Nyköping is perfect. Its underrated charms include an excellent museum in and around the ruins of its thirteenth-century **castle**, and a thriving harbour – a regular target for the Stockholm yachting set – that bustles with life in summer.

Arrival and information

The **train station** is ten-minutes' walk west of the winding Nyköpingsån River. Although it's not widely known, handy direct trains run to Nyköping from Gävle, Uppsala and Arlanda airport via Stockholm; these services are the easiest way to travel between Arlanda and Skavsta airports. From Skavsta **airport**, 7km northwest of Nyköping, buses #515 and #715 run to the bus station on Västra Kvarngatan, just 500m south of the train station which is on Järnvägsgatan. To reach the centre from the train station, it's an easy dog-leg walk of around ten minutes, first south along Järnvägsgatan, then east on Repslagaregatan, then south again on Brunnsgatan. Conveniently, all the town's sights lie between the stations and the river, or by the river itself. The harbour is at the other end of town from the stations, but the distance is easily walkable in around twenty minutes.

The central and enthusiastic **tourist office** (June–Aug daily 11am–8pm; Sept–May Mon & Wed–Fri 9.45am–6.45pm, Tues 11.30am–6.45pm; ☎0155/ 24 82 00, ⓦ www.visitnykoping.se) is in Rådhuset, the only hideous building on the otherwise graceful Storatorget. Bikes are available to rent here (100kr a day). They also have internet access.

Accommodation

Staying in Nyköping is remarkably good value and significantly cheaper than Stockholm. There's a good selection of budget options as well as one or two more upmarket choices and advance booking is not needed.

Clarion Collection Kompaniet Folkungavägen 1 ☎0155/28 80 20, ⓦ www.choice.se. Near the harbour and overlooking the river, this huge structure of curving red brick is the most stylish and well-appointed hotel in town and has surprisingly competitive rates. The rooms are airy, neutrally decorated and have wooden floors. ❹/❸

Connect Skavsta General Schybergs väg 23, Skavsta airport ⓦ www.connecthotels.se. Located opposite the terminal building at Skavsta, 7km from town, this brand new, modern design hotel is perfect for early morning departures or late arrivals. Regular buses (see above) run into town (and Stockholm) from opposite the hotel. ❷

Lanterna Östra Längdgatan 8 ☎0155/45 50 30, ⓦwww.hotellanterna.se. A delightful newly built family-run hotel overlooking the harbour that's done out in cosy, country-home style with floral wallpaper, wooden flooring, draped curtains and flower vases. No weekend or summer reductions. ❸

Railway Hostel Södra Bangårdsgatan ☎0155/28 29 20, ⓦwww.railway.nu. This new hostel is located at the train station and comprises a number of dorms sleeping a maximum of five, and double rooms. The bus to Skavsta airport leaves from right outside the hostel. Dorm beds 175kr, double room ❶

Strandstuvikens Camping Strandstuviken ☎0155/978 10, ⓦwww.strandstuvikencamping.se. Located in a mature pine forest 7km southeast of Nyköping on the Baltic coast; open all year.

Wiktoria Fruängsgatan 21 ☎0155/21 75 80, ⓦwww.hotelwiktoria.com. Cheap, basic and close to the town's picturesque theatre. Rooms are rather cramped though the central location is a bonus. ❸

The Town

Opposite the tourist office stands the vast **St Nicolai kyrka** (Mon–Fri 10am–4pm, Sat & Sun 10am–2pm), with its white, vaulted ceiling. The building dates from around 1260, although most of what you see is the result of sixteenth-century refurbishment. The pillars here are adorned with dozens of beautiful, heavily moulded silver candle sconces. It's the pulpit, though, that's the highlight of the church; crafted in Norrköping, it was modelled on the one in the Storkyrkan in Stockholm. Outside, standing proudly on a nearby rocky outcrop, is the red 1692 bell tower, the only wooden building not destroyed in 1719 when the town's worst fire struck.

The castle

From the tourist office, it's just a couple of minutes' wander south, down Slottsgatan with the river to your left, to Kungsgatan. Here you'll see the museum complex and beyond it, the **King's Tower**. A late twelfth-century defensive tower, built to protect the trading port at the estuary of the Nyköping river, it was subsequently converted into a **fortress** by King Magnus Ladulås. It was here in 1317 that the infamous **Nyköping Banquet** took place: one of Magnus's three sons, Birger, invited his brothers Erik and Valdemar to celebrate Christmas at Nyköping and provided a grand banquet. Once the meal was complete, and the visiting brothers had retired to bed, Birger had them thrown in the castle's dungeon, threw the key into the river and left them to starve to death. In the nineteenth century, a key was caught by a boy fishing in the river; whether the rusting item he found, now on display in the museum, really is the one last touched by Birger, no one knows.

In the sixteenth century, Gustav Vasa fortified the castle with gun towers; his son Karl, who became duke of Södermanland, converted the place into one of Sweden's grandest Renaissance palaces. A fire here in the 1660s reduced all lesser buildings to ash and gutted the castle. With no money forthcoming from the national coffers, it was never rebuilt; only the King's Tower was saved from demolition and became used as a granary. Today, the riverside tower and the adjoining early eighteenth-century house built for the county governor form a **museum complex** (mid-June to mid-Aug daily 10am–5pm; mid-Aug to mid-June Tues–Sun 11am–5pm; free). Wandering through the original gatehouse beneath Karl's heraldic shield, you reach the extensively restored King's Tower. On the first floor, a stylish job has been done of rebuilding the graceful archways that lead into the Guard Room. The rest of the museum is fairly uninspiring, with the best exhibition being a display of medieval shoes and boots.

Boat trips from Nyköping

From mid-June to mid-August the veteran M/S Labrador steams out of the town's tiny harbour (Tues 9am; 170kr return) bound for the countless rocks, skerries and islands that make up the Nyköping archipelago, much as she has for the past twenty-odd years. After just an hour, the boat puts in at the **Stendörren nature reserve**, which is by far the best place to jump ashore and explore. An unspoilt haven of smooth rocks, ideal for sunbathing, and secluded bays, the reserve is home to arctic tern, eider ducks, oyster catchers and white-tailed eagles as well as elk, roe deer and mountain hares. Stendörren is also the destination of the popular evening dinner cruises (May–Sept Wed–Sat 7pm; 280kr) which also leave from the main harbour. A buffet of prawns, cheese, bread and dips is served on the journey and is included in the price. Book tickets on ☎0155/26 71 00 or at ⓦ www.mslabrador.se.

Eating and drinking

Most of Nyköping's **eating** and **drinking** options are, unsurprisingly, at the harbour. Outside the summer season, though, the scene moves to the town centre where, curiously for a modestly sized town, there's a good range of choice to suit all pockets.

4

Hamnmagasinet Skeppsbron 1 ☎0155/26 92 92. A classy brick-walled establishment that stands out as the leading harbourside restaurant, with a large open-air terrace. Plenty of no-nonsense grilled fish and meat dishes 100–150kr. Open May–Aug.
Hellmanska Gården Västra Trädgårdsgatan 24. From Storatorget, head down Västra Storgatan and turn left. Set in a converted grain warehouse dating from the 1700s with a lovely summer courtyard, it attracts a young, relaxed crowd and serves great sandwiches, fruit flans, quiches and light lunches.
🏃 **Lamduan Thai Food** Östra Storgatan 27 ☎0155/21 61 11. The lurid green walls and adorning pictures of Thai royals notwithstanding, the genuinely tasty food here is worth seeking out: mains are around 120kr. The lunch buffet at 80kr is also good.
Mickes Skafferi Västra Storgatan 29 ☎0155/26 99 50. Nyköping's finest restaurant, set in a former barber's saloon complete with mirrors and shaving equipment in the glass cupboards. Sophisticated

and nicely presented Swedish food is on the menu such as reindeer steak, whitefish roe and char. Mains are 159–269kr.
M/S Linné Skeppsbron ☎0155/45 44 40. The elegant white ship moored in the harbour is the location for an agreeable waterborne restaurant serving fish stew (169kr), salmon kebab (159kr) and pork fillet (169kr). Sat or Sun lunch is 129kr. Open May–Aug Wed–Sun.
Oliver Twist Fruängsgatan 28 ☎0155/21 63 05. Close to the bus station, this popular wood-panelled English pub does a good range in food as well as drink: chicken curry (145kr), fried sole (169kr) and salads (from 69kr) are all available.
🏃 **Rökeriet** Östra Skeppbron 7 ☎0155/21 38 38. The red warehouse standing beside the roundabout north of the harbour. This fish smokery and fine restaurant with outside eating is a Nyköping institution and renowned for its excellent lunch menu of smoked salmon, mackerel and gravadlax for 150kr. Late April to early Sept only.

Gotland

Tales of good times on **GOTLAND** are rife. Wherever you are in Sweden, one mention of this ancient Baltic island 90km from the mainland will elicit a typical Swedish sigh, followed by an anecdote about what a great place it is. You'll hear that the short summer season is an exciting time to visit; that the place is hot, fun and lively. These claims are largely true: the island has a distinctly youthful feel, with young, mobile Stockholmers deserting the capital in summer for a boisterous time on its beaches. The flower-power era still makes its presence felt with a smattering of elderly VW camper vans lurching off the ferries, but shiny Saabs outnumber them fifty to one. During summer, the bars, restaurants and campsites are packed, the streets swarm with revellers, and the sands are awash with bodies. It's not everyone's cup of tea: to avoid the hectic summer altogether, come in late May or September when, depending on your

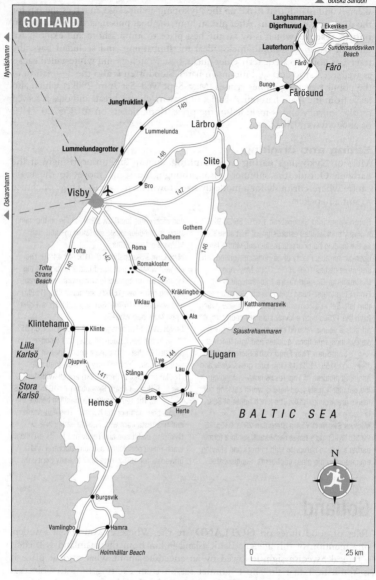

level of bravado, you might still manage to swim in the waters around the island. To experience the setting at its most frenetic, come in August during **Medieval Week** (see p.265), when people put a huge effort into dressing the part.

Visby, Gotland's capital, has always been the scene of frenetic activity of some kind. Its temperate climate and position attracted the Vikings as early as the sixth century, and the lucrative trade routes they opened, from here through to Byzantium and western Asia, guaranteed the island its prosperity. With the ending of Viking domination, a "golden age" followed, with Gotland's inhabitants maintaining trading posts abroad and signing treaties as equals with European and Asian leaders. However by the late twelfth century, their autonomy had been undermined by the growing power of the **Hanseatic League**. Under its influence, Visby became one of the great cities of medieval Europe, as important as London or Paris, famed for its wealth and strategic power. A contemporary ballad had it that "The Gotlanders weigh their gold with twenty-pound weights. The pigs eat out of silver troughs and the women spin with golden distaffs." Today, all the revelry which keeps Visby buzzing from late June to the end of August takes place against the spectacular backdrop of its medieval architecture; two hundred or so Hanseatic warehouses are dotted among stone and wooden houses, the whole lot nestled within its ancient walls.

There is a real charm to the **rest of Gotland** – rolling green countryside, forest-lined roads, fine beaches and small fishing villages. Everywhere the rural skyline is dominated by **churches**, the remnants of medieval settlements destroyed in the Danish invasion. Nowhere else in Scandinavia holds such a concentration of medieval churches, and 93 of them are still in use, displaying a unique Baltic Gothic style and providing the most permanent reminder of Gotland's ancient wealth. Churches aside, however, very few people bother to explore the island, perhaps because of Visby's magnetic pull; consequently, the main roads around Gotland are pleasingly free of traffic and minor roads positively deserted – **cycling** is a joy. As you travel, keep an eye out for the waymarkers erected in the 1780s to indicate the distance from Wisby (the old spelling of the town's name), calculated in Swedish miles – one of which is equivalent to 10km.

Visby

VISBY is much older than its medieval trappings suggest: its name comes from *vi*, "the sacred place", and *by*, "the settlement", a derivation that reflects its status as a Stone Age sacrificial site. After the Gotlanders had founded their trading houses in the eleventh and twelfth centuries, the Hansa or **Hanseatic League**

Getting to and around Gotland

Ferries to Gotland are numerous and, in summer, packed, so try to plan well ahead. Two mainland ports serve the island, Nynäshamn and Oskarshamn, and crossings take about three hours. Prices depend on season with the cheaper tickets for departures outside the summer peak: one-way tickets start at 180kr in the low season and 245kr for mid-June to mid-August sailings. Buy tickets online at ⓦwww .destinationgotland.se.

Flights to Gotland are good value if booked early. Skyways (ⓦwww.skyways.se) operate from both Arlanda and Bromma airports in Stockholm; Gotlandsflyg (ⓦwww .gotlandsflyg.se) have services from Bromma and Skavsta and several provincial airports. Cheapest single tickets are 328kr.

Transport on Gotland

For **getting around** the island, it's hard to resist the temptation to **rent a bike**, given the flat terrain and empty roads. See p.260 for rental outlets in Visby. Bikes can also easily be rented at various towns to the south of the capital, less so further north. As for Gotland's **buses**, services are pretty sparse; outside Visby, services tend to run only twice daily – morning and evening – though will takes bikes. Timetables are at ⓦwww.gotland.se/kollektivtrafiken.

was created, comprising a group of towns that formed a federation to assert their interests and protect their seaborne commerce. Following the foundation of Lübeck in the 1150s, German merchants began to expand into the eastern Baltic area in order to gain access to the coveted Russian market. A trading agreement between Gotlanders and the League in 1161 gave the islanders the right to trade freely throughout the whole Saxon area, while Germans were able to settle in Visby, which became the League's principal centre and the place where all lines of Baltic trade met. As Visby metamorphosed from Gotlandic village to international city, it was the Germans who led the way in form and architecture, building warehouses up to six storeys high with hoists facing the street, still apparent today.

In 1350 the **Black Death** swept through Gotland, creating ghost towns of whole parishes and leaving more than eight thousand people dead. Eleven years later, during the power struggle between Denmark and Sweden, the Danish king Valdemar III took Gotland by force and advanced on Visby. The burghers and traders of the city, well aware of the wealth here, shut the gates and sat through the slaughter which was taking place outside, only surrendering when it was over. Hostilities and piracy were the hallmarks of the following two centuries. In 1525, an army from Lübeck stormed the much-weakened Visby, torching the northern parts of the town. With the arrival of the Reformation and the weakness of the local economy, the churches could no longer be maintained, and Visby's era of greatness clanged to a close.

Visby is a city made for wandering and lingering over coffees and slices of cake. Whether climbing the **ramparts** of the surrounding walls, or meandering up and down the warren of cobbled, sloping streets, there's plenty to tease the eye. If you feel like something more educational, head for the fine **Fornsal museum**, which covers pretty well all there is to know about Gotland, and Visby in particular – and there's a rather good art gallery close by.

Arrival, information and orientation

Visby **airport** is 3km north of town and a five-minute ride by **taxi** into the centre (not more than 135kr). All the **ferries** serving Visby dock at the same terminal, just outside the city walls; for the centre, turn left out of the terminal and keep walking for five minutes.

The main **tourist office** (May to mid-June & mid- to end Aug Mon–Fri 8am–5pm, Sat & Sun 10am–4pm; mid-June to mid-Aug daily 8am–7pm; Sept Mon–Fri 8am–5pm, Sat & Sun 11am–2pm; Oct–April Mon–Fri 8am–noon & 12.30–4pm; ☏0498/20 17 00, ⓦwww.gotland.info) is within the city walls at Skeppsbron 4–6, conveniently en route between the ferries and the old city, and has plentiful maps and information brochures. There's also a selection of **tours** available, one of which, the walking tour of the town (mid-June to mid-Aug 2–3 times a week; 85kr), is worth considering, especially if time is short.

Visby's main square, **Storatorget**, is signposted from most places. The town is best seen on foot; despite its warren-like appearance, it's a simple matter to get the hang of the narrow, crisscrossing cobbled streets. Modern Visby has spread beyond the limits defined by its old city walls, and today the new town gently sprawls from beyond **Österport** (East Gate), a few minutes' walk up the hill from Storatorget. Here, in **Öster Centrum**, is the **bus terminal**, used by the buses serving the entire island; the tourist office has free timetables.

Bikes can be rented just outside the ferry terminal from Gotlands Cykeluthyrning, Skeppsbron 2 (from 75kr per day; ⓦwww.gotlandscykeluthyrning.com). Rental is also possible at several outlets near Österport on Östervägen: Visby Hyrcykel at no. 1 and Team Sportia at no. 17. There are no **internet** cafés in

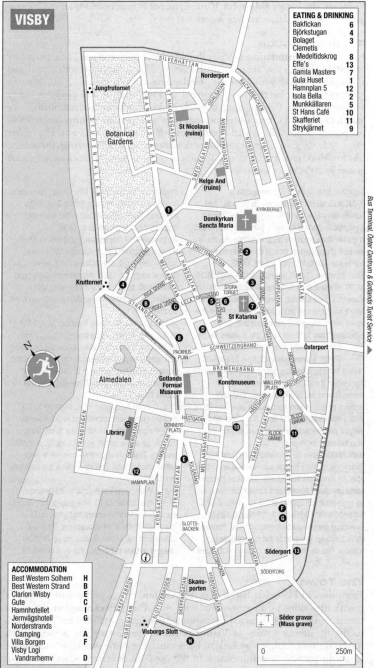

VISBY

▲ **A**   ▲ *Airport*

EATING & DRINKING

Bakfickan	6
Björkstugan	4
Bolaget	3
Clemetis Medeltidskrog	8
Effe's	13
Gamla Masters	7
Gula Huset	1
Hamnplan 5	12
Isola Bella	2
Munkkällaren	5
St Hans Café	10
Skafferiet	11
Strykjärnet	9

SILVERHÄTTAN

Norderport

Jungfrutornet

St Nicolaus (ruins)

Botanical Gardens

Helge And (ruins)

KYRKBERGET

Domkyrkan Sancta Maria

Kruttornet

St Katarina

Österport

PACKHUS-PLAN

Almedalen

Gotlands Fornsal Museum

Konstmuseum

WALLERS PLATS

BREMERGRÄND

HÄSTGATAN

DONNERS PLATS

Library

KLOCK-GRÄND

BLOCK GRÄND

HAMNPLAN

SLOTTS-BACKEN

Söderport

SÖDERTORG

Söder gravar (Mass grave)

Skans-porten

Visborgs Slott

ACCOMMODATION

Best Western Solhem	H
Best Western Strand	B
Clarion Wisby	E
Gute	C
Hamnhotellet	I
Jernvägshotell	G
Norderstrands Camping	A
Villa Borgen	F
Visby Logi Vandrarhemv	D

0   250m

▼ **⓵**, Ferry Terminal & Gotlandsresor (Room Booking Service)

Visby, but the library (Mon–Fri 10am–7pm, Sat & Sun noon–4pm) at Cramer-gatan 5, by Almedalen has free access.

Accommodation

Finding **accommodation** in Visby should seldom be a problem. There are plenty of **hotels** (though few are particularly cheap), several campsites with cabins, and a couple of good youth hostels. Gotlandsresor (℡0498/20 12 60, ⓦwww .gotlandsresor.se), by the ferry terminal at Färjeleden 3, and Gotlands Turist Service (Mon–Fri 9.30am–6pm; ℡0498/20 33 00, ⓦwww.gotlandsturistservice .com), Österväg 3A, near Österport, can help with **private rooms** (from 300kr per person, doubles ❶), as well as **cottages** both in and outside Visby. The higher price code we give below is for the peak summer season (May–Aug), the second one for Monday to Friday during the rest of the year (non-summer weekends are generally 200–300kr less).

Best Western Solhem Solhemsgatan 3 ℡0498/25 90 90, ⓦwww.hotellsolhem.se. Just outside the city walls at Skansporten, this large, comfortable chain hotel has a basement sauna and is quieter than the more central options. Rooms are modern, if uninspiring, though do vary in size so ask to see one before you accept. ❻/❹

Best Western Strand Strandgatan 34 ℡0498/25 88 00, ⓦwww.strandhotel.net. A rather glamorous place in a quiet cobbled street in the heart of town, with a sauna, steam bath, indoor pool and a stylish atmosphere. Altogether more luxurious, and expensive, than its sister hotel, the *Solhem*. ❻/❺

🏃 **Clarion Wisby** Strandgatan 6 ℡0498/25 75 00, ⓦwww.wisbyhotell.se. Splendid, central hotel in a building dating back to the Middle Ages when it was used as a merchant's store-house. Rooms are beautifully decorated with wooden panelling, soft lighting and period furniture. With a sumptuous pool to boot, this is the most elegant and the best option in town, though it's also the most expensive. ❼/❻

Gute Mellangatan 29 ℡0498/20 22 60, ⓦwww .hotellgute.se. Very central and reasonably comfort-able. All rooms are individually decorated though some are overly flowery and fussy. Reductions may be possible if you appear at the last minute. ❺/❹

Hamnhotellet Färjeleden 3 ℡0498/20 12 50, ⓦwww.gotlandsresor.se/boende/hh.asp. Housed in three buildings perched on the hill opposite the harbour. Rooms, though perfectly comfortable, are

modern and blocklike with little charm. However, it is perfect for early-morning ferries back to the mainland. Breakfast is served in the separate restaurant building from 5am. ❹/❸

Jernvägshotell Adelsgatan 9 ℡0498/20 33 00, ⓦwww.gotlandsturistservice.com/SVE/Boende /Wisby_Jernvagshotell. Although train services on Gotland ceased in 1960, this former railway hotel, now a youth hostel, is still in operation with modern, comfortable rooms, though with no dorms. Double rooms ❶.

Norderstrands Camping Österväg 3A ℡0498/21 21 57, ⓦwww.norderstrandscamping.se. Barely 800m outside the city walls – follow the cycle path that runs through the Botanical Gardens along the seafront, though reception is at Gotlands Turist Service (see above). Open June–Aug only. Has cabins for rent (❷).

Villa Borgen Adelsgatan 11 ℡0498/20 33 00, ⓦwww.gotlandsturistservice.com/SVE/Boende/ Villa_Borgen/index.htm. Attractive family hotel in the middle of the action, yet with lovely, peaceful gardens. Tastefully decorated en-suite, though rather small, rooms. There's a sauna and solarium too. ❺/❹

🏃 **Visby Logi Vandrarhem** St Hansgatan 31 ℡070/752 20 55. Five cosy double rooms decorated in tasteful whites and greys make up this youth hostel in an atmospheric old house dating from the 1600s. Rooms are up to 250kr cheaper outside the peak June–Aug period. ❸

The Town

From the old Hanseatic harbour at **Almedalen**, now a public park, all of the town's attractions are a few minutes' walk away. Pretty **Packhusplan**, the oldest square in the city, is bisected by curving Strandgatan, which runs southwards to the fragmentary ruins of **Visborgs Slott**, overlooking the harbour. Built in the fifteenth century by Erik of Pomerania, the castle was blown up by the Danes in the seventeenth century. In the opposite direction, Strandgatan runs northwest towards the sea and the lush **Botanical Gardens** (no set hours; free), just beyond which is the **Jungfrutornet** (Maiden's Tower), where a local goldsmith's daughter was walled up alive – reputedly for betraying the city to the Danes. Today, you can climb the tower for the fine view.

Strolling around the twisting streets and atmospheric walls is not something that palls quickly, but if you need a focus, aim for **Norra Murgatan**, above the cathedral, once one of Visby's poorest areas. The end of the street nearest Norderport enjoys the best view of the walls and city rooftops. Alternatively, head for the water's edge, where **Studentallén** is a popular late-evening haunt and the sunsets are magnificent – brilliant fiery reds, glinting mirrored waters and bobbing sailing boats in the distance.

Strandgatan itself is the best place to view the impressive **merchants' houses** looming over the narrow streets, with storerooms above the living quarters and cellars below; most notable among these is the clearly signposted **Burmeisterska huset** in Donnerplats, which is attractive and in good condition. One of the most picturesque buildings on the street is the old pharmacy, **Gamla Apoteket**, a lofty old place with gloriously higgledy-piggledy windows; it's at the corner of Strandgatan and Lybska gränd.

Gotlands Fornsal museum

At Strandgatan 14 is the outstanding **Gotlands Fornsal museum** (Historical Museum of Gotland; June to mid-Sept daily 10am–6pm; mid-Sept to May Tues–Sun noon–4pm; 75kr; ⓦ www.lansmuseetgotland.se), a must-see for anyone interested in **Viking history**. Housed in a mid-eighteenth century distillery, it comprises five storeys of exhibition halls covering eight thousand years of history, plus a good café and bookstore. Among the most impressive of the displays is the **Hall of Picture Stones**. Dating mostly from the fifth to seventh centuries, these large, keyhole-shaped stones are richly ornamented. The earlier ones are covered in runic inscriptions and are more intriguing, with vivid depictions of people, animals, ships and houses.

However, it's the **Viking Treasury** on the first floor that really steals the show. Gotland's wealth of gold and silver objects is unique; more hoards of Viking-age treasure have been found on the island than anywhere else in the world, clearly a sign of its economic and social importance. On display are hundreds of shiny coins and trinkets – some brought to Gotland from as far afield as Samarkand, Persia and Afghanistan, others from England. In a room off the treasury, the world's largest find of Viking-age silver, the **Spillings Hoard**, is proudly exhibited in a vast glass cabinet. Discovered in a farmer's field in the north of Gotland in 1999, the hoard, which lay buried for 1130 years, is truly breathtaking. It comprises 87kg of silver and bronze, including over 14,000 coins (the earliest dating from 539AD), neck rings, armbands and spiral rings. Elsewhere in the museum, look out for the two skeletons displayed in glass cases. The occupant of one, a 40-year old man buried in foetal position with two pieces of antler and flint arrows, is, at roughly 8000 years old, one of the oldest in Sweden.

Other rooms trace the history of **medieval Visby**; look out for the original trading booth, the sort of place where the burghers of Visby and foreign merchants would have dealt in commodities – furs, lime, wax, honey and tar – brought from all over northern Europe. Gotland's ecclesiastical history is also well covered with an impressive exhibition of ornate wooden carvings of bishops, Mary Magdalene and a truly magnificent triptych dating from the early sixteenth century from Vall church on the island.

A couple of streets up at St Hansgatan 21, Gotland's **Konstmuseum** (Art Musuem; mid-June to mid-Aug daily 11am–5pm; mid-Aug to mid-June Tues–Sun noon–4pm; 50kr; ⓦ www.lansmuseetgotland.se) has some innovative temporary exhibitions of contemporary painting and sculpture, and installations which tease the eye. Though for the most part much less exciting, the permanent collection on the top floor is given over to twentieth-century Gotlandic art; among the few notable classics is Axel Lindman's 1917 oil of Visby from the beach, showing brilliant dabs of sun before a storm. The eye is also drawn to a stunning picture by William Blair Bruce of his wife, the sculptress Carolina. The painting, from 1891, shows her at work, and the lifelike qualities of the style are remarkable.

The town wall and Valdemar's Cross

The oldest of the towers in Visby's town wall is the dark, atmospheric **Kruttornet** (Gunpowder Tower) by Almedalen, built in the eleventh century to protect the old harbour and offering some grand views of Visby. The **wall** itself, a three-kilometre circuit enclosing the entire settlement, was built around the end of the thirteenth century for a rather different purpose: it was actually aimed at isolating the city's foreign traders from the locals.

Just outside the walls to the east of Söderport (South Gate), **Söder gravar** is a mass grave, excavated in the twentieth century, of two thousand people; more than half were women, children and invalids who were slaughtered when Danish king Valdemar attacked the town in 1361. There's a cross here, erected by the survivors of the carnage; the inscription reads: "In 1361 on the third day after St James, the Goths fell into the hands of the Danes. Here they lie. Pray for them."

A section of the wall near Söderport was broken down to allow Valdemar to ride through as conqueror. **Valdemar's Breach** is recognizable by its thirteen crenellations representing, so the story goes, the thirteen knights who rode through with the Danish king. Valdemar soon left, in possession of booty and trade agreements, and Visby continued to prosper while the countryside around it stagnated, its people and wealth destroyed.

Visby's churches

At the height of its power, Visby maintained more **churches** than any other town in Sweden – sixteen in all, most of which are dramatic ruins today. However, one, the **Domkyrkan Sancta Maria** (Cathedral of St Mary; Mon–Wed, Fri & Sun 8am–9pm, Thurs & Sat 8am–6.30pm), is still in use. Constructed between 1190 and 1225, it was built for visiting Germans, becoming the German Parish Church when they settled in the city. In 1300, a large Gothic chapel was built to the south, the eastern tower was elevated and the nave was raised to create storage space; this was where the burghers kept their money, papers and records. It's been heavily restored, and about the only original fixture left is the thirteenth-century sandstone font inside. Most striking are its **towers**, a square one at the western front end and two slimmer eastern ones, standing sentry over the surrounding buildings. Originally each had spires, but following an eighteenth-century fire, they were crowned with fancy Baroque cupolas, giving them the appearance of inverted ice-cream cones. Inside, have a look beneath the pulpit, decorated with a fringe of unusually ugly angels' faces.

Seventeenth- and eighteenth-century builders and decorators found the smaller churches in the city to be an excellent source of free limestone, tiles and fittings – which accounts for the fact that most are ruins today. Considering the number of tourists clambering about them, it's surprising that the smaller church ruins manage to retain a proud yet abandoned look. Best of what's left is the

4

Medieval Week

During the second week of August, Visby becomes the backdrop for a boisterous re-enactment of the conquest of the island by the Danes in 1361. **Medieval Week** (Ⓦwww.medeltidsveckan.com) sees music in the streets, medieval food on sale in the restaurants (no potatoes – they hadn't yet been brought to Europe) and on the Sunday a procession re-enacting Valdemar's triumphant entry through Söderport to Storatorget. Here, people in the role of burghers are stripped of their wealth, and the procession then moves on to the Maiden's Tower. Locals and visitors alike really get into the spirit of this festival, with a good fifty percent of people dressed up and on the streets. There are weekly **jousting tournaments** throughout July and early August.

great **St Nicolaus** ruin, just down the road from the Domkyrkan. Destroyed in 1525, its part-Gothic, part-Romanesque shell hosts a week-long **chamber music festival** (Ⓦwww.gotland-chamber-music-festival.info), starting at the end of July; tickets cost 160kr for most events and are available from the tourist office. One of the loveliest ruins to view at night is **St Katarina** in Storatorget; its Gothic interior is one of the finest in Visby, having belonged to one of the town's first Franciscan monasteries, founded in 1233. This church was built in 1250; at night its glorious arches, lit creamy yellow, frame the blue-black sky.

The tourist office gives away a reasonably informative English-language **guide**, *The Key to all of Gotland's Churches*, which lists the key features of all the island's churches in alphabetical order. This can sometimes also be found in the churches themselves.

Eating, drinking and nightlife

Adelsgatan is lined with **cafés** and **snack bars**. At lunchtime, the eating places at Wallérsplats, the square at Adelsgatan's northern end, and Hästgatan, the street leading off the square to the southwest, are particularly busy; Strandgatan is the focus of Visby dining in the evening, though Hästgatan also boasts a number of places for dinner. For inexpensive fare at night, lively **Donnersplats** has lots of stalls selling takeaway food during summer.

Youthful **nightlife** is mainly down at the harbour. *Hamnplan 5* at the northern end offers old rock hits and folk music, both live and recorded. One place to try within the city walls is *Effe's*, Adelsgatan 2, built into one of the defence towers just inside the city walls at Söderport, which generally has plenty of live bands.

Cafés

Björkstugan Speksgränd 6. In a fabulous, lush garden on Visby's prettiest cobbled street, this little café serves tasty pies, sandwiches and coffee. Open till 10pm.

Gula Huset Tranhusgatan 2. Close to the Botanical Gardens and a favourite amongst locals: a cosy garden café outside a vine-covered cottage, deservedly well known for delicious port-wine cake with cream and fruit.

Skafferiet Adelsgatan 38. Appealing, characterful café in a lovely eighteenth-century house with coarsely hewn timber walls, chequered curtains and a lush garden at the back. Baked potatoes, great cakes and vast, generously filled baguettes which suffice for a full meal.

St Hans Café St Hansplan 2. Between May and Sept this café has outdoor seating in the rear garden amid a series of atmospheric medieval church ruins – for atmosphere it's hard to beat. Terrific cakes, muffins and pies as well as light lunches.

Restaurants and bars

Bakfickan Storatorget 1 ☏0498/27 18 07. A quiet, relaxed little restaurant with a tiled interior that specializes in some of the best seafood in town. The fried Baltic herring with mashed potato (128kr) is superb, so, too, fish soup with aioli (145kr). Starters from 69kr.

Bolaget Storatorget 6 ☏0498/21 50 80. A delightful, though extremely small French bistro right on the main square: confit de canard (189kr), bouillabaisse (155kr) and a delicious warm goats cheese starter (89kr) are all good bets.

Clematis Medeltidskrogen Strandgatan 20 ☎0498/21 02 88. Set in the vaulted cellars of a thirteenth-century house, this is Visby's most atmospheric and evocative restaurant. Candles provide the lighting, mead is served in flagons and the food comes in rough ceramic bowls or on wooden platters. Summer only.

Gamla Masters Stora Kyrkogatan 10 ☎0498/21 66 68. A justifiably popular bistro decked out with mosaic tiles serves everything from solid Swedish home cooking (meatballs 152kr, whitefish roe 168kr) to more upmarket, sophisticated meat and fish dishes (185–252kr). A great place, too, for an after-dinner drink.

Isola Bella Södra Kyrkogatan 20 ☎0498/21 87 87. Great Italian trattoria, with a superb vaulted cellar restaurant to the rear hung with gilt mirrors. Pasta, for example tortelloni stuffed with asparagus and ricotta, from 110kr, pizzas from 112kr as well as great meat dishes, especially Gotland lamb with tarragon risotto and cider mustard, from 195kr.

Munkkälleren Lilla Torggränd 2 ☎0498/27 14 00. This vast place in one corner of the main square is massively fashionable, and consequently crowded. There's an extensive array of grilled meats and fish, for example salmon and halibut, from 180kr. They also serve bar snacks including burgers (132kr) and cheese nachos (110kr).

Strykjärnet Wallersplats 3 ☎0498/28 46 22. This fantastic low-ceilinged crêperie is squeezed into the narrowest of triangular buildings at the corner of Adelgatan and Hästgatan (it's named "the iron" for its shape). A wide range of savoury gallettes (including vegetarian options) from 78kr; sweet crêpes from 39kr.

Central Gotland: Roma, Romakloster and around

Just fifteen kilometres southeast of Visby on Route 143, the small settlement of **ROMA** (bus #11 from Visby; timetable available from the tourist office) actually has nothing to do with Rome, but instead takes its name from "room" or "open space" – this was the original location of ancient Gotland's courthouse. The place looks something of a ghost town as its century-old sugar-beet factory, to the right of the main road as you approach from Visby, has recently closed, and the early twentieth-century cottages fronting Route 143 are also deserted (they can't be demolished, though, as they're protected for their rarity value). The church here, dating from 1215, is large and pretty; the three-aisled nave gives it a surprisingly Romanesque appearance, and because of this the church is known as the False Basilica.

Just 1km further down the road, the Cistercian cloister ruins of **Romakloster**, in the hamlet of the same name, are the real draw of the area; follow the sign left down a long avenue of beech trees. The crumbling Roma monastery, dating from 1164, lacks both apse and tower, being Romanesque in design; it would once have comprised a church with three wings built around a rectangular cloister. What is left is sturdy stuff – big arches of grey stone blocks so regular they could be breeze blocks. The multitude of spotlights set in the ground here make it very dramatic as a backdrop for night-time **theatre** (Shakespeare performances are staged each summer), though they detract from the site's timeless character by day. The ruin is not the isolated site one might expect, as it's behind the cream-stucco **manor house**, Kungsgården, built in the 1730s for the county governor. Part of the monastery was in fact destroyed by the Danish crown during the Reformation of the early sixteenth century, and it was further ruined when the governor used materials from it in the building of the house.

Temporary art exhibitions are held within the manor house (20kr), and there's a **café**, *Drängstugan*, serving delicious sweet pies and sandwiches (May & Sept Sat & Sun 10am–6pm; June & mid- to end Aug daily 10am–6pm; July to mid-Aug daily 10am–9pm).

Gotland's best beaches

Within easy striking distance of Visby, the sandy beaches at *Snäck* (a 5km cycle ride north of the town) and **Tofta strand** (take bus #10 south from Visby) are two of the island's most popular beaches, and ideally suited to families with children, since the water is relatively shallow and warm. For a perfectly formed sandy bay, head for **Sudersandsviken** on Fårö; take bus #20 from Visby to the ferry at Fårösund, then a taxi to the beach itself (book on ☎0498/20 20 00). Alternatively, in the south of the island, **Holmhällar** is surrounded by wild, unspoilt countryside and limestone *raukar*; bus #11 will take you here. However, by far the best beach on the entire island is the vast, unsullied stretch of coastline between **Sjaustrehammaren** and **Ljugarn** on the east coast; backed by pine forest, the southern section is popular with **naturists**. Get here on bus #41 to Gammelgarn from where it's a fifteen-minute cycle ride along the road to Ljugarn and then follow one of the narrow forest tracks which lead down off left to the shore. All beaches are marked on the map on p.258.

Practicalities

For cheap and basic **accommodation**, Peter Doolk provides rooms in his manor-house home dating from 1790 at the hamlet of Viklau (bus #11 from Visby), 5km south of Roma (☎0498/512 12; 100–150kr). This very affable and knowledgeable Gotlander will also take you round the island by arrangement – a good choice if time is limited. *KonstnärsGården* (☎0498/550 55) is a complex of art galleries at Ala, 15km southeast of Roma just off Route 143; the main reason to come here, though, is to eat at the appealing and popular **restaurant** (☎0498/550 55; mid-May to late Aug daily noon–9pm) round the back, serving filling meals including excellent fish and meat dishes for around 150kr. There's also a **café**, offering the usual baguettes and cakes.

Southern Gotland: Hemse to Ljugarn

The so-called "capital" of the south, **HEMSE**, around 50km from Visby along Route 142 (buses #10, #11 and #12), is little more than a main street. There's a good local café and bakery, *Jonassons Bageri & Konditori* at Storgatan 54, and you can rent **bikes** from *Endrells*, Ronevägen 4, which is the cheapest place in town (☎0498/48 03 33).

Taking Route 144 east from Hemse, signposted for Burs, you'll find the countryside is a glorious mix of meadows, ancient farms and dark, mysterious forest. One of the most charming villages just a couple of kilometres further on, **BURS** has a gorgeous thirteenth-century saddle church, so-called because of its low nave and high tower and chancel. There's a fabulously decorated ceiling, medieval stained-glass windows and ornately painted pews. A couple of kilometres further, the sandy **beach** at **HERTE** is one of the best on the island. For a really friendly, locals' **café**, the nearby *Burs Kafé* in Burs (June–Aug daily noon–10pm; Sept–May Tues–Sun 4–9pm) serves cheap, filling meals like beef stroganoff, or hamburgers made with Gotland beef for around 50kr.

Ljugarn

For Gotland's best beach (see box above), and the nearest thing it has to a resort, the lively and charming town of **LJUGARN** makes a good base. You can get here from Roma by heading straight down Route 143 for around 30km. Though full of restaurants and obviously aimed at tourists, Ljugarn no longer has a tourist office. It's famous for its *raukar* – tall limestone stacks rising up from the sea.

From the main street, it's only 100m to the town **beach**. A delightful cycle or stroll down Strandvägen follows the coastline through woods and clearings carpeted in *blåelden* (viper's bugloss), the electric-blue flowers for which the area is known. The *raukar* along the route stand like ancient hunched men, their feet lapped by the waves.

Ljugarn has a range of eating places and accommodation to suit most tastes. Rooms are advertised in appealing-looking cottages all over town, and Ljugarn's STF **youth hostel** (☎0498/49 31 84, ✉ljugarn@gotlandsturist.se; dorm beds 180kr, double rooms ❷; mid-May to Aug), at Storgatan 1, is located in a former customs house from the 1850s. For a splendid **café**, *Espegards Konditori* at Storvägen 58 is a must, serving some of the best cakes around – try their almond and blueberry tart. Their famously good breads, in particular *ljugarslimpa*, a dark, slightly chewy loaf, have been made here and shipped to the mainland since the 1930s. The place is very popular, so expect a queue in summer. The best place in town, though, is the lovely ✴ *Ljugarns Strandcafé & Restaurang*, located on the beach itself at Strandvägen 6 (☎0498/49 33 78; June–Aug daily 10am–midnight), serving delicious, top-notch Mediterranean-style mains, such as lamb Provençale with garlic confit and goats cheese cream (220kr); its large, open-air terrace is beautifully placed for a drink right on the sand.

Northern Gotland: the Lummelundagrottor to Bunge

Thirteen kilometres north of Visby on Route 149, or by bus #61, are the **Lummelundagrottor** (daily: May 10am–3pm; June to end–Aug daily 10am–4pm; July 9am–6pm; late Aug to mid-Sept 10am–2pm; 100kr; ⓦwww .lummelundagrottan.se): limestone caves, stalagmites and stalactites that are disappointingly dull and damp despite being marketed as Gotland's most visited tourist attraction. The cave adventures here are of interest if you enjoy clambering around in the damp, and are not recommended if you suffer from claustrophobia (minimum age 15).

There's a more interesting natural phenomenon 10km to the north, where you'll see the highest of Gotland's coastal *raukar* (see p.229). The remnants of reefs formed over four hundred million years ago, the fact that the stacks are now well above the tide line is proof that sea levels were once much higher. This particular stack, 11.5m high and known as **Jungfruklint**, is said to look like the Virgin and Child – something you'll need a fair bit of imagination to discern.

Instead of taking the coastal road from Visby, you could head around 10km inland along Route 148 towards the village of **BRO**, which has one of the island's most beautiful **churches**. Several different stages of construction are evident from the Romanesque and Gothic windows in its tower. The most unusual aspect is the south wall, with its flat-relief picture stones, carved mostly with animals, that were incorporated from a previous church that once stood on the site. On the whole, though, it's better to press on further into the eminently picturesque north, where many of the secluded cottages are summer-holiday homes for urban Swedes.

At the village of **BUNGE**, it's worth visiting the bright fourteenth-century fortified church, and the open-air museum of seventeenth- to nineteenth-century buildings (mid-May to mid-Aug daily 10am–6pm; 30kr).

Fårö

Just five minutes by ferry from Fårösund (essentially a continuation of Bunge), most of **Fårö** island is flat limestone heath, with shallow lakes and stunted pines much in evidence. In winter (and sometimes in summer, too) the wind whips over the Baltic, justifying the existence of the local windmills – and of the sheep shelters, with their steeply pitched reed roofs modelled on traditional Fårö houses.

The best place to head for is the five-kilometre arc of white sand at **Sudersandsviken** (see box, p.267), or alternatively, for more swimming, try **Ekeviken**, on the other side of the isthmus. The rest of the coastline is rocky, spectacularly so at **Lauterhorn** and, particularly, **Langhammars**, where limestone stacks are grouped together on the beach. At Lauterhorn you can follow the signs for **Digerhuvud**, a long line of stacks leading to the tiny fishing hamlet of Helgumannen, which is no more than a dozen shacks on the beach, now used as holiday homes. Continuing along the same rough track brings you to a junction; right runs back to the township of Fårö; left, a two-kilometre dead-end road leads to Langhammars.

You can get to Fårö by taking a bus from Visby to the town of **Fårösund** and making the ferry crossing from there (daily every 15–30min; 5min; free). There's a down-at-heel but surprisingly good **café** in town, *Fårösund Grill*, which serves excellent sandwiches, almond tart, and good, cheap coffee. Just opposite is Bungehallen, a very well-stocked supermarket (daily till 10pm). You can take a four-person **chalet** at *Fårösunds Semesterby*, Strandvägen 80 (☎0498/22 16 94, ⓦwww.farosundssemesterby.se; from 300kr per night; mid-April to mid-Sept).

Gotland's other islands: Stora and Lilla Karlsö

The two islands of **Stora Karlsö** and **Lilla Karlsö**, 16km offshore of Klintehamn, have been declared nature reserves: both have **bird sanctuaries** where razorbills, guillemots, falcons and eider duck breed; on Lilla Karlsö you'll also see the unique horned Gute sheep. Bit it's Stora Karlsö which really steals the show, for its perpendicular cliffs and range of **birdlife**: more than 230 species have been recorded on the tiny island. Orchids also flourish here in the damp sea air. It's possible to reach Stora Karlsö from Klintehamn, some 30km south of Visby on Route 140; tickets are available from the harbour office (May & Aug 9.40am & 2pm; June & July 9.30am, 11.30am & 4.10pm; 225kr

▲ Limestone stacks, Langhammars

Ingmar Bergman

Since the mid-1960s, Sweden's best-known film director and screenwriter, **Ingmar Bergman**, has lived for much of the time on Fårö. He was born in Uppsala in 1918, the son of a Lutheran pastor. The combination of his harsh upbringing, his interest in the religious art of old churches, and the works of August Strindberg inspired Bergman to constantly consider the spiritual and psychological conflicts of life in his films. The results – he made forty feature films between 1946 and 1983 – are certainly dark, and for many, deeply distressing and/or depressing. He made his first breakthrough at the Cannes Film Festival in 1944, winning the Grand Prix for his film *Hets* (*Persecution*), based on his school life. Among his best-known movies are *The Seventh Seal* (1957), starring Max von Sydow, and *Wild Strawberries* (also 1957). The two most prevalent themes in his films were marriage and the motives for marital infidelity, and the divide between sanity and madness. One of his finest films, *Fanny and Alexander* (1982), portrays bourgeois life in Scandinavia at the turn of the twentieth century; it's actually based on the lives of his own maternal grandparents and is the last major film he made. Bergman married five times, divorcing all but the last of his wives, who died in 1995.

return; ☎0498/24 04 50, ⑩www.storakarlso.com). As we went to press there was no boat service to Lilla Karlsö; check with the tourist office in Visby or call ☎0498/48 52 48. Should services resume, you can use the small **hostel** here near the pier (☎0498/24 00 10, ⓔwarfsholm@telia.com; dorm beds 250kr; double rooms ❶). The only **accommodation** on Stora Karlsö is at the STF **youth hostel**, which puts guests up in tiny fishermen's huts sleeping up to four (☎0498/24 05 00, ⓔboka@storakarlso.se; dorm beds 250kr, double rooms ❶; May–Aug); it's picturesque but extremely basic, with no showers, though there is a restaurant. Camping is not allowed on the islands.

Travel details

Trains

Jönköping to: Gothenburg (5 daily; 2hr).
Kalmar to: Gothenburg (2 daily; 4hr); Malmö (8 daily; 3hr); Växjo (11 daily; 1hr).
Norrköping to: Malmö (hourly; 3hr 10min); Nyköping (hourly; 40min); Stockholm (hourly; 1hr 15min).
Nyköping to: Stockholm (hourly; 1hr); Arlanda airport (hourly; 1hr 30min).
Örebro to: Luleå (1 daily; 16hr); Gothenburg (6 daily; 2hr 50min); Stockholm (10 daily; 2hr).
Växjö to: Gothenburg (6 daily; 3hr); Kalmar (11 daily; 1hr).

International trains

Kalmar to: Copenhagen via Kastrup airport (8 daily; 4hr).
Norrköping to: Copenhagen via Kastrup airport (2 daily; 4hr).

Buses

Kalmar to: Oskarshamn (2 daily; 2hr); Stockholm (2 daily; 6hr).
Norrköping to: Jönköping (8 daily; 3hr); Gothenburg (6 daily; 5hr); Kalmar (2 daily; 4hr); Stockholm (11 daily; 2hr).
Vadstena to: Stockholm (2 per week; 4hr).

Ferries

Nynäshamn to: Visby (mid-June to mid-Aug 5 daily; 3hr; rest of the year 2 daily; 3hr).
Oskarshamn to: Visby (mid-June to mid-Aug 2 daily; 3hr; rest of the year 1 daily: 3hr).

International ferries

Nynäshamn to: Gdansk, Poland (3–4 per week; 18hr).

The Bothnian coast:
Gävle to Haparanda

Highlights

CHAPTER 5

✳ **Stone architecture, Sundsvall** Admire the grand avenues of this vibrant northern city, lined with elegant turn-of-the-twentieth-century stone buildings.
See p.283

✳ **Högbonden, High Coast** A night in the former lighthouse on this unspoilt island, complete with shore-side sauna, is unbeatable.
See p.292

✳ **Elk farm, Bjurholm** Come face to face with the elusive "King of the Forest" at this fascinating farm outside Umeå. See p.300

✳ **Pite Havsbad, Piteå Northern** Sweden's premier beach resort is renowned for long hours of sunshine and warm waters.
See p.303

✳ **Gammelstad, Luleå** Four hundred and fifty knarled wooden cottages make up Sweden's most extensive church town, offering an insight into the country's religious past. See p.307

✳ **Luleå archipelago** Take a boat trip to one of the dozens of pine-clad islands at the very top of the Gulf of Bothnia. See p.308

▲ Gammelstad

5

The Bothnian coast: Gävle to Haparanda

S weden's east coast, bordering the **Gulf of Bothnia** (Bottenhavet), forms a corridor of land that is quite unlike the rest of the north of the country; the forest, so apparent in other parts of the north, has been felled here to make room for settlements. Although the entire coastline is dotted with towns and villages that reveal a faded history – some, like **Gävle** and **Hudiksvall**, still have their share of old wooden houses, though sadly much was lost during the Russian incursions of the eighteenth century – it is cities like **Sundsvall**, **Umeå** and **Luleå** that are more typical of the region: modern, bright and airy metropolises that rank as some of northern Sweden's liveliest and most likeable destinations.

All along the coast you'll find traces of the religious fervour that swept the north in centuries past; **Skellefteå** and particularly **Luleå** (included on the UNESCO World Heritage List) both boast excellently preserved **kyrkstäder** or church towns – clusters of old wooden cottages dating from the early eighteenth century, where villagers from outlying districts would spend the night after making the lengthy journey to church in the nearest town. Working your way up the coast, perhaps on the long train ride to Swedish Lapland, it's worth breaking your trip at one or two of these places.

The highlight of the Bothnian coast is undoubtedly the stretch known as the **Höga Kusten**, or the High Coast (see p.289), north of Härnösand: for peace and quiet, this is easily the most idyllic part of the Swedish east coast. Its indented coastline is best seen from the sea, with shimmering fjords that reach deep inland, tall cliffs and a string of pine-clad islands that make it possible to island-hop up this section of coast. The weather here may not be as reliable as further south, but you're guaranteed clean beaches (which you'll often have to yourself), crystal clear waters and some of the finest countryside for walking.

Getting around

Unlike southern Sweden, travel anywhere in the north of the country requires careful planning. Many **trains**, including the SJ departures to Swedish Lapland, only operate once daily and **bus** services to destinations off the beaten track can be skeletal – particularly between mid-June and mid-August when, arguably, the need for transport is greatest. Before setting off, make sure you check all travel

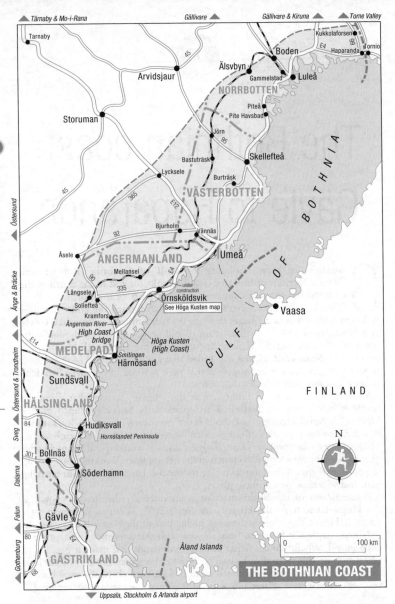

Tärnaby & Mo-i-Rana ▲   **Gällivare** ▲   **Gällivare & Kiruna** ▲   ▲ **Torne Valley**

Tarnaby

Kukkolaforsen
Haparanda — Tornio
Boden
Älsvbyn
Gammelstad — Luleå
Arvidsjaur
NORRBOTTEN
Storuman
Piteå
Pite Havsbad
Jörn
Skellefteå
Bastuträsk
Lycksele
Burträsk
VÄSTERBOTTEN
Bjurholm
Vännäs
Åsele
ÄNGERMANLAND
Umeå
Mellansel
under construction
Långsele
Örnsköldsvik
Sollefteå
See Höga Kusten map
Kramfors
Ångerman River
High Coast bridge
Vaasa
Höga Kusten
(High Coast)
MEDELPAD
Smitingen
Härnösand
G U L F   O F   B O T H N I A
Sundsvall
HÄLSINGLAND
F I N L A N D
Hudiksvall
Hornslandet Peninsula
Bollnäs
Söderhamn
N
Gävle
Åland Islands

0   100 km

GÄSTRIKLAND

THE BOTHNIAN COAST

◀ Östersund   ◀ Ånge & Bräcke   ◀ Östersund & Trondheim   ◀ Sveg   ◀ Dalarna   ◀ Falun   ◀ Gothenburg

▼ *Uppsala, Stockholm & Arlanda airport*

details thoroughly: two good places to start are the SJ and Resplus websites,
Ⓦ www.sj.se and Ⓦ www.resplus.se.

Buses and trains

The **train** route north from Uppsala hugs the **coast** from Gävle until
Sundsvall, where northbound services currently terminate. However, upon

completion of Botniabanan, the new coastal railway line north of Sundsvall, trains should continue up to Umeå from late 2010. Until then you'll need to catch one of the **Kustbussen** coaches to reach either Umeå or Luleå, where you can connect back onto the train. From Sundsvall trains run **inland** to Östersund via Ånge and Bräcke where you can connect with services operating on the main line to Swedish Lapland and on to the Norwegian port of Narvik. There are also several bus services running inland from Umeå and Skellefteå, which can whisk you up into the mountains of Swedish Lapland, should you wish to head inland from further up the Bothnian coast.

Ferries

Along the High Coast, island-hopping north of Härnösand via Högbonden, Ulvön and Trysunda (see p.294) is a wonderful way to make your way north and to take in one of northern Sweden's most beautiful regions at the same time. **Ferry** tickets here are good value; see p.292 for details. Once again, though, you'll need to carefully check departure times to make sure you're not left stranded either on the islands or the mainland; the general pattern of services is given in the text.

Gävle and around

It's only ninety minutes north by train from Stockholm to **GÄVLE** (pronounced "Yerv-luh", and confusingly similar to a much-used Swedish swearword), capital of the district of Gästrikland. Gävle is also the southernmost city of **Norrland**, the region – comprising almost two-thirds of Sweden – which represents wilderness territory in the minds of most Swedes. To all intents and purposes, Norrland, Sweden's main reservoir of natural resources with vast forests and large ore deposits, means everything north of Uppsala; crossing into here from Svealand (which together with Götaland makes up the southern third of the country) is – as far as the Swedish psyche is concerned – like leaving civilization behind.

Gävle's town charter was granted as long ago as 1446, a fact that's at variance with the modernity of the centre's large squares, broad avenues and proud monumental buildings. The city was almost completely rebuilt after a devastating fire in 1869 and its docks and warehouses reflect the heady success of its late nineteenth-century industry, when Gävle was the export centre for locally produced iron and timber. Today, the city is more famous as the home of **Gevalia coffee** ("Gevalia" being the old Latinized name for the town), which you'll no doubt taste during your time in Sweden and certainly smell in the air in Gävle.

Arrival and information

The city centre is concentrated in the grid of streets spreading southwest from the **Resecentrum** on Centralplan containing both the train and bus stations. A ten-minute walk from here is the **tourist office** at Drottninggatan 9 (Mon–Fri 9am–7pm, Sat 10am–4pm, Sun noon–4pm; ℡026/14 74 30, Ⓦwww.gastrikland.com) inside the Gallerian Nian shopping centre. If you need **internet** access, head for Sidewalk Express in the Resecentrum.

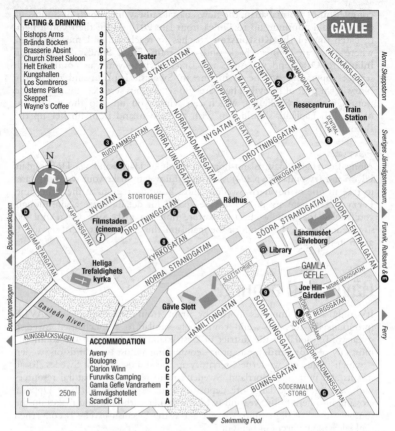

EATING & DRINKING

Bishops Arms	9
Brända Bocken	5
Brasserie Absint	C
Church Street Saloon	8
Helt Enkelt	7
Kungshallen	1
Los Sombreros	4
Österns Pärla	3
Skeppet	2
Wayne's Coffee	6

GÄVLE

Teater
Resecentrum
Train Station
Rådhus
Filmstaden (cinema)
Heliga Trefaldighets kyrka
Gävle Slott
Länsmuséet Gävleborg
Library
GAMLA GEFLE
Joe Hill-Gården

STAKETGATAN
N. CENTRALGATAN
SÖDRA ESPLANADGATAN
FÄLTSKÄRSLEDEN
HATTMAKARGATAN
NORRA KÖPMANGATAN
NYGATAN
NORRA KÖPPARSLAGERGATAN
DROTTNINGGATAN
CENTRAL PLAN
RUDDAMMSGATAN
NORRA RÅDMANSGATAN
NORRA KUNGSGATAN
KYRKOGATAN
STORTORGET
NYGATAN
SÖDRA STRANDGATAN
SÖDRA CENTRALGATAN
KAPLANSGATAN
DROTTNINGGATAN
KYRKOGATAN
SLOTTSTORGET
NEDRE BERGSGATAN
NORRA STRANDGATAN
ÖVRE BERGSGRÄND
NEDRE BERGSGATAN
BYGGMÄSTARGATAN
Gaveån River
HAMILTONGATAN
SÖDRA KUNGSGATAN
SÖDRA RÅDMANSGATAN
KUNGSBÄCKSVÄGEN
BUNNSSGATAN
SÖDERMALM-STORG

Norra Skeppsbron
Sveriges Järnvägsmuseum,
Furuvik, Rullsand &
Ferry

0   250m

ACCOMMODATION

Aveny	G
Boulogne	D
Clarion Winn	C
Furuviks Camping	E
Gamla Gefle Vandrarhem	F
Järnvägshotellet	B
Scandic CH	A

Swimming Pool

Boulognerskogen

Accommodation

Gävle has a good selection of accommodation and reservations are rarely necessary as the town isn't often overrun with visitors. The best place to stay is the city centre where you're within easy walking distance of the restaurants and bars.

Aveny Södra Kungsgatan 31 ☏026/61 55 90, ⊛www.aveny.nu. A small and comfortable family-run hotel south of the river, whose brightly painted rooms are hung with wall paintings and have nice wooden floors. ④/③

Boulogne Byggmästargatan 1 ☏026/12 63 52, ⊛www.hotellboulogne.com. Cosy, basic hotel, with breakfast brought to your room on a tray. Freshly brewed coffee available every evening. Close to Boulognerskogen park. ②

Clarion Winn Norra Slottsgatan 9 ☏026/64 70 00, ⊛www.clarionwinngavle.se. A large, smart hotel with 200 rooms, its own pool, sauna and sunbeds. Rooms are tasteful, if characterless and rather dark, with neutral decor and wooden floors.

The extensive breakfast buffet is one of the best in northern Sweden. ④/③

Furuviks Camping Södra Kungsvägen, Furuvik ☏026/17 73 00, ⊛www.camping.se/x12. Gävle's campsite is located by the amusement park, off Östnäsvägen, out at Furuvik (see p.279), a bus ride away on #838, which leaves roughly every 30min. Also has cabins for rent (①)

Gamla Gefle Vandrarhem Södra Rådmansgatan 1 ☏026/62 17 45, ℮stf.vandrarhem@telia.com. Beautifully located in the cobbled old town. It's worth timing your arrival carefully as reception is not staffed from 10am–5pm. Dorm beds 210kr, double room ①

Järnvägshotellet Centralplan 3 ☏026/12 09 90, ⊛www.jarnvagshotellet.nu. The cheapest hotel in

Gävle; fine, though most rooms aren't en suite, and it's located on a busy corner opposite the Resecentrum. Rooms in the annexe section have private facilities and cost around 200kr more. ❷ **Scandic CH** Nygatan 45 ☎026/495 84 00, ⓦwww.scandic-hotels.se. One of the smartest hotels in town, with old-fashioned en-suite rooms decorated in different colours on different floors. The "red floor" rooms with their bold wallpaper designs in reds and pinks are particularly attractive. ❺/❹

The Town

Although Gävle is one of the bigger towns in Norrland, you can comfortably see everything in a day. Your first point of call should be **Gamla Gefle**, the old town district, where you'll also find the town's two museums, **Joe Hill-Gården** and **Länsmuséet Gävleborg**. Nearby, the **Heliga Trefaldighets kyrka** is a riot of seventeenth-century woodcarving and makes a pleasant stop en route to Gävle's city park, **Boulognerskogen**, a vast expanse of forested parkland ideal for a picnic or a leisurely stroll.

Gamla Gefle

It's only a ten-minute walk from the train station, across the Gavleån river, to the district of **Gamla Gefle**, which escaped much of the fire damage and today passes itself off as the authentic old town. Unfortunately, though it's the most interesting part of the city, it doesn't amount to much. The few remaining narrow cobbled streets – notably Övre Bergsgatan, Bergsgränd and Nedre Bergsgränd – boast pastel-coloured wooden cottages, window boxes overflowing with flowers in summer and old black lanterns. It's all very attractive and quaint and the jumbled lanes now house the odd craft shop and a café or two.

For a glimpse of social conditions a century ago, visit the **Joe Hill-Gården** at Nedre Bergsgatan 28 (June–Aug daily 10am–3pm; free; other times by arrangement on ☎026/61 34 25), the birthplace of one Johan Emanuel Hägglund in 1879. He emigrated to the United States in 1902, changed his name to Joe Hill, and became a working-class hero – his songs and speeches became rallying cries to comrades in the International Workers of the World, a Utah-based syndicalist organization, which runs the museum today. Its collection of pictures and belongings is given piquancy by the inclusion of the telegram announcing his execution in 1915 – he was framed for murder in Salt Lake City – and his last will and testament.

On the northern edge of Gamla Gefle on the riverside, the county museum, **Länsmuséet Gävleborg**, at Södra Strandgatan 20 (mid-June to mid-Aug Mon–Fri 11am–5pm, Sat & Sun noon–4pm; mid-Aug to mid-June Tues–Fri 10am–4pm, Wed until 9pm, Sat & Sun noon–4pm; 50kr; Wed free; ⓦwww .lansmuseetgavleborg.se). has displays of artwork by some of the great Swedish artists from the seventeenth century to the present day, including Nils Kreuger and Carl Larsson. Also on display is the work of a local artist, Johan-Erik Olsson (popularly known as "Lim-Johan"), whose vivid imagination and naive technique produced some strange childlike paintings.

Gävle Slott and Heliga Trefaldighets kyrka

Follow the river west from the museum to the double bridges of Rådmansbron and Kungsbron and you'll come to **Gävle Slott**, the seventeenth-century residence of the county governor, which lost its ramparts and towers years ago and now lurks behind a row of trees like some minor country house. However, it's not open to the public.

From here, a short walk west following the river leads to a wooden bridge, across which is Kaplansgatan and the **Heliga Trefaldighets kyrka**, the Church of the Holy Trinity, a seventeenth-century masterpiece of **woodcarved** decoration: check out the pulpit, towering altarpiece and screen, each the superb work of the German craftsman, Ewardt Friis.

Central Gävle and Boulognerskogen park

The modern city lies north of the river, its broad streets and avenues designed to prevent fires from spreading. A slice through the middle of the centre is comprised of parks, tree-lined spaces and fountains, running north from the spire-like **Rådhus** to the beautiful nineteenth-century theatre designed by Axel Nyström. All the main banks, shops and stores are in the grid of streets on either side of Norra Kungsgatan and Norra Rådmansgatan; the **Resecentrum** is about 700m to the east. From the train station, look across the tracks and you'll see the beginnings of an industrial area. Home to three parallel streets of old dock-side **warehouses**, off Norra Skeppsbron just by the river, it's a reminder of the days when ships unloaded coffee and spices in the centre of Gävle. To get to the warehouses, use the subway to head under the railway tracks, and walk east to the riverside. Today, with company names emblazoned on the red, wooden fronts of the empty buildings, the area feels more like a Hollywood movie set than a Swedish town. Continue to the far eastern end of the warehouses and the heady smell of roasting coffee becomes ever stronger: Gevalia has its production centre here right next to the harbour at Nyhamn, north off Norra Skeppsbron.

On a rainy day (or even a fine one) you may find yourself contemplating the **Sveriges Järnvägsmuseum** or Swedish Railway museum, at Rälsgatan 1 (June–Aug daily 10am–4pm; Sept–May Tues–Sun 10am–4pm; 40kr; ⓦ www .jarnvagsmuseum.se). It's less than half an hour's walk: from the station cross Islandsbron bridge, then head south along Fältskärsleden which later becomes Upplandsgatan; turn right onto Österbågen, right again into Växelgatan and finally left into Rälsgatan. Located in what used to be Gävle's engine shed, it's a train enthusiast's paradise, stuffed to the gills with really old locomotives and information on SJ's pride and joy, the X2000; a simulator allows you to test drive the train for five minutes. The highlight is the hunting coach dating from 1859; one of the world's oldest railway carriages, it once belonged to King Carl XV.

Boulognerskogen park and swimming complex

West of the city centre and a twenty-minute stroll down picturesque Kungsbäcksvägen, a narrow street lined with brightly painted wooden houses beginning at Heliga Trefaldighets kyrka, you'll come to the rambling nineteenth-century park, **Boulognerskogen**. It's a good place for a picnic and a spot of sunbathing or a visit to the music pavilions, open-air **café** or the sculpture, by Carl Milles, of five angels playing musical instruments.

Beyond the sculpture, on the southern edge of the park, Västra Ringvägen slices south through the well-tended streets of suburban Gävle to the equally enticing Fjärran Höjderbadet **swimming complex** at Lantmäterigatan 5. Downstairs is an impressively large – and often deserted – pool and Jacuzzi plus an outdoor pool, whilst upstairs is a health suite with a couple of saunas (100kr entrance fee covers everything).

Eating and drinking

There's a fair choice of **eating places** in Gävle, with the best options in the central grid of streets around Stortorget and up and down the streets running from Rådhus to the theatre. The roomy Stortorget, just west of the central esplanade formed by Drottinggatan and Nygatan, has an open-air **market** that's worth visiting for its fruit and vegetable (Mon–Sat 9am–4pm).

Bishops Arms Södra Kungsgatan 7. A 15min walk from the centre, this pseudo-English pub comes complete with heavy floral wallpaper and even brass coal scuttles and chamber pots hanging from the ceiling. With outdoor seating in summer, it's *the* place to do your boozing.

Brända Bocken Stortorget ☎026/12 45 45. Young and fashionable, with outdoor seating in summer, plus an upstairs terrace. Inventive, modern menu featuring chicken breast stuffed with sundried tomatoes and tarragon aioli and salmon baked with gnocchi and pesto for 142kr. Also a popular place for a drink.

Brasserie Absint Norra Slottsgatan 9 ☎026/64 70 00. A delightful French brasserie with lots of mirrors and black tiling right in the heart of Gävle; it's attached to the Clarion Winn hotel. A wide range of dishes ranging from burgers (99kr) and spaghetti carbonara (69kr) to Wiener schnitzel (129kr), herb rack of lamb (195kr) and beef with onions (145kr).

Church Street Saloon Kyrkogatan 11 ☎026/12 62 11. A fun American saloon diner complete with riding boots, bridles and saddles and an American flag in the window. Plenty of Wild West grills on the plates and dancing on the tables. Meaty mains from around 150kr.

Helt Enkelt Norra Kungsgatan 3 ☎026/12 06 04. Modern Swedish mains (95–179kr) dominate the menu at this winning restaurant: smoked salmon,

chicken breast stuffed with feta, swordfish or lamb fillet are all worth trying. A few vegetarian dishes available, too.

Kungshallen Norra Kungsgatan 17 ☎026/18 69 64. A smart pizzeria serving mammoth pizzas from 65kr, steaks from 119kr and salads from 74kr, as well as a selection of excellent value chicken dishes for 89kr.

Los Sombreros Norra Slottsgatan 7 ☎026/10 10 92. Gävle's very own Mexican restaurant with plastic cacti in the windows and sombreros hanging over every table. They serve fajitas (129kr), burritos (109kr) as well as a wide range of grilled meats (from 139kr).

Österns Pärla Ruddammsgatan 23 ☎026/51 39 68. A stylish Asian restaurant with brushed metal interior walls decorated with bamboo poles. A good selection of Thai, Chinese, Japanese and vegetarian options, such as pork in sweet and sour sauce (118kr). Three set Thai dishes with dessert goes for 105kr.

Skeppet Nygatan 45 ☎026/12 99 50. Located in the basement below the *Scandic CH* and serving fine fish and seafood dishes amid tasteful maritime decor; main courses start from 200kr.

Wayne's Coffee Drottningatan 16. As always with this chain café, excellent coffees and cakes make this the best and busiest café in Gävle, centrally located in the main square. It's on the first floor where there's also access to outdoor seating.

Around Gävle

If the sun's shining, you'll find locals catching the rays at the sandy beach of **Rullsand**, about 25km east of town, which is also popular with naturists. To get here from Gävle, first take the train to Skutskär and then connect to bus #962 which runs all the way to the beach (bus times are at Ⓦwww .ul.se). Alternatively, at Furuvik (the train stop before Skutskär), you'll find the **Furuvik amusement park** (daily: late May to mid-June & mid-Aug to late Aug 10am–5pm; mid-June to mid-Aug 10am–7pm; entry is 120kr plus a further 150kr for an *åkband* ticket covering the attractions; Ⓦwww.furuvik.se). The place boasts a zoo, fairground, parks and playgrounds.

Northeast of Gävle, the beaches at **Engeltofta** or **Engesberg** are also within easy striking distance without your own transport; catch bus #95 from the Rådhus. From Engesberg, the bus continues to **Bönan**, where an old lighthouse marks a good spot for swimming. Other enjoyable beaches are on the island of **Limön**, connected by a summer ferry, **MS Drottning Silvia** (Ⓦwww.swed.net/drottning-silvia), from Norra Skeppsbron, reached by heading east along the banks of the Gavleån River from behind the Resecentrum (3 daily; 40min; 40kr), calling at Engeltofta on the way, if required.

Hudiksvall and around

On the first leg of the coastal journey further into Norrland, train services are frequent. Along this stretch of coast, **Hudiksvall** makes for a leisurely stop en route to the bigger towns and tourist centres further north. Hudiksvall's wood-panelled architecture and convenience for visiting the natural beauty of the nearby **Hornslandet peninsula**, jutting out into the Gulf of Bothnia, are the main draws.

Hudiksvall

Granted town status in 1582 by King Johan III and accordingly the second oldest town in Norrland, **HUDIKSVALL** has seen its fair share of excitement over the years. Though the original settlement was built around what had been the bay of Lillfjärden, at the mouth of the Hornån river, the harbour began to silt up, and so it was decided in the early 1640s to move the town to its current location: the old bay is now a lake, connected to the sea by a small canal.

The town has suffered no less than ten **fires**, the worst occurring in 1721 when Russian forces swept down the entire length of the Bothnian coast, burning and looting as they went. Then an important commercial and shipping centre, the town bore the brunt of the onslaught; only its **church** (June–Aug Mon–Fri 10am–4pm; Sept–May Mon–Thurs 11am–3pm), still pockmarked with cannonball holes today, remained standing. Although St Jakob's white stone exterior topped with a green onion dome is elegant enough, it's the interior that really impresses; unusually ornate for the Swedish Orthodox church, nineteenth-century renovators opted for brown marble hand-painted wall decoration, delicately lit by ornate candle-bearing chandeliers. The incongruous cannonball by the steps to the pulpit is a replica of the original fired by the Russians at the church. A further blaze, east of Rådhustorget, in 1792 led to a rethink of the town's layout, and so the street plan which exists today was conceived.

Turn right out of the train station and cross the narrow canal, Strömmingssundet ("Herring Sound"), and you'll soon see the small old **harbour** on the right; this area is known as **Möljen**. Here the wharfside is flanked by a line of red wooden fishermen's cottages and storehouses, all leaning into the water; it's a popular place for locals to while away a couple of hours in the summer sunshine, dangling their feet into the water. The back of the warehouses hides a run of handicraft studios and the tourist office (see below). More impressive and much larger than Möljen, **Fiskarstan** (Fishermen's Town), beyond the *First Hotel Statt* down Storgatan, contains neat examples of the so-called "Imperial" wood-panel architecture of the late eighteenth and nineteenth centuries. It was in these tightly knit blocks of streets, lined with beautiful wooden houses and fenced-in plots of land, that the fishermen used to live during the winter. Take a peek inside some of the little courtyards – all window boxes, flowers and cobblestones.

The history of these buildings is put into context in the excellent **Hälsinglands Museum** at Storgatan 31 (Mon noon–4pm, Tues–Fri 9am–4pm, Sat 11am–3pm; free; Ⓦwww.halsinglandsmuseum.se), which traces the development of Hudiksvall as a harbour town since its foundation. The museum's real showstoppers, however, are the ornately decorated **Malsta rune stone**, from around 1000 AD, ornately engraved with the letter-less Helsinge runic script – ask at the museum reception for a translation of the inscription – and the quite breathtaking collection of **medieval church art** kept in a dimly lit room, just to the right of the reception desk. From altar screens to intricately carved wooden figures of Sweden's saints, this astounding array of outstanding craftsmanship is sure to impress; the centrepiece is the sixteenth-century figure of the Madonna by renowned local artist, Haaken Gulleson from the village of Enånger in Hälsingland. Whilst here, be sure also to see the paintings by **John Sten** on the ground floor: born near Hudiksvall in 1879, he moved to Paris at the age of 30, where he was greatly influenced by Gauguin. Tragically, Sten died of dysentery at the age of 42 in Bali; like many artists of his day he travelled extensively in Southeast Asia collecting impressions and designs, and became one of the first to work with Cubism, from which his work extends towards a more decorative fanciful style.

Undoubtedly the best time to visit Hudiksvall is during the beginning of July, when the town hosts the **Musik vid Dellen**, a multifarious cultural ten-day festival, including folk music and other traditional events (for more information, contact the tourist office or see ⓦ www.misikviddellen.se), held in churches and farms in the surrounding countryside.

Practicalities

The **train** and **bus stations** are opposite each other on Stationsgatan. It takes two minutes to walk from either, along Stationsgatan, to the town centre around Möljen. Here, on the main street, the **tourist office** (mid-June to mid-Aug Mon–Fri 9am–6.30pm, Sat & Sun 10am–3pm; mid-Aug to mid-June Mon–Fri 10am–4.30pm; ⓣ0650/191 00, ⓦ www.halsingland.com) at Storgatan 33 has maps of the town and other useful information. For **internet** access, head for the library inside Folkets Hus, opposite the First Hotel Statt on Storgatan, or Hälsinglands Museum.

Accommodation

The **youth hostel** (ⓣ0650/132 60, ⓦ www.malnbadenscamping.com; dorm beds 225kr, double room ❶) is out at the Malnbaden **campsite**, 3km from town. Bus #5 runs there hourly in summer (10am–6pm); at other times you'll have to get there by taxi. For **hotel** accommodation, there's *Hotell Temperance* (ⓣ0650/311 07, ⓦ www.hotelltemperance.se; ❹), a cheapish place at Håstagatan 16, near the train station, which has utilitarian rooms (some are ensuite and cost 200kr more); there are also youth hostel dorm beds here for 350kr per person. The swishest hotel in town is the 1878 *First Hotel Statt*, at Storgatan 36 (ⓣ0650/150 60, ⓦ www.firsthotels.se; ❺/❸). It was here that the barons of the timber industry did their best to live up to the town's nickname of "Glada Hudik" ("Happy Hudiksvall"), a phrase coined in the first half of the nineteenth century, when the people here became known for their lively social life and generous hospitality.

Eating and drinking

Today, Hudiksvall continues its sociable tradition with a few decent eating and drinking places, though none are likely to form the highlight of a trip to Sweden.

For **snacks** and cakes, try *Dackås Konditori* at Storgatan 34, a Hudiksvall institution that's been here since the 1950s – with decor to match. A popular **restaurant** is *E Lounge & Matsal* (ⓣ0650/165 50) at Storgatan 49, whose warm wooden interior is the perfect place to enjoy modern Swedish home-cooking, such as ovenbaked pike-perch with salade Niçoise (mains 80–200kr). Alternatively, try the superb 🍴 *Hot Chili* (ⓣ0650/757 50), at Hamngatan 5 near the station, where the chefs rustle up magnificent Asian stirfries before your eyes for 79kr (also takeaway). The one and only **bar** is the *Pub Tre Bockar* at Bankgränd 1, opposite the fishermen's warehouses at Möljen, with occasional evening jazz. For those empty afternoons or evenings, you'll find the **cinema** at Drottninggatan 1 and the **swimming pool** at Norra Kyrkogatan 9B.

The Hornslandet peninsula

For a day-trip, head southeast out to the beautiful and unspoilt **Hornslandet peninsula**, renowned for its quaint fishing villages of red wooden cottages and sandy **beaches**. This egg-shaped chunk of land is the geological result of continuous land rise since the last Ice Age; as recently as the Viking era, the Arnösund sound, which once separated Hornslandet from the mainland, was easily navigable and remained an important channel for seafarers until the tenth century. Today, though, the sound has silted up and the peninsula is effectively an extension of the Bothnian coast. This whole area is rich in flora and fauna, as well as being ideal for swimming, fishing and walking; there are two villages to head for in particular: **Hölick** and **Kuggörarna**.

Located at the southern tip of the peninsula, **HÖLICK**, the larger of the two villages, traces its history back to the sixteenth century when a small fishing community became established here. Although there are no sights to speak of, the main purpose for coming here is to enjoy the plentiful peace and tranquillity on the very edge of the Gulf of Bothnia; a set of wooden steps lead up from the pilot boat station (*lotsstation*) in the centre of the village onto the rocks from where there are unsurpassed **views** out over the sea. A seven-kilometre circular **walking path** (allow around 2hr) will take you through the surrounding nature reserve to some of the peninsula's finest **beaches**: from the village the path leads southeast out to the Hornslandsudden promontory – there are sandy stretches of coast all the way to the furthest point of the promontory – from where it cuts inland, heading over a series of low hills, back towards Hölick. Heading in the opposite direction and following the road out of Hölick back towards Arnöviken and Hudiksvall, you'll come to another popular beach (near Arnöviken), frequented by **naturists** (ask as the campsite for precise directions).

If you want to stay here, **accommodation** is restricted to *Natura Hölick Resort & Camping* (T0650/56 50 32, Wwww.naturaholick.se; late May to mid–Sept), at Arnöviken 84 which also has **cabins** (❸) for rent; look out for the signs where the road into the village ends. Hölick also boasts one **restaurant**, *Sjöboa* (T0650/56 50 02; late May to mid–Sept), whose fish buffet for 130kr is truly superb.

Tiny **KUGGÖRARNA**, actually located on a small island, is joined to the rest of the peninsula by a narrow bridge across the dividing sound. Once again, it's for solitude and great sea vistas that most visitors come here, although the hamlet does have a couple of things worth seeking out: the eighteenth-century **chapel** up on the hill above the houses is worth a quick look (you'll find the key hanging by the door), and, just to the north of the cluster of houses, is a well-preserved stone **labyrinth**, a collection of winding walkways delineated by large stones on the ground, used in centuries past by superstitious fishermen to ensure a good catch. There's neither accommodation nor eateries here.

Getting to the Hornslandet peninsula by public transport is only possible in summer: take bus #37 (mid-June to mid-Aug, 2 daily; Wwww.xtrafik.se) which runs from the bus station via Hölick (40min) to Kuggörarna (1hr), otherwise, with your own transport, Route 778 leads to Kuggörarna from Hällby, just north of Hudiksvall.

Sundsvall

The capital of the tiny province of Medelpad, **SUNDSVALL** is often referred to as "Stone City", for the simple reason that most of its buildings are made of stone – a fact that distinguishes it immediately from other coastal towns here. Once home to a rapidly expanding timber industry, the whole city burned to the ground the day after Midsummer in June 1888. A spark from the wood-burning steamboat *Selånger* (promptly dubbed "The Arsonist") set fire to a nearby brewery, and the rest, as they say, is history – so much so that the remark "that hasn't happened since the town burned down" is now an established Sundsvall saying. Nine thousand people lost their homes in the resulting blaze. The work of rebuilding the city began at once, and within ten years a new centre had been constructed, entirely of **stone**. The result is a living document of turn-of-the-twentieth-century urban architecture, designed and crafted by

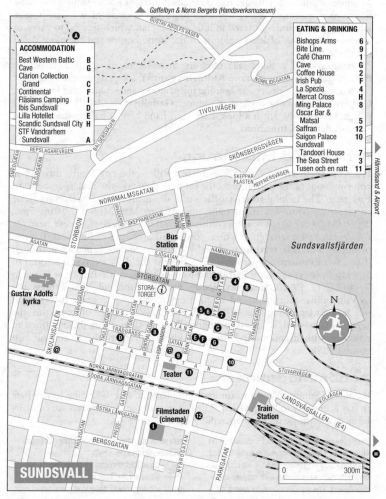

Gaffelbyn & Norra Bergets (Handsverksmuseum)

ACCOMMODATION

Best Western Baltic	B
Cave	G
Clarion Collection Grand	C
Continental	F
Fläsians Camping	I
Ibis Sundsvall	D
Lilla Hotellet	E
Scandic Sundsvall City	H
STF Vandrarhem Sundsvall	A

EATING & DRINKING

Bishops Arms	6
Bite Line	9
Café Charm	1
Cave	G
Coffee House	2
Irish Pub	F
La Spezia	4
Mercat Cross	H
Ming Palace	8
Oscar Bar & Matsal	5
Saffran	12
Saigon Palace	10
Sundsvall Tandoori House	7
The Sea Street	3
Tusen och en natt	11

Härnösand & Airport

SUNDSVALL

architects who were involved in rebuilding Stockholm's residential areas at the same time. Wide streets and esplanades that would serve as firebreaks in the event of another fire formed the backbone of their work. These thoroughfares are home to 573 residential buildings, all of which went up in four years; the centerpiece is the house that dominates the main square, Storatorget.

The reconstruction, however, was achieved at a price: the workers who had laboured on the city's refurbishment became the victims of their own success. They were shifted from their old homes in the centre and moved out south to a run-down suburb – the glaring contrast between the wealth of the new centre and the poverty of the surrounding districts was only too obvious. When **Nils Holgersson**, a character created by the children's author Selma Lagerlöf (see p.162), looked down from the back of his flying goose (see the picture on 20kr notes), he remarked: "There was something funny about it when you saw it from above, because in the middle there was a group of high stone houses, so impressive that they hardly had their equal in Stockholm. Around the stone houses was an empty space, and then there was a circle of wooden houses, which were pleasantly scattered in little gardens, but which seemed to carry an awareness of being of lesser value than the stone houses and therefore dared not come too close."

Having gawped at Sundsvall's imposing architecture, most visitors make for the city's other main attraction: **Kulturmagasinet**, a superb museum complex located right in the city centre housing the paintings and sculptures of local artist, Carl Frisendahl, amongst others. In summer, **Gaffelbyn**, Sundsvall's outdoor craft village, is definitely worth a look – try your hand here at baking the northern Swedish flatbread, **tunnbröd**.

Arrival and information

From the **train station**, it's a five-minute walk to the city centre; turn left as you come out of the station, cross the car park then take the underpass beneath Parkgatan. The helpful **tourist office** is in the main square, Storatorget (June to mid-Aug Mon–Fri 10am–6pm; mid-Aug to May Mon–Fri 10am–5pm; ℡060/61 04 50, Ⓦwww.sundsvallturism.com). For **internet access** head for Pressbyrån at Esplanaden 2 where you'll find a couple of Sidewalk Express terminals. The **bus station** is close by at the bottom of Esplanaden, though if you want information or advance tickets for the daily express bus south to Stockholm, north to Umeå, or inland to Östersund, visit Y-Bussen at Sjögatan 7 (℡060/17 19 60, Ⓦwww.ybuss.se). For the Lapplandspilen express bus to Vilhelmina, Storuman and destinations to Klippen contact ℡0940/150 30, Ⓦwww.lapplandspilen.se. The **airport**, 24km north of town on the way to Härnösand, is linked to Sundsvall by an airport bus (80kr), timed to coincide with flights to and from Stockholm; alternatively, a taxi will cost around 225kr.

Accommodation

Rooms in Sundsvall, even in summer, are plentiful, and so finding somewhere to stay is unlikely to be a problem. The majority of the city's **hotels** are centrally located, and throw up some incredibly good bargains.

Best Western Baltic Sjögatan 5 ℡060/14 04 40, Ⓦwww. baltichotell.com. Centrally located, near the Kulturmagasinet and the harbour, with tastefully decorated rooms with carpets and chandeliers. The smaller economy rooms off reception are several hundred *kronor* cheaper and excellent value. ⑤/③

🏃 **Cave** Rådhusgatan 11 ℡060/61 33 12, Ⓦwww.cavehotell.com/default.html. Airy, bright and charmingly decorated in shades of light grey and off-white, the nine doubles and two singles at this newly renovated, family-owned hotel are justifiably popular. All rooms have a flat-screen TV. ❸

Clarion Collection Grand Nybrogatan 13 ☏060/64 65 60, ⓦwww.choice.se. The sauna and Jacuzzi suite and gym are excellent and included in the room rate; the rooms, however, are on the small side, though are nicely decorated in classic, modern Swedish style with wooden floors and smart furnishings. Tremendous value in summer when doubles go for less than 600kr. ❺/❸

Continental Rådhusgatan 13 ☏060/15 00 60, ⓦwww.continentalsundsvall.se. A fairly cheap centrally located hotel offering basic, en-suite rooms with cable TV, and a sun terrace. There's twenty percent off food at the *Irish Pub* (see below) for all guests. ❸/❷

Fläsians Camping Västra långgatan 69A ☏060/55 44 75, ⓦwww.camping.se/y2. Open mid-May to Aug, Sundsvall's campsite is 4km south of town, close to the E4. The tourist office can help with directions. Also has two-bed cabins for rent (❶).

Ibis Sundsvall Trädgårdsgatan 31–33 ☏060/64 17 50, ⓦwww.ibishotel.se. All rooms are en suite and some even have baths. Worth trying, especially

if the cheaper hotels are full; breakfast is an extra 70kr. Book well in advance on the net and a double room can be as little as 400kr. ❷

Lilla Hotellet Rådhusgatan 15 ☏060/61 35 87, ⓦwww.lilla-hotellet.se. Built one year after the great fire, this fine old hotel has lots of charm: high ceilings, period furniture and ornate chandeliers. One of the most reasonably priced hotels in town with just eight rooms, all of which are en suite. Smaller budget rooms costs 300kr less and are a great bargain. ❸/❷

Scandic Sundsvall City Esplanaden 29 ☏060/785 6200, ⓦwww.scandic-hotels.se. Newly renovated and more stylish than ever, with gorgeous nature prints covering entire walls of the rooms. This chain hotel boasts saunas, sunbeds and a good breakfast, too, with prices to match the opulence. Book early though and prices fall by one price code. ❻/❹

STF Vandrarhem Sundsvall Gaffelbyvägen, Norra Berget ☏060/61 21 19, ⓦwww.gaffelbyn.se. The youth hostel is a 30min walk north of town at Norra Berget, the mountain overlooking the city. Accommodation in cosy en-suite cabins. Any bus for Norra Berget from the bus station also comes here. Dorm beds 210kr, double rooms ❶

The City

As you walk in from the train station, the sheer scale of the rebuilding here after the 1888 fire is clear to see. **Esplanaden**, the wide central avenue, cuts the grid of streets in two; towards its northern end it's crossed by **Storgatan**, the widest road in town. **Storatorget**, the central square, is a delightfully roomy shopping and commercial centre, home to the city hall, various impromptu exhibitions and displays, as well as a fresh fruit and veg market (May to early Sept Mon–Sat from 8am). The limestone and brick buildings are four- and five-storey palatial structures. As you stroll the streets, you can't help but be amazed by the tremendous amount of open space that surrounds you, even in the heart of the city; Sundsvall is unique among Swedish cities in this respect, yet it's the most densely populated metropolis in northern Sweden.

Several of the buildings in the centre are worth a second look, not least the sturdy **Kulturmagasinet** (Mon–Thurs 10am–7pm, Fri 10am–6pm, Sat & Sun 11am–4pm; June–Aug 20kr, Sept–May free), housed within two blocks of late nineteenth-century warehouses, spanned by a glass roof, at Packhusgatan 4, down by the harbour. The buildings stood empty for twenty years before a decision was taken to turn them into what's now the Kulturmagasinet, comprising museum, library and café. The museum is actually built over an old street, Magasinsgatan, once boasting train tracks running between the warehouses to carry coffee and rice to export. Deserving of a quick look, the museum does its best to depict the history of Sundsvall and the province of Medelpad. Upstairs, the art exhibition warrants a few minutes of your time: the works of twentieth-century Swedish artists are on show here, in particular, those of the local artist and sculptor Carl Frisendahl (1886–1948) whose early style is heavily influenced by Rodin. At the age of 20, Frisendahl studied in Paris where he met his wife, Marie Barbaud. Forsaking his native Sweden for a studio in

Montparnasse, he began painting in the 1920s; his works, which often depict animals and mythological figures in combat, clearly show inspiration from Delacroix and Orthon Friesz.

Continue west along the main pedestrian street, Storgatan, and at the far end you'll come across a soaring red-brick structure, **Gustav Adolfs kyrka** (June–Aug daily 11am–4pm; Sept–May Mon–Sat noon–3pm) which marks the western end of the new town. The church's interior looks like a large Lego set, its pillars, vaults and window frames all constructed from smooth bricks, making an eye-pleasing picture of order.

Norra Berget and Gaffelbyn

Beyond the city's design, the most attractive diversion is the tiring three-kilometre climb to the heights of **Gaffelbyn** on **Norra Berget**, the hill that overlooks the city to the north; walk up Storgatan, cross over the main bridge and follow the sign to the youth hostel. If you'd prefer to spare your legs, any bus for Norra Berget will take you there.

The view on a clear day is fantastic, giving a fresh perspective on the city's planned structure and the restrictive nature of its location, hemmed in on three sides by hills and the sea. From here you can see straight across to Södra Berget, the southern hill, with its winter ski slopes. The best views can be had from the top of the **viewing tower** which has stood on this spot since 1897. Originally made entirely from wood, the tower fell victim over the years to the Swedish winter. By the 1930s it was in such poor condition that during one particularly severe autumn storm, the entire thing blew down; the present concrete replacement, 22m high, dates from 1954. The nearby **Norra Bergets Hantverksmuseum** (daily 11am–5pm; 20kr) is an open-air handicrafts museum with the usual selection of twee wooden huts and assorted activities, though you can often try your hand at baking some *tunnbröd*, the thin bread that's typical of northern Sweden. The idea is to roll out your dough extra thin, brush off as much flour as you can, slip the bread into the oven on a big, wooden pizza-type paddle, and count slowly to five.

Eating and drinking

Restaurants have mushroomed in Sundsvall over the last couple of years, and there's a good choice of places to eat and cuisines to choose from, including unusual options such as Vietnamese, Spanish and Indian – something you may want to make the most of if you're heading further north, where culinary options are limited. There are a handful of inexpensive pizza places and restaurants on Storgatan, most offering daily lunches. **Bars** in the city generally have a good atmosphere, and there are several places serving cheap beer.

Bite Line Köpmangatan 20 ☎ 060/61 00 29. Fun American pizza joint serving genuine deep-pan pizzas from 95kr for a two-person number. Also has salad options for 65kr. Football matches are shown live on the big screen here. There's an eat-as-much-as-you-can Taco buffet every evening until 9pm.

Café Charm Storgatan 34. Very much of the old school, this café is bedecked with chandeliers and has a quiet and refined seating area at the rear. A good choice for coffee and cake, sandwiches, pastries and naughty-but-nice cream concoctions.

Cave Rådhusgatan 11 ☎ 060/61 33 12. Tasty and expertly prepared Lebanese food is the order of the day at this elegant hotel restaurant. A wide variety of hot and cold meze (55kr) as well as more substantial fish and meat dishes such as marinated grilled lamb (210kr) or chicken on a skewer (195kr).

Coffee House Storgatan 31. At the far end of Sundsvall's main street, a small and agreeable modern café with Swedish coffee, tea, sandwiches, and newspapers.

La Spezia Sjögatan 6 ☎ 060/61 12 23. Long-established pizzeria serving decent bargain-basement pizzas from 45kr; also has a takeaway service.

Ming Palace Esplanaden 10 ☎060/61 53 00. The best Chinese restaurant in Sundsvall with a range of dishes, including beef with bean sprouts, from 85kr, to eat in, or take away.

Saffran Nybrogatan 25 ☎060/17 11 07. An authentic and much-praised Spanish restaurant whose fare includes a selection of tapas, such as patatas bravas and serrano ham, for 45–55kr. Mains include pork with walnuts (219kr), rack of lamb (229kr) and salmon tournedos (209kr).

Saigon Palace Trädgårdsgatan 5 ☎060/17 30 91. Vietnamese restaurant with good-value beef and chicken dishes from 78kr – try the delicious chicken in peanut sauce for 91kr.

The Sea Street Sjögatan 9 ☎060/17 30 31. Genuine Japanese sushi restaurant, which has taken Sundsvall by storm and is exceptional value for money. Mix and match: 9 pieces for 75kr, 11 for 99kr and 15 for 135kr.

🏃 **Sundsvall Tandoori House** Kyrkogatan 12 ☎060/17 59 59. In stylish new premises replete with open-air roof terrace, this is one of Sweden's best Indian restaurants serving up first-class meals, including lots of tandoori specialities, for around 120–150kr per main course.

Tusen och en natt Köpmangatan 7 ☎060/61 28 16. This place has all your Greek favourites, from tzatziki to souvlaki, as well as good pizzas and a few other Mediterranean specialities. Main courses from 130kr.

Bars

Bishops Arms Storgatan 13. Yet another Swedish attempt to create a traditional British wood-panelled pub in Norrland. The result is not bad though, and it's a fine place to sample a wide selection of British ales and beers.

Irish Pub Nybrogatan 16. This Irish pub not only brews its own beer in the basement, but also has a broad selection of traditional ales, beers, and stouts, plus bar meals, music and darts. There's twenty percent off food if you're staying at the *Continental*.

Mercat Cross Esplanaden 29. Attached to the Scandic Sundsvall City at the southern end of Esplanaden, this Scottish theme pub complete with heavy wood panelling and a life-size knight in full armour serves just about every variety of whisky you can think of.

Oscar Bar & Matsal Bankgatan 11. A good, lively Euro-loungebar with retro floral wallpaper and leather chairs and sofas. It's one of Sundsvall's most popular places for a drink and is packed to the rafters on Fri and Sat nights.

Härnösand

Full of architectural delights, including a number of old wooden cottages dating from the 1730s, the town of **HÄRNÖSAND** is definitely worth a stop on the way north. An hour's trip along the coast from Sundsvall, Härnösand marks the beginning of the stunningly beautiful region of **Ångermanland** – one of the few areas in Sweden where the countryside resembles that of neighbouring Norway.

A pleasant little place at the mouth of the Ångerman River, **Härnösand** was founded in 1585 by King Johan III. In 1647, the town was selected as the capital of the second most northerly diocese in Sweden and, accordingly, the new bishop decreed that the old stone church, which already stood in the town, be enlarged into a cathedral. The town has since had more than its fair share of disasters: in 1710, flames tore through the town after drunken churchgoers accidentally set fire to a boathouse; just four years later, Härnösand fell victim to a second great fire, started by a group of school students. Newly rebuilt, the town was razed by a third blaze in 1721, during the Great Northern War, when invading Russian forces burnt every house to the ground, bar one (see p.289).

Striking **architecture** awaits at every turn in Härnösand, notably around the harmonious main square, **Storatorget**, and winding **Östanbäcksgatan** with its eighteenth-century wooden houses painted in gentle pastel shades. A short walk from the town centre, the extensive open-air museum at **Murberget** showcases vernacular architecture from around the country. If you tire of buildings head out of town to the peninsula and some of the region's best **beaches**.

Arrival and information

Buses and **trains** operate from the new Resecentrum on Järnvägsgatan. From here, the **tourist office** at Storatorget 2 is five-minutes' walk away, located in a corner of the main square (June–Aug Mon–Fri 9am–6pm, Sat & Sun 10am–3pm; Sept–May Mon–Fri 8am–5pm; ☏0611/881 40, ⊛www.harnosand.se/turism). It has free maps, bus times and **internet access**.

Accommodation

Härnösand is not a big town and accordingly doesn't have a great choice of **accommodation**. However, you shouldn't have any problems getting a room, even in the height of summer.

First Stadt Härnösand Skeppsbron 9 ☏0611/55 44 40, ⊛www.firsthotels.se. The biggest and plushest of the town's hotels with a perfect waterside location and well-appointed, if rather staid, rooms. ⑤/③

🏃 **Östanbäcken Logi** Östanbäcksgatan 14, ☏0611/155 60 00, ⊛www.ostanbackenlogi.com. These cute red-and-white wooden cottages hidden in a charming garden off Östanbäcksgatan are a real find. Pine interiors, en-suite bathrooms and a fully fitted kitchen make them the number one place to stay. ③

Royal Strandgatan 12 ☏0611/204 55, ⊛www.hotelroyal.se. Perfectly located for the Resecentrum, this rather basic pile is the cheapest hotel in Härnösand, though rooms are perfectly comfortable. ④/③

Sälstens Camping Sälsten ☏0611/181 50. This waterfront campsite also has a small selection of four-bed cabins (①) per night. It's around 2km northeast of the town centre, next to a string of pebble beaches; to get there, take Storgatan off Nybrogatan and follow the road as it swings eastwards along the coast. Open mid–May to Aug.

STF Vandrarhem Härnösand Frantzéngatan 14 ☏0611/243 00, ℮mitti@telia.com. Located beside the cathedral in a charming building from 1844, the town's newly opened youth hostel is modern, clean and a great money saver. Dorm beds 210kr, double room ①.

The Town

For a provincial place, Härnösand reeks of grandeur and self-importance, each of its proud civic buildings a marker of the confidence the town exudes. The main square, **Storatorget**, was once declared by local worthies as the most beautiful in Sweden and it's easy to see why: the western edge of the square is proudly given over to the governor's residence, built in Neoclassical style using local brick by the court architect, Olof Tempelman; it rubs shoulders with the Neo-Renaissance former provincial government building on the southwestern edge. From the square take a stroll up Västra Kyrkogatan to the heights of the Neoclassical **Domkyrkan** (daily 10am–4pm), the smallest cathedral in the country. Dating from the 1840s, it incorporates elements from earlier churches on the site; the Baroque altar is from the eighteenth century, as are the VIP boxes in the nave.

From the Domkyrkan, turn right and follow the road round and back down the hill until you come to the narrow old street of **Östanbäcksgatan**, with its pretty painted wooden houses from the 1730s. This is one of the oldest parts of town, Östanbäcken, where the houses were among the first to be built after the Russian incursions. For a further taste of the town's architectural splendour, take a walk up the hilly main street, **Nybrogatan**, to its junction with Storgatan: the Neoclassical pastel orange **Rådhuset** here, complete with white semicircular portico, originally served as a school and home to the diocesan governors; while further up the hill, at the corner of Brunnshusgatan, the headquarters of the regional administration is particularly beautiful, housed in a Neo-Baroque and Art Nouveau building with a yellow ochre facade. From the top of Nybrogatan, there are good **views** back over the town and the water.

Murberget and the beaches

Whilst in town it's worth retracing your steps back down Nybrogatan to the train station, from where Stationsgatan (turning into Varvsallén) turns right, passing through the docks on its way to the impressive **open-air museum** at **Murberget** (late June to early Aug Tues–Sun 11am–5pm; free), the second biggest in Sweden after Skansen (see p.79). It's a thirty-minute walk up here from the town centre, or, alternatively buses #2 and #52 run from Nybrogatan in front of the Rådhuset.

The first building to take up its location here was a bell tower, which was moved from the village of Ullånger on the High Coast to its current position in 1913. There are around eighty other buildings, most notably traditional Ångermanland farmhouses and the old Murberget church, once a popular venue for local weddings. Look out for the Rysstugan, the one and only wooden building to escape the devastating fire caused by the Russians in 1721. The nineteenth-century **Spjute Inn** here is still home to a restaurant, and also contains a skittle alley dating from 1910, where you can have a game.

If the weather's good it's definitely worth heading in the opposite direction, east across the Härnön peninsula to **Smitingen**, barely 5km out of Härnösand, to some of the best **sandy beaches** in the whole of Norrland; undoubtedly the best way to get here is to **hire a boat** (the tourist office has details) and sail around the peninsula. It's also possible to take **bus** #14 from the Resecentrum. There are also **pebble beaches** near the Sälsten campsite, within walking distance of the town centre.

Eating and drinking

Make no mistake, Härnösand may be an architectural feast, but its culinary prowess most certainly isn't. Eating places are thin on the ground and, sadly, rather uninspiring. What follows is the pick of the best.

New China Restaurant Storgatan 34 ℡0611/136 06. A run-of-the-mill Asian restaurant with a decent range of predictable Chinese mains (from 86kr) as well as better Indonesian ones (from 120kr).

O'Leary's Storgatan 28 ℡0611/183 00. The omnipresent sports bar is here, too, with its TexMex mains and light bar meals.

Östanbäckens Pizzeria Östanbäcksgatan 1 ℡0611/125 00. A good bet for tasty pizzas costing around the 75kr mark.

Ruom Thai Storgatan 34 ℡0611/55 60 42. Next door to *New China*, this new and rather cavernous Thai restaurant is head and shoulders above any other restaurant in Härnösand: mains here, such as green chicken curry, go for 85–119kr. There's takeaway service, too.

Rutiga Dukan Västra Kyrkogatan 1. A snug and cosy café below the cathedral that's a great place for a cup of coffee and good home-baked pastries.

Höga Kusten – the High Coast

Designated a UNESCO World Heritage Site in late 2000, **HÖGA KUSTEN** (ⓦwww.visitmidsweden.com and ⓦwww.highcoast.net), or the High Coast, is the highlight of any trip up the Bothnian coast. This stretch of striking coastline north of Härnösand is elementally beautiful: rolling mountains and verdant valleys plunge precipitously into the Gulf of Bothnia, and the rugged shoreline of sheer cliffs and craggy outcrops gives way to gently undulating pebble coves. The dramatic landscape is the result of the isostatic uplift that has occurred since the last Ice Age; as the ice melted, the land, no longer weighed down by ice up to three kilometres thick, rose by 286 metres. There's nowhere in the world

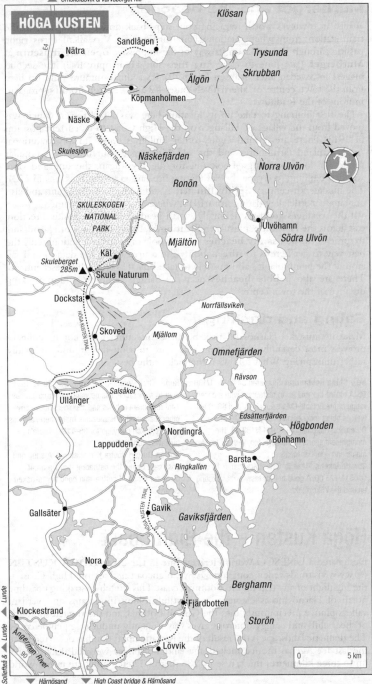

HÖGA KUSTEN

Örnsköldsvik & Varvsberget hill

Klösan

Sandlågen

Nätra

E4

Trysunda

Skrubban

Älgön

Köpmanholmen

Näske

Näskefjärden

Norra Ulvön

Skulesjön

Ronön

HÖGA KUSTEN TRAIL

SKULESKOGEN
NATIONAL
PARK

Mjältön

Ulvöhamn

Södra Ulvön

Käl

Skuleberget
285m

Skule Naturum

Docksta

Norrfällsviken

HÖGA KUSTEN TRAIL

Skoved

Mjällom

Omnefjärden

Rävson

Ullånger

Salsåker

Edsätterfjärden

Högbonden

Nordingrå

Bönhamn

Lappudden

Barsta

Ringkallen

HÖGA KUSTEN TRAIL

Gallsäter

E4

Gavik

Gaviksfjärden

Nora

Berghamn

Fjärdbotten

Klockestrand

Storön

Ångerman River

90

Lövvik

0   5 km

Sollefteå & ◄ Lunde

◄ Lunde

▼ Härnösand   ▼ High Coast bridge & Härnösand

where the uplift has been so great as in this part of Sweden, and, in fact, it is still rising at a rate of eight millimetres every year.

Off the Höga Kusten are dozens of islands, some no more than a few metres square in size, others much larger and covered with dense pine forest. It was on these islands that the tradition of preparing the foul-smelling **surströmming** is thought to have begun (see p.293). A trip here is a must for anyone travelling up or down the Bothnian coast; from out at sea, you'll get the best view possible of the coastal cliffs which (as the very name High Coast suggests) are the tallest in the country. The islands themselves are havens of peace and tranquillity, offering the chance to get away from it all. Among the most beautiful in the chain are, from south to north: **Högbonden**, **Ulvön** and **Trysunda**. Each of these islands can be visited using a combination of buses and boats; before setting off, make sure you've understood the boat timetables (available at tourist offices), which are in Swedish only and can be confusing.

Another enjoyable way to see the coastline at close quarters, remaining on the mainland, is to walk **Höga Kusten Leden**, a long-distance hiking trail that stretches 130km north from the new bridge over the Ångerman River, skirting the Skuleskogen National Park, to Örnsköldsvik.

Travel practicalities

The **boats** that serve the islands here operate only in summer, except for the *M/S Ulvön*, which sails for Ulvön all year round. For the latest bus and ferry times, check out ⓦ www.dintur.se. All boats accept bicycles, though cars are not transported on these passenger vessels.

Travelling between Härnösand and Örnsköldsvik along the E4 will involve crossing over the Ångerman River via the stunning High Coast **bridge** (no tolls). One of the longest suspension bridges in the world, with a span of 1210m, it has dramatically shortened the journey by cutting out a lengthy detour upriver to the old bridge between Lunde and Klockestrand (though this route is still used by some buses). Reaching a height of 180m above the water, the bridge is only 70m shorter than San Francisco's Golden Gate Bridge, which it closely resembles.

Högbonden

After a mere ten-minute boat ride from Bönhamn on the mainland, the steep sides of the tiny island of **Högbonden** rise up in front of you. Although the island can feel a little overcrowded with day-trippers in peak season (July to mid-Aug), at its best the place is a wonderfully deserted, peaceful haven. There are no shops – so bring any provisions you'll need with you – and no hotels on the island; in fact the only building here is a former lighthouse, now converted into a **youth hostel** (see p.292). It's situated on a rocky plateau at the island's highest point, where the pine and spruce trees, so prominent elsewhere on the island, have been unable to get a foothold; Högbonden's flora also includes rowan, sallow, aspen and birch trees, as well as various mosses that compete for space with wild bilberries.

You'll only get to know the special charm of Högbonden if you stay a couple of nights and take time to explore: a narrow gorge runs north–south across the island, and there are also forested hillsides and a shoreline where eider ducks glide by with their young. The **views** out across the Gulf of Bothnia are stunning; on a sunny day you could easily imagine you're in the middle of the Mediterranean. At any time, you can head for the traditional **wood-burning sauna** down by the sea, two-minutes' walk from the jetty (it's signposted "bastu" off the island's one and only path); you'll need to book your slot with the youth hostel staff, who keep the sauna's key (40kr). Afterwards, you can take a quick skinny-dip in the cool waters of the Gulf of Bothnia. The sunsets, seen from the boardwalk in front of the sauna, are truly idyllic.

Practicalities

Sailing from the mainland village of **Bönhamn**, *M/S Högbonden* makes the ten-minute trip out to Högbonden (mid-June to mid-Aug daily 10am, noon, 3pm & 6pm; 150kr return). To get to Bönhamn by car, turn off the E4 at Gallsäter onto the minor road leading there via Nordingrå. To get to Bönhamn on public transport **from Härnösand**, take the 11am Kustbussen to Ullånger, where you change for a connection at 12.35pm to Nordingrå; once there, catch the connecting bus at 12.55pm to Bönhamn (check times at ⓦwww.dintur.se).

Högbonden's **youth hostel** 🏠 is in the former lighthouse (ⓣ0613/230 05, ⓦwww.hogbonden.se; May–Oct; dorm beds only 300kr; breakfast costs 70kr), reached by several sets of steep wooden steps from the path that begins at the jetty. Inside the main building there is a kitchen, two bathrooms and two decent sized dorms (with creaking floorboards) though if the hostel is full, you may find that the separate-sex rule which normally applies is waived to accommodate as many guests as possible. To add to the novelty of sleeping in a converted lighthouse, the building's clifftop vantage point affords sweeping sea views from the kitchen and the dorms.

Ulvön

ULVÖN (ⓦwww.ulvon.com), 20km northeast of Högbonden and 12km southwest of Trysunda, is really two islands, Norra and Södra Ulvön, their combined area making it the largest in the High Coast archipelago. The southern island is uninhabited, separated from its northern neighbour by a narrow channel, Ulvösund, which provides a well-protected harbour. During the seventeenth and eighteenth centuries, Ulvön became home to the High Coast's biggest fishing community, as fishermen from Gävle came here to exploit the rich fishing grounds off the island; in subsequent centuries, though, many islanders moved to the mainland, especially after World War II, when the industry started to decline. Today, there are only around fifty permanent residents.

Ulvön is famous for its production of **surströmming**, fermented Baltic herring (see box opposite); two of the firms involved, Söderbergs Fisk and Ruben Madsén, are based in the main village of Ulvöhamn (see below) and it's possible to buy the locally produced stuff in the island's shops.

Travel practicalities

To reach Ulvön **from Härnösand**, take the 8.15am bus to the village of **Docksta** (50min) and alight at the jetty, from where the *M/S Kusttrafik* leaves at 10.15am (June–Aug daily; ⓣ0613/105 50, ⓦwww.hkship.se; 125kr one-way, 175kr day return), arriving in **Ulvöhamn**, on Ulvön, at 11.30am, heading back to the mainland at 3pm.

Ulvön is easily reached **from Trysunda** on the mainland, on the *M/F Ulvön* (ⓣ0660/29 90 21, ⓦwww.dintur.se; 30kr one-way). Sailings are roughly twice daily at 9.40am and 6.25pm. When there are no direct sailings, connections can be made via Köpmanholmen on the mainland.

Ulvöhamn

All boats to the island dock at the main village, **ULVÖHAMN**, a picturesque one-street affair with red-and-white cottages and tiny boathouses on stilts snuggling up eave to eave. Walking along the waterfront, you'll pass the pretty fishermen's chapel, dating from 1622 and now the oldest wooden building in Ångermanland (June–Aug daily 1.45–2.15pm); inside, its walls are covered with flamboyant eighteenth-century murals. The church was established by Gävle fishermen, who began summer fishing forays up the Baltic coast in the sixteenth century. Its detached bell tower was once used to signal that it was time to assemble for the daily fishing trip. To get to the **beaches**, follow the sign marked "Strandpromenaden" from the village shop (see below); it's about ten minutes by bike past small sandy coves to the harbour entrance and a promontory of red rocks, Rödharen, beyond which lie several pebbly stretches. The unusual red rock here is a granite known by its Finnish name, **rappakivi**.

The **tourist office** is in a tiny wooden hut (mid-June to mid-Aug daily noon–3pm; ℡0660/430 38), about 250m from the quay where the *M/S Kusttrafik* from Docksta puts in. You can **rent bikes** here and pick up information about the **Ulvön Regatta**, an annual gathering for ostentatious yachting types that takes place in mid-July. The island's only **hotel**, *Ulvö Skärgårdshotell*, is just to the right of the quay as you come off the boat at Hamngatan 1 (℡0660/22 40 09, Ⓦwww.ulvohotell.se; ❸; May–Sept); it has cosy, modern rooms with good views of the sea (those in the annexe cost 100kr less). At the other end of the road from the hotel is the village **shop**. To get to the non-STF **youth hostel**, about 2km from the harbour, take the road, just beyond the chapel midway between the jetties, that leads uphill to the right (℡0660/22 41 90; dorm beds 175kr; late June to late Aug). Four four-bed pine **cabins** with cooking facilities and fantastic views out over the harbour can be rented at Färjeläget, just by the village shop (℡0660/22 41 57; 775kr per night Sun–Thurs, 875kr for Fri or Sat); there are ten other four-bed cabins at Fäbodvallen, a ten-minute walk up the hill behind the harbour (700kr per night Sun–Thurs, 800kr Fri or Sat). Residents at the latter can use the **hälsohus**, a small health spa, containing a sauna, Jacuzzi and solarium.

For **eating**, there's the *Almagränd* restaurant (℡0660/22 41 32), with its limited menu, near the tourist office; and the excellent restaurant at *Ulvö Skärgårdshotell*,

Surströmming

Mention the word *surströmming* to most Swedes and they'll turn up their noses in disgust. It's best translated as "fermented Baltic herring" – though to the non-connoisseur, the description "rotten" would seem more appropriate. The tradition of eating the foul-smelling stuff began on Ulvön sometime during the sixteenth century when salt was very expensive; as a result just a little was used in preserving the fish, a decision which inadvertently allowed it to ferment.

The number of **salthouses** producing the herring has dwindled from several hundred early in the twentieth century to around twenty to thirty manufacturers now. Today, *surströmming* is made in flat tins containing a weak salt solution. Over the course of the four- to ten-week fermentation process, the tins blow up into the shape of a soccer ball under the pressure of the odious gases produced inside. Restaurants refuse to open the tins on the premises because of the lingering stink that's exuded, not unlike an open sewer; the unpleasant job has to be done outside in the fresh air.

The **season** for eating *surströmming* begins on the third Thursday in August, ending around two to three weeks later, when supplies run out. The fish can be accompanied with the yellow, almond-shaped variety of northern Swedish potatoes and washed down with beer or *akvavit*; alternatively it's put into a sandwich, perhaps with onion or tomato, all rolled up in a piece of *tunnbröd*, the thin unleavened bread traditional in this part of the country.

with main courses around 150kr and a good-value buffet for 175kr. If you are self-catering, the village shop, at the southern end of Ulvöhamn's main street, has a decent array of provisions. There's a pleasant **pub** below the hotel that buzzes in summer. Out of season, you'll have no choice but to cook for yourself since all eating places close down for the winter.

Trysunda

The charming fishing village of **TRYSUNDA**, on the tiny island of the same name, is the best preserved in Ångermanland, hemmed in around a narrow U-shaped harbour, with forty or so red-and-white houses right on the waterfront. The village's wooden chapel, which is usually unlocked, is one of the oldest on the Bothnian coast, dating from around 1655. Like the church on neighbouring Ulvön, the interior is decorated with colourful murals.

Trysunda is crisscrossed with walking paths, leading through the forests of dwarf pine that cover the island – many of which have become gnarled and twisted under the force of the wind. The island's gently sloping rocks make it ideal for bathing, and you'll find plenty of secluded spots where you can do so. There's a **sandy beach** at **Björnviken**, a bay on the eastern part of the island, and some smooth rocks on the north coast, just to the east of **Bockviken**. An easily walked path from the village will take you to both beaches and round the entire island in an hour or two. To continue east from Björnviken, don't be tempted to strike off round the headland, as the rocks there are impassable; instead, stay on the path, which cuts inland, and follow the signs for Storviken.

As you approach or leave the island, you might be lucky enough to catch a glimpse of elk on the neighbouring island, the volcanic and uninhabited **Skrubban**. Although the island has been a nature reserve since 1940, every year some hunting is allowed to control the animal population and prevent unnecessary suffering from starvation, a practice followed elsewhere in Sweden too.

▲ Trysunda

Practicalities

Heading here from **Högbonden**, you'll need to get to **Köpmanholmen**, from where you can catch the twice-daily ferry to Trysunda. From Högbonden take the 1.15pm bus from Bönhamn to Nordingrå, where you change for the 2pm bus to Ullånger. There's a connection at 3.20pm from Ullånger to Bjästa where you change again to catch the bus to Köpmanholmen at 4.35pm, from where the ferry leaves for Trysunda at 5.15pm (30kr; 50min). The journey isn't as complicated as it may sound; in fact every bus on your route will know you're coming because each driver is informed by radio of connecting passengers.

For **accommodation** on Trysunda, there are seven rather cramped double rooms located right by the harbour (℡0660/430 38, ✉trysunda@gmail.com; double room ❶; May to Sept). There is also a village **shop**, where you can buy bare necessities, including fresh and smoked fish, and the dreaded **surströmming**. Ask at the shop for their free map of the island.

The High Coast Trail and Skuleskogen National Park

It's possible to walk the entire length of the High Coast along **Höga Kusten Leden**, or High Coast Trail, which stretches 127km from the High Coast bridge at the mouth of the Ångerman river to **Varvsberget**, the hill overlooking the centre of Örnsköldsvik, a dreadfully dull place where you'd do well not to get stuck. The trail is divided into thirteen stages, which vary in difficulty and 7–15km in length. There's accommodation at each break between stages, mostly in the form of cabins. The buses between Härnösand and Örnsköldsvik stop very close to several stages along the way: Lappudden, Ullånger, Skoved, Skule Naturum (for Skuleberget) and Köpmanholmen. For more **information** on the trail, contact the tourist office in Härnösand (see p.288), which sells the excellent *Small Map Book for the High Coast*, which includes not only good maps of the region but also detailed descriptions of the trail.

Skuleskogen National Park

The High Coast Trail takes in the eastern edge of the magnificent, 26-square-kilometre **Skuleskogen National Park**, noted for its dense evergreen forests, coastal panoramas and deep ravines. Its main sight is the gorge known as Slåtterdalsskrevan, located at the eastern edge close to the coast; though only 200m long and 7m wide, it's 40m deep.

The park is home to a rich mix of **flora and fauna**, including many varieties of bird. Woodpeckers thrive here, alongside the grey-headed, black, three-toed, lesser spotted, greater spotted and even the rare whitebacked woodpecker. All four of Sweden's forest game birds, namely the capercaillie, hazelhen, black grouse and willow grouse, are also found here, along with other birds such as the wren, coal tit and crested tit. Among the numerous forest animals in the park are elk, roe deer, lynx, fox, gopher, stoat, pine marten, mink, mountain hare and red squirrel. Spruce is the dominant tree here; some of the large, mature specimens have regenerated naturally after logging ended one hundred years ago. Half of the park consists of bare stone outcrops, home only to a few gnarled and stunted pines – some of these trees are over five hundred years old. You'll also see the slow-growing long beard lichen (**Usnea longissima**), which is entirely dependent on old spruce trees, on whose branches it's found.

Leading inland through the park are a number of well-marked paths off the High Coast trail that take you past some wonderful, if very steep, countryside. You can also go **mountain climbing** in Skuleskogen; trails up **Skuleberget** (285m), near Docksta, afford stunning views from the top, and anyone in normal shape can make it safely to the summit; for the less energetically minded a **cable car** (June–Aug daily 10am–5pm, July till 7pm; 80kr) also makes the ascent. Skule Naturum nature centre at the foot of the mountain rents out equipment for serious climbing and offers sound advice from experts.

Umeå and around

UMEÅ is the biggest city in the north of Sweden, with a current population of 110,000 people which means that an astonishing one in ten of the residents of Norrland live here. Demographically speaking, it's probably Sweden's youngest city, a notion borne out by taking a stroll round the airy modern centre: you'll form the impression that anyone who's not in a pushchair is pushing one, and that the cafés and city parks are full of teenagers. Indeed one in five people are in their twenties, figures that are partly due to the presence of Norrland University. Its youthfulness may well be responsible for the fact that Umeå is the only town or city in northern Sweden where there's an air of dynamism: new restaurants and bars are opening all the time, there's a thriving cultural scene, and by late 2010, the **Botniabanan** high-speed rail link to Stockholm should be completed, making it possible to reach the capital in just five and a half hours.

With its fast-flowing river – a feature few other Swedish coastal cities enjoy – and wide, stylish boulevards, Umeå is an appealing metropolis. It would be no

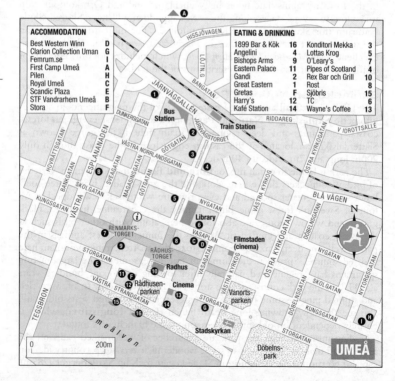

ACCOMMODATION

Best Western Winn	**D**
Clarion Collection Uman	**G**
Femrum.se	**I**
First Camp Umeå	**A**
Pilen	**H**
Royal Umeå	**C**
Scandic Plaza	**E**
STF Vandrarhem Umeå	**B**
Stora	**F**

EATING & DRINKING

1899 Bar & Kök	16	Konditori Mekka	3
Angelini	4	Lottas Krog	5
Bishops Arms	9	O'Leary's	7
Eastern Palace	11	Pipes of Scotland	4
Gandi	2	Rex Bar och Grill	10
Great Eastern	1	Rost	8
Gretas	F	Sjöbris	15
Harry's	12	TC	6
Kafé Station	14	Wayne's Coffee	13

bad idea to spend a couple of days here, sampling some of its bars and restaurants – the variety of which you won't find anywhere else in Norrland.

Arrival and information

Trains arrive at the **train station**, at the northern end of the city centre on Järnvägsallén. Opposite is the long-distance **bus station** used by services from Dorotea, Vilhelmina and Östersund, and by the Kustbussen to and from Haparanda. The city centre is a ten-minute walk south from here. Six kilometres south of the city is Umeå's busy **airport**, with direct flights to and from Stockholm, Kiruna and Östersund; it's linked with the centre by airport buses (35kr) and taxis (145kr). RG Line ferries from Vaasa in Finland dock at Holmsund, 20km from Umeå, from where connecting buses run inland to Umeå.

The city centre is easy to get around on foot, and many of its streets are pedestrianized, including the main east–west drag, Kungsgatan. A good first stop is the **tourist office** in Renmarkstorget (Oct–April Mon–Fri 10am–5pm; May to mid-June & mid-Aug to Sept Mon–Fri 10am–6pm, Sat 10am–2pm; mid-June to mid-Aug Mon–Fri 8.30am–7pm, Sat 10am–4pm, Sun noon–4pm; ☏090/16 16 16, ⊛www.visitumea.se), a concrete square whose ugliness is at odds with its romantic name, meaning "reindeer-country square". From the train and bus stations it's a ten-minute walk down the main north–south thoroughfare, Rådhusesplanaden, to the square. Umeå has a couple of **internet** points: Sidewalk Express is in McDonalds at Västra Rådhusgatan 7, whilst the tourist office also has a couple of terminals.

Accommodation

Umeå has a good selection of central **hotels**, the like of which you won't experience anywhere north of here; in short, splash out and treat yourself.

Best Western Winn Skolgatan 64 ☏090/71 11 00, ⊛www.winnhotel.se. Smart, comfortable and everything you would expect from a chain hotel – though lacking character. A bonus is its extremely central location which is ideal for nearby restaurants, bars and shops. ❺/❹

Clarion Collection Uman Storgatan 52 ☏090/12 72 20, ⊛www.choice.se. Located in the grand former home of the city's chief medical officer, this cosy place, decked out with a medical theme, really is a home from home, with afternoon coffee, cakes and an evening buffet for all guests included in the price. ❺/❸

🏃 **Femrum.se** Kungsgatan 93 ☏090/10 99 10, ⊛www.femrum.se. As the Swedish name suggests, just five rooms make up this cosy little guesthouse, though each has been tastefully and individually decorated to create a real sense of home from home. Bright colours and wood panelling add to the charm. ❸

First Camp Umeå Nydalasjön 2, Nydala ☏090/70 26 00, ⊛www.firstcamp.se/umea. Umeå's campsite is located 5km from town on the shore of a lake; take buses #2, #6, #7 or #9, get off at Nydala and walk for around 5min towards

Nydalabadet, which is signposted. It has cabins for two people (❸), individual double rooms in other cabins (❶) and trätält (tiny two-bed huts; ❶).

Pilen Pilgatan 5 ☏090/14 14 60, ⊛www.hotellpilen.se. One of the smaller, cheaper hotels, with newly renovated rooms whose cosy interiors have been redesigned to reflect the style of the building which dates from the turn of the last century. ❸

🏃 **Royal Umeå** Skolgatan 64 ☏090/10 07 30, ⊛www.royalhotelumea.com. A modern, centrally located hotel that's decorated throughout with pictures of Hollywood stars. There's free room service as well as access to a sauna, Jacuzzi, solarium and the hotel's own cinema which shows free films every night. ❺/❸

Scandic Plaza Storgatan 40 ☏090/205 63 00, ⊛www.scandic-hotels.se/plazaumea. For a treat, head for this very smart place which is popular with business travellers. Rooms are stylish to a T, decorated in the latest Scandinavian designs. There are superb views from the fourteenth-floor sauna suite which is worth a stay here in itself. ❻/❹

STF Vandrarhem Umeå Västra Esplanaden 10 ☏090/77 16 50, ⊛www.umeavandrarhem.com. With bright and airy en-suite rooms, this centrally located hostel, just 450m from the stations, is one of Sweden's best. Dorm beds 190kr, double room ➊.

Stora Storgatan 46 ℡090/77 88 70, ⓦwww.storahotelletumea.se. One of the city's oldest hotels, which opened in 1894 and is still full of many of the original features such as a grand, sweeping staircase, ornate chandeliers and period furniture. Every room is individually decorated in keeping with the building, and many have fine views out over the city or the river. ➏/➍

The City

The sound of the **rapids** along the Ume River gives the city its name: **uma** means "roar". Umeå is sometimes also referred to as the "City of Birch Trees", after the trees that were planted along every street following a devastating fire in 1888. Most of the city was burnt to the ground in the blaze, and two-thirds of the town's three thousand inhabitants lost their homes. In the rebuilding which soon began apace, two wide esplanades, one of which is Rådhusesplanaden, were constructed to act as fire breaks and help prevent such a disaster happening again. A decree was then handed down stating that the birch was the most suitable tree to add life to the town's newly reconstructed streets; even today, the city council places ads for free trees in the local papers and provides free birch saplings every spring to anyone who wants them.

Most visitors to Umeå make an immediate beeline for the city's excellent museum complex, **Gammlia**, home to a terrific collection of exhibitions on everything from photojournalism to skiing. In summer, the open-air section even has people dressed in period costume going about their daily tasks much as their predecessors did several centuries ago. Whilst in Umeå don't miss the opportunity, though, to take a trip to the **elk farm** in nearby Bjurholm where you can come face to face with these elusive creatures.

Gammlia

The highlight of Umeå is undoubtedly its terrific museum complex, **Gammlia** (late June to late Aug daily 10am–5pm; ⓦwww.vasterbottensmuseum.se; free), which merits a good half-day's exploration. It's a twenty-minute walk from the train or bus stations: head east along Järnvägsallén and turn left into Östra Kyrkogatan, crossing under the railway tracks. After the bridge, turn right into Hemvägen, which after its junction with Rothoffsvägen becomes Gammliavägen, leading to the museum.

Gammlia grew out of the **Friluftsmuseum**, an open-air cluster of twenty regional buildings, the oldest of which is the seventeenth-century gatehouse you pass on the way in. The grounds are home to the customary farmyard animals – cows, pigs, geese and the like – and the guides dressed in period costume are very willing to tell you about life in their mock town. It all helps to create a rural ambience including a windmill, church, two threshing floors and a smokehouse for pork. At the bakery there are demonstrations of how to make the thin unleavened bread, *tunnbröd*, which used to be baked in people's homes. You can also take a ride through the grounds in a horse-drawn carriage (free), an experience that's bound to entertain kids. The indoor **Västerbottens Museum** (mid-June to mid-Aug daily 10am–5pm; mid-Aug to mid-June Tues–Fri 10am–4pm, Sat noon–4pm, Sun noon–5pm; free; ⓦwww.vasterbottensmuseum.se) houses Gammlia's main collection: three exhibitions that canter through the county's past, from prehistoric times (the section on this period contains the oldest ski in the world, over five thousand years old) to the Industrial Revolution. It's all good stuff, well laid out and complemented by an array of videos and recordings; a useful English guidebook is available at reception.

Housed in the same building as Västerbotten Museum but run by Umeå university is the **Bildmuséet** (mid-June to mid-Aug Wed–Sun noon–5pm; mid-Aug to mid-June Tues–Sat noon–4pm, Sun noon–5pm; free; ⓦ www.bildmuseet.umu.se), which houses interesting displays of contemporary Swedish and international art, photojournalism and visual design.

Back outside, you can resume your exploration of provincial history in the separate **Fiske och Sjöfartsmuseum** (Fishing and Maritime Museum; late June to late Aug daily noon–5pm; late Aug to late June Tues–Sat noon–4pm, Sun noon–5pm; free), which tries its best to be a regional maritime museum: the tug, *Egil*, which once operated in the Ume River together with several fishing and rowing boats are squeezed into the small hall which also has a brief display about seal hunting in the region.

Winter activities

Visiting Umeå in winter can be a wonderful experience. What gives the city the edge over many smaller places further north is not only easy access by both plane and train, but also the chance to experience the northern winter right on the city limits by day and Umeå's extensive range of bars and restaurants by night.

During the coldest winter months the Ume River freezes over providing a ready opportunity to take **snow-scooter safaris** upriver. The easiest way to arrange this is to book through the *Scandic Plaza* who charge around 800kr per person (minimum five people) for a three-hour trip, which ends with a dip in a wooden hot pot (an additional 200kr) right on the riverbank. Another wintertime attraction here is the **northern lights**; January and February are both good months for observing this phenomenon – most spectacularly from a snowmobile.

Eating, drinking and entertainment

Eating and **drinking** opportunities are varied and generally of a high standard in Umeå, partly because of the size of the city and partly due to the large student population. Most restaurants and cafés are centred around the main pedestrianized Kungsgatan or Rådhusesplanaden. For fresh fruit and vegetables try the daily market in the main square, Rådhustorget, outside the old town hall.

Cafés

1899 Bar & Kök Stadskajen. Located on the Vita Björn boat moored off Västra Strandgatan and a great place to sit on deck with a cup of coffee and enjoy a view over the river.

Kafé Station Östra Rådhusgatan 2L. Handily located next to the Filmstaden cinema. Rough brick walls, wooden floors and a wide selection of sandwiches as well as great coffee and cheesecake. A firm favourite with all Umeåites.

Konditori Mekka Rådhusesplanaden 15. Close to the train station, this long-established café is known for its delicious cakes, especially its mouthwatering blueberry, carrot and squidgy *kladdkaka* cakes.

Wayne's Coffee Storgatan 50. With stylish halogen lighting and 1960s retro plastic stools, this branch of *Wayne's* is one of the best in Sweden, with a fantastic range of excellent coffee as well as sandwiches and muffins.

Restaurants

Angelini Rådhusesplanaden 14 ☎ 090/13 41 00. Style is high on the agenda at this Italian-American restaurant with mosaic walls, wooden floors and burnt-orange velvet chairs. The menu is equally tasty: burgers (119kr), ribeye steak (235kr), clam chowder (125kr) and seafood spaghetti (149kr) are all good bets, though they also do pizzas (105kr).

Eastern Palace Storgatan 44 ☎ 090/13 88 39. Tucked away in a courtyard accessed from Thulegatan, off Storgatan. Really good Japanese and Thai food has finally made it to Norrland; teriyaki salmon for 145kr or Thai mains 95–148kr. The weekday lunch buffet is excellent value at 79kr.

Gandi Rådhusesplanaden 17C ☎ 090/17 50 75. Located opposite the train station in Järnvägstorget, this place is worth seeking out. Despite the dingy basement location, the Indian food is excellent with good-value dishes, including tandoori specialities, for around 110kr.

Great Eastern Magasinsgatan 17 ☏ 090/13 88 38. The best Chinese restaurant in Norrland. Very popular lunch buffet as well as evening chicken and beef dishes from 92kr as well as a Mongolian barbecue for 159kr. Also has a few Thai dishes from 92kr.

Gretas Skolgatan 62 ☏ 090/10 07 35. Inside the *Royal Umeå* in Vasaplan, very smart and chi-chi grill restaurant with black floor tiles and white walls specializing in traditional Swedish dishes given an international flavour, such as snow grouse, elk tenderloin and Kalix whitefish roe. Mains 127–225kr. Two/three course set Norrland menu for 325/425kr respectively.

Lottas Krog Nygatan 22 ☏ 090/12 95 51. Pub-restaurant that does a roaring trade and is well established as one of the town's most popular eating places. The extensive menu is a mix of Swedish and World food: Mexican fajitas (159kr), fish and chips (159kr), pizzas and pasta are also available (92–125kr). Also has some sixty different beers, including Boddingtons.

🏃 **Rex Bar och Grill** Rådhustorget ☏ 090/12 60 50. Probably the most popular place to eat in Umeå complete with a stuffed elk head and suspended motorbike for decoration. *Rex* is two restaurants in one but it's best to avoid the fussy à la carte menu offering northern Swedish specialities at sky-high prices served in the French bistro (reindeer steak at 298kr) and choose instead from the bar meals priced from 115kr.

Rost Rådhusesplanaden 4B ☏ 090/13 58 00. A superb and justifiably popular vegetarian restaurant decked out in mosaic tiles. There's a small outdoor seating area that fills up fast when the sun is shining. All food is freshly prepared and they even produce their own cheeses: mains are 70–120kr.

Sjöbris Kajplats 10 ☏ 090/77 71 23. An excellent gourmet fish restaurant on board an elegant old white steamer built in 1915 and now moored off Västra Strandgatan. Well prepared fish dishes such as gravadlax, grilled char or salmon from 135kr. Open during the summer season (dates vary).

TC Vasaplan ☏ 090/15 63 21. Short for Teatercafé, this is a firm favourite among all age groups. It's the best place in town for top-quality northern Swedish specialities such as reindeer fillet with morel mushrooms (242kr) and the excellent black grouse terrine (125kr). There's outdoor seating in summer.

Bars

Umeå buzzes at night, with plenty of stylish and friendly **bars** to choose from, most of them British-style pubs or brasseries. The city centre is most lively during termtime when students are around.

Bishops Arms Renmarkstorget 8. Umeå's attempt at an English-style pub and consequently one of the most popular places to be seen and to do the seeing in – always packed. There's outdoor seating in summer, and for those chilly evenings, blankets and free-standing gas heaters.

Harry's Västra Rådhusgatan 1. One of the busiest bars in Umeå and attached to the *Stora* hotel. Identical in design to every other *Harry's* in Sweden, though with outdoor seating in summer. There's a nightclub here on Fri & Sat.

Lottas Nygatan 22. Another of the British-style pubs the Swedes love so much, with heavy wooden panelling and carpets. Always a good choice for either a pre- or post-dinner drink. A *storstark* here is just that: beer is always served here in big 50cl glasses, not the smaller 40cl seen elsewhere.

O'Leary's Kungsgatan 50A. A popular pub with large video screens showing various sports. Also has dancing in the nightclub on Fri and Sat nights.

Pipes of Scotland Rådhusesplanaden 14. Umeå's newly opened Scottish pub really pulls the crowds with its After Work specials on food and drink. It's a fun place for a drink, though, at any time and a good place to meet the city's student population.

Around Umeå

Umeå is ideally placed for a jaunt to the Älgens hus **elk farm** (early June to mid-Aug Tues–Sun noon–6pm; rest of year by advance booking on ☏ 0932/500 00; 120kr; ⓦ www.algenshus.se) at Väster Nyliden 23 in **Bjurholm**, a small village 65km west. Driving around Sweden you may well have caught the briefest glimpse of the "King of the Forest", Europe's largest land animal, as tall as a horse but with antlers. The farm, though, provides an excellent opportunity to come face to face with these cumbersome looking beasts and to learn all about their behaviour from the knowledgeable staff, who also make cheese from elk milk – a rare and inordinately expensive delicacy. You can reach Bjurholm by bus (daily: every 1–2hr; 1hr) from Umeå. Incidentally, elk love bananas, so you may wish to pack a few for your visit.

Skellefteå

There used to be a religious fervour about the town **SKELLEFTEÅ**, 140km northeast of Umeå. In 1324, an edict in the name of King Magnus Eriksson invited "all those who believed in Jesus Christ or wanted to turn to him" to settle between the Skellefte and Ume rivers. Many heeded the call, and parishes mushroomed on the banks of the Skellefte River. By the end of the eighteenth century, a devout township was centred around the town's monumental church, which stood out in stark contrast to the surrounding plains and wide river. Nowadays, though, more material occupations, including computer and electronics industries, and the mining of gold and silver, support the town. If you're heading north for Swedish Lapland, Skellefteå can make an appealing stop on the way. There are enough attractions to keep you busy for a day or so, particularly its superb church town, **Bonnstan**, an engaging collection of battered log cottages gathered together around the proud Neoclassical **church**, which houses one of Norrland's proudest exhibits – the **medieval carving** of the Virgin of Skellefteå.

Nearby, the rickety **Lejonströmsbron** is Sweden's oldest wooden bridge, offering elevated views of the Skellefte River. Skellefteå is also well placed for jaunts into the Swedish inland with good bus connections to Arvidsjaur and Arjeplog.

Arrival, information and accommodation

The small centre is based around a modern paved square flanked by the streets Kanalgatan and Nygatan; at the top of the square is the **bus station** and, at the bottom, the **tourist office** (end June to early Aug Mon–Fri 10am–6pm, Sat 10am–3pm, Sun noon–3pm; rest of year Mon–Fri 10am–5pm, Sat 10am–2pm; ℡0910/73 60 20, ⓦwww.skelleftea.se), at Trädgårdsgatan 7 which also has **internet** terminals.

The **youth hostel**, at Brännavägen 25 (℡0910/72 57 00, ⓦwww.stiftsgardenskelleftea.com; dorm beds 280kr, double room ❷), a rustic red two-storey building by the banks of the Skellefte River, half an hour's walk from the centre, is well worth seeking out though it only takes advance bookings. Head west along Nygatan (which later becomes Brännavägen) until the junction with Kyrkvägen, where the hostel is on the corner. Of the central **hotels**, the cheapest is *Hotell Victoria* at Trädgårdsgatan 8 (℡0910/174 70, ⓦwww.hotelvictoria.se; ❶/❷), a family-run establishment on the top floor of one of the buildings on the south side of the main square. Virtually next door at Torget 2, *Best Western Malmia* (℡0910/73 25 00, ⓦwww.malmia.se; ❹/❸) has perfectly adequate rooms and is the place to try for last-minute special deals. For **campers**, *Skellefteå Camping* is about 1.5km north of the centre on Mossgatan, just off the E4 (℡0910/73 55 00, ⓦwww.skecamp.mammon.se); you can rent two-bed **cabins** here for 350kr per night per cabin. The site also has a heated outdoor swimming pool, wave machine and Jacuzzi.

The Town

Since there's little to see in the town centre you would fare better concentrating on nearby **Bonnstan**, comprising Skellefteå's **church** and **kyrkstad** (church town). A fifteen-minute walk west from the centre along Nygatan brings you to the **Nordanå Kulturcentrum**, a large and baffling assortment of old wooden buildings that's home to a theatre, a traditional grocer's store (*lanthandel*) and a rather dire **museum** (Tues–Sun noon–4pm; Ⓦ www.skellefteamuseum.se; 40kr), containing three floors of mind-numbing exhibitions on everything from the region's first settlers to swords. Tucked away to the side of the grocer's store is a pleasant **restaurant**, *Nordanå Gårdens Värdshus*, with outdoor seating in summer.

Bonnstan

Skellefteå's church and **church town**, known as **Bonnstan**, are within easy striking distance of the centre: walk west along Nygatan and keep going for about fifteen minutes. An evocative sight, the **kyrkstad** (see box below) here comprises five long rows of weather-beaten log houses, with battered wooden shutters. The houses are protected by law: any renovations, including the installation of electricity, are forbidden. You can take a peek inside, but bear in mind that these are privately owned summer houses today.

Next to these cottages is the **landskyrka** (daily 10am–4pm), a proud white Neoclassical church which so enthused Leopold von Buch, a traveller who visited here in the nineteenth century, that he was moved to describe it as "the largest and most beautiful building in the entire north of Sweden, rising like a Palmyra's temple out of the desert". Its domed roof is supported by four mighty pillars along each of the walls; inside, there's an outstanding series of medieval sculptures. Look out too for the 800-year-old **Virgin of Skellefteå**, a walnut **woodcarving** immediately behind the altar on the right – it's one of the few remaining Romanesque images of the Virgin in the world. Nearby, on the Skellefte River, the islet of **Kyrkholmen**, reached by a small wooden bridge, is a pretty place to sit and while away an hour or two. It's home to an outdoor **café** that's handy for a cup of coffee and simple sandwiches (mid-June to mid-Aug).

Sweden's church towns

After the break with the Catholic Church in 1527, the Swedish clergy were determined to teach their parishioners the Lutheran fundamentals, with the result that, by 1681, church services had become compulsory. There was one problem with this requirement, though – the population in the north was spread over considerable distances, making weekly attendance impossible. The clergy and the parishes agreed a compromise: it was decreed that those living within 10km of the church should attend every Sunday; those between 10km and 20km away, every fortnight; and those 20–30km away, every three weeks. The scheme worked, and within a decade, **church towns** (*kyrkstäder*) had appeared throughout the region to provide the travelling faithful with somewhere to spend the night after a day of praying and listening to powerful sermons.

Of the 71 church towns Sweden originally had, only eighteen are left today, predominantly in the provinces of **Västerbotten** and **Norrbotten**. Each *kyrkstad* consists of rows of simple wooden houses grouped tightly around the church. The biggest and most impressive, at **Gammelstad** near Luleå (see p.307), is included on the UNESCO World Heritage List. Today, they are no longer used in the traditional way, though people still live in the old houses, especially in summer, and sometimes even rent them out to tourists.

From the church you have two walking routes back to the centre: either take Strandpromenaden along the river's edge, interrupted by barbecue sites and grassy stretches; or cross **Lejonströmsbron**, the longest wooden bridge in Sweden, beneath the hill where the church stands. Dating from 1737, the bridge was the scene of mass slaughter when Russian and Swedish forces clashed there during the War of the Hats, which started in 1741. Once on the south side of the river, you can stroll back to Parksbron, past the occasional boat and silent fisherman.

Eating and drinking

For all its contemporary go-ahead industry, modern Skellefteå is quiet and retiring; however, its restaurants and bars come as a pleasant surprise since they are among the best in Norrland.

For a **café**, try the popular *Lilla Mari* at Köpmangatan 13, set in an old-fashioned wooden cottage in a small courtyard off the main drag. The best **restaurant** in town is *Balzac*, (☏0910/156 05) attached to the *Best Western Malmia* at Torget 2, the most fashionable place in town with its retro floral wallpaper and modern Swedish cooking at 165–268kr per dish. An excellent choice for Greek food is the *Stekhus Kriti* (☏0910/77 95 35) at Kanalgatan 51, with steaks from 219kr, moussaka at 120kr and lamb cutlets for 215kr; there's also a decent **bar** here. Otherwise **drinking** is best done at the traditional-English-style *Old Williams Pub* in the main square at Trädgårdsgatan 13–15.

North to Norrbotten: Pite Havsbad

From Skellefteå it's another 70km north on the E4 to the superb sandy **beaches** and swimming complex of **Pite Havsbad**, northern Sweden's main beach resort in the province of Norrbotten at the head of the Gulf of Bothnia. The location, so far north, may come as a pleasant surprise but Havsbadet, as it's known locally, is renowned for its long hours of summer sunshine, relatively warm water temperatures and long sweeping strands of golden sand that are well looked after, friendly and a great place to unwind after the long journey up from the south. There's even an official **nudist beach**, quite a rarity in northern Sweden, given that you can sunbathe nude more or less anywhere you choose away from the crowds. The best way to find it is to follow the side of the main building of the swimming complex down to the sea, turn left along the beach and look out for a large rock, with the words "Naturist Bad" painted on, approximately where the caravan park ends, or look for another sign on the red toilet block around here; the beach runs as far as the wooden post marked "Här slutar naturistbad".

Back at the **swimming complex**, you'll find open-air pools with water slides, and the indoor Äventyrsbadet (☏0911/327 31; late June to late Aug daily 10am–8pm; late Aug to late June Mon–Fri 4pm–8pm, Sat & Sun 10am–6pm; summer 140kr, otherwise Sun–Fri 80kr, Sat 120kr), with fun pool, Jacuzzis, saunas, steam room and yet more water slides. If you're here in winter don't miss the fabulous **icebreaker tours** onboard the *Arctic Explorer* which sails from Piteå out into the frozen expanses of the Gulf of Bothnia. The two-hour tours operate from mid-January to March on Saturdays only at 11am; contact Pite Havsbad for booking and more information.

For **accommodation** here try the on-site *Hotell Pite Havsbad* (☏0911/327 00, ⓦwww.pite-havsbad.se; ❺/❷) with its modern rooms, or next door, right on the beach, there are four-bed **cabins** (same contact details; from 490kr per night), though you'll need to book at least three weeks ahead to be sure of getting one.

You can get here easily from Skellefteå on the Kustbussen **bus** which stops here en route to Luleå and Haparanda (50min).

Luleå and around

When **LULEÅ**, 65km from Pite Havsbad up the E4, was founded in 1621 it had at its centre a church town (see p.302) and medieval church. Numerous trading ships would load and unload their goods at its tiny harbour, reflecting the importance of trade with Stockholm even in those days. The harbour soon proved too small, thanks to the growth in business, and so, by royal command, the settlement was moved to its present site in 1649; only the church and church town, today part of Luleå's **Gammelstad** (Old Town), remained in situ. Up until the end of the eighteenth century, Luleå was still little more than a handful of houses and storage huts; indeed Linnaeus, Sweden's famous botanist, who passed through here in 1732 on his journey to Swedish Lapland, described Luleå as a village. Though the town had started to become something of a shipbuilding centre in the nineteenth century, it wasn't until the construction in 1888 of the Malmbanan, the railway built to transport iron-ore from the Gulf of Bothnia for wintertime export at the ice-free Norwegian port of Narvik, that Luleå's fortunes really started to flourish. Luleå was at one end of the line, and its port was vital for lucrative iron exports (the main ironfields were – and are – around Kiruna and Gällivare).

Although shipping is still important today, in recent years Luleå has become the hi-tech centre of the north, specializing in metallurgy; it also has an important **university**. The town's wide streets and lively, friendly atmosphere

make Luleå immediately likeable, and if you're heading north for the wilds of the Torne valley, Gällivare and Kiruna, or to the sparsely populated regions of Swedish Lapland, Luleå represents your last chance to enjoy a decent range of restaurants and bars. Be mindful of the weather, though: Luleå is built on a peninsula which takes the full brunt of the northerly winds. If you're here in summer (see p.309 for times), taking a boat out into the **archipelago** makes a wonderful day-trip – departures are daily and there's a whole array of islands in the Gulf of Bothnia to choose from: beaches, walking trails and plenty of peace and solitude are the main draws.

Arrival and information

The **train** and **bus stations**, five-minutes' walk apart, are at the eastern end of the central grid of streets. The **tourist office** is in Kulturens Hus, Skeppsbrogatan 17 (mid-June to mid-Aug Mon–Fri 9am–7pm, Sat & Sun 10am–4pm; mid-Aug to mid-June Mon–Fri 10am–6pm; ☏0920/45 70 00, ⓦwww.lulea.se). The busy **airport** lies 10km west of the city, with buses (45kr) and taxis (180kr) linking it with Luleå; there are flights to and from Gothenburg, Pajala, Sundsvall and Stockholm Arlanda. For **internet** access head to Sidewalk Express at Pressbyrån, Storgatan 67.

Accommodation

Given Luleå's thriving economy and popularity as a conference centre, demand for rooms can be high, hence, it's a good idea to book **accommodation** well in advance. Weekend and summer rates at all hotels in Luleå represent excellent value for money and a substantial saving on regular weekday rates.

Amber Stationsgatan 67 ☏0920/102 00, ⓦwww.amber-hotell.se. A small and cosy family-run place in an old wooden building close to the train station. Rooms are individually decorated in modern styles: all are airy with high ceilings and large windows. ④/②

Aveny Hermelinsgatan 10 ☏0920/22 18 20, ⓦwww.hotellaveny.com. Great emphasis is placed on creating a home-from-home atmosphere at this cosy hotel whose corridors are decorated to resemble shopping streets and small alleyways. Rooms are pleasantly, though simply, furnished. ④/②

Best Western Arctic Sandviksgatan 80 ☏0920/109 80, ⓦwww.arctichotel.se. This smart little hotel, very handy for the train station, has cosy rooms with wooden floors and chic Nordic decor in bold reds and greens. Contemporary in feel, though still rather homey. ⑤/③

Elite Luleå Storgatan 15 ☏0920/27 40 00, ⓦwww.lulea.elite.se. The most northerly hotel in the Elite chain and over a hundred years old. This grand old place is right in the centre of town and is the most elegant of all the city's hotels, with old-fashioned rooms, kitted out with drapes and large armchairs, and a huge breakfast buffet. ⑤/③

First Camp Luleå Arcusvägen 110, Karlsvik ☏0920/603 00, ⓦwww.firstcamp.se/lulea. Boasts a superb waterside location with views back towards Luleå. To get there, take bus #6 from Smedjegatan in the city centre (every 1–2hr; 20min). Also has cabins for rent (④).

Luleå Vandrarhem & Minihotell Sandviksgatan 26 ☏0920/22 26 60, ⓦhttp://web.telia.com/~u92017710. Luleå's non-STF hostel is 15min walk from the centre and open all year round, though it is located beside a busy main road and can be noisy. Dorm beds 165kr, double room ❶

Park Kungsgatan 10 ☏0920/21 11 49, ⓦwww.parkhotell.se. With a choice of rooms with private and shared bathrooms, this newly renovated place, the cheapest of Luleå's hotels, is perfectly acceptable. We've given the non-en-suite prices; add around 100–200kr for private facilities. ③/②

The City

Just to the south of **Storgatan**, the main street, lies Luleå's main square, **Rådhustorget**, with the **Domkyrkan** (late June to mid-Aug Mon–Fri 10am–6pm; rest of the year Mon–Fri 10am–3pm; free) in the corner. The medieval incarnation of the cathedral disappeared centuries ago and the present one, built in 1893 on the same spot as its predecessor, is a modern barrage of copper chandeliers hanging like Christmas decorations. Unusually for northern Sweden, it's built of brick, in late-Gothic style to the design of the architect Adolf Emil Melander. The interior was completely renewed in 1938 when the original wooden walls and fittings were removed, revealing the brickwork underneath which was then painted white. Northeast of the Domkyrkan, **Kulturens Hus** at Skeppsbrogatan 17 is not only home to the tourist office and the city library but also **Konstens Hus Arts Centre** (Mon–Fri 10am–6pm, Sat noon–4pm; free) and worth a look, with interesting displays of changing work from modern Swedish artists and sculptors. There's more local art and **handicrafts** on sale at *Konst & Hantverk*, a treasure trove of a store, closeby at Smedjegatan 13, that sells everything from handmade coat hooks in the shape of rams' horns to the seemingly obligatory "Välkommen" sign which no Swedish summer cottage is complete without.

Back at the main square, walk 300m west along Köpmangatan, and you'll come to the **Norrbottens Museum** at Storgatan 2 (Mon–Fri 10am–4pm, Sat & Sun noon–4pm; closed Mon in winter; free; ⓦ www.norrbottensmuseum .se). Although most of the collection is a rather dull resumé of county history and the effects of the 1809 war with Russia, the museum's worth a look mainly for the informative displays and exhibitions on **Sámi** life and culture that predominate northwest of Luleå. Don't leave without seeing the superb hour-long **film**, *Herdswoman* (in Swedish with English subtitles) about three generations of *Sámi* women from Nordmaling near Umeå and their ground-breaking court case in 2006 to establish traditional indigenous grazing rights for their reindeer herds. The museum also has a pleasant **café**.

When the weather's good, it's worth heading to the oddly named **Gültzauudden**, a wooden promontory that has a great **beach**; it was named after the German shipbuilder, Christian Gültzau, who helped to make Luleå a shipbuilding centre. It's easily reachable on foot from the centre: head north from the cathedral along Rådstugatan, which later changes its name to Norra Strandgatan and veers northwest past the Norrbotten theatre to the junction with Fagerlindsvägen. Turn right and follow the road down to the beach. Another good bet on a warm day is the long sandy beach at **Lulviksbadet**, just south of the airport, which also has a naturist section. To get here take the airport bus all the way to the airport and then walk south for a further fifteen minutes, following the main road, until you come to the beach on your left hand side.

Eating and drinking

While the city often has a busy feel in summer, Luleå is much more lively when the university is in session. **Drinking** is generally done at the main restaurants listed below; the most lively and interesting **places to eat** are all found along Storgatan.

Baan Thai Kungsgatan 22 ☏ 0920/23 18 18. Authentic and extensive Thai menu with chicken, beef and pork dishes for 109kr and rice and noodle mains from 95kr. Take the steps at the entrance to reach the restaurant which is located upstairs. The eat-as-much-as-you-like buffet costs just 75kr. Don't miss it or the kitsch pink interior complete with hideous mosaic pillars.

Bakfickan Storgatan 11 ☏ 0920/22 72 72. At last a decent Mediterranean-style restaurant has made it to northern Sweden: the grilled tuna with scallops (245kr) is delicious, or, alternatively, there's a range of northern Swedish dishes such as ptarmigan (268kr) and reindeer fillet with cep mushrooms (242kr).

Bar Bistro Brygga Skeppsbrogatan ☏ 0920/22 00 00. Known colloquially as BBB, this floating pontoon and boat comprise Luleå's most enjoyable outdoor restaurant, open from late May to early Sept: lots of summer grill dishes such as salmon, char and ribs for around 150–250kr, as well as seafood specials such as moules marinières and bouillabaisse (around 190kr).

Bishops Arms Storgatan 15. Attached to the Elite Stadshotellet, this pseudo-English pub with its bookshelves of battered old novels is undoubtedly the most popular place for a drink in town and is always busy with hotel guests and locals alike.

Cook's Krog Storgatan 17 ☏0920/20 10 25. Intimate and cosy, this is the best place in Luleå for steak and reindeer cooked over a charcoal grill, for 155–263kr. The five-course set Northern Swedish speciality menu at 565kr, which includes reindeer and whitefish roe, is definitely worth considering.

Corsica Nygatan 14 ☏0920/158 40. The dark and dingy interior notwithstanding at this none-too-authentic French bistro, there are some good-value items on the menu: pasta dishes are just 89kr, pizzas go for 79kr, whilst a choice of steaks can be had for 169kr. Arguably though, pasta is the safest bet.

Roasters Storgatan 43. Perfectly located on the main drag, this is best café in Luleå with magnificent espressos, cappuccinos and lattes. Also has a good selection of sandwiches, light snacks, quiches and salads. Very popular outdoor seating area in summer.

Zan Smedjegatan 10 ☏0920/104 41. A great Persian restaurant with red lanterns suspended from the ceiling and a menu featuring lots of skewered meats and meze (85kr for a plateful). Alternatively, there's marinated beef or chicken with rice and grilled tomato for 195kr. Pizzas and pasta, too (from 75kr).

Gammelstad church town

One of the most significant places of historical interest north of Uppsala, **GAMMELSTAD** (ⓦwww.lulea.se/gammelstad), the original settlement of Luleå and 11km northwest of the present city, is included on UNESCO's World Heritage List. The **Nederluleå kyrka** here (June to mid-Aug daily 8am–6pm; mid-Aug to June Mon–Fri 10am–2pm; free) was completed at the end of the fifteenth century; originally intended to be a cathedral, it's one of the largest churches in Norrland, and among the most impressive in the whole of Sweden. On the outside are decorative brick and plaster gables and there's an opening above the south door through which boiling oil was poured over unwelcome visitors. The high altar, made in Antwerp, is adorned with finely carved biblical scenes; the decorated choir stalls and ornate triptych are other medieval originals. Have a close look at the sumptuous 1712 pulpit, too, a splendid example of Baroque extravagance, its details trimmed with gilt cherubs and red-and-gold bunches of grapes, made by local craftsman Nils Fluur.

When Luleå moved to the coast, a handful of the more religious among the townsfolk stayed behind to tend the church, and the attached **church town**, the largest in Sweden, remained in use. It comprises over four hundred **cottages**, which can only be occupied by people born in Gammelstad (even people from Luleå must marry a local to gain the right to live here). Down the hill from the cottages is **Friluftsmuséet Hägnan** (June to mid-Aug daily 11am–5pm; free; ⓦwww.lulea.se/hagnan) an open-air heritage park, whose main exhibits are two old farmstead buildings from the eighteenth century. During summer, it plays host to displays of rural skills, such as sheep-rearing, making traditional wooden roof slates and baking of northern Sweden's unleavened bread, *tunnbröd*.

Practicalities

Gammelstad, 10km northwest of the modern city centre, is readily reached by **bus** from Luleå: bus #9 runs every 1–2hr leaving from Smedjegatan in the town centre. The **tourist office** is right by Nederluleå kyrka at Kyrktorget 1 (June–Aug daily 9am–6pm; rest of the year Tues–Thurs 10am–noon & 1–4pm; ☏0920/45 70 10, ⓦwww.lulea.se-gammelstad) and the staff organize guided walks (June–Aug hourly 10am–4pm) around the village and have brochures telling you all about the historical significance of the place. For a place to **eat**, there's ⌘ *Kyrkbyns kök* (℡0920/25 40 90), widely regarded as one of the best restaurants in the entire north of Sweden, at Lulevägen 1, close to the old church; among the exquisite fare it serves up are Norrbotten delicacies like reindeer and Arctic char for around 265kr.

The Luleå archipelago

Luleå's **archipelago** (Ⓦwww.lulea.se/english) is the only one in the world surrounded by brackish water (the Atlantic Ocean off the Norwegian port of Narvik contains ten times more salt than this part of the Gulf of Bothnia). Made up of over 1700 islands and skerries, most of which are uninhabited and unexploited, it's well worth a visit; the islands are renowned for rich bird-life and a profusion of wild berries: lingonberries, blueberries and raspberries are very common, with arctic raspberries, cloudberries, wild strawberries and seabuckthorns also found in large numbers. The **islands** mentioned below are among the most **popular** destinations in the archipelago; being served by once-daily passenger boats from Luleå, they're also the most accessible. With a few notable exceptions, the islands are relatively small – no more than a couple of square kilometres in size – and are therefore ideal for short **walks**. Few are inhabited year-round and, hence there are barely any facilities – you should take all provisions with you and shouldn't count on being able to buy anything once you leave the boat. Although it's perfectly feasible to take a tent and camp on the islands, other **accommodation** is severely limited (we have listed where cabins exist) and most visitors to the islands are day-trippers.

The wildest and most beautiful of all the islands is **Brändöskär**. Located far out in the Gulf of Bothnia, the island can often be very windy; its best features are some terrific upland scenery and smooth rocks along the coast, ideal for sunbathing. There are three **cottages** for rent (400kr per night; bookable through the tourist office in Luleå).

People have lived and worked on **Hindersön**, one of the bigger islands here, since the sixteenth century. Then, fishing, farming and catching seals were the main occupations; today, this is the only island north of Arholma in the Stockholm archipelago which is still farmed.

Kluntarna has a little of everything – small fishing villages, dense pine forest and thousands of seabirds – and is a good choice, especially if you've only time to visit one island. You can rent a simple **cottage** here (book at Luleå's tourist office; ❶), and there's a sauna for your use as well.

South of Luleå in the outer archipelago is **Rödkallen**. Site of an important lighthouse, this tiny island offers fantastic sea and sky views; parts of it have been declared a nature reserve.

Klubbviken, a bay on the island of **Sandön**, is the place to come for good sandy beaches, and has the added advantage of regular boat connections to Luleå. Walking paths crisscross the island, taking in some terrific pine moorland scenery. **Cabins** (❷) on Klubbviken can be booked at the tourist office.

Småskär is characterized by virgin forest, flat clifftops and countless small lakes. The island traces its history back to the seventeenth century, when it was a base for Luleå's fishermen. Its small chapel, dating from 1720, was the first to be built in the archipelago. There are a few small **cottages** available for rent here (❶) – book through the tourist office in Luleå.

Boats leave Södra Hamnen for the various islands in the archipelago from late June to early August, with a reduced service running from late early to late June and from early August to early September; routes and times change from year to year but the latest timetable can be found at Ⓦwww.lulea.se/english or by contacting the tourist office in Luleå. A single ticket to Klubbviken is 50kr, 100kr to any of the other islands.

Haparanda and around

Right by the Finnish border, at the very northern end of the Gulf of Bothnia, **HAPARANDA** is hard to like. The signpost near the bus station reinforces the fact that the town is a very long way from anywhere: Stockholm, 1100km away; the North Cape in Norway, 800km; and Timbuktu 8386km. Viewed from the south, Haparanda is at the end of a very long road to nowhere. However, turn the map upside down, look a little wider and it's easy to see why IKEA took a strategic risk in late 2006 and opened its most northerly store in the world in Haparanda – a town of barely 10,000 people. The gamble paid off and shoppers from the whole of northern Scandinavia, even from as far afield as Murmansk in Russia, now travel here to get their hands on those famous flatpacks. Other companies have followed the retailer's lead and set up business here giving the local economy a long overdue kickstart.

Some history
The key to Haparanda's late coming of age is the neighbouring Finnish town of **Tornio**. Finland was part of Sweden from 1105 until 1809, with Tornio an important trading centre, serving markets across northern Scandinavia. Things began to unravel when Russia attacked and occupied Finland in 1807; the Treaty of Hamina followed, forcing Sweden to cede Finland to Russia in 1809 – thereby losing Tornio. It was decided that Tornio had to be replaced, and so in 1821, the trading centre of Haparanda was founded on the Swedish side of the new border, which ran along the Torne River. However, the new town was never more than a minor upstart compared to its neighbour across the water – until recently. With both Sweden and Finland now members of the European Union, Haparanda and Tornio have declared themselves a **Eurocity** – one city made up of two towns from different countries. The inhabitants of Haparanda and Tornio are bilingual and use both the euro and the Swedish *krona*; roughly half of the children in Haparanda have either a Finnish mother or father. Services are also shared between the two: everything from central heating to post delivery is centrally coordinated. If a fire breaks out in Tornio, for example, Swedish fire crews from Haparanda will cross the border to help put out the flames.

The Town
Other than the new IKEA store, there are only two real sights in town. The **train station**, a grand-looking structure built in 1918, was the result of the town's aspirations to be a major trading centre after World War I and still dominates the suburban streets of southern Haparanda from its location on Järnvägsgatan. Constructed from red brick and complete with stone tower and lantern, it provided Sweden's only rail link to Finland until 1992 when it became another victim of SJ closures. From the platforms, you'll be able to

discern two widths of track – Finnish trains run on the wider, Russian, gauge. Indeed, plans are now being finalized to upgrade the track between Haparanda and Luleå to once again allow trains to operate via this route to Tornio in Finland, though it's likely to be some time yet before services resume. Until then, the empty sidings, overgrown with weeds and bushes, backed by the towering station building, with its vast roof of black tiles and chimneys, give the place a strangely forlorn air. The only other place worthy of some attention is the peculiar copper-coloured **Haparanda kyrka** on Östra Kyrkogatan, a monstrous modern construction that looks like a cross between an aircraft hangar and an apartment building. When the church was finished in 1963, its design caused a public outcry: it even won the prize for being the ugliest church in Sweden.

Practicalities

Haparanda is the terminus for the **Kustbussen** services which run up the Bothnian coast from Sundsvall. Arriving by bus, you'll be dropped at the **bus station** at the northern end of Haparanda's main street, Stationsgatan, which runs parallel to the Torne River (the buildings you can see here across the river are in Finland). From here it's a five-minute walk south along Storgatan to the main square, Torget. The **tourist office** (Finnish time: June to mid-Aug Mon–Fri 7am–7pm, Sat & Sun 10am–6pm; mid-Aug to May Mon–Fri 8am–5pm; ℡0922/120 10, ⓦwww.haparandatornio.com), is actually in Finland in the Green Line Welcome Center and also has information about Tornio and the rest of Finland; there are two phone lines in the office, one for calls from Sweden, the other with enquiries from Finland; staff switch effortlessly from one language to another depending on which line is ringing. To get here from the bus station head towards the "Finland" signs on the nearby bridge; there are no border formalities, and so you can simply walk over the bridge to Finland and wander back whenever you like. It's worth remembering that **Finnish time** is one hour ahead of Swedish time and that Haparanda and Tornio have different names in Swedish (Haparanda and Torneå) and Finnish (Haaparanta and Tornio).

The cheapest beds in town are at Haparanda's STF **youth hostel**, a smart riverside place at Strandgatan 26 (℡0922/611 71, ⓦwww.haparandavandrarhem .se; dorm beds 180kr, double room ❶), affording good views to Finland. The only other option is *Haparanda Stadshotel* at Torget 7 (℡0922/614 90, ⓦwww .haparandastadshotell.se; ❺/❸), an elegant and sumptious hotel dating from 1900 with wooden floors and opulent chandeliers; some rooms even have their own sauna. From late June to mid-Aug a double here can be had for 590kr, though can't be booked in advance.

As far as eating, drinking and nightlife go, you're better off in Tornio in every respect. Friday nights there are wild, the streets full of people trying to negotiate the return leg over the bridge; meanwhile, Haparanda sleeps undisturbed. It used to be the case that Tornio was much cheaper than Haparanda, but prices are now roughly the same, although drinking is still a little less expensive in Finland. For **eating** without trekking over to Finland, *Hasans Pizzeria* (℡0922/104 40) at Storgatan 88, close to Torget, has pizzas for 44kr. Another option is *Leilani* (℡0922/107 17) at Köpmansgatan 15, which has Thai (from 128kr) and Chinese dishes (from 92kr) as well as pizzas (from 56kr). Across in Tornio, your best bet is the riverside *Umpitunneli* at Hallituskatu 15, a restaurant, bar and nightclub all rolled into one that serves Arctic char and grilled chicken for around €15 and a half-litre of beer for €4.

Around Haparanda

Having travelled so far to reach Haparanda, the northernmost point on the Swedish east coast, it seems churlish to leave without making at least one foray into the surrounding area. Other than popping over the Finnish border into Tornio, there are a couple of other diversions worth exploring, notably a day-trip to one of several nearby **islands** or, inland, to the impressive rapids at **Kukkolaforsen** at the start of the Torne Valley.

Twenty-four kilometres to the southwest and attached to the mainland by a slender road-bridge, you'll find the sandy island of **Seskarö** (Ⓦ www.seskaro .nu), a favourite refuge for windsurfers and swimmers. There's a **campsite** here (Ⓣ 0922/201 50, Ⓔ anders.borg@haparanda.se), at Industrivägen 1 with five cabins for two people available (❶), as well as cycle and boat rental. To get to the island, take **bus** #322 from the bus station in Haparanda (Mon–Fri 4 daily).

Fifteen kilometres north of Haparanda, reached on buses #53 and #54 to Pajala, the impressive rapids at **Kukkolaforsen** are best visited during the **Sikfesten** (whitefish festival), held on the last weekend in July. The **whitefish**, a local delicacy grilled on large open fires, are caught in nets at the end of long poles, fishermen dredging the fast, white water and scooping the fish out onto the bank. The festival celebrates a sort of fisherman's harvest, centuries old, although it's now largely an excuse to get drunk at the beer tent, with evening gigs and dancing the order of the day. If you fancy staying here, book the on-site cabins with cooking facilities (Ⓣ 0922/310 00, Ⓦ www.kukkolaforsen.se; ❷).

To get out onto the water, **river rafting** down the rapids can be arranged through the tourist office in Haparanda or at the campsite at Kukkolaforsen – 390kr per person for the gear and a short trip downriver.

Travel details

Trains

Gävle to: Falun (2 hourly; 1hr); Hudiksvall (hourly; 1hr 15min); Kiruna (1 daily; 15hr); Luleå (2 daily; 14hr); Östersund (3 daily; 5hr); Stockholm (hourly; 1hr 20min); Sundsvall (hourly; 2hr); Umeå (1 daily; 9hr 30min); Uppsala (hourly; 45min).

Hudiksvall to: Gävle (hourly; 1hr 15min); Stockholm (hourly; 2hr 30min); Sundsvall (hourly; 50min); Uppsala (hourly; 1hr 50min).

Luleå to: Gällivare (3 daily; 3hr); Gävle (2 daily; 14hr); Kiruna (3 daily; 4hr); Stockholm (2 daily; 14hr); Umeå (1 daily; 4hr 45min); Uppsala (2 daily; 13hr 15min).

Sundsvall to: Gävle (hourly; 2hr); Hudiksvall (hourly; 45min); Östersund (8 daily; 2hr 30min); Stockholm (hourly; 3hr 30min).

Umeå to: Gävle (1 daily; 9hr); Luleå (1 daily; 5hr 30min); Stockholm (1 daily; 11hr); Uppsala (1 daily; 10hr).

Buses

The reliable Kustbussen services run five times daily between Sundsvall and Luleå, generally connecting with trains to and from Sundsvall; three of the five departures continue to Haparanda. From Sundsvall, the buses call at Härnösand, Gallsäter, Ullånger, Docksta, Umeå, Skellefteå and Luleå. Supplementary services also run from Umeå to Haparanda calling additionally at Pite Havsbad.

Other bus services run from the coast into central northern Sweden, often linking up with the Inlandsbanan.

Haparanda to: Pajala (Mon–Fri 2–3 daily, Sat & Sun 1 daily; 3hr 30min).

Luleå to: Arvidsjaur (Mon–Fri & Sun 2 daily, Sat 1 daily; 3hr); Jokkmokk (Mon–Fri & Sun 2 daily, Sat 1 daily; 3hr); Pajala (Mon–Fri & Sun 2 daily, Sat 1 daily; 3hr 30min).

Skellefteå to: Arjeplog (2 daily; 3hr 15min), Arvidsjaur (2 daily; 2hr).

Umeå to: Storuman and Tärnaby/Hemavan (Mon–Sat 3 daily, Sun 1 daily; 3hr 40min to Storuman, 6hr to Tärnaby/Hemavan); Östersund (2 daily; 6hr 30min).

International trains

Luleå to: Narvik, Norway (2 daily; 7hr).

International buses

Haparanda to: Tornio, Finland (hourly; 5min).
Skellefteå to: Bodø, Norway (Mon–Fri & Sun 1 daily; 9hr).
Umeå to: Mo-i-Rana, Norway (1 daily; 8hr).

International ferries

Umeå to: Vaasa, Finland (1 daily; 4hr).

Food and drink

With the freshest of ingredients and a tremendous variety of local specialities – everything from reindeer steaks to Arctic cloudberries – eating in Sweden is invariably a pleasure, and the country's chefs tend toward the innovative, too. Restaurants can be expensive, but you can lessen the blow to your pocket by filling up at hotel breakfast buffets, and by choosing a lunchtime *Dagens Rätt* (daily special) as your main meal. When it comes to drinking, locally produced beers and *akvavit*, rather than wine, are the mainstays.

The smorgasbord

An enormous buffet table groaning with everything from fish and seafood to sausages, cold meats, salads, pastries, fruit and cheeses, the **smorgasbord** is Sweden's best-known culinary treat. Pace yourself and return to the table as many times as you like. Although the smorgasbord doesn't come cheap, it's perfect for a special occasion – the delicious spread served up in the opulent surrounds of the *Grand Hotel* in Stockholm (see p.64) is one of the best.

Swedish specialities

Whether marinated, doused in mustard sauce or even flavoured with blackcurrant, the quintessential Swedish food is **herring** (*sill*). Herring features heavily in any smorgasbord spread and, served with mashed potatoes and chopped dill, is one of the country's staples at the

Meat balls ▲
Fish dish ▼

Filling up without breaking the bank

Start the day by eating your fill from your hotel's **breakfast buffet** – it's included in the room rate. There's everything from cereals to cheese and salad to salami, plus coffee, tea and juice. Swankier venues like the *Mayfair* in Malmö (see p.194) also offer porridge, herring, yoghurt and fruit alongside hot food such as bacon, scrambled egg and sausages. Otherwise, choose a lunchtime **Dagens Rätt** as your main daily meal. Served from Monday to Friday between 11am and 2pm, these cost 65–85kr and consist of a main dish (usually two or three choices) plus salad, bread or crispbread, a soft drink (*läsk*) or light beer, and unlimited coffee.

▲ Menu board

▼ Akvavit

dinner table. A superb accompaniment is crunchy *knäckebröd*, a rye-based **crispbread**. Another lunchtime favourite is the **smorgas** open sandwich: a single piece of white or rye bread piled high with an elaborate variety of toppings such as slices of boiled egg with anchovies, prawns in mayo, or meatballs with beetroot.

Swedish home cooking

▼ Smorgasbord

Swedish **home cooking** (*husmanskost*) has its origins in the simple but tasty country dishes prepared by past generations using the few ingredients they had to hand. Today, these old favourites are back in vogue – and Swedes can't get enough of them. Try **Janssons frestelse**, for example, delicious potato and anchovy bake with cream and onions. Other goodies are **pytt i panna**, a no-nonsense pork and potato fry-up with beetroot and a fried egg on top; and **plättar**, thin pancakes eaten with jam as a main course, or with **ärtsoppa**, a pea soup with thyme and marjoram.

F12 restaurant, Stockholm ▲

Swedish beer ▼

Northern delicacies

Reindeer (*ren*) is the most obvious northern dish to try; it has a delicious flavour when smoked and is akin to beef in taste and texture, but with virtually no fat. When not dished up as a fillet (*reninnanlår*), it's often cut into strips, flash-fried and served with a creamy sauce of chanterelle mushrooms and parsley. **Elk** (*älg*, pronounced "elly"), with a taste somewhere between beef and venison, is another local favourite. Much more tender and flavoursome, **venison** (*hjort*) is a staple of stews, and is sometimes accompanied by *klyftpotatis*, tasty potato wedges sprinkled with salt. The lakes of northern Sweden are known for their vast amounts of **Arctic char** (*röding*), a succulent freshwater fish with tender, pinky flesh usually pan-fried and served with boiled potatoes and a dill sauce.

Buying alcohol

Sweden's state-run alcohol store – **Systembolaget** – was put in place with the aim of cutting alcohol consumption. Often tucked away in an obscure location, the Systembolaget is made as unattractive as possible to its punters, and advertisements are forbidden under Swedish law. Walking into a Systembolaget – if you can find one – really is a trip into the twilight zone. The first thing to do is take a numbered ticket from the machine by the door. In stores with counter service, you select your bottles by number (each bottle in the cabinets has its number displayed alongside) and quote this to the cashier, who then scuttles off to retrieve your booty. Although the Systembolaget undoubtedly limits alcohol consumption, illicit moonshine production is still widespread and many Swedes stock up with cheap booze when they go abroad.

Central Sweden

CHAPTER 6

Highlights

✳ **Riding the Inlandsbanan** A chance to see Sweden's vast forests and fast-flowing rivers close up without leaving the comfort of your train seat. See p.318

✳ **Orsa Grönklitt bear park, Dalarna** Northern Europe's largest bear park offers a unique chance to see these shy animals at close quarters. See p.325

✳ **Hiking in the Härjedalen mountains** Get back to nature and experience the wild side of central Sweden in this remote mountainous province. See p.333

✳ **Klövsjö, Jämtland** A haven of flower meadows and log cabins, this tranquil mountain village has been voted the most beautiful in Sweden. See p.336

✳ **Årets Näck, Hackås** This fun riverside competition featuring naked male fiddle players has its roots in Swedish folklore. See p.337

✳ **Monster spotting, Östersund** Go hunting for Sweden's version of the Loch Ness monster in this appealing lakeside town. See p.341

▲ Huskies, Dalarna

6

Central Sweden

In many ways, the long wedge of land that comprises **central Sweden** – the sparsely populated provinces of Dalarna, Härjedalen and Jämtland – encompasses all that is most typical of the country. This vast area of land is really one great forest, broken only by the odd village or town. Rural and underpopulated, it epitomizes the image most people have of Sweden: lakes, log cabins, pine forests and wide, open skies. Until just one or two generations ago, Swedes across the country lived in this sort of setting, taking their cue from the people of these central lands and forest, who were the first to rise against the Danes in the sixteenth century.

Dalarna, centred around **Lake Siljan**, is an intensely picturesque – and touristy – region, its inhabitants maintaining a cultural heritage (echoed in contemporary handicrafts and traditions) that goes back to the Middle Ages. You won't need to brave the crowds of visitors for too long, as even a quick tour around one or two of the more accessible places here gives an impression of the whole: red cottages with a white door and window frames, sweeping green countryside, water that's bluer than blue and a riot of summer festivals. Dalarna is *the* place to spend midsummer, particularly **Midsummer's Eve**, when the whole region erupts in a frenzy of celebration.

The privately owned **Inlandsbanan**, the great Inland Railway, cuts right through central Sweden and links many of the towns and villages covered in this chapter. Running from **Mora** in Dalarna to Gällivare, above the Arctic Circle, it ranks with the best of European train journeys, covering an enthralling 1067km in two days; the second half of the journey, north of Östersund (where you have to change trains), is covered in the Swedish Lapland chapter; see p.349. Buses connect the rail line with the mountain villages that lie alongside the Norwegian border, where the surrounding Swedish *fjäll*, or mountains, offer some spectacular and compelling hiking, notably around **Ljungdalen** and **Tänndalen** in the remote province of **Härjedalen**. Marking the halfway point of the line, **Östersund**, the only town of any size along it and the capital of the province of **Jämtland**, is situated by the side of Storsjön, the great lake that's reputed to be home to the country's own Loch Ness monster, Storsjöodjuret. From here trains head in all directions: west into Norway through Sweden's premier **ski** resort, **Åre**, south to Dalarna and Stockholm, east to Sundsvall on the Bothnian coast and north into the wild terrain of Swedish Lapland.

315

Dalarna

A sizeable province, **DALARNA** takes in not only the area around **Lake Siljan** but also the ski resorts of **Sälen** and **Idre**, close to the Norwegian border. The area holds a special misty-eyed place in the Swedish psyche and should certainly be seen, although not to the exclusion of places further north. Tiny countryside villages and rolling meadows sweet with the smell of summer flowers make up most of Dalarna, a rural idyll given a handsome backdrop by the land to the northwest of Lake Siljan, which rises slowly to meet the chain of mountains that forms the border with Norway. One small lakeside town can look pretty much like another, so if time is short, restrict yourself to visiting just one or two: **Leksand** and **Mora** are the best options, and the latter is also the starting point for Sweden's most beautiful train journey, along the **Inlandsbanan** to the Arctic Circle.

If you're staying in the area for a few days or more and tire of the predominantly folksy character and tourist crowds of the lakeside settlements, the industrial town of **Falun** can provide relief. North of Mora, the province becomes more mountainous and less populous, the only place of note here being **Orsa**, with its fascinating **bear park**. There's no need to worry about **accommodation** in the province: you'll find numerous hotels, hostels and campsites around.

Paradoxically, in summer, when Dalarna is inundated with visitors, its **bus** system is down to a skeleton service; services to some places, like Idre and Sälen, are reduced to one or two buses a day then. It's worth picking up a timetable from the tourist office and organizing your route before you go,

▲ Reindeer

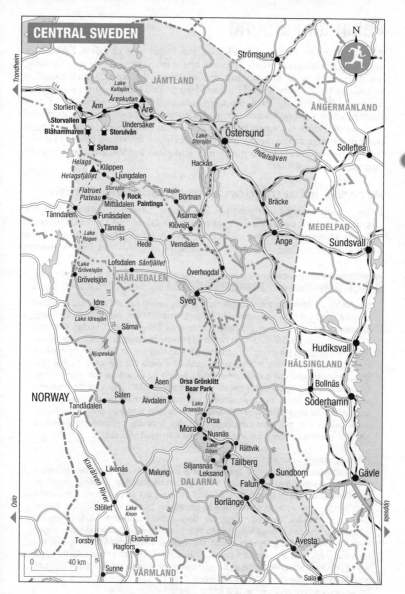

or you could find yourself facing a very long wait for your next connection. Mora is one of the main interchanges in Dalarna's bus network; the only way to get to Sälen or Idre by public transport is by bus from here, and if you want to visit both, you'll be forced to retrace your steps back to Mora to get from one village to the other, adding about five hours to your journey. A good way to get about locally, especially around Lake Siljan, is to rent a **bike** from one of the tourist offices.

Falun and around

About 220km northwest of Stockholm and 90km west of Gävle, **FALUN** is essentially an industrial town – a pleasant one at that – known for copper mining, which began here in the eleventh century; today, the mines, which closed as recently as 1992, can be visited on hour-long guided tours. Falun is also known for a sobering event: in 1994, the town witnessed Sweden's worst case of mass murder, when a young soldier, inflamed with jealousy after seeing his girlfriend with another man, ran amok and shot dead seven local people; there's a simple stone monument to the event, bearing an inscription to "young people killed by meaningless violence", at the junction of Parkgatan and Vasagatan between the hospital and train station.

Arrival, information and accommodation

Falun is easily reached by train from Stockholm, Arlanda airport and Uppsala, and there are also useful through services from Gävle and Örebro. The **train** and **bus stations** are to the east of the centre; follow the "Centrum" signs, hugging the train line, and you'll soon reach Trotzgatan and Falun's **tourist**

The Inlandsbanan

SJ and locally operated **trains** (all accepting rail passes) call at Falun and at all the towns around Lake Siljan, terminating in Mora; north of here, the privately operated **Inlandsbanan**, the great Inland Railway that links Dalarna with Swedish Lapland, takes over. With special guides on board to provide commentaries and information about places along the route, it's certainly a fascinating way to reach the far north of the country; however, the Inlandsbanan today is a mere shadow of its former self. Spiralling costs and low passenger numbers forced SJ to sell the line, and the last state-run trains trundled down the single-line track in 1992. Trains on the southern section between Mora and Kristinehamn had ceased running several years earlier, and part of the track there was dismantled. The railway was then sold to the fifteen municipalities that the route passes through, and a private company, Inlandståget AB, was launched to keep the line going – and with great success.

Inlandsbanan practicalities

The Inlandsbanan is now only operated as a tourist venture in summer, generally between June and August. The latest timings can be found at ⓦwww.grandnordic .se. **Timetables** are only approximate, and the train will stop whenever the driver feels like it – perhaps for a spot of wild-strawberry picking or to watch a beaver damming a stream. Currently there are daily trains north from Mora at around 2.35pm, but this can change from year to year (in previous years, for example, departures have been at 7am). Done in one go, the whole journey (Mora–Gällivare; 1067km) lasts two days, with an overnight stop in Östersund. Take it at a more relaxed pace, with a couple of stops along the route (you can break your journey as many times as you like on one ticket), and you'll get much more out of it. More details of Inlandsbanan services are given in the text and in "Travel Details", p.346.

All trips **cost** 1.23kr per kilometre, with tickets bought on the train; Mora–Östersund, for example, costs 395kr and takes six hours. InterRail and Scanrail passes are valid on the Inlandsbanan. Alternatively, you can buy the **Inland Railway Card** (normal price 1395kr), which gives unlimited travel during the entire period of operation. Seat reservations are best made at least 24 hours in advance and cost 50kr per seat. Two children under 15 can travel free if accompanied by an adult; otherwise they pay half price. Bicycles can be carried on board if space allows.

office (mid-June to mid-Aug Mon–Fri 9am–7pm, Sat 9am–5pm, Sun 11am–4pm; mid-Aug to mid-June Mon–Fri 10am–6pm, Sat 10am–2pm; ☎023/830 50, ⓦwww.visitfalun.se), at nos. 10–12, opposite the *First Hotel Grand*, which also has **internet access**.

The nearest **youth hostel** (☎023/105 60, ⓦwww.stfvandrarhemfalun.com; dorm beds 190kr, double rooms ❶) is at Vandrarvägen 3, 3km from the centre in the Haraldsbo part of town (take bus #701 from the centre to Korsnäs, and get off at the stop for *Koppartorget*). The swankiest **hotel** in town is the central *First Hotel Grand* at Trotzgatan 9–11 (☎023/79 48 80, ⓦwww.firsthotels .se; ❺/❸), whose rooms are sumptuous to say the least. For a more homely feel, try *Clarion Collection Bergmästaren* (☎023/70 17 00, ⓦwww.choice.se; ❺/❹), at Bergskolegränd 7 near the train station, which has a superb sauna suite complete with Jacuzzi and sunbeds. The nearest **campsite** (☎023/835 63, ⓦwww.falun.se/lugnet) is up at Lugnet by the National Ski Stadium, 1.5km from the town centre.

The Town and around

Falun grew in importance during the seventeenth and eighteenth centuries, when its **copper mines** produced two-thirds of the world's copper ore. Commensurate with its status as what was then the second largest town in Sweden, Falun acquired grand buildings and an air of prosperity. The few old, wooden houses that survive (in 1761, two fires wiped out virtually all of central Falun) are worth seeking out to gain an idea of the cramped conditions mine workers had to live in; you'll find these buildings in the districts of **Elsborg** (southwest of the centre), Gamla Herrgården and Östanfors (both north of the centre).

By far the most interesting attraction in Falun is its **mines** (ⓦwww .kopparberget.com), reached from the centre along Gruvgatan – head along this street for around a kilometre, right to the far end. Mandatory **guided tours** (May–Sept daily 9.30am–4.30pm; Oct–April daily noon–4pm; 150kr; English commentary available), lasting around an hour, are organized on the site, beginning with an elevator ride 55m down to a network of old mine roads and drifts. The temperature down below is only 6–7°C, so make sure you bring warm clothing; try also to wear old shoes, as your footwear is likely to come out tinged red.

The site has a worthy **museum** (same hours as above; 50kr), recounting the history of Falun's copper production. Conditions below ground in the mines were appalling, said by the botanist Carl von Linné to be as dreadful as hell itself. One of the most dangerous aspects of eighteenth-century copper mining was the presence everywhere in the mines of **vitriol** gases, which are strong preservatives. It's recorded that the body of a young man known as *Fet Mats* (Fat Mats) was found in the mines in 1719; though he'd died 49 years previously in an accident, his corpse was so well preserved when discovered that his erstwhile fiancée, by then an old woman, recognized him immediately. Be sure not to miss peering into the **Great Pit** (Stora Stöten), just nearby, which is 100m deep and 300–400m wide. It suddenly appeared on Midsummer Day in 1687, when the entire pit caved in – the result of extensive mining and the unsystematic driving of galleries and shafts.

Back in Falun's centre, the riverside **Dalarnas Museum** (Tues–Fri 10am–5pm, Sat & Sun noon–5pm; Sept–May Wed until 9pm; free; ⓦwww.dalarnasmuseum .se), Stigaregatan 2–4, makes for a worthwhile visit. Containing sections on the province's folk art, the Dala horse, dresses and music, it includes a reconstruction, on the ground floor, of the dark, heavily wood-panelled study where the author

Selma Lagerlöf worked when she moved to Villavägen 34 in Falun in 1897, as well as a number of black-and-white photographs of her and her home; a copy of Lagerlöf's books, including her most famous work *Nils Holgerssons underbara resa genom Sverige* ("The wonderful Adventures of Nils"), are displayed on the bookshelves (for more on Lagerlöf, see p.162).

Around Falun: Sundborn

"It was here I experienced the unspeakably delightful feeling of seclusion from all the world's noise and din".

Carl Larsson's words on living in Sundborn.

The delightful **Carl Larssongården** (May–Sept daily 10am–5pm; Oct–April Mon–Fri guided tours at 11am; 100kr), once the home of the artist **Carl Larsson**, lies in the village of **SUNDBORN**, 13km from Falun; to get there, take bus #64 from Falun's train station (hourly; 20min). One of Sweden's most visited tourist attractions, the cottage was at first the summer dwelling of Carl and his wife Karin, later becoming their permanent home. The artist's own murals and portraits of his children form part of the decor, as do the embroidery and tapestries of his wife. At the start of the twentieth century, when the Larssons had done the place up, the house represented an entirely new decorative style for Sweden, its bright, warm interior quite unlike the dark and sober colours used until that time. The artist is buried in the churchyard just outside.

Eating, drinking and nightlife

The variety and quality of the places to **eat** and **drink** in Falun, all of them in or around the main square, Storatorget, far outstrip the selection in the other towns around Lake Siljan.

Bars and restaurants

Bakfickan Slaggatan 2. One of *the* places to be seen, as far as Falun's young and trendy are concerned, this bar is at its busiest on Fri and Sat nights. It also serves light bar snacks (89–159kr), such as a juicy open sandwich with prawns for 89kr.

Banken Åsgatan 41 ☏023/71 19 11. A trendy bistro with a grand stuccoed ceiling which takes its name from the former bank which once stood here. Modern Swedish dishes make up the menu here, for example ovenbaked char and steaks (185kr), although there are also burgers and pasta dishes available.

The Kings Arms Falugatan 3 ☏023/71 13 44. A cosy and popular pub with a heavy wooden interior and models of rigged sailing ships in the windows.

Light bar meals such as burgers (99kr) and pasta dishes (125kr) are available as well as heftier steak and fish meals (from 145kr).

Hammars Åsgatan 28. The best café in town, with wide variety of open sandwiches, delicious cakes and a home-from-home interior featuring old clocks on the mantelpiece and olde-worlde chandeliers. Closed Sun.

Rådhuskällaren Slaggatan 2 ☏023/254 00. Located under the Rådhus in Storatorget, this is an atmospheric place to indulge in delicious Swedish food given an international twist. Mains including salmon fillet with grilled vegetables or grilled veal start at 159kr. There's also a three-course set menu for 535kr featuring reindeer steak and whitefish roe.

Around Lake Siljan

Things have changed since Baedeker, writing in 1889, observed that "Lake Siljan owes much of its interest to the inhabitants of its banks, who have preserved many of their primitive characteristics. In their idea of cleanliness they are somewhat behind the age." Today it's not the people who draw your attention but the setting. **Lake Siljan**, created millions of years ago when a meteorite crashed into the earth, is what many people come to Sweden for, its gently rolling surroundings, traditions and local handicrafts weaving a subtle spell on the visitor. There's a lush feel to much of the region, the charm of the forest heightened by its proximity to the lake, all of which adds a pleasing dimension to the low-profile towns and villages that interrupt the rural scenery. Only **Mora** stands out as being bigger and busier, with the hustle and bustle of holidaymakers and countless caravans crowding the place in summer.

Leksand

Perhaps the most traditional of the Dalarna villages, **LEKSAND**, about 50km northwest of Falun, is certainly worth making the effort to reach at midsummer, when it stages festivals recalling age-old dances performed around the **maypole** (Sweden's maypoles are erected in June – in May the trees here are still bare and the ground can be covered with snow). The celebrations culminate in the **church boat races**, a waterborne procession of sleek wooden longboats, which the locals once rowed to church on Sundays. Starting on Midsummer's Day in nearby **Siljansnäs** – take the roughly hourly bus #84 from Leksand – and continuing for ten days at different locations around the lake, the races hit Leksand on the first Saturday in July. Leksand's tourist office will have details of the arrangements for each summer's races.

Another event you should try to catch is **Musik vid Siljan** (ⓦwww .musikvidsiljan.se), nine days of musical performances in lakeside churches, the stunning former limestone quarry, Dalhalla, and at various locations out in the surrounding forest. The range of music covered is pretty wide, including chamber music, jazz, traditional folk songs and dance-band music. It all takes place during the first week of July, with proceedings starting in the early morning and carrying on until late evening every day.

There's little else to do in Leksand other than take it easy for a while. A relaxing stroll along the riverside brings you to **Leksands kyrka** (daily 9.30am–3.30pm), one of Sweden's biggest village churches; it has existed in its present form since 1715, although the oldest parts of the building date back to the thirteenth century. The church enjoys one of the most stunning locations of any in the land, its peaceful churchyard lined with whispering spruce trees and looking out over the lake to the distant shore. Next door is the region's best open-air **Hembygdsgård** (Homestead Museum; no set hours; free) – about a dozen old timber buildings grouped around a maypole, ranging from simple square huts used to store hay during the long winter months to a magnificent *parstuga*, which forms the centrepiece of the collection. Built in 1793, this two-storey dwelling, constructed of thick circular logs, is notable because buildings of the period were rarely more than one storey in height, since timber was expensive. From directly behind the museum a narrow track leads down to the lake, where there's a recon-struction of a church boathouse used to house the *kyrkbåtar* boats for which Dalarna is known throughout Sweden.

Whilst in Leksand, it's worth taking one of the **cruises** on Lake Siljan aboard the lovely old steamship *M/S Gustaf Wasa*, built in Stockholm in 1876 (timetables vary; check sailing times with the tourist office or at ⓦwww .wasanet.nu), which depart between May and September from the quay near the homestead museum; take the track down to the reconstructed boathouse (see above) and turn left following the lakeside to the bridge and the quay. The excursions include a round-trip to Mora and back (150kr), or a two-hour cruise round a bit of the lake (100kr).

Practicalities

There are frequent **trains** between Mora and Stockholm in both directions, all of which stop at Leksand. The **tourist office** is at Norsgatan 40 (mid–June to mid-Aug Mon–Fri 10am–7pm, Sat & Sun 10am–5pm; mid-Aug to mid-June Mon–Fri 10am–5pm; ☎0247/79 61 30; ⓦwww.siljan.se), a ten-minute walk from the train station up Villagatan towards the centre of town, then left along Sparbanksgatan.

Leksand's cosy **youth hostel**, one of the oldest in Sweden, is around 2.5km from the train station, over the river at Parkgattu 6 (☎0247/152 50, ⓦwww .vandrarhemleksand.se; dorm beds 190kr, double rooms ❷); bus #58 will take you there. The lakeside **campsite**, *Leksands Camping & Stugby* (☎0247/803 13, ⓔkommunen@leksand.se) is at Siljansvägen 91, a twenty-minute walk from the tourist office along Tällbergsvägen. Four-bed **cabins** in the vicinity of Leksand are available (❷); you can book them at the tourist office, which is also where to head in the afternoon for any last-minute **hotel** deals. Comfortable rooms in log cabins are to be found at *Hotell Moskogen*, Insjövägen 50 (☎0247/146 00, ⓦwww.moskogen.com; ❹). But by far the best place to stay in Leksand is ⚞ *Korstäppens Herrgård* at Hjortnäsvägen 33 (☎0247/123 10, ⓦwww.korstappan .se; ❹), a wonderful hotel tastefully decked out in traditional Dalarna colours. Its sitting and dining rooms look out over the lake, whose lapping waters can be reached by a path behind the hotel.

A good place to **eat** is *Siljans Konditori*, in the main square; their summer terrace is a wonderful place from which to watch the world go by while sipping a cup of coffee. They serve up sandwiches with fantastic home-made bread, and salads and pies; make this place your first choice for lunch (they're not open in the eve). Alternatively, try *Bosporen* (☎0247/132 80) in the tiny pedestrianized centre of town; the village's main restaurant, it serves pizzas from 60kr as well as meat and fish dishes such as schnitzel or sole from 165kr. Chinese food can be had at *Lucky House* (☎0247/100 80) in the main square, with the usual array of dishes from 109kr. For a **drink**, try the downstairs cocktail bar in the *Bosporen* or the pub attached to the *Lucky House*.

Tällberg

If you believe the tourist blurb, then **TÄLLBERG**, all lakeside log cabins amid rolling hills, *is* Dalarna. Situated on a promontory in the lake 10km north of Leksand, this folksy hillside village, whose wooden cottages are draped with flowers in summer, first became famous in 1850 when the Danish writer Hans Christian Andersen paid it a visit; on his return to Copenhagen, he wrote that everyone should experience Tällberg's peace and tranquillity, and marvel at its wonderful lake views. Ever since, hordes of tourists have flooded into the tiny village to see what all the fuss was about – prepare yourself for the crowds that unfortunately take the shine off what is otherwise quite a pretty little place. Tällberg today is also a prime destination for wealthy middle-aged Swedes, who come to enjoy the good life for a few days, savour the delicious food dished up by the village's hotels, and admire the fantastic views out over Lake Siljan. To escape the crowds, walk down the steep hill of Sjögattu, past the campsite, to the calm lapping water of the lake and a small sandy beach; keep going through the trees to find a couple more secluded spots.

Tällberg is on the main **train** line round Lake Siljan; the **station** is a ten- to fifteen-minute walk from the village. There's no tourist office here. For **accommodation**, avoid the expensive hotels and walk down ⚞ Sjögattu to *Siljansgården* (☎0247/500 40, ⓦwww.siljansgarden.com; ❷) at no. 36, a wonderful old wooden farm building with a cobbled courtyard and a fountain, and rooms that are comparable to those in youth hostels – it's one of the best deals in Dalarna. Alternatively, head for the **campsite** (T0247/503 01), a little further along from *Siljansgården* – head down to the lakeshore and turn left.

Mora and around

At the northwestern corner of the lake, 60km from Leksand, **MORA** is the best place to head for on the lake, handy for onward trains on the Inlandsbanan (see p.318) and for moving on to the ski resorts of Idre (see p.327) and Sälen (see p.328). An appealing, laidback town, the main draw here are two excellent museums, one dedicated to the painter Anders Zorn, and the other to Vasaloppet ski race.

Arrival and information

For the centre of town, you should leave the **train** at Mora Strand station (which consists of little more than a platform), one stop after the main Mora station on trains coming from the south; the Inlandsbanan begins at Mora Strand before calling at Mora station. The **bus station** is at Moragatan, close to Mora Strand and just off the main Strandgatan. The **tourist office** (mid-June to mid-Aug Mon–Fri 10am–7pm, Sat & Sun 10am–5pm; mid-Aug to mid-June Mon–Fri 10am–5pm; T0250/59 20 20, Wwww.siljan.se), opposite Mora Strand station at Strandgatan 14, has all the usual literature, including a map of the Vasaloppsleden hiking route, which you can follow north from Mora to Sälen (see p.328).

Accommodation

Although Mora sees a sizeable influx of tourists for the Vasaloppet race and during the summer season, there's a surprising lack of choice in terms of places to **stay**. Hence, it pays to book ahead from mid-June to mid-August in particular.

Best Western Mora Strandgatan 12 T0250/59 26 50, Wwww.morahotell.se. Mora's biggest and best hotel, opposite Mora Strand station, with both modern and old-fashioned rooms hung with Zorn pictures. There's also a first-class sauna suite and gym with pool and Jacuzzi. ④/❸
Kristineberg Kristinebergsgatan 1 T0250/150 70, Wwww.trehotell.nu. An annexe of the *Kung Gösta*, this is a plain and simple B&B-style alternative with dorm beds (130kr) as well as cramped en-suite double rooms. There's a kitchen for self-catering. ❷
Kung Gösta Kristinebergsgatan 1 T0250/150 70, Wwww.trehotell.nu. Close to the main train station and handy for early-morning departures. Although this is a modern hotel with identikit

rooms, there's a choice between bathrooms with bathtubs or showers. There's an excellent swimming pool here, too. ④/❸
Mora Parken Parkvägen 1 T0250/276 00, Wwww.moraparken.se. A comfortable modern hotel catering for families with children; there's a playground nearby as well as a lake for swimming. They also have a selection of cottages for rent (❶). It's a 10min walk from the centre along Hantverkaregatan, which begins near the bus station. ❺/❸
Youth hostel Fredsgatan 6 T0250/381 96, Wwww.maalkullann.se. A comfortable STF hostel in the heart of Mora at the finishing line for the Vasalopp race, with double rooms (❷) as well as dorm beds (230k).

The Town

The main attraction in Mora is the outstanding **Zorn Museum** at Vasagatan 36 (mid-May to mid-Sept Mon–Sat 9am–5pm, Sun 11am–5pm; mid-Sept to mid-May Mon–Sat noon–5pm, Sun 1–5pm; 35kr; Wwww.zorn.se), showcasing the work of Sweden's best-known painter, **Anders Zorn** (1860–1920), who moved here in 1896. Most successful as a portrait painter, he worked in both oil and watercolour and spent periods living in both St Ives in Britain and in Paris. Zorn even went to the United States to paint American presidents Cleveland, Theodore Roosevelt and Taft. At the museum, look out for his larger-than-life self-portrait dressed in wolfskin from 1915 and the especially pleasing *Midnatt* (Midnight) from 1891, which depicts a woman rowing on Lake Siljan, her hands blue from the cold night air. The artist's remarkable silver collection containing four hundred pieces ranging from tankards to teaspoons is also on display. You might also want to wander across the museum lawn and take in his home, **Zorngården** (mid-May to mid-Sept Mon–Sat 10am–4pm, Sun 11am–4pm; mid-Sept to mid-May daily, hourly guided tours at noon–3pm; 60kr), where he and his wife Emma lived during the early twentieth century. What really makes the place unusual is its cavernous ten-metre-high hall with a steeply V-shaped roof, entirely constructed from wood and decked out in traditional Dalarna designs and patterns, where the couple lived out their roles as darlings of local society.

The other museum in town worth considering is the **Vasaloppsmuséet** (Ski Museum; mid-June to mid-Aug Mon–Wed & Fri–Sun 10am–5pm, Thurs 10am–3pm; mid-Aug to mid-June Mon–Wed & Fri 10am–5pm, Thurs 10am–3pm; 30kr; ⓦ www.vasaloppet.se); it's east of the Zorn Museum, on the other side of Vasagatan, and covers the history of the ski race, Vasaloppet, held on the first Sunday in March. The event commemorates King Gustav Vasa's return to Mora after he escaped from the Danes on skis; two men from Mora caught up with him and persuaded him to come back to their town, where they gave him refuge. The longest cross-country ski race in the world, the competition was the idea of a local newspaper editor, who organized the first event in 1922; it was won by a 22-year-old from Västerbotten who took seven and a half hours to complete the course. Today, professionals take barely four hours to cover the 90km. Although the Vasaloppet enjoys royal patronage (the current Swedish king has skied it), it does have a somewhat chequered past, since women were forbidden from taking part until 1981. Whilst here, make sure you watch the half-hour **film** (with English subtitles) about the race – the impressive aerial shots really help to portray the massive scale of the competition.

Eating and drinking

Mora is no gastronomic nirvana. However, there are one or two places worth seeking out in town which we've listed below. Outside the summer months, expect all of them to be rather empty.

China House Strandgatan 6 ⓣ0250/152 40. The food here isn't overly authentic but this is the only Chinese restaurant for miles around. There are both Chinese and Thai dishes on the menu, with mains starting at 136kr (three-course set menu 225kr). Alternatively there are steaks, from 145kr.

Claras Vasagatan 38 ⓣ0250/158 98 40. They don't come cuter than this homely place which is back up and running after a devastating fire. Akin to eating in your grandmother's dining room, it's been rebuilt and decorated with classic Dalarna wallpaper and fittings. A great location for fine dining at respectable prices: steaks from 179kr and pasta dishes from 89kr.

MålkullAnns Vasagatan 19. Mora's best and most atmospheric café, set in a snug old timber building done out in traditional nineteenth-century style. There's a good choice of sandwiches, home-baked bread and cakes, as well as light lunch dishes.

Pizzeria Prima Fridhemsplan ⓣ0250/120 11. The interior may be plain and simple, but the pizzas here are tasty and the range on offer impressive. Reckon on around 70kr per pizza.

Wasastugan Tingnäsvägen 6 ⓣ0250/177 92. Set within a huge log building between the main train station and the Vasaloppsmuséet and serving up Cajun dishes such as blackened salmon (148kr), tuna fishcake (68kr) and a massive barbecue-burger (109kr) which really hits the spot. Also open for lunch; May–Aug evening meals.

The Dala Horse

No matter where you travel in Sweden, you'll come across small wooden figurines known as **Dala horses** (*dalahästar*). Their bright red colour, stumpy legs and garish floral decorations are, for many foreigners, high kitsch and rather ugly; the Swedes, however, adore bright colours (the redder the better) and so love the little horses – it's virtually an unwritten rule that every household in the country should have a couple on display. Two brothers from the town of **Nusnäs**, Nils and **Jannes Olsson**, began carving the horses in the family baking shed in 1928, when they were just teenagers. Though they were simply interested in selling their work to help their cash-strapped parents make ends meet, somehow the wooden horses started catching on – Swedes are at a loss to explain why – and soon were appearing across the country as a symbol of rural life.

Around Mora: Nusnäs

Whilst in Mora you might want to consider a visit to **Nusnäs**, just east of town on the lakeside, where you'll find **Grannas A. Olssons Hemslöjd** (mid-June to mid-Aug Mon–Fri 9am–6pm, Sat & Sun 9am–4pm; mid-Aug to mid-June Mon–Fri 9am–4pm, Sat 10am–1pm; free; ⓦ www.grannas.com), the **workshop** of the Olsson brothers, creators of Sweden's much-loved **Dala horses** (see box above). Skilled craftsmen carve the horses out of wood from the pine forests around Lake Siljan and then hand-paint and varnish them. You can get to Nusnäs from Mora on bus #108 (Mon–Fri 3 daily; 20min).

Orsa and the bear park

A dull little place barely 20km from Mora, sitting aside Lake Orsasjön, a northerly adjunct of Lake Siljan, **ORSA**'s draw is its location – right in the heart of Sweden's bear country – and its fascinating bear park. It's reckoned that there are a good few hundred **brown bears** roaming the dense forests around town, though few sightings are made in the wild. The nearby **Orsa Grönklitt björnpark** (Bear Park; mid-June to mid-Aug daily 10am–6pm; mid-Aug to mid-June daily 10am–3pm; 160kr; ⓦ www.orsagronklitt.se) is the biggest **bear park** in Europe. The bears here aren't tamed or caged, but wander around the 255-thousand square metres of the forested park at will, much as they would in the wild. It's the human visitors who are confined, having to clamber up viewing platforms and along covered walkways.

The bears are fascinating to watch: their behaviour is amusing, and they're gentle and vegetarian for the most part (though occasionally they're fed the odd dead reindeer or elk that's been killed on the roads). Trying hard not to be upstaged by the bears are a few lynx, wolves and wolverines, the other three Swedish predators – although you'll be lucky to spot the wolves in particular; in fact, it's a good idea to bring along a pair of binoculars to help you pick out any rustlings in the undergrowth. In addition, the park has a couple of Siberian tigers, two truly enormous Kamchatka bears from eastern Russia (the male weighs a whopping 900kg) and a pair of Eurasian eagle owls, the largest owl in the world, and found throughout Sweden's forests.

The bear park is located 16km from Orsa, and can be reached by taking bus #118 (Mon–Fri 2 daily, Sun 1 daily) from Orsa bus station; from Mora, take #104 or #245 to Orsa and then change. From late autumn to early spring the park closes, when the bears hibernate (Nov–April) in specially constructed lairs, monitored by closed-circuit television cameras.

The **train station** for Inlandsbanan arrivals and departures is right in the centre of town on Järnvägsgatan, opposite the **bus station**. Nearby, at Dalagatan 1, the **tourist office** (mid-June to mid-Aug Mon–Fri 10am–7pm, Sat & Sun 10am–5pm; mid-Aug to mid-June Mon–Fri 10am–5pm; ☎0250/55 25 50, ⓦwww.siljan.se), can help with local accommodation. Right in the centre near the station at Järnvägsgatan 4 is the *Orsa* **hotel** (☎0250/409 40, ⓦwww.orsahotell.se; ❸), built in 1894 to serve the new-fangled railway, and today a decent enough place with modern rooms, though it's a much better bet to head for the beautifully located **youth hostel** (☎0250/421 70; ⓦwww.orsavandrarhem.se; dorm beds 280kr, double rooms ❶), Gillevägen 3, 1km west of the centre by the side of Orsasjön lake. However, should you want to stay up at the bear park there's also a second, well-equipped hostel at Grönklitt (☎0250/462 00, ⓦwww.orsagronklitt.se; no dorms, double rooms ❷); the hostel and the park are easily reached on the #118 bus from Orsa bus station. There are filling meals available on site at the *Wärdshuset* restaurant next door (☎0250/462 31); pork ribs or grilled trout with salad here is just 110kr.

Northwestern Dalarna

The area to the northwest of Mora offers travellers approaching from the south a first taste of what northern Sweden is really all about. The villages in this remote part of Dalarna lie few and far between, separated by great swathes of coniferous forest which thrive on the poor sandy soils of the hills and mountains which predominate here. On its way to the Norwegian border, **Route 70**, the main artery through this part of the province, slowly climbs up the eastern side of the Österdalälven river valley. After the tiny village of Åsen, the road leaves the river behind and strikes further inland towards the mountains which mark the border between Sweden and Norway. Buses to Särna, Idre and Grövelsjön follow this route, whereas services to Sälen only travel as far as Älvdalen before heading west towards Route 297.

It is predominantly to ski (in winter) or to hike (in summer) that most visitors come to this part of Dalarna. Indeed, **Sälen** and **Idrefjäll** are two of Sweden's most popular **ski resorts** and, in season, the slopes and cross-country trails here are busy with Swedes from further south, where snowfall is less certain. In summer, though, **Grövelsjön** makes a better destination than its sleepy neighbours, thanks to some superb hiking trails through the surrounding mountains which begin here.

Sälen

Considered as one entity, **SÄLEN** and the surrounding resorts of Lindvallen, Högfjället, Tandådalen, Hundfjället, Rörbäcksnäs and Stöten constitute the biggest **ski centre** in the Nordic area, with over a hundred pistes and guaranteed snow from November to May. It isn't unreasonable to lump all these places together, as each of the minor resorts, despite having its own ski slope, is dependent on Sälen for shops (not least its Systembolaget) and services. Novice skiers can take advantage of Sälen's special lifts, nursery slopes and qualified tuition; there are also plenty of intermediate runs through the densely forested hillsides and, for advanced skiers, twenty testing runs as well as an off-piste area. To get the best value for money, it's really worth buying a package rather than trying to book individual nights at local hotels; prices are high and in season they're packed to capacity. During the **summer**, Sälen specializes in assorted **outdoor activities** – fishing, canoeing and beaver safaris are all available, and the hills, lakes and rivers around the town will keep you busy for several days. There's also some fantastic hiking to be had in the immediate vicinity (see box below).

Bus #95 heads from Mora to Sälen (see Ⓦwww.dalatrafik.se for times). Heading here from further south, first take the train to Borlänge, where you change to a train to **Malung**, from where bus #157 takes an hour to reach Sälen. The bus calls at each resort in turn, terminating at Stöten. Sälen's **tourist office** is on the straggly main street that runs through the village (late April to late June & mid-Aug to Nov Mon–Thurs 9am–6pm, Fri 10am–6pm, Sat 10am–2pm; late June to mid-Aug & Dec to late April Mon–Thurs 9am– 6pm, Fri 10am–6pm, Sat & Sun 9am–4pm; ℡0280/187 00, Ⓦwww.salen .se). **Accommodation** is best at the wonderfully situated *Högfjällshotellet*, at Högfjället (3–4 buses daily from Sälen; ℡0280/870 00, Ⓦwww.salen-hotell .se; ❼), just in the tree line; it has a restaurant and a bar with fantastic panoramic views, though is only open during the ski season. There's also a superb sauna suite in the basement, and a swimming pool with whirlpool and jet streams. To be out in the wilds, head for the **youth hostel** at Gräsheden, near Stöten (℡0280/ 820 40, Ⓦwww.salensvandrarhem.se; dorm beds 200kr, double rooms ❶); buses from Sälen to Stöten will drop you close by, though you need to reserve ahead before heading out here. Breakfast can be ordered in advance and there's a kitchen, laundry room and sauna.

Idre, Idrefjäll and around

The two daily buses (#170) from Mora follow the densely forested valley of the Österdalälven on their three-hour journey to **IDRE** – one of Sweden's main **ski resorts** and home to the country's southernmost community of reindeer-herding *Sámi*. However, if you're expecting wooden huts and reindeer herders dressed in traditional dress, you'll be disappointed – the remaining six herding families live in conventional houses in the area around Idre, and dress like everyone else.

Hikes around Sälen

The route taken by skiers on the first Sunday in March during the annual **Vasaloppet race**, the **Vasaloppsleden** from Sälen to **Mora** (90km) is equally rewarding to explore on foot. The path starts just outside Sälen, in **Berga**, and first runs uphill to Smågan, then downhill all the way to Mora via Mångsbodarna, Risberg, Evertsberg, Oxberg, Hökberg and Eldris. For **accommodation**, there are eight **cabins** along the route, each equipped with a stove and unmade beds; it's also possible to stay in a number of the hamlets on the way, too – look out for *rum* or *logi* signs. A detailed map of the route is available from the tourist offices in Sälen and Mora.

Another hike to consider is the little-known **southern Kungsleden** (for the main Kungsleden, see p.379). It starts at the *Högfjällshotellet* on **Högfjället**, one of the slopes near Sälen, and leads to **Drevdagen**, a thirty-minute drive west of Idre off Route 70 (bus #128 runs once daily Mon–Fri between Idre and Drevdagen), where it continues to Grövelsjön and all the way north to **Storlien**. With the notable exception of the Grövelsjön to Tänndalen stretch (see p.332), it doesn't pass through particularly beautiful scenery, and although it's an easy path to walk it's best suited to serious walkers who are not averse to covering large distances and camping – there's no accommodation on the Högfjället–Drevdagen stretch.

The continental climate here – Idre is located at one of the wider points of the Scandinavian peninsula, and thus isn't prone to the warming influence of the Atlantic – means that the summers are relatively dry; consequently Idre, like its fellow ski resort, Sälen (see p.326), offers plenty of seasonal **outdoor activities**. Its tourist office can help arrange fishing trips, horseriding, mountain biking, tennis, climbing and golf. There are some good sandy beaches along the western shore of **Idresjön**, a lake that's a kilometre east of town; to go canoeing, you can rent a boat through the tourist office, where staff can also advise on local hiking routes, many of the best of which are in nearby Grövelsjön (see p.328).

Continuing up the mountain (two daily buses; 20min), you'll come to the ski slopes at **IDREFJÄLL**, one of the most reliable places for snow in the entire country, with particularly cold winters. Although not quite on the scale of Sälen, Idre's ski resort Idrefjäll manages to be Sweden's third largest and one of the most important in the Nordic area, with 34 lifts and 42 slopes. In winter the place is buzzing – not only with skiers but also with reindeer, who wander down the main street hoping to lick the salt off the roads.

With your own transport, it's an easy day-trip from Idrefjäll to see the stunning waterfall, **Njupeskär**, near the village of Särna. Alternatively, you can continue by bus to **Grövelsjön**, where there's some of the best hiking anywhere in central Sweden waiting right outside the comfortable fell station accommodation.

Practicalities

Idre is a tiny one-street affair; if you come in summer, it's where you should stay, rather than up at Idrefjäll, which will be completely void of life. The main street, where the bus drops you, is where you'll find everything of any significance, including a supermarket and bank. The **tourist office** (mid-June to mid-Aug daily 10am–7pm; mid-Aug to mid-June Mon–Fri 9am–5pm; ☏0253/59 82 00, ⓦwww.destinationidre.se), in a turf-roofed building at Framgårdsvägen 1, off the main Byvägen, is near the entrance to the village when approaching from Mora. Nearby, at Byvägen 2, there's a small and comfortable **hotel**, the *Idregården* (☏0253/208 60, ⓦwww.idregarden.com; ❸). When it comes to **eating and drinking**, there's precious little choice: you can either go to the *Idregården's* restaurant for traditional Swedish home cooking, or *Restaurang Lodjuret* (☏0253/200 12), next to the tourist office at Framgårds-vägen 1, which does pizzas and pasta dishes for around 150kr.

Idrefjäll's main **hotel** is the *Pernilla Wiberg* (☏0253/59 30 00, ⓦwww .pernillawiberghotel.se; ❼/❷), named after one of Sweden's most successful downhill skiers. In addition to the surrounding ski slopes and lifts, the hotel also boasts a state-of-the-art sauna suite. Room prices are fiendishly complicated and vary almost week to week through the season, depending on when Stockholmers take their holidays (don't just turn up here in winter and expect to find a room – you won't). You can get a much better rate if you book a package for a week or so; contact the tourist office down in the village for details.

Around Idre

From Idre, it's well worth a trip to **Särna**, 30km away, to see the impressive **Njupeskär waterfall**, Sweden's highest, with a drop of 125m. In winter it's particularly popular with **ice climbers**, as the waterfall freezes completely. An easy, circular **walking route** is clearly signposted from the car park to the waterfall and back, making for a good two-hour hike. There's no public transport from Idre; by **car**, take the main road to Särna, then turn right following signs for Mörkret and later for Njupeskärsvattenfall.

Surrounded by nature reserves and national parks, **GRÖVELSJÖN**, 45km northwest of Idre and reachable by bus #170 from Mora via Idre is where the road ends and the mountains and wilderness really start. The area is renowned throughout Sweden for its stark, beautiful mountain scenery; in summer, the pasture around here is home to hundreds of grazing reindeer. Virtually the only building here is the ✝ STF Grövelsjön *fjällstation* (☎0253/59 68 80, ⓦwww .stfgrovelsjon.com; dorm beds 360kr, double room ❷; closed late April to mid-June & Oct to early Feb, but open Christmas & New Year), with a variety of rooms and prices depending on the season; it boasts a restaurant, kitchen, sauna, massage room and solarium. The *fjällstation* makes an ideal base for **hikes** (summer only) out into the surrounding countryside, with a variety of routes available, some lasting a day, others several days.

Among the established **day-hikes** is the clearly marked route (16km round-trip) from the *fjällstation* up to Storvätteshågnen (1183m), with fantastic views over the surrounding peaks and across the border into Norway. Another worthwhile hike starts with a short walk from the *fjällstation* to Sjöstugan on Lake Grövelsjön (roughly 1500m away), from where you take the morning boat to the northern (Norwegian) end of the lake. You can now return along the lake shore to the *fjällstation* (9km) by way of the Linné path, following in the footsteps of the famous botanist who walked this route in 1734. It's possible to do the whole route in the opposite direction, heading out along the Linné path in the morning and returning by boat in the late afternoon; ask at the *fjällstation* for details of boat departure times. A third option is to strike out along the path leading northwest from Sjöstugan, heading for the Norwegian border and Salsfjellet (1281m) on the other side of it (16km round trip). There's no need to take your passport with you as the border is all but invisible; people wander back and forth across it quite freely.

Härjedalen

From Mora and Orsa, the Inlandsbanan trundles through the northern reaches of Dalarna before crossing the provincial border into **Härjedalen**, a sparsely populated fell region stretching north and west to the Norwegian border, and containing some of the best scenery anywhere in Sweden. Indeed, the region belonged to Norway until 1645, and the influence of the Norwegian language is still evident today in the local dialect. Härjedalen got its name from the unfortunate Härjulf Hornbreaker, a servant to the Norwegian king, who mistakenly killed two of the king's men and was banished from the court. He fled to Uppsala, where he sought protection from King Amund, but after falling in love with Amund's cousin, Helga, and arousing the king's fury he was forced to make another hasty exit. It was then he came across a desolate valley in which he settled and which he named after himself: Härjulf's dale, or Härjedalen, as it's known today.

From the comfort of the Inlandsbanan, you'll be treated to a succession of breathtaking vistas of vast forested hill and mountainsides (Härjedalen boasts more than thirty mountains of above 1000m) – these are some of the emptiest tracts of land in the whole country, also home to the country's largest population of bears. Although the sleepy provincial capital, **Sveg**, holds little of appeal, it's from here that **buses** head northwest to the remote mountain villages of **Funäsdalen** and **Tänndalen**, both with easy access to excellent and little-frequented **hiking trails** through austere terrain which features a handful of shaggy musk oxen that have wandered over the border from Norway. Nearby, across the lonely **Flatruet plateau**, with its ancient rock paintings, tiny **Ljungdalen** is the starting point for treks to Sweden's southernmost glacier, **Helags**, on the icy slopes of Helagsfjället (1797m).

Sveg and around

Around three hours and 140km north of Mora by the Inlandsbanan, **SVEG** is the first place of any significance after Lake Siljan. With a tiny population of just 3500, the town is far and away the biggest in Härjedalen – though that's not saying much. Even on a Friday night in the height of summer you'll be hard pushed to find anyone on the streets. But though there's not an awful lot to do or see, Sveg's a pretty enough place: the wide streets are lined with grand old wooden houses, and the beautiful Ljusnan River runs through the centre of town. There are a couple of diversions worthy of attention, the first of which is ideally located for arrivals by both train and bus: on permanent display inside the train station building on Järnvägsgatan (which is also used as the bus station) is a free **exhibition** of the life and times of the Inlandsbanan, in old photos and maps. Unfortunately the text and captions are only in Swedish but it's pretty evident that without the railway Sveg probably wouldn't be here at all. The town's lifeblood since 1909, when the line to Orsa was opened by King Gustaf V and Queen Viktoria, the Inlandsbanan not only brings visitors to the region during the short summer months, but also provides a means of transporting timber and peat pellets (see opposite) to southern Sweden.

From the station, your next port of call should be the parish church, **Svegs kyrka**, on Vallarvägen; head to the right from the station on Järnvägsgatan and walk to the T-junction with Fjällvägen, then turn left into this road, which later becomes Vallarvägen. A church has stood on this spot since the latter part of the eleventh century when Sveg was also the site of an ancient Viking *ting*, or parliament. In 1273 a border treaty between Sweden and Norway was hammered out here, when the church was part of the bishopric of Trondheim. Sadly, though, the glory days are long gone. The present building only dates from 1847 and contains few of the fittings which once made its predecessors so grand; it's predominantly the woven textiles inside that catch the eye today.

In front of the church, beside the main crossroads in town, looms the world's largest **wooden bear**, a mammoth and weirdly ominous structure reaching 13m in height; it's meant as a reminder to passers-by that this is bear country – it's estimated there are around 1200 animals in Härjedalen and neighbouring Jämtland. Sveg's final attraction is the newly opened **Kulturcentrum Mankell** (Mon–Fri 10am–5pm; 40kr), opposite the bear inside the Folkets Hus at Ljusnegatan 1. Here you'll find a simple museum dedicated to Sveg's most famous son, Henning Mankell, who's one of Sweden's best known novelists. Translated into everything from Faroese to Chinese, a collection of Mankell's books are available inside for persual.

At the western end of Fjällvägen, a pleasant **walk** of twenty to thirty minutes takes you across the road and train bridge on Brogatan to the riverbank, ideal for a picnic and a bit of skinny-dipping. Once over the bridge, just beyond the point where the railway line veers left and leaves the road, head right over a little stream into the forest, all the time walking back towards the river's edge. Hidden from the road by the trees is a wonderful sweet-smelling open flower meadow, but don't forget your mosquito repellent – the countryside around Sveg is made up of vast tracts of uninhabited marshland and countless small lakes, ideal breeding grounds for the insect. However, Sveg has the surrounding swamps to thank for its livelihood; Härjedalen's biggest factory, on the outskirts of town, turns the peat into heating pellets which are then transported down the Inlandsbanan to Uppsala.

Practicalities

The **train** and **bus stations** are on Järnvägsgatan. The **tourist office** at Ljusnegatan 1 in the Folkets Hus building (Mon–Fri 10am–5pm; ℡0680/107 75, Ⓦwww.herjedalsporten.se) has leaflets about local hiking routes, useful for their maps even if you don't understand Swedish; to get here from the train station, walk east along Gränsgatan for around ten minutes.

For a place to **stay**, try the very welcoming *Hotell Härjedalen* (℡0680/103 38, Ⓦwww.hotellharjedalen.se; ❷), a ten- to fifteen-minute walk from the station at Vallarvägen 11, near the main square, Torget. With comfortable and spacious rooms, this place dates from the late 1800s and has been run for the past fifty years by the endearing, though slightly hard-of-hearing, Svea af Trampe. Otherwise there's the overpriced and unfriendly *Hotell Mysoxen* (℡0680/170 00, Ⓔhotell@mysoxen.se; ❹/❸), Fjällvägen 12, just the other side of the main square, which also doubles as the town's **youth hostel** (same contact details; dorm beds 250kr, double rooms ❶). The campsite (℡0680/130 25) is by the riverside, a stone's throw from the tourist office, and also has two-berth cabins (❶).

Most of Sveg's **eating places** are of poor standard. A notable exception is the nameless Thai restaurant at Älvgatan 8 (℡0680/102 84) whose dishes, expertly prepared by Thai chefs, are delicious (125kr for a main course). Otherwise, the dreary *Knuten* pizzeria (℡0680/130 15), off the main square at Berggatan 4, serves standard pizzas and salads for 65kr and the tired, rather gloomy hotel restaurant at the *Mysoxen* churns out fish dishes from 130kr and steaks for 168kr.

Tännäs and Funäsdalen

Although Sveg may be shy, retiring and void of major attractions, what it does have is some blockbuster scenery right on its doorstep. It's worth leaving the Inlandsbanan at Sveg to travel into the far reaches of Härjedalen and explore one of Sweden's least visited and most rewarding landscapes, where compelling views of the vast, uninhabited forest unfold at every turn. From Sveg, **bus** #633 (Mon–Fri 1 daily at 3.40pm) winds its way northwest towards the tiny village of Lofsdalen, from where a connecting service continues to the remote outpost of **TÄNNÄS**, at the junction of Routes 311 and 84, remarkable for its **church town**, a handful of gnarled wooden cottages clinging to the south-facing valley-side where, quite unbelievably for such a high altitude and latitude location, corn was once grown. Should you want to stay here, the well-equipped **youth hostel** (℡0684/240 67, Ⓔinfo.tannasgarden@herjenet.net; dorm beds 200kr, double rooms ❶) lies just to the west of the main road junction at Bygatan 51; it's open all year though advance booking is required in May and November.

From here the bus heads a further 15km west to reach the pretty mountain resort of **FUNÄSDALEN**, which is surrounded by kilometres of superb hiking trails. Curling gracefully around the eastern shore of Funäsdalssjön lake, this appealing little village, barely 30km from the Norwegian border, enjoys some fantastic views of the surrounding mountains. It's best seen from the top of the sheer Funäsdalsberget mountain (977m), which bears down over the village and is reached by **chairlift** (50kr) – you can get to the base-station by walking ten minutes along the road signed to Ljungdalen at the eastern end of the village. The main thing to do in Funäsdalen is visit **Härjedalens Fjäll-museum**, the province's mountain museum (same times as tourist office, see below; 80kr), at Rörosvägen 30, which has a short slide-show about the province as well as informative explanations of how the mountain farmers of these parts managed to survive in such a remote location; transhumance (the practice of moving animals to higher ground during summer to fatten them on the fresh lush pasture) is given particular prominence. The adjacent outdoor **Fornminnesparken** homestead museum (unrestricted access; free), the oldest in Sweden and established in 1894 by a local trader, contains the usual collection of old timber buildings, plus a former customs house from the early nineteenth century used to regulate cross-border trade with Norway.

Practicalities

The best place for advice on the dozens of local **hiking trails** is the **tourist office** at Rörosvägen 30 (late June–Sept Mon–Fri 9am–6pm, Sat & Sun 10am–6pm; Oct to mid-June Mon–Fri 9am–5pm; ☎0684/155 80, ⓦwww .funasdalen.com), which also has useful information about **canoe rental**. The top place to **stay** in the village is *Hotell Funäsdalen* (☎0684/214 30, ⓦwww .hotell-funasdalen.se; ❻/❶), the huge red building with the green roof down by the lakeside on Strandvägen, which has comfortable modern rooms with unsurpassed views out over the lake; in the winter high season, when prices shoot up, bookings are only accepted for long weekends or one week. Alternatively, two-person **cabins** are available at *Norrbyns Stugby* (☎0684/212 05, ⓦwww .norrbyns-stugby.nu; ❶), by the chairlift at Vallarvägen 25, with terrific views out over Anåfjället mountain; once again, in winter bookings are by the week only. *Veras Stekhus & Pub* (☎0684/215 30), Rörosvägen 23, opposite the tourist office on the main road, is the best place to **eat**, not only for its delicious Arctic char and grilled meats, including reindeer (around 200kr), but also its wonderful views of the lake.

Tänndalen

From Funäsdalen, Route 84, covered by **bus** #623, climbs steeply uphill bound for dramatic **TÄNNDALEN**, an altogether better destination if you want to get out and do some proper hiking rather than just take in the mountain scenery. Considerably smaller than its easterly neighbour, consisting of a dozen or so houses strung out along a main road which crosses this highland plateau, the village boasts Sweden's highest **hotel** and **youth hostel**, *Skarvruet* (☎0684/221 11, ⓔskavruetfjallhotell@telia.com; dorm beds 215kr, double rooms ❶) at 830m above sea level. The hotel is made up of one main building with double rooms, a sauna and restaurant, as well as a number of smaller two-person cabins (❶) which function as the youth hostel – all with breathtaking views of Rödfjället mountain (1243m). In winter, Tänndalen is

From Tänndalen there are two main hiking routes, both along the **southern Kungsleden**. Heading **south**, the stretch to **Grövelsjön** in Dalarna (see p.329) makes an excellent hike, taking three to four days to complete (76km) and beginning with an ascent of Rödfjället. For much of the time the route passes through sparse pine forest relatively untouched by modern forestry; an eight-kilometre stretch also runs alongside Lake Rogen, known for its rich birdlife and unusual moraine formations. Between Tänndalen and the lake, you might be lucky enough to see the only herd of **musk oxen** in Sweden. They spend the winter in the mountain area between Storvålen and Brattriet before nipping over the border into Norway's Femundsmarka national park (close to the western edge of Lake Rogen) for the summer months. It's wise to keep your distance should you come across them, as musk oxen can be ferocious creatures; also bear in mind they're one of the few animals which can run faster uphill than downhill. The route then crosses the provincial border from Härjedalen into Dalarna to the east of Slagufjället, skirts round Töfsingdalens National Park and finally goes over the reindeer-grazing slopes of Långfjället. This hike takes in three STF **cabins** (all closed mid-April to early July & late Sept to mid-Feb) at Skedbro (21km from Tänndalen), Rogen (17km from Skedbro) and Storrödtjärn (16km from Rogen and 22km to Grövelsjön), with about twenty beds each and selling provisions. These cabins cannot be booked in advance; a dorm bed costs 310kr per person and is payable to the warden on arrival.

Heading **north**, the trail leads to **Storlien** (see p.345), first heading to the ski slopes of Ramundberget (20km from Tänndalen), then climbing steeply towards Helagsfjället and Sweden's southernmost **glacier**; at an altitude of 1796m, it's disappointingly small, only a couple of square kilometres in size. From Helags it's possible to either descend 18km to **Ljungdalen** and pick up bus #613 to Åsarna and Östersund (see p.337) or continue north towards Storlien via the *fjällstation* at **Sylarna** and Blåhammaren and the youth hostel at **Storvallen** outside Storlien (see p.385), a magnificent fifty-kilometre stretch across central Sweden's most enchanting mountain range.

There are several places for overnight **accommodation**: Fältjägaren cabin (late Feb to early May & late June to late Sept), 15km from Ramundberget; Helags cabin at the foot of the glacier (late Feb to early May & late June to late Sept), 12km from Fältjägaren; Sylarna STF *fjällstation* (☎0647/722 00, ⓦwww.stfsylarna.com; late Feb to early May & late June to late Sept), 19km from Helags; STF Blåhammaren *fjällstation* at 1086m (☎0647/722 00, ⓦwww.stfblahammaren.com; late Feb to early May & late June to late Sept), 19km from Sylarna and 12km from Storvallen youth hostel (see p.345) just outside Storlien, from where there are trains to Östersund. Again, the cabins cannot be booked in advance; a dorm bed at all of them costs 310kr per person (other than Helags, where the fee is 445kr), payable to the warden on arrival.

surrounded by 300km of prepared cross–country ski tracks (there's another 450km of marked expedition trails up on the surrounding mountains), the most extensive anywhere in the world, as well as a variety of downhill slopes; **ski rental** is available in the village from *Tänndalens Skiduthyrning* (☎0684/222 25) – ask at the hotel for directions. In summer, though, it's the extensive **hiking** routes which attract people here. One of the better routes is outlined in the box above. **Buses** from Tänndalen leave for Funäsdalen, where there are direct connections to Östersund via Klövsjö and Åsarna (see p.335) or, with a change in Lofsdalen, back to Sveg. There are no buses, however, over the border into Norway or to Ljungdalen.

The Flatruet plateau and around

From Funäsdalen, an unnumbered road, actually the highest in the country, heads north for the bumpy ascent to the hamlet of Mittådalen and beyond to the **Flatruet plateau** (975m), a bare stretch of desolate, rocky land, punctuated only by electricity poles and herds of grazing reindeer. The plateau is renowned for its 4000-year-old Stone Age **rock paintings** (*hällmålningar* in Swedish) at the foot of the Ruändan mountain at the eastern edge of this extensive upland area; get here by turning right in Mittådalen for another hamlet, Messlingen, where you should leave your vehicle. East of the settlement, a track off to the left leads towards Byggevallen and Ruvallen; from the latter a footpath then leads to the paintings – from the road it's a walk of 5–6km. Fashioned from a mix of iron ochre and animal fat and etched into slabs of rock, the twenty or so figures show, in remarkable clarity, elk, reindeer and even bears.

Once over the plateau, the road descends steeply towards the charming village of **LJUNGDALEN**, hemmed in on three sides by high mountains, occupying an area of flat grassland near the head of the Ljungan River. Though the fifty or so wooden houses are pleasant enough, it's as a base from which to reach the **Helags glacier** that Ljungdalen really comes into its own. From the ICA supermarket in the centre of the village, take the road signed for "Helags/Kläppen" which leads to a car park after 6km, from where the hiking trail starts. Before the car park though, the road passes a small settlement, Kläppen, where you should take Kläppenvägen uphill, following the signs. Once at the car park it's 12km to the STF mountain cabin at Helags. For details of this and the route towards Storlien see the box on p.333.

Practicalities

Ljungdalen's **tourist office** (Mon–Wed 10am–5pm, Thurs & Fri 10am–7pm; ☎0687/200 79, ⓦ www.ljungdalen.com) occupies a red-painted wooden house in the centre of the village. They have good advice about hiking to Helags and about onward travel possibilities; there's no bus over the plateau to Funäsdalen, though it is possible to hike there; see the box on p.333 for details.

Ljungdalen is an excellent place to rest up for a few days. The *Dunsjögården* **youth hostel** (☎0687/202 85; dorm beds 220kr, double rooms ❶) also has a swimming pool and sauna nearby for relaxing those aching muscles after hiking. You can cook here, but the best **eating** alternative in the village is *Restaurang Fjällsippan* (☎0687/200 14), in the centre of the village, which serves good pizzas (70kr) and Swedish dishes (around 150kr).

Southeast to Åsarna

From Ljungdalen, one of the most beautiful journeys anywhere in northern Sweden unfolds. Although the 110-kilometre trip to Åsarna certainly requires stamina – the road is in a truly appalling condition, unsurfaced all the way to the border with Jämtland and with some alarmingly large ruts and potholes – it offers a real taste of wild Sweden. The switchback road cuts through some of the most spectacular mountain and lakeside landscapes you'll witness in the north, threading its way around serpentine bends and across narrow isthmuses between the extensive areas of swampland and spruce forest that characterize this forgotten corner of the country,.

Curiously for such a remote route, it is served by **bus**: the #613 runs from Ljungdalen to Åsarna (bus times at ⓦ www.lanstrafiken-z.se) providing a rare insight for anyone without their own transport into life in backwoods Sweden – as the bus trundles through the tiny villages, you'll notice how the lumberjack culture is alive and well in these parts. Indeed, the stretch of road between the Härjedalen/Jämtland border and the village of **Börtnan** (1hr 10min from Ljungdalen) runs through one of the region's most important forestry areas; mountains of timber line the roadside awaiting transport to the nearest railhead.

Jämtland

Stretching from just north of Sveg to the border with Lapland, a distance of around 250km, the province of **JÄMTLAND** is centred round one of Sweden's greatest lakes, **Storsjön**, and its associated watercourses. Altogether more pastoral than its wilder and more mountainous neighbour to the south, Härjedalen, it was the plentiful supply of fish from the lake coupled with successful cultivation of the rich lands around its shores that enabled the region's first settlers to eke out an existence so far north – Stockholm, for example, is 550km to the south. Although the province can trace its history back to the early Iron Age, Jämtland has only been Swedish since 1645, before which it was part of Norway. The people here have a strong sense of regional identity and, in recent years, have even called (albeit rather half-heartedly) for independence from Sweden. Spend any length of time here and you'll soon encounter the tremendous pride the locals have in their villages, forests and lakes.

Approaching from the south, it's the cross-country skiing centre of **Åsarna** and the pretty village of **Klövsjö** that you'll reach first. Just beyond here, **Hackås** is the location for the wildly entertaining *Årets Näck* competition, which sees a group of naked male fiddle-players compete for the prestigious title. The most enjoyable town in the province is the provincial capital of **Östersund**, situated on Storsjön lake, whose murky waters reputedly hide Sweden's own version of the Loch Ness monster. West of Östersund, **Åre** is Sweden's most popular ski destination for foreign tourists, whilst nearby **Storlien** has some great summer hiking right on its doorstep.

Åsarna and around

From Sveg, the Inlandsbanan veers eastwards in order to skirt the vast area of marshland north and east of the town. The train line finally swings west at Överhogdal, where the Viking Age tapestries now on display in Östersund were discovered (see p.338), before crossing the provincial border into Jämtland and continuing north to **Åsarna**. From here, **buses** run southwest to **Klövsjö** before crossing back into Härjedalen, where, close to the provincial border, **Vemdalen** is deservedly known for its eighteenth-century Rococo wooden church.

Åsarna

Blink and you'll miss **Åsarna**, a tiny one-street affair 109km north of Sveg that serves as a diminutive service centre for the southern part of Jämtland. Other than the railway station, a filling station and a hotel, all lined up along the nameless main road, there's nothing to recommend an overnight stay here. Even the all-year **Skicenter** (see below), at the southern end of the town (to the left of the railway station as you exit) holds little appeal. Established by four of the region's many skiing champions – Tomas Wassberg, Torgny Mogren, Jan Ottosson and Hans Persson – the centre organizes cross-country skiing in winter and provides advice on hiking in summer. If, however, you're waiting for a bus to nearby Klövsjö, the real reason for breaking your journey at Åsarna, you may want to check out its **ski museum** (daily: June–Aug 8am–10pm; Sept–May 8am–8pm; free), which has worthy displays of the Åsarna ski club's Olympic and World Championship medals and equipment, as well as photographs of famous Swedish skiers and a couple of video exhibits.

For a stroll or an afternoon picnic in summer, wander past the campsite cabins behind the ski centre and down to the river; turn right here and follow the age-old Kärleksstigen ("Lover's Lane") along the water's edge – you can cross the river over an old stone bridge, further upstream by the rapids, and return on the opposite bank along a minor road. The smooth, low rocks by the bridge make an ideal spot to fish or catch a few rays of sunshine.

Åsarna's Skicenter (daily: June–Aug 8am–10pm; Sept–May 8am–8pm; ☏0687/302 30, ⓦwww.asarnaskicenter.se) has limited amounts of **tourist information**. While it's virtually impossible to **stay** in Åsarna in winter without an advance booking, in summer you can just turn up and find a room. The Skicenter's **youth hostel** (☏0687/302 30, ⓔinfo@asarnaskicenter.se; dorm beds 180kr, double rooms ❶) and **campsite** (same contact details as youth hostel) are down by the river's edge, with a small bathing pool and a sauna. The **restaurant** at the Skicenter is hard to beat for cheap meals (closes around 8pm, June–Aug 10pm), with breakfast, *Dagens Rätt* until 6pm and evening meals for 85kr.

Klövsjö and Vemdalen

Åsarna is well placed for a quick jaunt out to charming **KLÖVSJÖ**. The village has gained the reputation as Sweden's most beautiful, with some justification: the distant lake and the forested hills that enclose Klövsjö give it a special, otherworldly feeling: the flower meadows, streams, wooden barns and the smell of freshly mown hay drying on frames in the afternoon sun cast a wonderful spell.

The ten farms here work the land in much the same way as in medieval times: ancient grazing rights, still in force, mean that horses and cows are free to roam through the village. Once you've taken a look at **Tomtangården** (July to mid-Aug daily; free), a preserved seventeenth-century farm estate, there's not much else to do except breathe in the biting, clean air and admire the beauty. Unfortunately there's nowhere to stay in the village, but the **tourist office** (Mon–Fri 10.30am–5pm, Sat 9am–noon; ☏0682/41 36 60, ⓦwww.klovsjo.com) on the main road has cabins for rent in the vicinity (around 500kr a day). Bus #164 from Åsarna continues to Funäsdalen (where you can change for Tänndalen and hike along the southern Kungsleden to Grövelsjön; see p.326), passing within fifteen-minutes' walk of *Klövsjö fjällhotell* (tell the driver if you wish to go here), a comfortable, modern place (☏0682/41 31 00, ⓦwww.klovsjofjall.se; ❺/❸); rooms here are popular in winter with the skiers making the most of the thirteen ski slopes nearby.

The road from Klövsjö to Funäsdalen is especially worth travelling. Once beyond the turn for the hotel, the route crosses the provincial border back into Härjedalen and follows the ancient track used by the region's merchant farmers through the **Vemdalsskalet pass**. Bound for **VEMDALEN**, the road descends sharply and offers clear views of another of Härjedalen's mighty peaks: the impressive sugarloaf-shaped **Sånfjället** mountain (1278m) to the southwest. Back in the 1900s the forest and fell terrain around the mountain was declared a national park in an attempt to maintain its delicate ecosystem – with great success, since the park is now a favourite habitat for Härjedalen's bear population. Once through the pass and down into Vemdalen, you'll find a stunning octagonal **wooden church** right by the roadside in the centre of the village. Built in Rococo style in 1763, eight years after its separate onion-domed bell tower, the church supports a deep two-stage roof and a central onion turret. Inside, the work of a couple of local craftsmen is proudly displayed: the pulpit, with its bowing cherrywood panels, was made in Ljungdalen, whilst the altar was carved by a carpenter from Klövsjö. From Vemdalen, **bus** #164 continues to Tännäs and Funäsdalen; in the opposite direction it runs back to Åsarna and Klövsjö, continuing on to Östersund.

Hackås

One of the most intriguing and quintessentially Swedish events you'll witness takes place in **HACKÅS**, just 35km north of Åsarna, around the middle of July as part of the town's summer celebrations, *Hackåsdagarna*. The **Årets Näck** competition (⑩www.näck.nu), usually staged on the second Thursday in July, attracts not only a huge crowd of onlookers but also media interest from right across Sweden, and features a succession of naked male fiddle players who compete for the prestigious title of *Årets Näck* (rough translation: Nudie of the Year) by sitting in the unflatteringly chilly waters of the local river, Billstaån, to play their instruments. The roots of this eye-opening spectacle of public nudity are to be found in the mists of Swedish folklore where the *näck*, a long-haired, bearded, naked water sprite, would sit by a river rapid or waterfall and play his fiddle so hauntingly that women and children from miles around would be lured to him, only to drown in his watery home. Today, competitors are judged on how successfully they capture the spirit of the *näck* and, naturally, on their musical skills. The event usually begins around 9pm on the island of Gaveriholmen near Strömbacka kvarn – to get there, just follow the crowds. The Inlandsbanan reaches Hackås at around 7.30pm on its way to Östersund, otherwise buses #161, #163 and the Inlandsexpressen #45 call here several times daily.

Östersund

Just 45km north of Hackås and sitting gracefully on the eastern shore of the mighty **Storsjön** (Great Lake), **ÖSTERSUND** is the only large town along the Inlandsbanan (until Gällivare inside the Arctic Circle, another 750km further north), and is well worth a stop. King Gustav III gave the town its charter two hundred years ago with one thing in mind: to put an end to the lucrative trade that the region's merchant farmers carried out with neighbouring Norway. Travelling through the Vemdalsskalet pass (see above), they bartered and sold their goods in Trondheim before returning back over the mountains to the Storsjön region. Although rival markets in Östersund gradually stemmed the trade, it took

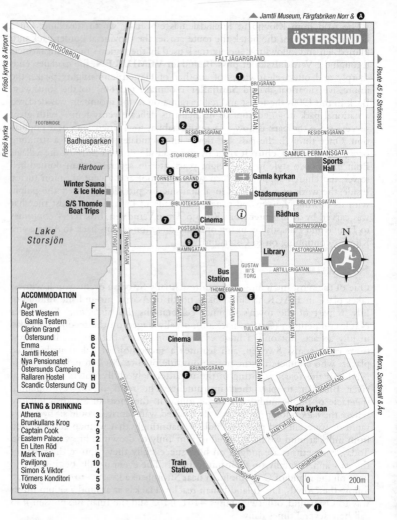

▲ Jamtli Museum, Färgfabriken Norr & **Ⓐ**

ÖSTERSUND

FRÖSÖBRON

FÄLTJÄGARGRÄND

BROGRÄND

❶

FÄRJEMANSGATAN

❷

RESIDENSGRÄND

❸ **Ⓑ**

❹

STORTORGET

RESIDENSGRÄND

SAMUEL PERMANSGATA

Sports Hall

Badhusparken

FOOTBRIDGE

Harbour

Winter Sauna & Ice Hole

S/S Thomée Boat Trips

Lake Storsjön

❺

TÖRNSTENS GRÄND **Ⓒ**

❻

BIBLIOTEKSGATAN

❼

POSTGRÄND

❽

HAMNGATAN

Gamla kyrkan

Stadsmuseum

BIBLIOTEKSGATAN

Cinema

i

Rådhus

MAGISTRATSGRÄND

Library

PASTORGRÄND

❾

Bus Station

GUSTAV III'S TORG

ARTILLERIGATAN

Ⓓ

Ⓔ

THOMÉEGRÄND

❿

Cinema

BRUNNSGRÄND

Ⓕ

Ⓖ

GRÄNSGATAN

TULLGATAN

STUGUVÄGEN

Stora kyrkan

N. HANTVÄGEN

Train Station

N

ACCOMMODATION

Älgen	**F**
Best Western Gamla Teatern	**E**
Clarion Grand Östersund	**B**
Emma	**C**
Jamtli Hostel	**A**
Nya Pensionatet	**G**
Östersunds Camping	**I**
Rallaren Hostel	**H**
Scandic Östersund City	**D**

EATING & DRINKING

Athena	3
Brunkullans Krog	7
Captain Cook	9
Eastern Palace	2
En Liten Röd	1
Mark Twain	6
Paviljong	10
Simon & Viktor	4
Törners Konditori	5
Volos	8

0   200m

▲ Frösö kyrka & Airport

▲ Frösö kyrka

▶ Route 45 to Strömsund

▶ Mora, Sundsvall & Åre

▼ **Ⓗ**   ▼ **Ⓘ**

another century for the town's growth to really begin, heralded by the arrival of the railway from Sundsvall in 1879.

Today, Östersund is a major **transport hub**: the E14 runs through on its way to the Norwegian border; the Inlandsbanan stops here (the town is 6hr north of Mora by this line); and other trains run west to Åre, Storlien and Trondheim in Norway, east to Sundsvall (a very beautiful run which hugs lakeshore and riverbank the entire way) and south to both Stockholm and Gothenburg, through some of Sweden's most stunning primeval forest. Coming from Swedish Lapland, train connections can be made for Östersund in nearby Bräcke.

Most visitors head straight for Östersund's top attraction, **Jamtli**, home to the beautiful **Överhogdal Viking tapestries**; the adjoining **open-air museum** expertly – and enjoyably – brings to life Östersund from years past.

Reached by bridge from the town, the nearby island of **Frösön** is also worth checking out for the oldest rune stone in Sweden and its elaborate wooden church. However, it's for its lake **monster**, the Storsjöodjuret, that Östersund is perhaps best known.

Arrival and information

From the **train station** on Strandgatan, it's a five-minute walk north to the town centre; the **bus station**, on Gustav IIIs Torg, is more central. The town's **airport** with flights from Stockholm Arlanda and Umeå, is on Frösön, an island 11km west of town, from where buses (connecting with flights; 60kr) and taxis (305kr) run to the centre. A couple of blocks north of the bus station, at Rådhusgatan 44 opposite the minaret-topped Rådhus, is the **tourist office** (early June Mon–Fri 9am–7pm, Sat & Sun 10am–3pm; late June & July Mon–Fri 9am–8pm, Sat & Sun 9am–7pm; Aug Mon–Fri 9am–5pm, Sat & Sun 10am–3pm; Sept–May Mon–Fri 9am–5pm; ☎063/14 40 01, ⊛www.turist.ostersund.se). Here you can obtain the **Östersundshäftet** (valid March–Oct; 125kr), a booklet of coupons giving free or discounted museum entry and boat trips as well as reductions in the town's shops and restaurants. Pressbyrån at the train station has internet access.

Accommodation

Unlike many other places in central northern Sweden, Östersund has good-quality **hotels** at reasonable prices; you won't find their like north of here until Gällivare. There are also a couple of **hostels** in town and a **campsite**, just outside the centre.

Älgen Storgatan 61 ☎063/51 75 25, ⊛www.hotelalgen.se. Handy for the train station, this small, central hotel has plain and comfortable en-suite rooms with rather uninspiring modern furnishings. ❹/❸

Best Western Gamla Teatern Thoméegränd 20 ☎063/51 16 00, ⊛www.gamlateatern.se. The most atmospheric hotel in town, housed in a turn-of-the-twentieth-century theatre with sweeping wooden staircases. The Art Nouveau rooms are snug and cosy, and many have delightful pieces of period furniture. Choose carefully, though, because some are rather worn. ❺/❸

Clarion Grand Östersund Prästgatan 16 ☎063/55 60 00, ⊛www.choice.se. This business-oriented hotel is Östersund's finest – the very best rooms have their own marbled hallway, sitting room and sumptuous double beds. Book early and the discounted rates are definitely worth the splurge though the cheaper rooms are much less glamorous. ❹/❸

Emma Prästgatan 31 ☎063/51 78 40, ⊛www.hotelemma.com. Eighteen tastefully decorated rooms with high ceilings, wooden floors, old tiled corner stoves and lots of chequers and bold colours, all en suite, in a perfect location on the main drag. ❹/❸

Jamtli Hostel Rådhusgatan, inside the Jamtli museum ☎063/12 20 60, ⊛www.jamtli.com. Housed in an old timber building within the Jamtli museum complex and a wonderfully atmospheric choice. Dorm beds 190kr, double rooms ❶.

Nya Pensionatet Prästgatan 65 ☎063/10 20 05, ⊛www.nyapensionatet.se. Near the train station and the cheapest place in town, this tastefully decorated guesthouse dating from around 1900 has just six rooms; all have washbasins, but the bathrooms are shared. ❷

Östersunds Camping Krondikesvägen 95C ☎063/14 46 15, ⊛www.camping.se/plats/z11. Located a couple of kilometres south of the town centre and perfect for the fantastic indoor swimming complex, Storsjöbadet.

Rallaren Hostel Bangårdsgatan 6 ☎063/13 22 32, ⊛www.rallarens.se. Accessed from the platform at the train station, this hostel has dorm beds in rooms sleeping 2–6 for 150kr per person. Bear in mind that the noise from passing goods trains in the night may disturb your sleep.

Scandic Östersund City Kyrkgatan 70 ☎063/57 57 00, ⊛www.scandic.se. A massive modern hotel with 126 rooms; high on Scandinavian design and quality – with wooden floors and leather armchairs – but rather impersonal and low on charm. ❻/❹

▲ Östersund town hall

The Town

Östersund's **lakeside** position lends it a seaside-holiday atmosphere, unusual this far inland, and it's an instantly likeable place. In addition to the youthful buzz about town, there's an air of commercialism here, too (lacking in most other inland towns), since Östersund is also a centre for the engineering and electronics industries, as well as the Swedish armed forces, who maintain two regiments here – witness the numerous military aircraft flying overhead.

A stroll through the pedestrianized centre reveals an air of contented calm – take time out to sip a coffee around the wide-open space of the main square, Stortorget, and watch Swedish provincial life go by, or amble along one of the many side streets that slope down to the still, deep waters of the lake. In winter, though, temperatures here regularly plummet to -15°C; the modern apartment buildings you'll see lining the town's gridded streets are fitted with quadruple-glazed windows to keep the winter freeze at bay.

The main thing to do in Östersund is visit the impressive **Jamtli open-air museum** (late June to late Aug daily 11am–5pm; late Aug to late June closed Mon; 110kr late June to late Aug, otherwise 60kr; Ⓦ www.jamtli.com), a quarter of an hour's walk north of the centre along Rådhusgatan. It's full of people milling around in nineteenth-century costume, farming and milking much as their ancestors did. Everyone else is encouraged to join in – baking, tree felling, grass cutting and so on. The place is ideal for children, and adults would have to be pretty hard-bitten not to enjoy the enthusiastic atmosphere. Intensive work has been done on getting the settings right: the restored and working interiors are authentically gloomy and dirty, and the local store, Lanthandel, among the wooden buildings around the square near the entrance, is suitably old-fashioned. In the woodman's cottage (presided over by a bearded lumberjack, who makes pancakes for the visitors), shoeless and scruffy youngsters snooze contentedly in the wooden cots. Beyond the first cluster of houses is a reconstructed farm, **Lillhärdal**, where life goes on pretty much as it did in 1785, when the land was ploughed using horses, and crops were sown and harvested by hand – even the roaming cattle and the crop varieties are appropriate to the period.

The indoor **museum** on the same site is the place to get to grips with Östersund's **monster**. Ask to see the fascinating film (with English subtitles) about the creature, which contains a series of telling interviews with local people who claim to have seen it; one very Swedish thing leaps out at you – having witnessed something unusual out on the lake, many people took several months, even years, to talk about their experience for fear of ridicule. Having seen the film, head downstairs for a further display of monster-catching gear, alongside what's claimed to be a pickled embryo of a similar monster found in the lake in 1895; this quite grotesque thing is kept in a small glass jar on a shelf next to the foot of the stairs. However, the museum's prize exhibits are the awe-inspiring Viking **Överhogdal tapestries**, crowded with brightly coloured pictures of horses, reindeer, elk and dogs, and different types of dwellings. Dating from the ninth and tenth centuries, most of the tapestries were discovered by accident in an outhouse in 1910. One piece was rescued after being used as a doll's blanket – rumour has it the child had to be pacified with a 2kr reward to hand it over.

Close to Jamtli at Infanterigatan 30, the newly opened **Färgfabriken Norr** (Thurs & Fri noon–5pm, Sat & Sun noon–4pm; free) is an excellent modern art museum with constantly changing and thought-provoking exhibitions. Housed in a former military building, the spacious exhibition hall can easily be visited on the way to Jamtli.

Back in the town centre, the **harbour**, where a fleet of tiny boats bob about on the clean water, makes a pleasant place to stroll. Immediately to the north of the harbour is the tiny **Badhusparken**, an extremely popular sunbathing spot in summer; in winter the adjoining waterfront is the place for a quick dip in the invigorating waters of Lake Storsjön – a hole in the ice is kept open here for this purpose (mid-Jan to late March). Once you're out of the water, head straight for the nearby mobile **sauna** or you'll be covered in frost faster than you can say

Storsjöodjuret – the "Great Lake Monster"

The people of Östersund are in no doubt: **Storsjöodjuret** is out there, in their lake. Eyewitness accounts – there are hundreds of people who claim to have seen it – speak of a creature with a head like a dog, long pointed ears and bulging eyes, that sweeps gracefully through the water, sometimes making a hissing or clucking sound, often several hundred metres away from the shore; each summer sees new reports of sightings. Although several explanations have been given that dispel the myth – a floating tree trunk, a row of swimming elk, the wake from a passing boat, a series of rising water bubbles – the monster's existence is taken so seriously that a protection order has now been slapped on it, using the provisions of paragraph fourteen of Sweden's Nature Conservation Act. For most people, though, the monster will be at its most tangible not in the lake, but on the web (ⓦwww.storsjoodjuret.com).

In 1894, the hunt for this sinister presence began in earnest, when King Oscar II founded a special organization to try to catch it. Norwegian whalers were hired to do so, but the rather unorthodox methods they chose proved unsuccessful: a dead pig gripped in a metal clasp was dangled into the water as bait, and large, specially manufactured pincers were on hand to grip the creature and pull it ashore. Their tackle is on display at Jamtli, together with photographs that claim to be of the creature.

If you fancy a bit of monster-spotting, consider taking a **steamboat cruise** on the lake on board *S/S Thomée*, a creaking 1875 wooden steamship. Routes and timetables vary, but in general the boat does a two-hour trip (90kr) round the lake leaving from the harbour in town. Also available are trips out to the island of **Verkön**, where there's a nineteenth-century castle (5hr 30min; 110kr).

"Storsjöodjuret". This is also the place to rent skates to go long-distance **skating** on the lake (℡070/231 49 19; 150kr per day), which freezes over each winter.

Frösön

Take the footbridge across the lake from Badhusparken, or the road bridge a little further north, and you'll come to the island of **Frösön**. People have lived here since prehistoric times; the name comes from the original Viking settlement, which was associated with the pagan god of fertility, Frö. There's plenty of good walking on the island, as well as a couple of historical sights. Just over the bridges, in front of the red-brick offices, look for the eleventh-century **rune stone** telling of Östmaður ("East Man"), son of Guðfast, the first Christian missionary to the area. From here, you can clamber up the nearby hill of Öneberget to the fourth-century settlement of **Mjälleborgen**, where a pleasant walking trail of around 4km leads through the area.

Five kilometres west of the bridges, along the island's main road and up the main hill, is the beautiful **Frösö kyrka** (bus #3 from the centre comes here), an eleventh-century church with a detached bell tower. In 1984, archeologists digging under the altar came across a bit of old birch stump surrounded by animal bones – bears, pigs, deer and squirrels – evidence of the cult of ancient gods, who were known as *æsir*. Today, the church is one of the most popular in Sweden for weddings – to tie the knot here at midsummer, you have to book years in advance.

Eating and drinking

Gastronomically, there's more **choice** in Östersund than for a long way north, with good Swedish, Thai, American and even Australian food. Most of the city's eating places, many of which double as bars, are to the south of Stortorget.

Athena Stortorget 3 ℡063/51 63 44. Tucked away in one corner of Stortorget, this rather dingy place serves tasty, authentic pizzas from 70kr, as well as steaks for around 198kr. The house speciality are lamb chops marinated in rosemary served with fried mushrooms and Greek salad for 215kr.

Brunkullans Krog Postgränd 5 ℡063/10 14 54. This old-fashioned, home-from-home restaurant, with polished lanterns and a heavy wooden interior dating from the 1880s, offers traditional modern Swedish dishes, such as elk burger (129kr) and cod in mustard (151kr), as well as "snapas" – three tapas and three schnapps for 159kr.

Captain Cook Hamngatan 9 ℡063/12 60 90. This moderately priced place has a selection of delicious Australian-style specials that really draw in the crowds – try the Bushman sandwich with bacon and coleslaw (98kr) or an Aussie burger (118kr). Other favourites are the reindeer fillet in port (235kr) and the salmon skewer (189kr).

Eastern Palace Storgatan 15 ℡063/51 00 15. The town's best Chinese restaurant with an enormous central aquarium and giant Ming vases, with the usual dishes from 80kr. They also have a number of Szechuan mains for 115kr and an evening Mongolian barbecue and Korean buffet at 129kr.

En Liten Röd Brogränd 19 ℡063/12 63 26. A cosy neighbourhood restaurant with a good choice of meat dishes from 198kr; their chocolate fondue for two people at 145kr is the stuff dreams are made of. There's also a cheese fondue for two at 198kr and a delicious seafood fondue for four people (395kr each). All fondues should be ordered one day in advance.

Mark Twain Biblioteksgatan 5 ℡063/12 33 20. A noisy American-style bar and restaurant, with winning dishes such as clam chowder (74kr), spring rolls with lobster and asparagus (82kr), pesto pasta with blackened chicken breast (129kr) and a fantastic key lime pie (65kr).

Paviljong Prästgatan 50B ℡063/13 00 99. The modest interior decor may suggest otherwise, but this is the best Indonesian/Thai restaurant in central Sweden – make the most of it, and try the excellent Massamam chicken curry (129kr) or chicken with garlic chilli and Thai basil (both 129kr).

Simon & Viktor Prästgatan 19 ℡063/10 12 14. An English-style pub with carpets, wooden wall panels and chandeliers overlooking the main square with upmarket pub food, such as a Big Ben burger (95kr), reindeer fillet with Jämtland cheese (215kr) and bouillabaisse (110kr).

Törners Konditori Storgatan 24. A modern Euro-café rather than a traditional Swedish *konditori* with a good selection of cakes, pastries, sandwiches and quiches; this is the best café in town.

Volos Prästgatan 38 ☏063/51 66 89. Simple yet popular Greek restaurant and pizzeria with an array of authentic dishes such as pork souvlaki (149kr) and a Greek burger with tzatziki (119kr) as well as steaks and a couple of fish dishes (all around 159kr). Takeaway is available.

West to Åre and Storlien

Heading west from Östersund, the **E14** and the **train** line follow the course trudged by medieval pilgrims on their way to Nidaros (now Trondheim in Norway) over the border, a twisting route that threads its way through sharp-edged mountains rising high above a bevy of fast-flowing streams and deep, cold lakes. Time and again, the eastern Vikings assembled their armies beside the holy Storsjön lake to begin the long march west, most famously in 1030, when King Olaf of Norway collected his mercenaries for the campaign that led to his death at the Battle of Stiklestad. Today, although the scenery is splendid, the only real attractions en route are the winter skiing and summer walking centres of **Åre**, 98km west of Östersund, and **Storlien**, a further 60km.

Åre

The alpine village of **Åre** is Sweden's most prestigious ski resort, with forty lifts, 100 ski slopes and guaranteed snow between December and May; it can be reached from Östersund either by **train** or on **bus** #155. During the skiing season, rooms here are like gold dust and prices sky high: book accommodation for this period well in advance through the tourist office or, better yet, take a package trip. Equipment isn't that expensive to rent: downhill and cross-country gear starts at 290kr per day from *Skidåkarna* (☏0771/84 00 00) and *Hanson* (☏0647/520 00) both in the main square. To walk up to the square from the train station, take Stationsvägen uphill for around two minutes from opposite the station building.

In summer, the village is a quiet, likeable haven for ramblers, sandwiched as it is between the Åresjön lake and a range of craggy hills that's overshadowed by Sweden's seventh highest peak, the mighty **Åreskutan** mountain (1420m). A network of tracks crisscrosses the hills; the tourist office has endless information about **hiking routes** in the nearby mountains and further afield – ask them for the excellent *Hikebike.se and Sommarguiden* booklets, which will tell you all you need to know. A popular route south of nearby Storlien is the **Jämttriangle**, from Sylarna STF *fjällstation* mountain lodge (☏0647/722 00, ⓦwww.stfsylarna.com; ❷) via the one at Blåhammaren (☏0647/722 00, ⓦwww.stfblahammaren.com; ❷) to Storulvån (☏0647/722 00, ⓦwww.stfstorulvan.com; ❷), which takes in fantastic wilderness scenery close to the Norwegian border and involves overnight stays in the mountain lodges.

A cable car, the **Kabinbanan** (110kr return), whisks you from just behind Storlien's main square to the viewing platform (1274m) and *Stormköket* restaurant, some way up Åreskutan. The ride takes just seven minutes, and it'll take you a further thirty minutes to clamber to the summit. Wear sensible shoes and warm clothes, as the low temperatures are intensified by the wind, and it can be decidedly nippy even in summer. From the top the view is stunning – on a clear day you can see over to the border with Norway and a good way back to Östersund. There's a tiny wooden **café** at the summit, serving coffee and extortionately priced sandwiches. Even the shortest route back down to Åre (2hr) requires stamina; other, longer,

▲ Kungsleden

paths lead more circuitously back down to the village. One word of warning: there are phenomenal numbers of **mosquitoes** and other insects up here in July and August, so make sure you are protected by repellent. The mountains around Åre are also as good a place as any to go **mountain biking**; the tourist office can help sort out a bike for you and has information about a series of trails, known collectively as Åre Bike Park.

Back in the centre, Åre's **kyrka** (use the key hanging on a hook outside the door to get in), just above the campsite, is a marvellous thirteenth-century stone building: inside, the simple blue decoration and the smell of burning candles create a peaceful ambience.

Practicalities

The **tourist office** is in the impressive new train station building known as Station Åre at St Olavsväg 35 (May to mid-June & early Sept to mid-Dec Mon–Fri 9am–5pm, Sat & Sun 10am–3pm; mid-June to early Sept & mid-Dec to April daily 9am–6pm; ℡0647/177 20, ⓦwww.visitare.se), and has free **internet** access. Station Åre also contains a supermarket, cash machines and the library. **Accommodation** in the village, of which there's plenty, is packed in winter; in summer, however, most places are either closed or only take groups, but it's worth asking the tourist office about fixing up a **private room** (from around 250kr per person), almost all of which will have a kitchen, shower and TV. The cheapest place to stay is the unofficial **youth hostel**, known as *Åre Torg Hotell*, in the park below the square (℡0647/515 90, ⓦwww.hotellaretorg.se; dorms beds 190kr in summer, from 240kr in winter) with bright, airy dorms sleeping 4–5 people. Alternatively, for something a little more luxurious, there's the newly built *Holiday Club* (℡0647/120 00; ❻), opposite the train station at Årestrand. A whole resort in itself, this lakeside hotel comprises top-notch Scandinavian-design rooms and apartments as well as a swimming pool, spa and bowling alley.

Åre's not up to much in terms of **food**, but there are several cheap options around the square for pizzas and more substantial meals of reindeer, fish or steak (200–250kr); stylish *Weréns* (℡0647/66 55 60) with its walls of white tiles is extremely popular. Near the cable car, *Dahlbom på Torget* (℡0647/508 20) is a smart brasserie offering porcini pasta, Asian salad with chicken and other international fare. Next door, *O'Leary's* is a popular pub with a menu of standard meat and fish dishes (open from 5pm). However, the best food in town can be sampled at ⚔ *Villa Tottebo* (℡0647/506 20), a former wood-panelled hunting lodge from 1897 opposite the train station at Parkvägen 1, which cooks up gourmet meat and fish dishes, including pike-perch, reindeer and duck for 240–285kr.

Storlien

Just six kilometres from the Norwegian border and linked to Åre by infrequent train, **tiny STORLIEN** is an excellent place to stop if you're into hiking, surrounded as it is by rugged, scenic terrain. The **southern Kungsleden** (see p.333) starts here and winds its way south via Sweden's southernmost glacier on the slopes of Helagsfjället, continuing on to Tänndalen and Grövelsjön, terminating on the hills above Sälen. Storlien is also prime berry-picking territory (the rare cloudberry grows here); mushrooms can also be found in great numbers hereabouts, in particular the delicious chanterelle.

Storlien is little more than a couple of streets and a supermarket amid open countryside. The best place to stay is the Storvallen **youth hostel**, a four-kilometre walk across the tracks from the train station to the E14 then left down the main road to Storvallen (℡0647/700 50, ⓦwww.stfstorvallen .se; dorm beds 225kr, double rooms ❷). **Eating** and **drinking** opportunities in Storlien are very limited. The best bet is *Le Ski* (℡0647/701 51), a restaurant and bar at the station, which has cheapish eats for lunch and dinner; otherwise, breakfast, coffee, pizzas and burgers are available at *Sylvias Kanonbar* (℡0647/702 12) in the main square in front of the station.

Travel details

Trains

Falun to: Gävle (2 hourly; 1hr); Stockholm
(2 hourly; 2hr 45min); Uppsala (2 hourly; 2hr).
Mora to: Leksand (2 hourly; 40min); Stockholm
(2 hourly; 3hr 50min); Uppsala (2 hourly; 3hr).
Östersund to: Åre (3 daily; 1hr 45min); Gothenburg
(1 daily; 12hr); Stockholm (3 daily; 5hr 30min);
Storlien (3 daily; 2hr); Sundsvall (2 hourly;
2hr 15min).

The Inlandsbanan

Timetables change slightly from year to year, but
the following is a rough idea of Inlandsbanan
services and times. The Inlandsbanan runs in two
sections from early June to Aug. Northbound trains
leave Mora daily at 2.35pm calling at Orsa, Sveg
and many other wayside halts en route for
Östersund. From Östersund, trains leave daily for
Gällivare at 7.15am, and another leaves at 7.10am
daily for Mora.

International trains

Östersund to: Trondheim (2 daily; 4hr).
Åre to: Trondheim (2 daily; 2hr 30min).

Buses

The Inlandsexpressen (#45) runs north from
Mora to Östersund via Orsa, Sveg and Åsarna.
It operates daily all year, leaving Mora daily
at 8am, and Mon–Sat 2pm & Sun 4.05pm for
Östersund. Heading south, two daily buses leave
Östersund for Mora at 7am and 12.20pm; there's
an additional departure Mon–Fri & Sun at 5.05pm
to Sveg.
Funäsdalen to: Östersund (Mon–Sat 2 daily, Sun
1 daily; 3hr 30min).
Mora to: Orsa (hourly; 25min).
Åsarna to: Klövsjö (2–3 daily; 15min); Östersund
(Mon–Sat 2 daily, Sun 1 daily; 1hr 20min).
Östersund to: Umeå (2 daily; 6hr).

Swedish Lapland

CHAPTER 7 # Highlights

✳ **Lapland delicacies, Klippen**
The hotel restaurant in this isolated village is the place to taste delicious local cuisine: reindeer, elk and ptarmigan are all on the menu. See p.358

✳ **Lappstaden, Arvidsjaur**
The square timber huts and cabins at this *Sámi* church town offer an insight into the life of Sweden's indigenous people. See p.362

✳ **Kungsleden trail, Jäkkvik**
Walk one of the quietest and most beautiful sections of the north's premier hiking trail through the Pieljekaise national park. See p.365

✳ **The Arctic Circle, Jokkmokk**
Crossing the magic line is a real sense of achievement and undoubtedly the best place to see the Midnight Sun. See p.367

✳ **Icehotel, Jukkasjärvi** Spend a night in a thermal sleeping bag in this awe-inspiring hotel constructed from snow and ice, where the interior temperature hovers at a chilly -5C. See p.377

✳ **Northern Lights, Abisko**
Witness one of the most breathtaking sights in the world in the far north of Swedish Lapland. See p.380

▲ Sámi travelling by reindeer

Swedish Lapland

wedish Lapland, the heartland of the indigenous **Sámi** people, is Europe's last wilderness, characterized by seemingly endless forests of pine and spruce, thundering rivers that drain the snow-covered fells, and peaceful lakeside villages high amongst the hills. The irresistible allure of this vast and sparsely populated region is the opportunity to experience raw nature at first hand. This unsullied corner of the country is a very long way away for many Swedes; in terms of distance, Gothenburg, for example, is closer to Venice than it is to Kiruna. The reputation of the local people for speaking their mind or, alternatively, not speaking at all, has confirmed the region's image within Sweden: remote, austere yet still rather fascinating.

One constant reminder of how far north you've come is the omnipresent **reindeer** that are still fundamental to the livelihood of many families here, but the enduring *Sámi* culture, which once defined much of this land, is now under threat. Centuries of mistrust between the *Sámi* and the Swedish population have led to today's often tense standoff; *Sámi* accusing Swede of stealing his land, Swede accusing *Sámi* of scrounging off the state. Back in 1986, the Chernobyl nuclear accident led to a fundamental change in *Sámi* living patterns: the fallout affected grazing lands, and even today the lichen (the reindeer's favourite food) in certain parts of the north is unfit for consumption, a fact which the *Sámi*, perhaps understandably, are keen to play down. The escalating problems posed

Lapland, Lappland or Sápmi

Whilst Lapland's strong cultural identity is evident in every town and village across the north, it's a much trickier task to try to pin down the region geographically. The word **Lapland** means different things to different people. Mention it to a Swede (the Swedish spelling is **Lappland**) and they'll immediately think of the northern Swedish province of the same name which begins just south of Dorotea, runs up to the Norwegian and Finnish borders in the north, and stretches east towards (but doesn't include) the Bothnian coast. For the original inhabitants of the north, the *Sámi*, the area they call **Sápmi** (the indigenous name for Lapland) extends from Norway through Sweden and Finland to the Russian Kola peninsula, an area where they've traditionally lived a semi-nomadic life, following their reindeer from valley bottom to fell top. Most foreigners have a hazy idea of where Lapland is; for the sake of this guide, we've assumed Swedish Lapland (the English spelling) to be located within the borders of the administrative province of Lappland but have included all of Route 342 – The Wilderness Way, or Vildmarksvägen – beginning in Strömsund (see p.351), which crosses into Lappland, as well as the Torne Valley, which also lies partly within the province.

by tourism – principally the erosion of grazing land under the pounding feet of hikers – have also made the *Sámi*'s traditional existence increasingly uncertain.

The best way to discover more about *Sámi* culture is to drive the 320-kilometre-long Wilderness Way from **Strömsund**, a notable canoeing centre, over the barren Stekenjokk plateau to isolated **Fatmomakke**, a church town of dozens of traditional wooden *kåtor* (huts) beside the steely waters of Kultsjön lake. The road terminates at **Vilhelmina**, another tiny church town which makes an interesting diversion on the way north. **Storuman** and neighbouring **Sorsele** have handy train and bus connections that are useful access points for a small handful of charming mountain villages close to the Norwegian border, where hiking is the main draw. More accessible **Arvidsjaur**, reached by the Inlandsbanan, also offers a worthwhile insight into indigenous culture at its *lappstad*, a diverting collection of religious dwellings and storehuts.

However, it's **Jokkmokk**, just north of the **Arctic Circle**, that is the real centre of *Sámi* life – not least during its Winter Market when thousands of people brave the chill to buy and sell everything from reindeer hides to Wellington boots. Moving further north, the iron-ore mining centres of **Gällivare** (where the Inlandsbanan ends) and **Kiruna** share a rugged charm, though it's undoubtedly the world-famous **Icehotel** in nearby **Jukkasjärvi** that is the real winter draw. Beyond, the rugged **national parks** offer a chance to hike and commune with nature like nowhere else: the **Kungsleden trail** runs for 500km from the tiny village of **Abisko** – oddly, yet reassuringly for hikers, the driest place in all of Sweden – to **Hemavan**, northwest of Storuman, through some of the most gorgeous stretches anywhere in the Swedish mountains.

Strömsund and routes north

At quarter past seven every morning between June and August (check the timetable for the exact season, which changes from year to year), the Inlandsbanan sets out from Östersund (see p.337) on its fourteen-hour journey to Gällivare, north of the Arctic Circle. Just outside Östersund, the train crosses the Indalsälven River, one of Sweden's greatest natural sources of power, the first sure sign that civilization is slowly being left behind and only the wilds of nature lie ahead. Indeed, it's a good hour and a half before the train makes the first stop of any significance: Ulriksfors, the wayside halt for the small waterside town of **Strömsund**, which is the starting point for Route 342, the **Wilderness Way** (*Vildmarksvägen*), a circular road looping out towards the Norwegian border. The route passes through stunning scenery more than worthy of its name, rejoining the main Inlandsvägen in Vilhelmina which, in turn, is directly linked to Strömsund via the appealing little town of **Dorotea**.

Getting around Swedish Lapland

Covering a whopping 110,000 square kilometres – an area only fractionally smaller than the whole of England – getting from one place to another in Swedish Lapland is inevitably going to take up a lot of time. During the short summer months, the **Inlandsbanan** provides the easiest and most enjoyable form of transport. Slowly snaking its way across the northern hinterland, the train often has to stop so that elk and reindeer – and occasionally bears – can be cleared from the tracks, and it often stops at least once by a lake, weather permitting, for everyone to take a quick dip, usually at Varjisträsk (1hr 30min north of Arvidsjaur). At the **Arctic Circle** it stops again, so that everyone can jump off and take some photos. The train terminates in Gällivare, 100km north of the Arctic Circle, where there are mainline train connections linking most of the major centres and attractions.

Route 45 – the **Inlandsvägen** – is the best **road** north through Swedish Lapland; from Östersund, it sticks close to the train line on its way to Gällivare. It's easy to drive and well surfaced for the most part, although watch out for reindeer with a death wish – once they spot a car hurtling towards them they seem to do their utmost to throw themselves in front of it. You could drive from Östersund to Gällivare in a day if you left very early and put your foot down, but you're better off taking it in stages. The **Inlandsexpressen** (see p.352), the daily **bus** service that runs from Östersund to Gällivare, follows Route 45; it's not as much fun as the train, but is faster and very comfortable.

Strömsund and around

Built on a narrow isthmus of land between Russfjärden lake and the extensive **Ströms Vattudal** network of **waterways** that stretches to the northwest, **STRÖMSUND** is a shy and retiring sort of place. It consists of no more than a couple of parallel streets sporting the odd shop or two, and is of interest mainly as a centre for **canoeing** along the surrounding rivers and lakes. The tourist office (see below) can rent out canoes (180kr per day) and also provide information – walking routes, details of places to stay and maps – on the road known as the **Wilderness Way** (see below), which starts here.

The town's other claim to fame is its proximity to the impressive **Stone Age rock paintings** (*hällmålningar* in Swedish) at **Fångsjön**, around 10km southeast along Route 345. The easiest way to get here without your own transport is to rent a bicycle from the tourist office (110kr per day); get precise directions before setting off. The paintings, created by hunter-gatherers around 2500BC, were a plea to their gods for plentiful hunting.

Practicalities

Although there's no actual train station in Strömsund, you can get off at nearby Ulriksfors and walk the 4km into town or take a **taxi** (pre-booking essential on ☏020/45 00 45; 100kr). Strömsund's **tourist office** (late June to early Aug daily 9am–4pm; mid-Aug to late June Mon–Fri 9am–4pm; ☏0670/164 00, ⓦwww.stromsund.se) is in the centre of town at Storgatan 6. The Inlandsexpressen **bus** #45 stops in the town itself. For a **place to stay**, the **campsite** (☏0670/164 10, ⓦwww.stromsundscamping.com; open June–Aug) is just on the outskirts of town – about 1km out – on the way to Östersund, and also has **cabins** (❶). Otherwise, good **hotel** accommodation is available at the *Nordica*, Ramselevägen 6 (☏0670/61 10 00, ⓦwww.hotelnordica.se; ❹/❺). **Eating** opportunities in this pint-sized town are few, but the best option is *Pizzeria Granen* (☏0670/61 44 48), opposite the tourist office at Storgatan 7, which serves the usual array of pizzas (75kr) as well as a few steak dishes (around 150kr).

Vildmarksvägen: the Wilderness Way

From Strömsund, **Route 342**, the **Wilderness Way** (**Vildmarksvägen**), strikes out northwest towards the mountains at Gäddede, before hugging the Norwegian border and crossing the barren Stekenjokk plateau. It then swings inland again, joining Route 45 at Vilhelmina. The route ranks as one of the most beautiful and dramatic in Sweden, passing through great swathes of **virgin forest**, tiny forgotten villages and true wilderness. It's also the part of Sweden with the densest population of **bears**. If you're driving, stop wherever you can, turn off the engine and listen to the deep silence, broken only by the calls of the birds and the whisper of the forest.

There are plenty of **lakes** along the way ideal for nude bathing – you can choose whichever one you want to make your own as there'll be nobody else there. One of the most beautiful stretches of rocky beach is just south of the tiny village of Alanäs on the beautiful Flåsjön lake, before you get to Gäddede.

If you have your own transport, you should turn left at **Bågede** and follow the minor, very rocky road along the southern shore of **Fågelsjön lake** to reach **Hällsingsåfallet**, an impressive **waterfall**. Sweden's answer to Niagara Falls, it has an 800-metre-long canyon, into which the falls plummet, that's getting longer every year due to continuing erosion.

The only town along the route is **Gäddede**, whose name means "the spot where the northern pike can no longer go upstream". The name may be cute

The #425 **bus** runs from **Strömsund** to **Gäddede**. There's one daily service and two buses on Fridays (ⓦwww.lanstrafiken-z.se). Travelling on a Friday is best since you can stock up with picnic delights in Strömsund, catch the earlier of the two buses (3.25pm), get off wherever you like (just tell the driver to stop), and spend the late afternoon and early evening walking or chilling out by the side of a lake. You can then catch the evening bus on to Gäddede; alternatively on Monday to Friday the bus connects in Gäddede with the #472 to Stora Blåsjön and Anakarde, beside the pretty Stora Blåsjön lake, arriving at 6.40pm and 6.55pm respectively. Unfortunately from here there's no bus connection from Stora Blåsjön over the Stekenjokk plateau to **Klimpfjäll**, from where bus #420 runs down to Saxnäs and Vilhelmina (Mon–Fri 2 daily, Sat & Sun 1 daily; ⓦwww.tabussen.nu); on weekdays the last bus from Klimpfjäll goes at 3.30pm. However, there are three options to cross into Lappland: take a **taxi** from Stora Blåsjön (☎0672/201 53); **hitch** between the two places – there are a lot of German and Dutch camper vans on this stretch of the road who may be able to help out with a lift over the plateau; or **hike** from Ankarede towards Raukasjön lake before heading north up over the Norra Borgafjällen mountains for Slipsiken lake and down into Klimpfjäll – a distance of approximately 40km, best covered over two days.

but the place certainly isn't; give it a miss and instead turn off the main road and follow the road signed "Riksgränsen" (National Border) for a few kilometres to the long and empty sandy beaches of **Murusjöen lake**, right on the border with Norway (the beach is in Sweden, the water in Norway). You'll be hard pushed to find a more idyllic spot: the silence is total, the deep blue water still and calm, and the mountains in the distance dark and brooding.

Stora Blåsjön, a lake 50km to the north of Gäddede, is surrounded by blue mountains; the village of Stora Blåsjon is where the road starts to climb above the tree line to cross the desolate, boulder-strewn **Stekenjokk plateau** into the province of Lappland. Just outside Stora Blåsjön, look out for the minor road leading to **Ankarede**, an age-old meeting place for the local *Sámi*; even today, families from Sweden and Norway get together here at midsummer and again in the autumn. Its old wooden **church** dates from 1896 and is located by the lake, between the two rivers. In addition there are around twenty circular *Sámi* wooden huts – *kåtor* – close by. The Stekenjokk plateau is the temporary summer home of several *Sámi* families, who tend their reindeer on the surrounding slopes, including those of the magnificent peak of **Sipmeke** (1424m) to the west of the road.

After dropping into the minuscule village of **Klimpfjäll** (the stretch of road over the plateau between Leipikvattnet lake and Klimpfjäll is open mid-June to mid-Oct only), the Way continues east. Taking the first turn to the left, after about 12km and then following the signs, you'll reach **Fatmomakke**, a fascinating *Sámi* **church town** made up of eighty *kåtor*, gathered neatly around the church, and twenty log cabins lined up by the side of Kultsjön lake. The first church on the site was built in 1790, but the *Sámi* met together here long before that for special religious celebrations including marriages, christenings and funerals, travelling vast distances on skis, horseback or by boat to reach here. The huts are made out of birch wood, with a hole in the roof to let the smoke out, and birch twigs on the floor to sit on. Everything inside is orderly, the fireplace in the middle, the cooking area at the back; there's a strict code of behaviour as well – you must first wait in the entrance before being invited to enter. Look out for the signposted *visningskåta*, the "show hut" near the church, and have a peek inside.

SAXNÄS, about 20km further east, has a **youth hostel** at Kultsjögården on the main road (☎0940/700 44, ⓦwww.kultsjogarden.se; dorm beds 195kr, double rooms **①**), next door to a luxury **hotel** complex, ⚓ *Saxnäsgården* (☎0940/377 00, ⓦwww.saxnas.se; **❹**; simpler rooms in the annexe **①**). The hotel also has lakeside **cabins** for rent, each sleeping up to eight people, with open fireplaces and a sauna (**❹**).The place also doubles up as a **health complex**: surrounded by water and situated at the foot of the Marsfjällen mountains, it is quite literally an oasis in the surrounding wilderness and a wonderful place to pamper yourself for a day.This alcohol-free spot boasts a divine 34°C swimming pool, herbal health baths, massage facilities, saunas, a fitness centre and sports hall. It also rents out mountain **bikes**, **canoes**, **fishing tackle** and **motor boats**. In summer the hotel runs a boat service to the Fatmomakke *Sámi* village as well as a **seaplane** up into the mountains for **hiking**. In winter, **dog-sledding** trips can be arranged by the hotel, which also has **snow scooters** for hire.

Opposite the *Saxnäsgården*'s front door, the **Marsfjällen Naturum nature centre** (no fixed hours; if it's closed ask at the hotel for the key) is worth a quick look; try to ignore the cheesy mobile of stuffed snow grouse revolving from the ceiling and look instead for the impressively large dropping of one of the bears resident in the nearby Marsfjällen nature reserve. Between mid-October and mid-April, whilst in their lair, bears neither eat nor defecate, hence the size (the length of a child's arm) of this first movement, which was collected close to the exit of the bear's lair – the surrounding tracks, each measuring a whopping 30cm in length and 22cm in width, give an idea of the mighty size of this male bear.

North to Dorotea

Avoiding the Wilderness Way detour, it's possible to head directly north from Strömsund both along the Inlandsbanan and the Inlandsvägen to tiny **DOROTEA**, 71km north, a journey of around an hour by rail or road. A textbook example of a linear village, its houses and shops strung out in a long line either side of the main road, Dorotea has a few attractions which merit a stop on the long journey north. Firstly, it has the biggest **bear** population in Sweden; bears regularly wander into town during the night to rummage through rubbish bins for scraps of food. Sweden's bear population stretches from northern Värmland to the furthestmost reaches of Lapland and is currently estimated at 2500–3000 animals.

At the top of the village, in the same building as the tourist office at Storgatan 46, the **Jakt och Fiskemuseum** (Hunting and Fishing Museum; mid-June to mid-Aug Mon–Fri 9am–8pm, Sat & Sun 11am–6pm; mid-Aug to mid-June Mon–Fri 9am–5pm; 40kr) is a taxidermist's dream: inside, there's a varied collection of stuffed local wildlife, everything from a bear to a wolverine, as well as a tired exhibition of glass boxes containing a motley group of butterflies, grasshoppers and beetles. More interesting, however, is the adjacent **aquarium** where there are live specimens of the bream, perch, pike, trout and Arctic char found in vast numbers in the surrounding lakes.

Whilst in Dorotea, make sure to see the powerful Björn Martinius group **sculpture** of the Last Supper. Housed in a small chapel in the church graveyard on a low hill just off the main road, the life-size wooden figures sit around three long trestle tables – the very size of the sculpture, filling an entire room, the striking bright colours used to paint the figures, as well as the intense expressions, create a sense of life and motion that's enough to send a shiver down the spine of the most ardent agnostic.

Practicalities

Dorotea's **tourist office** (May–Aug Mon–Fri 9am–5pm, Sat & Sun 11am–6pm; Sept–April Mon–Fri 9am–5pm; ☎0942/140 63, ⓦwww.dorotea.se) is located at the top of the village, at Storgatan 46, a ten-minute walk along the main road from the train station. As well as booking bear-spotting tours, they also have good advice on local **hiking routes** and **fishing trips**. The only **hotel** is the swanky *Dorotea* (☎0942/477 80, Ⓦwww.hotelldorotea.se; ❹/❸) at Bergsvägen 2. However, a much more agreeable option is *Doro Camp Lappland* (☎0942/102 38, Ⓦwww.dorocamp.com), beautifully situated beside the Bergvattenån River. As well as four-bed **cabins** (❶), it has a number of simple hostel-style double rooms (❶) with access to showers and a sauna in the nearby service building. A popular café for locals to swap gossip in is *Görans Konditori*, at Parkvägen 2, which serves set lunch for 75kr as well as a number of open sandwiches and cakes. More substantial meaty **meals**, including pizzas and a daily *Dagens Rätt*, are available at *Ankis Bar & Pizzeria* at Storgatan 37, opposite the bank. For **internet** access, head to the tourist office or the library on Storgatan opposite *Görans Konditori*.

Vilhelmina

The Inlandsvägen and the Wilderness Way meet up again in the pretty little town of **VILHELMINA**, 54km north of Dorotea. Once an important forestry centre, the timber business has now moved away and one of the main sources of employment is a telephone booking centre for the package tour company, Fritidsresor. The town, a quiet little place with just one main street, is named after the wife of King Gustav IV Adolf, Fredrika Dorotea Vilhelmina (as is its southerly neighbour, Dorotea). The principal attraction is the **church town**, nestling between Storgatan and Ljusminnesgatan, whose thirty-odd wooden cottages date back to 1792 when the first church was consecrated. It's since been restored, and the cottages can be rented out via the tourist office (see below). The **museum** here, at Storgatan 7 (daily June–Aug 10.30am–3pm; 20kr), contains a mind-numbingly dull display of local history from prehistoric times to the present day; give it a miss and instead have a look inside the *Sámi* **handicraft store**, *Risfjells Sameslöjd*, nearby at Storgatan 8.

Practicalities

The **tourist office**, Storgatan 9 (mid-June to mid-Sept daily 8am–7pm; mid-Sept to mid-June Mon–Fri 9.30am–5pm; ☎0940/152 70, Ⓦwww.sodralappland .se), is located in the middle of the church town, a ten-minute walk from the **train station** (which also serves as the **bus** arrival and departure point); turn left along Järnvägsgatan, then left again into the main street, Volgsjövägen, then finally right into Fjällgatan to its junction with Storgatan. There are two **hotels** in town: the showy *Wilhelmina*, Volgsjövägen 16 (☎0940/554 20, Ⓦwww.hotell.vilhelmina.com; ❺/❸), where each room (and the sauna) has stunning views out over Volgsjön lake and the distant mountains; and the simpler and friendlier *Lilla* (☎0940/150 59, Ⓦwww.lillahotellet.vilhelmina .com; ❸), at Granvägen 1. During the summer months, it's possible to book a double **room in the church town** through the tourist office (❶). The **campsite**, *Saiva Camping* (☎0940/107 60, Ⓦwww.saiva.se), has two- to six-berth cabins for rent (290–650kr depending on size) and a great sandy **beach**; to get there, walk down the main Volgsjövägen from the centre and take a left turn after about ten minutes, just before the Volvo garage.

Eating and **drinking** doesn't exactly throw up a multitude of options: for coffee and cakes, there's *Stenmans Konditori*, Volgsjövägen 21B, or for something more upmarket, try the traditional northern Swedish dishes at *Hotell Wilhelmina*, which also offers a *Dagens Rätt* for 75kr. Otherwise, there's the plain *Pizzeria Lascité* (℡0940/550 34), Volgsjövägen 38, for cheap pizzas or *krogen* (℡0940/108 88), in the main square at Torget 3, which has simple dishes such as pasta carbonara and meatballs for 59kr, and is also a popular place for a **drink** or two.

Storuman, Tärnaby and around

The one defining factor that unites the small settlement of **Storuman** with its northwesterly neighbours, **Tärnaby** and **Hemavan**, is the **Blå vägen** (Blue Way) or E12, as it is less poetically known, running through all three villages. This major artery, one of northern Sweden's better roads, is so named because it follows the course of the great Ume River that flows down from the mountains of southern Lappland to Umeå on the Bothnian coast. Water is omnipresent hereabouts, not only in Storuman, a dreary little town which sits on the banks of the eponymously named lake, best used as an access point to the mountains, but also all the way up to Tärnaby, a small-time skiing centre, and Hemavan, the start of Sweden's longest and best hiking trail, the Kungsleden, leading 500km north to Abisko.

Storuman

In 1741, the first settler arrived in what was to become **STORUMAN**, 68km north of Vilhelmina. His first neighbours didn't appear until forty years later and even by World War I, Storuman, then called Luspen (the *Sámi* name for a river which emerges from a lake) numbered barely forty inhabitants working just eight farms. Things changed, though, with the arrival of the railway in the 1920s; today Storuman is an important centre for the generation of hydro-electric power. That said, there's not much to the town: the centre consists of one tiny street that supports a couple of shops and banks. You can head off into the mountains west of here for some good **hiking** and **fishing**; ask at the tourist office for maps and information. If you find yourself at a loose end whilst waiting for buses or trains, one diversion is the worthwhile short walk signed "Utsikten" from the main square, which leads up to a wooden **viewing platform** from where there are fantastic views out over the surrounding lakes and forest towards the mountains which mark the border with Norway; it's around a two-kilometre uphill walk to the platform from the town centre. Otherwise, the only sight in town, if indeed it can be called such, is the town's emblem, **Wildman**, a giant-sized red figure who stands near *Hotell Toppen* (see below) madly brandishing a club, a traditional symbol for Lapland encapsulating strength, riches and determination.

Practicalities

An hour by the Inlandsbanan from Vilhelmina, Storuman is a **transport hub** for this part of southern Lapland. From here, **buses** run northwest up the E12, skirting the Tärnafjällen mountains to Tärnaby and Hemavan, before wriggling through to Mo-i-Rana in Norway; in the opposite direction, the road leads down to Umeå via Lycksele, from where there are bus connections to Vindeln and Vännäs on the main coastal train line. A direct bus, **Lapplandspilen** (ⓦwww.lapplandspilen.se), links Storuman with Stockholm.

The **tourist office** (late June to mid-Aug Mon–Fri 9am–8pm, Sat & Sun 10am–5pm; mid-Aug to late June Mon–Fri 9am–5pm; ℡0951/333 70, ⓦwww .entrelappland.se) is at Järnvägsgatan 13, 50m to the right of the **train station**, and can supply a handy map of town and a few brochures; **buses** from Vilhelmina (Ⓦ www.tabussen.nu) stop outside the station. While you're here, check out the wonderful old **railway hotel**, diagonally opposite the tourist office, which now houses the library; built in association with the Inlandsbanan, the wide-planked wooden exterior hides an ornate interior, complete with wrought-iron chandeliers, that's well worth a peek.

The **youth hostel** (Ⓣ 0951/333 80; no dorms, double rooms ❶) is in the same building as the tourist office. At the same address, Järnvägsgatan 13, there's also **hotel** accommodation at the friendly 🅰 *Luspen* (Ⓣ 0951/333 70, Ⓦ www .hotelluspen.se; ❸), which is excellent value for money. The engaging owner, Tord, is a font of local knowledge and only too ready to help with advice and information on Storuman and the rest of Lapland. Alternatively, *Hotell Toppen* (Ⓣ 0951/777 00, Ⓦ www.hotelltoppen.se; ❺/❸), with pine and birchwood rooms, is altogether more luxurious and correspondingly expensive; to get here, walk up the hill from the station to Blå Vägen 238. In the middle of the local **campsite**, by the lakeside at Vallnäsvägen (Ⓣ 0951/106 96, Ⓦ www.storuman .se), is a church built in the style of a *kåta*, a traditional *Sámi* hut; there are also **cabins** here for rent (❷). The **restaurant** at *Hotell Toppen* should be your first choice for **food**, with a 75kr lunch buffet; alternatively, *Kitas Restaurang Piccolo* (Ⓣ 0951/100 15), opposite the train station at Järnvägsgatan 20C, has Swedish and Italian food, pizzas and lunch for much the same prices. During the day, *Café Akkan* at Skolgatan 23 is a good place for coffee and cakes.

Tärnaby and around

Buses (Ⓦ www.tabussen.nu) make the two-hour drive northwest from Storuman to the tiny mountain village of **TÄRNABY**, the birthplace of Sweden's greatest skier, Ingemar Stenmark. A double Olympic gold medallist, he occasionally spiced up his training with a spot of tightrope walking and monocycling. It's a pretty place: yellow flower-decked meadows run to the edge of the mountain forests, the trees felled to leave great empty swathes that accommodate World Cup ski slopes. Since there's not much to do in Tärnaby itself, it's a much better idea to explore the surrounding countryside: a popular **walk** leads across the nearby mountain, **Laxfjället**, which affords fantastic views down over the village – it can be reached by chair lift from either of the two hotels listed below. Another good walk for a sunny day leads to the beach at **Lake Laisan**, though the water is rarely warm enough to swim even in the height of summer; to get there, take the footpath that branches off right from the main Sandviksvägen past the campsite or ask the tourist office for precise directions.

The **tourist office** on the one main road (mid-June to mid-Aug Mon–Fri 9am–7pm, Sat & Sun 10am–6pm; mid-Aug to mid-June Mon–Fri 9am–5pm; Ⓣ 0954/104 50, Ⓦ www.tarnaby.se), at Västra Strandvägen 1, can supply advice about local **fishing**, which is excellent. For accommodation, the **campsite** (Ⓣ 0954/100 09, Ⓦ www.tarnabycamping.se) at Sandviksvägen 4 also has dorm beds for 120kr per person and **cabins** (❶). The **youth hostel**, *Åkerlundska gården* (Ⓣ 0954/104 20, Ⓦ www.tarnabyfjallhotell.com; dorm beds 230kr, double rooms ❶; July–Sept), is 2km east of the village at Östra Strandvägen 16. Otherwise, the best place **to stay** is the smart *Tärnaby Fjällhotell*, next door (Ⓣ 0954/104 20, Ⓦ www.tarnabyfjallhotell.com; ❻/❸). For something to **eat** the best bet is the *Tärnaby Wärdshus* (Ⓣ 0954/103 95), opposite the tourist office at Västra Strandvägen 2B, serving decent pizzas and some good Swedish home-cooking; there's also a tolerable **bar** here.

Buses continue from Tärnaby on to **HEMAVAN**, 18km northwest, which marks the beginning and the end of the five-hundred-kilometre **Kungsleden** trail (for more information on the trail and hiking in general, see p.379). The village is also reachable from Stockholm on direct flights (℡0951/305 30, Ⓦwww.hemavansflygplats.nu; journey time 1hr 45min). This tiny, nondescript village, straddling the main road, is totally devoid of attractions. It's purely and simply a service centre which provides accommodation and eating opportunities to hikers starting and ending the trail here. Hemavan can be busy during the peak summer season (mid-June to mid-Aug) and at this time it's therefore wise to book a bed in advance to be sure of somewhere to stay.

There's an STF **youth hostel**, *Hemavans Kursgård* (℡0954/300 02, Ⓦwww .hemavanskursgard.se; dorm beds 185kr, double rooms ❶), on the main road at Renstigen 1–8; it's always busy with hikers, so it's essential to book ahead all year. You'll find a swimming pool, sauna, steam room, Jacuzzi and even a climbing wall on site.

Although there's a greasy spoon, *Sibylla Grill*, in Hemavan, when it comes to **eating** you're much better catered for in neighbouring **KLIPPEN**, just 6km away and reachable by **bus**. This tiny village sheltering beneath the bulk of Artekenvalle mountain (1188m) is an unlikely location for one of Sweden's top restaurants. Housed in the gay-friendly ⚥ *Hotell Sånninggården* (℡0954/330 00, Ⓦwww.sanninggarden.com; ❸), the kitchen is renowned across the north of the country for culinary excellence. In fact, it's worth making a special journey here just to eat in the award-winning **restaurant**, as the northern Swedish delicacies they serve up – everything from fillet of reindeer with potato cakes and parsnip purée (239kr) to Arctic char with warm potato salad and Västerbotten cheese and dill pesto (169kr) – really are some of the best you'll find. Everything on the menu is locally produced – even the wild goose is likely to have come from the lakes around Tärnaby. Make sure you try the various local *akvavits* – the angelica (akin to fennel in flavour) is particularly good. In addition to the extensive à la carte menu there's an all-day lunch buffet for 99kr. Although the cuisine here is world-class, the accommodation, unfortunately, is not – rooms, although adequate, are cramped and share facilities. *Sånninggården* is the last stop for the Lapplandspilen bus to and from Stockholm as well as a destination on the Umeå to Mo-i-Rana service.

Sorsele and around

The next major stop on the Inlandsbanan north of Storuman (also served by bus from Storuman) is **SORSELE**, 76km away – a pint-sized, dreary town on the **Vindelälven River**. The town became a *cause célèbre* among conservationists in Sweden when activists forced the government to abandon its plans to build a hydroelectric power station, which would have regulated the river's flow. Consequently, the Vindelälven remains in its natural state today – seething with rapids – and is one of only four rivers in the country that hasn't been tampered with in some way or other.

During the last week in July, the river makes its presence felt with the **Vindelälvsloppet**, a long-distance running race that sees hundreds of competitors cover, in stages, over 350km from nearby Ammarnäs (see p.360) down to Vännäsby, near Umeå. It's quite a spectacle, but needless to say accommodation at this time is booked up months in advance. The other big event here is the **Vindelälvsdraget**, a dog-sled race held over the same course in the third week of March. Sorsele is an ideal base for **fly-fishing**: the Vindelälven and the other local river, Laisälven, are teeming with grayling and brown trout, and there are a number of local lakes stocked with char. Ask at the tourist offices for details.

The town's only other attraction is the Inland Railway **museum**, in the same building as the tourist office (mid-June to mid-Sept Mon–Fri 9am–6pm, Sat & Sun 11am–4pm; mid-Sept to mid-June Mon–Fri 8.30am–11.30am; 20kr), detailing the life and times of the Inlandsbanan; the labelling here is in Swedish only, though there is an English-language factsheet available, which will help make sense of the evocative black-and-white photographs of German troops travelling up and down the line during World War II; during the height of the conflict, 12,000 German soldiers and significant amounts of war material were moved every week between Narvik and Trondheim in occupied Norway, travelling via Gällivare and Östersund along the Inlandsbanan in supposedly neutral Sweden.

Practicalities

The **tourist office** (end June to Aug Mon–Fri 9am–6pm, Sat & Sun 11am–4pm; end Aug to end June Mon–Fri 8.30am–11.30am; ☎0952/140 90, Ⓦwww.sorsele.se/turist) at the **train station**, Stationsgatan 19, has information about local activities such as fishing and **canoe rental**; **buses** stop outside. Free **internet** access is available at the village library at Storgatan 11. For **accommodation**, there are **cabins** at the riverside **campsite** (☎0952/310 41, Ⓦwww.lapplandskatan.nu; ❶) which is also the location of the small STF **youth hostel** (☎0952/100 24; dorm beds 225kr, double rooms ❶) at Torggatan 3, just 500m from the station. The only **hotel** in town is *River* (☎0952/121 50, Ⓦwww.sorseleriverhotel.se; ❹/❸), Hotellgatan 2, a smart place featuring tasteful rooms with wooden floors and modern furnishings as well as a superb sauna and Jacuzzi suite; to walk here from the train station (around a ten-minute journey), turn left into Stationsgatan, right into Södra Esplanaden, left again into Vindelvägen and finally right into Hotellgatan.

Eating choices in Sorsele are scant, too, although what food is on offer is cheap, with few dishes costing more than 70kr. At lunchtime, head for the *River* hotel, which has tasty local fare, or *Grillhörnan Bar*, near the station at Södra Esplanaden 6, which has burgers, pizzas and beer; there's a café, *Älvan*, in the Folkets Hus at Stationsgatan 16. The gourmet restaurant at the *River Hotel* is open in the evenings for northern Swedish delicacies at around 200kr per dish.

Around Sorsele: Ammarnäs

The tiny mountain village of **AMMARNÄS**, with a population of just two hundred and fifty, lies ninety-minutes' bus ride northwest of Sorsele; the road only reached this remote corner of Sweden in 1939. Set in a wide river valley by the side of the **Gautsträsk lake** and at the foot of the towering **Ammarfjället mountains**, the village offers peace and tranquillity of the first order. This is **reindeer** country (one-third of the villagers here are reindeer herders), and for hundreds of years the local *Sámi* are known to have migrated with their animals from the coast to the surrounding fells for summer pasture.

The first settlement began here in 1821 when two *Sámi* brothers, Måns and Abraham Sjulsson, were granted permission to set up home at Övre Gautsträsk. When they failed to keep the terms of their agreement, a new tenant, Nils Johansson, took over. He eked out an existence by cultivating the land and is responsible for *Potatisbacken* or Potato Hill, adjacent to the church at the eastern end of the village at the junction of Kyrkvägen and Nolsivägen (get here by

There's some excellent **hiking** to be had around Ammarnäs, not least along the Kungsleden (see p.379), which passes through the village. For the less adventurous, **Mount Kaissats (984m)** is ideal for a day spent in the mountains; to get there, take the road at the western end of the village that leads to the lake of **Stora Tjulträsk**, from where a marked trail for Kaissats (not particularly difficult) leads off to the right (8km). Even less strenuous is taking a **chair lift** from the village and up **Näsberget**, from where trails lead back down into Ammarnäs. Another hiking possibility is along the road up to the village of **Kraipe**; this small turning, to your left before you reach Ammarnäs on Route 363, is one of the steepest in Sweden. From Kraipe you can easily reach the surrounding summits, and if you take the route in September you may well encounter the marking and slaughtering of reindeer at Kraipe corrals. From any of these bare mountain tops, the spectacular views look out over some of the last remaining wilderness in Europe – mountains and dense forest as far as the eye can see.

following Nolsivägen from opposite the *Ammarnäsgården* hotel, signed "Norra Ammarnäs"), where the northern Swedish potato (a sweet, yellow variety), is grown – unusual for a location so far north. With the founding of a postal station in 1895, the village changed its name from Gautsträsk (*gaut* is a *Sámi* word meaning "bowl" – an accurate description of its valley-bottom location) to Ammarnäs – the foreland between the Tjulån and Vindelälven rivers. A stone plinth now stands in Nils Johansson's memory across from the church on Strandvägen.

The **Sámi church town**, near the potato hill on Nolsivägen, was built in 1850, and was moved to its present site in 1911. The dozen or so square wooden huts, which are perched on horizontal logs to help keep them dry, are still used today. Three times a year *Sámi* families gather here, much as they have done for centuries, to celebrate important **festivals**: the *Sámi* festival (Sun before midsummer), Vårböndagshelgen (spring intercession day, on the first Sun in July) and Höstböndagshelgen (autumn intercession day, on the last Sun in Sept). The nearby **Samegården** (*Sámi* museum; mid-June to mid-Aug Mon–Fri 9am–2pm) on Strandvägen has a simple display of *Sámi* history and traditions.

Adjoining the tourist office on Tjulträskvägen is the **Naturum Vindelfjällen** (Nature Centre; mid-June to mid-Sept daily 9am–5pm,; free), which has information about the local geology, flora and fauna, and an unflattering selection of stuffed animals, including bear, lynx and wolverine. It also shows a 1940s film of bears in the woods along the Vindelälven – just ask them to put it on. Look out also for the model of the surrounding peaks, which will give you an idea of just how isolated Ammarnäs is, locked in on three sides by mountains.

Practicalities

Buses take an hour to reach here from Sorsele, and will drop you along the main road, Tjulträskvägen, where you'll find the **tourist office** (mid-June to mid-Sept daily 9am–5pm; ☎0952/600 00, Ⓦwww.ammarnasby.com). They have plenty of maps and brochures on the surrounding countryside, and useful information on hiking, and can also help with the renting of **dog sleds** and **snowmobiles** in winter, and rides on **Icelandic ponies**.

Virtually opposite the tourist office at Nolsivägen 6 is the STF **youth hostel** (☎0952/600 24, Ⓔammarnas.fiskecentrum@telia.com; dorm beds only 230kr). The only **hotel** is the busy and popular *Ammarnäsgården* (☎0952/600 03, Ⓦwww.ammarnasgarden.se; ❸), on the main road, which has rather simple en-suite rooms aimed at hikers walking the Kungsleden; its decent sauna and pool complex in the basement makes up for the lack of creature comforts in the rooms. There are also basic youth hostel dorms (170kr) in a separate building. For **eating** and **drinking**, your only option is the hotel's bar and restaurant.

Arvidsjaur and around

An hour and forty-five minutes and 89km north of Sorsele by Inlandsbanan, **ARVIDSJAUR** was for centuries where the region's **Sámi** gathered to trade and debate. Their presence was of interest to Protestant missionaries, who established the first church here in 1606. The success of this Swedish settlement was secured when silver was discovered in the nearby mountains, and the town flourished as a staging point and supply depot. While these developments unfolded, the *Sámi* continued to assemble on market days and during religious festivals. At the end of the eighteenth century, they built their own church town of simple wooden huts. Today, out of a total population of five thousand, there are still twenty *Sámi* families in Arvisdjaur who make their living from reindeer husbandry, and the town is a good place to get a real hands-on experience of *Sámi* life.

Arvidsjaur is not one of Sweden's more attractive towns – its streets of drab houses strung out either side of the main drag lined with a dozen or so shops make a pretty depressing impression on any first-time visitor. However, although the modern town is decidedly unappealing, it hides one of northern Sweden's top attractions in the traditional *Sámi* village of **Lappstaden**.

Arrival, information and accommodation

The **train station** is on Järnvägsgatan. Five-minutes' walk away, up Stationsgatan, is the **tourist office** (mid-June to mid-Aug Mon–Fri 9.30am–6pm, Sat & Sun noon–4.30pm; mid-Aug to mid-June Mon–Fri 8.30am–4.30pm; ℡0960/175 00, ⓦwww.polcirkeln.nu) at Östra Skolgatan 18C, just off Storgatan. The **bus station** is in the centre of town at Västlundavägen, just behind the Konsum supermarket. Flights from Stockholm's Arlanda airport land at the modern **airport** terminal, 15km east of town, which has been designed to resemble a *Sámi* wooden *kåta*; you can get from here to the centre by taxi (℡0960/104 00; 65kr). For **internet** access, head for the tourist office or the library in Medborgarhuset, Storgatan 12.

For inexpensive accommodation there's also a cosy private **youth hostel**, *Lappugglan*, conveniently situated at Västra Skolgatan 9 (℡0960/124 13; dorm beds 145kr, double rooms ❶). The tourist office will fix you up with a **private room** from 400kr, or the **campsite**, *Camp Gielas* (℡0960/556 00), has waterside **cabins** for 695kr with TV, shower and running water (495kr without water). It sits beside one of the town's dozen or so lakes, Tvättjärn, with its bathing beaches; there's a sports hall here, too, as well as a gym, sauna, tennis courts and mini-golf. The site is a ten-minute walk from the tourist office (head south down Lundavägen, left along Strandvägen and left again into Järnvägs-gatan). More upmarket is *Lapland Lodge* at Östra Kyrkogatan 18 (℡0960/137 20, ⓦwww.laplandlodge.eu; ❸), a comfortable bed and breakfast place near the church, whereas the sole **hotel** in town, ⚒ *Laponia*, Storgatan 45 (℡0960/555 00, ⓦwww.hotell-laponia.se; ❷/❹), is a much larger affair with 200 comfort-able, modern en-suite rooms and a swimming pool; some rooms have a small kitchen and private sauna. Although the hotel is full of (male) test drivers from Europe's leading car companies between December and April, who come to the area to experience driving on the frozen lakes, there is no men-only sauna, only a small shared one. If you're planning to visit Arvidsjaur during the winter (when the higher price code applies), it's imperative to book well in advance to secure a room, especially in February and March.

Lappstaden

A good way to find out more about the *Sámi* culture (which manifests itself more and more as you travel north from here) is to visit **Lappstaden** (free; daily tours mid-June to mid-Aug at 10.30am & 6pm, 30kr), reached by walking west along Storgatan and turning right into Lappstadsgatan. Although you probably won't meet any *Sámi* here, you will at least be able to see how they used to live in traditional huts or *kåtor*. About eighty of these huts in the eighteenth-century *Sámi* **church town** have survived, and are clumped unceremoniously next to a yellow, modern apartment building. The design of these square wooden buildings supporting a pyramid-shaped roof is typical of the Forest *Sámi* who lived in the surrounding forests, constructing their homes of indigenous timber. Local *Sámi* schoolteacher, Karin Stenberg, made it her life's work to preserve Lappstaden and, the huts are still used today during the last weekend in August as a venue for a special **festival**, Storstämningshelgen.

Eating and drinking

For **snacks**, coffee, fresh pastries and bread, try *Greya Knut* at Stationsgatan 20, which also has cheap lunches, sandwiches (often filled with reindeer meat) and salads; there's outdoor seating here in summer. Arvidsjaur also has a small selection of **restaurants**: you can sit down to Mediterranean food at *Afrodite*, Storgatan 10 (☎0960/173 00), with averagely priced lunches, pizzas, meat and fish dishes and a few Greek dishes for around 150kr; next door at Storgatan 8, *Cazba* (☎0960/215 24) serves up pizzas for the same price but has less atmosphere. The latest arrival in Arvidsjaur is *The Square*, Storgatan 34 (☎0960/212 50), a stylish gourmet restaurant where the delicious à la carte meals include local reindeer and other Lapland delicacies (mains around 250kr).

Around Arvidsjaur: Båtsuoj Sámi Center

Seventy kilometres to the west of Arvidsjaur, in the village of **GASA**, the **Båtsuoj Sámi Center** (☎0960/130 14 or 070/642 31 66, ⓦwww.algonet .se/~same-id), Hedgatan 40, is a good place to get to grips with the everyday life

---

Summer activities in and around Arvidsjaur

From July to early August, an incredibly popular **steam train**, pulling vintage coaches from the 1930s, runs from Arvidsjaur along sections of the Inlandsbanan. The trips head west to **Slagnäs** on Fridays and Saturdays (5.45pm; 190kr, under-16s free; bookings on ☎0771/53 53 53) stopping at Storavan beach for swimming and a barbecue. Alternatively, you can strike out through the surrounding countryside on your own steam on a **rail-inspection trolley** (a bike with train wheels; *dressin* in Swedish), which can be booked through the tourist office (70kr for up to 5hr, 160kr for 24hr). Each trolley can carry two people, with camping gear provided. Thus equipped, you can cycle along the disused rail line from Arvidsjaur 75km southeast to **Jörn** – a stopping-off point for trains on the main coastal route – though there's an extra 250kr fee if you leave the trolley in Jörn. In July and August **whitewater rafting** trips (☎070/260 05 83, ⓦwww.laplandraftingcafe.se; 445kr) are possible on the Piteälven River, 45km north of Arvidsjaur. The starting point (reachable by bus) is the Burmabron bridge where Route 45 crosses the river.

of the *Sámi*. Here, you'll not only come face to face with **reindeer** (*båtsuoj* in *Sámi*) but also meet real reindeer herders, who'll teach you about their religion and way of life, including the way to milk a reindeer and the tricks of baking their traditional bread; frozen reindeer meat is also available for purchase.

A short visit to Båtsuoj of around an hour or so costs 200kr and includes a chance to taste dried reindeer meat sitting around the fire in a *kåta*; a longer half-day trip, including dinner of reindeer cooked over an open fire as well as information about the *Sámi* way of life, is 500kr. From late June to early July you can go on **branding** trips here, which generally take place in the evenings (500kr). The centre also arranges all-day **cloudberry-picking** and medicinal herb-gathering expeditions (Aug; 600kr); the rare cloudberries grow in the most inaccessible of northern Sweden's marshlands – hence the hefty price. To get to Båtsuoj from Arvidsjaur, head west on Route 45 until the village of Slagnäs, from where you take the unnumbered minor road 19km north towards Arjeplog. You can reach Slagnäs by Inlandsbanan, from where Båtsuoj staff will collect you if you book in advance.

Arjeplog and around

Stretching northwest of Arvidsjaur out towards the Norwegian border, the municipality of **Arjeplog**, roughly the size of Belgium, supports a population of just three and a half thousand – half of whom live in the eponymous lakeside town, 85km from Arvidsjaur. It's one of the most beautiful parts of Sweden, with nearly nine thousand lakes and vast expanses of mountains and virgin forests. The air is clear and crisp, the rivers clean and deep and the winters mighty cold – in 1989 a temperature of -52°C was recorded here. January and February, in particular, are bitter, dark and silent months, but it's during winter that Arjeplog is at its busiest: hundreds of test drivers from Korea, Australia, Germany, Britain, Italy, America and France descend on the town to put cars through their paces in the freezing conditions, with brakes and road-holding being given a thorough examination on the frozen lakes. In summer, Arjeplog is a likeable little place away from the main inland road and rail routes, where **hiking**, **canoeing** and **fishing** are all popular activities, each offering the chance of blissful isolation, be it by the side of a secluded mountain tarn or in a clearing deep in the pine forest. In late July you can go **cloudberry picking** in the surrounding marshland, and in the autumn you can hunt for lingonberries, blueberries and wild mushrooms.

Arjeplog town itself is a tiny, unassuming sort of place, barely one main street leading to what passes as a main square, but is really only a car park between the tourist office and the **Silvermuséet** (Silver Museum; Mon–Fri 10am–4pm, Sat 10am–2pm; 50kr; ⑩www.silvermuseet.arjeplog.se), the only sight in town. Housed in a yellow wooden building opposite the tourist office, it's home to fascinating collections of *Sámi* silver, including several ornate silver collars that were handed down from mother to daughter; if a mother had several daughters she would divide her chain amongst them. Whilst in the museum, make sure to visit the newly constructed cinema in the basement, where you can see a **slide show** about the surrounding countryside and nature and how people in this remote part of Sweden learnt to adapt to the harsh climate.

Practicalities

There are daily **buses** to Arjeplog from Arvidsjaur. The **tourist office** is in the main square (mid-June to mid-Aug Mon–Fri 8am–7pm, Sat 10am–5pm, Sun noon–5pm; mid-Aug to mid-June Mon–Fri 8am–5pm; ☏0961/222 30,

ⓦwww.polcirkeln.nu) and can help with local hiking trails, fishing and **bike rental**. The best-value **accommodation** is the central and palatial **youth hostel** at Lugnetvägen 4 (ⓣ0961/612 10, ⓔinfo@hotellyktan-arjeplog.se; dorm beds 150kr, double rooms ❶; May–Nov), where every room sleeps a maximum of four and has en-suite facilities. The hostel is part of *Hotel Lyktan* (ⓣ0961/612 10, ⓦwww.hotellyktan-arjeplog.se; ❷/❹), which offers comfortable modern rooms of the highest standard. At *Hotell Silverhatten* (ⓣ0961/315 10, ⓦwww.kraja.se; ❷/❹), 1500m up Öberget hill from the centre (a 30min walk), the cosy rooms have fantastic views over the village and surrounding lake. Ten-minutes' walk along Silvervägen, the lakeside **campsite**, *Kraja* (ⓣ0961/315 00, ⓦwww.kraja.se) has simple **cabins** (❷); there's also an outdoor swimming pool which is open to non-residents (free). Bear in mind that in winter, accommodation hereabouts is often booked months in advance by the major car manufacturers.

Eating and **drinking** in the centre of Arjeplog isn't a joy. There are two cut-price options: the basic *Mathörnan* (ⓣ0961/614 44), Drottninggatan 4, which serves up moderately priced reindeer, Arctic char and traditional Swedish home-cooking amid hideously tacky decor; next door, the cavernous *Pizzeria Verona* (ⓣ0961/108 00), with an equally dingy 1970s interior, offers salads, pizzas and not overly authentic Thai and Asian food at similar prices. For gourmet food head for *Kraja Värdshus* (ⓣ0961/315 00) at the campsite, where you can tuck into fillet of elk or saddle of reindeer.

Around Arjeplog

From Arjeplog, the **Silvervägen** (Silver Way; Route 95) strikes out for the craggy chain of mountains which marks the border with Norway. The **views** on this stretch of the road are stunning – unlike in so many other parts of Swedish Lapland, the forest here is set back from the road, rising and falling over the surrounding hills, giving an awe-inspiring sense of the scale of the uninhabited territory you're passing through. The **Silverexpressen** bus #200, running

The Kungsleden in one day: Jäkkvik–Adolfström

One of the quieter sections of the Kungsleden trail begins in **Jäkkvik** to the northwest of Arjeplog and leads through the hauntingly beautiful Pieljekaise National Park. From the village shop, walk back along the main road to the sign for Kungsleden car parking. The trail begins at the car park, climbing first through mountain birch forest before emerging on bare upland terrain dominated by **Mount Pieljekaise** (1138m), which is said to look like a large ear (hence its name, which means just that in *Sámi*). From here, the views over the surrounding mountains are truly spectacular. The trail winds round the mountain and descends below the tree line into virgin birch woodland, carpeted with stately flowers like the northern wolfsbane, alpine sow-thistle and angelica. Pieljekaise National Park is also home to elk, bear, Arctic fox, wolverine, golden eagle and the gyrfalcon. It's a moderate 27-kilometre hike from Jäkkvik to Adolfström (all downhill after climbing out of Jäkkvik; allow 6–7hr). Cabin **accommodation** can be rented in Adolfström at *Adolfströms Handelsbod och Stugby* (ⓣ0961/230 41, ⓦwww.adolfstrom.com; ❶) and *Johanssons Fjällstugor* (ⓣ0961/230 40, ⓦwww.fjallflygarna.se; ❶); there's an old-world village shop at the former. Buses usually only leave Adolfström (the post box serves as the bus stop) once daily, at 2pm on Monday, Tuesday & Wednesday for **Loholm** (the junction with Route 95, change here for Arjeplog and Arvidsjaur), so time your hike carefully and check the bus information on ⓣ020/47 00 47 before setting out.

between Skellefteå and Bodø in Norway, via Arvidsjaur and Arjeplog, is the only public transport on this section of the road (daily except Sat). Thirty minutes northwest of Arjeplog, the bus reaches the minuscule settlement of **JÄKKVIK**, little more than a cluster of houses dependent on the tiny shop and petrol station which doubles as the bus station. From here, one of the least walked sections of the Kungsleden trail (see box opposite) heads across to **Adolfström**, a tiny village on Lake Gautosjön, 27km away, where the summer air is sweet with the smell of freshly scythed hay. The route makes an ideal day's hike through the beauty of the **Pieljekaise national park**, just south of the Arctic Circle and containing the least disturbed flora and fauna in the entire Swedish mountains. There are **cabins** in Jäkkvik at the *Stugby* (℡0961/211 20 and 0961/211 22; ❶) or simple hostel-style double rooms and a **campsite** at *Kyrkans Fjällgård* (℡0961/210 39, ⓦwww.kyrkansfjallgardjakkvik.com; ❶).

Jokkmokk and around

During his journey in Lapland, the botanist Carl von Linné said "If not for the mosquitoes, this would be earth's paradise". His comments were made after journeying along the river valley of the Lilla Luleälven during the short summer weeks, when the mosquitoes are at their most active. Along this valley is the town of **JOKKMOKK**, its name deriving from one particular bend (*mokk* in *Sámi*) in the river (*jokk*). The densely forested municipality through which the river runs is the size of Wales and has a tiny population: just 6500.

The town is a welcome oasis, although not an immediately appealing one. At one time winter quarters for the *Sámi*, by the beginning of the seventeenth century the site had a market and church, which heralded the start of a permanent settlement. Today, as well as being a well-known handicraft centre, Jokkmokk functions as the capital of the *Sámi* and is home to Samernas Folkhögskola, the only further education college in Sweden using the *Sámi* language, teaching handicraft-making, reindeer husbandry and ecology.

Arrival and information

From Arvidsjaur, 161km away, it's a three and a half-hour journey to Jokkmokk on the Inlandsbanan, or just over two hours on the Inlandsexpressen **bus**. If you're arriving here for the Winter Market (when the Inlandsbanan isn't running), take the **train** to Murjek (between Boden and Gällivare), from where bus #43 runs west to Jokkmokk. Jokkmokk's **tourist office**, **with internet access**, is at Stortorget 4 (mid-June to mid-Aug daily 9am–7pm, Sat & Sun 10am–6pm; mid-Aug to mid-June Mon–Fri 8.30am–noon & 1–4pm; during the Winter Market Thurs–Sat 9am–6pm, Sun noon–4pm; ℡0971/222 50, ⓦwww.turism.jokkmokk.se), five-minutes' stroll from the train station along Stationsgatan. You pass some of the prettiest houses and shops in Jokkmokk, oddly reminiscent of small-town America. The tourist office has all sorts of literature useful for planning a hike in the region.

Accommodation

Since **accommodation** options in Jokkmokk are rather limited, it's a good idea to book ahead, particularly during the summer months when the Inlandsbanan is running, as well as during the Winter Market, when a reservation is required at least two years in advance (if Jokkmokk is full, try looking for

A brief look at the Sámi

Among the oldest people in Europe, the **Sámi** – erroneously known to many as "Lapps" – are probably descended from the original prehistoric inhabitants of much of Scandinavia and northern Russia. Today there are around 58,000 *Sámi*, stretched across the whole of the northernmost regions of Norway, Sweden, Finland and Russia; traces of their nomadic culture have even been discovered as far south as Poland. In Sweden itself – though the population is declining – they number around 17,000 (ten percent of the population of northern Sweden), their domain extending over half the country, stretching up from the northern parts of Dalarna.

The *Sámi* **language** is a rich one, strongly influenced by their harmonious natural existence. There are no words for certain alien concepts (like "war"), but there are ninety different terms to express variations in snow conditions. One of the Finno-Ugric group of languages, which also contains Finnish and Hungarian, the *Sámi* language is divided into three dialects which are not mutually comprehensible. In Sweden you'll come across two words for *Sámi*: the politically correct *Sámi* (as used by the *Sámi* themselves), and, more commonly, the Swedish corruption *Same* (plural *Samer*). **Reindeer**, of which there are estimated to be 238,000 in Sweden, have been at the centre of *Sámi* life and culture for thousands of years, with generations of families following the seasonal movements of the animals. Accordingly, the *Sámi* year is divided into eight separate seasons, ranging from early spring, when they traditionally bring the reindeer cows up to the calving areas in the hills, through to winter, when they return to the forests and the pastures.

The *Sámi* were dealt a grievous blow by the **Chernobyl** nuclear disaster of 1986, which contaminated not only the lichen that their reindeer feed on in winter, but also the game, fish, berries and fungi that supplement their own diet. Contamination of reindeer meat meant the collapse of exports of the product to southern Scandinavia, Germany, America and the Far East; promises of government compensation came late in the day and failed to address the fact that this disaster wasn't just on an economic level for the *Sámi*, their traditional culture being inseparably tied to reindeer herding. However, perhaps as a consequence of Chernobyl, there has been an expansion in other areas of *Sámi* culture. Traditional **arts and crafts** have become popular and are widely available in craft shops, and *Sámi* **music** (characterized by the rhythmic sounds of *joik*, a form of throat-singing) is being given a hearing by fans of world music. On balance, it would appear that the *Sámi* are largely managing to retain their culture and identity in modern Sweden. For more on the *Sámi* in Sweden, visit Ⓦ www.sametinget.se.

---

rooms in Arvidsjaur and Gällivare). That said, the tourist office arranges simple dormitory accommodation in the local school for around 250kr per person, and puts together a list of **private rooms** at 500kr per person.

Gästis Herrevägen 1 ☏ 0971/100 12, Ⓦ www.hotell-gastis.com. Handily situated in the town centre, close to the train station, the simple brightly decorated en-suite rooms here are clean and tidy if lacking in character. There's an attractive sauna suite. ❹/❸

Jokkmokk Solgatan 45 ☏ 0971/777 00, Ⓦ www.hoteljokkmokk.se. In a pretty lakeside location, rooms here (ask for one with a lake view) are modern and comfortable. The restaurant, designed in the shape of a *kåta* and with great views of the lake, contains stuffed reindeer for authenticity. The sauna suite of red and white tiles in the basement is one of the best in northern Sweden. ❻/❹

Jokkmokk Camping Center Notudden ☏ 0971/123 70, Ⓦ www.jokkmokkcampingcenter .com. Located by the Lule River, 3km southeast of town off Route 97 towards Luleå, this pleasant campsite also has cabins (❷). The best way to get here is to rent a bike from the youth hostel per day.

Youth hostel Åsgatan 20 ☏ 0971/559 77, Ⓦ www.jokkmokkhostel.com. This wonderful old house, surrounded by a pretty garden, has a great central location and cosy double rooms (❶) as well as dorms (175kr). However, it fills fast so it's wise to book well in advance.

The Town

Jokkmokk's fascinating **Ájtte museum** (*ájtte* means storage hut in *Sámi*) is the place to really mug up on the *Sámi* (May to mid-June & mid-Aug to mid-Sept Mon–Fri 10am–4pm, Sat & Sun 11am–3pm; mid-June to mid-Aug daily 9am–6pm; mid-Sept to Aug Tues–Fri 10am–3pm; 50kr; ⓦ www.ajtte.com); it's a brief walk east of the centre at Kyrkogatan 3, which is off the main street, Storgatan. The displays and exhibitions recount the tough existence of northern Scandinavia's original settlers, and show how things have slowly improved over time – today the modern *Sámi* are more dependent on snow scooters and helicopters to herd their reindeer than on the age-old methods employed by their ancestors. The collection of traditional costumes and silver spoons, which gave the owner prestige and were a symbol of social status, is particularly engaging. The museum also has an impressive collection of stuffed eagles and owls; the enormous golden eagle is truly impressive.

Close to the museum on Lappstavägen, the **Fjällträdgård** (Alpine Garden; early June to mid-Aug Mon–Fri 11am–5pm; July to mid-Aug also Sat & Sun noon–5pm; 25kr, 50kr including Ájtte) is home to moor-king, mountain avens, glacier crowfoot and other vegetation that's found on the fells around Jokkmokk. There's also a small section of edible plants which the *Sámi* have traditionally used for medicinal purposes. Also worth a quick look is **Naturfoto** (July & Aug Mon–Fri 10am–6pm, Sat & Sun 10am–3pm; at other times by arrangement on ☎0971/557 65), in Klockartorget square near the corner of Klockarvägen and Storgatan; it's an exhibition of work by the local

---

The Arctic Circle and the midnight sun

Just 7km south of Jokkmokk, the Inlandsbanan finally crosses the **Arctic Circle**, the imaginary line drawn around the earth at roughly 66°N, which links the northernmost points along which the sun can be seen on the shortest day of the year. Crossing into the Arctic is occasion enough for a bout of whistle-blowing by the train, as it pulls up to allow everyone to take photos. However, the painted white rocks that curve away over the hilly ground here, a crude delineation of the Circle, are completely inaccurate. Due to the earth's uneven orbit, the line is creeping northwards at a rate of 14–15m every year; the real Arctic Circle is now around a kilometre further north than this line. It won't be for another ten to twenty thousand years that the northward movement will stop – by which time the Circle will have reached 68°N – and then start moving slowly south again.

Thanks to the refraction of sunlight in the atmosphere, the **midnight sun** can also be seen south of the Arctic Circle – Arvidsjaur marks the southernmost point in Sweden where this happens – for a few days each year. The further north you travel, the longer the period when the phenomenon is visible, and conversely the longer the polar winter. True midnight sun occurs when the entire sun is above the horizon at midnight. The following is a list of the main towns and the dates when the midnight sun can be seen; remember, though, that even outside these periods, there is still 24-hour daylight in the north of Sweden in summer, since only part of the sun ever dips below the horizon.

Arvidsjaur and Haparanda	June 20/21
Arjeplog	June 12/13 to July 28/29
Jokkmokk	June 8/9 to July 2/3
Gällivare	June 4/5 to July 6/7
Kiruna	May 28/29 to July 11/12
Karesuando	May 26/27 to July 15/16
Treriksröset	May 22/23 to July 17/18

wilderness photographer, Edvin Nilsson, and a good place to pick up a few postcards or posters.

Have a look, too, at the **Lapp kyrka** (daily 8am–4pm, until 6pm early June to early Aug) off Stortorget, a recent copy of the 1753 church on the same site (the original burnt down in 1972). The octagonal design, curiously shaped tower and colours inside the church represent *Sámi* styles; outside, notice the space in between the coarsely hewn timbers which was used to store coffins during winter, waiting for the thaw in May when the *Sámi* could go out and dig graves again (temperatures in this part of Sweden regularly plunge to -30°C and below).

During the summer, Talvatissjön, the lake behind *Hotel Jokkmokk*, is the preferred spot for catching Arctic char and rainbow trout. To **fish** here you'll need a **permit** (*fiskekort*), available from the tourist office. There's a barbecue on the lakeside behind the hotel, should you catch anything. It's also possible to go **canoeing** on the unspoilt surrounding lakes and rivers as well as **hiking** in the nearby national parks. For more information and bookings, contact Jokkmokkguiderna (☎0971/122 20, ⓦwww.jokkmokkguiderna.com) who're based in the village of Skabram, 3km west of Jokkmokk. They'll collect you from Jokkmokk once you've made a firm booking.

The Winter Market

Known simply in Swedish as *Jokkmokks marknad*, the town's 400-year-old **Great Winter Market** (ⓦwww.jokkmokksmarknad.com) traces its origins back to 1602, when King Karl IX decreed that a series of market sites should be set up in the north to help extend Swedish territory and increase taxes to fund his many wars. A chapel, a parsonage and a row of market sheds were built in Jokkmokk, and the rest is history. Today the market is held on the first Thursday to Sunday of each February, when thirty thousand people force their way into town – ten times the normal population. It's the best (and coldest) time of year to be here; with lots of drunken stallholders trying to flog reindeer hides and other unwanted knick-knacks to even more drunken passers-by, there's a Wild West feeling in the air at this time. Held on the frozen Talvatissjön lake behind *Hotell Jokkmokk* (see p.366), the **reindeer races** run during the market can be a real spectacle, as man and beast battle it out on a specially marked-out ice track. The reindeer, however, often have other ideas and every now and then veer off with great alacrity into the crowd, sending spectators fleeing for cover. A smaller, historical market is held on the proceeding Monday to Wednesday, when people dress in traditional costume and put on various theatrical performances.

Eating and drinking

Jokkmokk's range of **eating** and **drinking** possibilities isn't huge, and as there's no proper pub or bar here, the restaurants double as drinking dens. At the cheap and cheerful *Restaurang Kowloon* (☎0971/100 56), Föreningsgatan 3, lunch is 65kr and Chinese meals start at 99kr at other times. *Restaurang Opera* (☎0971/105 05), Storgatan 36, is the cheapest place in town for reindeer meat, which is usually available at lunchtime, though there are also pizzas, salads and a rather uninspiring range of meat and fish à la carte dishes. For traditional Swedish and *Sámi* home cooking, head for the restaurant inside the Ájtte museum at Kyrkogatan 3 (☎0971/170 70), where lunch deals go for 70kr; there are also a couple of reindeer dishes on the menu. For pastries and a cup of coffee, try *City Konditoriet* at Storgatan 28, which also serves up good sandwiches.

Gällivare and around

Seven hundred and fifty kilometres north of Östersund, the Inlandsbanan finally reaches its last stop, **GÄLLIVARE**, two and a quarter hours up the line from Jokkmokk. Although the town is not immediately appealing, it is one of the few relatively sizeable ones in this part of northern Sweden, and it's a good idea to spend a day or two here enjoying the relative civilization before striking out in the wilds beyond – Gällivare is a good starting point for walking in the national parks, which fill most of the northwestern corner of the country (see p.371). The town is also one of the most important areas for iron ore in Europe – if you have any interest in seeing a working mine, don't wait until Kiruna's tame "tourist tour" (see p.376); instead, take a trip down the more evocative mines here.

Arrival and information

The **train station** is on Lasarettsgatan, next door to the **tourist office** at Centralplan 3 (mid-June to mid-Aug daily 8am–10pm; mid-Aug to mid-June Mon–Fri 8am–5pm; ☎0970/166 60, ⓦwww.visit.gellivare.se), which has good free maps, hiking information and internet access. Gällivare is an easy place to walk around, with nearly everything you could want located east of the train line

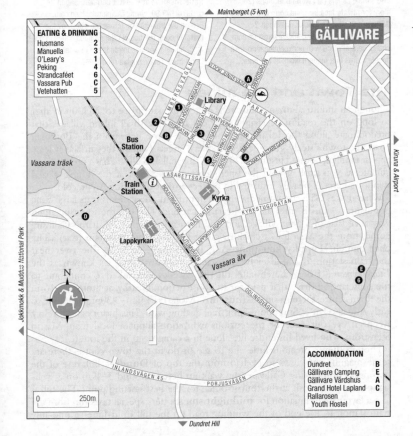

▲ Malmberget (5 km)

GÄLLIVARE

EATING & DRINKING

Husmans	2
Manuella	3
O'Leary's	1
Peking	4
Strandcaféet	6
Vassara Pub	C
Vetehatten	5

Library

Bus Station

Vassara träsk

Train Station ⓘ

Kyrka

Lappkyrkan

Vassara älv

N

▲ Jokkmokk & Muddus National Park

▲ Kiruna & Airport

ACCOMMODATION

Dundret	B
Gällivare Camping	E
Gällivare Värdshus	A
Grand Hotel Lapland	C
Rallarosen Youth Hostel	D

0   250m

▼ Dundret Hill

(except the youth hostel, which is west of the tracks). The main sight in town, **Lappkyrkan**, is barely five minutes on foot from the centre. Outside Gällivare in Malmberget, the mines are easily reached on bus #1 and #2.

Accommodation

Advance bookings for places to **stay** in Gällivare are a good idea from mid-June to mid-August, when, thanks to its strategic location at the junction of two major rail routes, the town receives trainloads of backpackers. It's a wonderful place to stay in winter when the Vassara träsk lake is frozen and snow scooters whizz up and down its length under the eerie northern lights, which are clearly visible in Gällivare.

Dundret Per Högströmsgatan 1 ℡ 0970/550 40, ⓦ www.hotelldundret.se. A small, friendly guesthouse with just eight comfortable rooms and shared facilities. ❸

Gällivare Camping Malmbergsvägen 2 ℡ 0970/100 10, ⓦ www.gellivarecamping.com. Open all year and close to the centre by the river, off Porjusvägen (Route 45 to Jokkmokk). There are also simple cabins (❶) with no facilities (200kr more for private facilities) and dorm beds (180kr).

Gällivare Värdshus Klockljungsvägen 2 ℡ 0970/162 00, ⓦ www.gellivarevardshus.com. A cheap, central place with unexceptional no-frills double rooms in a modern block of red brick

resembling a school, close to the swimming pool. There's also a sauna on site. ❹/❸

Grand Hotel Lapland Lasarettsgatan 1 ℡ 0970/77 22 90, ⓦ www.grandhotellapland.com. The best of the bunch in the town centre, with smart, tastefully decorated rooms and a good restaurant (see opposite); sit in the sauna and enjoy views of the station and the main street below. ❻/❹

Rallarrosen youth hostel Barnhemsvägen 2A ℡ 0970/143 80, ⓔ info@explorelapland.com. Behind the train station (cross the tracks by the metal bridge), the hostel offers a good sauna in the main buiding and accommodation in small cabins. Dorm beds 150kr, double rooms ❶

The Town and the mines

Though an industrial town, Gällivare is quite a pleasant place to fetch up in after so long on the road; it's certainly a far cry from the small inland villages that predominate along the Inlandsbanan. If you've come here from the Bothnian coast, the town's steely grey mesh of modern streets will, on the surface at least, appear familiar. Located just north of the 67th parallel, Gällivare has a pretty severe climate: as you stroll around the open centre, have a look at the double-glazed windows here, all heavily insulated to protect against the biting Arctic cold.

What makes Gällivare immediately different from other towns is its large *Sámi* population – this is, after all, the heart of Lapland. The site the town occupies was once that of a *Sámi* village, and one theory has it that the name Gällivare comes from the *Sámi* for "a crack or gorge (*djelli*) in the mountain (*vare*)". The *Sámi* church, **Lappkyrkan** (June–Aug 10am–3pm), down by the river near the train station, is a mid-eighteenth-century construction; it's known as the *Ettöreskyrkan* ("1 öre" church) after the sum Swedes were asked to contribute to the subscription drive that paid for its construction. Nearby, at Storgatan 16 in the town centre, there's a simple **museum** (Mon–Fri 11am–3.30pm, late June to early Aug also Sat & Sun noon–2pm; free) dealing with *Sámi* history and forestry. Keep an eye out, too, for the curious exhibition about a local man, Martin Stenström, who lived his entire life alone in a cabin deep in the forest.

Though there's precious little else to see or do in the town centre, there are some magnificent views to be had from the top of **Dundret** hill, one of the two peaks dominating Gällivare; the walk up here is around 3–4km on a well-signposted path – ask at the tourist office for the best starting point. The hill is also a favourite destination for **midnight sun** spotters; special taxis run from the train station to the end of the winding road up the hill (mid-June to mid-July

daily 11pm; mid-July to end July daily 10pm; early to mid-Aug daily 9.30pm).
Tickets, available from the tourist office, cost 140kr return.

The mines at Malmberget

Tucked away at **Malmberget**, the other hill that overlooks the town, the
modern mines and works are distant, dark blots down which the tourist office
ferries relays of tourists in summer. There are two separate tours, both running
from mid-June to mid-August: one of the underground *LKAB* **iron-ore mine**
(daily 9.30am; 250kr), the other to the open-cast **copper mine** known as *Aitik*
(Mon, Wed & Fri 2pm; 220kr), the largest of its kind in Europe (and also
Sweden's biggest gold mine – the metal is recovered from the slag produced
during the extraction of the copper). The ear-splitting noise produced from the
mammoth-sized trucks (they're five times the height of a human being) in the
iron-ore mine can be quite disconcerting in the confined darkness.

Around Gällivare

To dip into *Sámi* culture – meet (and taste) reindeer, and see how the *Sámi*
make their handicrafts and throw lassoes – you can visit the nearby Purnu **Sámi
camp** with Arctic Light Safari whose office in Gällivare is at Klockaregatan 5
(T070/547 30 65; W www.arcticlightsafari.se). You're likely to return smelling of
wood smoke after sitting around an open fire inside a traditional *kåta*, so don't
wear your best gear.

Eating and drinking

If you're arriving from one of the tiny villages on the Inlandsbanan, the wealth
of **eating** possibilities in Gällivare will make you quite dizzy; if you're coming
from Luleå, grit your teeth and bear it.

Husmans Malmbergsvägen 1 T0970/170 30. A
simple cafeteria-style place with various Swedish
home-style dishes on the menu, plus a variety of
burgers and sausages: lunch here is served all day.
Manuella Storgatan 9 T0970/123 80. A busy
though quite small Italian restaurant serving a
range of pizzas (55kr) and pasta dishes (60kr) as
well as a couple of steaks (69kr).
O'Leary's Per Högströmsgatan 9 T0970/77 22 80.
Having closed down in neighbouring Kiruna,
O'Leary's are now open in Gällivare with the usual
sports bar atmosphere and range of burgers and
other TexMex pub grub.
Peking Storgatan 21B T0970/176 85. A long-
established and reasonable Chinese restaurant with

mains from 110kr, as well as pizzas from 85kr.
Closed Mon.
Strandcaféet Malmbergsvägen 2. Beautifully
located campsite café right by the graceful Vassara
river with a small range of open sandwiches and
cakes. Open until 10pm, but closed Sept–May.
Vassara Pub Lasarettsgatan 1 T0970/77 22 90.
Although a little pretentious and expensive, this
bar-restaurant does a range of good lunches and
serves excellent local delicacies such as Arctic
char and reindeer. There's a range of Swedish
home cooking classics every evening.
Vetehatten Storgatan 16. A Gällivare institution,
right in the town centre and serving up a selection
of sandwiches and gooey cakes.

Swedish Lapland's national parks

It's not a good idea to go **hiking in the national parks** of northern Sweden on
a whim. Even for experienced walkers, the going can be tough and uncomfortable
in parts, downright treacherous in others. The best **time to go** hiking is from late
June to September: during May and early June the ground is still very wet and
boggy as a result of the rapid snow melt. Once the snow has gone, wild flowers
burst into bloom, making the most of the short summer months. The weather is

The Laponia World Heritage Area

"It is one of the last and unquestionably largest and best preserved examples of an area of transhumance, involving summer grazing by large reindeer herds", said the UNESCO World Heritage Committee when they established **Laponia** as a **heritage area** in 1996. Covering a vast area of 9400 square kilometres, including the Padjelanta, Sarek and Stora Sjöfallet **national parks**, Laponia is the home and workplace of Forest and Mountain **Sámi** families from seven different villages, who still tend their reindeer here much as their ancestors did in prehistoric times. The Forest *Sámi* move with their herds within the forests and the Mountain *Sámi* follow their animals from the lichen-rich forests, where they spend the winter, up to the tree line by the time spring comes, then on into the mountains for summer; in August they start making their way down. Come September, many animals will be slaughtered either at the **corrals** in Ruokto, on the road between Porjus and Kebnats, or at highland corrals between Ritsem and Sitasjaure.

very changeable – one moment it can be hot and sunny, the next it can be cold and rainy – and snow showers are not uncommon in summer.

Mosquitoes are a real problem: it's difficult to describe the utter misery of being covered in a blanket of insects, your eyes, ears and nose full of the creatures. Yet the beautiful landscape here is one of the last wilderness areas left in Europe – it's one vast expanse of forest and mountains, where roads and human habitation are the exception rather than the norm. **Reindeer** are a common sight, as the parks are their breeding grounds and summer pasture, and **Sámi** settlements are dotted throughout the region – notably at **Ritsem** and **Vaisaluokta**.

The hiking trails in the five **national parks** (ⓦwww.fjallen.nu) here range in difficulty from moderately challenging to a positive assault course. Four of the parks lie about 120km northwest of Gällivare in the tract of Swedish wilderness edging Norway, whereas easy **Muddus** national park lies between Gällivare and Jokkmokk. The low fells, large lakes and moors of **Padjelanta**, **Stora Sjöfallet** and **Abisko** parks (see p.383 for more on the latter) act as the eyebrows to the sheer face of the mountainous and inhospitable **Sarek** park (ⓦwww.fjallen.nu /parker/sarek.htm). Classed as "extremely difficult", Sarek (not covered in this book) has no tourist facilities, trails, cabins or bridges; the rivers are dangerous and the weather rotten – in short, you need good mountaineering experience to tackle it. For coverage of the Kungsleden hiking trail, see p.379.

Muddus national park

Recommended for novice hikers, **Muddus national park** (ⓦwww.fjallen .nu/parker/muddus.htm) is a five-hundred-square-kilometre pine-forested and marshland park between Jokkmokk and Gällivare, hemmed in by the Inlandsbanan on one side and the train line from Luleå to Gällivare on the other. Muddus is home to bears, lynx, martens, weasels, hares, elk and (in summer), also reindeer; among birds, the whooper swan is one of the most common sights. The terrain here is gently undulating, consisting of bog and forest, though there are clefts and gorges in the southern stretches. The park's western edges are skirted by Route 45; the easiest approach is to leave the highway at **Liggadammen** (there are also buses here from Gällivare) and then follow the small road to **Skaite**, where an easy hiking **trail** begins; two suggested routes are Skaite–Muddusfallet–Måskoskårså–Skaite (24km) or Skaite–Mudduaeluobbal–Manson–Skaite (44km). There are cabins along the trail (April–Sept; rest of the year keys can be obtained from Jokkmokk and

Gällivare tourist offices), and a campsite at Muddus Falls. There are no outlets for buying food or provisions en route.

Padjelanta and Stora Sjöfallet national parks

Padjelanta (@www.fjallen.nu/parker/padje.htm) is the largest of Sweden's national parks; its name comes from *Sámi* and means "the higher country", an apt description for this plateau that lies almost exclusively above the tree line. The **Padjelanta trail** (150km) runs from **Vaisaluokta** through the **Laponia World Heritage Area** (see box opposite) south to **Kvikkjokk**, and is suited to inexperienced walkers – allow at least a week to finish it. You can get to Vaisaluokta by taking a **bus** from Gällivare to Ritsem (which will take you through the beautiful **Stora Sjöfallet** national park (@www.fjallen.nu/parker /storasjo.htm) with its luxuriant forests and sweeping vistas, from where a boat takes you across Akkajaure lake to Vaisaluokta (details at @www.stfturist.se /ritsem). To get to Kvikkjokk, hop on a bus in Jokkmokk; times are at @www .ltnbd.se. There's also a helicopter service, operated by Lapplandsflyg, between Kvikkjokk, Staloluokta and Ritsem (late June to early Sept daily; 1530kr per person over whole route, 850kr over part of route; ☏0971/210 40, @www .lapplandsflyg.se).

For **accommodation**, there's an STF mountain cabin at Ritsem (☏0973/420 30, @www.stfturist.se/ritsem; dorm beds 345kr; mid-Feb to early May & mid-June to late Sept) and a **youth hostel** at the end of the trail, in Kvikkjokk (☏0971/210 22, @www.stfturist.se/kvikkjokk; dorm beds 375kr; Feb–April & mid-June to Sept); simpler **cabins** can be found elsewhere along the route and wardens have information about the nearest **food** stores.

Kiruna and around

One hundred and twenty-three kilometres northwest of Gällivare, **KIRUNA** (the town's name comes from the *Sámi* word "Giron", meaning "ptarmigan") was the hub of the battle for the control of the iron-ore supply during World War II; ore was transported north from here by train to the great harbour at Narvik, over the border in Norway. Much German firepower was expended in an attempt to interrupt the supply to the Allies and wrest control for the Axis. In the process, Narvik suffered grievously, whilst Kiruna – benefiting from supposed Swedish neutrality – made a packet selling to both sides. Today the train ride to Kiruna, 200km north of the Arctic Circle, rattles through sidings, slag heaps and ore works, a bitter contrast to the surrounding wilderness.

Partly due to its proximity to the world-famous **Icehotel** in the nearby village of **Jukkasjärvi**, and partly because it's the most northerly town in Sweden, Kiruna has become *the* destination in Swedish Lapland, the place that everyone wants to visit. However, don't come here expecting monumental architectural delights, tree-lined avenues and big-city sophistication – it has none of that, at least not for the time being. All that, however, could change when the town ups sticks and moves location for, indeed, that is what is set to happen over the next decade. Due to severe **subsidence** from the mines over one kilometre below the town, Kiruna is sinking. In January 2007 plans were formalized to move the entire city to the northwest of its current site, near Luossavaara hill. First to relocate will be the railway station and the E10 highway, followed by individual houses, which will be loaded onto trailers for transportation. Oddly, local people seem unperturbed by the enormity of the task ahead, perhaps because they are painfully aware that without the iron-ore mines on which Kiruna is dependent, the place would cease to exist.

Ahead of the move, the present town still retains a strangely likeable down-to-earth feel. Although there are a few sights, it's attractive as a base from which to visit this corner of northern Lapland, with rail connections northwest to the start of the Kungsleden trail (see p.379) and Riksgränsen, as well as bus connections into the Torne Valley (see p.384). Sweden's highest mountain, **Kebnekaise** (2114m), is also within easy reach of Kiruna. It's accessed from the tiny village of **Nikkaluokta**, the departure point for ambitious ascents of the peak.

Arrival and information

The **train** station is at Bangårdsvägen, from where it's a brisk ten-minute walk up the steep road, Konduktörsgatan, to the **tourist office** (mid-June to Aug Mon–Fri 8.30am–8pm, Sat & Sun 8.30am–5pm; Sept to mid-June Mon–Fri 8.30am–5pm, Sat 8.30am–3pm; ℡0980/188 80, ⊛www.lappland.se) in Folkets Hus, on the central square off Mommagatan where there's also internet access. The **bus station** is at the corner of Biblioteksgatan and Hjalmar Lundbohmsvägen. Served by flights from London Heathrow (winter only), Stockholm and Umeå, the **airport**, 10km away to the east, is linked to town by bus (June to mid-Sept only; 40kr); taxis (250kr) run all year round. There is also an airport bus to and from Narvik, over the border in Norway (⊛www.flybussen.no).

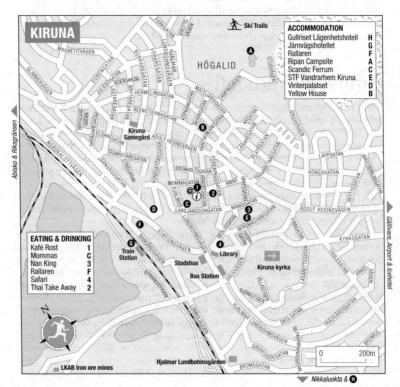

Accommodation

Kiruna is not overburdoned with accommodation choices. It pays, therefore, to book in advance, especially during the winter season when the town is at its busiest; many people combine an overnight stay in town with a trip to *Icehotel*.

Gullriset Lägenhetshotell Bromsgatan 12 ☎0980/109 37, ⒲www.fabmf.se/gullriset. A good choice of modern apartments for one to four people costing 450–790kr depending on size, perfect for self-catering. All have private bathrooms and kitchens.

Järnvägshotellet Bangårdsvägen 7 ☎0980/844 44, ⒲www.jarnvagshotellet.com. Located on the main platform of the train station, this rambling old timber building (totally no-smoking) has been restored as a hotel. Rooms are comfortable and spacious, though plainly decorated – noise from the passing iron-ore trains can be a problem. ❸

Rallaren Bangårdsvägen 4 ☎0980/611 26, ⒲www.hotelrallaren.se. Snug, individually decorated rooms in *Sámi* colours and styles in an old wooden structure down by the railway. There are also two *kåtor* for rent immediately outside. ❸/❺

Ripan campsite Campingvägen 5 ☎0980/630 00, ⒲www.ripan.se. Located up in the Högalid part of town (a 20min walk from the centre), this pleasant campsite also has four-berth cabins (❹/❺) and ice igloos (Dec–April; ❻).

Scandic Ferrum Lars Janssongatan 15 ☎0980/39 86 00, ⒲www.scandichotels.se/ferrum.

By far the most expensive place in town, with characterless chain-hotel rooms and indifferent staff, but the palatial sauna suite on the top floor is a wonderful place to relax and watch the midnight sun. ❹/❺

STF Vandrarhem Kiruna Bergmästaregatan 7 ☎0980/171 95, ⒲www.kirunahostel.com. Dorm beds (in rooms sleeping up to ten people) at 210kr are the best option at this centrally located youth hostel since double rooms are rather pricey ❸. Boasting its own sauna, it fills quickly and reservations are necessary at any time of year.

Vinterpalatset Järnvägsgatan 18 ☎0980/677 70, ⒲www.vinterpalatset.se. A listed building with wooden floors, large double beds and rooms decorated with antique furniture. There's also a superb sauna and Jacuzzi suite on the top floor. You'll find four cheaper, more basic rooms in the annexe. ❸/❺

Yellow House Hantverkaregatan 25 ☎0980/137 50, ⒲www.yellowhouse.nu. Budget hotel-cum-youth hostel with dorm beds (140kr) and double rooms sharing facilities. Linen is not included in the room rate but is available for 50kr extra per stay. ❶

The Town

When Swedish pioneers first arrived in what is now Kiruna in the early 1600s, they found the *Sámi* already in place here. Completely ignoring the indigenous population, the Swedes opened their first mine in 1647 at nearby Masugnsbyn ("Blast Furnace Village"), but it wasn't until the beginning of the following century that the **iron-ore** deposits in Kiruna itself were finally discovered. Exploratory drilling began in the 1880s, which nicely coincided with the building of the **Malmbanan**, the iron-ore railway between Luleå and Narvik in Norway, and the first train laden with iron ore trundled out from Malmberget in Gällivare in March 1888. In 1900, the settlers braved their first winter in Kiruna, a year which is now regarded as the town's birthday. Built on a hill to try to keep the temperature up (warm air rises), Kiruna was planned to withstand the coldest snaps of winter – even the streets are curved as protection against the biting polar wind. Sadly, though, much of the wooden architecture of Kiruna's early days, gloriously painted in reds, greens and yellows, was ripped down to make way for today's unprepossessing concrete structures; the town even won an award in the 1960s for its out-with-the-old-in-with-the-new policy.

Not surprisingly, most sights are firmly wedded to iron in one way or another. The tower of the **Stadshus** is a strident metal pillar, designed by Bror Marklund and harbouring an intricate latticework clock face and 23 sundry bells that chime raucously; incomprehensibly, the Stadshus won an award in 1964 for being the most beautiful Swedish public building. Inside, there's a tolerable art collection and, in summer, occasional displays of *Sámi* handicrafts.

Sunrise and sunset in Stockholm and Kiruna

	Stockholm		Kiruna	
	Sunrise	Sunset	Sunrise	Sunset
January	8.47am	2.55pm	24hr darkness	
February	8.01am	4.01pm	8.59am	2.45pm
March	6.48am	5.12pm	7.02am	4.41am
April	6.17am	7.26pm	5.52am	7.33pm
May	4.52am	8.37pm	3.43am	9.29pm
June	3.47am	9.44pm	24hr daylight	
July	3.40am	10.02pm	24hr daylight	
August	4.35am	9.13pm	3.02am	10.29pm
September	5.46am	7.50pm	5.08am	8.10pm
October	5.54am	5.21pm	5.53am	5.04pm
November	7.08am	3.54pm	7.50am	2.55pm
December	8.19am	2.54pm	10.14am	12.41pm

The **mines**, ugly brooding reminders of Kiruna's prosperity, still dominate the town, much more depressingly so than in Gällivare; despite its new central buildings and open parks, Kiruna retains a grubby industrial feel. The tourist office arranges **guided tours** around the mines (mid-June to mid-Aug 4 daily; early June & late Aug 2 daily; 280kr), on which visitors are bussed down into the *InfoMine*, a closed-off section of the rabbit warren of tunnels comprising a working mine. Inside you'll see facilities such as petrol stations and a workers' canteen, and mining paraphernalia, including trains for transporting ore and equipment, and mills for crushing the ore-bearing rock.

Back in town, **Kiruna kyrka**, on Kyrkogatan (daily 11am–4.45pm), causes a few raised eyebrows when people see it for the first time: built in the style of a *Sámi* hut and the size of a small aircraft hangar, it's an origami-like creation of oak beams and rafters. LKAB, the iron-ore company (and the town's main employer) which paid for its construction, was also responsible for the **Hjalmar Lundbohmsgården** at Ingenjörsgatan 1 (Tues, Thurs & Fri 8am–4pm, Wed 10am–4pm; 35kr), fifteen-minutes' walk away (take Gruvvägen south, turn left at Hjalmar Lundbohmsvägen, then right into Ingenjörsgatan). The displays in this country house, once used by the former managing director of LKAB, who was the town's "founder", consist mostly of early twentieth-century photographs featuring the man himself and his personal study, much as he left it. Try to visit the house in order to get a perspective on the town's history before going down the mine; you'll be all the more aware afterwards how, without the mine, Kiruna would be a one-reindeer town instead of the thriving place it is today – quite a feat when you consider its location on the map (don't be surprised to see snow on the slag heaps in the middle of June).

For the most rewarding exhibition of *Sámi* culture in town, head for the handi-craft centre, **Kiruna Samegård**, at Brytaregatan 14 (Mon–Fri 7am–noon & 1–4pm; 20kr). The handicrafts you'll see here may well be familiar by now; what probably won't be is its small but impressive display of *Sámi* art featuring scenes from everyday life in the north. It also has a souvenir shop, where you can pick up a piece of antler bone or reindeer skin.

Eating and drinking

Eating and **drinking** in Kiruna is not a joy. Restaurants and bars are few and far between, and in summer you may even find several closed: frustratingly, the staff take their holidays just when the town is full of tourists. That said, Kiruna is a good place to try some traditional *Sámi* delicacies such as reindeer.

Kafé Rost Located inside Folkets Hus in the main square, off Mommagatan. This open-plan first-floor café serves up decent sandwiches, including reindeer in pitta bread, as well as baked potatoes and pasta salads. It's also a good place from which to take in Kiruna's goings-on, with an outside terrace in summer.

Mommas Lars Janssonsgatan 15 ☎ 0980/39 86 07. Inside the Scandic Ferrum hotel, this American-style steakhouse with wooden booths, serves up good burgers (135kr), steaks (210kr) and sautéed reindeer with mash and lingonberries (145kr).

Nan King Mangigatan 26 ☎ 0980/174 80. This friendly little restaurant is the most northerly Chinese restaurant in Sweden, serving – besides the expected fare – pizza and spaghetti. Main dishes, for example Szechuan fried beef with bamboo shoots, from 110kr. Closed Mon.

Rallaren Bangårdsvägen 4 ☎ 0980/611 26. *The* place for northern Swedish food in Kiruna, with a menu featuring reindeer steak in red wine sauce (225kr), game meat gratin (149kr) and thinly sliced reindeer and elk meat with mashed potatoes (99kr).

Safari Geologgatan 4. A charming café with elegant wallpaper and wooden floors that's easily the best choice in town for tea, coffee, sandwiches, salads and baked potatoes, with outdoor seating in summer and a curiously continental feel.

Thai Take Away Föreningsgatan 17 ☎ 0980/608 44. At last, decent Thai food has arrived in Kiruna, albeit lacking the fire of the original. A good selection of vegetarian (95kr) and meat mains, such as green pork curry, from 125kr, though the lunch buffet of three or four dishes is arguably the best deal.

Jukkasjärvi and Icehotel

An obvious destination for any tourist travelling around Kiruna in winter is the tiny village of **JUKKASJÄRVI** (known locally simply as "Jukkas"), 17km east of Kiruna and 200km north of the Arctic Circle, and the location for Swedish Lapland's blockbuster attraction: **Icehotel**. What's effectively the world's largest igloo, *Icehotel* is built every year by the side of the Torneälven river in late October, from when it stands proudly until temperatures rise definitively above zero in May, and it finally melts away back into the river.

Jukkasjärvi village

Although *Icehotel* totally dominates tiny Jukkasjärvi from its position at the entrance to the village, it's worth taking a stroll down the main (and only) road, Marknadsvägen, passing a handful of simple dwellings owned by locals – not all of whom are in favour of the changes that the hotel has brought to their village. A much more traditional sight awaits at the end of the dead-end road: an old wooden *Sámi* **church** (daily: June–Aug 8am–10pm; rest of the year 8am–8pm), parts of which date from 1608, making it the oldest surviving church in Lapland. Check out the richly decorated altarpiece by Uppsala artist Bror Hjorth, depicting the revivalist preacher, **Lars Levi Laestadius** (see p.387), alongside the woman who inspired him to rid Lapland of alcohol, Maria of Åsele. The triptych was given to the church in 1958 by the mining company, LKAB, who were then celebrating their 350th anniversary.

Under the floor are the mummified remains of villagers who died here in the eighteenth century (not on display). The sandy ground and frost are thought to have been responsible for keeping the bodies, including that of a woman dressed in a white wedding dress and high-heel shoes, so remarkably well preserved. The organ above the door is made from reindeer horn and birch wood; the artwork in the centre of the organ, suspended over the pipes, symbolizes the sun rising over the Lapporten (see p.381), the two U-shaped mountain tops near Abisko which are one Lapland's most enduring images. Across the road from the church, the wooden houses of the tedious **Hembygdsgården** (Homestead

Museum; daily 10am–5pm; 90kr) contain the usual suspects: a stuffed reindeer, an old sleigh, a rickety spinning wheel and other equally dull paraphernalia.

Icehotel

The brains behind **Icehotel** belong to Yngve Bergqvist, a southern Swede who moved to Lapland thirty-odd years ago. In 1989, he built an igloo – barely sixty square metres in size – as an art gallery to showcase local *Sámi* crafts and design. Visitors asked to sleep in the igloo, and the concept was born. Today, covering a colossal 5000 square metres, *Icehotel* is constructed of thirty thousand tonnes of snow and four thousand tonnes of ice (cut from the Torne River); its exact shape and design changes from year to year, though there's always a chapel, in which couples can marry. From the entrance hall there's usually one main walkway filled with ice **sculptures**, from which smaller corridors lead off to the bedrooms and suites (all with electric lights, and beds made out of blocks of compact snow covered with reindeer hides) which make up the bulk of the hotel.

There are two reception areas – one for cold accommodation (*Icehotel* itself) and another for warm accommodation (double rooms and cabins); simply follow the direction signs. Staff in the cold reception will dish out warm clothing and general information about how to survive a night in sub-zero temperatures. When it's time to go to bed, you should leave your valuables and most of your clothes in lockers provided close to reception (where there are also heated bathrooms with showers and a sauna) and then make a run for it from here to your room (wearing as little as possible; see below) and dive into your sleeping bag as quickly as you can – the temperature inside the hotel is –5C, outside it's generally around –20 or –30C. Guests are provided with specially made, tried-and-tested **sleeping bags** of a type used by the Swedish army, who have used the hotel for Arctic survival training; the bags are supposed to keep you warm in temperatures down to -35°C. However, as they enclose your entire body and head (bar a small area for your eyes and nose) they are rather claustrophobic. You should take off all the clothes you're still wearing and sleep naked to prevent sweating; stuff your clothes into the bottom of the sleeping bag to keep them warm and place your shoes on the bed with you to stop them freezing. Don't expect to sleep – you won't – it's simply too cold and uncomfortable. In the morning, you can refresh yourself with a sauna and have a hearty breakfast at the restaurant across the road, though you'll soon notice from people's faces that nobody else has slept a wink either.

Whilst there is no doubt that this is one of the most unusual places in the world to spend a night, simply seeing *Icehotel* is an experience in itself and it's possible to visit the structure and take a tour of the adjoining **ice factory** without staying here; **day visitors have access to** *Icehotel* until 6pm daily. One-hour tours (295kr) take in both the hotel and the fascinating ice factory – it's here that the collosal blocks of ice that will be used to construct the following year's hotel are stored after being carved out of the Torne River each February and March.

Practicalities

Icehotel is open from early December until it thaws, and the dubious pleasure of spending a night in the freezer doesn't come cheap – we've given the high-season Thurs–Sun prices (less expensive rates Mon–Wed), which apply from January to mid-April; the low-season rate is applicable for most of December, including Christmas. Special prices apply at New Year and over Valentine's Day. The simplest double rooms, known as **snow rooms**, cost 3800kr per night, while a more stylish ice room decorated with furniture made of ice and adorned with ice carvings and ornaments, is 4900kr; a similar, though larger ice suite is 5800kr, and a top-of-the-range **deluxe suite** with more sculptures than you can shake an ice pick at is 7000kr. As for warm accommodation, prices are identical (3395kr per night) where you choose a regular double room, known as *kaamos* (Finnish for twilight or polar night) and beautifully designed in modern Scandinavian style, or a more homely **cabin** complete with kitchen (Dec–April ❻; May–Nov ❹). Warm and cold accommodation can be booked through *Icehotel*, Marknadsvägen 63 (☎0980/668 00, 🌐www .icehotel.com); you should book in advance, especially in the January–March peak season.

Organized **activities** include a dog-sledding trip through the neighbouring forests with a short stop for coffee and cake (1595kr; 1hr 30min); an accompanied daytime drive on snow scooters down the Torne River and into the wintry forests (895kr; 1hr 30min); or a night-time snow-scooter spin to see the northern lights (1750kr; 4hr). In **summer** there's generally organized fishing and hunting tours as well as canoeing, though exact details change from year to year and prices are available on the website.

You can **eat** all meals across the road at *Icehotel Restaurant* (winter only; ☎0980/668 84) which has a good selection of tasty northern Swedish specialities in the range of 200–300kr; there are also two **bars** here, one attached to the restaurant and one in the basement. The cosier *Old Homestead* restaurant (open all year), housed in the former village school from 1768, is less expensive but serves an equally tasty range of local specialities. The outdoor terrace, open in summer, has good views of the Torne River. For **provisions**, you'll find a small supermarket in the village.

To get to Jukkasjärvi from Kiruna, take bus #501 (🌐www.ltnbd.se; 20min). Undoubtedly the best way to arrive, though, is by **dog sledge** from Kiruna airport; for a hefty 5900kr (price includes up to four people) you can be met at your plane and pulled all the way to your room; you can arrange this via *Icehotel*.

Nikkaluokta and Kebnekaise

Nikkaluokta, 66km west of Kiruna and reached on the twice-daily bus, is the starting point for treks towards and up Sweden's highest mountain, **Kebnekaise** (2114m). From the village, a nineteen-kilometre trail leads to the **fjällstation** mountain lodge at Kebnekaise (☎0980/550 00, 🌐www.stfkebnekaise.com; dorm beds 410kr, double room ❷; mid-Feb to early May & mid-June to mid-Sept) at the foot of the mountain. The mountain was first conquered in 1883 by a Frenchman, Charles Robot; today it can be reached in 8–9 hours by anyone in decent physical condition. Two paths lead to the peak: the eastern route goes over Björling glacier, includes some climbing and is only recommended for experts; the western route is much longer and is the one most people opt for.

The Kungsleden

The **Kungsleden** (literally "King's Trail") is the most famous and popular hiking route in Sweden. A well-signposted, five-hundred-kilometre path from **Abisko** in the north to **Hemavan**, near Tärnaby (see p.358), it takes in Sweden's highest mountain, **Kebnekaise** (2114m), en route. If you're looking for splendid isolation, this isn't the trail for you; it's the busiest in the country, though it's the section from Abisko to Kebnekaise that sees most hikers (one of the least busy sections is between Jäkkvik and Adolfström).

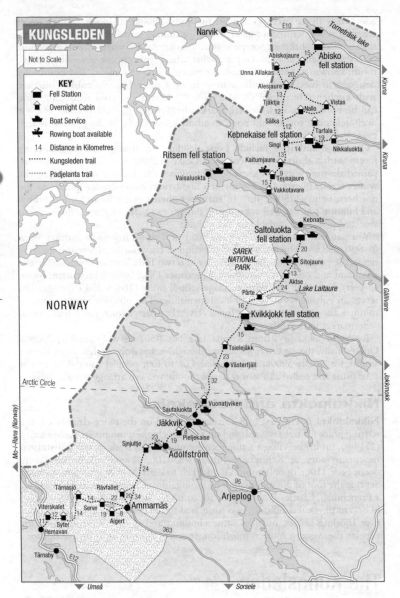

KUNGSLEDEN

Not to Scale

KEY

■ Fell Station
▲ Overnight Cabin
⛴ Boat Service
⛵ Rowing boat available
14 Distance in Kilometres
···· Kungsleden trail
-- Padjelanta trail

Narvik

E10

Torneträsk lake

Abiskojaure 15
Abisko fell station

Unna Allakas
20

Alesjaure
13

Tjäktja
12

Nallo

Vistas

Sälka
12

Kebnekaise fell station

Tarfala
19

Nikkaluokta

Singi
14

Ritsem fell station

Kaitumjaure
13

9
Teusajaure
15
Vakkotavare

Vaisaluokta

Kebnats

Saltoluokta fell station

SAREK NATIONAL PARK

20
Sitojaure

13

Aktse

Lake Laitaure

NORWAY

Pårte
24

16

Kvikkjokk fell station

15

Tsielejåkk
23
Västerfjäll

32

Sautaluokta
7
Vuonatjviken

Jäkkvik
8
Pieljekaise

Sjnjultje
23
19

Adolfström
24

95
Arjeplog

Arctic Circle

Tärnasjö
Rävfallet
22
20 34

Viterskalet
12
14
Serve
19
8
Aigert
Ammarnäs

Syter
11
Hemavan

Tärnaby
E12

363

Mo-i-Rana (Norway)

Kiruna

Kiruna

Gällivare

Jokkmokk

Umeå

Sorsele

Abisko and around

Leaving Kiruna, it's 98km northwest along the E10 to **ABISKO**. Although accessible by both rail and road, it's by **train** that most people arrive at the start of the Kungsleden trail. The train line from Luleå, via Kiruna, to Narvik, known as the **Malmbanan**, is Europe's northernmost line, and would never have been built had it not been for the rich deposits of iron ore around Gällivare and Malmberget. The idea to construct the Malmbanan, which connects the Bothnian coast with the Atlantic coast (170km), passing through some of the remotest and most inhospitable parts of Europe, was talked about on and off throughout the nineteenth century, when the only means of transporting the ore was by reindeer and sleigh. Finally, in 1884, an English company was awarded the contract to build it; by 1888, the line had reached Gällivare from the Bothnian coast and the company was bankrupt. Ten years passed before the state took over the project; in July 1902, the navvies – who'd been subject to temperatures of -30°C and lower and incredibly harsh conditions – finally shovelled their way through deep snow at Riksgränsen to cross the Norwegian border. A year later the line was officially opened by King Oscar II.

Arriving by train from Kiruna, the first stop, Abisko Ö (short for Östra, meaning east) is the location of the tiny village of Abisko itself, nothing more than a couple of residential streets that are of little interest to visitors. Instead, stay on the train for another five minutes and alight at the next stop, **Abisko Turiststation**, the name of the eponymous STF establishment (T 0980/402 00, W www.abisko.nu; dorm beds 310kr, double rooms ❸), the only **accommodation** option hereabouts (booking ahead is wise), superbly located beside the vast Torneträsk lake. There are 300 beds in both private rooms and two-berth cabins, a great basement sauna suite, and a restaurant and bar with views over the lake. There's also a food store which hires out hiking equipment. The friendly staff have expert knowledge of the Kungsleden and surrounding area and more than compensate for the lack of a dedicated tourist office.

Even if you don't intend to walk the Kungsleden, there are a couple of attractions right on Abisko's doorstep. Departing from directly opposite the *Turiststation*, you can take a **chairlift** (140kr return) 500m up Nuolja mountain (1169m), from where there are fantastic views of the surrounding wilderness including the seventy-kilometre-long Torneträsk lake and the spectacular U-shaped mountaintops of **Lapporten**, which have come to represent the gateway to Lapland and are used as landmarks by the *Sámi* for guiding their reindeer between their summer and winter grazing land; and the vast wooded land. Tucked away in one corner of the **café** at the end of the chairlift, the **Aurora Sky Station** is the best place for miles around to observe the **northern lights**; Abisko lies in a rain shadow and

Reaching the Kungsleden by public transport

You can get to **Abisko** pretty easily by **train**; it's just before the Norwegian border on the Kiruna–Narvik run. The **Inlandsbanan** will get you to Jokkmokk, from where you can get a bus to Kvikkjokk, another point on the trail.

There are also several useful **bus** routes that you can take to link up with the trail, listed below; most of these services are run by Länstrafiken Norrbotten and Länstrafiken Västerbotten (W www.ltnbd.se & W www.tabussen.nu). The buses operate a *bussgods* service, which allows you to send your pack ahead to your destination or, alternatively, back to your starting point, sparing you the effort of lugging your stuff around; ask about this service at bus stations or on the bus.

#31: Hemavan to Umeå

#47: Jokkmokk to Kvikkjokk

#92: Kiruna to Nikkaluokta (19km from Kebnekaise fell station)

#93: Gällivare to Ritsem (passes through Vakkotavare and Kebnats for the boat to Saltoluokta)

#200: Arjeplog to Jäkkvik

#341: Ammarnäs to Sorsele

the sky is consequently often free of cloud. Containing all kinds of equipment to measure and hear the lights (they often emit a series of hisses and clicks), it's a perfect introduction for the non-initiated into this most compliated of scientific phenomena since experts are on hand to explain what you're seeing and hearing. The Aurora Sky Station is open in connection with special organized tours to see the lights, which depart from the *Turiststation* – usually Tuesday, Thursday & Saturday late February to mid-March and late August to late September.

Alternatively, Nuolja is also the starting point for an easy walking path (7km; 2–3hr) leading downhill to nearby **Björkliden**, 9km away by road, comprising nothing more than a few houses gathered around the railway station. From here, the **Navvy Road** (Rallarvägen) leads to Rombaksbotn, near Narvik, in Norway; the road was built alongside the Malmbanan, then under construction, in order to transport materials needed for the line. Today it provides a walking or mountain-biking route between Abisko and Narvik – though it can be fairly narrow and rough going in parts.

Riksgränsen

From Abisko and Björkliden, the train line and the E10 continue on to **RIKSGRÄNSEN**, 34km from Abisko, a self-contained mountain ski and spa resort 400km north of the Arctic Circle in the shadow of the Norwegian border. The proud claim of Riksgränsen is that plentiful precipitation means there's never any need for artificial snow; you can ski and snowboard until midsummer. Although the minuscule settlement consists of barely a couple of houses supplemented by a top-notch **hotel**, the *Riksgränsen* (☎0980/400 80, ⓦwww .riksgransen.nu; ❹/❺) opposite the train station, it's the chance to explore the only high alpine area in Sweden – sixty peaks over 1350m – that brings trainloads of people here, predominantly during the winter season (mid-Feb to late June). The hotel certainly buzzes in season: it's one of the Swedes' favourite ski destinations, despite its isolated location, and advance booking is therefore essential. As well as its rooms, the *Riksgränsen* has three- to eight-bed self-catering **apartments** (❼) which, although adequate, are a little cramped.

In addition to the ski trails here, the hotel also boasts a well-appointed **spa centre** complete with five massage rooms, gym, Jacuzzi and outside hot tubs from where there are breathtaking views over the Vassijaure lake; this is certainly one of the best places in the whole of Sweden to completely chill out. During the summer months, there's some great **fishing** and **hiking** to be had in these parts; the hotel can supply detailed information as well as rent **mountain bikes** (330kr) to cycle along the Rallarvägen (see above) or **canoes** for use on the lake here (220kr). Bear in mind, though, that Riksgränsen is one of the wettest places in the entire country in summer, subject to frequent heavy downpours due to its proximity to the mountains which form the border with Norway.

Along the Kungsleden trail

As Sweden's premier hiking trail, there is no doubt that the **Kungsleden**, particularly its northern stretches, can be busy with trekkers. However, it's not difficult to get away from the crowds. Most people start the trail at Abisko, but it's equally feasible to begin further south – see the box on p.381 for possible starting points and how to get to them.

There are basic **cabins** (all open late Feb to April & late June to mid-Sept; dorm beds 360kr; advance bookings not possible) along the entire route, and from Abisko to Saltoluokta, north of the Arctic Circle, and in the south between Ammarnäs and Hemavan, and also better equipped STF *fjällstationer*, or

▲ Cycling the Kungsleden

mountain lodges. The ground is easy to walk, with bridges where it's necessary to ford streams; marshy ground has had wooden planks laid down to ease the going, and there are either boat services or row-boats with which to get across several large lakes. The route, which passes through the national parks (see p.371), is traditionally split into the five segments described below. For the distances between the places mentioned on each segment, see the map on p.380; the best map to have of the entire area is Lantmäteriet Kartförlaget's *Norra Norrland* (scale 1:400,000).

Abisko to Kebnekaise: 6 days, 105km

From its starting point at Abisko Turiststation, the Kungsleden winds through the elongated **Abisko National Park** (Ⓦ www.fjallen.nu/parker/abisko.htm), which contains some of the most lush and dense vegetation of the trail, including beech forest lining the valley bottom. From the Alesjaure cabins, perched on a mountain ridge 35km from the start, you'll get a fantastic view over the open countryside below; there's a sauna here, too. The highest point on this segment is the Tjäktja pass (1105m), 50km from the start, from where there are also wonderful views. There are **cabins** en route at Abiskojaure, Alesjaure, Tjäktja (before the pass), Sälka and Singi.

At the end of this section of cabins lies **Kebnekaise** *fjällstation* mountain lodge (see p.379), from where it's possible to leave the main trail and head to Nikkaluokta (see p.379), 19km away (served by buses to Kiruna).

Kebnekaise to Saltoluokta: 3 days, 51km

One of the quietest sections of the trail, this segment takes in beech forest, open fells and deep valleys. First of all you backtrack 14km to **Singi**, before heading south again with an unobstructed view of the hills and glaciers of Sarek National Park. You then paddle across the river at **Teusajaure** and climb over a plateau, from where you drop steeply through more beech forest to **Vakkotavare**. Here a bus runs to the quay at Kebnats, and then a short boat trip brings you to **Saltoluokta** *fjällstation* mountain lodge (Ⓣ0973/410 10, Ⓦ www.stfsaltoluokta .com; dorm beds 395kr, double room ❶; late Feb early May & late June to mid-Sept) and the start of the next section. There are **cabins** en route at Singi, Kaitumjaure, Teusajaure and Vakkotavare.

Saltoluokta to Kvikkjokk: 4 days, 73km

This segment involves crossing two lakes and also passes through a bare landscape edged by pine and beech forests. A long uphill climb of around five to six hours leads first to **Sitojaure**, on a bare high fell. The shallow lake here, which you have to cross, is choppy in the strong wind; take the boat service operated by the cabin caretaker. You then cross the wetlands on the other side of the lake, making use of the wooden planks laid down here, to **Aktse**, where there's a vast field of yellow buttercups in summer. Using the row-boats provided, row across **Lake Laitaure** for Kvikkjokk; as you approach you'll see pine forest. There are **cabins** en route at Sitojaure, Aktse, and Pårte; at **Kvikkjokk** there's a *fjällstation* mountain lodge.

Kvikkjokk to Ammarnäs: 8 days, 166km

Not recommended for novices, this is one of the most difficult stretches of the trail (distances between cabins can be long, and there are four lakes to cross); it is, however, one of the quietest. From **Kvikkjokk** you take the boat over Saggat lake and walk to the first cabin at **Tsielejåkk**. It's 55km to the next cabin at **Vuonatjviken**.

You then take the boat across Riebnesjaure and walk to Hornavan for another boat across to the village of **Jäkkvik**; there are cabins available here (see p.364). It's a short hike of 8km to the next cabin, then on to the village of **Adolfström**, where once again there is accommodation (see p.364). Then you get another boat over Iraft lake and on to the cabins at **Sjnjultje**. From here there's a choice of routes: 34km direct to Ammarnäs, or 24km to Rävfallet and then another 20km into Ammarnäs. **Accommodation** en route is at Tsielejåkk, Vuonatjviken, Jäkkvik village, Pieljekaise, Adolfström village, Sjnjultje, Rävfallet and Ammarnäs.

Ammarnäs to Hemavan: 4 days, 78km

This is the easiest part of the trail: you'll pass over low fells and heather-covered moors and through beech forests and wetlands, the horizon lined with impressive fell peaks. The only steep climb is 8km long between **Ammarnäs** and **Aigert**, where there's an imposing waterfall and a traditional steam sauna in the cabin. On the way to the **Syter** cabin, 48km from Aigert, you'll pass a network of bridges, which cross the various lakes in what is called the **Tärnasjö archipelago**. There are no fell stations on this stretch of the trail; cabins en route are at Aigert, Serve, Tärnasjö, Syter, Viterskalet and Hemavan.

The Torne Valley

Along the border with Finland, the lush, gentle slopes of the **TORNE VALLEY** (*Tornedalen* in Swedish) are among the most welcoming sights in northern Sweden. Stretching over 500km from the mouth of the Gulf of Bothnia to Sweden's remote northern tip, the three rivers, Torne, Muonio and Könkämä, mark out the long border between Sweden and Finland. The valley is home to Swedes, Finns and *Sámi*, who speak an archaic Finnish **dialect** known as *tornedalsfinska* (Torne Valley Finnish, an official minority language), though Swedish is widely understood and is the language of choice for the youth. Refreshingly different from the coast and the heavily wooded inland regions, the area is dotted with small villages, bordered by flower meadows. To either side of Route 400, the main road along the valley, lie open fields providing much-needed grazing land for the farmers' livestock. Arriving from Gällivare or Kiruna, you can enter the valley by **bus** at its midway point, **Pajala**. From the south, buses also run daily from Haparanda (see p.309).

Arriving from Gällivare or Kiruna, you can enter the valley by **bus** at its midway point, **Pajala**. From the south, buses also run daily from Haparanda (see p.309).

Pajala

Over time we understood that Pajala didn't actually belong to Sweden... we'd made it by chance. A northerly appendage, desolate swampland where a few people just happened to live, who only partly managed to be Swedish ... no roe deer, hedgehogs or nightingales. Just interminable amounts of mosquitoes, Torne Valley Finnish swearwords and Communists.

Popular Music, Mikael Niemi, on growing up in Pajala during the 1960s and 1970s.

The valley's main village is pretty **PAJALA**, a place that has earned itself a reputation and a half throughout Sweden on two counts: firstly, the inordinately successful book, and now film, *Popular Music*, is set here (see p.418), and secondly, the locals' need of women. The predominance of heavy labouring jobs in the north of Sweden has produced a gender imbalance here – around three men to every woman (a fact which also explains the ridiculously macho behaviour that seems to prevail in these parts). So, to celebrate the village's four-hundredth anniversary in 1987, the local council placed advertisements in the national papers inviting women from the south of the country up to Lapland to take part in the birthday festivities. Journalists outside Sweden soon heard of the ads, and articles about the unusual invitation began to appear in newspapers across Europe. Before long, busloads of women from all over the continent were heading for the village. The anniversary festivities proved to be a drunken, debauched bash that tiny Pajala wouldn't forget in a long time, but they did help to redress the gender problem: dozens of East European women lost their hearts to gruff Swedish lumberjacks, and began new lives north of the Arctic Circle. Naturally a succession of winters spent in darkness and in temperatures of -25°C takes its toll and some women have already left; to date, though, about thirty have stayed the course.

Taking place in the last week in September, the **Römpäviiko** ("romp week") cultural festival, featuring live music and street stalls selling food and handicrafts, is undoubtedly the liveliest time to be in the village. However, the second weekend after midsummer is another good time to visit, when up to forty thousand people flood into town for the Pajala **market**, one of the biggest in northern Sweden selling everything from chorizos to reindeer antlers; it's an excellent opportunity to pick up a few *Sámi* handicrafts.

In order to appreciate Pajala's other claim to fame, you really need to have read *Popular Music* (one in eight Swedes own a copy of the book) or seen the film, which recently played to sell-out audiences in cinemas across the country. Based around the life of Matti, a teenage boy who dreams of becoming a rock star, the book offers a rare insight into the psyche of the northern Swede and life in the remote Torne Valley. Dotted across town, striking yellow signposts proudly point the way to some of the most infamous locations which feature in the dramatization: Vittulajänkkä, Paskajänkkä and slightly more sedate Strandvägen, all plotted on the free map available from the tourist office.

Having dealt with Pajala the film location, there's little else to do in this unprepossessing town other than rest up for a day or so – take a walk along the riverside, or head off in search of the great grey **owl** (*strix nebulosa*) that sweeps through the nearby forests. The huge wooden **model** of the bird in the bus station will give you an idea of its appearance: lichen grey, with long, slender tail feathers and a white crescent between its black and yellow eyes. Close by, on Torggatan, is the largest **sundial** in the world, a circular affair with a diameter of 38m which tells the real solar time – always 18–25min different to that of a regular watch or clock.

Laestadius and the demon drink

No other man has made a greater impression on northern Scandinavia than **Lars Levi Laestadius**, the Swedish revivalist preacher who dedicated his life to saving people in three countries from the perils of **alcoholism**. Born in Jäkkvik in 1800 and educated in Kvikkjokk, the young Laestadius soon developed a close relationship with the indigenous *Sámi*, many of whom had turned to drink to escape the harsh reality of their daily lives. It was while the priest was working in Karesuando (1826–49) that he met **Mary of Åsele**, the *Sámi* woman who inspired him to steer people towards a life of total purity. Following Laestadius's death in Pajala in 1861, the movement continued under the leadership of Juhani Raattamaa before splitting into two opposing branches: a conservative western group in Sweden and Norway, and a more liberal eastern one in Finland. Today tens of thousands of teetotal Swedes, Finns, Norwegians and *Sámi* across the Arctic area of Scandinavia still follow Laestadius's teachings; they're not allowed to have flowers or curtains in their homes, nor are they permitted to wear a tie, listen to the radio or watch TV. Drinking, of course, is totally out of the question.

While you're in Pajala, make an effort to visit the **grave** of the revivalist preacher, **Lars Levi Laestadius** (see box above), who came to Pajala in 1849. Although he strived throughout his life to rid Lapland of alcohol abuse, he was rarely popular hereabouts since many workers were paid for their toils in hard liquor. He died in Pajala in 1861, and his grave is located in the middle section of the old graveyard next to Pajala kyrka on Kyrkallén. Close by, on Prästgårdsallén, **Laestadiuspörtet** (mid-June to mid-Aug daily 10am–6pm; 60kr) is the simple unassuming house he once lived in; the entrance fee includes a guided tour and coffee.

Practicalities

The **bus station**, right in the centre of town, contains the **tourist office** (May–Aug Mon–Fri 9am–5pm; mid-June to mid-Aug also Sat & Sun 11am–5pm; Sept–April Mon–Fri 8am–4pm; ☎0978/100 15, ⓦwww.pajalaturism.bd.se).

For central **accommodation**, the *Bykrogen Hotell*, close by at Soukolovägen 2 (☎0978/108 15, ⓦwww.bykrogen.se; ⑤/③) has cosy little rooms with a nice old-fashioned feel, while *Lapland River*, Fridhemsvägen 1 (☎0978/108 15, ⓦwww.laplandriverhotel.se; ⑥/③), features more modern en-suite rooms; it's a ten-minute walk from the centre, east along Tornedalsvägen and then right into Kengisgatan. The best place to stay, however, is out of town in the quiet village of Junosuando (57km northwest; take bus #53 towards Kiruna): ⚓ *Aurora Retreat* (☎0978/300 61, ⓦwww.auroraretreat.se; ⑤ with full board), at Prästgården, is an eco-friendly haven of stripped pine and potted plants in the former vicarage dating from 1928. Rooms here are airy and spacious and the emphasis is on minimal environmental impact.

For **eating** and **drinking**, head for the *Bykrogen Hotell* where there's a decent Thai restaurant (mains for 79–89kr), which becomes a sports bar by night. Alternatively, the *Tre Kronor* pizzeria in the centre of town at Tornedalsvägen 11 serves pizzas (from 65kr), burgers (65kr) and steaks (from 79kr). Across the road at no. 2, *Kafé Nedan* is a good place for sandwiches and salads.

Karesuando and around

Sweden's northernmost village, **KARESUANDO**, 180km north of Pajala, is a surprisingly likeable little place that you can reach from Pajala by bus by changing in nearby **Vittangi**, where, incidentally, there's a great **elk park** (June–Aug daily 10am–5pm; call ahead at other times on ☎070/247 69 06, ⓦwww.moosefarm.se; 100kr);

follow the "Algpark" signs from the town centre. This far corner of Sweden is as good a spot as any to take stock of just where you've reached: the North Cape is barely 500km away, you're as far north as Canada's Baffin Island and the northern tip of Alaska, and the tree line slices through the edge of the village. **Winters** up here can be particularly severe; the first snow falls at the end of September or early October and stays on the ground until late May, when the Muonioälven, the river which curls around the village, also melts. Just a few centimetres beneath the surface, the ground is in the grip of **permafrost** all year round. Summer here is short and sweet – but the region becomes a mosquito paradise in the warmer and lighter months. Karesuando is right in the midst of *Sámi* heartland; reindeer husbandry, particularly in the nearby villages of Övre, Nedre Soppero and Idivuoma, where many herders live, is of primary importance to the local economy.

The only sight to speak of in Karesuando is beyond the tourist office: the wooden cabin here was once the rectory of **Lars Levi Laestadius**, the village's most famous son (see box opposite). Complete with simple wooden pews, it was used as a meeting place while Laestadius was rector in Karesuando, and is now a simple **museum** (no set hours; free) of his life and works. Also worth a quick look, along the road to the campsite, is the village **museum** (Mon–Fri 8am–4pm; 30kr), known as Vita Huset, containing a few atmospheric black-and-white photographs from 1944, when Karesuando was inundated by Finns fleeing the approaching German forces – with their cattle. Look in particular for the picture of Olga Raattamaa, known locally as Empress Olga, who once lived in nearby Kumma-vuopio, and single-handedly saved the lives of dozens of Finns by rowing them across the Könkämä river to safety in neutral Sweden.

With your own transport, it's well worth the short drive south along Route 400 for fantastic **views** over the surrounding tundra: some five or ten minutes after leaving the village, take the right turn marked "Kaarevaara" and continue past a small lake, whereupon the road begins to climb up past a TV mast and eventually

Treriksröset

Heading north for **Treriksröset** – the **three-nation marker post** where Sweden, Norway and Finland all meet – walk over the bridge to Kaaresuvanto in Finland, from where a daily bus leaves at 2.35pm (Finland is an hour ahead of Sweden) for **Kilpisjärvi** (journey time 2hr). From June to mid-September a second daily bus leaves at 4.25pm for Tromsø in Norway, travelling via Kilpisjärvi. From Kilpisjärvi, there are two ways to get to Treriksröset. One of these is a hike of 11km down a track which passes through an area of dwarf woodland before running around a small lake to reach Sweden's northernmost point, marked by a yellow bell-shaped piece of concrete, suspended in a lake and surrounded by wooden walkways; don't forget your camera and mosquito repellent. The path then continues (14km) towards the **northernmost peak** in Sweden, **Pältsan** (1445m); the going here is rocky in parts. The STF **cabins** (advance booking not possible; mid-March to April & mid-July to mid-Sept; dorm beds 360kr) at the foot of the mountain, two of Sweden's most northerly buildings, boast thirty beds and a sauna. There's an easy hike (40km) from the Pältsa cabins back to **Keinovuopio** (see below), then cross the river to the village of Peera, on the main E8 road in Finland, where you can catch the bus back towards Karesuando (daily; approximately 1.45pm, also June to mid-Sept daily at 11.25am; check Finnish bus times at ⓦ www.matkahuolto.fi).

Alternatively, you can reach Treriksröset from Kilpisjärvi by getting a **boat ride** across the Bajit Gilbbesjávri on board *M/S Malla*, which shortens the hike to just 3km. The boat requires at least four passengers if it's to sail (late June to early Aug 10am, 2pm & 6pm Finnish time; 45min; €16 return); for boat information ask at the tourist office in Karesuando or call the Finnish number ☏ 00358/400 669 392.

ends in a small car park. On a clear day you can see for miles across the Swedish and Finnish tundra from up here. The vast tract of land you'll see stretching away to the northwest contains **Treriksröset**, the point where Sweden, Finland and Norway meet (see box, p.387).

Practicalities

The **tourist office** (June–Sept daily 9am–6pm; Oct–May Mon–Fri 9am–3pm; ℡0981/202 05, Ⓦwww.karesuando.se) is in the customs house on the bridge across to Finland. There are various **accommodation** options, including *Karesuando Camping* (℡0981/201 39, Ⓦwww.karesuandokonst.com; June to mid-Sept), a two-kilometre walk past the church, heading out of the village along the main road towards Pajala. A number of four-berth **cabins** are available at the campsite; those with a simple kitchen go for 375kr, those without are a little smaller and cost 275kr. There's a separate toilet and shower block. On the same road, five-minutes' walk before the campsite, the **youth hostel** (℡0981/203 30 or 0981/203 70, Ⓔarctic.tours@telia.com; dorm beds 190kr, double rooms ❷; April to mid-Sept) enjoys a fantastic waterside location and is the best place to stay in the village. Immediately opposite, *Hotell Karesuando* (℡0981/203 30, Ⓦwww.artictours.se; ❹/❸) has modern rooms decked out in *Sámi* colours. To get away from it all, there are **cabins** in the wilds (℡0981/202 12; ❶) at **Keinovuopio**, a tiny settlement that's home to just fifteen people, right on the Konkämä River in the far northwestern corner of Sweden. To reach Keinovuopio, cross the river to **Karesuvanto** in Finland, and then take a Finnish bus towards **Kilpisjärvi**, from where there's a footbridge back over the river to Swedish Keinovuopio.

There are just two **eating** places in Karesuando, a greasy-spoon grill-restaurant, *Karesuando Lunch & Grill*, at the opposite end of the village to all accommodation options, between the Statoil and OK filling stations and, altogether better, the restaurant attached to *Hotell Karesuando*. For **provisions** go for the ICA supermarket opposite Statoil.

Travel details

Trains

The Inlandsbanan runs from Mora to Gällivare via Östersund, generally from early June to late Aug although this is subject to change from year to year. Northbound trains leave Östersund daily for Gällivare at 7.15am calling at Ulriksfors (for Strömsund), Dorotea, Vilhelmina, Storuman, Sorsele, Arvidsjaur, the Arctic Circle, Jokkmokk and Gällivare. Southbound trains leave Gällivare daily at 6.50am for stations to Östersund. For details of the Mora–Östersund stretch, see "Travel details" for Central Sweden (p.346).

Abisko to: Gällivare (2 daily; 2hr 20min); Kiruna (2 daily; 1hr 20min); Narvik (2 daily; 1hr 30min); Riksgränsen (2 daily; 40min); Stockholm (1 daily; 18hr).

Gällivare to: Kiruna (3 daily; 1hr); Luleå (3 daily; 2hr 20min); Narvik (2 daily; 2hr); Stockholm (1 daily; 15hr 30min).

Kiruna to: Luleå (3 daily; 3hr 20min); Narvik (2 daily; 3hr); Stockholm (1 daily; 16hr 30min).

Riksgränsen to: Abisko (2 daily; 40min); Gällivare (2 daily; 3hr); Kiruna (2 daily; 2hr); Narvik (2 daily; 1hr); Stockholm (1 daily; 19hr).

International trains

Abisko to: Narvik (2 daily; 1hr 30min)
Gällivare to: Narvik (2 daily; 2hr)
Kiruna to: Narvik (2 daily; 3hr)
Riksgränsen to: Narvik (2 daily; 1hr)

Buses

The Inlandsexpressen (#45) runs north from Östersund to Strömsund, Dorotea, Vilhelmina, Storuman, Sorsele, Arvidsjaur, Jokkmokk and Porjus. It operates daily all year round.

Contexts

Contexts

History

Sweden has one of Europe's longest documented **histories**, but for all the upheavals of the Viking times and the warring of the Middle Ages, the country has, in modern times, seemed to delight in taking a historical back seat. For a brief period in 1986, when Prime Minister Olof Palme was shot dead, Sweden was thrust into the limelight. Since then, the country has regained some of its equilibrium, though political infighting and domestic disharmony often threatens the one thing that Swedes have always been proud of, and that other countries aspire to: the politics of **consensus**, the potential passing of which is arguably of far greater importance than even the assassination of their prime minister.

Early civilizations

It was not until around 6000 BC that the **first settlers** roamed north and east into Sweden, living as nomadic reindeer hunters and herders. By 3000 BC people had settled in the south of the country and were established as farmers; from 2000 BC there are indications of a development in burial practices, with **dolmens** and **passage graves** found throughout the southern Swedish provinces. Traces also remain of the **Boat Axe People**, named after their characteristic tool and weapon, shaped like a boat. The earliest horse riders in Scandinavia, they quickly held sway over the whole of southern Sweden.

During the **Bronze Age** (1500–500 BC) the Boat Axe People traded furs and amber for southern European copper and tin – large finds of finished ornaments and weapons show a comparatively rich culture. This was emphasized by elaborate burial rites, the dead laid in single graves under mounds of earth and stone.

The deterioration of the Scandinavian climate in the last millennium before Christ coincided with the advance across Europe of the Celts, which halted the flourishing trade of the Swedish settlers. With the new millennium, Sweden made its first mark upon the Classical world. In the *Historia Naturalis*, Pliny the Elder (23–79 AD) mentioned the "island of Scatinavia" far to the north. Tacitus was more specific: in 98 AD he mentioned a powerful people who were strong in men, weapons and ships, the *Suinoes* – a reference to the **Svear**, who were to form the nucleus of an emergent Swedish kingdom by the sixth century.

The Svear settled in the rich land around Lake Mälaren and became rulers of most of the territory comprising modern Sweden, except the south. They gave Sweden its modern name: *Sverige* in Swedish or *Svear rik*, the kingdom of the Svear. More importantly, their first dynastic leaders had a taste for expansion, trading with Gotland and holding suzerainty over the Åland Islands.

The Viking period

The Vikings – raiders and warriors who dominated the political and economic life of Europe and beyond from the ninth to the eleventh centuries – came from all parts of southern Scandinavia. But there is evidence that the **Swedish Vikings** were among the first to leave home, the impetus being rapid population growth, domestic unrest and a desire for new lands. Sweden being located on the eastern part of the Scandinavian peninsula, the raiders largely turned their attention further eastwards, in the knowledge that the Svear had already reached the Baltic. By the ninth century, the trade routes were well established, with Swedes reaching the Black and Caspian seas and making valuable trading contact with the **Byzantine Empire**. Although more commercially inclined than their Danish and Norwegian counterparts, Swedish Vikings were quick to use force if profits were slow to materialize. From 860 onwards Greek and Muslim records relate a series of raids across the Black Sea against Byzantium, and across the Caspian into northeast Iran.

The Vikings were settlers as well as traders and exploiters, and their long-term influence was marked. Embattled Slavs to the east gave them the name **Rus**, and their creeping colonization gave one area in which the Vikings settled its modern name, Russia. Russian names today – Oleg, Igor, Vladimir – can be derived from the Swedish – Helgi, Ingvar, Valdemar.

Domestically, **paganism** was at its height; dynastic leaders would claim descent from Freyr, "God of the World". It was a bloody time: nine **human sacrifices** were offered at the celebrations held every nine years at Uppsala. Adam of Bremen recorded that the great shrine there was adjoined by a sacred grove where "every tree is believed divine because of the death and putrefaction of the victims hanging there".

Viking **law** was based on the **Thing**, an assembly of free men to which the king's power was subject. Each largely autonomous province had its own assembly and its own leaders: where several provinces united, the approval of each *Thing* was needed for any choice of leader. For centuries in Sweden, each newly elected king had to make a formal tour to receive the homage of each province.

The arrival of Christianity and the early Middle Ages

Christianity was slow to take root in Sweden. Whereas Denmark and Norway had accepted the faith by the turn of the eleventh century, the Swedes remained largely heathen. Missionaries met with limited success: no Swedish king was converted until 1008, when **Olof Skötonung** was baptized. He was the first known king of both Swedes and Goths (that is, ruler of the two major provinces of Västergötland and Östergötland), and his successors were all Christians. Nevertheless, paganism retained a grip on Swedish affairs, and as late as the 1080s the Svear banished the then king, Inge, when he refused to take part in the pagan celebrations at Uppsala. By the end of the eleventh century, though, the temple at Uppsala had gone and a Christian church was built on its site. In the 1130s, Sigtuna – the original centre of the Swedish Christian faith – was replaced by Uppsala as the main episcopal seat, and in 1164 Stephen, an English monk, was made the first archbishop.

The whole of the early Middle Ages in Sweden was characterized by a succession of struggles for control of a growing central power: two families, the Sverkers and the Eriks, waged battle against each other throughout the twelfth century. **King Erik** was the first Sverker king to make his mark: in 1157 he led a crusade to heathen Finland, but was killed in 1160 at Uppsala by a Danish pretender to his throne. Within 100 years he was to be recognized as patron saint of Sweden, and his remains interred in the new Uppsala cathedral.

Erik was succeeded by his son **Knut**, whose stable reign lasted until 1196, a period marked by commercial treaties and strengthened defences. Following his death, virtual civil war weakened royal power. As a result, the king's chief ministers, or **jarls**, assumed much of the executive responsibility for running the country, so much so that when Erik Eriksson (last of the Eriks) was deposed in 1229, his administrator **Birger Jarl** assumed power. With papal support for his crusading policies, he confirmed the Swedish grip on the southwest of Finland. He was succeeded by his son, Valdemar, who proved a weak ruler and didn't survive the family feuding after Birger Jarl's death.

In 1275, Valdemar's brother, **Magnus Ladulås**, assumed power. He earned his nickname "Ladulås" ("Barn-lock") from his having prevented the nobility from claiming maintenance at the expense of the peasantry, who travelled from estate to estate. Magnus's reign represented a peak of Swedish royal might that wasn't to be repeated for 300 years. While he was king, his enemies dissipated; he forbade the nobility to meet without his consent, and began to issue his own authoritative decrees. He also began to reap the benefits of conversion: the clergy became an educated class upon whom the monarch could rely for diplomatic and administrative duties. By the thirteenth century, there were ambitious Swedish clerics in Paris and Bologna, and the first stone churches were appearing in Sweden, the most monumental of which is the early Gothic **cathedral** built at Uppsala.

Meanwhile, the nobility had come to constitute a military class, exempt from taxation on the understanding that they would defend the crown. In the country the standard of living was still low, although an increasing population stimulated new cultivation. The forests of Norrland were pushed back, more southern heathland turned into pasture, and crop rotation introduced. Noticeable, too, was the increasing **German influence** within Sweden as the Hansa traders spread. Their first merchants settled in Visby and, by the mid-thirteenth century, in Stockholm.

The fourteenth century – towards unity

Magnus died in 1290, power shifting to a cabal of magnates led by **Torgil Knutsson**. As marshal of Sweden, he pursued an energetic foreign policy, conquering western Karelia to gain control of the Gulf of Finland and building the fortress at Viborg, only lost with the collapse of the Swedish Empire in the eighteenth century.

Magnus's son Birger came of age in 1302 and soon quarrelled with his brothers Erik and Valdemar, who had Torgil Knutsson executed. They then rounded on Birger, who was forced to divide up Sweden among the three of them. An unhappy arrangement, it lasted until 1317 when Birger had his brothers arrested and starved to death in prison – an act that prompted a shocked nobility to rise against Birger and force his exile to Denmark. The Swedish nobles restored the principle of elective monarchy by calling on the 3-year-old **Magnus** (son of a Swedish duke, and already declared Norwegian king) to take the Swedish crown. During his minority, a treaty was concluded in 1323 with Novgorod in Russia to define the frontiers in eastern and northern Finland. This left virtually the whole of the Scandinavian peninsula (except the Danish provinces in the south) under one ruler.

Yet Sweden was still anything but prosperous. The **Black Death** reached the country in 1350, wiping out whole parishes and killing around a third of the population. Subsequent labour shortages and troubled estates meant that the nobility found it difficult to maintain their positions. German merchants had driven the Swedes from their most lucrative trade routes: even the copper and iron-ore **mining** that began around this time in Bergslagen and Dalarna relied on German capital.

Magnus soon ran into trouble, and was threatened further by the accession of Valdemar Atterdag to the Danish throne in 1340. Squabbles concerning sovereignty over the Danish provinces of Skåne and Blekinge led to Danish incursions into Sweden; in 1361, Valdemar landed on Gotland and sacked **Visby**. The Gotlanders were refused refuge by the Hansa merchants, and massacred outside the city walls.

Magnus was forced to negotiate and his son **Håkon** – now king of Norway – was married to Valdemar's daughter Margaret. When Magnus was later deposed, power fell into the hands of the magnates who shared out the country. Chief of the ruling nobles was the Steward **Bo Jonsson Grip**, who controlled virtually all Finland and central and southeast Sweden. Yet on his death, the nobility turned to Håkon's wife **Margaret**, already regent in Norway (for her son Olof) and in Denmark since the death of her father, Valdemar. The nobles were anxious for union across Scandinavia, to safeguard those who owned frontier estates and strengthen the crown against any further German influence. In 1388 she was proclaimed "First Lady" of Sweden and, in return, confirmed all the privileges of the Swedish nobility. Called upon to choose a male king, Margaret nominated her nephew, **Erik of Pomerania**, who was duly elected king of Sweden in 1396. As he had already been elected to the Danish and Norwegian thrones, Scandinavian unity seemed assured.

The Kalmar Union

Erik was crowned king of Denmark, Norway and Sweden in 1397 at a ceremony in **Kalmar**. Nominally, the three kingdoms were now in union but, despite Erik's kingship, real power remained in the hands of Margaret until her death in 1412.

Erik was at war with the Hanseatic League throughout his reign. He was vilified in popular Swedish history as an evil and grasping ruler, and the taxes he raised went on a war that was never fought on Swedish soil. He spent his time instead directing operations in Denmark, leaving his queen Philippa (sister to Henry V of England) behind. Erik was deposed in 1439 and the nobility turned to **Christopher of Bavaria**, whose early death in 1448 led to the first major breach in the union.

No one candidate could fill the three kingships satisfactorily, and separate elections in Denmark and Sweden signalled a renewal of the infighting that had plagued the previous century. Within Sweden, unionists and nationalists skirmished, the powerful unionist **Oxenstierna** family opposing the claims of the nationalist **Sture** family, until 1470 when **Sten Sture** (the Elder) became "Guardian of the Realm". His victory over the unionists at the **Battle of Brunkeberg** (1471) – in the centre of what's now modern Stockholm – was complete, gaining symbolic artistic expression in the **statue of St George and the Dragon** that still adorns Storkyrkan in Stockholm.

Sten Sture's primacy fostered a new cultural atmosphere. The first **university** in Scandinavia was founded in Uppsala in 1477, with Sweden's first printing press appearing six years later. Artistically, German and Dutch influences were great, traits seen in the decorative art of the great Swedish medieval churches. Only remote **Dalarna** kept a native folk art tradition alive.

Belief in the union still existed though, particularly outside Sweden, and successive kings had to fend off almost constant attacks and blockades emanating from Denmark. With the accession of **Christian II** to the Danish throne in 1513, the unionist movement found a leader capable of turning the tide. Under the guise of a crusade to free Sweden's imprisoned archbishop Gustav Trolle, Christian attacked Sweden and killed Sture. After Christian's coronation, Trolle urged the prosecution of his Swedish adversaries (who had been gathered together under the pretext of an amnesty) and they were found guilty of heresy. Eighty-two nobles and burghers of Stockholm were executed, their bodies burned in what became known as the **Stockholm Bloodbath**. A vicious persecution of Sture's followers throughout Sweden ensued, a move that led to widespread reaction and, ultimately, the downfall of the union.

Gustav Vasa and his sons

Opposition to Christian II was vague and disorganized until the appearance of the young **Gustav Vasa**. Initially unable to stir the locals of the Dalecarlia region into open revolt, he was on his way to Norway, and exile, when he was chased on skis and recalled, the people having had a change of heart. The chase is celebrated still in the **Vasaloppet** race, run each year by thousands of Swedish skiers.

Gustav Vasa's army grew rapidly. In 1521 he was elected regent, and subsequently, with the capture of Stockholm in 1523, king. Christian had been deposed in Denmark and the new Danish king, Frederick I, recognized Sweden's de facto withdrawal from the union. Short of cash, Gustav found it prudent to support the movement for religious reform propagated by Swedish Lutherans. More of a political than a religious **Reformation**, the result was a handover of Church lands to the Crown and the subordination of Church to state. It's a relationship that is still largely in force today, the clergy being civil servants paid by the state.

In 1541 the first edition of the Bible in the vernacular appeared. Suppressing revolt at home, Gustav Vasa strengthened his hand with a centralization of trade and government. On his death in 1560, Sweden was united, prosperous and independent.

Gustav Vasa's heir, his eldest son **Erik**, faced a difficult time, not least because the Vasa lands and wealth had been divided among him and his brothers Johan, Magnus and Karl (an uncharacteristically imprudent action of Gustav before his death). The Danes, too, pressed hard, reasserting their claim to the Swedish throne in the inconclusive **Northern Seven Years' War**, which began in 1563. Erik was deposed in 1569 by his brother, who became **Johan III**, his first act being to end the war by the **Peace of Stettin** treaty. At home, Johan ruled more or less with the goodwill of the nobility, but matters were upset by his Catholic sympathies: he introduced a new Catholic liturgy, familiarly known from its binding as the *Red Book*, which the clergy accepted only under protest. On Johan's death in 1592, his son and heir, Sigismund (who was Catholic king of Poland) agreed to rule Sweden in accordance with Lutheran practice, but failed to do so. When Sigismund returned to Poland, the way was clear for Duke Karl (Johan's brother) to assume the regency, a role he filled until declared King **Karl IX** in 1603.

Karl, the last of Vasa's sons, had ambitions eastwards but was routed by the Poles and staved off by the Russians. He suffered a stroke in 1610 and died the year after. His heir was the 17-year-old Gustav II, better known as **Gustav II Adolf**.

The rule of Vasa and his sons made Sweden a nation, culturally as well as politically. The courts were filled with and influenced by men of learning; art and sculpture flourished. The **Renaissance** style appeared for the first time in Sweden, with royal castles remodelled – Kalmar being a fine example. Economically, Sweden remained mostly self-sufficient, its few imports being luxuries like cloth, wine and spices. With around eight thousand inhabitants, Stockholm was its most important city, although **Gothenburg** was founded in 1607 to promote trade to the west.

Gustav II Adolf and the rise of the Swedish Empire

Sweden became a European power during the reign of **Gustav II Adolf**. Though still in his youth he was considered able enough to rule, and proved so by concluding peace treaties with Denmark (1613) and Russia (1617), the latter pact isolating Russia from the Baltic and allowing the Swedes control of the eastern trade routes into Europe.

In 1618, the **Thirty Years' War** broke out. It was vital for Gustav that Germany should not become Catholic, given the Polish king's continuing pretensions to the Swedish crown and the possible threat Germany could pose to Sweden's growing influence in the Baltic. In 1629, the Altmark treaty with a defeated Poland gave Gustav control of Livonia and four Prussian seaports, and the income this generated financed his entry into the war in 1630 on the Protestant side. After several convincing victories, Gustav pushed on through Germany, delaying an assault upon undefended Vienna. The decision cost him his life: Gustav was killed at the **Battle of Lützen** in 1632, his body stripped and battered by the enemy's soldiers. The war dragged on until the **Peace of Westphalia** in 1648.

With Gustav away at war for much of his reign, Sweden ran smoothly under the guidance of his friend and chancellor, **Axel Oxenstierna**. Together they founded a new Supreme Court in Stockholm (and did the same for Finland and the conquered Baltic provinces); reorganized the national assembly into four Estates of nobility, clergy, burghers and peasantry (1626); extended the university at Uppsala (and founded one at Åbo – modern Turku in Finland); and fostered the mining and other industries that provided much of the country's wealth. Gustav had many other accomplishments, too: he spoke five languages and designed a new light cannon which assisted in his routs of the enemy.

The Caroleans

The Swedish empire reached its territorial peak under the **Caroleans**. Yet the reign of the last of them was to see Sweden crumble. Following Gustav II Adolf's death and the later abdication of his daughter Kristina, **Karl X** succeeded to the throne. War against Poland (1655) led to some early successes and, with Denmark espousing the Polish cause, gave Karl the opportunity to march into Jutland (1657). From there his armies marched across the frozen sea to threaten Copenhagen; the subsequent **Treaty of Roskilde** (1658) broke Denmark and gave the Swedish empire its widest territorial extent.

However, the long regency of his son and heir, **Karl XI**, did little to safeguard Sweden's vulnerable position, so extensive were its borders. On assuming power in 1672, Karl was almost immediately dragged into war: beaten by a smaller Prussian army at Brandenberg in 1675, Sweden was suddenly faced with war against both the Danes and the Dutch. Karl rallied, though, to drive out the Danish invaders, and the war ended in 1679 with the reconquest of Skåne and the restoration of most of Sweden's German provinces.

In 1682, Karl XI became **absolute monarch** and was given full control over legislation and *reduktion* – the resumption of estates previously alienated by the Crown to the nobility. The armed forces were reorganized too: by 1700, the Swedish army had 25,000 soldiers and twelve regiments of cavalry; the naval fleet had expanded to 38 ships and a new base had been built at **Karlskrona** (which was nearer to the likely trouble spots than Stockholm).

Culturally, Sweden began to benefit from the innovations of Gustav II Adolf. *Gymnasia* (grammar schools) continued to expand, and a second university was established at **Lund** in 1668. A national **literature** emerged, helped by the efforts of **George Stiernhielm**, father of modern Swedish poetry. **Olof Rudbeck** (1630–1702) was a Nordic polymath whose scientific reputation lasted longer than his attempt to identify the ancient Goth settlement at Uppsala as Atlantis. Architecturally, this was the age of **Tessin**, both father and son. Tessin the Elder was responsible for the glorious palace at **Drottningholm**, work on which began in 1662, as well as the cathedral at **Kalmar**. His son, Tessin the Younger, succeeded him as royal architect and was to create the new royal palace at Stockholm.

In 1697, the 15-year-old **Karl XII** succeeded to the throne; under him, the empire collapsed. Faced with a defensive alliance of Saxony, Denmark and Russia, there was little the king could have done to avoid eventual defeat. However, he remains a revered figure for his valiant (often suicidal) efforts to take on the rest of Europe. Initial victories against Peter the Great and Saxony led him to march on Russia, where he was defeated and the bulk of his army destroyed. Escaping to Turkey, where he remained as guest and then prisoner for four years, Karl watched the empire disintegrate. With Poland reconquered by Augustus of Saxony, and Finland by Peter the Great, he returned to Sweden only to have England declare war on him.

Eventually, splits in the enemy alliance led Swedish diplomats to attempt peace talks with Russia. Karl, though, was keen to exploit these differences in a more direct fashion. Wanting to strike at Denmark, but lacking a fleet, he besieged Fredrikshald in Norway (then united with Denmark) in 1718 – and was killed by a sniper's bullet. In the power vacuum thus created, Russia became the leading Baltic force, receiving Livonia, Estonia, Ingria and most of Karelia from Sweden.

The Age of Freedom

The eighteenth century saw absolutism discredited in Sweden. A new constitution vested power in the Estates, who reduced the new king **Frederick I**'s role to that of nominal head of state. The chancellor wielded the real power, and under **Arvid Horn** the country found a period of stability. His party, nicknamed the "Caps", was opposed by the hawkish "Hats". The latter forced war with Russia in 1741, a disaster in which Sweden lost all of Finland and had its whole east coast burned and bombed. Most of Finland was returned with the agreement that **Adolphus Frederick** (a relation of the crown prince of Russia) would be elected to the Swedish throne on Frederick I's death. This duly occurred in 1751.

During his reign, Adolphus repeatedly tried to reassert royal power, but found that the constitution had been strengthened against him. The Estates' power was such that when Adolphus refused to sign any bills, they simply utilized a stamp bearing his name. The resurrected "Hats" forced entry into the **Seven Years' War** in 1757 on the French side, another disastrous venture, as the Prussians were able to repel every Swedish attack.

The aristocratic parties were in a state of constant flux. Although elections of sorts were held to provide delegates for the *Riksdag* (parliament), foreign sympathies, bribery and bickering were hardly conducive to democratic administration. Cabals continued to rule Sweden, the economy was stagnant, and reform delayed. It was, however, an age of **intellectual and scientific advance**, surprising in a country that had lost much of its cultural impetus. **Carl von Linné**, the botanist whose classification of plants is still used, was professor at Uppsala from 1741 to 1778; **Anders Celsius** initiated the use of the centigrade temperature scale; **Carl Scheele** discovered chlorine. A royal decree of 1748 organized Europe's first full-scale **census**, a five-yearly event by 1775. Other fields flourished, too. The mystical works of **Emmanuel Swedenborg**, the philosopher who died in 1772, encouraged new theological sects; and the period encompassed the life of **Carl Michael Bellman** (1740–95), the celebrated Swedish poet whose work did much to identify and foster a popular nationalism.

With the accession of **Gustav III** in 1771, the Crown began to regain the ascendancy. A new constitution was forced upon a divided *Riksdag* and proved a watershed between earlier absolutism and the later aristocratic squabbles. A popular king, Gustav founded hospitals, granted freedom of worship and removed many of the state controls over the economy. His determination to conduct a successful foreign policy led to further conflict with Russia (1788–90) in which, to everyone's surprise, he managed to more than hold his own. But with the French Revolution polarizing opposition throughout Europe, the Swedish nobility began to entertain thoughts of conspiracy against a king whose growing powers they now saw as those of a tyrant. In 1792, at a masked ball in Stockholm Opera House, the king was shot by an assassin hired by the disaffected aristocracy. Gustav died two weeks later and was succeeded by his son **Gustav IV**, with the country being led by a regency during his minority.

The wars waged by revolutionary France were at first studiously avoided in Sweden but, pulled into the conflict by the British, Gustav IV entered the **Napoleonic Wars** in 1805. However, Napoleon's victory at Austerlitz two years later broke the coalition, and Sweden found itself isolated. Attacked by Russia the following year, Gustav was later arrested and deposed, and his uncle was elected king.

A constitution of 1809 established a liberal monarchy in Sweden, responsible to the elected *Riksdag*. Under this constitution **Karl XIII** was a mere caretaker, his heir a Danish prince who would bring Norway back to Sweden – some compensation for finally losing Finland and the Åland Islands to Russia (1809) after 500 years of Swedish rule. On the prince's sudden death, however, Marshal Bernadotte (one of Napoleon's generals) was invited to become heir. Taking the name of **Karl Johan**, he took his chance in 1812 and joined Britain and Russia to fight Napoleon. Following Napoleon's first defeat at the Battle of Leipzig in 1813, Sweden compelled Denmark (France's ally) to exchange Norway for Swedish Pomerania.

By 1814 Sweden and Norway had formed an uneasy union. Norway retained its own government and certain autonomous measures. Sweden decided foreign policy, appointed a viceroy and retained a suspensive (but not absolute) veto over the Norwegian parliament's legislation.

The nineteenth century

Union under Karl Johan, or **Karl XIV** as he became in 1818, could have been disastrous. He spoke no Swedish and just a few years previously had never visited either kingdom. However, under Karl and his successor **Oscar I**, prosperity ensued. Construction of the **Göta Canal** (1832) helped commercially, and liberal measures by both monarchs helped politically. In 1845, daughters were given an equal right of inheritance. A Poor Law was introduced in 1847, restrictive craft guilds reformed, and an Education Act passed.

The 1848 revolutions throughout Europe cooled Oscar's reforming ardour, and his attention turned to reviving **Scandinavianism**. It was still a hope, in certain quarters, that closer cooperation between Denmark and Sweden–Norway could lead to some sort of revived Kalmar Union. Expectations were raised with the **Crimean War** of 1854: Russia as a future threat could be neutralized. But peace was declared too quickly (at least for Sweden) and there was still no real guarantee that Sweden would be sufficiently protected from Russia in the future. With Oscar's death, talk of political union faded.

His son **Karl XV** presided over a reform of the *Riksdag* that put an end to the Swedish system of personal monarchy. The Four Estates were replaced by a representative **two-house parliament** along European lines. This, together with the end of political Scandinavianism (following the Prussian attack on Denmark in 1864 in which Sweden stood by), marked Sweden's entry into modern Europe.

Industrialization was slow to take root in Sweden. No real industrial revolution occurred, and development – mechanization, introduction of railways, etc – was piecemeal. One result was widespread **emigration** amongst the rural poor, who had been hard hit by famine in 1867 and 1868. Between 1860 and 1910 over one million people left for America (in 1860 the Swedish population was only four million). Given huge farms to settle, the emigrants headed for land similar to that they had left behind – to the Midwest, Kansas and Nebraska.

At home, Swedish **trade unionism** emerged to campaign for better conditions. Dealt with severely, the unions formed a confederation (1898) but largely failed to make headway. Even peaceful picketing carried a two-year prison sentence. Hand in hand with the fight for workers' rights went the **temperance movement**. The level of alcohol consumption was alarming and various abstinence programmes attempted to educate the drinkers and, if necessary, eradicate the stills. Some towns made the selling of spirits a municipal monopoly – not a big step from the state monopoly that exists today.

With the accession of **Oscar II** in 1872, Sweden continued on an even, if uneventful, keel. Keeping out of further European conflict (the Austro-Prussian War, Franco-Prussian War and various Balkan crises), the country's only worry was growing dissatisfaction in Norway with the union. Demanding a separate consular service, and objecting to the Swedish king's veto on constitutional matters, the Norwegians brought things to a head, and in 1905 declared the union invalid. The Karlstad Convention confirmed the break and Norway became independent for the first time since 1380.

The late nineteenth century was a happier time for Swedish culture. **August Strindberg** enjoyed great critical success and artists like **Anders Zorn** and **Prince Eugene** made their mark abroad. The historian **Artur Hazelius** founded the Nordic and Skansen museums in Stockholm; and the chemist, industrialist and dynamite inventor **Alfred Nobel** left his fortune to finance the Nobel Prizes. It's an instructive tale: Nobel hoped that the knowledge of his invention would help eradicate war, optimistically believing that humankind would never dare unleash the destructive forces of dynamite.

The two World Wars

Sweden declared strict neutrality on the outbreak of **World War I**, influenced by much sympathy within the country for Germany that stemmed from longstanding cultural, trade and linguistic links. It was a policy agreed with the other Scandinavian monarchs, but a difficult one to pursue. Faced with British demands to enforce a blockade of Germany and with the blacklisting and eventual seizure of Swedish goods at sea, the economy suffered grievously; rationing and inflation mushroomed. The **Russian Revolution** in 1917 brought further problems to Sweden. The Finns immediately declared independence, waging civil war against the Bolsheviks, and Swedish volunteers enlisted in the White Army. But a conflict of interest arose when the Swedish-speaking Åland Islands wanted a return to Swedish rule rather than stay under the victorious Finns. The League of Nations overturned this claim, granting the islands to Finland.

After the war, a liberal–socialist coalition remained in power until 1920, when **Branting** became the first socialist prime minister. By the time of his death in 1924, franchise had been extended to all men and women over 23, and the state-controlled alcohol system (Systembolaget) set up. Following the Depression of the late 1920s and early 1930s, conditions began to improve after a Social Democratic government took office for the fourth time in 1932. A **welfare state** was rapidly established, offering unemployment benefit, higher old-age pensions, family allowances and paid holidays. The **Saltsjöbaden Agreement** of 1938 drew up a contract between trade unions and employers to help eliminate strikes and lockouts. With war again looming, all parties agreed that Sweden should remain neutral in any struggle, and so the country's rearmament was negligible, despite Hitler's apparent intentions.

World War II was slow to affect Sweden. Unlike in 1914, there was little sympathy in the country for Germany, but Sweden again declared neutrality. The Russian invasion of Finland in 1939 brought Sweden into the picture, with the Swedes providing weapons, volunteers and refuge for the Finns. Regular Swedish troops were refused, though, the Swedes fearing intervention from either the Germans (then Russia's ally) or the Allies. Economically, the country remained sound – less dependent on imports than in World War I and with no serious shortages. The position became stickier in 1940 when the Nazis marched into Denmark and Norway, isolating Sweden. Concessions were made – German troop transit allowed, iron-ore exports continued – until 1943–44, when Allied pressure had become more convincing than the failing German war machine.

Sweden became the recipient of countless refugees from the rest of Scandinavia and the Baltic. Instrumental in this process was **Raoul Wallenberg**, who rescued Hungarian Jews from the SS and persuaded the Swedish government to give him diplomatic status in 1944. Anything up to 35,000 Jews in Hungary were sheltered in "neutral houses" (flying the Swedish flag), and fed and clothed by Wallenberg.

But when Soviet troops liberated Budapest in 1945, Wallenberg was arrested as a suspected spy and disappeared; he was later reported to have died in prison in Moscow in 1947. However, unconfirmed accounts had him alive in a Soviet prison as late as 1975; in 1989 some of his surviving relatives flew to Moscow in an unsuccessful attempt to discover the truth about his fate.

The end of the war was to engender a serious crisis of conscience in the country. Though physically unscathed, Sweden was now vulnerable to **Cold War** politics. The Finns had agreed to let Soviet troops march unhindered through Finland, and in 1949 this led neighbouring Sweden to refuse to follow the other Scandinavian countries into **NATO**. The country did, however, much to conservative disquiet, return into Stalin's hands most of the Baltic and German refugees who had fought against Russia during the war – their fate is not difficult to guess.

Postwar politics

The wartime coalition quickly gave way to a purely Social Democratic government committed to welfare provision and increased defence expenditure – now non-participation in military alliances did not mean a throwing-down of weapons.

Tax increases and a trade slump lost the Social Democrats seats in the 1948 general election, and by 1951 they needed to enter into a **coalition** with the Agrarian (later the Centre) Party to survive. This coalition lasted until 1957, when disputes over the form of a proposed extension to the pension system brought it down. An inconclusive referendum and the withdrawal of the Centre Party from government forced an election. Although the Centre gained seats and the Conservatives replaced the Liberals as the main opposition party, the Social Democrats retained a (slim) majority.

Sweden regained much of its international moral respect (lost directly after World War II) through the election of **Dag Hammarskjöld** as secretary-general of the United Nations in 1953. His strong leadership greatly enhanced the prestige (and effectiveness) of the organization, which under his guidance participated in the solution of the 1956 Suez crisis and the 1958 Lebanon–Jordan affair. He was killed in an air crash in 1961, towards the end of his second five-year term.

Domestic reform continued unabated throughout the 1950s and 1960s. It was during these years that the country laid the foundations of its much-vaunted social security system, although at the time it didn't always bear close scrutiny. A **National Health Service** gave free hospital treatment, but only allowed for small refunds on doctor's fees and the costs of medicines and dental treatment – hardly as far-reaching as the British system introduced immediately after the war.

The Social Democrats stayed in power until 1976, when a **non-Social Democrat coalition** (Centre–Liberal–Moderate) finally unseated them. In the 44 years since 1932, the socialists had been an integral part of government in Sweden, their role tempered only during periods of war and coalition. It was a remarkable record, made more so by the fact that modern politics in Sweden has never been about ideology so much as detail. Socialists and non-socialists alike share a broad consensus on foreign policy and defence matters, even on the need for the social welfare system. The argument in Sweden has instead been about economics, a manifestation of which is the issue of **nuclear power**. A second non-Socialist coalition, formed in 1979, presided over a referendum on nuclear power (1980); the pro-nuclear lobby secured victory, the result being an immediate expansion of nuclear power generation.

Olof Palme

The Social Democrats regained power in 1982, subsequently devaluing the *krona*, introducing a freeze on prices and cutting back on public expenditure. They lost their majority in 1985, having to rely on Communist support to get their bills through. Presiding over the party since 1969, and prime minister for nearly as long, was **Olof Palme**. He was assassinated in February 1986 (for more on which, see p.76), and his death threw Sweden into modern European politics like no other event. Proud of their open society (Palme had been returning home unguarded from the cinema), Swedes were shocked by the gunning down of a respected politician, diplomat and pacifist. The country's social system was placed in the spotlight, and shock turned to anger and then ridicule as the months passed without his killer being caught. Police bungling was criticized and despite the theories – Kurdish extremists, right-wing terror groups – no one was charged with the murder.

Then the police came up with **Christer Pettersson**, who – despite having no apparent motive – was identified by Palme's wife as the man who had fired the shot that night. Despite pleading his innocence, claiming he was elsewhere at the time of the murder, Pettersson was convicted of Palme's murder and jailed. There was great disquiet about the verdict, however, both at home and abroad. Pettersson was eventually acquitted on appeal; it was believed that Palme's wife couldn't possibly be sure that the man who fired the shot was Pettersson, given that she had only seen the murderer once, on the dark night in question, and then only very briefly. The police appear to believe they had the right man all along, but in recent years some convincing evidence of the involvement of the South African secret services has come to light (Palme having been an outspoken critic of apartheid).

Carlsson and Bildt

Ingvar Carlsson was elected prime minister after Palme's murder, a position confirmed by the **1988 General Election** when the Social Democrats – for the first time in years – scored more seats than the three non-socialist parties combined. However, Carlsson's was a minority government, and with a background of rising inflation and slow economic growth, the government announced an **austerity package** in January 1990. This included a two-year ban on strike action, and a wage, price and rent freeze – strong measures which astounded most Swedes, used to living in a liberal, consensus-style society.

The **General Election of 1991** merely confirmed that the consensus model had finally broken down. A four-party centre-right coalition came to power, led by **Carl Bildt**, which promised tax cuts and economic regeneration, but the recession sweeping western Europe did not pass Sweden by. Unemployment hit a postwar record and in autumn 1992 – as the British pound and Italian lira collapsed on the international money markets – the *krona* came under severe pressure. In an attempt to steady nerves, Prime Minister Bildt and Carlsson, leader of the Social Democratic opposition, made the astonishing announcement that they would ignore party lines and work together for the good of Sweden – and then proceeded with drastic **public expenditure cuts**.

The fat was trimmed off the welfare state – benefits were cut, health care was opened up to private competition and education was given a painful shake-up.

But it was too little, too late. Sweden was gripped by its worst **recession** since the 1930s and unemployment had reached record levels of fourteen percent – the days of a jobless rate of one or two percent were well and truly gone. Poor economic growth coupled with generous welfare benefits, runaway speculation by Swedish firms on foreign real estate and the world recession all contributed to Sweden's economic woes.

The return of the Social Democrats

A feeling of nostalgia for the good old days of Social Democracy swept through the country in September 1994, and Carl Bildt's minority Conservative government was booted out. Swedes voted in massive numbers to return the country's biggest party to power, headed by **Ingvar Carlsson**. He formed a government of whom half the ministers were women.

During 1994, negotiations on Sweden's planned **membership of the European Union** were completed and the issue was put to a referendum, which succeeded in splitting Swedish public opinion right down the middle. The *Ja till EU* lobby argued that little Sweden would have a bigger voice in Europe and would be able to influence pan-European decisions if it joined. *Nej till EU* warned that Sweden would be forced to lower its standards to those of other EU countries, unemployment would rise, drug trafficking would increase, and democracy would be watered down. But in November of that year, the Swedes followed the Austrians and the Finns in voting for membership from 1 January 1995 – by the narrowest of margins, just five percent.

Following membership the *krona* fell to new lows as money-market fears grew that the minority government wouldn't be able to persuade parliament to approve cuts in state spending. However, the cuts were duly introduced – the welfare state was trimmed back further and new taxes were announced to try to rein in the spiralling debt. Unemployment benefit was cut to 75 percent of previous earnings, benefits for sick leave were reduced, and lower state pension payments also came into force; a new tax was also slapped on newspapers. To try to keep public support on his side, Finance Minister **Göran Persson** reduced the tax on food from a staggering 21 percent to just 12 percent.

Just when everything appeared under control, Carlsson resigned to be replaced by the bossy Persson, known to friends and enemies alike as HSB – short for *han som bestämmer*, he who decides. As the new millennium approached, the Swedish government concentrated its efforts on turning the economy round and experts argue this quiet period was necessary to muster strength to face the challenges to come.

Sweden today

Sweden's export-led **economy** has rendered the country extremely susceptible to changes in world finances. As globalization has gathered momentum since the turn of the millennium, Sweden has faced a number of difficult choices which would have been unthinkable during the heady days of Social Democracy. Privatizations, mergers and general cost-cutting measures within the much-cherished welfare state have brought Sweden more into line with countries that went through equally painful economic change decades ago. Some economists argue it is this enforced shaking up of the business environment from outside, rather than any direct government measures, that is responsible for Sweden's improved economic fortunes since 1998 – although **unemployment** remains stubbornly above government targets.

In September 2003, as Swedes prepared to hold a public referendum on adopting the **euro**, the nation was thrown into shock by the **murder** of the former foreign minister, **Anna Lindh**, one of Sweden's most popular politicians, who was tipped to become the country's first female prime minister. Lindh was stabbed repeatedly by a man with a history of psychiatric problems whilst she was out shopping; she later died of massive internal bleeding. **Mijailo Mijailovic**, born in Sweden to Serbian parents, is now serving a life sentence for her murder.

The perceived bungling of aid to Swedes caught up in the **tsunami disaster** in December 2004 cost Persson dear in September 2006 when he lost the general election to the Conservative, Fredrik Reinfeldt, who has since slashed the welfare state even further in an attempt to stimulate the economy and create jobs. The bête noire of past governments, Sweden's appalling record of sick leave was tackled head on in new legislation in 2008 which will mean that no person is allowed to claim sick leave for over a year – unthinkable in most other countries, but all too common in Sweden where many people earn more than their regular salary by claiming an array of social welfare benefits including sick pay.

Swedish architecture

The all-encompassing Swedish preoccupation with **design** and the importance attached to the way buildings interact with their wider environment
have provided Sweden with a remarkable wealth of buildings, both domestic
and commercial, during the past century. Despite this, planning for a
perceived shortage of affordable housing has also meant that almost every town of
any size is blighted with a plethora of faceless postwar apartment blocks which can
look more Soviet than Scandinavian. To really get the most out of Sweden's hugely
rich architectural history, it's invariably worth seeking out the historic heart of a
settlement – from small country towns to larger commercial cities.

There are rich pickings in terms of **Romanesque** and **Gothic** buildings,
particularly ecclesiastical and royal ones, and the number of **Renaissance** and
Baroque buildings is quite remarkable. But Sweden's architectural heritage is
not always so grand; the more vernacular constructions – from rural cottages to
fisherman's homes – provide a fascinating insight into how Swedes have lived
and worked for centuries.

Prehistoric buildings

Discussion of **prehistoric** building in Sweden is mostly a matter of conjec-
ture, for the only structures to have survived from before 1100 are ruined or
fragmentary. The most impressive structures of **Bronze Age** Sweden are the
numerous grassy burial barrows and the coastal burial sites (particularly apparent
on the island of Gotland) that feature huge boulders cut into the shapes of a
prow and stern. One of the best known of the latter type is at **Ales Stennar** on
the South Skåne coast – a Swedish Stonehenge set above windy cliffs.

More substantial are the **Iron Age** dwellings from the **Celtic** period (c. 500 BC
to 800 AD). The best example of a fortification from this era is at **Ismantorp** on
the Baltic island of Öland. Dating from the fifth century AD, this remarkable site
has limestone walls up to fifteen feet high and some eighty foundations arranged
into quarters, with streets radiating like spokes of a wheel.

From the remnants of pre-Christian-era houses, a number of dwelling types
can be identified. The open-hearth hall, for example, was a square house with
an opening in the roof ridge by which light entered and smoke exited. The
two-storey gallery house had an open upper loft reached via an exterior stair,
while the post larder was a house on stilts allowing for ventilation and protection from vermin.

Romanesque to Gothic

The Christianization of Sweden is dated from 1008, the year St Sigfrid is said to
have baptized King Olof. In the eleventh and twelfth centuries the Church and
the monastic orders were the driving force behind the most significant building
projects, with the most splendid example of Romanesque architecture being
Lund Cathedral. Consecrated in 1145, when Lund was the largest town in
Scandinavia and the archepiscopal see, this monumental building was designed

as a basilica with twin western towers, and boasts some tremendously rich carvings in the apsidal choir and vast crypt. The chief centre of Romanesque church building, however, was the royal town of **Sigtuna** to the northwest of Stockholm. Apart from boasting Sweden's oldest street, Sigtuna has the ruins of three eleventh-century churches – one of which, St Peter's, features the country's oldest groin vault.

Round arches, a distinctive feature of Romanesque architecture, flourished wherever limestone and sandstone were found – principally in regions of southern and central Sweden, such as Västergötland, Östergötland and Närke, as well as Skåne. An easy supply of both types of stone was to be found on the Baltic island of Gotland, from where numerous baptismal fonts and richly carved sandstone decorations were exported to the mainland both to the west (Sweden proper) and the east (Swedish-controlled Finland).

Of the great monastic ruins from this period, the finest is **Alvastra Monastery** (1143), just south of Vadstena near the eastern shores of Lake Vättern. A portion of the huge barrel-vaults can still be seen, though much of the graceful structure was carted off by Vasa to build his castle at Vadstena.

Gothic architecture emerged in the thirteenth century, one of the finest early examples being the **Maria Church** in Sigtuna (1237), which with its red-brick step gables is markedly unlike the austere grey-stone churches of a century earlier. The cathedral at **Strängnäs**, due east of Stockholm, is another superb piece of Gothic brick architecture, while in Malmö, the German-inspired **St Peter's Church** survives as a fine example of brick Gothic, a style often known as the Hanseatic Style. The cathedral at Uppsala (the largest in Scandinavia) is another intriguing specimen, designed by Parisian builders as a limestone structure to a French High Gothic plan, but eventually built in brick in a simpler, **Baltic Gothic** form. A good example of late Gothic is **Vadstena Convent Church**; begun in 1384, this austere limestone and brick hall was built exactly as decreed by St Birgitta, the founder of the church, and is flanked by her monastery and nunnery. However, the most rewarding place to explore Sweden's Gothic architecture is **Gotland** – the countryside is peppered with almost one hundred richly sculpted medieval churches, while the island's capital, the magnificently preserved Hanseatic seat of **Visby**, is replete with excellent domestic as well as ecclesiastical Gothic.

Few examples of the castles and fortifications of this period exist today. One of the best examples, **Varberg's Fortress** in Halland, just south of Gothenburg, was built by the Danes, while the best Swedish-built medieval fortifications are in Finland, a Swedish province until the early nineteenth century. One stark and beautifully unmolested example of a fortification in Danish-controlled Skåne is the castle of Glimmingehus; dating from around 1500, it was built by Adam van Duren, who also supervised the completion of the cathedral of Lund.

Renaissance and Baroque architecture

Gustav Vasa (1523–60) could not have had a more pronounced effect on Swedish architecture. In 1527, with his reformation of the Church, Catholic properties were confiscated, and in many instances the fabric of monasteries and churches was used to build and convert castles into resplendent palaces. Wonderful examples of such Renaissance palaces are **Kalmar Castle**, in the south of Småland, and

Vadstena's Castle – though, unlike Kalmar, the latter's interior has been stripped of its original furnishings. Another magnificent Vasa palace, a glorious ruin since a nineteenth-century fire, is **Borgholm Castle** on the Baltic island of Öland.

While few churches built in this period enjoyed much prominence, one of outstanding elegance is the **Trefaldighetskyrkan** (Trinity Church) in Kristianstad, Danish king Christian IV's model Renaissance city in Skåne. With its tall windows, slender granite pillars and square bays, it is the epitome of sophistication and simplicity.

By the time Gustav II Adolf (Gustavus Adolphus) ascended the throne in 1611, a greater opulence was becoming prevalent in domestic architecture. This tendency became even more marked in the **Baroque** area, which in Sweden commenced with the reign of Queen Kristina, art-loving and extravagant daughter of Gustav II Adolf. The first wave of Baroque was largely introduced by the German Nicodemus Tessin the Elder, who had spent much time in Italy.

The most glorious of palatial buildings from this era is **Drottningholm** outside Stockholm, a masterpiece created by Tessin for the Dowager Queen Hedvig Eleonora. Tessin's other great creation was **Kalmar Cathedral**, the finest church of the era and a truly beautiful vision of Italian Baroque. Nicodemus Tessin the Younger followed his father as court architect and continued his style. He designed the new **Royal Palace at Stockholm** following the city's great fire of 1697 and the two contrasting **Karlskrona** churches: the domed rotunda of the Trefaldighetskyrkan (Trinity Church) and the barrel-vaulted basilica of the Fredrikskyrkan (Fredrik's Church). Karlskrona, like **Gothenburg**, is a fine example of regulated town planning, a discipline that came into being during this era.

The eighteenth century

In the eighteenth century **Rococo** emerged as the style favoured by the increasingly affluent Swedish middle class, who looked to France for their models. This lightening of architectural style paved the way for the Neoclassical elegance which would follow with the reign of Gustav III, who was greatly impressed by the architecture of classical antiquity. Good examples of this clear Neoclassical mode are the **Inventariekammaren** (Inventory Chambers) at Karlskrona, and the **King's Pavilion at Haga**, designed for Gustav III by Olof Temelman, complete with Pompeiian interiors by the painter Louis Masreliez.

Another, and quite distinct aspect of late eighteenth-century taste, was the fascination with **chinoiserie**, due in large measure to the power and influence of the Gothenburg-based Swedish East India Company, founded in 1731. The culmination of this trend was the **Kina Slott** (Chinese Pavilion) at Drottningholm, a tiny Palladian villa built in 1763 and now beautifully restored.

The nineteenth century

Two vast projects dominated the Swedish architectural scene at the beginning of the nineteenth century: the remarkable **Göta Canal**, a 190-kilometre waterway linking the great lakes of Vänern and Vättern, Gothenburg and the Baltic; and the **Karlsborg Fortress** on the western shores of Vättern, designed to be an inland retreat for the royal family and the gold stocks, but abandoned ninety years later in 1909.

By the mid-nineteenth century, a new style was emerging, based on Neoclassicism but flavoured by the French-born king's taste. This **Empire Style** (sometimes referred to as the Karl Johan Style) is most closely associated with the architect **Fredrik Blom** of Karlskrona, whose most famous building is the elegant pleasure palace **Rosendal** on Djurgården, Stockholm.

During the reign of Oskar I (1844–59), while the buildings of Britain's manufacturing centres provided models for Sweden's industrial towns, the styles of the past couple of centuries began to reappear, particularly Renaissance and Gothic. One of the most glamorous examples of late nineteenth-century neo-Gothic splendour is **Helsingborg Town Hall**, built around 1890 as a riot of fairy-tale red-brick detail. The names which crop up most often in this era include Fredrik Scholander, who designed the elaborate **Stockholm Synagogue** in 1861, and Helgo Zetterwall, whose churches of the 1870s and 1880s bear a resemblance to neo-Gothic buildings in Britain and Germany.

The twentieth century to the present

Some of the most gorgeous buildings in Sweden's cities are the result of a movement which germinated in the final, resurgent years of the nineteenth century – **National Romanticism**, which set out to simplify architecture and use local materials to create a distinctive Swedish style. Its finest example, which was much influenced by the Arts and Crafts movement in Britain, is **Stockholm City Hall**, built in 1923 from plain brick, dressed stone and rustic timber. Another luscious example is Lars Israel Wahlmann's **Tjolöholm Castle**, just south of Gothenburg – a city in which some of the finest apartment buildings are those produced in the associated Art Nouveau style, known in Sweden as **Jugendstil**. One beautifully renovated building in full *Jugendstil* form is the theatre in Tivoli Park in **Kristianstad**, a town otherwise known for its Renaissance buildings. Stockholm's 1910-built *Hotel Esplanade* is a fine example, though the cities of Gothenburg, Malmö and Lund amongst others are rich in the heritage. The small town of Hjö on the western shores of Lake Vättern has a fine clutch of Jugendstil houses.

In the second quarter of the century a new movement – **Functionalism** – burst onto the scene, making great use of "industrial" materials such as stainless steel and concrete. The leading architect of his generation was **Gunnar Asplund**, famed for Stockholm City Library (mid-1920s) and his contribution to many other buildings – his interior of the law courts in **Gothenburg's Rådhus** is a mecca for architecture students and enthusiasts today. Asplund was also responsible for the famed **Woodland Cemetery** in Stockholm, a magnificent project that also involved another designer, **Sigmund Lewerentz**.

The creation of the welfare state went hand in hand with the ascendancy of a functionalist approach to architecture, which rejected many of the individualistic features of traditional Swedish design. By the 1960s, the faceless **International Style** had gained dominance in Sweden, as town planning gave way to insensitive clearance of old houses and their replacement with bland high-rises.

The late 1980s and early 1990s saw restoration becoming the order of the day with areas that had been left to decay – such as the old working-class neighbourhood of **Haga** in Gothenburg – gently gentrified and preserved. More recently the emphasis has shifted towards environmentally sympathetic architecture.

Intrinsically Nordic in their tone, these new buildings are often low-level structures constructed from locally sourced wood, with vast areas of glass capitalizing on natural light. A wonderful example of this sympathy with Sweden's natural habitat is on the Bohuslän coast where the **Nordic Water-Colour Museum** (Akvarellmuséet) explores the interplay between a sizeable constructed space and the surrounding wild landscape. A little further south, in Gothenburg, the natural science museum, **Universeum** is a splendidly organic building – all rough-hewn wood, glass and concrete reflecting in the pools of water outside. One of the highest profile projects of the last decade is the **Modern Museum** and **Museum of Architecture** (Moderna Muséet and Arkitekturmuséet) on the island of Skeppsholm, in Stockholm Harbour. Designed by the Spaniard **Rafael Moneo**, the building eloquently complements the diverse structures of the city's waterfront without trying to overshadow them.

Geography and wildlife

Sweden is known above all else for its forests and lakes, yet the sheer diversity of its terrain is less familiar. While there are indeed a vast number of **lakes**, the largest – Vättern and Vänern – home to a wide variety of fish, and swathes of forest blanket vast tracts of the country, the southern shores are fringed with sandy **beaches**, and the east and west coasts are a myriad of rocky islands forming **archipelagos**. The Baltic islands of Gotland and Öland provide an entirely different habitat to anywhere on mainland Sweden, with limestone plateaus, dramatic sea-stacks and a variety of flora found nowhere else in Scandinavia.

Reindeer are the most celebrated **animals** associated with Sweden, and are a common sight – especially in the province of Lapland – though the rarest mammals, such as brown bears, lynx and wolverines, are found as far south as northern Värmland.

Geography

The appearance of Sweden's terrain owes most to the last **Ice Age**, which chafed the landscape for 80,000 years before finally melting away 9000 years ago. Grinding ice masses polished the mountains to their present form, a process particularly evident in scooped-out U-shaped mountain valleys such as **Lapporten** near Abisko, in the extreme north of the country. Subsequent to the thaw, the landmass rose, so that former coastlines are now many kilometres inland, manifested by the form of huge plains of rubble, while the plains of Sweden were created by the deposition of vast quantities of silt by the meltwater.

The northwest of the country is dominated by **mountains**, which rise well above the timber line. Deciduous trees are most prevalent, except in the most southerly regions, where coniferous forest predominates. Sweden also boasts some of Europe's most impressive **archipelagos**, such as the dramatically rugged Bohuslän coast on the west, and Stockholm's own archipelago of 24,000 islands, many covered in meadows and forest, on the east.

The country is also known for its **lakes**, which number more than 100,000. These support rich aquatic life, mostly salmon and salmon trout, although the coastlines are where most of the country's fishing takes place.

The north

Sweden's mountainous north is home to many of the country's national parks. The mountains here are part of the **Caledonian range**, the remains of which are also to be found further south in Europe, notably in Scotland and Ireland. Formed around 400 million years ago, the range is at its highest at **Kebnekaise** and **Sarek**, both above 2000m, in the extreme northwest of Sweden. Ancient spruce, pine and birch forest extends continuously along most of the 1000-kilometre range, providing an unspoilt habitat for birds such as the golden eagle. The treeline here lies at around 800m above sea level; higher up are great expanses of bare rockface and heathland, the latter often covered in wild orchids.

Central Sweden

The most extensive of Sweden's plains is in the **central Swedish lowlands**, a broad belt spanning from the Bohuslän coast in the west to Uppland and Södermanland in the east. Divided by steep ridges of rock, this former seabed was transformed by volcanic eruptions that created rocky plateaus such as Ålleberg and **Kinnekulle** (Flowering Mountain) to the west of Lidköping. The latter is Sweden's most varied natural site, comprising deciduous and evergreen woodland, meadows and pastures, and treeless limestone flats. Particularly notable among the flora here are cowslips, lady's-slipper orchids, wild cherry trees and, in early summer, the unusual and intensely fragrant bear-garlic.

Stretching some 160km north from Gothenburg up to the Norwegian border, the rough and windswept **Bohuslän coast** possesses a considerable **archipelago** of around three thousand islands. Most of these are devoid of trees – any which existed were cut down to make into boats and houses during the great fishing era of the eighteenth century. This low coastal landscape is peppered with deeply indented bays and fjords, interspersed with islands and peninsulas. To the north of the region, the waves have weathered the pink and reddish granite, and the resulting large, smooth stone slabs with their distinctive cracks are characteristic of the province. Inland from this stretch of coast are steep hills and plateaux which are separated from one another by deep valleys, the inland continuations of the fjords. Long, narrow lakes have developed here, the Bullaren lakes being the largest.

One of the region's most splendid areas of virgin forest is **Tiveden National Park**, around 50km northeast of Karlsborg and just to the northwest of **Lake Vättern**, one of the two enormous lakes in this part of Sweden, the other being **Vänern**. Fishing being a major sport in Sweden, Vänern and Vättern attract thousands each year who wish to try their luck. Around 1300 tonnes of fish are taken from Vänern alone each year, with commercial fisheries accounting for around eighty percent of the catch. The lake's waters were once the most productive for salmon in Sweden, but the construction of hydroelectric dams ruined the spawning grounds, and by the 1970s salmon was almost extinct here. In an effort to complement natural reproduction, salmon and brown trout have been raised in hatcheries and released into the lake with considerable success.

The south

The southernmost third of Sweden, the country's most highly populated and industrialized region, is a mixture of highlands (in the north), forests, lakes and cultivated plains. In southeastern Sweden, the forests of **Småland** have kept the furnaces of the province's glass factories alight since the seventeenth century. In the south, where the highlands give way to a gently undulating landscape, the combination of pastures and fields of rape and poppy makes for some glorious summertime scenery in **Skåne**. Though this province has a reputation for being monotonous and agricultural (true of much of its southwest), it also boasts tracts of conifers, a spectacular coastline and lush forests of beech, best seen in the first weeks of May. The province also boasts dramatic natural rock formations at **Hovs Hallar**, a stunning castellation of red-rock sea-stacks on the northern coast of the Bjäre peninsula.

To the east of Skåne, the **Stenshuvud National Park** has rocky coastal hills surrounded by woods of hornbeam and alder and moorlands full of juniper. Animals untypical of Sweden live here, such as tree frogs, sand lizards and dormice.

Öland and Gotland

Sweden's two largest islands, **Gotland** and **Öland**, lying in the Baltic Sea to the east of the mainland, have excited botanists and geologists for centuries. When Carl von Linné first arrived in Öland in the mid-eighteenth century, he noted that the terrain was "of an entirely different countenance" from the rest of the country, and indeed the island's limestone plateaus – known as **alvar** – are unique in Sweden. In southern Öland, **Stora Alvaret** (Great Limestone Plain) is a thin-soiled heathland with vividly colourful flora in spring and summer.

Gotland is the more dramatic of the two great islands, thanks to its tall sea-stacks (*raukar*), the remains of old coral reefs which loom like craggy ghosts along the island's shoreline. Like Öland, Gotland sustains rich floral life, including at least 35 species of orchid.

Fauna

Stretching over two thousand kilometres from the northern temperate zone into the Arctic Circle, Sweden is unsurprisingly home to a considerable diversity of flora and **fauna**. To see endangered species from Sweden in conditions approaching those in the wild, it's worth visiting **Nordens Ark**, near Lysekil on the Bohuslän coast. A not-for-profit breeding park, it's home to wolves, wolverines and lynxes, as well as to lesser pandas and snow leopards from the Himalayas.

Sweden's attitude to wild animals is in marked contrast to that of, say, Britain, in that Swedes deeply concerned with animal rights will often also be in support of **hunting**, regarding the practice as working hand in hand with nature conservation. Elk, bear, deer, fox and grouse are all hunted during specified seasons.

Mammals

The animal with the highest profile in Sweden is the **reindeer**: road signs warning of reindeer are common in northern Sweden, as is serious damage to vehicles involved in collisions with them. Throughout the year, reindeer are to be seen not just on mountainsides but also in the wooded valleys and lowlands throughout the north.

The most common deer in the country is the **roe deer**, one of the smaller breeds; these number around a million in Sweden. Roe deer are much more likely to be seen in the south and the centre of the country than the north. One of the best places to see them, as well as **red deer** and (in particular) **elk** (a close relation of the American moose) is the plateau of Hälleberg, just south of Vänersborg in Västergötland. Used as a royal hunting ground for elk since the 1870s, Halleberg has around 140 of these creatures in winter and 200 in summer. The elk, which is the largest species of deer in the world, can be over 2m tall and weigh up to five hundred kilograms. The best times to see elk and deer are dawn and dusk, when they emerge to seek food in cleared areas.

Also seen in this area are Swedish **woodland hare**, **badgers** and even **lynx** – the only member of the cat family living in the wild in Sweden. It lives off roe deer and hare, and is characterized by its triangular tufted ears. Although it's a rare practice today, some provinces still organize small-scale hunting of the creature.

Sweden's **wolves** have been hunted almost to extinction. A rare few – believed to be fewer than forty – still live in the north and west. Thanks to intensive efforts at conservation, however, the wolf population is slowly beginning to recover. Also found in the north are **Arctic foxes**, which have adapted to the conditions of extreme cold; they live only in the mountain regions above the tree line. Although the animals were common in Sweden at the beginning of the twentieth century, excessive hunting for their fur has reduced numbers dramatically. Ironically, the recent minor decline in the **fur trade**, due in part to animal rights activism, has posed a danger to Arctic foxes. A project aimed at conserving the Arctic fox in Sweden and Finland has found that where red foxes (also hunted for their fur) are left uncontrolled, they dominate over Arctic foxes, even preying on juvenile Arctic foxes.

Far closer to extinction than the Arctic fox are **wolverines**, placed under protection in 1969; there are now under one hundred individuals left in Sweden, entirely found in the north and mountain regions. One of their difficulties is that they depend on offal left by other predators, mainly wolves. The near demise of the wolf has clearly put considerable pressure on wolverines and recently they have been known to damage the tame reindeer herds owned by the *Sámi* people.

The Swedish **brown bear** can grow to 2.3 metres in length and weigh around 350 kilograms. Though rarely seen, they still live in the forests between Lappland and northern Värmland – their densest concentration is in the province of Härjedalen.

Birds

While Sweden is not particularly noted for its avian wildlife, the variety of **native birds** is considerable, and as a staging post for great numbers of **migratory birds** there is some spectacular viewing as they make their way between the far north and hotter climes.

Unsurprisingly, the country's coastlines are thick with seagulls, ducks and herons, while swans make beautiful additions to inland lakes and coastal inlets. Kingfishers and dippers can be found around the country's rivers and streams. The mountain regions of Sweden are home to capercaillie, mountain grouse, black grouse, and a range of owls as well as snow bunting and golden plovers, while the woodlands support willow grouse and bluethroat, among other species.

Two varieties of **eagle** are seen throughout the country, though their numbers are small, while hawks and buzzards make an occasional appearance. Many of these birds are threatened with extinction, and so the hunting of all birds of prey is forbidden.

Among the finest bird areas in the country is **Getterön Nature Reserve**, a few kilometres north of Varberg on the west coast of Halland. The area is seen as hugely valuable for bird-life, due to its large mosaic of wetlands in an otherwise exploited region. The mix of open water and dramatic clumps of reeds and rushes here make an ideal home for **nesting birds**. Among the rare birds which nest at Getterön are the black-tailed godwit and the southern dunlin; also found here are lapwings, redshanks, skylarks and yellow wagtail. Bird-life is also rich and varied on Öland. The **Öland goose**, one of the oldest domesticated breeds in the country, originated here from interbreeding with wild geese. **Ottenby**, on the island's southern point, is Öland's largest nature reserve, supporting golden oriole as well as fallow deer, which have lived here since the time when the entire island was a royal hunting ground. Nearby, off Gotland's western shores, **Stora Karlsö** is an island breeding ground for guillemot and razorbill.

The number of birds peaks in April and May (though spring migration begins as early as Feb) and from August to October. Every April, for example, thousands of cranes briefly settle in the potato fields just to the south of Sweden's most famous lowland lake, Hornborgasjon, southeast of Lidkoping. At this time of the year, the lake boasts 120 species of wetland birds, many on their migration to the northern marshes, whilst Lake Vanern is home to nesting seabirds such as the turnstone, water pipit and Caspian tern. The last waders head northwards in June, while female curlews and spotted redshanks meet them heading south. This latter southbound migration goes on through July and August. The plains of central Sweden are dotted with lakes, and many wetland and migratory birds shelter here. **Kvismaren**, near Örebro, is an area of reed marsh and open waters where geese and ducks live in their thousands.

In autumn, Canada geese and greylag geese arrive. During the winter months it's possible to see white-tailed eagles; peregrine falcons are seen all year. During the wintertime some of the best bird-viewing can be found at Lake Åsnen in southern Småland, where up to ten thousand goosanders and the rare white-tailed eagles have made a spectacular sight.

Fish and reptiles

Fish play an important role in Swedish life, with fishing a national sport and almost every restaurant boasting about its local, fresh fish. Pike perch, roach, bream and carp are the most common types in all but northern Swedish lakes, which are home to salmon trout and char. Lake Vättern, being particularly cold for its latitude, is also rich in Arctic char. The country's rivers are filled with trout, salmon and salmon trout, whilst offshore waters are home to shoals of herring, mackerel, Baltic herring, spiny dogfish and some sharks. **Shellfish** also appear on thousands of tables throughout the land, with crab, lobster, crayfish and oyster all harvested from offshore waters.

The only poisonous **snake** found in Sweden is the **viper**, its bite comparable to the sting of a wasp. **Grass snakes** tend to live near the water's edge; in Sweden, neither grass snakes nor vipers reach more than 1m in length. **Frogs** and **toads** are very common, particularly in southern and central Sweden.

Books

English-language books on Sweden are remarkably scant. Although Swedish publishing houses are producing quality titles – particularly fiction – remarkably few find their way into English.

Travel and general

James William Barnes Steveni *Unknown Sweden* (Hurst & Blackett, o/p). A fascinating account of journeys through Sweden in the early years of the twentieth century. With its excellent illustrations, this book is a superb social record.

Mary Wollstonecraft *A Short Residence in Sweden, Norway and Denmark* (Penguin). A searching account of Wollstonecraft's three-month solo journey through southern Scandinavia in 1795.

History and politics

Sheri Berman *The Social Democrat Movement* (Harvard University Press). A comparison between the Swedish and German social democratic systems between World War I and World War II. Whilst Sweden placed itself at the forefront of the drive for democratization after the Great Depression, Germany lacked direction and opted for Hitler.

H.R. Ellis Davidson *The Gods and Myths of Northern Europe* (Penguin). This "Who's Who" of Norse mythology, which includes some useful profiles of the more obscure gods, displaces the classical deities and their world as the most relevant mythological framework for northern and western European culture.

Eric Elstob *Sweden: A Traveller's History* (Boydell & Brewer). An introduction to Swedish history from the year dot to the twentieth century, with useful chapters on art, architecture and cultural life.

Bridget Morris *St Birgitta of Sweden* (Boydell & Brewer). A comprehensive and intelligently researched book offering a rounded perspective of

Sweden's first female saint and her extraordinary life. Accessible and educational without being over-academic in approach.

Lee Miles *Sweden and European Integration* (Ashgate Publishing Limited). A political history of Sweden comparing the period 1950–66 with the accession to the European Union in 1995.

Michael Roberts *The Early Vasas: A History of Sweden 1523–1611* (Cambridge University Press, o/p). A clear account of the period. Complements the same author's *Gustavus Adolphus and the Rise of Sweden* and *The Age of Liberty: Sweden 1719–1772* (Cambridge University Press), which, more briefly and enthusiastically, covers the period from 1612 to Gustav's death in 1632.

Jan-Öjvind Swahn *Maypole, Crayfish and Lucia – Swedish Holidays and Traditions* (The Swedish Institute). This little edition is superbly written and informative about how and why Swedish traditions have evolved. In contrast to the pictures, the prose is historically accurate and both entertaining and frank about what makes Sweden tick.

Franklin Daniel Scott *Sweden, The Nation's History* (Southern Illinois University Press). A good all-round account of Sweden's history from a poor, backward warrior nation to the prosperous modern one of today.

Art, architecture and design

Henrik O. Andersson and Fredric Bedoire *Swedish Architecture 1640–1970* (Swedish Museum of Architecture). With superb colour plates, this is the definitive survey of the subject, with parallel English/Swedish text.

Katrin Cargill *Creating the Look: Swedish Style* (Frances Lincoln; Pantheon Books). A great book to help you create cheerful Swedish peasant interiors. Includes lots of evocative photographs by Christopher Drake and a long list of stockists of the materials you'll need. A practical guide, the book includes some background information to place the designs in context.

Görel Cavalli-Björkman and Bo Lindwall *The World of Carl Larsson* (Simon & Schuster, US). A charming and brilliantly illustrated volume, charting the life and work of one of Sweden's most admired painters.

Barbro Klein and Mats Widbom *Swedish Folk Art* (Abrams). A lavishly illustrated and richly documented history of its subject, relating ancient crafts to modern-day design ideas.

Mereth Lindgren, Louise Lyberg, Birgitta Sandström and Anna Greta Wahlberg *A History of Swedish Art* (Coronet, US). A fine overview of Swedish painting, sculpture and, to a lesser extent, architecture, from the Stone Age to the present. Clear text and good, mostly monochrome, illustrations.

Nils-Olof Olsson *Skåne Through The Artist's Eye* (Fårgtrappan AAA) A likeable, cleverly balanced illustrated book encompassing everything from the prehistoric to the present day in its coverage of the country's southernmost province. Steering clear of the usual demarcations in art history, it shows how much contemporary artwork can help with our understanding of history.

Lars Sjöberg and Ursula Sjöberg *The Swedish Room* (Frances Lincoln; Pantheon Books). An exceptionally well-documented journey through developments in the design of Swedish homes, covering the period from 1640 through to the nineteenth century (stopping short of National Romanticism, Art Nouveau and Functionalism). The book sets design patterns in their historical and political context, and includes beautiful photographs by Ingalill Snitt. There's also a section on achieving classic Swedish decor effects, and a good list of suppliers of decorative materials, though without exception all are in America.

Håkan Sandbring & Martin Borg *Skåne – Wide Horizons* (Salix Förlag, Lund). A glorious visual study of Skåne – the ultimate coffee-table tome for anyone who loves the sort of beauty at which Sweden excels. From country scenes to urban visions and all the quirks of Swedish life in between, these brilliantly hued photographs will keep you absorbed for hours.

Literature

Hugh Beach *A Year in Lapland* (University of Washington Press). As a young man, Beach went to live with the *Sámi* reindeer herders of Jokkmokk. In later life he returns to the Arctic Circle to chart the fascinating changes that have occurred to northern Sweden and its traditionally nomadic inhabitants.

Frans G Bengtsson *The Long Ships: A Saga of the Viking Age* (HarperCollins). A real gem of historical fiction, bringing the Viking world vividly alive with solid background on arcane Norse traditions such as "trollcraft", "gold-luck" and "the Ale-death". This marvellously pacy adventure story is literally laugh-out-loud funny.

Marikka Cobbold *Frozen Music* (Orion). Cobbold – who is herself Swedish, though lives in England – paints a very true-to-life picture of Swedish mannerisms and way of life. This novel about the relationship between a Swedish architect and an English woman is set on a very well-drawn Swedish island.

Stig Dagerman *A Burnt Child* (Quartet, UK). One of the author's best works, this intense short narrative concerns the reactions of a Stockholm family to the death of the mother. A prolific young writer, Dagerman had written short stories, travel sketches, four novels and four plays by the time he was 26; he committed suicide in 1954 at the age of 31.

Kerstin Ekman *Blackwater* (Vintage; St Martin's Press). A tightly written thriller by one of Sweden's most highly rated novelists. Set in the forests of northern Sweden, the plot concerns a woman whose lover is murdered; years later, she sees her daughter in the arms of the suspect.

Kerstin Ekman *Under the Snow* (Vintage). In a remote Lapland village, a police constable investigates the death of a teacher following a drunken brawl. The dark deeds of winter finally come to light under the relentless summer sun.

Robert Fulton *Preparations for Flight* (Forest Books, UK). Eight Swedish short stories from the last 25 years, including two rare prose outings by the poet Niklas Rådström.

Lars Gustafsson *The Death of a Beekeeper* (New Directions Press). Keenly observed novel structured around the journal of a dying schoolteacher-turned-beekeeper.

Pers Christian Jersild *A Living Soul* (Norvik Press; Dufour). The work of one of Sweden's best novelists, this is a social satire based around the "experiences" of an artificially produced, bodyless human brain floating in liquid. Entertaining, provocative reading.

Selma Lagerlöf *The Wonderful Adventures of Nils* (Floris, Edinburgh; Dover, New York). Lagerlöf is Sweden's best-loved children's writer. The tales of Nils Holgren, a little boy who flies all over the country on the back of a magic goose, are continued in *The Further Adventures of Nils* (Tomten, US).

Sara Lidman *Naboth's Stone* (Norvik Press; Dufour). A novel set in 1880s Västerbotten, in Sweden's far north, charting the lives of settlers and farmers as the industrial age – and the railway – approaches.

Ivar Lo-Johansson & Rochelle Wright *Peddling My Wares* (Boydell & Brewer). An intriguing exploration of life for a young, self-educated Swede. This autobiographical tale is written by the last surviving member of the "Thirties Generation" and is as popular today in Sweden as when it appeared in 1953.

Torgney Lindgren *Merab's Beauty* (HarperCollins). Short stories capturing the distinctive flavour of family life in northern Sweden.

🏃 **Vilhelm Moberg** *The Emigrants* (Minnesota Historical Society, US). From one of Sweden's greatest twentieth-century writers, this is one of four novels depicting Karl Oskar and Christina Nilsson as they struggle their way from Småland to Minnesota. It's a highly poignant story dealing with the emigration of Swedes to the US.

🏃 **Michael Niemi** *Popular Music* (Flamingo). The enchanting tale of two boys, Matti and Niila, growing up in Pajala in northern Sweden in the 1960s and 1970s. Dreaming of an unknown world beyond the Torne Valley, they use their fantasy to help take them there. Winner of the *August Prize* for Sweden's best novel in 2000.

Leo Perutz *The Swedish Cavalier* (Harvill; Arcade). Two men meet in a farmer's barn in 1701 – one is a thief, the other an army officer on the run. An adventure story with a moral purpose.

Agneta Pleijel *The Dog Star* (Peter Owen, UK). By one of Sweden's leading writers, *The Dog Star* is the powerful tale of a young girl's approach to puberty. Pleijel's finest novel yet, full of fantasy and emotion.

Clive Sinclair *Augustus Rex* (Andre Deutsch, UK). August Strindberg dies in 1912 – and is then brought back to life by the Devil in 1960s Stockholm. Bawdy, imaginative and very funny treatment of Strindberg's well-documented neuroses.

August Strindberg *Plays: One* (including *The Father*, *Miss Julie* and *The Ghost Sonata*); *Plays: Two* (*The Dance of Death*, *A Dream Play* and *The Stronger*) (both Methuen). The major plays by the country's most provocative and influential playwright, analysing the roles of the sexes both in and out of marriage. Only a fraction of Strindberg's huge output has been translated into English.

Bent Söderberg *The Mysterious Barricades* (Peter Owen; Dufour). A leading Swedish novelist writes of the Mediterranean during the wars – a part of the world in which he's lived for many years.

Hjalmar Söderberg *Short Stories* (Norvik Press; Dufour). Twenty-six short stories from the stylish pen of Söderberg (1869–1941). Brief, ironic and eminently suited to dipping into.

Biography

Peter Cowie *Ingmar Bergman* (Andre Deutsch; Scribner; both o/p). A fine critical biography of the great director. Bergman's major screenplays are published by Marion Boyars.

Michael Meyer *Strindberg* (Oxford University Press). The best and most approachable biography of the tormented genius of Swedish literature.

Andrew Oldham, Tony Calder and Colin Irwin, *Abba* (Pan; Music Book Services). The last word on the band, here described as the "greatest composers of the twentieth century".

Alan Palmer *Bernadotte* (John Murray, o/p). A lively and comprehensive biography of Napoleon's marshal, who later became King Karl XIV Johan of Sweden.

Language

Language

Swedish

F or most foreigners, **Swedish** is nothing more than an obscure, if somewhat exotic, language spoken by a few million people on the fringe of Europe, and whose most famous speaker is the Swedish chef from TV's *The Muppet Show*. Many travellers take their flirtation with the odd hurdy-gurdy sounds of the language no further than that, since there is no need whatsoever to speak Swedish to enjoy a visit to Sweden – recent surveys have shown that 95 percent of Swedes speak English to some degree. However, Swedish deserves closer inspection, and if you master even a couple of phrases you'll meet with nothing but words of encouragement.

Despite what you might think, Swedish is one of the easiest languages for English-speakers to pick up; its grammar has developed along similar lines to that of English and therefore has no case system to speak of (unlike German). Many everyday words are common to both English and Swedish, having been brought over to Britain by the Vikings, and anyone with a knowledge of northern English or lowland Scottish dialects will already be familiar with a good number of Swedish words and phrases. Your biggest problem is likely to be perfecting the "tones", different rising and falling accents which Swedish uses (the hurdy-gurdy sounds you're no doubt already familiar with).

Swedish is a Germanic language and, as such, related to English in much the same way as French is related to Italian. However, its closest cousins are fellow members of the North Germanic group of tongues: Danish, Faroese, Icelandic, Norwegian. Within that subgroup, Swedish is most closely linked to Danish and Norwegian, and the languages are mutually intelligible to quite an extent. A knowledge of Swedish will therefore open up the rest of Scandinavia to you; in fact Swedish is the second official language of Finland. Unlike Danish, for example, Swedish spelling closely resembles pronunciation, which means you stand a sporting chance of being able to read words and make yourself understood.

Basics

Swedish **nouns** can have one of two **genders**: common or neuter. The good news is that three out of four nouns have the common gender. The **indefinite article** precedes the noun, and is *en* for common nouns and *ett* for neuter nouns. The **definite** article, as in all the other Scandinavian languages, is suffixed to the noun, for example, *en katt*, a cat, but *katten*, the cat; *ett hus*, a house, but *huset*, the house. The same principle applies in the plural: *katter*, cats, but *katterna*, the cats; *hus*, houses, but *husen*, the houses. The plural definite article suffix is therefore *-na* for common nouns and *-en* for neuter nouns (and confusingly identical with the definite article suffix for common nouns).

Forming **plurals** is possibly the most complicated feature of Swedish. Regular plurals take one of the following endings: *-or*, *-ar*, *-er*, *-r*, *-n*, or no ending at all. Issues like the gender of a word, whether its final letter is a vowel or a consonant, and stress can all affect which plural ending is used. You should learn each noun with its plural, but to be honest, the chances are you'll forget the plural ending and get it wrong. Swedes have no apparent difficulty in forming plurals and can't understand why you find it so hard. Show them the plurals section in any grammar and savour their reaction.

Adjectives cause few problems. They generally precede the noun they qualify and agree in gender and number with it; *en ung flicka*, a young girl (ie no ending on the adjective); *ett stort hus*, a big house; *fina böcker*, fine books. The *-a* ending is also used after the definite article, irrespective of number, *det stora huset*, the big house, *de fina böckerna*, the fine books; and also after a possessive, once again irrespective of number, *min stora trädgård*, my big garden, or *stadens vackra gator*, the town's beautiful streets.

Verbs are something of a mixed blessing. There is only one form for all persons, singular and plural, in all tenses, which means there are no irksome endings to remember: *jag är* – I am, *du är* – you (singular) are, *ni är* – you (plural) are, *han/vi är* – we are, *de är* – they are. All verbs take the auxiliary *att ha* (to have) in the perfect and pluperfect tenses (eg *jag har gått* – I have gone, *jag har talat* – I have spoken; *jag hade gått* – I had gone, *jag hade talat* – I had spoken). The price for this simplicity is unfortunately four different conjugations which are distinguished by the way they form their past tense. Verbs are always found as the second idea in any Swedish sentence, as in German, which can often lead to the inversion of verb and subject. However, in Swedish, there are no "verb scarers" which are responsible for the suicidal pile-up of verbs which often occurs at the end of German sentences.

How to say "you" in many Germanic languages poses considerable problems – not so in Swedish. In the 1960s a wave of liberalism and equality swept through the language and the honorific form, *ni* (the equivalent of *sie* in German), was dropped in favour of the more informal *du*. However, the change in the language has left many elderly people behind, and you'll often still hear them using *ni* to people they don't know very well. In modern Swedish *ni* is really only used to express the plural of you (the equivalent of both *ihr* and plural *sie* in German). Sadly, though, in recent years it has made a limited comeback in the service industry where staff seem intent on making the customer feel respected and important by using the honorific *ni*.

Pronunciation

Rest assured – you're never going to sound Swedish, for not only can **pronunciation** be difficult, but the sing-song **melody** of the language is beyond the reach of most outsiders. Swedish uses two quite different **tones** on words of two or more syllables – one rises throughout the entire word, while the other falls in the middle before peaking at the end of the word. It's this second down-then-up accent which gives Swedish its distinctive melody. Unfortunately, identical words can have two different meanings depending on which tone is used. For example, *fem ton* with a rising accent throughout each word means "five tons", whereas *femton* where the accent dips during the *fem-* and rises throughout the *-ton* means "fifteen". Equally, *komma* with a rising tone throughout means "comma", whereas *komma* with a falling tone followed by a rising tone is the verb "to come". In short, try your best, but don't worry if you get it wrong. Swedes are used to foreigners saying one word but meaning another and will generally understand what you're trying to say.

Vowels can be either long (when followed by one consonant or at the end of a word) or short (when followed by two consonants). Unfamiliar or unusually spelt vowels are as follows:

ej as in m**ate**

y as in **ewe**

å when short, as in h**o**t; when long, sort of as in r**aw**

ä as in g**e**t

ö as in f**ur**

Consonants are pronounced approximately as in English except:

g before e, i, y, ä or ö as in **y**et; before a, o, u, å as in **g**ate; sometimes silent

j, dj, gj, lj as in **y**et

k before e, i, y, ä or ö approximately as in **sh**ut and similar to German **ch** in "ich", otherwise hard

qu as in k**v**

rs as in **sh**ut (also when one word ends in r and the next begins with s, for example *för stor*, pronounced "fur shtoor")

s as in **s**o (never as English z)

sj, skj, stj approximately as in **sh**ut (different from soft k sound and more like a sh-sound made through the teeth but with rounded lips – this sound takes much practice; see below)

tj approximately as in **sh**ut and with same value as a soft **k**

z as in **s**o (never as in **z**oo)

The soft sound produced by **sj, skj** and **stj** is known as the **sj-sound** and is a peculiarity of Swedish. Unfortunately it appears widely and its pronunciation varies with dialect and individual speakers. To confuse matters further there are two variants, a back sj-sound formed by raising the back of the tongue and a front sj-sound formed by raising the middle or front of the tongue. Gain instant respect by mastering this Swedish tongue twister: *sjuttiosju sjuksköterskor skötte sju sjösjuka sjömän på skeppet till Shangai*, meaning "seventy-seven nurses nursed seven seasick sailors on the ship to Shanghai".

Books

Swedes are always keen to practise their English, so if you're intent on learning Swedish, perseverance is the name of the game. The excellent *Colloquial Swedish* by Philip Holmes and Gunilla Serin (published by Routledge) is the best **textbook** around and should be your starting point – it will guide you through everything from pronunciation to the latest slang. Make sure you buy the companion cassette so you get a chance to hear the spoken language.

Of the handful of **grammars** available, by far the most useful is the six-hundred-page *Swedish: A Comprehensive Grammar* by Philip Holmes and Ian Hinchliffe (Routledge), which is head and shoulders above anything else on the market. An abridged version, *Essentials of Swedish Grammar* (Routledge), is handy as a first step on the road to learning the language.

Until just a couple of years ago, it was virtually impossible to buy an English–Swedish **dictionary** outside Sweden; now most bookshops will supply the *Collins Gem Swedish Dictionary*, perfect for checking basic words whilst travelling around. It's also available in Sweden under the title *Norstedts engelska fickordbok* but costs twice as much. Incidentally, the Swedish word for dictionary, *ordbok* – meaning "wordbook" – is a good example of how Swedish builds new words from existing ones.

Of the **phrasebooks**, the most useful is *Swedish Phrase Book and Dictionary* (Berlitz).

Useful words and phrases

Basic phrases

yes/no	ja/nej	open/closed	öppet/stängt
hello	hej/tjänare	women/men	kvinnor/män
good morning	god morgon	toilet	toalett
good afternoon	god middag	bank/change	bank/växel
good night	god natt	post office	posten
today/tomorrow	idag/imorgon	stamp(s)	frimärke(n)
please	tack/var så god	where are you from?	varifrån kommer du?
here you are/ you're welcome	var så god	I'm English	jag är engelsman/ engelska
thank you (very much)	tack (så mycket)	Scottish	skotte
		Welsh	walesare
where?/when?	var?/när/hur dags?	Irish	irländare
what?/why?	vad?/varför?	American	amerikan
how (much)?	hur (mycket)?	Canadian	kanadensare
I don't know	jag vet inte	Australian	australier
do you know? (a fact)	vet du ...?	a New Zealander	nyzeeländare
		what's your name?	vad heter du?
could you ...?	skulle du kunna ...?	what's this called in Swedish?	vad heter det här på svenska?
sorry/excuse me	förlåt/ursäkta	do you speak English?	talar du engelska?
here/there	här/där		
near/far	nära/avlägsen	I don't understand	jag förstår inte
this/that	det här/det där	you're speaking too fast	du talar för snabbt
now/later	nu/senare		
more/less	mera/mindre	how much is it?	hur mycket kostar det?
big/little	stor/liten		

Getting around

how do I get to ...?	hur kommer jag till ...?	what time does it arrive in ...?	hur dags är det framme i ...?
left/right	till vänster/till höger		
straight ahead	rakt fram	which is the road to ...?	vilken är vägen till ...?
where is the bus station?	var ligger busstationen?	where are you going?	vart går du?
the bus stop for ...	busshållplatsen till ...	I'm going to ...	jag går till ...
railway station	järnvägsstationen	that's great, thanks a lot	jättebra, tack så mycket
where does the bus to ... leave from?	varifrån går bussen till ...?	stop here please	stanna här, tack
is this the train for Gothenburg?	åker detta tåg till Göteborg?	ticket to	biljett till
		return ticket	tur och retur
what time does it leave?	hur dags går det?		

Accommodation

where's the youth hostel?	var ligger vandrarhemmet?
is there a hotel round here?	finns det något hotell i närheten?
I'd like a single/ double room	jag skulle vilja ha ett enkelrum/dubbelrum
can I see it?	får jag se det?
how much is it a night?	hur mycket kostar det per natt?
I'll take it	jag tar det
it's too expensive	det är för mycket, jag tar det inte
I don't want it now	
can I/we leave the bags here until …?	kan jag/vi få lämna väskorna här till …?
have you got anything cheaper?	har du något billigare?
with a shower?	med dusch?
can I/we camp here?	får jag/vi tälta här?

Days and months

Sunday	söndag	March	mars
Monday	måndag	April	april
Tuesday	tisdag	May	maj
Wednesday	onsdag	June	juni
Thursday	torsdag	July	juli
Friday	fredag	August	augusti
Saturday	lördag	September	september
		October	oktober
January	januari	November	november
February	februari	December	december

The time

what time is it?	vad är klockan?	one forty	tjugo i två
it's ….	den/hon är …	one forty-five	kvart i två
at what time …?	hur dags …?	one fifty-five	fem i två
at …	klockan …	two o'clock	klockan två
midnight	midnatt	noon	klockan tolv
one in the morning	klockan ett på - natten	in the morning	på morgonen
ten past one	tio över ett	in the afternoon	på eftermiddagen
one fifteen	kvart över ett	in the evening	på kvällen
one twenty-five	fem i halv två	in ten minutes	om tio minuter
one thirty	halv två	ten minutes ago	för tio minuter sedan
one thirty-five	fem över halv två		

Numbers

1	ett	9	nio
2	två	10	tio
3	tre	11	elva
4	fyra	12	tolv
5	fem	13	tretton
6	sex	14	fjorton
7	sjö	15	femton
8	åtta	16	sexton

17	sjutton	70	sjuttio
18	arton	80	åttio
19	nitton	90	nittio
20	tjugo	100	hundra
21	tjugoett	101	hundraett
22	tjugotvå	200	två hundra
30	trettio	500	fem hundra
40	fyrtio	1000	tusen
50	femtio	10,000	tio tusen
60	sextio		

Swedish sayings

Just two generations ago, Sweden was a predominantly rural country which had yet to experience the Industrial Revolution. As a result the language is still full of **phrases and expressions** which refer to the Swedish countryside. When something goes wrong, you'll often hear *det gick åt skogen*, literally "it went to the forest", the implication being that the uncivilized world began at the forest edge; hence also *dra åt skogen!*, "be off to the forest!", which is a polite way of telling someone to leave you alone. Animals also feature in Swedish phrases: *gå som katten kring het gröt* is "cats walking around hot porridge", as opposed to the hot tin roofs familiar to their English cousins. Equally, every good Swede is told *sälj inte skinnet förrän björnen är skjuten*, "don't sell the skin before the bear is shot". Swedes don't talk of the devil, but instead of the trolls (the Swedish word for "devils", *djävlar*, is one of the worst swear-words in the language). When they're in a crowd, Swedes are never packed like sardines but *packade som sillar* – like herrings. If a Swede is singularly unimpressed about something, it's definitely *ingenting att hänga i julgran*, literally "nothing to hang on the Christmas tree".

Food and drink terms

Basics and snacks

ägg	egg	peppar	pepper
bröd	bread	pommes	fries
bulle	bun	ris	rice
glass	ice cream	salt	salt
grädde	cream	senap	mustard
gräddfil	sour cream	småkakor	biscuits
gröt	porridge	smör	butter
kaka	cake	smörgås	sandwich
keks	biscuits	socker	sugar
knäckebröd	crispbread	sylt	jam
olja	oil	tårta	cake
omelett	omelette	vinäger	vinegar
ost	cheese	våffla	waffle
pastej	paté		

Meat (kött)

älg	elk	kyckling	chicken
biff	beef	lammkött	lamb
fläsk	pork	lever	liver
hjort	venison	oxstek	roast beef
kalvkött	veal	renstek	roast reindeer
korv	sausage	rådjursstek	roast venison
kotlett	cutlet/chop	skinka	ham
köttbullar	meatballs		

Fish (fisk)

ål	eel	makrill	mackerel
ansjovis	anchovies	räkor	shrimps/prawns
blåmusslor	mussels	röding	arctic char
fiskbullar	fishballs	rödspätta	plaice
forell	trout	sardiner	sardines
hummer	lobster	sik	whitefish
kaviar	caviar	sill	herring
krabba	crab	sjötunga	sole
kräftor	freshwater crayfish	strömming	Baltic herring
lax	salmon	torsk	cod

Vegetables (grönsaker)

ärtor	peas	rödkål	red cabbage
blomkål	cauliflower	sallad	lettuce/salad
brysselkål	Brussels sprouts	spenat	spinach
bönor	beans	svamp	mushrooms
gurka	cucumber	tomater	tomatoes
lök	onion	vitkål	white cabbage
morötter	carrots	vitlök	garlic
potatis	potatoes		

Fruit (frukt)

äpple	apple	hjortron	cloudberry
ananas	pineapple	jordgubbar	strawberries
apelsin	orange	lingon	lingonberry/red whortleberry
aprikos	apricot		
banan	banana	persika	peach
citron	lemon	päron	pear
hallon	raspberry	vindruvor	grapes

Culinary terms

ångkokt	steamed	filé	fillet
blodig	rare	friterad	deep fried

genomstekt	well done
gravad	cured
grillat/halstrat	grilled
kall	cold
kokt	boiled
lagom	medium

pocherad	poached
rökt	smoked
stekt	fried
ungstekt	roasted/ baked
varm	hot

Drinks

apelsinjuice	orange juice
chocklad	hot chocolate
citron	lemon
fruktjuice	fruit juice
grädde	cream
kaffe	coffee
lättöl	light beer
mellanöl	medium-strong beer
mineralvatten	mineral water
mjölk	milk

öl	beer
rödvin	red wine
saft	juice
skål	cheers!
starköl	strong beer
storstark	large strong beer
te	tea
vatten	water
vin	wine
vitt vin	white wine

Swedish specialities

ål	eel, smoked and served with creamed potatoes or scrambled eggs (äggröra)
ärtsoppa	yellow pea soup with pork, spiced with thyme and marjoram; a winter dish traditionally eaten on Thursdays
bruna bönor	baked, vinegared brown beans, usually served with fried pork
filmjölk	soured milk
fisksoppa	fish soup usually including several sorts of fish, prawns and dill
getost	goat's cheese
glögg	mulled wine, usually fortified with spirits to keep out the cold, and drunk at Christmas
gravad lax	salmon marinated in dill, sugar and seasoning; served

	with mustard sauce and lemon
hjortron	a wild, orange-coloured berry (the cloudberry), served with fresh cream and/or ice cream. Also made into jam
Janssons frestelse	a potato and anchovy bake with cream
kryddost	hard cheese spiced with seeds, sometimes caraway seeds or cloves
köttbullar	meatballs served with a brown creamy sauce and lingonberries
kräftor	crayfish, often served with hryddost, and eaten in August
lingon	lingonberry (sometimes known as red whortle-berries), a red berry made into a kind of jam and served with meat dishes as well as on

	pancakes and in puddings eaten at Christmas	semla	sweet bun with almond paste and whipped cream; associated with Lent
långfil	a special type of soured milk from northern Sweden	sillbricka	various cured and marinated herring dishes; often appears as a first course in restaurants at lunchtime
lövbiff	sliced, fried beef with onions		
matjessill	sweet-pickled herring		
mesost	brown, sweet whey cheese; a breakfast favourite	sjömansbiff	sailors' beef casserole: thin slices of beef baked in the oven with potatoes and onion topped with parsley
ostkaka	curd cake made from fresh curds and eggs baked in the oven served with jam or berries		
		smultron	wild strawberries, known for their concentrated taste
pepparkakor	thin, spiced gingerbread biscuits popular at Christmas	strömming	Baltic herring
plättar	thin pancakes, often served with pea soup	surströmming	Baltic herring fermented for months until it's rotten and the tin it's in buckles – very smelly and eaten in very, very small quantities. Not for the faint-hearted!
potatissallad	potato salad, often flavoured with dill or chives		
pytt i panna	cubes of meat and fried potatoes with a fried egg and beetroot		

L

LANGUAGE | Food and drink terms

Glossary

älg elk
ångbad steamroom
ångbåt steamboat
ankommande arriving
ankomst arrival
avgående departing
avgång departure
bad swimming (pool)
bastu sauna
berg mountain
biljett ticket
bio cinema
björn bear
bokhandel bookshop
bro bridge
brygga jetty/pier
båt boat/ferry
cyckelstig cycle path
dagens rätt dish of the day
dal valley
domkyrka cathedral
drottning queen
ej inträde no entrance
extrapris special offer
färja ferry
färjeläge ferry terminal/berth
gamla old
gamla stan old town
gata (g.) street
gränd alley
hamn harbour
hembygdsgård homestead museum
hiss lift
järnvägsstation railway station
kapell chapel
klockan (kl.) o'clock
kung king

kyrka church
liggvagn couchette car
lilla little
muséet museum
öppet open
öppettider opening hours
pressbyrå newsagent
rabatt discount
rea sale
ren reindeer
restaurang restaurant
riksdagshus parliament building
rådhuset town hall
rökning förbjuden no smoking
simhall swimming pool
sjö lake
skog forest
slott palace/castle
storstark strong beer
smörgåsbord spread of different dishes
sovvagn sleeping car
spår track
stadshus city hall
stora big
strand beach
stuga cottage
systembolaget alcohol store
stängt closed
torg square/market place
tunnelbana underground (metro)
turistbyrå tourist office
tåg train
tältplats campsite
universitet university
vandrarhem youth hostel
väg (v.) road
vrakpris bargain

Travel
store

Available from all good bookstores

For more information go to www.rough guides.com

ROUGH GUIDES

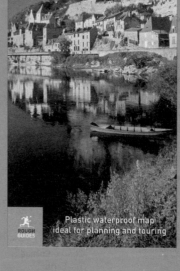

www.roughguides.com

nformation on over 25,000 destinations around the world

- **Read** Rough Guides' trusted travel info
- **Access** exclusive articles from Rough Guides authors
- **Update** yourself on new books, maps, CDs and other products
- **Enter** our competitions and win travel prizes
- **Share** ideas, journals, photos & travel advice with other users
- **Earn** points every time you contribute to the Rough Guide
  community and get rewards

Small print and

Index

A Rough Guide to Rough Guides

Published in 1982, the first Rough Guide – to Greece – was a student scheme that became a publishing phenomenon. Mark Ellingham, a recent graduate in English from Bristol University, had been travelling in Greece the previous summer and couldn't find the right guidebook. With a small group of friends he wrote his own guide, combining a highly contemporary, journalistic style with a thoroughly practical approach to travellers' needs.

The immediate success of the book spawned a series that rapidly covered dozens of destinations. And, in addition to impecunious backpackers, Rough Guides soon acquired a much broader and older readership that relished the guides' wit and inquisitiveness as much as their enthusiastic, critical approach and value-for-money ethos.

These days, Rough Guides include recommendations from shoestring to luxury and cover more than 200 destinations around the globe, including almost every country in the Americas and Europe, more than half of Africa and most of Asia and Australasia. Our ever-growing team of authors and photographers is spread all over the world, particularly in Europe, the USA and Australia.

In the early 1990s, Rough Guides branched out of travel, with the publication of Rough Guides to World Music, Classical Music and the Internet. All three have become benchmark titles in their fields, spearheading the publication of a wide range of books under the Rough Guide name.

Including the travel series, Rough Guides now number more than 350 titles, covering: phrasebooks, waterproof maps, music guides from Opera to Heavy Metal, reference works as diverse as Conspiracy Theories and Shakespeare, and popular culture books from iPods to Poker. Rough Guides also produce a series of more than 120 World Music CDs in partnership with World Music Network.

Visit www.roughguides.com to see our latest publications.

Rough Guide travel images are available for commercial licensing at www.roughguidespictures.com

Rough Guide credits

Text editor: Helena Smith
Layout: Nikhil Agarwal
Cartography: Richard Marchi
Picture editor: Sarah Cummins
Production: Rebecca Short
Proofreader: Helen Castell
Cover design: Chloë Roberts
Editorial: Ruth Blackmore, Andy Turner, Keith Drew, Edward Aves, Alice Park, Lucy White, Jo Kirby, James Smart, Natasha Foges, Róisín Cameron, Emma Traynor, Emma Gibbs, Kathryn Lane, Christina Valhouli, Monica Woods, Mani Ramaswamy, Harry Wilson, Lucy Cowie, Helen Ochyra, Alison Roberts, Joe Staines, Peter Buckley, Matthew Milton, Tracy Hopkins, Ruth Tidball; **Delhi** Madhavi Singh, Karen D'Souza, Lubna Shaheen
Design & Pictures: **London** Scott Stickland, Dan May, Diana Jarvis, Mark Thomas, Nicole Newman, Emily Taylor; **Delhi** Umesh Aggarwal, Ajay Verma, Jessica Subramanian, Ankur Guha, Pradeep Thapliyal, Sachin Tanwar, Anita Singh
Production: Vicky Baldwin

Cartography: **London** Maxine Repath, Ed Wright, Katie Lloyd-Jones; **Delhi** Rajesh Chhibber, Ashutosh Bharti, Rajesh Mishra, Animesh Pathak, Jasbir Sandhu, Karobi Gogoi, Alakananda Bhattacharya, Swati Handoo, Deshpal Dabas
Online: **London** George Atwell, Faye Hellon, Jeanette Angell, Fergus Day, Justine Bright, Clare Bryson, Aine Fearon, Adrian Low, Ezgi Celebi, Amber Bloomfield; **Delhi** Amit Verma, Rahul Kumar, Narender Kumar, Ravi Yadav, Debojit Borah, Rakesh Kumar, Ganesh Sharma, Shisir Basumatari
Marketing & Publicity: **London** Liz Statham, Niki Hanmer, Louise Maher, Jess Carter, Vanessa Godden, Vivienne Watton, Anna Paynton, Rachel Sprackett, Libby Jellie, Laura Vipond, Vanessa McDonald; **New York** Katy Ball, Judi Powers, Nancy Lambert; **Delhi** Ragini Govind
Manager India: Punita Singh
Reference Director: Andrew Lockett
Operations Manager: Helen Phillips
PA to Publishing Director: Nicola Henderson
Publishing Director: Martin Dunford
Commercial Manager: Gino Magnotta
Managing Director: John Duhigg

Publishing information

This fifth edition published June 2009 by
Rough Guides Ltd,
80 Strand, London WC2R 0RL
14 Local Shopping Centre, Panchsheel Park, New Delhi 110017, India
Distributed by the Penguin Group
Penguin Books Ltd,
80 Strand, London WC2R 0RL
Penguin Group (USA)
375 Hudson Street, NY 10014, USA
Penguin Group (Australia)
250 Camberwell Road, Camberwell, Victoria 3124, Australia
Penguin Group (Canada)
195 Harry Walker Parkway N, Newmarket, ON, L3Y 7B3 Canada
Penguin Group (NZ)
67 Apollo Drive, Mairangi Bay, Auckland 1310, New Zealand
Cover concept by Peter Dyer.

Typeset in Bembo and Helvetica to an original design by Henry Iles.

Printed and bound in China

© James Procter and Neil Roland 2009

No part of this book may be reproduced in any form without permission from the publisher except for the quotation of brief passages in reviews.

448pp includes index

A catalogue record for this book is available from the British Library

ISBN: 978-1-84836-024-2

The publishers and authors have done their best to ensure the accuracy and currency of all the information in **The Rough Guide to Sweden**, however, they can accept no responsibility for any loss, injury, or inconvenience sustained by any traveller as a result of information or advice contained in the guide.

1   3   5   7   9   8   6   4   2

Help us update

We've gone to a lot of effort to ensure that the fifth edition of **The Rough Guide to Sweden** is accurate and up-to-date. However, things change – places get "discovered", opening hours are notoriously fickle, restaurants and rooms raise prices or lower standards. If you feel we've got it wrong or left something out, we'd like to know, and if you can remember the address, the price, the hours, the phone number, so much the better.

Please send your comments with the subject line "**Rough Guide Sweden Update**" to ®mail @roughguides.com. We'll credit all contributions and send a copy of the next edition (or any other Rough Guide if you prefer) for the very best emails.

Have your questions answered and tell others about your trip at
®community.roughguides.com

Acknowledgements

James Proctor would like to thank Philippa Sutton at the Sweden Travel and Tourism Council for organisation of the first order. Special thanks, too, to ACC in Gothenburg and Jan Svensson at SJ in Stockholm. Also, to staff at tourist offices up and down Sweden who provided invaluable local help, including: Elisabet Corengia in Malmö, Sara Lood in Helsingborg, Susanne Gustavsson and Tomas Jönsson in Karlstad, Joakim Kihlberg in Östersund, Cecilia Enerud in Sundsvall, Tatjana Summermatter in Sveg, Erja Back in Umeå, Marie Almqvist and Lasse Svesson in Uppsala, Petra Nordström and Mickan Flink in Nyköping, Gunn-Viol Kattilakoski in Örebro, Sara Ståhle in Varberg, Eva Holmgren in Växjö, Johanna Andersson in Halmstad, Margareta Svensson-Hjorth in Sydkoster, Maria Kjelsson in Lysekil, Marie-Louise Svensson in Stockholm, Lina Gahnström in Visby and Dan Björk in Jukkasjärvi.

ROUGH GUIDES

SMALL PRINT

Photo credits

All photos © Rough Guides except the following:

Title page
Sunset over lake © C Parker/Axiom

Full page
Lighthouse © Jeppe Wikstrom/Getty Images

Introduction
Elk road sign © SCPHOTOS/Alamy
Reindeer, Lapland © Ullamaija Hnninen/Getty Images
Stockholm © Ellen Rooney/Axiom Photo Agency
Ornate door © Jeppe Wikstrom/Getty Images
Hiking the Kungsleden Trail © Doug McKinlay/Axiom
Tanumshede rock paintings © Gallo Images/Getty Images
Swedish church © Hakan Hjort/Getty Images
Maypole celebrations © Chad Ehlers/Alamy
Man skiing © Scott Markewitz/Getty Images
Husky © Simon Roberts/Axiom
Aurora Borealis © Doug McKinlay/Axiom
Pine forest © Roine Magnusson/Getty Images

Things not to miss
01 Snowmobiling © Nick Hanna/Alamy
02 Sámi man © Bryan & Cherry Alexander Photography/Alamy
03 Lund Cathedral © isifa Image services/Alamy
04 Girls swimming in lake © Nordic Photos/Alamy
05 Kalmar buildings © imagebroker/Alamy
06 Smorgasbord © Bo Zaunders/Corbis
07 Vasa ship © R1/Alamy
08 Kungsleden trail © Mediacolours/Alamy
09 Family on south coast beach © Johan Furusjo/Alamy
10 Smögen © Jon Arnold Images/Alamy
11 Kayakers exploring the Koster Archipelago/Alamy
13 Konstmuseum, Gothenburg © Neil Roland
14 Gammelstad © Robert Harding/Alamy
15 Birka © ayimages/Alamy
16 Brown bear © Arctic Images/Alamy
17 Rafting Klarälven © Arctic Images/Alamy
18 Bohuslän coast © Lucky Look/Alamy
19 Jokkmokk market © Bryan & Cherry Alexander Photography/Alamy
20 Boat ride © Bo Lind/Visit Sweden
21 Visby © Peter Grant/Visit Sweden
22 Inlandsbanan © Kai-Uwe Och/Alamy
23 Icehotel © tbkmedia.de/Alamy
24 Arctic Circle sign © Arco Images GmbH/Alamy
25 Gamla Stan © Jon Arnold Images/Alamy
26 Sauna © Pictorium/Alamy
27 Hikers in Lapland © Andy Sutton/Alamy
28 Midnight sun © LOOK Die Bildgentur der Fotografen GmbH/Alamy

Food and drink colour section
Swedish open sandwich © Macduff Everton/Corbis
Restaurant chalk board © David Sanger/Alamy
Akvavit label © Murt Michael Westermann/Corbis

The Swedish winter colour section
Man jumping into ice hole © Romilly Lockyer/Getty Images
Winter mountain biking © Peter Ros/Visit Sweden
Traditional winter footware © Henrik Trygg/Getty Images
Man braving the winter © Michael Dwyer/Alamy
Icehotel bar © Chad Ehlers/Alamy
Car on icy road © Tommy Nilsson/Getty Images
Snowboarding © Goran Assner/Swedish Travel & Tourism
Skiing © Henrick Trygg/Visit Sweden
Snow-covered trees © Jason Lindsey/Alamy

Black and whites
p.51 View of Old Town, Stockholm © Chris Fredriksson/Alamy
p.72 Stockholm National Museum © Chad Ehlers/Alamy
p.80 The Vasa ship © Jon Sparks/Alamy
p.103 Gripsholms Castle © International Photobank/Alamy
p.118 Tram in Gothenburg © Paul Thompson/Getty Images
p.128 Sightseeing boat in Gothenburg © Mikael Utterstrom/Alamy
p.163 Selma Lagerlöf house © Interfoto Pressebildagentur/Alamy
p.166 Halland, Varberg © Chris Fredriksson/Alamy
p.195 Café on Lilla Torg © Barry Mason/Alamy
p.198 Öresund Bridge © Woodystock/Alamy
p.220 Stortorget square © FAN Travelstock/Alamy
p.244 Castle in Vadstena © Picturesbyrob/Alamy
p.269 Raukar © Ladi Kirn/Alamy
p.272 Gammelstad © Juliet Ferguson/Alamy
p.294 Trysunda © Pixonnet/Alamy
p.314 Dog sled © Juniors Bildarchiv/Alamy
p.316 Reindeer © RBO Nature/Alamy
p.340 Östersund town hall © Arco Images GmbH/Alamy
p.344 Kungsleden Trail © Pixonnet/Alamy
p.348 Sámi and reindeer © Bryan & Cherry Alexander Photography/Alamy
p.383 Mountain biking in Lapland © Vario Images GmbH & Co.KG/Alamy

Index

Map entries are in colour.

Map symbols

maps are listed in the full index using coloured text

– – –	Chapter boundary	🔥	Waterfall
–––·	International boundary	👁	Lighthouse
— ··	Provincial boundary	*(i)*	Tourist office
▬▬▬	Motorway	⊠	Post office
===	Major road	@	Internet access
===	Minor road	★	Transport stop
⊞⊞⊞	Steps	Ⓣ	T-bana station
▬▬	Pedestrianized street	✈	Airport
– – – –	Path	🅿	Parking
— —	Ferry route	⊞	Hospital
———	Railway	⊙	Statue
———	Inlandsbanan railway	🏊	Swimming pool
———	Waterway	🎿	Ski trail
———	Wall	☗	Lodge
◆	Point of interest	⚐	Church (regional maps)
∴	Ruins	✚	Church (town maps)
▲	Mountain peak	▮	Building
♟	Castle	⬭	Stadium
⛫	Stately home	✝	Cemetery
⚘	Gardens		Park
⚑	Museum		Beach

We're covered. Are you?

ROUGH GUIDES Travel Insurance

Visit our website at www.roughguides.com/website/shop or call:

COLUMBUS
Travel Insurance

ROUGH
GUIDES

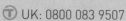 UK: 0800 083 9507

Spain: 900 997 149

Australia: 1300 669 999

New Zealand: 0800 55 99 11

Worldwide: +44 870 890 2843

USA, call toll free on: 1 800 749 4922

Please quote our ref: **Rough Guides books**

Cover for over 46 different nationalities and available
in 4 different languages.